Gamble

in The Devil's Chalk

Caleb Pirtle III

Text: Caleb Pirtle III
Editing/Design: Linda Greer Pirtle
Cover Design: Jutta Medina

Manufactured in the United States of America

Second Printing

What is history but a fable agreed upon.

--Napoleon Bonaparte

1

*R*einhardt Richter was a man of the earth. If nothing else, he knew and understood the curious mysteries that lay beneath the Texas farmlands sprawling at his feet.

He had studied the good earth and could read the empty landscape as easily as last year's edition of the *Farmer's Almanac.* Every furrow, crop row, creek bottom, bald knob, and ravine was as familiar as the lines in the palm of his hand.

Richter had knelt in his pastures on many an early morning and held up a fistful of dirt, watching as the winds slowly and surely separated the sand from the rocks.

The rocks scattered across the undulating pasturelands just north of Giddings and south of Dime Box intrigued him. They were of the ages, as ancient and as common as time itself, and the stories they could tell remained, more or less, untold.

The dirt was an old friend indeed.

It buried, then nourished, his seed, gave him a harvest and grew the tall grasses that kept his cattle fed, often with sunburnt stalks. Dirt ran shallow above those great folds of Austin Chalk, hiding the complexities of a puzzle that only he and he alone had been able to unravel.

Reinhardt Richter was known by many and understood by few, none of whom ever admitted it.

There were those in Lee County who said privately and over a beer or two that Richter was a little different, not quite like the rest of the folks, and not all of them were quite right either. He was not a tall man, standing only about five feet and ten inches, but he was wide, broad-shouldered, and carved with solid muscle, known far and wide for his ungodly strength.

Richter lived on a farm that had been in his family for more than a century, and by the 1970s, he was working on a vacuum truck that generally took at least two and more likely three men to load. Richter would wander on down to the road in the early morning hours and load it by himself.

Didn't ask for any help.

Didn't need to.

Didn't particularly want it.

Never complained.

Never showed up late or sick.

He had already been on the earth for more than seven decades.

Reinhardt Richter might or might not have a lot, depending entirely on who happened to be talking down at the City Meat Market in Giddings, but he had his land, and God had given him enough, probably as much as he deserved, and, what's more, he possessed a secret so vital, so crucial that others dared not believe it even when he slowly and carefully explained it to them.

Why, he said, a bunch of damn good preachers had made a damn good living for a long damn time sermonizing on the fate of mankind that Reinhardt Richter knew was absolute gospel.

But preachers did not really know the source of their anguish and admonitions.

Reinhardt Richter did.

He had devoted himself to demystifying the strange enigma of those boiling masses of fire and brimstone, bristling with fury and damnation far beneath the crust of the earth. He wasn't interested in the eruptions or the cinder-cone craters left behind when flames and smoke, dust and ash, lava and magma came bursting violently through those fractures and fissures in a great subterranean vault, flowing like molten molasses down the side of a mountain suddenly rising above a crevice on flat ground.

No, he said, others seemed to have a pretty good grasp on whatever geologic explosion happened to be occurring on top of the landscape.

Reinhardt Richter was drawn to the underworld. That was his fate. That was the one lingering circumstance of his life. Hard work. German beer. Harder work. More beer. Couldn't out work him. Couldn't out think him. Couldn't out drink him.

The sum of it all gave him, Richter said, a vast wealth of geologic knowledge unknown to lesser men in the field, and he kept his faith and his studies directed toward places he had never seen and certainly never gone – the deep and hidden sanctuaries far below the earth.

Volcanologists believed there was no way to define an active volcano, which could raise its ugly head in a lifespan ranging from several months to several million years.

Richter knew better.

Volcanoes, he said, never lost their fire, and they were all connected – every last one of them – by an inner linking network of tunnels filled with molten lava that spread throughout the netherworld.

They wormed their way like a maze through the hard-rock recesses of the earth, and together they possessed more energy, more radiation, and certainly more heat than the sun.

Thousands of volcanoes from every corner of the globe were emptying their assorted magma into one great ocean of fire and brimstone that was near enough to the surface of the ground for mankind to reach down and touch it.

Only Reinhardt Richter knew the location. It's there, he said, nodding as astutely as any scholar would.

Where?

He grinned, an old man with an old and wizened grin. In the ground beneath my farm, he said. You can hear them rattle sometimes when the day grows dark.

What?

The gates of hell, he said, and the grin lost its bite.

The howling of the condemned will sometimes keep you awake at night.

His face turned to stone.

Then again, it might have been the beer.

2

*I*t was a battle for hard ground, fought in the devil's chalk by a curious assortment of men who dared to defy those fractured layers of an ancient limestone that impacted the earth far beneath a land that had historically refused to give up its oil, provided any reservoirs of crude did exist in the notorious Austin Chalk.

Major oil companies stayed away. Some had been burned before. Dry holes were a curse of the chalk. Only a small band of independent operators stabbed their drill bits into the vast fields of burnt cotton and brittle peanut vines. They did not have a lot of money. Some said they had even less sense.

Most of them were new to the oil game: Irv Deal, a real estate developer facing the sudden wrath of hard times. Max Williams, a real estate broker watching various and assorted land deals crumble around him. Pat Holloway, a lawyer who operated drilling funds but had never drilled in the devil's chalk. Jimmy Luecke, a highway patrolman who kept law and sometimes order atop land rich with oil. Bill Shuford, right out of college and more interested in finding the next beer joint than his next job. Clayton Williams, the only big-time oilman in the bunch.

They had far more hope than experience, and the Austin Chalk would break them or make them rich. They fought the land, dueled before judges, and battled each other in the field of broken hearts. They spilled more money than blood, but the scars ran deep. For some, the scars would last a lifetime. They drilled toward a confluence of volcanic channels, if Reinhardt Richter had been right, and stopped just short of the howling voices from hell. In time, the howling voices sounded a lot like their own.

●

Max Williams gazed through the dusty windshield of his Chevy Blazer, his eyes scanning the far country as it sprawled defiantly around him. A few rises that passed for hills. Mostly flat. A few trees clustered together here and there, mostly there. Tall grasses burned and wilted by an unforgiving sun. Weathered homesteads, the last known will and testament of stubborn farmers who fought the land, watered the crop rows with their own sweat, were too proud to ever even think about quitting, and considered it a good year if they broke even. Once the fields held cotton, then peanuts, always peanuts, and farmers cursed it and condemned it but could never quite convince themselves to turn it loose.

The land was called worthless by those who plowed it, godforsaken by those who could neither sell it nor live on it, and barren by the few speculators who, with more grit than sense, perhaps, jammed a drill bit down into the ancient layers of Austin Chalk, searching for hidden pools of oil. Then again, Williams thought, maybe the whole bunch of them was wrong. All it would cost him to find out was a little time.

Giddings intrigued him, although, he figured, the town was probably nothing more than some little hole-in-the-wall, dying cluster of decrepit buildings by the side of the road. He had never been there, had never wanted to go, or thought about going.

But Giddings had suddenly become the only place in Texas occupying his every thought. What did Giddings know that no one else in the chalk had learned, he asked himself, and how tightly was the little town holding on to its secret? Could the big chalk well be the gateway to an undiscovered field, or just a one hit wonder.

The Austin Chalk had a lot of those.

The noted geologist Everett DeGolyer had once said, "The greatest single element in all prospecting – past, present, and future – was the man willing to take a chance." He might as well have been talking about Max Williams.

Williams knew there were a lot of places he should be that spring afternoon, and Lee County probably wasn't one of them. He had driven south out of Dallas, letting the hours pass by with the long miles, on a quixotic, maybe even foolhardy, search for a mythical oil well, a *big chalk well*, that he had heard a lot of roughnecks, roustabouts, wildcatters, and geologists talk about, even though they claimed it was a rich orphan in ground that bore the remnants of rusting oil pipe and the wounds of dry holes.

They all possessed the logs, the production reports, the shared research, but most believed that oil only flowed in great amounts from beneath the mythical well, the *big chalk well*. The remaining acreage would only take their money and give them back faint traces of oil. It had happened before. It would happen again. They had, from time to time, simply looked over the mythical well, shook their heads, and quietly driven away. A lot of big dreams had been burned in the chalk and blown like ashes with the wind.

The land simply wasn't worth the trouble, they said. The well was in the chalk, they said. The chalk's cold-blooded. It'll tempt you and lie to you. The chalk will take your money, then turn its back on you. If one well was out there running oil, lost, or misplaced somewhere on the fringe of an out-of-the-way town known as Giddings, it was probably running the only oil in the chalk. A one-in-a-million well, they said. That's all it was. The other scattered holes in the ground were simply holes in the ground. Dry. Empty. Hard enough to break you and your drill bit both. Too deep or too shallow. And there was absolutely no need to regret or worry about the cold cash a man poured into the chalk holes. It wasn't coming back out. Maybe it would spit a little oil at you from time to time, but that was about all, and it was hardly ever anything to speak of, much less take to the bank.

Williams had heard it all before. The oilfield, wherever it might be, was always rampant and often corrupt with gossip, lies, rumors, and hope. A good oil operator, he knew, was someone who could separate fact from fiction and never believe too much in the fiction, no matter how good it sounded, and it almost always sounded good.

●

It had not seemed nearly so promising when a weary Chuck Alcorn drove through the biting wind and dust of a land as dry as the bones of cattle that had fallen victim to a hard drought settling down upon the barren landscape of Lee County.

Chuck Alcorn had a job to do, and his work was never easy, seldom lucrative, and usually a pain in the ass. His was a face well known throughout the oilfield, and company men always dreaded that singular, self-loathing moment when they knew it was time to pick up the phone and call him. His name officially was C. W., but everyone called him Chuck. He was a junior. But nobody cared from which branch of the family tree he had descended. He made his money, what little of it there was, from a various assortment of failures and misfortunes encountered on a rig site. As he always said, "I managed to build the rough edges of my career on the unromantic side of the oil business."

Chuck Alcorn, in the shank of another long, unforgiving day, standing up to his ankles in mud, his face splattered with streaks of oil and grease, thought he would kill for the outside chance of being a genuine, authentic, down-home wildcatter who owned his own oil well or maybe a field full of them. He learned about the intricacies and pitfalls of the business during his early years at Gulf Oil. Simple realities: The rich got richer, and the poor boy operations went busted, and so many of the fields wound up as graveyards for rusting pipe, burned out pumps, empty holes, and hopes gone awry.

By 1973, he owned his own oil well salvage company down in Victoria. However, Chuck Alcorn, it appeared, had never been destined to explore new fields, shoot and read seismographs, track down investors, negotiate with bankers, patch together leases and a drilling crew, and finally search down hole for a pool or a river of crude. He had, more or less, been condemned to the task of buying up old wells and attempting to rejuvenate them with a special treatment that the industry referred to as *acidizing*.

He took the old, the tired, the worn out and tried like hell to make them profitable. A few breathed a little life, but, sooner or later, the dead usually stayed dead.

He was, many believed, the oil business equivalent of a used car dealer.

Sometimes there was a little oil left smoldering in the ground. At a humiliating price of four dollars a barrel, it didn't amount to much. Often more trouble than it was worth. Breaking even was becoming more difficult all the time.

Mostly he merely salvaged the pipe and equipment left abandoned in the field and sold it for scrap or to some little two-bit oil company trying to scrape by and maybe strike it rich with glorified leftovers from Chuck Alcorn's personal junkyard.

●

He was forty years old, had hair turning gray long before its time, and stood six feet, four inches tall. Some of the ladies thought he had a boyish face, and others thought he was downright handsome, and none paid a lot of attention to the oil dirt buried beneath his fingernails.

He was a working man. That's all. A working man with the face of a boy and the hardened eyes of a man who understood the tribulations of disappointment.

Chuck Alcorn could be white collar when he needed to be, even put on a pin-stripe business suit when necessary, but he felt more at home in his khaki shirt, khaki pants, and brown cowboy boots, usually crusted with dried mud. In the field, he wore a battered cowboy hat with a narrow, curled brim and drove a four-door Ford pickup truck. Good on the road, off the road, in cow pastures, from one creek bank to another, and into terrain where only the brave dared to go and only the lucky came back out again with their sanity intact. Pot holes. Chug holes. Post holes. Didn't matter. Chuck Alcorn, sooner or later, drove across them all.

It was not the best of days, growing dark, and the sun hadn't even set. Chilly even for October. And the clouds above the narrow Lee County road were gray and beginning to turn black, fringed with shades of purple, and full of wind. He waited for the rains to fall and figured he wouldn't have to wait long. Chuck Alcorn was the son of an independent drilling contractor, a third generation interloper in the Texas oil patch. He had graduated from The University of Texas with a degree in geology, dutifully paying for his education by working long hours as a roughneck during the summer months.

Chuck Alcorn remained a fixture in the oilfield even when times grew hard and virtually impossible for men who hitched their dreams and borrowed money to a frayed hole in the ground. He watched the world around him become glutted with foreign oil. He saw the price of crude tumble to four dollars a barrel and sensed a serious shift in the economy for the worst, always the worst, when drilling activity sank to a twenty-year low. Major oil companies were re-thinking their long-range strategies and casting their hopes and a bulk of their dwindling finances on offshore drilling, content to sell their onshore operations for pennies on the dollar and suffer the losses and the consequences.

Work was difficult to find. New and old fields alike were dying for lack of funds, lack of interest, lack of gumption. A man might be willing to gamble, but only as long as he still had a few chips left to wager. The only difference between a wildcatter and a bum was the number of empty beer bottles sitting on the table in front of him. The wildcatter didn't have any.

Chuck Alcorn was grateful for any scrap of salvage business that came his way. Someone had drilled on promise and potential. Someone had gone broke. Dry hole. Disappointing hole. The money ran short. The money ran out.

The phone call came. The well would be his baby now, provided he wanted it, and Chuck Alcorn hated to ever say he didn't. Some of the wells he bought outright. Some he bought on credit, hoping to turn a profit before the note came due. Some he bought so low he felt like he had stolen them.

In some, the oil was so scarce he felt as though he had been swindled. No time to fret. No reason to worry. All in a day's work. Chuck Alcorn understood simple realities. He hadn't lost the dream. He still wanted an oil well. Any well. Any place. As long as it kept on producing. He wasn't a greedy man. One good well just might be enough, although enough was never enough in the oil patch where, during tough times, a man could run out of money and friends at about the same time.

That was the reason why Chuck Alcorn was heading in the general direction of Giddings on such a dreary afternoon. He turned on the radio in his pickup truck, and, amongst the static, the news kept spitting out bursts of information about the Israeli and Arab war. Deadly. Brutal. Frightening consequences. Only the Good Lord had any idea about what the conflict might do to the oil business, which was already hanging on with broken fingernails. Chuck Alcorn shook his head. The business had always been a sordid kind of gamble where men bet their lives, their fortunes, their futures on a stacked deck. Now he had begun to wonder if there was anyone left who could afford the ante. A pair of deuces in a game of two-handed poker was no hand at all.

Chuck Alcorn passed the rolling hills, the hardwood timber stands, the grazing cattle, the peanut fields that needed the rain a lot more than he did. The oilfield business was difficult enough dry. Wet, it could be a nightmare unless, of course, it was wet with oil. Early that morning, his tool pusher, Alfred Baros, had called to let him know that the Halliburton crew he had hired was on site and getting ready to pump acid down the gullet of the old City of Giddings No. 1 that afternoon. The well, for better or worse, now belonged to Chuck Alcorn, lock, stock, and barrel. He had already spent as much money as the salvage was worth. Good money. Maybe even good money after bad. Did he have any interest in driving up and seeing for himself whether or not a heavy dose of acidized mud could awaken the last, best, and probably only hope in the Giddings field?

"What do you think?" Alcorn asked.

"Might be pretty good."

"It's in the chalk."

"They think it has a little promise."

"Oil?"

"No, just a little promise."

Chuck Alcorn laughed and didn't know why.

"The chalk's fickle."

"It blew a lot of oil before."

"Maybe she spit out all she's had, and there's nothing left."

"I got a good feeling about this one."
"The chalk will lie to you."
"Today might be different."

●

Chuck Alcorn grinned. In the oil business, every day was always different. Good, maybe. Bad, perhaps. But always different. In recent months, however, the bad days had far outnumbered the good ones, and he had no reason to raise his expectations about the drive to Giddings. So often, the bottom of the hole revealed little more than the bottom of a hole. The task awaiting him was, at best, just another routine salvage job. Another day. Another dollar. Nothing more. Probably less.

The City of Giddings well had been drilled in the dastardly Austin Chalk Trend back in 1960 by Union Producing Company, which in time, would find itself as a branch of Pennzoil. Union Producing had discovered far too quickly that the Austin Chalk was a breaker, the kind that drove sane men mad and mad men to ruin. It broke bits. It broke spirits. It broke men. It broke bank accounts. It broke hearts. Lots of hearts.

The chalk trend was a great underground formation extending up from Mexico, spreading across South Texas, and spilling down toward the gulf coast of Louisiana. For eons, it had remained there untouched, a fine-grained limestone and calcite crystal cast containing fossilized shells of microscopic foraminifers, mollusks, echinoids, and other marine organic debris, some of it, perhaps, even left behind by the great flood. The Upper Cretaceous Austin Chalk sprawling beneath Giddings was renowned and roundly cursed for being a foreboding and demanding formation, at least a hundred feet thick beneath Burleson County and layered more than eight-hundred-feet thick in places below Lee County – a buffer between the peanut farms, the ranch lands, and old Reinhardt Richter's chambers of hell.

The gardens of chalk confronted and confounded oilmen with a proposition that only the devil could have devised. They knew the trend encased great amounts of oil, but the chalk was a tight formation, the oil trapped in the dense rock. It was a limestone beast interwoven with elusive fractures that if found and penetrated would allow the crude to travel to the wellbore. No fractures. No oil. No production.

When Union Producing Company decided to take a chance with the chalk, its geologists had no magic bullet to pinpoint those cracks. Finding oil was little different from tracking down the proverbial needle in a haystack. How many fractures were there? How far apart were they? How deep did they go? And how large were they? The size of a boxcar or the eye of a needle?

The wildcatter going straight down with a vertical well knew he was drilling blind. Far too often, a well had a habit of coming in with a bang and soon going out with a whimper.

On that fateful afternoon in 1960, the City of Giddings No. 1, in fact, had erupted with a hundred barrels of oil a day, indicating that it could make a fair amount of natural gas as well. Union Producing was ecstatic. The company egotistically believed that it had obviously cracked the code of the chalk.

Two other wells, however, were hastily drilled in the southern acreage of Lee County, but their production had been marginal at best. The oil making its way to the top was worth a great deal less than the cost of a drill bit going down.

●

The cranky City of Giddings well, on the other hand, had all the significant signs of becoming a big winner in a field littered with losses. A hundred barrels a day seemed like the mother lode of the chalk, and, even more intriguing, the oil flowing to the surface had a much different color and consistency from the raw crude that had risen reluctantly from the depths of Union Producing's Preuss No. 1 and Jenke wells. It wasn't black and full of tar. Not this oil. Not this time. It was lighter and bore a distinctive hint of gold. It was, the drilling crew agreed without argument, the rich color of honey.

They shook hands, slapped each other on the back, shared a drink or two of hard whiskey in a bar outside of Giddings, and went to sleep that night with visions of riches far greater than any of them had imagined.

Disaster descended upon the cursed gardens of chalk almost immediately. Union Producing killed the flow of the City of Giddings well so that its crew would be able to remove the drilling rig and install the proper production equipment. It was time-honored, and time-approved standard operating procedure. The hole was dutifully plugged with several thousand gallons of drilling mud.

Nothing unusual about that. The crew had done the procedure at least a hundred times before, maybe more. Finally, as the day neared an end, the mud pack was punctured, and the crew waited for production to begin.

But something was wrong. Dreadfully wrong. The flow was sluggish, with oil reaching the surface at a much slower rate than it had before, falling far short of a hundred barrels a day. The well had barely been born, and already it lay dying.

No gusher. No hole full of riches. Just a hole.

In desperation, a pump jack was quickly installed, but the City of Giddings well was only coughing up five barrels a day, ten barrels if the crew got lucky, and luck had always been a stranger in the gardens of chalk. The mother had lost its lode.

The Crew was baffled. Union Producing was devastated. It had looked so good for such a short period of time, then production faded away like a candle's flame in a wet summer wind. Saner heads searched for an explanation. That's just the chalk, they said. Promises you the world. Doesn't give you a doggone thing. Makes your heart race. Then breaks it. The chalk is a lying sonuvabitch. There are more oilmen than rocks busted around here.

It was easy for Union Producing to blame the chalk. Everybody blamed the damnable old chalk. It was tricky. It was fraught with frustrations. Drilling through those tightly laced layers was no different from driving a ten-penny nail through a concrete block.

The Austin Chalk that held the City of Giddings well was eight hundred feet thick, but a crew was forced to drill down somewhere between eight to nine thousand feet to even reach it. And down below, in the great, unknown stratum of cracked and fossilized limestone, near Reinhardt Richter's personal chambers of hell, the oil was trapped and locked tight inside a maze of faults.

The chalk may have been saturated with oil – everyone knew it was – and the oil had a history of spilling out into fractures both large and small, mostly small, but few had managed to locate enough porosity and permeability in the limestone to pull a big payday's worth of crude to the surface,

Still, the chalk continued to tempt and taunt those wildcatters who were tough enough, determined enough, or sometimes drunk enough to think they could find their way down to vast and uncharted caverns of oil.

The caverns, the reservoirs, the great pools of oil had never been there, but, in the beginning, no one knew it.

They only hoped, which was a precarious, unstable way to do business. Only independent oilmen, the little guys in the business, dared to defy the chalk. They were poor boy operators, drilling on a shoestring, not much to invest. Not much to lose. A few had lost it all before anyway.

The major oil companies had long ago washed their hands of the Austin chalk fields. Maybe there was oil in the ground. Maybe not. But it was certainly too costly for them to haul a crew out to Giddings and find out.

●

Wildcatters, searching for unknown and undeveloped fields, had ventured out into the chalk back during the 1930s. They possessed no maps, few, if any, seismographs to read, and attached their hopes to geologists who had never been able to understand the chalk or decipher the fractures. The boom struck South and Central Texas hard, although the term "boom" might be somewhat misleading.

The wells came in with all the fury of a Roman candle and quickly fizzled out. No one, not even the learned scholars of geology and petroleum engineering, could figure out why the wells kept acting in such a strange and mischievous manner.

Give a little. Take it back. A few barrels. A few drops. And the wells rapidly lapsed back into a coma.

After battling the sun-baked farmlands for far too many months, the weary and slump-shouldered oilmen all came to the same final and basic conclusion. The Austin Chalk bled a little oil from time to time, but there wasn't enough crude in the ground to fill a good-sized wheelbarrow. They turned their backs on the good earth surrounding

Giddings and drove away. They ignored the field, but none of them ever forgot it.

What Union Producing decided it was willing to sell Chuck Alcorn in 1972, officials said, were "two old chalk dogs," which was the term they used to describe the Preuss and City of Giddings wells. It was all worthless property to them.

Maybe Alcorn could sell the scrap metal for enough money to make it worth his while. Maybe not. Union Producing did not care one way or another. The company had already invested the last dollar it ever wanted to spend in the chalk, and it was willing to accept a check, cash, or money order for $27,500, an amount they figured just about covered the salvage value of the abandoned production equipment they had left behind.

Let Chuck Alcorn ante up a few dollars, then see if he could somehow manage to turn a profit, even a small one, while inheriting the headaches that went with the territory. Hell, he was used to it.

Chuck Alcorn, however, had a far different idea rattling around in his mind. He had hired a Halliburton crew to pump as much as ten thousand gallons of hydrochloric acid down the holes and shock the wells in an effort to kick-start production. Just maybe the acid would be able to clean out some of the crevices and fractures in the rock, giving the oil more room to push its way to the top. Sometimes it worked. Sometimes it didn't. But, Lord, if he was just able to coax another twenty or thirty barrels of oil a day out of the ground, Chuck Alcorn would indeed be a happy man. Not rich, perhaps. But happy.

He glanced briefly at the four-sided clock tower atop the red brick Lee County Courthouse as he drove through downtown Giddings, heading south on U.S. 77 and leaving behind a little community of twenty-five hundred hard-working, God-fearing, straight-laced souls, most of them German Lutherans.

Before the day came to an end, he would ignite the process that, in time, would change his life and their lives forever. He turned off onto FM 448 and bounced his way steadily toward the old Giddings Airport property. A gravel road finally led him to the well, and he witnessed an odd and curious sight, almost surreal in nature, unfolding before him.

His red trailer, loaded down with a well-worn workover rig, had been backed in alongside the old Union Producing pump jack, still in place, but its silver paint, streaked and fading, was beginning to show the wear and tear of weather and time. The head of the embattled pump jack, for some reason, had been sheared off, and it lay in a clump of weeds like a decapitated old warhorse that had been slain, left unburied, and forgotten. Closer to the rig itself sat Halliburton's "Big Red" pumping unit truck and transport trailer, both being prepared for another standard light acid job. A lot of mud. A little acid. A little sweat. A short turn around. Wouldn't take long, and the crew would be back on the road and headed again toward Houston long before darkness descended on the gardens of chalk.

Chuck Alcorn frowned. The hookup at the wellhead bothered him. There wasn't anything particularly normal about it. The nipple valve did not dangle just a foot or two off the drilling platform floor as it should have. The damn thing was hanging at least ten good feet in the air, and the flexible steel acid hose curled out of it like the long, coiled stem of an ancient Oriental pipe, the kind used to smoke tobacco and sometimes marijuana, if one were so inclined.

Chuck Alcorn opened the door of the pickup truck and stepped out. A cool wind crept across the empty prairie and kicked up dust against his boots. The sudden, ominous sound of metal clanging against each other startled him. He jerked his head around, and his gaze swept swiftly across the well site. Trouble made its own peculiar brand of noise, and he had heard trouble rumbling his way before. That was the oil business, the nature of the beast. Hope for the best. Expect the worst.

The ground-level flow lines that connected the well to the storage tanks were shaking violently, threatening to tear themselves loose at any moment. The cylindrical separator unit was flaring gas, rocking with turbulence back and forth, looking and sounding for all the world like the beginning of a small war.

Chuck Alcorn had no idea what was going through the lines. But he knew it was moving with a powerful force. Hang on, he thought. Don't let it get away from you. Ride it out. Volcanoes had erupted with less intensity. He watched as his tool pusher leaped from the rig and rushed toward him. "What's wrong?" Chuck Alcorn asked.

"You ain't gonna believe it," Alfred Baros said, his breath coming in short bursts.

"Ain't gonna believe what?"

"That dadgummed thing is flowing with fifteen hundred pounds of pressure."

Chuck Alcorn ran to toward the derrick, climbing up the metal arms of the rig so he could read the gauge at the top of the nipple valve, trapped in the air far higher than it should have been. Sure enough, he discovered, the well was flowing with fifteen hundred pounds per square inch, an enormous and extraordinary amount of pressure. Chuck Alcorn held on and prayed the well wouldn't blow with him still hanging on the rim of the derrick.

●

If Chuck Alcorn had expected a great plume of oil to burst from the earth and come roaring through the top of the crown, he was sorely disappointed. Instead, the City of Giddings well merely delivered a massive overdose of crude. It wasn't sticky. It wasn't black. It was free of tar. It had less viscosity and possessed a higher gravity than black oil. A spray of oil bathed his hands, and he slowly shook his head, muttering to himself, it's the honey-colored oil. Damn, if it's not the honey-colored oil. Just like the crude that Union Producing had found and lost.

If the hole was dry then, it certainly wasn't now. And the golden oil was almost good enough to pump straight into his Ford Pickup without ever having to go through the rigors of a refinery.

By the time Chuck Alcorn crawled down from the derrick and jumped off the rig floor, the storage tanks had already collected forty barrels of oil, and, as near as anyone could figure, the City of Giddings well would deliver more than three hundred barrels before the day shut down on them.

Chuck Alcorn laughed out loud. Sonuvabitch, he thought, it hadn't been an old chalk dog after all. His wallet didn't feel nearly as empty as it had been. He had wanted a producing well. Now, from all outward appearances, he had himself one.

"We've got a problem," Alfred Baros told him.

"Doesn't look like a problem to me."

"The well came in a whole lot quicker than we thought it would," Baros said. "And it came in strong, as strong as a straight flush. Nobody expected this to happen. Not in a million years, we didn't. I'm afraid the crew didn't have time to remove the acid hose and install our production equipment."

"So what are you telling me?"

"It looks like we'll have to kill the well so they'll be able to go back in and rig up the equipment like it's supposed to be."

Chuck Alcorn frowned. His face hardened. He glanced back at the oil flowing wildly into the storage tank. "You'll have to kill me first," he said.

Union Producing had made a fatal mistake in shutting down the flow in 1960 and virtually ruining the oil well. Even then, a basic, hand-me-down superstition held by old wildcatters hung heavy over the City of Giddings well. For decades they had said, based on their own experiences, never kill an Austin chalk well because it'll never come back.

The chalk is too unpredictable, too treacherous. If you get lucky, leave well enough alone. If you get the oil flowing, don't mess with it. Chuck Alcorn had no reason to tempt fate. He would not make the same tactical error that Union Producing had made a dozen years earlier. "Leave everything the way it is," he told Baros.

Chuck Alcorn realized immediately that the valve and hose connection was not right for producing oil. Hell, it probably wasn't even safe if he left it the way it was for too long. There was even a real danger of the hose suddenly coming loose and spraying a frenzy of uncontrollable oil all over the place, triggering a gusher that could drown them or burn them alive if it caught fire. Chuck Alcorn squared his shoulders and sighed. That, he decided, was a risk well worth taking. He had a well. A damn fine well. He did not want to lose it.

●

During his two decades in the business, Chuck Alcorn had always been highly skeptical of the Austin Chalk. He had heard tales of untold riches flowing like quicksilver from the depths of the limestone. Hard to grasp. Harder to hold. Gone before you knew it was leaving. Had he beaten the chalk? Or was the chalk merely setting him up for failure at another time and in another place? Chuck Alcorn wasn't sure exactly what he had or what, if anything, he might find next.

Within days, he gave in to his better judgment, knew he was probably making a serious, perhaps fatal, mistake, and temporarily shut down the City of Giddings well. He didn't have mud pumped down the hole. Instead, he used a special freezing process to stop the flow, a daring move that gave him the time he needed to gingerly remove the workover rig and hook up production equipment that wasn't nearly so hazardous. The nipple valve was still dangling precariously above him, but Chuck Alcorn was far too superstitious to think about lowering it. That's where it was hanging when the oil came rushing in. That's where it would remain.

He built a metal tower around the pipe, then implemented steel hose to connect the valve to the flow lines on the ground. Unorthodox, perhaps, but it had not been the first time that Chuck Alcorn had to dredge up the hand-me-down skills of a backyard, shade-tree mechanic in a desperate attempt to resuscitate or rescue a well. There was no blueprint for his plan. Just a gut feeling, and gut feelings didn't always pay off.

Chuck Alcorn stepped back, squared his shoulders, and waited, as nervous, he said, as a frog in a hot skillet. He nodded. Alfred Baros turned the valve. Nothing at first, then oil began to flow again. He had met the chalk on its own terms, and, at least for the moment, he breathed the rarified air of a survivor.

And there it would sit, an orphan well, nothing around it but parched and empty land, a one-of-a-kind well, producing more than three hundred barrels of oil a day, every day, week after week, year after year, as regular as clockwork. Reliable. Dependable. Old Faithful. For Chuck Alcorn, it seemed to have an endless supply of oil coming out of a bottomless pit, the honey-colored residue, perhaps, from Reinhardt Richter's chambers of a volcanic hell. Defying the odds. Defying the chalk. Chuck Alcorn grinned every time he thought about it. Owning the big well was better than owning the bank. *The big well. The big chalk well.* Just sitting all alone out in the middle of nowhere, hovering over the gates of hell, producing one barrel after another and waiting for Max Williams to find it.

3

Max Williams had been, for as long as he could remember, a man unafraid to take risks – but cautious and calculated in the risks he took. He was an athlete, a wizard with a basketball, a three-time All-Southwest Conference point guard under the guidance of the legendary Doc Hayes at SMU. He had been the man working behind the scenes to raise the money necessary to bring professional basketball to Dallas. He had worked to build a successful franchise for the Dallas Chaparrals in the old red, white, and blue basketball days of the ABA. He had won big in the Dallas real estate market during the furious and fortuitous dirt-dealing days of the early 1970s, then watched as a sudden and unexpected economic downturn snatched the fortunes away from them all as quickly as the shadows of a black Texas thunderhead turned to night. No dusk. No lingering shades of daylight. No hint or even the promise of a full moon. Just darkness. Out of nowhere. Darkness. Pure, unadulterated darkness.

But black was the color of oil, and Max Williams did not hesitate to change gears in either his life or his business. For him, good, raw land had always been the promise. He had sold the top of it and watched developers raise tall buildings, shopping centers, and home estates on dirt that had been transformed from five thousand dollars an acre to a hundred grand for the same patch of dirt. He had decided that he might as well find out what lay far beneath the surface of the good earth. As he often thought, if you want to make real money, you have to get into a business where the money is.

For all practical purposes, the nation, if you believed what you read, might be operating on the gold standard. In reality, however, the good, old U.S. of A. was running on the oil standard. Oil just happened to be where the gold was.

●

Before leaving Dallas, Williams had placed a Texas map across his desk and began tracking the highways and farm roads that crisscrossed their way like a broken spider's web through the sprawling landscape east of Austin.

The collection of towns seemed to be scattered and plentiful, small and smaller. Just dots on the map. He circled each of them. *Taylor. Rockdale. Elgin. Bastrop. LaGrange. Lexington. Serbin. Caldwell. Somerville. Dime Box. Fedor. Giddings.*

There it was. Didn't look like much on the map. The key said it had a little over two thousand people, probably with as many tractors as cars, and he doubted if any of them had been affected by either oil or wealth. Williams leaned back and closed his eyes, letting his thoughts ramble from Dallas to a town blessed, for whatever reason, with a *big chalk well.*

It had no business being there, not in the chalk anyway.

Something, he thought, wasn't quite right. Then again, maybe some poor boy operator in Giddings had beaten the odds and finally gotten it right. Driving seven hours south on a gut hunch was crazy. It might be a wild goose chase, the longest of long shots. But he would never know unless he found out for himself.

Max Williams shrugged and reached for the keys to his Blazer. Six hours later, he found himself driving south, some nine thousand feet above the gardens of chalk, easing softly across a parched and dying landscape that seldom ever felt the cool perspiration of rain on the furrows of its farmlands.

He still looked like the athlete he had always been. He was in his mid-thirties. His crew cut had long ago begun to thin on top. He wore denim jeans and boots, mostly a gentle smile and never a scowl. Williams thought a man played the game for only one reason, and that was to win, whether he was in business or the sporting arena. Moral victories didn't count. Losses were unacceptable.

He had drilled a little down in the rigid limestone formations of the Frio County oilfield, and the scoreboard had shown mixed results. Won a few. Broke even on a few. Found a little oil but not nearly enough of it. The gamble wasn't particularly bad, but he had definitely not been able to exceed his expectations. The Austin Chalk was a cruel and foreboding opponent even when everything went perfect, and it hardly ever did.

Around him, across unbroken pasturelands, scattered herds of cattle grazed on scattered patches of grass. Peanuts fought to survive in soil where stunted cotton had once withered and perished. Aging farmhouses and weathered barns sat back on the rocky knolls beneath stands of post and blackjack oak, pecan, elm, and mesquite trees. Blackberry vines lined the ditches beside barbed wire fences. The sun bore down harshly on the road, and the heat rose up in dizzying waves above the clay and sand that, more or less, held Lee County together. The winds tortured the earth like a furnace whose coals were smoldering embers.

He crossed Yegua Creek and headed toward Giddings, his eyes scanning the horizon for anything that might resemble the near or distant presence of oil. A derrick. A pump jack. A stack of pipe. A rig. A tank. A truck stained the color of crude.

Max Williams adjusted his sunglasses and stared down an empty road. It appeared to him that he could well be the only living soul around, not counting the cattle, the goats, the coyotes, or the turkey vultures hanging on a power line. Williams wasn't quite sure what he was searching for or exactly where it might be located, but he had been told that somewhere out there within the near reaches of the town limits was *the big chalk well,* the damndest well any of them had ever heard about. If the rumors were right, the well sat upon an uncharted and unforgiving field that had broken the hearts and emptied the pocket books of wildcatters for generations.

All alone, it sat. A single well. The one-in-a-million well. Remote. Isolated. An orphan. If he could track down *the big chalk well*, Max Williams reasoned, he might be able to drill another one just like it, provided, of course, he could raise the funds and there was any oil encased in the thick, unyielding creases of the Austin Chalk.

Geologists swore there was. Geologists said the chalk was rife with oil. But geologists, at least the smart ones, never spent their hard-earned money to drill and find out. A few wildcatters, too stubborn to listen to reason, had discovered just enough crude to tempt them, taunt them, and condemn their worthless souls to wander an oil patch perched just on the sane side of purgatory. The oil struck with fury, then, a few days later, barely leaked out of the hole in the chalk. A promise. A disappointment. A lie. The great lie. Max Williams was undeterred. He no longer had any interest in Dallas real estate ventures. Those days had passed him by. Those days were dead. The market had cured him.

But there were investors still around in the financial shadows who understood the burgeoning potential of the oil business. Well, perhaps they did not really understand the complex, complicated, and unpredictable inner workings of mapping anomalies and anticlines beneath the ground with odd little voodoo boxes and drilling an oil well.

But, make no mistake, they were quite aware of the riches that could be attained by coaxing crude by the barrel from the holy inner sanctum of the earth. And they liked the *gamble.*

No. They were obsessed with the *gamble.* The roll of the loaded dice. The turn of a roulette wheel, which was little different from the rotation of a drill bit down amidst the final resting place of the dinosaur. Deep sand. Shallow sand. Quicksand. Mud. Clay. Rock. And the devil's own, the Austin Chalk.

The chalk just might be the death of them all. It was all the same. That final spin of the wheel, that final six-figure bet, always triggered within them a greater sense of exhilarating fear than those first coins on a poker table. But that last dollar, good or bad, was the only one remembered. But then again, it was only money.

●

There were many sane and rational economic speculators who argued that oil, at least in the vast undiscovered, untapped Texas fields, just might be the safest bet left on the board.

The ages-old conflict between Israel and Egypt had abruptly spilled over into war. Egypt had been the aggressor. Israel struck back, swiftly and with dead certainty.

The Arabs blamed the West for building Israel's military power and, in retaliation, began slowly tightening the screws on production throughout their massive oil domains.

The Organization of the Petroleum Exporting Countries, better known as OPEC, announced an immediate five percent cut in October of 1973, promising that additional cuts would be made each month until Israel again retreated back inside its 1967 border.

The cartel also implemented an embargo on oil shipments to the United States and the Netherlands. Oil dependent nations felt the sharp and sudden pain of an energy crisis, driving them closer to the precipice of chaos and even panic.

Texas was unshaken. But then, as an oilman said over a short glass of Chivas and ice one night, what's best for the rest of the nation is good for Texas.

The price of crude had been ratcheted up from three dollars a barrel to ten dollars a barrel, and wildcatters turned their eyes and their rigs toward great unknown reservoirs of oil which, according to rumors, were still untouched beneath the raw lands of a state that boasted a single white star in its flag.

Sure, oil had its risks. Sure, there were no guarantees. Pocket change was made from guarantees. Real wealth came from real risks. Win some. Lose some. That was their motto and, for many, the dictates of their religion. Just make sure, they said, you win a few more than you lose. It was, they knew, the difference between sipping champagne and draining a warm beer.

●

Max Williams gently tapped the brakes of his Blazer as he eased into downtown Giddings, dissected sharply by the crossing of Highway 290, which connected Austin to Houston, and Highway 77, which connected somewhere north with somewhere south and not much to speak of in between, including Giddings. The past had not deserted the town. The past had never left at all.

Giddings looked much as it had in the 1950s when it looked much as it had in the 1930s. Not a lot had changed except the license plates, the red light hanging above the intersection and, of course, the price of barbecued ribs. Giddings was a typical small-town Texas farming community, a down-home concoction of pickup trucks, gimme caps, cowboy hats, tobacco cans stuffed in the back pocket of patched and faded denim jeans, and frayed overalls, bleached by the sun. Stooped shoulders. Hard eyes. Square jaws. Boots shuffling along the edge of a dusty street. Backbones that were gun barrel straight. Burnt, rawboned faces that bore the unmistakable scars of long hours and hard work in the glare of the blistering heat.

Driving past them, as they walked along the sidewalk, Max Williams could not tell the rich from the poor if, perhaps, there was any difference between the two. They all looked alike and dressed alike, and a few could hit a moving cat at twenty-five paces with a well-timed spit of tobacco juice.

Giddings may not have been dying, but decay had set in, and its farmers were too worried about today to be concerned with tomorrow or, God forbid, any day beyond that. They were the salt of the earth, the roots of Lee County, the sweaters. They sweated over the price of hogs and cattle. They sweated over their peanut crops. They sweated over the lack of rain that condemned their crops and the hailstones that ruined them. They sweated over the cost of a second-hand pickup truck, a tractor that had plowed its last field and burned out its last engine, a water well gone dry, and another business closing its doors. Sweat and work. Sweat and worry. That was pretty much all they did. In Giddings, there was enough sweat to go around for them all.

A highway stretched out belly flat in all four directions, straight lines and main lines across the gardens of chalk. Max Williams glanced ahead, then into his rearview mirror, and only an occasional oak or pecan tree blocked his line of sight. No derrick. No rig. No stack of pipe. No truck stained the color of crude. Surely, he thought, the reliable and unreliable sources hadn't all been wrong or mistaken. Those unregulated rumors passed along in the cafes and bars of Frio County described a *big chalk* well in terms usually reserved for rainbows and pots of gold.

Were all of them talking about the same well? Was one real and one a myth? Which one had been drilled below the rocky landscape of Giddings? Or would the big chalk well turn out to be a myth, too?

The big well.

If it were as good, as predictable, as productive as the report indicated it was, *the big well* could change his luck and his fortune. Max Williams was sure of it.

But where in hell was it?

And what was the well of the world doing down in the gardens of chalk, out on a God-forsaken patch of ground that hovered above the howling innards of hell itself?

4

*G*iddings looked for all the world like a ghost town that had not yet given up the ghost when Max Williams turned beside the City Meat Market and drove slowly past a row of old brick buildings, heavily weathered with age, the proud and stoic remains of an earlier century, a faded collection of brick portraits from better days when the town had a soda water bottling works, a couple of mills, a creamery, a blacksmith shop, and a processing plant that shipped out untold carloads of turkeys each year. Railroads came roaring through Giddings from all directions, but by the 1960s, they no longer had any reason to stop and left the remnants of three grand old depots decayed and dying in their wake. The downtown economy took it hard and had never quite recovered. About all the Chamber of Commerce ever dared to brag about was being the home of the oldest peanut company in Texas. Not much, perhaps. But better than nothing.

Casting a broad shadow over Giddings was the Romanesque Revival Lee County Courthouse, fashioned from red brick, laced with white sandstone, and featuring corner porches held in place by great blue granite columns. It was an architectural masterpiece of James

Riely Gordon, who had acquired a growing reputation for designing grand and grandiose courthouses throughout Texas.

Based on his traditional cruciform plan, it had been his intention, he said, to give the structure lines similar to those found in the New York State Capitol and in several buildings on the campus of Harvard University.

James Riely Gordon, after all, had become a man of national stature, acclaimed for his work as the supervising architect for the famed U. S. Treasury in Washington D. C. His Lee County center for county government had been created with an exceptional sense of drama and theater, critics said, even though it was an anomaly that in no way reflected the homespun, hardscrabble character of a hard-working region that had little money and absolutely no pretense at all.

In reality, the regal building had been created to replace the first courthouse, destroyed by fire in 1879 because firefighters did not have ladders tall enough to reach the upper floors of a structure engulfed by flames. They did what they could to rescue important papers from the shelves but watched as the blaze left their symbol of government in ashes.

Like the original, however, the new Lee County Courthouse rose up above Giddings on the top of a divide separating the Colorado and Brazos River Basins. In its yard was the giant Courthouse live oak tree, whose limbs were used, the law said, to hang anybody who needed hanging.

The town had been named for the prosperous and influential Jabez Deming Giddings, who taught school, practiced law, served as the district clerk, established the first bank in Brenham, and was instrumental in building the Houston and Texas Central Railroad. His brother Giles had marched into battle with General Sam Houston at San Jacinto, and on the eve of the final and fateful attack, he wrote his family:

I was born in a land of freedom. And rather than to be driven out of the country, I may leave my bones to bleach on the plains of Texas. If I fall, you will have the satisfaction that your son died for the rights of men ... If I should see you no more, remember Giles still loves you.

As the smoke of battle blackened the field, he fell mortally wounded, dying a few days later.

General Houston decreed that every soldier taking part in the routing of Santa Ana's Mexican army would receive a league of Texas land. Jabez Deming Giddings, with a heavy heart, took the league his brother had bought with blood and staked his claim on land just south of the Brazos River bottom. Around him would grow the communities of Serbin, Dime Box, Fedor, Evergreen, Lexington, and, of course, Giddings.

In time, a syndicate from Houston, headed by William Marsh Rice, who gave his name and his money to build the foundation for Rice University, purchased the entire township and methodically began selling off town lots to the pioneer Anglo-Saxon, German, Norwegian, Czech, Hispanic, African American, and Wendish Lutheran families who had fled their past of social unrest and were betting their hopes on the beckoning farmlands rolling without end on both sides of the east, middle, and west branches of Yegua Creek.

The Wends even went so far as to establish a respected German-language newspaper, named *Giddings Deutsches Volksblatt*, and build a Serbin church that held closely to Old World traditions. Men gathered in the balcony, and women sat with their children on the downstairs pews. The pulpit, however, was located on the balcony level. Men received the full brunt of the sermon, and wives heard only those sanctified words that fell to the bottom floor.

The streets of Giddings were a hundred feet wide and lined with a Methodist Church, Masonic Lodge, a saddle and harness shop, the Granger Store, a millinery shop, and, of course, a saloon or two. The town became and remained a farming community, surrounded with cotton fields, with several gins, an opera house, a bank, and a depot built especially for the San Antonio and Aransas Pass Railway. Freed slaves from farms and plantations had pointed their wagons to the sparse region as soon as gunfire from the War Between the States began fading from their memories.

By 1915, as many as two thousand fortunate souls were basking in the glow of an electric light company, and only twenty some odd miles to the north, the town of Lexington had pinned its fragile hopes on a brick kiln, a tomato packing shed, and pickle, butter, and ice cream factories. Commerce had become just about as good as it could possibly get in Lee County.

●

When Max Williams drove through town in the spring of 1976, the population of Giddings still hovered near two thousand, give or take a few old soreheads, some staying, and some just drifting through. Almost forty years earlier, the first parade of wildcatters began venturing into the empty farmlands in search for oil. None of them knew anything about the cursed and defiant Austin Chalk.

Most merely hoped to stumble across a salt dome because common wisdom in the oil patch, handed down for generations, said oil was seldom found anywhere else.

The country was being battered, its resources drained and emptied, by the Great Depression. The price of cotton had dropped from thirty cents to six cents a pound, and some landowners were on the verge of losing everything they had. A lot had already packed up and left, although few had any idea about where they were going or if life would be any better when they arrived. They were merely looking for a job, any job, good or bad, and the chance for employment in Lee County was as futile as the hope for rain. Men and women both earned ninety-cents a day picking cotton, and the good pickers could bring in three hundred pounds by sundown. Long lines of wagons circled the gins, and farmers were beginning to talk about re-plowing their fields with peanuts, grain sorghum, and corn. A few were even running cattle, horses, and hogs. For them, money was scarce and drying up. Rain could make a difference, but the skies had all turned dry. Trees lost their shade, and even the clouds drifted elsewhere for lack of interest.

The ground of Lee County possessed a lot of secrets. It was rumored that a lead mine lay hidden in the earth; a few farmers down in Serbin did sell plenty of lead for bullets during the Civil War. Somewhere on Yegua Creek near Hranice, a Spanish pack train loaded with the gold payroll for forts and missions had been ambushed, and in the face of certain death, a few of the soldiers buried the gold. Only one survived. He never returned. An *R* was said to mark the revered spot where as much as ninety thousand dollars worth of gold had been left behind in a hole stained the color of blood. The hard ground also held the mystery of William P. Longley's bones. An outlaw, a highwayman, a man with a short temper and no regard for those who lived around him, he had been hanged after a jury in Giddings ruled that it did not approve of a renegade guilty of murdering thirty-two men. A crowd of four thousand expectant souls gathered on a misty morning to watch as a Catholic priest chanted a prayer. Longley asked for forgiveness and gave a loud and hardy goodbye as the black hood was slipped over his head. Some said he was buried in the chalk. Others said he had survived the fall from the gallows and had ridden away. They only knew that the sheriff soon left with a pocketful of money and was murdered in Chicago.

The ground of Lee County did indeed possess a lot of secrets. Maybe a reservoir of oil was one of them. At least, that's what the farmers thought during those harsh and unforgiving days of the 1930s. The promise was so bright that Texas Osage, founded as a cooperative royalty pool when the stock market crashed in 1929, came hard into Lee County and began buying up mineral tracts, as many as they could acquire, from the landowners. Bad times loomed on the horizon, and most farmers were willing to sell almost anything they owned for a few extra dollars. They wanted to keep their land if possible. Mineral rights on acreage that had never yielded any minerals were worthless.

Rigs were brought in. Holes were drilled, and this was not an easy drill. A little oil splashed here and there among the crop rows. But most of the holes were dry or soon dry. Wildcatters had come face to face with the Austin Chalk, and they left with a little more wisdom and a lot less money in the bank than when they rode into town to outwit the land. Hard ground. Hard times. Hard luck.

It was shortly after two o'clock in the early afternoon when Max Williams pulled into an Exxon service station. He was looking for oil, low on gas, and lost. Well, he knew where he was. He wasn't quite sure he knew where he was going.

And that's how he met Walter Schneider. "I understand there's a big chalk well around here," Williams said.

Schneider nodded. "I don't just pump gas here at the station," he said. "I also go out and pump that big well for Chuck Alcorn."

"I hear it's pretty good."

"It's the best well we've got around here," Schneider said. "Of course, it's about the only one we have, too. Others went dry, but that old City of Giddings Well, it just keeps right on flowing and hasn't shown any slack yet."

"Can you tell me where it is?"

"South of town." Schneider paused a moment, grinned, and said, with a shrug, "If you can wait awhile, I'll go out there with you. Show you where it's at."

"How long?"

"Won't be but a minute or two."

Max Williams, guided by the directions of Walter Schneider, bounced across the potholes and down the old, narrow country road that led past the rusting, rotting remains of the airport. The terminal had already been torn down. The runway was latticed with dirt and scattered patches of grass, mostly weeds. Planes were landing somewhere else now, coming into a newer airport that had not been sprayed or speckled with old oil.

Through the windshield of his Blazer, Max Williams gazed for the first time at *the big chalk well*. He could barely hide the excitement boiling up inside of him, but he kept his feelings to himself. The well, the one-in-a-million well, wasn't a myth after all. It was pretty much where the rumors said it would be. The scene before him was far different from the one he had imagined. Something wasn't quite right.

Chuck Alcorn had left the tanks overturned and lying on their sides. The rusting rods and old pipes had fallen next to the pumping unit. They remained untouched and undisturbed. Chuck Alcorn had been a superstitious man. He found a fortune at the bottom of an old clunker, and he refused to tempt fate. Nothing had been removed. The well site remained unchanged on a blistered landscape, surrounded with brittle brush stands and strewn with broken collections of rock.

Walter Schneider folded his arms and leaned back in the Blazer. "I hear that she's already made three hundred thousand barrels," he said. "Maybe more. I have no idea how deep or wide the pool is, but that old string of pipe just keeps sitting there and bringing the oil back up. Don't look like she's ever gonna quit."

"Why do you think there aren't any more wells like it around here?" Williams wanted to know.

"It's the chalk." Walter Schneider laughed. "There may be a dozen or so holes in the ground, and some have been here a long time. Nothing worthwhile in any of them. If a well had as much as a thimble full of oil, it's long gone by now."

Max Williams frowned. The field did not make sense to him. "What makes this well so good?" Williams asked.

"Chuck Alcorn – he's the man who figured out how to make it work – is one lucky sonuvabitch," Schneider said. "This field's probably got one good well, and he's found it. Made him a rich man, too. Well, maybe not quite so rich, but he hasn't been worrying about his next meal for some time."

Walter Schneider laughed again. He felt a close and sometimes reverent kinship with the well, too. He kept it pumping, rain or shine, and it kept right on producing, night or day. The City of Giddings No. 1 had not made him a rich man either, but, on payday, it certainly helped ease the pain.

"What's the chance of a man buying up a little lease acreage around here?" Williams asked.

"There's plenty of it available."

"Cheap?"

The grin on Schneider's face broadened. "I doubt if it would cost you a lot," he said. "I just hope you've got a lot of money."

"Why?"

"The chalk's gonna take ever last bit of it," he said.

5

Max Williams had always felt a strong kinship with the great open stretches of unspoiled land that bore few footprints and even fewer traces of civilization. That was an integral part of his West Texas birthright.

He had grown to manhood in the Humble Oil Camp of Avoca, Texas, his face blistered by the sand that dust devils, whirling dervishes, and windstorms raked across the empty, troubled wastelands far below the Caprock. It had been a great time for the oil business, and hard-working families attached their hopes and daily livelihood to a company town that was destined to survive only as long as the pump jacks continued to pull great amounts of crude out of the ground. For a time, the Williams family lived in Guthrie where the high school occupied one room, and Max's sister single-handedly formed the entire fifth grade. No restrooms. No running water. No cafeteria. No gym. Williams always said that if his family had remained in Guthrie, he would probably have been a roper.

Two years later, the family moved back to Avoca, a town too small even to field a six-man football team. Williams would never forget the small community where drifters were treated as neighbors and neighbors like family. Avoca was nestled back amidst a rough-hewn, hard-rock, and mesquite-thorn landscape of scarred beauty and enduring serenity.

It was, he said, a place where common decency and honesty prevailed, where neighbors stuck together whether times were tough or prosperous, where a man's full worth was judged by his character, not by how much money he had or didn't have in the bank.

Max Williams had something of an idyllic childhood. Hard work. Few problems. Didn't have a lot of money, but neither did any other family in the camp or the town. When you don't know anybody who is rich, you don't have any idea who might be poor. During his thirteenth year, however, the carefree world as he had known it suddenly crumbled around him. His father Claude died after a struggle with cancer, and the pleasantries of childhood scattered with the winds across the prairie. His father had been the family anchor, a good man who never bowed nor bent under the weight of hard work, and now he was gone.

The boy, who would become a man long before his allotted time, stood alone in the backyard of his home wearing a T-shirt, faded jeans, and the best $12.95 cowboy boots that money could buy. There was a scarred, leather basketball in his hand, an old hoop hanging ten feet above him, and, even though his heart was breaking, he refused to shed a tear because he had never seen his father cry. As a melancholy sun dropped below the treetops, with a hot wind stinging his face, his jaws clenched and his eyes unflinching, Max Williams shot basket after basket, soft one-handed jump shots, hour after hour, until darkness tumbled down around his shoulders and night brought an uneasy chill but no relief and little comfort. It was a dark and apprehensive time for the Williams family.

His mother Willie Mae, proud, stubborn, and undaunted, took the life insurance money and completed her education, becoming a teacher. His older sister Theresa had always been his best friend, his confidante, and she became his rock when he needed one. She, probably more than anyone, understood the grief boiling down inside him, the grief he kept to himself when his only outlet was hard work, either on a basketball court or in the oilfield.

By age fifteen, Williams was working for farmers during the summer break, and three years later, while waiting on college, he took a job for Humble Oil and Refining Company to help ease the financial burdens shouldered by his mother.

Basketball, however, always basketball, became his salvation and his road out of a lonely town. Randy Galloway wrote in his *Dallas Morning News* column: *Back in the mid-fifties, there was this great basketball player named Max who lived so far out in the West Texas bush that he thought Sweetwater was Dallas. Avoca, forty miles north of Abilene as the tumbleweed blows, was his home court. The town's population was, and is, 150. But for some strange reason, Avoca was once a breeding ground for hoop heads. With the smallest enrollment of any UIL school in the state (only twelve in Max's senior class, including nine boys), this dot on the map was known throughout West Texas as a giant killer. The Mustangs took on the big boys in San Angelo, Abilene, and Fort Worth Poly and drummed them. And this Max, he was something. The son of a widowed schoolteacher, he handled the ball like a transfer student from a New York playground. It was Showtime when Max hit the floor – passes came from behind his back and over the bus. He appeared to prefer dribbling between his legs, and he had that weird one-handed jump shot in an era when the two-handed set was still the only way to put it up.*

Max Williams was the first Texas high-school player to ever be chosen All-State for three consecutive years. He ended his high school career as the all-time leading scorer in Texas schoolboy history, racking up 3,360 points. He led the Avoca Mustangs to a state championship, was voted the Most Valuable Player in the 1956 High School All-Star Game, and became the only Texan to make high school All-American his senior year. There were several occasions when he scored as many as fifty or sixty points in a game, and sometime the long-range bomber personally outscored the other team. Just Max, the ball, and nothing but net.

The Avoca post office had difficulty handling the mail that came pouring in with college scholarship offers from one end of the country to the other. He was, in the eyes of America's great basketball coaches, a wanted man. Max Williams, however, was a good Methodist. That good Methodist University in Dallas, SMU, was coached by Doc Hayes, and Hayes had a well-deserved reputation for building a national basketball power in a conference better known for its football teams. Williams politely told the rest of the coaches, including Kentucky's Adolph Rupp, "Thanks, I'm honored that you wrote me, but no thanks." He had been a Mustang in high school, so he might as well go ahead and play his college ball for the Mustangs as well. Doc Hayes finally made it official by heading down the long, straight-shot road to Avoca and buying Williams a steak dinner. The deal was sealed, medium rare.

On a basketball court, he was a sleight-of-hand magician Here you see the ball. Now you don't. Moves as unpredictable as a sand storm dancing across the prairie lands around his home. He became the biggest gate draw in the Southwest Conference, the point guard, the deadly assassin, whom every coach feared. Couldn't guard him. Could not stop him. If SMU beat you, it was Max Williams coming down the lane with a dagger in his hand. He brought a little razzle and a lot of dazzle to a game that had traditionally relied more on hard-nosed, eyeball-to-eyeball, elbow-in-the-gut defense.

Doc Hayes, his own coach, simply said, "If he were six foot, ten, he'd hit the rafters every time he jumped. He is the most unusual player I ever saw. He has more native ability, he has the quickest reactions, he jumps the highest, he is the cleverest dribbler, and he has more ways of passing the ball than Bob Cousy. I saw Cousy as a senior at Holy Cross, and he couldn't do what Max can do with a basketball. You couldn't change a natural talent like Williams. You just lived with it."

Williams led SMU to a stunning victory over Kentucky and Adolph Rupp when the Wildcats were ranked number one in the nation and destined to win the NCAA championship, then spearheaded wins over Georgia Tech and Vanderbilt, both rated among the country's top ten teams. It was little different from his days at Avoca. The bigger they were, the more he enjoyed cutting them down.

He was called a high-flying Houdini with a basketball, a player who could build two points in mid-air and out of thin air. He was the driving force that helped engineer a Southwest Conference championship. Williams, however, did have one major obstacle confronting him. Size. Or, at least, lack of it. The proud NBA, even then, frowned on ball players who stood less than six feet tall, no matter how high they could jump. Williams quietly put his basketball aside, buckled down, earned a business degree at SMU while taking a class in geology simply because he needed a course in science. Growing up in an oilfield camp, he had more than a passing interest in the ancient earth around him. After graduation, he took a job selling insurance, but detested every minute of it. There must be a better way, he thought, and if there was, Max Williams was determined to find it.

●

Max Williams had no avowed intention of going into business for himself until George Smith met with him one afternoon and offered him a chance to potentially earn a small fortune by importing mercury from the badlands of Mexico. "I'll handle the deal with the miners on the other side of the Rio Grande," Smith said casually, "and you can make arrangements for the sale of the mercury on the United States side of the border."

"Is it legal?" Williams asked.

Smith grinned wryly. "By the time it gets to U.S. customs, it will be," he said.

"It sounds a little like smuggling."

"Don't worry," Smith assured him. "If it wasn't on the up and up, I wouldn't be involved. It's just business. That's all. The United States needs all of the mercury it can get its hands on. Mexico has the mercury to sell. You and I are just the middle men."

George Smith's role was to acquire the mercury. He knew his way around the cinnabar mines of Chihuahua and Sonora. Williams would be responsible for finding the money necessary to pay for the mercury when it reached U.S. customs. There would be as many as three hundred flasks of mercury, and it would all be sold to Associated Metals. Smith and Williams would split the profits. It was a clean and simple deal, and it might go on forever.

But as the months passed, Williams, on a lonely stretch of highway south of San Antonio, decided he was giving up a lot more than he was earning. He was giving away his time in Dallas, time he would never be able to recover during those long days and weeks away from his wife Carolyn, daughter Laura, and son Wayne, who had just entered the first grade. He thought, why have a family if you become a stranger in the house? It was, he knew, the right time to leave. He was driving across those endless miles for the final time. It was just as well. During the Christmas holidays, the cinnabar mines shut down. No more flasks. No more trips to Laredo. He had imported his last flask of mercury. Might as well stay around Dallas and home, which, in retrospect, became a wise decision.

●

In the midst of the holidays, Max Williams received an unexpected phone call from Jim Hammond, who had played basketball with him at SMU. Hammond was working with the All Sports Association of Dallas, and, he said, the organization had a serious interest in pursuing a franchise with the newly created American Basketball Association. Would Max like to investigate the possibility of making such a project a reality? Williams grinned. Might as well, he thought. He knew a lot more about basketball than mercury.

Williams telephoned Roland Spaeth, whose brother had originated the ABA and who was on the road, desperately seeking to secure new franchises. Yes, he said, Dallas was definitely on the list of potential cities. Yes, he would be happy to fly to Dallas and outline the league's strategy for moving forward.

All Dallas needed to do, Spaeth said at a clandestine meeting in the Chaparral Club, was come up with an investment of three hundred thousand dollars, which, if the league's figures were correct, would certainly be enough money to run a basketball team for a year. Last a season and build for the future. That was the formula, and it did not seem to be a complicated venture. Dallas would need to submit a formal application for a franchise to the league, but, with three hundred thousand dollars in ready cash, how could the ABA turn Dallas down?

Williams immediately made arrangements to meet with Bob Folsom, a good friend and a successful real estate developer, the last four-sport letterman to graduate from SMU. He outlined the plan for obtaining professional basketball. All Dallas had to do was raise three hundred thousand dollars.

Folsom nodded. "We've tried to land a franchise in the past," he said, "and this might be as good a chance as we'll get. Here's what you need to do to get your money. Find thirty guys who'll give you ten thousand dollars apiece." Folsom had raised money before. He continued, "I'll draw up a list of potential investors. You just call them and tell them that I asked you to call. Then tell them what you want and why you want it. These are good men. They'll do anything they can to support Dallas."

Within two weeks, Max Williams had his three hundred thousand dollars, and Dallas had its franchise. If Bob Folsom wanted a deal done, to no one's surprise, it was done. There was, however, one stipulation from those who had handed Williams their ten thousand dollar checks. Bob Folsom would take over as president of the franchise. No vote. No need to vote. No opposition.

Bob Folsom would look after their money.

From day one, it was a struggle. The league didn't have the history, the notoriety, or the fan base of the NBA. It had difficulty signing the nation's top players if any team in the NBA wanted them, and, for the most part, league owners didn't even know who the nation's top players were. Williams spent days on the phone with college coaches scattered across the country, scanning basketball magazines, searching out seniors who might have the potential to play.

He compiled an unofficial list and sent their names – posted from A to Z – to Roland Spaeth, who erroneously thought Max Williams had assembled a scientific draft order with the best player written in first and the worst player penciled in at the bottom.

The Dallas Chaparrals thus drafted names as they appeared in alphabetical order. Matthew Aitch from Michigan was the first name called and Charlie Beasley the second.

The Chaparrals were a week away from their opening game and still didn't have a radio contract. No one had thought about going out and finding one. The general manager and advertising director for KRLD Radio showed up at Williams' office and asked about the possibility of his 50,000-watt, clear channel station broadcasting the games. For Max Williams, it was an under-the-wire godsend.

KRLD, however, expected the Chaparrals to provide their own play-by-play announcer.

Williams turned to Terry Stembridge, who had just signed on to work with him in the business office. In the back of his mind, Williams remembered that the young man had previously broadcast Kilgore High School and Kilgore College basketball games. Was pretty good at it, too. He had heard the tapes. Williams leaned back in the chair behind his desk and told Stembridge, "You're it."

"I'm what?"

"Our radio voice."

Terry Stembridge did not merely broadcast games. He was a master storyteller. He painted word pictures, and it sometimes seemed that the ninety-feet of action, from basket to basket, was more of a theatrical stage than a sporting contest.

With Stembridge behind the microphone, Chaparral fans did not hear the game on radio. They watched the game on radio as surely as if they had been seated in the stands.

The Chaparrals, frankly, were not viewed as the city's number one attraction. Interest lagged. Attendance was poor and, on some nights, virtually non-existent even though the Chaparrals finished second and reached the 1968 Western Division finals before losing to the New Orleans Bucs.

The club ran out of money four times, and four times Williams managed to scrape together just enough cash, pledges, or IOUs to keep the franchise from failing apart. He endured four hard, grueling, and disappointing years.

The bleeding had not stopped, and the Chaparrals were bled dry. In desperation, the owners sold the franchise to a group in New Jersey, but the league refused to approve the deal. The money was right. But, alas, the potential new owners, according to rumors, had ties to the Mafia. Good for New Jersey, maybe. Bad for the ABA. Terry Stembridge was even told, in a quiet and private conversation, "When you pack up your microphone and head to New Jersey, you'd be a lot better off carrying a machine gun than a suitcase." As a last resort, owners leased the Chaparrals to San Antonio for a dollar as long as San Antonio guaranteed operating expenses. The team's name was changed to the Spurs, and they became the hottest draw in town. Terry Stembridge loaded up his microphone and became the only member of the front office to move south with the team. The tamales sounded a lot more enticing than a New Jersey machine gun, and he broadcast Spurs games for the next six years.

Four years at the helm of the Chaparrals had been taxing for Max Williams, and he began toying with the idea of branching out into the petroleum business. His wife's uncle, Glenn Cooper, owned a small oil company in the West Texas town of Seymour, and Williams already had experience working in the oil patch during his summers with Humble. Bob Folsom thought otherwise.

"This isn't the right time," he told Williams. "Companies are only allowed to produce thirteen or fourteen days a month. The price is low, and a few dry holes will drive you out of the oil patch. There's just not a whole lot you can do with oil these days. If you want to go where the money is, go into real estate with a good broker like Claude McClennahan. He'll teach you a lot."

Williams recognized sound advice when he heard it. If nothing else, Bob Folsom knew real estate. He had made several fortunes developing raw land. Max Williams went knocking on Claude McClennahan's door and again entered a high-powered, pressure-cooker world of business.

His job, on the surface, was simple enough. Max Williams tracked down pieces and parcels of raw land and negotiated deals for real estate developers who were building shopping centers, office buildings, industrial parks, warehouses, retail stores, and homes, creating a new suburbia on empty farmlands, primarily north of Dallas. Property selling for ten thousand dollars an acre was suddenly worth as much as eighty thousand dollars an acre.

Money was flowing like fine wine, and the intensity behind a man's assignment to find new land and new deals was suffocating.

At the time, Williams began a working relationship with Randy Stewart, fresh out of law school and working as a commercial real estate closer. For several years, Williams would handle the intricacies of placing a buyer together with the seller, the right land with the right developer. He took responsibility for financing the real estate packages, then stepped aside and turned the deals over to Stewart to hammer out the fine print and handle the legal work of each transaction.

Williams liked satisfied clients and big commission checks. Stewart made sure that the deals were tightly tied together and would go through the legal process without a hitch. Max Williams admired the young man's grit and energy.

Stewart was smart, and he had no problem with working long hours on short notice. Williams knew there would always be a place for Randy Stewart.

●

During the halcyon days of the early 1970s, Dallas was known as Big D for a reason. The city possessed a great deal of money, and Dallas had a lot of daring, high-rolling men and women who possessed a great deal of money. Dallas, the myth and the reality, was being nailed together with a handful of promises and an armload of good, honest, make-you or break-you entrepreneurial greed.

The right real estate wizard with the right vision on the right side of town could make greed both fashionable and socially acceptable. For many, deals were consummated in saloons, in taverns, in coffee shops, in back rooms, in board rooms, in hotels – illicit, illegal, immoral, or otherwise – on golf courses, beside tennis courts, at cocktail parties, over dinner, over phones, overnight, and with a handshake. Max Williams had become part of a business where a man's money kept score of his wins and losses

Within a year, Claude McClennahan's company had sold more commercial real estate than any other business in Dallas County. Max Williams did not have a magician's touch, nor did he ever intimate that he did. He made his fortune the old fashion way, which reflected his West Texas upbringing. He worked hard and endured long hours. He had no idea what the word *quit* meant. Max Williams tracked down the land, and money had an uncanny way of finding him. No razzle. No dazzle. No wild speculative ventures. His was a sound, reasonable voice in an easy-come, easy-go, run-away world of real estate.

6

*H*is company was known as I. C. Deal Investments, but everyone throughout the burgeoning Dallas real estate industry knew and respected him simply as Irv Deal. He was, he said, nothing more than a good businessman who had long ago manufactured the foundation for his success while still in college – going from door to door and selling pots and pans for Alcoa. He sold so many of them that the company finally decided to let him go. Goodbye. Good luck. Irv Deal was, officials feared, making more money on commission fees than the president earned by running the company.

Deal ran a tight ship. He had a reputation for hiring the right people and making the right decisions. He kept a hard, unflinching eye on the devil that was in the details, as well as on the money coming in and going out, making sure the bottom line never varied or wavered from the financial game plan he had established for each of his projects.

He was never known as a tyrant, but Irv Deal did maintain dictatorial control over every aspect, large or small, of his investment firm. He depended on his own ability as a real estate developer and never bothered himself with any sudden swings or shifts in an unpredictable economic climate. Thus far, the economic winds had always blown in a favorable direction.

It was all about to change.

As far as Irv Deal was concerned, raw land was simply an over-priced commodity necessary for building apartment buildings. Dallas was his base of operation, and he built as many as ten thousand units throughout the sprawling Metroplex.

But his influence and his holdings, during the mid-1960s, ranged from coast to coast, with apartments rising up alongside the streets of America's most prominent cities from San Francisco to Tampa by way of Lake Tahoe. His I. C. Deal Investments had become universally recognized as the second or third largest apartment builder in the United States, depending on whichever report happened to be the latest to hit his desk.

For years, Irv Deal remained firmly entrenched as a major player who had found his niche and parlayed it into a small, or large, fortune, depending on whether he was talking to his tax man or his banker. Irv Deal preferred working from behind a desk and on the telephone. He was smooth. He was eloquent. He possessed a boyish charm and the reassuring style of a businessman who had figured all of the angles and knew how to turn pennies into dollars, great amounts of them.

He liked to make deals, and he was good at it. In one shrewd market-changing venture, he sold sixty-five hundred apartment units to the Great Southwest Corporation for twenty million dollars. For Irv Deal, it was indeed the best of times. The worst of times, however, was swiftly approaching, and it would catch him long before he realized that sudden and unexpected economic erosion was on the way.

●

Those prolific, fruitful years in real estate were just about as tempting and as seductive as a fashionable, beautiful woman on some other man's arm, and just about as unpredictable. The good times had rolled in with minks and limousines and settled down around Dallas for good. No one doubted it, and no end lay in sight. There was plenty of raw land, and land begat money, and money begat fortunes, and fortunes begat Dallas. The power was intoxicating.

One morning, the elixir that had been so intoxicating left a bad taste and a hell of a hangover. Dallas Real Estate awoke and discovered that, virtually over-night, the good times had all loaded up and gone. No one had seen them slip out of town. A grand and glorious market had passed away sometime in its sleep, and not everyone at the funeral would be a pallbearer.

Real estate magnates called it building ahead of demand, but their crime had been to dramatically overbuild North Dallas and suddenly discover that banks no longer had construction loans to pass around. Interest rates were on the rise, and speculators were caught in a deadly financial trap, paying fourteen percent interest, and sometimes more, for property on which they were unable to build. Raw land became raw again. Dollar signs had faded from the fields of splintered promises. Boom to bust, riches to rags, power to poverty, good fortune to good riddance. The game of speculative real estate was simple. Buy land and flip it before they had to pay for it, and they all kept flipping it back and forth.

Each time the price grew greater, and the odds went up. Whoever got caught with the final flip of the land lost. A lot of men lost.

●

Irv Deal had been devastated by the sudden downturn of the real estate market. His world had crumbled around him, and the loss hit his personal life harder than his business life. He could ride out a slump. He had done it before.

But real estate in Dallas had unexpectedly turned south, then exploded in his face, and left him trying to develop luxury apartment complexes and shopping centers when the buyers had all left the sellers grimly holding their "For Sale" signs.

The ashes and debt were suffocating.

Money always had a curious way of finding Irv Deal. Money, he knew, wasn't out looking for him anymore. Money had dried up and left him scrambling for one more roll with somebody else's dice. His only salvation, he decided, would be to find another business where he could invest the funds he still had tucked away in the bank and crawl back to profitability again.

Irv Deal was standing at a financial crossroads filled with potholes and lined with detour signs, financial cul-de-sacs, and dead ends. What next? He wondered. He had no idea. But for a man who had mastered the science of running a sound and profitable business, something would turn up. It always did.

●

During Christmas of 1974, Irv Deal, with time on his hands and nothing better to do, wandered up to a holiday party hosted by Frank West. He ran across Pat Holloway, an attorney who ran with fast company and owned, or at least handled, the legal work for drilling funds. Deal and Holloway had been friends for years.

Well, they may not have been close friends, but they knew each other well enough to discuss the ups and downs of a business market gone awry.

Deal looked the way he felt, forlorn and downcast. What's worst, he was standing around and drinking far too much, and he was drinking alone, a sad predicament, which, throughout the Dallas business community, was generally frowned upon and regarded as an unforgivable sin.

In Dallas, when players got together for any occasion, the broke supped from the same cup as the rich, and it was virtually impossible to determine who had received their next check and who had written his last one, who had chicken and who was left with the feathers.

Holloway strode across the room. He was charismatic and had a commanding presence, especially at a social gathering. "What's wrong?" Holloway asked.

"The real estate business is just terrible," Deal answered, his shoulders slumped, his face shaded by the dim lights in the room. "I'm going broke," he said. "The business is out there dying and taking us down with it. I'm not sure I'll be able to hang on much longer."

"Real estate will bounce back," Holloway said.

"Maybe. Maybe not."

"It always does."

"I don't want to wait for it," Deal replied. "It looks to me like the oil business is the place where I need to be. The price is going up on a regular basis. There seems to be a lot of money to be made, and the rewards far outweigh the risks. I need to get myself in the oil business, Pat. It's as simple as that. The trouble is, I don't know how to get there. You run drilling funds. You're on the inside of the oil business. Tell me. How's the best way for me to become a player in the oil business?"

Holloway had no intention of encouraging a man down on his luck and looking for the next big play. It bordered on being criminal. A man like that was grasping for straws and easily tempted by the illusion of dollar signs.

Sure, the rewards of oil were greater than the risks. Always had been. But, as he would say, the inherent dangers of a man losing his financial ass were just as plausible and infinitely more probable. The hidden costs could strangle him.

Holloway said as kindly as possible, "Irv, you don't know a damn thing about the oil business. Let me tell you, it's an entirely different world from the one in which you've always lived and worked. Building apartments is one thing. You're damn good at it. Drilling for oil is quite another. Frankly, the oil business can eat you alive."

It was as though Irv Deal had not heard a word the attorney said. "I like oil," Deal replied. "Oil is money. And I can't say that about real estate these days."

Pat Holloway took a long, slow drink and let the warm whiskey slide down his throat.

"I think you might be making a big mistake," he said.

"Maybe I am." Deal smiled. "But I'm a big boy," he said. "I've made mistakes before. I'll ask you the same question again. How's the best way for me to get into the oil business?"

"Well, if you're dead set on making the biggest blunder you've ever made, you need to get yourself a good geologist," Holloway said. "Just do whatever he says, and let him find you some prospects. If you don't know what kind of shit you're looking for, you won't stand a chance. The oil patch has chewed up a lot of beginners and spit them out in all directions. Without a good geologist, you might as well be drilling a water well. Your only hope is to tie yourself to some old boy who knows what he's doing."

"Okay," Deal answered. "If I decide that oil is really the direction I want to go, that's exactly what I'll do."

Pat Holloway watched him walk away. He doubted seriously if Irv Deal would remember anything at all about the oil business by morning. Maybe he was wrong. But he just could not picture the suave, cosmopolitan Irv Deal out on a rig, his face spackled with mud, dirt, and grime. He laughed quietly to himself and poured another shot glass full of whiskey. Pat Holloway forgot all about Irv Deal.

●

Max Williams quietly and quickly began changing gears in his life and his business. He was still smitten with an unabashed and unbridled passion for raw land.

The surface of the landscape lying within the shadows of Dallas skyscrapers had been good to him for years, but now he was once again more interested in what he might find buried deep within the recesses of the good earth than what he might earn by selling the top of it.

A change of heart. A change of plan. A change, period.

When real estate in Dallas headed over the far edge of the earth, Max Williams began moving quietly in another direction. Business had turned sour. He hadn't.

He had seen others become depressed with a slumping economy that offered few promises and little hope. But, as he said long ago, sometimes something bad simply puts you in a place for something good to happen.

He had grown up with the smell of oil thick in his nostrils. To oil he would return. Oil had been good to a lot of people, but only if they knew where it was, how deep it lay, and were able to find it. Someone had once asked the legendary J. Paul Getty the secret of his success in discovering oilfields.

"It's simple," Getty said. "I just keep drilling holes."

Max Williams was already exploring the idea of branching off into the oil business when geologist Clayton Childress came to him, looking for some investors to back a few wells in the heralded Fort Worth Basin, particularly on some promising ranchlands tucked away within the tableau of knolls in Palo Pinto County. Good idea, Williams thought.

Probably a good area. At least, Childress thought it was. And the timing could not have been better.

Williams had known the geologist since their boyhood days in the West Texas oil patch and had no reservations about working with a man who, he remembered, was as honest as the day was long. But money throughout the marketplace was as tight as it had ever been. Those who still had cash were generally hanging onto to it for fear they might never find it again, and none of them had any idea about a precarious and unpredictable future looming before them like an ominous thunderhead. As a rule, the rich knew they were one bad and costly gamble removed from being poor.

Childress wasn't having any luck at all raising the money, and he turned to the only man he knew who had been involved in high-finance deals before.

Max Williams, it was said, ran in the right circles with the right crowd and rubbed shoulders with the real players of Dallas. Mostly in real estate. Seldom if ever in oil.

To Childress, it did not matter. Money was money. Childress needed it, and someone else had possession of it. Max Williams would probably know who did. Childress drove to Dallas and explained his plight to the man he had always called *Little Exxon* because of his childhood days in the Humble Oil Camp.

"I've been around a few years, drilled some wells, and seen my share of good locations," Childress said. "The basin looks to be a solid bet and a good prospect to drill."

"How much money do you need to raise?" Williams asked.

"Well, Little Exxon," the geologist told him, "I think we can drill several shallow wells for two hundred and sixty thousand dollars. We may even be able to drill them for less. Raise what you can. Any money we have left over is yours."

"How deep?"

"I'm figuring about four thousand feet."

"I don't know much about oil," Williams admitted.

"You know money."

Max Williams nodded. No argument there. If anything, he knew money. He had watched it flood Dallas, then leak out like the last drop of rain in a West Texas drought.

To Childress, especially during hard times when men were as depressed as their bank accounts, two hundred and sixty thousand dollars seemed like an imposing amount of money, and the challenge of raising it loomed over him like a formidable if not an impossible task.

In reality, Williams knew, it wasn't that much money at all. Not really. Long ago, Bob Folsum had given him the secret to fundraising. Line up a bunch of investors, take a few dollars from each of them, not enough to hurt anybody, and get them all involved in a deal that potentially offered a nice return.

Williams knew immediately what he needed. Twenty-six investors. Ten thousand dollars each. And he had his money. Of course, nothing was ever as easy as it looked when brainstorming an idea.

But he thought he had a good strategy that might just work in a far-ranging field known as the Fort Worth Basin.

7

*E*ven with most of the serious investment dollars being pigeon-holed away within the holy inner sanctum of the Dallas rich, Max Williams still had his share of influential friends. One of them was Irv Deal, who had been an old friend, a real estate developer who had made a fortune lining the nation's suburban streets with shopping centers and apartments, large and small. Deal had gone to Stanford University on an academic scholarship, and, Williams knew, he owned a brilliant, incisive, and decisive mind. He was an astute businessman blessed with common sense, which, in most high-finance circles, was a rarity.

Irv Deal wasn't a big man, standing only about five inches short of six feet. He was slightly built, and, at a quick glance, he appeared to be frail. But, as Williams was quick to point out, "Irv might not have been particularly strong physically, but mentally, he was a giant."

He was sophisticated and charming, a gentleman and a scholar, and Deal was always attuned to everything going on in Dallas, around the country, and across the globe, generally in the world of high-dollar real estate.

There were even rumors circulating that Deal, for the last few weeks, had been looking for one more good business opportunity. He didn't particularly care what the deal was as long as it could be played for big stakes. There was no reason for Deal to waste his time on any venture where the risks were small and the profits smaller. He had even made a few overt and oblique inquiries about the oil business.

Max Williams decided that, with real estate in the throes of death, he would give Irv Deal a chance to find out what the quest for oil was all about.

Why not?

They did not have to dig, drill, tromp around in the mud, or kick the dust off their boots or, in Deal's case, their loafers. They would simply remain as moneychangers. Bring it in. Throw a few dollars in a barrel. Hope that oil would fill it up.

Irv Deal may have appeared to be fragile to some, but he was a tough-minded, left-handed competitor, especially on the tennis courts. He and Max Williams played tennis together, and, for years, between sets at the club, they had talked about prospective business ventures, always wondering if they might some day partner up on a project at the far end of the rainbow.

Williams had sold Deal land in the past, and Deal had turned the land into a valuable commodity.

Now, as Max Williams talked, Irv Deal was gazing down at a worn-out land map, ragged, torn, and threatening to fall apart. He was staring at a myriad of possible drilling locations carefully marked in ink, and learning about a chance to strike it rich, or at least parlay a fistful of dollars into a handful of cash, somewhere out West in the Fort Worth Basin, which was nowhere near Fort Worth but in the middle of some ranch in the god-forsaken wasteland of Palo Pinto County.

The map meant absolutely nothing to him, Deal said. Oil and its terminology were a foreign and unfamiliar territory where he had never before traveled. And when it came to the technology of drilling a well, Deal, by his own admission, was clueless and trapped in the dark.

One thing was for certain.

There might or might not be oil in the ground. Irv Deal had been given no guarantees.

But Max Williams was a hell of a salesman.

One man, Irv Deal believed, might be able to enlighten him. He left the tennis courts and sat down with Frank West, a good friend, a respected petroleum engineer, who worked with Santa Fe Minerals and was the genius behind the Hanover Drilling Funds.

If anybody understood the good, the bad, and the ugly of the oil business, Frank West did. Deal was sure of it. He did not want an education. It was not important for him to understand the geological and geophysical nuances associated with drilling for oil or finding it. He could hire trained people to do the field work. Irv Deal was simply on the outside, looking on the inside, and searching for direction.

West patiently listened while Deal outlined the basic skeleton of the proposal that Williams had given him. West did not hesitate. "Go for it," he said. "It has controls."

Deal frowned. He was still in the dark.

"What does that mean?" he asked.

"Do you want the technical definition?"

"No."

"Simply put, it means you can drill it."

Irv Deal nodded. He called Max Williams. "Let's go for it," he said.

Irv Deal was suddenly in the oil business, and he had never before changed the oil in his own automobile. He was, however, aware of the fact that oil, as often as not, had big sums of money with a lot of zeros attached to them. The business he thought wasn't that much different from his years in real estate. It dealt with raw land. He had put apartments on top of it. He could dig holes beneath it. He had employed good contractors to build. He would hire good oilmen to drill. He had operated a big business before. And oil was definitely a big business. The only thing that would change was his business card.

He smiled. Pat Holloway had once told him that the oil business would eat him alive. Well, Pat Holloway did not know Irv Deal, not as well as he probably thought he did. Oil was a gamble. He would never argue that point. Any business deal with six or more zeroes attached was a big gamble. Irv Deal had played the game and faced the odds before. They did not frighten or concern him.

For most of his life, Irv Deal had been strongly attracted to money. What it could buy was inconsequential to him. But the ability to make it and a lot of it proved a man's worth in the hierarchy of a frantic Dallas business and social climate where too much, no matter how large it might be, was never quite enough. Max Williams had brought him one proposal. He went back to Williams with another.

Deal said, "I've got a little money to play with, and I've got some friends who still have a little money to play with. I'm not sure what it will take for us to get started in the basin, but I doubt that raising the money will be much of a problem for either one of us. Who knows? If there's any oil to be found down there, we've got as good a chance of finding it as anyone."

"What kind of arrangement are you thinking about?" Williams wanted to know.

"Let's put our two companies together," Deal said. "You raise half the money, and I'll raise the rest of it. Then when we hit something, we'll split the profits fifty-fifty." The arrangement was nice, clean, and devoid of a lot of fine print.

Max Williams went back to his office and thought it over. He would lose half of the profits if the wells happened to be good enough to earn any profits. Deal, on the other hand, would be shouldering half of the financial burden and fifty percent of the risk. It was definitely give and take, and Williams wondered if he were giving more in the long run than he would be able to take.

He finally took a deep breath, called Irv Deal back, and told him, "All right, we'll join up our two companies and do it."

The two men could have developed a new and single company. Irv Deal, however, didn't like the idea.

He would say, "I anticipated from the beginning that there would one day be animosity rising up between two entrepreneurs who were strong-willed, stubborn, and used to doing business their own way. We could probably work together for a little while. But I knew it wouldn't last. One of us would make a decision or a deal, and the other one wouldn't like it. That was simply the bitter end of human nature. I thought that Max and I would both be better off with our own individual companies. In reality, I was preparing to get divorced before we got married."

Irv Deal established Windsor Energy with less than a half million dollars of his own money. He named it after the street where he lived. Max Williams founded U.S. Operating and sold a third of the company to collect the revenue he would need to make his own set of footprints in the oil patch.

Both men were wheeler-dealers. It's just that they wheeled and dealed in different ways. They drilled jointly. They argued separately. They fumed inwardly.

Neither was the kind of man who took orders. They gave orders. Each liked to be in charge. Each marched to his own drumbeat. Neither owned the same drummer.

At the moment, however, with the wake never ending for real estate and a new day dawning in the oil business, they needed each other – two novices embarking in the turmoil and turbulence of a brave new world. Irv Deal and Max Williams squared their shoulders and readied themselves to confront the sprawling and empty ranchlands that would hold the shallow wells of Palo Pinto County. A few barrels of oil could salve a lot of wounds, even before they were carved into a man's flesh or his soul.

●

In real estate, men like Max Williams and Irv Deal had gone from riches to ruin between the rise and fall of a single day. Both were innocent strangers to the whims and wicked ways of the oil business. But it was tattooed with dollar marks. It couldn't be all bad. They realized that there was no future in looking back or wallowing in regret, so they picked up the dice and rolled them again. Williams promptly placed a call to Randy Stewart, who no longer had any real estate deals to close.

"I'd like to talk to you about a job," Williams said.

Stewart paused on the other end of the phone. He was out of work. There was no money coming in from anywhere. He was contemplating moving to Colorado to see if he could find a position teaching. Tomorrow had never looked so bleak.

"Sure," he said. "I'm interested." He tried not to sound desperate.

"How much money would you need to come work for us?" Williams asked.

"Who is us?"

"Irv Deal and myself."

Stewart knew that Williams and Deal, whatever the job might be, were starting from scratch, and their cash flow was non-existent. He tried to be fair. In his head, he figured out his house payment, car payment, and living expenses. He gave Williams a number. It was just enough dollars to cover his basic costs.

He heard a long pause on the phone before Williams spoke softly. "That's more money than I make," he said. "At the moment, I can't even afford to buy us lunch." He and Randy Stewart came to an agreement. Williams would pay him his expenses and a day rate. Nothing more.

"Here's what I want you to do," Williams said when the two men finally met. "I want you to go out to Graham, just on the other side of Fort Worth, and look over some oil and gas leases for us. Make sure they are clean and legitimate. If we drill on them, I want to be sure that the land titles are good."

Stewart nodded, but he had a look of concern in his eyes. "Frankly, I don't even know what an oil and gas lease looks like," he said.

"Don't worry." Williams grinned. "They print them, and they're all alike." He pulled a blank form from his desk drawer and handed it to the young attorney. "Welcome to the oil business," he said.

Randy Stewart headed west. He said, "I learned early that if you wanted to find some land to lease, you simply walked into the courthouse and threw yourself at the mercy of the oldest lady you could find. Chances were, she had worked there for a long time and knew which chunks of land were available and which had already been tied up by some other oil company."

The land across Young County had been heavily drilled, and only a few patches of scattered acreage remained. Stewart was growing desperate. He had to find land. He had to keep his job.

The money wasn't much, but it was better than going home broke at the end of the day. Armed with all the pieces of information he had gleaned from the oldest lady he could find in the courthouse, Randy Stewart drove down a narrow country road until he came to a farm that no one had bothered to lease.

In the heat of the day, he saw the farmer astride his tractor down in a pecan tree bottom.

Since Stewart was driving a four-wheel- drive pickup truck, he cut across a corner of land and drove up to the farmer.

The old man idled his tractor, leaned across the steering wheel, frowned, pushed his hat back on his head and asked, "What do you think I'm doing down here?"

"I have no idea."

"I'm shaking the pecans out of the trees."

"That's pretty damn clever," Stewart said.

The farmer's frown deepened. "Do you know how many pecans you just ran over coming out here with that damned truck?" he asked.

Stewart shuddered inside. It was not a good beginning. The farmer laughed. The beginning just got a little better. Stewart drove back to Dallas with the lease, and the farmer was richer by two dollars an acre. Max Williams and Irv Deal had a place to drill.

●

It did not take long for the financial package to be pieced together, and it took even less time for the drilling bit, under the guidance of Red Livingston, to cut its way into oil bearing sands. Williams and Deal earned a little money on the front end for raising the funds and took a quarter interest in the well.

The investors all got their money back, made a little profit, tasted the potential riches of oil, and lined up to participate in the drilling of another seven wells. Each came in as profitable as the first. The number of dollars spilling wildly across an oil patch was staggering. If an oilfield gambler was smart, diligent, and spent his money wisely, he could beat the odds or at least stand a better than average chance of winning as many dollars as he threw away. In the oil game, breaking even was for losers. Red Livingston drilled eight wells for Windsor Energy and U.S. Operating. Clayton Childress had chosen eight good locations. Williams and Deal banked eight winners.

Natural gas had become as prevalent as the oil. It was blowing wide open, and Irv Deal realized that he and Williams were losing a small fortune to the flares that were burning escaping gas throughout the days and nights.

A pipeline had not yet come to the forlorn back country of Palo Pinto County. It did not matter. Deal recalled, "At an oil supply house in the area, I saw miles of red pipe just lying stacked up on the ground.

The pipe wasn't doing anybody any good. It was just gathering rust. I talked it over with Max, and we bought as much of the pipe as anybody could locate and had it delivered out to the ranch. We strung red pipe on top of the ground, tied our wells together, gathered our own natural gas, sold it, and immediately had revenue."

In the midst of those harsh, unforgiving days while Red Livingston was battling the good earth for oil, the relationship between Irv Deal and Max Williams was already beginning to show faint signs of unraveling. As far as Max Williams was concerned, Irv Deal had not brought as much money to the table as he should have. And Deal was angry to learn that he and his partner were not on equal footing. It seemed to Irv Deal that, until the well reached a certain depth, both men were responsible for paying the drilling costs. If Livingston had to go any deeper to find oil, Windsor and Windsor alone paid the bill. At least, that was his fear. Williams, for the life of him, couldn't figure out how his partner could come up with such outlandish ideas.

Irv Deal didn't like the arrangement. He knew he should split the blanket with Max Williams, but he didn't. Williams was more than ready to dissolve his business deal with Windsor Energy. If he raised the most money, he reasoned, he deserved a bigger share of the earnings. But he didn't walk away. The trust between both men was rapidly withering away. But they had known each other too long. They may not have liked each other during the heat of searching for oil. But they respected each other. They would keep their personal and their business relationship patched together until the patches finally burst at the seams and flew apart. In the meantime, they worked together and grew rich together.

They sold their field of eight wells on the ranchlands of Palo Pinto to a German Company, and it would be a long time before either man would ever again be tempted by real estate. A lot of bitterness between them dissolved away with money in the bank. Now they were only interested in raw land that had oil beneath it.

8

*P*at Holloway was well versed in the practice of being disliked. Didn't bother him. Never had. He was, after all, a lawyer, who handled and repackaged truths as deftly as a sleight-of-hand magician. Now you see it. Now you don't. He was not afraid to break old rules or invent new ones. Holloway was tall, slender, had blue eyes, strawberry blond hair, and was considered quite handsome within the inner circles of Dallas society. Well, if not handsome, he was at least debonair and supremely confident. He was sure of who he was and where he was going although it was not unusual for him to keep changing directions at the oddest of times.

Attorneys, especially those who had the misfortune of opposing him, regarded Holloway as arrogant and abrasive. He could charm a man as easily as cut his heart out with some dusty law or precedent that the innocent had never heard about and the guilty didn't know was on the books. Holloway was a schemer – both brash and brilliant.

Some feared him. Others damned him. A few had threatened him. He worked hard and drank even harder, but said he never let an overabundance of alcohol cloud his good judgment. He passed off any bad judgment as bad luck. Holloway punctuated his sentences with intermittent explosions of profanity as though curse words, when cleverly pieced together, were the stuff of poetry. He almost always looked as if he had just walked off the cover of *Gentleman's Quarterly*, and he was recognized as one of the more flamboyant figures – lawyer or otherwise – to swagger down the hallways of the Dallas courthouse.

Pat Holloway loved the law. It was a chess game of the mind, a matching of wits, played out with briefs and pleadings, and it was his belief that whenever a legal matter was being discussed, debated, defended, disputed, denied, or negotiated, the best team always won. The facts be damned.

He was tenacious but could charm the fangs off a rattle snake. He had a deep aversion to losing. Did not like it. Never accepted it. Did not believe it had any place in his life or his profession.

No. It didn't bother him at all to be disliked. He expected it, even reveled in the rock-hard reputation that he had carved for himself. Holloway had long ago decided that angered accusations or condemnations – the wilder the better – merely came with the territory.

●

When Pat Holloway left the prestigious Dallas law firm of Thompson & Knight, he kept as a client his good friend Frank West. West had been a petroleum engineer with Continental Oil Company and had left to form his own petroleum consulting business. He was hired by the Wall Street firm of Hornblower, Weeks, Hemphill & Noyes to run its public drilling firm during the early 1970s, and he asked Holloway to work directly with the investment bankers, as well as their Wall Street and Washington lawyers, on all the various legal aspects of public drilling funds.

When Frank West decided to take Hornblower's offer, it was understood that he would not be required to help Wall Street brokers sell units in the drilling funds in an effort to raise money. The acquisition of capital was their job.

West's responsibility was to find drilling prospects, evaluate them, negotiate to secure them, get the wells drilled, supervise the production, and, in general, manage the exploration and production business required by the Hanover drilling funds.

In reality, Hornblower and its nationwide network of securities salesmen knew hardly anything about the oil business. They were having a difficult time explaining the funds to customers, and Hornblower prevailed on Frank West to come to just one meeting in a midwestern city to explain the drilling program to a roomful of potential prospects. One meeting. That's all. The securities salesmen would listen and learn. He would be teaching them while he was also pitching new customers.

Frank West was an authentic oilman. He knew and fully understood what he was talking about. His presentation was so successful and convincing that, in a short time, he found himself on the road day after day, week after week, traveling the country and moving among high-dollar circles from New York to San Francisco by way of Chicago. He turned the intricacies and details of Hanover and its drilling funds over to his attorney. Pat Holloway was no longer merely reviewing the deals. Now he was out developing the deals as well. When a critical decision needed to be made, Holloway made it. Often faced with demanding deadlines, Holloway did not have time to weigh his old friend's opinions on any matter or situation that he might confront. Frank West was never around. Frank West had left a void, and Holloway was filling it the best way he could.

He began evaluating, as well as negotiating, the numerous drilling deals that crossed his desk. He became the active face of Hanover before he even realized it. Wall Street knew it. Promoters knew it. Frank West began to suspect it. Pat Holloway did not slow down long enough to even think about it.

Holloway, however, was not a geologist, and he knew it. But, he had worked for and with geologists, and he believed that he had learned to read isopach and structure maps and could assess the potential risks and rewards of the drilling prospects as well as anyone. Holloway was convinced that he could read between the lines of the prospect brochures and determine, from a geologist's map, the risk associated with each possible venture. He was well versed in the way a deal could be structured and promoted, and he knew the best, most effective way to ascertain the potential profit of a prospect.

●

When Frank West was in town, it was customary for him and Pat Holloway to have lunch together at the Petroleum Club on Fridays, but never before they had at least two drinks at the bar. On one Friday in early 1974, they never left the bar.

In the midst of casual conversation, West suddenly announced, "Holloway, I'm having a real problem. You are practically running my damned company. People are beginning to talk about it, and I am afraid if those peckerwoods on Wall Street find out about it and see that you aren't making any bad mistakes, they may hire you as president and give me the full-time job of running around the country selling the drilling funds – which is something I hate to do and am doing only out of necessity. Those assholes can't sell their own drilling funds, and if I don't sell them, I won't have a company to run."

Holloway stared at West, his eyes hard, his voice soft. "Frank," he said, "you know that's bullshit. I am just your lawyer and, to the extent I have gone beyond that, I am only doing whatever I think you would do if you were here because you are not here and hardly ever here."

"Well, you aren't acting like just a lawyer," West snapped. "You are acting like you think you are some kind of geologist, for God's sake."

"Frank, I know I'm not a geologist," Holloway replied. "But then, neither are you. You are merely a reservoir engineer who happens to have a genius for both salesmanship and management. Nobody but a Wall Street banker would ever hire a reservoir engineer instead of a geologist to find oil. But somebody up there must have had sense enough to see that you are a born manager of people and a born salesman. Maybe because I am trained as a lawyer, I have some ability to sell people on things I believe in, but I am not and never will be a good manager of people like you are. As you well know, I am an arrogant asshole and not a good people person like you are. So you don't have to worry about me stealing either of your jobs, either running the drilling programs or selling them to the public. All this is just bullshit and alcoholic paranoia on your part. Let's have another drink and talk about something else. Like women we want to bed down or something more important."

Frank West laughed out loud. "Okay, Holloway," he said. "Maybe I am imagining or exaggerating things to some extent. But the truth is, you have been taking over part of my job, and the truth of the matter is you haven't made any bad mistakes, and you have been doing a fairly good job. And that has led me to another idea I want to lay out to you instead of talking about the wanton virtues of women right now."

West paused. He squared his shoulders. He leaned across the table and continued. "As you know," he said, "my business philosophy is not to put more than five percent of the drilling program into any one prospect, to spread the dry hole risk. Even without being geologists, you and I both know that if we spread the total available pool of money around twenty intelligent drilling prospects, enough of them are likely to hit and more than pay for the dry holes. Now, I am nearly always offered a larger part of virtually every drilling prospect I see than I can afford to take without breaking my five percent rule. So I need somebody who can take a piece of the deal. And, Holloway, that's where you come in."

Pat Holloway frowned. He thought he knew where West was heading, but he wasn't sure. He sat back and let Frank West talk. A good lawyer always knew when it was time to listen. This was one of those times.

West sat in silence for a moment, letting the conversation play out in his mind. He finally emptied one glass of whiskey, asked for another, and said, "I've been doing a lot of thinking, Pat. You do understand the business as well as anyone. You've been around oil for most of your life. Your grandmother was in the oil business. You've represented quite a few oil companies. Oil is what you know best. It makes sense to me that you should form your own private drilling funds. It would allow you to eliminate all of the SEC legal and accounting expenses that dilute a public drilling funds like Hanover, and you won't have to pay commissions to any securities salesmen like Hornblower does. It appears to me that no-load drilling funds should be pretty attractive to all of your rich friends."

Holloway shook his head. "I can't do it," he said.

"Why not?"

"I already have a drilling funds company for a client," Holloway said. "It would be unethical and a conflict of interest in the highest order if I went out and did my own deal. Wouldn't be fair to you."

West, for the first time all night, looked relieved. "It would not only be fair," he said, "but it would sure help me out a lot."

"How you figure that?"

"Well," West answered, "I hear about a lot of good oil deals, but I can't take them all. Most people bringing me a deal want their money and want to raise it the easiest way possible. " He continued, "They're asking me to take either half or all of them, and I have to spread my money among as many prospects as I can. Now if you had your own drilling funds, I could lay off an eighth or a fourth of a deal with you, and I could take the other eighth or fourth myself. It wouldn't be difficult for you, Pat, because you wouldn't have to go out and spend a lot of money hiring a bunch of high-priced engineers, geologists, or accountants. I already have them, either in the office or on retainer. And they'll all be at your disposal. You know – or at least think you know – everything else about this business that I know except maybe the geology and reservoir engineering. And, being the arrogant asshole you are, you may even trade tougher than I do. And I admit you can write up the deals better than I can. You may even know more oil, gas, and tax law than I do. I think you should follow my advice. If we're as smart as we think we are, both of our funds can do quite well. You will probably end up making a fortune. But even if you don't, at least I will get you out of my hair at Hanover. And I will get a partner for my drilling funds who is a good friend and someone I know I can trust. So think about it." Frank West shrugged. He downed his drink. He stood and headed for the dining room. "Now, we can talk about the women we've caught if you want to.

●

The more he thought about the idea, as the days passed, the better Pat Holloway liked it. Several of his wealthy and influential friends, from time to time, had asked about the possibility of investing in the Hanover drilling funds.

Holloway, however, had always been quick to discourage them, telling them bluntly, "I won't take your money. I don't think it would be entirely wise for you to invest in Hanover because the load is way too heavy. By the time payments are spread to Wall Street and investment banking firms, their accountants, their lawyers, and Security and Exchange Commission attorneys, as much as thirty percent of the public fund is already eaten up. That's not Frank's fault. He just has to deal with a bunch of rules, a lot of regulations, and more red tape than you'd care to wade through. That is simply the way the game is played. If you make a decision to invest in public drilling funds, Hanover is the best one around. But I can't personally justify a deal where only seventy percent of the money paid out by an investor is actually going into the ground in hopes of finding oil. The other thirty percent is overhead, as much as three hundred thousand dollars for a million-dollar deal."

Even Frank West would admit privately that he wouldn't invest any of his own money in Hanover.

But private drilling funds, Holloway realized, were a different story altogether. He was now being given the chance to develop a no-load investment opportunity where he made his own deals, wrote up the necessary battery of legal documents, would never need to hire a geologist or petroleum engineer, and had the ability to sink a hundred percent of the money in the ground.

Investors never had to worry about Wall Street expenses. There were none.

Holloway would earn his compensation by taking an override on the working interest of a well after the land and drilling costs had been paid out. No arguments. No complaints. No guarantees. Some wells hit. Some didn't. Pat Holloway knew better, but he assumed that all of his wells would come blowing in with gusto. He certainly would not make much money unless they did.

He made his way across Dallas, meeting with a dozen or more potential investors, including an old ally from Yale, William Browning, who preferred to be called Bill. Holloway and Browning's relationship, in fact, went back to their boyhood days as classmates at the prestigious St. Mark's of Dallas. The two men shared an affinity and passion for fast cars and exotic women. Or was it exotic cars and fast women? Browning was quick to tell him, "I'll be your first investor and chances are damn good that I'll be your largest investor."

Holloway knew that Browning probably had the most dollars, and he had never been shy about looking for a new and better deal. He was a sophisticated investor who owned, among other things, an automobile dealership, a plane dealership, and a boat dealership. Browning was a swashbuckling gambler at heart, having raced automobiles on the road course of Europe during an earlier time in his life, and he already understood the potential financial rewards of the oil business. He had taken a big chunk of acreage in the Slaughter Field, and some were known to whisper that his royalty payment balanced out around a half million dollars a month. Bill Browning had an affinity for oil. Oil had been good to him. With the influential William Browning now on board, other investors would start lining up to make their wager on oil as well. At the moment, it was the only gamble paying off in a tough economy. Pat Holloway would never have trouble tracking down investors, and they could always find the investment dollars. It was, he admitted, a deadly combination.

●

Pat Holloway resigned from Hanover with no further thought about his decision. He promptly moved his operation into a large home he had built in North Dallas as a hedge against inflation and failure. Late one evening over drinks, Holloway began verbally nailing together the legal points for his new drilling funds venture with Bill Browning after the two men had grown weary of discussing the obvious attributes of the women they knew or wished they had known.

In his mind, Pat Holloway had his strategic plan hammered in place. His idea was to form his own company, raise the money, oversee the drilling funds, locate and close the oil deals, and work with a geologist to choose the prospects. Nothing new. He had done it all before. He had spent years finding and separating out investors for Frank West and Wall Street's exploration and drilling endeavors. No longer would anyone be looking over his shoulder, and he liked it that way. Pat Holloway was the man in charge, not merely Frank West's surrogate and masquerading as boss.

Bill Browning suddenly dropped a bombshell into the conversation. It came out of the blue and was totally unexpected. He set his chin defiantly and said he not only wanted to invest in the company, he wanted to be president as well.

"Why?"

"I sure would like to be able to travel around the country and tell people I'm the president of a genuine oil company," he said. "There's a significant difference between a player and the man who runs the play."

"You won't be running the play," Holloway said.

Browning shrugged. "They'll think I am," he replied.

Holloway mentally departed the table and crawled back into the sanctity of his own mind. He sat deep in thought.

He and Bill Browning had known each other for a long time, and Browning would let him run the company anyway he wanted, as long as they found a little oil from time to time.

He did not want to run the risk losing the kind of investment funds that Browning could bring him, and he could not remember the two of them ever disagreeing, much less quarreling, on any deal or project where they worked together.

Besides, titles were cheap. Even the title of president was not worth much more than ink on a business card. Holloway grinned.

Browning, as was his nature, was simply buying another plaything. It might be a mistake, he thought, but it wouldn't be a big one.

"Okay," Holloway said at last. "Here's what I'm prepared to do, Bill. I will make you president of the exploration company. I've also decided to give Mike Starnes, your business manager, ten percent of the stock to handle all of our accounting needs and make sure the books are kept and audited properly. I won't have time to do it myself. That leaves me with the remaining ninety percent of the company. If it works for you, Bill, it works for me."

Browning nodded.

He was president. It worked for him.

Holloway recalled, "Because it was anticipated that Browning would be the largest single individual investor in my drilling funds, it seemed appropriate that Starnes watch over the management of Bill's investment by keeping our books. It allowed Starnes to participate in the profits the company made from his compensation for running the drilling funds. It could amount to a lot of money."

Pat Holloway and Bill Browning believed that the stock would give Mike Starnes a strong reason and incentive to help make the company as successful as possible.

Browning was relieved because he would not be obligated to increase his business manager's salary even though he was increasing the man's workload.

Bill Browning leaned back, smiled broadly, and poured himself another drink. He had what he wanted and all that he wanted. No negotiations. No hard feelings. No regrets. But one question did concern him. "What's the name of our company?" he asked.

Pat Holloway had been thinking about it for some time. He wanted a name that had immediate credibility and stature, one that did not belie the small size of a start up company that had not yet drilled its first well. "Humble Exploration Company," he said.

"Seems like I've heard that name Humble before."

"You have."

"What will the folks down in Houston think?"

"They don't use the name anymore. They'd rather be Exxon."

"Sounds impressive."

"It is."

"What's the next step?" Browning asked.

"Drill."

"Do we have any locations yet?"

Pat Holloway laughed. "We've got the whole world," he said.

Pat Holloway's original idea, when Humble Exploration was formed on May 31, 1974, was to organize and operate drilling funds that would take interests in prospects being generated by Robert Nance, a consulting geologist who was working with Frank West's Hanover Planning Company in Montana, the Dakotas, and the Red River play.

Holloway had long known that geologists were more important to the oil business than lawyers, even lawyers who bore the scars of working for two decades or more in oil and gas. He promptly issued fifty percent of Humble' stock to Nance for twelve hundred dollars. Holloway personally took forty percent of the stock for a thousand dollars. Ten percent of the stock was issued to Mike Starnes for two hundred and forty dollars.

Within a year, however, Frank West began fearing that his Wall Street bosses would decide that Nance, with all of that stock in his pocket, might have a tendency to favor Humble over Hanover when it came to locating prime prospects, After all. Humble had compensated Nance far more generously than Hanover, which did not share with him any of its promotion revenue on Nance's drilling deals. In reality, it was a mute point. West and Holloway knew from the beginning that it was not in Robert Nance's nature to show favoritism. He was honest. He was trustworthy. He could not be bought by Humble or anyone else. Those Wall Street bosses, however, were suspicious of almost everyone. For them, a conspiracy was being woven behind the scenes of every deal.

Nance, long before he became independent, had worked as a young geologist for Frank West's consulting firm. They had a strong father-son relationship, and Nance had no intention of ever doing anything improper if it might injure the familial relationship he had with his mentor.

Besides, Frank West was running a major public drilling funds, and he remained firmly entrenched as Nance's principal customer for drilling prospects.

Nonetheless, West, aware that the powers on Wall Street were forever looking down on the venture like vultures hanging on a tree limb, told Holloway and Nance that he would feel more comfortable if the geologist was not a stockholder in Humble. Both funds, in the eyes of many, were out in the market competing for the same prospects. West did not want any deal to even hint of impropriety. Robert Nance readily agreed. He doubted if Humble would ever amount to much anyway. Hanover was his bread and butter.

Without any hesitation, he endorsed his stock certificate over to Pat Holloway and mailed it from Billings, Montana. Holloway promptly sent him a check for twelve hundred dollars to repay the cost of Nance's twelve hundred shares.

No debate. No dispute.

Robert Nance was removed from Humble Exploration. He was no longer a stockholder who had any financial interest in the company.

Holloway immediately apprised Bill Browning of the transaction, explaining that, as far as Humble Exploration was concerned, nothing had really changed. Nance would continue to bring the company prospects, and Frank West was content to lay off to them any percentage of a deal he did not want to take.

It would be business as usual.

"Well, that sounds okay to me," Browning said, frowning, deep in thought. Then he broached a subject that had been long simmering in his head.

"But now that you own ninety percent of Humble's stock, he said, "don't you think you should give me part of the percentage you got back from Nance? After all, I shouldn't need to remind you that I am by far the largest investor you have."

His request was not a surprise. Holloway had been expecting it. "Here's the problem," he told Browning. "It would give you preferential treatment over all of the other investors in Humble's drilling funds, and that would not be fair to the other investors. If I give you some stock, those other investors might demand that I give them stock as well. I could end up with nothing for all of the work I've been doing. No stock. Not even a salary. And that would certainly not be fair."

Bill Browning only smiled.

He fired his next shot. "Well, Holloway," he said, "why don't you just call them all up and see if any of them have any objections to the biggest investor in Humble's drilling funds having a ten percent interest in the company. See if they demand any stock for themselves."

Holloway never made the call. He didn't have to. It wouldn't matter, and he knew it. The other investors would neither object nor demand any stock of their own. He had been running a failed bluff.

A few days later, over drinks, Holloway told Browning that he had mailed him a stock certificate representing two hundred and forty shares of stock. He now owned ten percent of the outstanding stock in Humble.

Holloway never asked for payment. And Bill Browning never bothered to pay his two hundred and forty dollars for the stock.

He simply kept what he was sent.

Soon after Pat Holloway formed Humble Exploration and resigned as attorney for Hanover, he and Frank West were approached by petroleum engineer John LaRue, who had a proposition for them to consider.

"I've found this kid who used to work for Texaco, and I want to hire him," LaRue said. "He works all the time, has a good head on his shoulders, and, from what I've been able to find out, he's one of the better geologists to come down the pike in a long time."

"So what's the problem?" West asked.

"I can't afford him unless I get a lot more business," LaRue answered, "and I don't want to lose him. I'd like for each of you to pay me a retainer each month, and I'll use the money to bring him on board. You'll have first call for his services any time you happen to need them."

"You think he's that good?"

"He's been all over Texas, Louisiana, Africa, Australia, and the Middle East." John LaRue shrugged and continued, "He's been around, and they tell me that when it comes to understanding what goes on in an oilfield, this kid is an absolute genius."

"You think he can find oil?"

"Always has."

"How much money do you need?"

"Four or five hundred dollars a month from each of you," LaRue said. "Won't hurt your checkbook any, and it would help me a lot. It'd be a real loss if the kid went somewhere else."

"What's his name?" Holloway asked.

"Ray Holifield."

Pat Holloway thought it over for a minute. He knew he wouldn't miss the money. Spent more than that on either a good or bad night at the Petroleum Club.

Besides, this Ray Holifield fellow might be able to go out and generate some new prospects for them. They already had a straight line to investors, and even with plenty of acres already sewn up, they were always looking for some new hot spot to drill.

He glanced at Frank West.

West nodded.

"It's a deal," Holloway said. "Now, let's find out if this Ray Holifield is as good as you say he is."

9

Max Williams made the decision to stay with oil exploration. The eight wells he and Irv Deal had found in Palo Pinto activated a mechanism in his brain that he figured was not unlike that of a high-stakes black jack player betting his life and most of his fortune on the next turn of the card, which might well be his last. Oil had seeped into his blood. It occupied his every waking hour.

Oil triggered good money, but it was slow money. He needed revenue to move forward. He could not wait on those royalty checks from his last wells before financing the drilling operation of his next well, provided, of course, either he or Irv Deal was able to track down the right lease on the right acreage that enclosed the right reservoir of crude.

Max Williams had sold a third of U.S. Operating to Dick and Alan Gold for a hundred and sixty-six thousand dollars. The funds gave him the working capital he so desperately needed. The Gold brothers owned a woman's clothing manufacturing company called Nardis of Dallas, and both admitted they knew absolutely nothing about the oil business. Dick Gold, however, wanted to be like Max Williams. He had invested in real estate with Williams. He wore cowboy boots, western shirts, and denim jeans similar to those Williams wore. And he played tennis with Max Williams every chance he got. The Gold brothers did not know whether oil was a good or a bad investment. They just wanted to be in business with Max Williams, and, in their minds, they were simply doing their friend a favor.

Williams needed some money. They happened to have some money. Deal done. No questions asked. Besides, they were also intrigued with the idea of being involved in the search for raw crude. It put them in the middle of a mythical Texas that had been built on cattle and oil.

It may not ever be as good as the movie *Giant*, but it was close. In the oil game, close sometimes counts.

●

Max Williams had known Edwin L. Cox for years. Cox was on the board at Southern Methodist University and had admired Williams' exploits on the basketball court and in the tenuous, ever-changing world of business. Several years earlier, while working as a real estate broker, Williams had sold him the sixty-seven-hundred-acre La Reata Ranch in the heart of the East Texas piney woods. They were more than casual acquaintances. The rumors of oil brought them closer together.

By all accounts, by all who knew him, Edwin Cox was an honest man but a hard trader, a long-time oilman, whose father had been a partner with Jake Hamon in the oil exploration business throughout Texas and Oklahoma. Oil was his birthright.

The storied career of Hamon's father had been cut short when a gunshot in an Ardmore, Oklahoma, hotel room took his life in 1920. Was it an accident, a suicide, or had he been murdered by his stenographer at the dastardly end of a scandalous love affair? Whispers, as always, were far more plentiful than the facts.

Jake Hamon, the second, dropped out of law school after his father's funeral and trekked to the oilfields around Ranger, Texas. A roustabout's life was no good at all, so a year later, he returned to Oklahoma, drilled his first well, partnered up with Edwin B. Cox, and had a bad run with dry stripper wells before hitting it big. The Hamon legacy in oil had been handed down from father to son just as it would be in the Cox family.

Edwin Cox, the son, had built a celebrated career in oil and gas production. He had made millions of dollars and invested them in oil, politics, and, above all, Southern Methodist University. But Max Williams did not want his investment dollars. Nor did he ask for them. Max Williams was far more interested in the knowledge that Cox possessed about the oil business. When the two men finally sat down, held together by their close bond at SMU, Williams told him succinctly enough, "I'd like to get more involved in the oil business."

"Been in it yet?"

"Yes, sir."

"Drill a few wells?"

"Yes, sir."

"Had any luck?"

"Yes, sir."

"Think you can do it again?"

"I'm willing to take that chance."

Cox laughed, then leaned back in his chair and said, "Oil can make you a rich man, Max. But it can whittle you away to nothing. Oil is a tough business. Not every hole has oil at the bottom of it."

Williams quietly and openly placed his cards on the table. He and Cox would be honest with each other if nothing else. "I've drilled a few wells in the Fort Worth Basin, out in Palo Pinto County to be more exact," he said. "My partner and I made some money from production, then sold the field to a German company. But I'm still just small time. I'd like to be an operator, and there's an awful lot I haven't learned yet." Williams paused, then asked softly, "Do you really think that somebody like me can be successful in the oil business?" The question was simple, heartfelt, and to the point.

"It's a good business," Cox replied. "Might even get better. You've got to be tough, but you know that. There are a lot of disappointments along the way, but I bet you've figured that out as well. If you find a good field, stick with it, hang in there even when everything looks like it might be falling apart around you, the amount of money you can make is staggering."

"Do you have any idea where I should go from here?"

"Do you have any acreage?"

"No, sir."

"Leases?"

"No, sir."

Cox thought it over, then suggested that Max Williams and his partner consider moving their operation down south, down into the Austin Chalk of Pearsall, Texas, where a new play had just gotten underway. The field had made more than a few good wells and had experienced a fair amount of success.

No one doubted that the chalk could be tricky, Cox said, but the fractures had oil in them, and his plan was to cut through the faults at an angle in order to encounter as many fractures as possible. It was vital for an operator to have a geologist smart enough to read the seismic log and cagey enough to find the crude, but, yes, he thought, Pearsall just might be as good a place as any for Williams to get a solid education about the hard knocks, hard luck, and hard cash of the oilfield.

"We have twenty-two locations in Frio County," Cox said. "They're all clustered together, and we don't plan to drill anywhere outside of the leases we already have. I have a feeling that you can pick up as much acreage in the Pearsall chalk as you want."

Edwin Cox may well have been plotting to explore and maybe even drill on locations far removed from Pearsall. If so, however, he did not bother to mention any of them. He pulled a map of the Pearsall field out of his desk, stretched it flat, and marked dots on those twenty-two key locations where he owned his leases. Max Williams was certainly welcome to wander around Pearsall and pick up as much acreage as he wanted. Frio County had other operators running around, probing the ground, but the field was wide open, and there was a lot of land that farmers hadn't yet turned loose. Good price. Good leases. Good luck. Godspeed.

Max Williams had met with a man he trusted. Irv Deal immediately went to see his Patron Saint of the oil business, Frank West. Like Williams, he was looking for advice. He wanted answers. He knew Frank West had them. Frank West always did.

"We drilled eight wells," Irv Deal said.

"Hit any oil?"

"They were all productive."

West grinned and shrugged. "Then what do you need from me?" he asked.

"What do I do now?"

"You need a good petroleum engineer," West said. "You need somebody to look over your shoulder and help guide your exploration efforts. If you have the right leases, you need somebody who knows how to find oil."

"Where do I find a good petroleum engineer?"

"Go meet John LaRue," West replied. "His firm is LaRue, Moore, and Schafer. It's located here in Dallas, and they have the best group of petroleum engineers and finest bunch of geologists you can find."

"Does John need a new client?"

"John's always looking for somebody who's looking for oil."

Max Williams and Irv Deal sat down in the well-appointed and prestigious Dallas office of John LaRue, Joe Moore, and Bob Schafer. Yes, the petroleum engineers said, they knew all about the historical incongruities of the Austin Chalk. They had heard the horror stories, most if not all of them. Certainly, it was their business to study the earth and understand the nuances of its anomalies.

John LaRue, however, was blunt and frank with them both, pointing out that his firm did not recommend any kind of oil venture down in the cursed Pearsall region. He possessed an unpublished and unprinted engineering study of the chalk and, in essence, it concluded: *Get the hell out of Pearsall.* And that's what he told them: "Stay the hell out of Pearsall."

Irv Deal and Max Williams, however, were determined to move forward in spite of the foreboding reputation hovering around the Pearsall field like a dark cloud devoid of any silver linings. The chalk might indeed be capricious. LaRue might be right in his assessment. But Edwin Cox was a respected oilman. He had operations in the chalk. He had recommended for them to buy leases in the chalk. And their minds were made up. At least, Max Williams was convinced that he could meet the chalk on its own terms and win. For him, it was Pearsall or bust.

The odds weighed heavily on bust.

John LaRue had dealt with stubborn men before. He leaned back in his chair and said, "We'll work with you although I want you to understand the risk involved. We'll take only a small amount of upfront money. We'll charge you twenty-five dollars an hour to handle any geological and engineering work we do. We normally charge fifty. And we'll ask for a two and a half percent override in case you beat the odds. You'll receive a discount on our hourly rate, but, otherwise, it's pretty much our standard deal."

Max Williams and Irv Deal looked at each other, then nodded. It sounded like a reasonable proposal.

"I assume you'll have a geologist assigned to us," Williams said.

"I will."

"He have a name?"

"Ray Holifield."

"Tell me about Holifield," Deal said.

"He's got an awful good resume," LaRue said. "He's young. He's energetic. He's a brilliant geologist who's worked in oilfields all over the world, especially in fractured reservoirs in the Middle East. He's about as you good as you can get."

The men all shook hands. They signed an agreement. John LaRue placed a call to Ray Holifield's office.

It was once written that "if you see a man walking down the street with oil on his shoes where it shouldn't be, no oil on his hair where it should be, that's an oilman. If he has a faraway look in his eyes and seems to be contemplating the depths of the Jurassic sandstone in Persia, that's a geologist. Have pity on him. He's just as lonesome as he looks ... (A geologist) draws on his total knowledge, experience, and the facts he has, says a prayer if he is a religious man, and then gives his best judgment. But the proof of whether he is right or wrong comes only when oil is found or not found."

As one old oilman said, "Little boys who pick up rocks either go to prison or become geologists." Ray Holifield had been picking up rocks for a long time, and he always had that faraway look in his eyes. Mostly, he studied and worked the oilfields alone. He was just as lonesome as he looked.

Ray Holifield had gone to college in 1955 with the sole intention of becoming a lawyer. It was a difficult task from day one. He had grown up as the inquisitive son of an Arkansas sharecropper in a ramshackle home tucked back in the Ozarks, not too far from Rector and a little closer to Piggott. About all his mother was ever able to give him was a strong work ethic. It would be enough, she said, to get him through life no matter what he chose to do. Determined to work his way through the University of Missouri in pursuit of a career in law, Holifield accepted a part-time job in the geology department. He recalled, "All of the professors had begun teaching during the Great Depression, and they understood the financial hardship I was facing. They sort of adopted me." Holifield could easily identify with his professors, who became his mentors, and they could empathize with him.

He often worked fifty hours a week, mostly at night, late at night, and earned a dollar an hour when the going rate for student employment generally topped out around fifty cents an hour. Somewhere between his duties of cleaning slides and pinpointing the dates for odd collections of rocks, Ray Holifield lost all interest in becoming a lawyer. The earth, he decided afforded him more complexities and enigmas than a courtroom.

By 1964, he had earned his Master's Degree in geology, sold a little insurance to keep his wife and three children fed, and was offered a job with Texaco. He worked for a time as a micro paleontologist, studying the age of rocks and identifying fossils, then was moved on to New Orleans where he began mapping the sands of the Gulf Coast, serving as a stratigrapher. He was walking across sands on the beach, he said, and was struck by the sudden realization that their appearance had not changed in the last ten million years. The old earth beneath his feet might shift around some from time to time. But, in reality, it never really changed. It simply grew older. That's all.

Holifield studied the currents flowing west to east at the mouth of rivers, both large and small, washing sediment far out to the deep. He was involved in finding sweet spots for offshore drilling beyond the coastline of Louisiana. In the late hours, he sat alone, looking closely at seismic readings, learning to recognize those distinct substrata characters that indicated a strong potential for oil. He was dispatched into the field to track down and buy oil leases, and Holifield collected the data that Texaco needed to make a major sale in 1967, earning the company hundreds of millions of dollars, not bad at all for a young, gangling geologist who wore thick, black sideburns, large, dark, horn-rimmed glasses, and earned $575 a month.

●

By 1970, Ray Holifield had walked away from Texaco and journeyed again to Texas, accepting a position with D. R. McCord & Associates in Dallas. Within weeks, he had been shipped out to foreign shores and assigned to conduct the geological evaluation of the vast oilfields being drilled in North Africa, Australia, Kuwait, Abu Dhabi, Saudi Arabia, and Iran. He buckled down – it was the chance of a lifetime, he said – working as many as eighty hours a week. Out in the field. On the desert. In the bars. Day and night.

Oil and water might not mix. But oil and whiskey certainly did. "I wasn't really an expert," Holifield said with a grin, "but I certainly made myself appear to be one, and nobody ever knew the difference."

The stern-faced Minister of Petroleum in Algeria came marching unannounced into Holifield's office one morning and dropped a map on his desk. He had marked the site of each well drilled in the country, and he asked a simple question that had occupied the minds of oilmen for generations. "Why are some of these good wells?" he asked. "And why are some of them bad?"

Ray Holifield did not have a ready answer. Wished he did. But he didn't. And it was not the time to bluff. He would spend the rest of his life searching for an answer to the riddle, even though, he knew, the geology of each field was hardly ever the same and almost always had to be interpreted differently. For decades, the industry had understood the basic strategy of drilling on and around salt domes or in traditional oil-bearing sands. The Middle East, however, remained an enigma. Holifield uncovered the fact that the old faults had been cemented together with limestone crystals. Oil might well be plentiful far below the sands, but it lay trapped inside the storage chambers of ancient rock. Calcite plugged the fissures. The oil couldn't get out. It couldn't be pumped. It defied anyone who tried to find it. The oil was a fortune entombed in compressed stone

Holifield made a fascinating discovery, and, to him, it generated a revolutionary concept. Eons ago, the pressure deep inside the earth had been so strong that the faults had a tendency to bend sharply at the edges of the desert, breaking the rocks and creating a fractured reservoir where the oil had been collected. Without those fractures, the field would have appeared to be barren. What an oil exploration company needed to do was frac the well and create its own fractures down in the faults. Special fluids were forced into the wellbore by a powerful hydraulic pump, shattering the limestone and opening up the fissures so hydrocarbons could flow more freely into the shaft of the bore. Otherwise, the fortune went to waste. Ray Holifield took the knowledge he learned and the data he had compiled from the hard rock, limestone formations beneath the desert floor and filed them away.

Holifield's geologic work and track record during his years in the Middle East oilfields were sterling. Some of the wells drilled on locations he had chosen were flowing a hundred thousand barrels of oil a day. He had a knack for reading the seismic data of the formations correctly. When he selected a location, it was usually a good one, even though some wells were better than others. He was in the field with the crew, a permanent fixture on the rigs. He survived massive blow-outs, including one that burned up forty thousand barrels of oil a day for six months before the famed Red Adair arrived from Houston and killed the flames by pumping cement down the hole. Those in high places kept a watchful eye on his successes in the field. Other geologists simply searched for oil, they whispered among themselves. Ray Holifield had a knack for knowing where it was buried.

The Minister of Petroleum in Saudi Arabia made him a quiet and private offer. If Holifield would agree to stay in the Middle East and direct the geology of the country's oil exploration efforts, he would be allowed to live in a small palace, have a special driver for his car, be given enough money to place his children in one of Europe's best schools, and earn a salary of $250,000 a year. Holifield accepted the proposal without hesitation. There really wasn't anything for him to consider. Back home, not even the presidents of major oil companies made that kind of money. Ray Holifield smiled to himself. He may not be king. But he was certainly close to one. Oil had a way of making a lot of people in power happy throughout Saudi Arabia, and, if nothing else, he could find oil.

Holifield promptly flew home, apologetically resigned his position at D. R. McCord, sold his Dallas home, took all of the shots necessary for living overseas, applied for his visa, and made sure that his passport was up to date. He was leaving nothing to chance. He viewed himself as an expatriate extraordinaire.

The phone rang. He wasn't expecting a call. It was the Minister of Petroleum on the other end of the line. He was speaking in hushed tones. "There appears to have been a slight problem," he said.

"What kind of problem?"

"Word has leaked out about how much money I offered you. Word has come down that it is far too much."

"We can certainly negotiate the money," Holifield said. "What's the new offer?"

"There isn't one. Everything has changed. The agreement we signed with you has been cancelled."

Silence. The phone went dead.

When he had crawled out of bed early that morning, Ray Holifield thought he would soon be living in a palace among royalty, working as the head geologist in one of the greatest oilfields in the world. Oil had made a lot of people wealthy. He had a chance to get rich as well.

Then the phone rang, and, within the space of a dozen well-chosen words, his new world had not only crumbled and fallen apart, it had been rudely and ruthlessly yanked out from beneath him. Holifield suddenly realized that he had absolutely nothing. No job. No salary. No home. Saved a little money. Not much. Tucked it away in a bank. For all practical purposes, however, he and his family were out on the streets. His tenuous and circuitous life had gone from rags to riches to rags again.

What a difference those dozen little words could make.

He sighed, squared his shoulders, and accepted the grim fact that he would have to begin again. Some company out there must need a good geologist with his experience. Who knows? He might even wind up in the Middle East for another tour of duty.

Holifield was right, and he was wrong. Someone did need a good geologist. The Middle East was out of the question. He had served his time and left his imprint on the desert for others who would follow.

●

Ray Holifield went to work for the geology firm of Larue, Moore & Schafer in Dallas, developing oil and gas prospects with an increased emphasis on low permeability sands and carbonates. The pay wasn't particularly good. He even heard that a couple of businessmen involved with some kind of oil fund were providing part of the money necessary to hire him. By now, Holifield had learned that the Middle East had made the decision to cut off much of the oil supplied to the United States, and he had a much better understanding of why the Minister of Petroleum had succinctly told him that everything had changed. It had indeed changed. Maybe even for the better.

The demand for domestic oil was rising, and so was the price for crude, inching up near eight dollars a barrel. It still took a good well delivering a high volume of oil on a consistent basis to make a decent payday, especially for the major companies.

For independent operators, the sudden real estate slump had made a lot of investors nervous. If they still had any money, most did not want to give it up, no matter how glamorous an oilfield prospectus might sound.

Holifield knew he wouldn't have any problem staying busy, but he wondered just how productive he could be when it seemed that all of the easy fields had already been discovered The only temptation beckoned from those out-of-the-way sections of empty acreage that had been passed over time and again. A few parcels of the land were even dotted with dry holes. Rig sites were overgrown with brush and weeds. Hopes had been dashed. Dreams had turned sour. Old truck roads had been swept away by the winds. Even the ruts had filled in.

If an investor did happen to be straying into the oil business, where would Ray Holifield find a deal that he could recommend with a clear conscience? He had no idea. He was about to find out.

The phone on his desk rang. He picked it up and heard John LaRue say, "I need you to come on down to my office. I have a couple of men I want you to meet. They're oilmen and relatively new in the game. They have some acreage leased and say they can raise the money to drill the wells. They need a geologist. I told them you were available."

A few minutes later, Ray Holifield walked down the hall and shook hands for the first time with Max Williams and Irv Deal. Holifield was a chain smoker, dressed with all the aplomb of an absent-minded professor, and had holes in his shoes. If he had made any money at all, it was obvious that Ray Holifield had not wasted it on the finer things of life. He began putting two and two together in a hurry. Max Williams and Irv Deal both had companies, which were little more than one-man operations. One was a basketball player turned real estate broker, and the other happened to be one of the largest builders of apartments in the country. He often wondered if either of them understood the oil business well enough to really know the difference between logging and fracking a well and whether or not either of them had ever figured the intangible costs involved with sinking a hole.

They had obviously made a lot of money, and their shoes had stepped in a puddle or two of oil, but those intangible costs had jumped up unexpectedly and far too often. They broke a lot of men. A genuine novice in the oil game was always one decision away from potential disaster. Holifield was staring at two genuine novices.

The geologist looked at Max Williams and Irv Deal with unwavering eyes and asked simply, "Where do you have leases?"

"Frio County," Williams replied. "Down in Pearsall."

"That's in the Austin Chalk."

"It is."

Ray Holifield shrugged. "You'd be better off to get yourselves some leases down on the coast or out in the Permian Basin of West Texas," he said. "The chalk's not where it's at. Never has been. Certainly isn't now. They don't call that worthless chalk the field of broken hearts for nothing."

Max Williams had no idea what to say. For a moment, he just stared at Holifield. Here he was, standing face to face with a man who had been hired to find him an oilfield in the Austin Chalk, and already Williams was being told that he had made a mistake, maybe even a grave mistake. A wiser man might have decided to cut and run. But Max Williams had never seen a game he didn't think he could win. Basketball. Raw land. Oil. It was all the same. Play it out, play as hard as you can, and let the scoreboard sort out the haves from the have nots. Irv Deal's mind was in a quandary.

Had he and Williams made a mistake? Had Edwin Cox led them astray? Did they have the wrong leases? On the wrong land? Or were they merely saddled with the wrong geologist?

●

Max Williams and Irv Deal decided to make their first tenuous foray into the Frio County brush country to confront the Austin Chalk. Williams was constantly on the road between Dallas and Pearsall and wherever the next investor might be.

Deal remained in Dallas, his eyes riveted on the business end of the venture.

He would never go to the trouble of embarking on those long seven-hour treks to the field, never see exactly where the oil leases had been located, preferred the slick pavement of city life to a harsh dust always blowing in the oil patch, and, somewhere along the way, neglected to raise great sums of money.

Irv Deal did have a couple of major deals working. Up north, he said. Up in Chicago. He wasn't interested in collecting small sums of money. Why bother with living on the telephone, dialing number after number, knocking on doors, chasing down one investor after another for a few thousand dollars here, a few thousand more there, when he could finance the whole operation with an investment from one high-dollar source?

Irv Deal was quite content to remain in his Dallas office, hire the right crew, make sure that Windsor/U.S. had good, hard-working drilling experts on the rigs, oversee the spiraling costs of production, keep an eye on the numbers, manage the money, and run the operation. He was not an oilman, Deal said. He was a businessman. He just happened to be in the oil business.

Besides, Max Williams was a good salesman. He knew how to promote the wells. He loved escorting potential investors across the brush lands around Pearsall, scuffing the top of the ground with his boots, and explaining how the ground far below held fractures filled with oil. Max Williams was a good fundraiser. Williams could bring in the quick money. Deal would make the companies run smoothly. In his mind, Irv Deal had it all worked out.

●

Those who invested with Max Williams knew absolutely nothing about the oil business, other than it was a precious and valuable commodity. But they all knew him, and, if they bought at all, they were buying Max Williams. There was W. O. Bankston, one of the largest automobile dealers in Dallas. As the years passed by, he would always be ready to provide Williams with investment funds, as well as a list of new names when those last, few dollars for drilling a well still needed to be raised.

Mary Kay Ash and her son, Richard Rogers, came on board, she driving her pink Cadillac in a lifelong quest to make women more beautiful. A little oil could pay for manufacturing a lot of cosmetics. Don Carter was not afraid of any investment as long as it didn't interfere with his Rolls Royce dealership or his trucking firms, cattle ranches, and hotels. He would one day sell Home Interiors & Gift, which his mother had founded, for $470 million and bring the Dallas Mavericks into the NBA. Harold Clark had firmly cemented his reputation and made his first fortune in the home development business.

D. Harold Byrd's father had married Mattie Carruth, whose family owned most of the land sprawling across North Dallas. When Dallas grew, their riches followed suit. D. H. Byrd, the father, had romanced the oil business once before. He journeyed to Overton in 1931 when Dad Joiner's Daisy Bradford No. 3 well ushered in the great East Texas boom because the crippled, old wildcatter had promised to sell him some of his land holdings. Byrd found Joiner asleep in his tent. He waited.

He was too late. H. L. Hunt wound up with the leases and the fortune. Not to be outsmarted by the likes of Dad Joiner, D. H. Byrd went ahead and drilled twenty-nine oil wells of his own. Twenty-eight of them had nothing at the bottom of the hole but more rocks. He became known far and wide as Dry Hole Byrd. But he married well. In North Dallas, dry dirt was about as valuable as oil.

To his eclectic collection of investors, Max Williams added Don and Corky Furr, who had made their considerable amount of money with Furr's Cafeteria, as well as Ben and June Collier, who had flown to Dallas from Montgomery Alabama, to determine how much it would cost them to play a game that paid off in oil. To them, a drilling rig was little more than a toy with a hefty price tag. June Collier was an entrepreneur who would ultimately be named as one of the country's top ten business women.

When Ford began developing its Mustang in 1964, she and Ben submitted the winning bid to build the wire harness for the snappy little sports car even though they did not own or have access to a manufacturing plant. Ben Collier, who had been a weight lifter at The University of Texas, weighed more than four hundred pounds, was extremely athletic in spite of his size, sold an assortment of auto parts, and was regarded as a great salesman. Ford was moving swiftly and ordered twenty thousand wire harnesses in case the Mustang was a success. Collier hastily built a plant and, before the year ended, had manufactured wire harnesses for more than three hundred thousand automobiles.

Max Williams had met Ben Collier while playing tennis in a Dallas tournament. He and June seemed to be quite impressed that Williams had dared venture into the oil business.

"That's what I want to do," Ben Collier said,

"What's that?"

"Run an oil company."

Max Williams grinned. "You can't run mine, he said, but I'll let you put some money in it."

Ben Collier nodded. That was close enough. He and June would be the first to step up and invest a million dollars in the oil exploration ventures of Max Williams, Irv Deal, and Windsor/U.S.

10

*F*or many, the search for oil was not merely a gamble. It was a game. And those with investment dollars believed in Max Williams. He shot straight with them, looked them squarely in the eyes when he spoke, always did what he said he would do, owned up to the mistakes he made, and began immediately to correct them. It sometimes cost him money. It never cost him his honor. An investor, who placed his faith and his money with Max Williams, said one Dallas banker, could go to bed and sleep well at night. Max took care of the dollars you gave him as though they were his own.

He had moved quietly into the harsh landscape of Pearsall, down where Interstate 35 reached toward the border with Mexico, about an hour's drive southwest of San Antonio. In appearance, the countryside was little different from the empty, sun-baked ranchlands that sprawled around his West Texas home. Pearsall had once been known as Frio Town when the International-Great Northern Railroad roared through in 1882. Its first brush with oil greatly changed the complexion of Pearsall during the 1930s, insuring that the town fared better than expected when the dark clouds of the Great Depression hovered above the nation. By the time drillers uncovered pockets of natural gas in 1945, the town had paved streets, a hundred and twenty-eight businesses, and more than five thousand hardy souls who endured a life that had always depended on the land – cotton farms and horse ranches long before oil was ever squeezed from the crevices in the Austin Chalk.

Max Williams was not timid about leaving his own imprint in the field. Ed Cox was moving his operation into the area, and Windsor/U.S. immediately dispatched Randy Stewart to Pearsall. His mission had not changed. Find land. And lease it.

Stewart drove to the Frio County Abstract Office, hid himself away in the clerk's records room, and began searching through oil and gas leases for names of landowners. He spent the nights in Devine, the closest town with a motel.

He was in a little cafe late one night, eating alone, as usual, and he heard raucous noise and laughter coming from the far corner of the dining room. Two men, obviously of Mexican heritage, had been drinking far too long, and each new word they uttered was louder and more profane than the last. They may not have been raising hell, but hell was simmering near the surface. One of them turned around and noticed Stewart. He waved. Come on over and have a drink with us, he said, his words slurred.

Stewart did. He was afraid not to join them. And Randy Stewart came face to face with the Trevino brothers. Good men. Hard working men. They owned a grocery store in Pearsall. And, more importantly, they owned fifty acres of land. By midnight, Stewart had leased all fifty acres sight unseen. It wasn't until the next day that he found out the land was wedged next to the city dump. It did not matter. Windsor/U.S. had land where they could drill their first well in the chalk. In time, Stewart was able to patch together leases on almost two thousand acres, just enough land to hold twenty wells if Max Williams had figured correctly.

Windsor/U.S. paid out ten dollars an acre, which, Williams and Deal thought, was pretty conservative, and they generously offered a twenty percent royalty on production. The company was relying on investors. It had not spent a great deal of its own money, and the farmers had earned a few unexpected dollars for land that seldom paid them anything. Irv Deal was handling the day-to-day business back in Dallas. Williams kept raising money, watching closely as their drilling crew dueled an unpredictable earth with time-worn, rock-battered drill bits. He was in and out of the field, managing investors, selling the deals, packaging the money, making the bets, and rolling the dice. Make it. Lose it. Throw it away. Whatever happened, his name was on the line, and Max Williams would have it no other way.

The drill bit tore into the fracture beneath the city dump. Thus began the struggle. From beginning to end, it was a fight. The oil came, but it did not come easy, and it came with a price.

●

Some in the oil patch described Max Williams, Irv Deal, and others as foolish for even daring to test the Austin Chalk. The firm of LaRue, Moore, and Schafer certainly did not recommend any kind of oil venture in the Pearsall region. The chalk was fickle. Demanding. Daunting. And erratic.

A lot of the wells in and around Pearsall had produced oil. No one disputed it. But no one, as of yet, had been able to bank any high-profit production. The miserly chalk, frankly, would not allow it. Max Williams and Irv Deal, however, had ignored the warnings and decided to take a chance. It was the first of their gambles in hard ground.

Both men believed that, with a little luck, they might be able to figure out the riddles of that ancient limestone formation. The oil must be down there somewhere in the chalk. Wildcatters had been catching tantalizing glimpses of it since 1930. Maybe those early day operators did not understand the formations or how to treat them properly. The formations were tight, and it was a slow, arduous process to merely cut through the chalk.

If the field had a chance to make it at all, Irv Deal told his partner, the team of LaRue, Moore, and Schafer might well make the difference. The Dallas firm certainly had a good reputation. The petroleum engineers knew what they were doing and how to do it. Besides, he and Williams now had access to a geologist of some renown named Ray Holifield. He had found oil in the deserts of the Middle East. Frio County was as much of a desert as any slab of distant sand in Saudi

Arabia. Maybe it was time to let some seasoned professionals tackle the chalk.

Across Frio County, Randy Stewart kept securing the leases that Windsor/U.S. needed and handling the legal work. Strike deals with landowners. Track down the heirs, living and deceased. Make sure the titles were clear. Build a pad. Haul in a rig. Put a crew in place. Then the drill bit could begin chewing into the earth.

Once. Twice. Three times. Windsor/U.S. found wells that were fairly productive, not great by any means, but they did spit out a few dollars. There was not enough oil to make them rich, but enough to keep them going on.

Back in Dallas, Ray Holifield was sadly shaking his head. Windsor/U.S. was wasting its time, he said. Its time and its money. Holifield had not yet trekked to Pearsall. He did not want his reputation, past or present, tainted and sullied by a field that had about as much life as a ghost town, one condemned with more chalk than oil. He could find locations all right, but he feared they would be a dead end. He kept meeting Irv Deal in his Dallas office and pleading with him: *Get the hell out of Pearsall.*

His logic was sound. If history were to be believed, and if history kept repeating itself, the chalk would ruin them. Williams and Deal had not yet grown wealthy in the Frio County field. But, then again, they had not been broken either.

Max Williams and Irv Deal decided that it might be wise to invest the money, and they met with a petroleum geologist who was in town preaching the gospel of a new fracking technique that just might turn Pearsall into a giant oil field.

The fractures in the chalk were small and narrow, some the size of blood vessels and veins. It was suggested that the wells could be fracked to make them larger. The method wasn't guaranteed, but it had been known to sometimes work.

Max Williams and Irv Deal decided that it might be wise to invest the money, and they met with a petroleum geologist who was in town preaching the gospel of a new fracking technique that just might turn Pearsall into a giant oil field.

Fred Skidmore was a self-styled geologist, a colorful character who claimed to be from South America and wore a .45 caliber pistol on his hip. He carefully outlined a new technology that had been developed to flush the oil from the fractures of the chalk in Pearsall. Skidmore said he could break open the limestone by pumping a lot of water under pressure and using a patented mixture of gel, sand, and mud to trigger a spectacular flow back. Oil was no longer a prisoner of the chalk. He had a convincing story, one that was simple enough for a pair of novices and more than a few veterans in the oil business to easily understand and embrace.

Fred Skidmore went to work with his new method of fracking a well. His was a procedure designed to clear the faults by pulsating water at timed intervals in order to turn the frac as it blasted through the formation. Water slurry and gel were slammed down the wellbore and into the formation through perforations in the pipe. Pumped under massive pressure, the mixture cracked the rock. Pump for thirty minutes, Skidmore said, then stop. Launch the attack again, and, if theory happened to be correct, the artificial frac turned and went in another direction, seeking out faults and fractures wherever they might be hidden. It was a good plan. It was based on sound science. It did not work.

Max Williams, Randy Stewart, and the crew grouped around Skidmore to watch the flow back on their first well. The water shot out of the hole with a tremendous force. Cheers rattled through the afternoon. By night, the water was no longer shooting its gusher of hope. As Stewart said, "It was barely peeing out of the end of the pipe." The men kept catching samples. They kept looking for oil. Only occasionally did they catch a trace. No one remembered the cheers.

Ray Holifield arrived in Pearsall late, selecting perforations on the last wells that Windsor/U.S. would drill in a faltering and cantankerous field. Until then, he said, his role primarily dealt with reviewing the production and economics of the wells that lay in hard, uncompromising ground. Holifield had absolutely no faith in the long-term benefits of the Austin Chalk in Pearsall. And he certainly had did not believe in

Skidmore's Kiel Frac technology, which had promised to crack the chalk and splash the ground with oil.

It had not been a technological breakthrough that would revolutionize a failing field. It had not cracked the tight formation of the chalk and had not splashed the ground with new oil. Another promise had bit the dust. The technology required a lot of horsepower, a squadron of pump trucks and mixing trucks, tons of sand, a number of command vans, company men, and engineers.

Randy Stewart remembered, "It didn't work, but, Lord, it was quite a show."

Ray Holifield drove away and turned his back on Pearsall for good. He was out searching for better prospects and new locations where Windsor/U.S. might at least have a fighting chance to drill and find oil. Holifield was young. He was ambitious. He was confident in his ability, and some even considered him arrogant. His reputation lay with his success in the great fields that had erupted from the sands of the Middle East. No one would be able to blame Holifield if the Pearsall chalk turned out bad. It always did. His advice to Irv Deal was: *You need to stop this insane drilling. Pearsall is a place that has no winners.*

The ancient limestone formations had turned rich men into paupers before.

As Ray Holifield recalled, "Max and Irv tackled the Austin Chalk below Pearsall as though their money was running out and their lives depended on it. In reality, there wasn't any kind of science involved. Just drill. Frac a well. And drill some more."

Max Williams and Irv Deal were conservative. They did not make a decision unless they knew all the facts, and they were never afraid to face the bad news and figure out some way to make the problems go away. Williams held on to his money. He wasn't particularly tight-fisted. He simply tried to spend it wisely. Irv Deal, on the other hand, thought big. No. Irv Deal thought huge. He always had. The one lesson he taught Ray Holifield again and again was: *Think big and don't worry about the cost. If it's any good, you can sell it.*

The wells came in producing a hundred and fifty barrels of oil a day. Good wells. Lot of money. Could make a poor man rich and a rich man happy. After the first month, production dropped to ninety barrels a day. Still good wells. Not quite as much money. No one was complaining, but everyone held his breath. At the end of two months, only thirty-five barrels of oil a day were flowing from the wells, which, at times, looked as though they had a serious need for life support. Not bad wells, not really. The money was still promising. Oilmen, however, knew what the chalk usually meant. *Don't go out and buy anything you can't afford, and you can't afford nearly as much today as you could have bought yesterday.*

The wells settled down and leveled off, making a mere six barrels a day. They were barely economical. Far-fetched dreams of immediate riches began to fade away. Irv Deal was concerned and had a right to be. He always thought big, and Pearsall might not be that big. At his request, John LaRue assigned engineer Dale Badgwell to prepare a study on the potential of the field, and the ultimate report indicated that oil and gas reserves were much lower than those previous projections developed by the industry.

His recommendation echoed Ray Holifield's original warning. LaRue told Irv Deal that Windsor/U.S. should immediately cease all drilling operations in the Pearsall field. Good money had no reason to go in a hole that had already swallowed the bad.

●

Maybe the field was somewhat worse than Max Williams believed it was, and the economics of drilling had all the earmarks of a funeral. Many an oilman left the pipes in the ground for a salvage company, turned his back on the holes, and rolled out of town. The wells that he and Deal had gambled on in Pearsall had managed to give each of them back only thirty thousand barrels of oil. It was time to look somewhere else.

The dreaded Austin Chalk had struck back once more. Ray Holifield understood the insanity of it all. Irv Deal and Max Williams had fallen victim to the chalk, and he was quick to remind them that their venture in Pearsall had been against his advice and consent. The oil patch, even on good days, had always been a bitter gamble, but Holifield believed that, in the right field, he had the ability to greatly reduce the odds and raise their chances for success.

Now and again, Max Williams would hear someone mention the big chalk well that had been producing several hundred barrels of oil a day for the last several years. Never been one quite like it, the rumors said. In cafes, around rigs, on street corners, beneath the neon sign of a Saturday night bar and grill, across a plate of barbecue ribs, at the desks of service companies, on the nearest pay phone, somebody, it seemed, was always talking about the big chalk well.

Must be a phantom well, Williams thought. Everybody knew about it. Nobody knew exactly where it was located, had taken the time to find it, or thought it was the harbinger of a major field. Everybody knew how much oil it was producing. Nobody remembered who had drilled it. Then again, Max Williams realized that rumors, both fact and fiction, ran rampant in the oil patch, any oil patch.

He and Clayton Childress had sat in roadside cafes on the edge of the Fort Worth Basin and overheard roughnecks, roustabouts, and tool pushers talking about the shallow wells that Windsor/U.S. had in the basin. He found out whether they were good or bad before he ever finished drilling them. Somebody always had an opinion that he passed off for gospel. After awhile, Williams did not believe any of the wild rumors. And, yet, he could not forget about the big chalk well. It was of mythical proportions, growing bigger and better with each new story that crept its way across Pearsall.

It was vital to ferret out the facts, he knew. Rumors were generally always based on the undertow of outlandish exaggerations, and a man could get in serious trouble if he wasted too much of his money chasing rumors that did not exist. He turned to Holifield, who sat hunched over a plate of enchiladas one night, and said, "We need to find us that big chalk well. If it's paying off as good as everybody around here claims it is, we should locate the well and see if we can figure out why it's making such a good payday."

Finding it should be no problem, Holifield said. Neither man would have to leave his office. All they had to do was start rummaging through those monthly reports sent out by the Texas Railroad Commission. It listed all of the wells in the state, their production, and their locations. The two men spread a map on the table and plotted all of the wells in the Austin Chalk trend. Ray Holifield agreed to start down south on the border in Maverick County and move northward. Williams chose to begin working his way back through East Texas and check the wells that edged down toward Pearsall. If the big chalk well had been drilled anywhere in the trend, they should be able to determine exactly where it had been positioned – city, county, hog pasture, farmland, dog run – wherever it might be.

The chalk remained an enigma wrapped in a riddle. Max Williams could keep on making nickel and dime wells, but suddenly mediocre wells weren't good enough. Others might want to throw away their time just talking about the big chalk well. As if on a Quixotic quest, he and Ray Holifield were determined to find it. The windmills wouldn't get in their way.

●

Terry Moore had worked with Max Williams as an agent for McClennahan, and when real estate fell into a deep slumber, he took his inordinate talent for salesmanship and moved into the oil game as a promoter and operator. Moore was no stranger to the risks and rewards of investing, and he considered himself a deal maker. He asked Williams, "Do you by any chance know Ted Clifford?"

"I can't say that I do."

"Well, he knows about your leases down in Pearsall, and he'd like to talk to you."

Max Williams grinned. "I'll talk to anyone," he said softly. "What does Ted have in mind?"

"Ted wants to make a deal on your Pearsall acreage."

"What kind of deal?"

"That's between you and Ted."

Ted Clifford was a Schedule D operator, which meant that, legally, he had to register with the Securities Commission before he could send out mailings or make calls in an effort to raise money. By registering, however, he was allowed to call on as many investors as it took to raise money as long as every aspect of the investment was included in the prospectus, including the pitfalls, the risks, and the uncertainties associated with oil exploration. Schedule D operators made sure that their brochures and phone calls pointed out the hard truth of it all. *The investment has no relationship to the ultimate cost of the well. This is a very speculative venture. The odds of making money are slim at best.* They also duly listed all of the best fields and best wells they had found, or at least named the great fields where they had drilled or owned a small percentage of a well, giving them the credibility and credentials they needed to be recognized as successful oil operators.

Some Schedule D operators might raise two or three times the actual cost to drill and complete a well from several hundred investors. Many of the investors bought shares for as little as five hundred dollars, which gave them less than one percent of the well, but everyone wanted to be part of an oil deal. Such Schedule D operators often ran bucket shops, single rooms full of telephones and telemarketers to man them. They placed calls from sun up to sundown, looking for small investors. The more, the better.

For many operators working on the shady side of the street, a well might indeed cost them two hundred thousand dollars to drill. By phone and by mail, tracking down hundreds of small-time, two-bit investors, they might generate a million dollars or more. It made no difference to them whether the well was good or bad. An operator had eight hundred thousand dollars he could carry the to bank.

It may not have been ethical. On some deals, it probably wasn't even legal. Max Williams and Irv Deal scorned the practice. It gave a lot of good, honest, decent operators a bad name. They both had known for a long time that a man's reputation might well be his greatest asset.

Terry Moore had been right when he said that Ted Clifford wanted to meet with Max Williams. Clifford was not a man who had time to waste. He had a job to do, and he was ready to get it done. He was blunt. He was up front. He never beat around the bush. "How many locations do you have?" he asked.

"We've already drilled several wells," Williams told him. "They're making a little money. And I have more locations if those wells turn out to be profitable."

Clifford stared out the window and scratched his face, deep in thought. He was not and had never been accused of being a dabbler in the oilfield. He wanted what was his, always trying to figure out a way to acquire what was somebody else's as well. "Tell you what I'll do," he said at last. "I'll take all of your leases, pay you fifty dollars an acre for them, and give you twenty-five percent of production. It's good money if the wells hit, and I'm betting I can make them hit."

Clifford caught Max Williams at exactly the right moment. He had grown weary of the day-to-day, phone-call-to-phone-call, time consuming chore of raising money, and he needed at least a few new investors to cover the production cost of every new well that went into the chalk. Williams kept close tabs on the total cost of drilling. He promoted but never oversold a well.

He and Irv Deal took their money and their profits only when they found oil. Dry holes could ruin them. There was no financial cushion. Drillers seldom ever agreed to send their drill bits down into the deep earth if the money wasn't there.

Ted Clifford would now be responsible for underwriting those costs. Williams never liked to lose control of a well, but Clifford's proposal was fair enough, he guessed. Under the circumstances, it might be the best deal he would get.

Max Williams pocketed his forty-dollar-an-acre profit for Windsor/U.S. on the twenty-two hundred lease acres, almost ninety thousand dollars, and took the road north toward Dallas. He was still wondering what the notorious Austin Chalk had in store for him. As far as he was concerned, Ted Clifford could fight it out in Pearsall on his own. Good luck, and God bless.

At the moment, Max Williams had the big chalk well on his mind.

11

*B*ack in Dallas, Max Williams spent the morning, reading through various and assorted production reports in an effort to better determine his position in the Pearsall chalk. Found a little oil. Made a little money. Not much. But a little. Could have been better. He stood and stared out the window toward the Dallas skyline. The next time in the next field, he vowed to himself, it would be.

At Preston Trails that afternoon, he ran into Jack Stroube. Nothing unusual about the chance encounter. Both men occupied offices in the Addison State Bank Building, and they saw each other virtually every day either at work or the country club.

Jack Stroube and his brother Bill were independent oil producers themselves, and they were well aware that Williams had been in Pearsall, tackling the chalk. Their father, H. R., had gained notoriety as a key figure behind the development of the famed Corsicana Oilfield during the 1920s.

H. R. Stroube had broken into the oil business as a boll weevil roughneck in the Burkburnett Field, but, by 1921, he was broke and, as his son recalled, was turning handsprings for hamburgers and hook slides for chili. All he had to his name was a junk pile, baling wire rig and a string of drill pipe. He hocked the pipe for money to ship his rig to the next promise of oil, a transaction that brought him to Corsicana. He hired his water, fuel, rig building, pit digging, and tool pushing people by giving them 1/256th interest in the wells he was drilling. He did not have any loose cash to pay them. His son Jack recalled, "It was so dead in Corsicana you could hear your hair grow on Main Street."

H. R. Stroube drilled the first of four wells on a two and a half acre lease. It came in, Jack Stroube said, flowing something that looked more like red barn paint than oil.

It would, however, make a hundred and seventy-five barrels of oil a day. Between 1924 and 1971, those four wells produced nine million barrels of oil.

Jack Stroube once wrote: *After well number two had averaged twenty thousand barrels per day for four days, daddy and Cornie found themselves oil poor – potentially rich but short on cash. They didn't know how long it takes to get titles cleared, division orders signed, and how pipeline companies love to ride on your money. They called Humble in Houston and told them they would like to draw a little on account, on account of they needed a little walkin' around money. The Humble people said sure, to meet their pipeline superintendent, Ralph Hanrahan, in Houston, and he would hand them a partial payment. Daddy caught the train to Houston, still in his oilfield clothes, lace top boots, and all. He toted up the bills on the ride down, figuring if Humble would advance them around $20,000, they could pay off most of their debts. When Hanrahan handed him the check, on first glance he thought it was $10,400. He told Hanrahan he was hoping for at least $20,000 and that $10,400 just wouldn't do it. Hanrahan told him to take another look at the check. It was for $104,000.*

When Jack and Bill Stroube settled into the oil business, they were only carrying on a family tradition.

It was said of the two brothers: Jack can spend more money at a funeral than Bill can at the State Fair. Jack Stroube would always be fascinated with the search for oil.

He sat down with Max Williams over lunch and said, "I hear you've been doing some operating of your own down in South Texas. We've drilled a few wells in and around Pearsall. The chalk's a bitch."

Max Williams grinned. He wouldn't disagree.

Stroube paused a moment, searched back through his memory, then asked, "Do you know anything about that big chalk well down near the airport in Giddings?"

"If you've been in the chalk at least a day or two, you've heard about it," Williams said. "That's about all anybody ever talks about. But no one I've met has ever mentioned it being in Giddings before. Maybe that's the well I've been looking for."

"From what folks who've been there keep telling me," Jack Stroube said, "it's the damndest thing you ever saw. Makes at little more than three hundred barrels a day as regular as a ticking clock."

"Might be worth me taking a look."

"I don't know what else is there or how big the field is," Stroube said as he shrugged his shoulders. "But that big chalk well is making somebody a lot of money."

Max Williams frowned, thought it over for a moment, then casually asked, "Where in the world is Giddings?"

"Somewhere east of Austin. Not far from LaGrange. A little west of Brenham."

Williams nodded and filed the information away in the back of his mind. Somewhere between noon and midnight, his mind was made up. Come morning, he would be on his way to Giddings.

The big chalk well, if it were indeed tucked back against the Giddings airport, had waited a long time for someone to stumble across it. He would not keep the well waiting much longer.

●

Ray Holifield had been asked by Max Williams and Irv Deal to find another oil play even before they drove away from Pearsall. The chalk continued to intrigue them, but the chalk stretched across Texas, through Louisiana, and down to the Mississippi coast.

As was his custom, Holifield began most days by diligently thumbing through a stack of information generated and published by the Texas Railroad Commission, the regulators of the oil industry in the state. The commission duly noted each well in Texas, marked its location, and divulged the amount of oil it was producing on a daily basis.

One well, however, intrigued him a great deal. He had originally been aware of its existence because of the rumors drifting from one oil rig to another. The well certainly did not occupy the heart of any great field. It was sitting perched on the edge of Giddings, drilled smack dab in the formidable chalk, and Holifield had always possessed a bad feeling about the chalk. It ground the bones of men into sand scattered by the winds. It offered paybacks and very few paydays.

The City of Giddings No. 1 was a perplexing conundrum, a lonesome well, an orphan well, situated out in the middle of nowhere, surrounded by untold acres of dry farmlands, dry creek beds, and dry holes.

Holifield had already circled the location on a worn Texas land map by the time Max Williams telephoned to say he thought he had tracked down the big chalk well that everyone had been talking about in Pearsall. "It's in Giddings near the airport," he said.

"That's the one," Holifield said.

"How do you know?"

"I have the data right here in front of me."

"Can we find another well just like it?"

Holifield sighed. "The odds say we can't."

"I'm not betting on the odds," Williams said. 'I'm betting on you."

He was on his way to Giddings, and he wanted Holifield to unearth as much data as he could on the old airport well. Was it any good? Was it worth chasing? Was Giddings, perhaps, the next great hope? Or the next great hoax?

Holifield already knew. But a little knowledge was a dangerous thing. It defied all logic, unexpected and unexplained. Some old boy had dabbled in the chalk and gotten rich, Holifield figured. The City of Giddings No. 1 had been a steady producer for a long time, flowing three hundred barrels of oil a day for at least the last four years. The field wasn't large, just a single big well next door to an abandoned airport and a handful of dry holes. There may have been only one well, and it was lodged firmly in the chalk, but it was a dandy.

●

Max Williams had driven down a lonesome highway past rolling farmlands, and only a bare horizon rose up in font of him. He gazed across an unbroken landscape that covered the chalk like the jacket on a book. The *big chalk well* was the stuff of legends. But not all legends were true. Max Williams grinned. He would find out soon enough.

By the time Williams reached Giddings, picked up Walter Schneider, and turned his Blazer toward the airport, he was convinced that his bare-boned strategy just might work. Find the best chalk well in Texas, which he believed he had. Lease a little land around it. Try to determine which way the faults or fractures ran in the chalk. Move in as close as possible to the City of Giddings No. 1. And drill an off-setting well. The oil was down there. No doubt about it. Trying to locate it with a string of drill pipe, battling through chalk that, at times, appeared to be impenetrable, and probing around ten thousand feet below the surface of the ground had never been an easy task.

One place to hit. An ungodly amount of places to miss.

●

The oil patch had forever been rife with a lot of odd theories about the locations where oil could be discovered and ways to discern where it might be. For more than a century, poor boy operators had met with mediums and spiritualists, used water witches, divining rods, and doodlebugs, outfitted with an array of electrical wires, dials, and bells.

A doodlebug was placed in a shrouded sedan chair and carried across empty pastures by four men. A wildcatter knew to drill on the spot where the bells caught life and began to ring. Some oilmen only chose to spud in their wells near cemeteries because tombstones always occupied the high ground, which might be a salt dome.

A few, H. L. Hunt among them, drilled near a creek or wouldn't drill at all. They were constantly searching for a faint trace of oil that might be coating the top of the water and were classified as *creekologists*. Others were more like H. R. Stroube, known as *closeologists*. They were adamant about trying their luck as close as they could get to a high-dollar, money-making well, so close, in fact, they could smell the strong aroma of oil coming out of the ground. Max Williams may not have realized it at the time, but he was quickly becoming a self-styled *closeologist*.

If Williams were right and Ray Holifield was as good a geologist as advertised, Giddings just might be on the threshold of becoming a town – no longer forgotten, no longer ignored or overlooked – that had the potential of changing many lives, not the least of which happened to be his own.

●

After surveying the rusting carcass of a dead well brought back to life, a well whose pulse had never weakened, Williams drove Walter Schneider back to his service station and talked again to Ray Holifield. He had seen the well.

The myth was as real as he had hoped it would be.

He needed for Holifield to track down the right locations and Randy Stewart to lease the right acreage. Irv Deal would handle the operation and put the crew together.

Williams would raise the money. His nerves were on edge. He wasn't for sure whether the gamble in hard ground around Giddings excited him, frightened him, or just made him wary. The difference between riches and financial disaster was often a single step, a single decision, right or wrong.

Ray Holifield, tucked away in his Dallas office, sat down with a lease map and began carefully marking the fault lines where he believed they extended away from the City of Giddings well. He handed the map to Randy Stewart and said, "Get me every available acre of land within those lines."

Back in the beginning, Stewart said he really had no idea what oil or gas looked like underground. He simply referred to himself as a legal mind getting paid for doing some legal work.

While Williams and Deal folded up their real estate businesses and began poking around for oil in Palo Pinto and Pearsall, Stewart found himself spending more and more time out of the office, on the road, and trying to piece together scraps of acreage that made up those elusive leases.

He pored through musty old records hour after hour, day after day, tracking down those who owned the land or the leases, and figuring out who, if anybody, possessed a clear title to the acreage.

He assembled it all. Names. Addresses. Phone numbers. Did the phone still work? Had that sacred patch of ground been abandoned, sold, passed on, settled during probate, or lost to hard times?

For him, it was always something different, but somebody always had a title or at least one that could be cleared up with a few legal dance steps. Family trees often had a few crooked limbs and split branches that the family chose not to speak about, not in public anyway. When Max Williams decided that he wanted land in a certain region, however, Randy Stewart had a knack for finding enough old records to make sure he got it. The search for a title often began like a wild goose chase, but Stewart considered himself to be a pretty decent goose hunter.

●

Stewart drove immediately to Giddings, booked a room at the Sands Motel, and headed directly to the County Clerk's office at the courthouse. He carefully checked through the records, which, he said, were poorly organized and kept in a cramped vault. It might not be impossible to find the information he wanted, but, then again, it might take him a lifetime to track down the data he needed.

Stewart quickly glanced through the telephone book and discovered that Lee County was at least large enough to have its own abstract company with records, the yellow pages ad said, that dated "back to the sovereign."

The company might be a godsend, and it was located directly across the street from the courthouse.

Stewart remembered, "That evening I went scouting. Having come up from Pearsall, which had a bustling oil play, I expected to find some activity around Giddings as a result of the City Well. I kept looking for the sight of rigs. Nothing. As darkness fell, I looked for rig lights. Again, nothing. It was after eight o'clock, night lay around the city, and Giddings had gone to bed. I drove past the City Well on county road 448 and eased out into the country toward Serbin. A few miles out of town, I turned around and headed back. My car window was down, and suddenly I heard the clanking of iron, the squeal of turning metal.

It was a *Eureka* moment. At last, I thought, someone is drilling just off to the west, just past a tree and brush line."

Randy Stewart parked, climbed out of his car, cloaked by the darkness of night, and waded into the tall grass. He pushed through the brush, ducked beneath low-hanging tree limbs, and stumbled out into the open. He expected to find a drilling pad, a rig, maybe even a pump jack. Instead, he found himself standing alongside the railroad right-of-way. And in front of him was a work car with workmen pounding their hammers into metal spikes as they repaired the tracks. To Randy Stewart, it sounded for all the world like a working drilling rig. Without a word, he turned back into the tall grass, walked to his car, and drove sheepishly back into the sleeping town.

The next morning, he walked into the Lee County Land and Abstract Company and met the Knox brothers, identical twins, John and Bob. Stewart introduced himself as a landman for a small oil company and said, "I'm looking for leases in certain areas in and around town." The Knox brothers glanced at each other. It was about time. No one had come looking for leases or oil in a long time.

Randy Stewart knew Giddings was small. He knew the town moved at a slow place. He quickly learned that morning that business in Giddings took place over coffee, and no one was in a hurry. He sipped coffee for two hours with the Knox brothers, talked about oil, discussed the fortunes and misfortunes of the chalk, and, somewhere between the first and second pot, they all became lifelong friends.

The title plant consisted of land maps that covered the length and breadth of Lee County, as well as copies of all recorded instruments affecting the land. The documents were organized and entered by survey and abstract, which were critical for any landman. The county records, on the other hand, had only been filed by name, and if Stewart did not happen to know the right name, which he didn't, he would never find the right survey or abstract. The Knox brothers had given him access to a gold mine, provided there was more than a single reservoir of oil beneath Giddings.

John and Bob Knox were petroleum geologists by profession, educated at The University of Texas, and they had prospected for oil, gold, and copper throughout the four corners of the American Southwest. They had returned to Giddings, their hometown, to take over the land and abstract business for their father, John Knox, Sr., who had also served as the Lee County surveyor until his death.

On numerous occasions, the brothers had been hired to lease acreage for various oil companies that had tried and failed to find oil in various formations of chalk beneath the town. Their going rate was a dollar an acre, and they always enjoyed seeing another landman walk through their front door.

A landman meant the potential for new business.

The Knox brothers may have believed there was indeed oil beneath their town, but they had never bothered to drill for it. They were quite content to lease the surface and let somebody else pour good money down holes that, for the most part, always came up dry. One of their clients happened to be Hughes and Hughes Petroleum down in Beeville, Texas.

When news of the City of Giddings well had reached him, Dan Hughes immediately called the Knox brothers and told them to keep leasing acreage on trend until he told them to stop.

The Knox brothers had no problem leasing land. For hardscrabble farmers, it was easy money. They had managed to lease seventeen thousand acres before Dan Hughes called it quits. His company had been led to drill a well on one of the tracts, which was owned, coincidentally, by John and Bob Knox. But it was just an old chalk well. Came in quick. Played out quick. Nothing more.

As John Knox explained to Randy Stewart with a wry grin, "Dan Hughes was left holding a disappointment and seventeen thousand acres of dog ass land."

Randy Stewart looked at his map. He checked Ray Holifield's fault lines. They were scrawled across the same land where Dan Hughes had drilled. Holifield's marks had been scribbled smack dab in the heart of those seventeen thousand acres. Dog ass acreage. That's all it was. But Randy Stewart had a job to do.

"How well do you know Dan Hughes?" he asked the brothers.

"We're pretty good friends," came the reply.

Stewart nodded and asked, "Will you call him and tell him that the company I'm working with would like to discuss a farm out on his Giddings acreage?"

"Sure. No problem."

Randy Stewart stood to leave.

Bob Knox stopped him. "There's one more thing we need to discuss," he said.

"What's that?"

"When we did the leasing for Dan," he said, "we took a one-sixty-fourth override in the acreage instead of our usual dollar per acre. And we think we should get a one-sixty-fourth from you boys as well, provided, of course, you put this deal together."

"Done," Stewart said.

He didn't even have to think it over. He knew Max Williams and Irv Deal would agree. No money up front. Everybody gambling on the back end. In the oil business, that was simply good business. Before the afternoon ended, Randy Stewart had scheduled an appointment in Beeville with Hughes and Hughes.

The company had drilled a few locations in the Giddings area with hardly any degree of success. Dan Hughes, when he took the call from John Knox, was sitting in his office with the rights to several thousand acres of farmland stuffed back in his files, and he had little if any interest at all in them. It had all been a waste of money, Hughes thought. He might as well have gone down to the bank, borrowed a couple of hundred thousand dollars, gone out to a barrow ditch on the south side of Giddings, and thrown it away among the weeds.

Randy Stewart placed a call to Max Williams back in Dallas. "How much acreage do you want in Giddings?" he asked.

"As much as you can lease."

"An oil company named Hughes and Hughes has most of it."

"They willing to lease?"

"As near as I can tell, they've given up on it."

On the surface, it appeared to Max Williams that the town of Giddings just might be the next hot spot. Of course, he knew, a lot of oil operators in the past had believed the same thing, and they had all been beaten and broken by the devil's chalk. He wasted little time in placing a call to Ray Holifield. "You might as well head south," he said.

"What's going on?"

"We're moving the Windsor/U.S. operation to Giddings."

"It's still the chalk."

"I'm not as afraid of the chalk as some people."

"What are your ideas about Giddings?" Holifield wanted to know.

"Same as it was," Williams said. "Drill as close to the big chalk well as I can get and see if we can locate the same fault. Maybe it has enough oil for several wells."

"Can Randy get us some good leases?"

"He says he can."

"Who has the leases now?"

"Hughes and Hughes," Williams said. "We probably can't get all of them, but maybe we can acquire enough acreage to get us started."

"You think Hughes and Hughes wants to get out from under them?"

"Randy thinks they're tired of the leases costing them money," Williams said. "From what I've been told, they've drilled their last well in Lee County. Didn't like it when they were there. They have no plans to go back."

Ray Holifield chuckled sardonically. "So you're dead set on investing good money in the same old ground that turned good money bad," he said.

"I've got a feeling about this one."

Oilmen always did. Even the broke ones. Holifield laughed again. "I doubt if Hughes and Hughes is willing to turn loose of more than a couple of hundred acres," he said. "And Randy's gonna have to do some hard bargaining to get those."

"You may be right."

"Can you drill on as little as two hundred acres?"

"If I have to, I can. If it's the right acreage, I can drill on forty."

Irv Deal, like his partner, held a deep fascination for the big chalk well and its consistent production on land that, over the years, had become a graveyard for dry holes. The acreage around it might be tough to negotiate, he thought, and since he ran the operation of the company, Deal strongly believed that he was better suited than anyone to make the right deal on the right patch of real estate. He chartered a Lear Jet and flew to Corpus Christi to keep Randy Stewart's appointment with Dan Hughes.

Hughes wasn't there.

Hughes was never there.

His office was in Beeville. Irv Deal had a good idea. He was in the wrong city.

Undaunted, he promptly rented a car and drove to Beeville.

He sat before Dan Hughes and told him, "We're planning to drill a couple of wells in Giddings, and I hear you have some property we can lease."

Hughes nodded. He studied Deal for a moment, then asked, "Are you an oilman?"

"No."

"What business are you in?"

"I made my money in real estate."

"Oil is a different game."

"Not really," Deal said.

Dan Hughes raised his eyebrow in surprise. "How do you figure that?" he asked.

"All I have to do is replace a building contractor with a drilling contractor, then use a geologist instead of an architect," Irv Deal replied. "Business is about people. It's always about putting the right people in place. I know how to do that."

"What makes you think you can find oil in Giddings?" Hughes asked.

"I can, and I will," Deal replied.

"It's a dead field."

"Somebody found oil." Deal shrugged. "I'm betting we can do the same," he said.

Dan Hughes thought it over.

He had no faith in Irv Deal as an oilman.

He had little faith in Giddings as an oil field. But who knows? There might still be an acorn left for a blind hog to find. "I'll lease you some land," Dan Hughes said, "but I want royalties on the back end in case you hit something."

"How much?"

"A quarter interest."

Irv Deal was in no mood to argue.

Dan Hughes was in no mood to negotiate.

"It was probably an outrageous demand," Irv Deal would recall. "But at the time, I didn't care about the terms. I just wanted the acreage."

He would send Randy Stewart down to clear the titles, lease all of the acreage he could, hammer out the details, and close the deal. Irv Deal slid behind the steering wheel of his rent car and headed back to Corpus Christi. Long drive. Open road. He silently cursed Beeville for not having an airport that would accommodate the jet.

●

Randy Stewart walked into the Beeville office of Hughes and Hughes. The lobby was a small room. It had no windows. The light was dim, and a simple bare table sat in the room with a telephone perched on top. The sign on the phone said: *Pick me up.*

Stewart did, and he waited to meet Dan Hughes. No one was expecting a lot, no one except Randy Stewart, who was working for expenses and maybe a small override, depending on whether he secured the leases and if the acreage held oil.

The wild goose had settled in Beeville. The wild goose wasn't so difficult to pluck this time.

Stewart drove back to Dallas, sat down with Max Williams, and said, "I have the acreage you wanted."

"How much?"

"Eight thousand acres."

Max Williams did not know whether to be elated or concerned. "What kind of deal did you get?"

"Hughes is pretty tough. Worked Irv over pretty good and didn't treat me any better."

"He has that reputation." Williams leaned back, folded his hands behind his head, and asked calmly, "Tell me, what are the leases gonna cost me?"

"Hughes wants you to take a farm out. You don't put any money up front, but you have to drill three wells during the next ninety days. If you don't get them all drilled, you lose the deal and the leases. Hughes will take his normal percentage."

"Which means he's taking a lot."

Randy Stewart shrugged apologetically. "It's always a lot," he said. "What he wants is a quarter interest on the back end. That's the deal Irv promised him."

"What options do I have?"

"Two. Take it or leave it."

Williams nodded. "Where are the leases located?" he asked.

Stewart was as precise as he could be. "They cover an area shaped like a half moon, lying from the city well north, south, and west of Giddings," he said.

Stewart unfolded a land map and handed it to Williams. On it, Dan Hughes had created a checkerboard for his total acreage in Lee County, eight thousand acres shaded in black and another eight thousand acres left white.

"Dan says you can have your pick," the young attorney said. "Black or white. Doesn't make any difference to him."

Max Williams stared at the back wall, trying to determine if he were in the middle of a dilemma, a shell game, or an opportunity. Houston Oil and Minerals had originally brought a rig into the chalk and drilled the Knox Number One. The bit never made it through the chalk. It broke off. It was throttled by the rock. Williams couldn't remember exactly what happened, but he knew that the well had blown out before anybody cashed a dollar's worth of oil. It might be risky, Williams thought.

Then again, Ray Holifield, who disliked the chalk as much or more than anyone, would tell him, "The field's full of faults, and some of those faults have fractured the chalk. Where the chalk is fractured, there's oil, and the fractures allow it to travel to the wellbore. That, you can bet on."

The problem was, the seismic was almost impossible to read. Looked like a bunch of hieroglyphics to most geologists. What should make sense didn't. And what didn't make sense was even more confusing. It could be that Houston Oil and Minerals, just like Hughes and Hughes, simply missed the fault beneath the well, provided, of course, any faults did actually exist down below the Knox Number One. "If there was," Holifield said, "he just might be the only man on earth who could find them."

Williams leaned over the desk and studied the map again. A checkerboard of squares. Some shaded black, and some left white. His pick. He sighed, looked up at Randy Stewart, and said, "We'll take the black."

12

*I*t did not take Ray Holifield long to realize that Max Williams and Irv Deal were both serious and focused. They had a game plan. Williams had access to money. He had done his homework. He was on a frantic pace, driving back and forth from his Dallas office to the chalk.

Irv Deal, on the other hand, was methodically setting up the business operation as Windsor/U.S. He watched the men pull up stakes in Pearsall and move northward to another chalk trend of broken hearts and empty bank accounts.

It marked the beginning of a venture that would force the two companies to invest more than four million dollars in the production of their first seven wells. They were all drilled, it seemed, within spitting distance of those dry holes that bore the last hopes and fortunes of good men, dry holes that had already been buried, if not forgotten, beneath a stack of rusting scrap metal.

Deal sent Charles Holbrook to the field to organize his venture into the well-lamented Austin Chalk. Holbrook had been in charge of construction for his apartment development, and Deal was convinced that supervising a team to drill for oil beneath the earth was little different from overseeing a crew hired to nail together buildings on top of it. Holbrook had been successful at one. Deal had no doubt that Holbrook, with his work ethic and organizational skills, would prove just as valuable in Giddings.

A veteran of the oil patch, Clarence Cheatham, came on board to handle the day-to-day field operation of each rig, and Red Livingston signed on to direct the drilling of the wells. Back in the Fort Worth basin, he seldom ever had to go farther down than four thousand feet to discover a positive show of oil. In the Giddings field, he would have to cut through as many as nine thousand feet to even reach the chalk.

Giddings was a brand new game.

Irv Deal thought big and sometimes bigger. That's what Ray Holifield liked about him. Shoot for the moon, and you might just hit it. In the oil business, go for broke, he said, and if you get there, you've made more money than either you or your ex-wives can spend. The conservative Max Williams kept his eyes steady on the details, always on the go, promoting and looking for investors, making sure the puzzle wasn't completed until all of the missing pieces were in place, trying to patch up any possible mistake before it occurred. Max Williams and Irv Deal would get a well. No doubt about it. But the chase for oil would be a wild ride, and both men hoped it wasn't a long ride and oil wells kept pumping money.

Deal had the assets banked, but he preferred to keep his assets for himself, and he kept alluding to the fact that he had some investors squirreled away up in Chicago. When the timing was right, the money would be right.

Max Williams kept patching together the financial end of the package with many of the Dallas connections he had made during his days at SMU and with the Chaparrals. He was a man who would not be denied and, as in basketball, he would never give up until the final shot had been taken.

The Fort Worth Basin had been all right for the tenuous, frayed partnership of Max Williams and Irv Deal. Nothing spectacular. But all right. Pearsall had given them some oil. Not a lot. But it hadn't given anyone else a lot either. Now Holifield was seated at a desk in the Sands Motel on the edge of Giddings, hovered over an old land map, barely visible or legible beneath the dim glow of a single naked light bulb, trying to pinpoint a drilling location on that confounded line between the Knox well, a failure, and the City of Giddings No. 1, still flushing out as many as three hundred barrels of oil a day.

Holifield carefully smoothed out the folds and wrinkles of the map. He took a pen and drew a straight line across the acreage that Randy Stewart had been able to secure from Hughes and Hughes, connecting the City of Giddings No. 1 to the old Knox well.

Somewhere along that line, he reasoned, would be the place to drill. Maybe a little seismic work would tell him exactly where the right pressure point had cracked the limestone, provided there was any money available for the seismic shots.

Otherwise, he realized, it would be more like probing the innards of the earth with his eyes closed.

Holifield was convinced that he had a definite edge in the Giddings field now that he was beginning to better understand it. Unlike most geologists, he had studied the nuances of similar faults and fractures before in the Middle East.

He knew exactly what he was looking for in the seismic logs, which generally looked as though they had been written down in ancient, unknown tongues, and those strange, wavy lines were no longer a mystery.

The process was not really a complicated one.

Crews set off a series of small dynamite explosions in designated areas of the field, precisely recording and timing the reflected waves or signals in order to determine the depth of the substrata. Basically, the shots did little more than vibrate the earth, but they were instrumental in turning the hit-and-miss art of oil exploration into a science-based methodology.

Ray Holifield always believed that seismograph technology was simply a bunch of shockwaves that gave eyes to the geologist and let him map the faults and fractures, anomalies and anticlines, domes, and broken strata beneath the crust of the earth where oil and gas might be accumulating. He smiled to himself. The logs were worthless if a geologist could not read them.

As of yet, no geologist in his right mind had been able to make heads or tales of the seismic data being spit out in the chalk.

They were still shooting in the dark at a moving target.

He adamantly told Max Williams that his particular understanding of the science had the ability to change the odds, and Williams saw no reason to doubt him.

●

Holifield was certain that he knew which direction the faults ran in the earth. Some things in textbooks, he said, were absolutes. He looked hard at the big chalk well. He measured distances. He calculated angles. He walked the acreage that bound together the City of Giddings and Knox wells, measuring the bleak lease lots again in yards, in feet, in inches. He did not have any existing science or technology available to him. His decision would be based more on experience and gut instincts than anything else. *Trendology,* following the direction set by successful wells, had long been an effective method for finding oil, However, two wells did not a trend make.

Holifield would have to gamble.

He knew how to read the earth. But no one had ever been able to read or unravel the puzzle of the Austin Chalk. The forbidden layers of limestone were as defiant in 1976 as they had been when that first renegade band of wildcatters came stomping through Lee County in the 1930s. The old school ways of exploring a field had never worked below Giddings.

However, Holifield was convinced that if someone came along with the right idea and the right application, he had a chance of making a large and important field. It would require a special understanding of the limestone formations and the utilization of unconventional methods of recovery because the oil was down there lying in wait. Ray Holifield could sense it. But what would it take to unlock the crude? Who had the magic wand? The old chalk definitely wasn't for amateurs; then again, maybe it was.

A geologist Parke A. Dickey had once written, "We usually find oil in new places with old ideas. But sometimes we find oil in an old place with a new idea. Several times in the past, we thought we were running out of oil when actually we were only running out of ideas." Ray Holifield had come to the chalk searching for a new idea.

He took a deep breath and selected the location for his initial venture into Lee County soil. No seismic readings. Just going down blind. Many had drilled on the land above the Austin Chalk trend. Only one well, after all of these years, remained standing. Flame outs. Blowouts. Dry outs.

The rest were little more than deserted holes in a deserted field. If he missed as others had, his name and reputation both would probably be nothing more than mere afterthoughts in the annals of Giddings. If he hit, however, if he could find some way to decipher the code of the chalk, he would be recognized for his discovery of a major oilfield that had long been blasphemed and abused, feared and ignored, bypassed and condemned, but never forgotten.

Ray Holifield thought he had it all figured out. He didn't. Historically, he knew, faults almost always ran back up from the coast at a forty-five degree angle. That's what he had been taught. That's what experience told him. Holifield was convinced, beyond any reasonable doubt, that he had been able to pinpoint the critical fault line that fed the City of Giddings No. 1. Drill. Hit it. Head to the bank.

He later recalled, "My science was all wrong in the chalk. I didn't realize it at the time, but I didn't have a clue. A seismic reading may have told me altogether something different. We'll never know. We simply drilled on a hunch. Mine."

●

It wouldn't be easy, and the venture got off to a rocky start. The Austin Chalk was tough enough, but it looked in the beginning as though red tape and city ordinances might present even worse problems. Ray Holifield had selected his prime location. Believed in it. Stood his ground. Wouldn't move.

The trouble was, however, his proposed drilling site lay inside the city limits of Giddings. By all rights, Windsor, which owned the permit, would not be allowed to drill without the city's cooperation.

As a community, Giddings was suffering much as it had during the Great Depression, and Lee County had always been recognized as poor and losing money every day. Giddings needed the well. Giddings needed the business. Before any drill bit touched the ground, Max Williams and Irv Deal needed approval from the Texas Railroad Commission and a permit from the Giddings city aldermen.

They received both in July of 1976, and the newspaper reported: *The well will be drilled on the H. T. Moore land. It will be located on the north side of Highway 77. Windsor Oil officials have repeated that once the work begins, they should know if there is oil within a month. The company has deposited in the city's name a total of $25,000 in lieu of a bond in the First National Bank of Giddings.*

●

Max Williams and Irv Deal drilled the M&K – named for landowners H. T. Moore, an African American shoe repairman in his late seventies, and James Krchnak, a traveling paint salesman of Czech descent – on acreage offset from the big chalk well. The men were staring hard at a drilling cost of about three hundred and twenty thousand dollars, which amounted to the total annual budget of both companies. The drill bit carved its way quickly through an overlay of eight thousand feet of soft earth, then bore heavily into the tight layers of limestone.

All or nothing. That was the creed of the chalk. All or nothing, with the emphasis almost always on nothing. The chalk was hard as concrete, and nobody ever knew exactly where the drill bit was. Ray Holifield may have been drilling for a precise spot, but there was a lot of wiggle in the chalk.

Jack Killigan was an investor who had worked with Irv Deal on building a shopping center, and he told Randy Stewart, "Finding oil in the chalk is like trying to open the lock on a car door with a coat hanger that's two blocks long."

Day after day, the long hours weaving themselves around him like a spider web, Max Williams watched the drill bit turn alongside Bill Walker, an investor from Arlington, Texas, who had earned his riches by hiring an artist to paint bright-colored murals on the sides of vans and created a whole new line of vehicles he called the "Good Time Machines." Walker needed a break. He had sold his business to his partner on a leveraged buyout, realized one day that the company was headed for the legal pitfalls of bankruptcy, and hoped he would one day see his money. Bill Walker was still waiting.

The string of pipe went deeper. The intensity around the well was so thick, Max Williams said, that it was often difficult to breath. Emotions were running the gamut from wild expectations to a belief that the M&K might be little more than a pipe dream with more chalk than oil. Lord, they needed the oil. Chalk was so cheap a man couldn't give it away.

The pipe suddenly shuddered, and the well kicked wildly out of control and wide open. Oil the color of honey came bursting out of the ground. The M&K hit exactly three years to the day after Chuck Alcorn brought in the City of Giddings No. 1.

Fate? Perhaps. A little luck? No doubt. Irony? If a man didn't have the good sense to be superstitious, he wouldn't be playing for high stakes in the oil game.

Max Williams stood with a face of stone, his eyes never wavering from the well as it painted the slush pits around him the color of honey gold. It had hit big, bigger than anyone had the right to expect or imagine. The rush he felt was overwhelming. It was, he said, better than hitting a fifteen-foot jump shot at the buzzer to beat Kentucky.

Bill Walker was beside himself. An oil well, he thought, came much closer to being a good time machine than a van any day of the week. Oil rushing through the pipes was not unlike the blood pulsating through his veins.

Williams, however, tried to temper his excitement with a hard dose of reality, which was always a bitter pill to swallow.

Wells had hit big in the chalk before. Would the M&K begin to slowly die out by morning? Would it be nothing more than a stagnant seep by the end of the month? One side of his brain was overcome with sheer, unadulterated emotion. The other side was numbed with concern. Wait and see, he told himself. It might be over by the end of the week. Then again, the M&K might go on for as long as Chuck Alcorn's famous old City of Giddings well. He caught sight of Ray Holifield walking across a dirt road stained with mud and grease. Holifield was grinning in spite of himself.

"How'd she come in?" Williams asked.

"Looks like about five hundred barrels a day."

"Any sign of her slowing down?"

Holifield shook his head. "She's still out of control," he said. "Just look at her. That's what you hope for. That's what you hardly ever get."

Williams glanced down at his hands. They were covered with good, honest dirt, spackled with a trace of oil. He sadly shook his head. Irv Deal had no idea what he was missing.

The M&K settled down to flow more than four hundred barrels a day without any signs of ever giving up or running out. It was, most conceded, the hottest well ever drilled in the chalk. Even the City of Giddings No. 1 paled somewhat by comparison. When the news reached Dan Hughes in his Beeville office, he was elated. He had missed out on the big chalk well, he knew. Maybe the M&K would make up for it and ease the pain. Such was the complexion of oil. Such was the nature of the business.

Max Williams wrapped his arm around Holifield's shoulder. "You must be a genius," he said. "You told me you could outsmart the chalk, and I believe you did."

Ray Holifield's grin grew broader. "Now what?" he asked.

"Well, we've got sixty days to drill two more wells," Williams said. "Otherwise, we lose the leases. We'll celebrate tonight. Tomorrow, it's back to work."

At the moment, Holifield was not worrying about tomorrow or the day after. He may have been grinning for all of the world to see, but the grin was a lie. A big lie. Ray Holifield was lucky, and he knew it.

The drill bit had hit the hard chalk and twisted off at a crooked angle. No one realized it during the chaos and frenetic activity on the rig, but the bit had badly lost its direction, strayed off course, and missed the critical fault that had been Holifield's primary target, the one based on the Knox No. 1 log.

Instead, it had driven quite accidentally into a greater fault that harbored a much larger fractured reservoir of oil. It was a mistake, perhaps, but a mistake worth millions. Holifield kept his secret to himself and basked in the glory of the moment. His face was streaked the color of honey. The residue on his lips tasted like oil.

Oil had never tasted so sweet.

13

*P*at Holloway pointed Humble Exploration out of Texas, headed northward to the high country, and targeted an expanding oil play in the Williston Basin of Montana and the Dakotas. The early going was rough, and it tested every facet of Holloway's resolve. Raising money was no problem at all. Being an oil operator, however, had its pitfalls and its drawbacks. If something could go wrong, it usually did. He was face to face with men and machines, and he preferred the machines.

But Holloway rode clear of the hard days and found production in six western states, then moved on down to Louisiana. He was a virgin no more.

Pat Holloway was still running production costs and figures on the Williston Basin when Mike Starnes called and asked him for a meeting. This afternoon would be fine. This morning would be even better. It must have something to do with the books, Holloway immediately thought.

But then, there was no way Starnes could be blaming him for anything. Numbers spoke for themselves, and Mike Starnes was keeping the books.

The two men seated themselves, and Starnes got right to the point. "It looks like your oil exploration business has a chance to be pretty good," he said.

"We've done all right coming out of the chute." Holloway smiled. "Montana. The Dakotas. Louisiana. That was only the beginning," he said as though he had just made the first bold move in a philosophical chess game.

Starnes nodded. "I believe that we may have a problem we need to correct," he said.

"What's that?"

"Well," Starnes continued, "you're making a lot of money for Bill, but all it's doing is increasing his estate taxes when he dies. We don't like to think about it, but that's sure to happen someday, and we need to start planning for the future if Humble Exploration continues to make as much money as it already has."

"What's your solution?" Holloway asked. He and Bill Browning had written a clean and simple deal. Both men knew where each other stood in the business. One owned ten percent of the company, was a stockholder, had President on his business card, and remained the largest single contributor to the drilling funds. The other owned eighty percent and ran the company. On the ground. At the rig. Making the decisions. Engineering the risks. Making it work. Pat Holloway owned the eighty percent. He was not comfortable with making revisions that would drastically change their agreement.

"We need to figure out some way for Browning's children to be alleviated of any potential estate problems," Mike Starnes replied. "What H. L. Hunt did was set up a trust for his children, and it seems to have worked pretty well. Pat, I think you should consider starting such a trust on Bill's behalf.

"He and his wife can put some money in it, you can go out and buy some leases for the trust, farm out the leases to the drilling funds, and then let Bill and the other high-income tax bracket investors drill the wells and get all of the income deductions. The drilling funds shouldn't be spending money buying leases anyway. Lease costs are not deductible, and the drilling funds are supposed to maximize income tax deductions. You and I will be the co-trustees, and our compensation can be set up like Humble's with a convertible overriding royalty interest instead of a salary or a percentage of the money invested. A trust will simply be a much more favorable deal for the children, for the family, and, in the long run, for Bill."

Pat Holloway had a gut feeling that was more like a stab of nausea. He didn't like the idea, and he didn't know why. On paper, it made perfect sense. As a lawyer, he knew well the estate consequences ultimately faced by the children of a wealthy man. In the high-finance world of business, a man was always looking for every break he could get, every loophole the law allowed him to find.

"Is that what Bill wants to do?" he asked.

Mike Starnes said that it was.

"I wish you had brought Bill with you," Holloway said.

Mike Starnes shrugged and smiled. "Bill leaves the accounting work to me."

Pat Holloway recalled, "I told Mike I would talk it over with Bill, and I did. He did indeed want to set up the trust."

Holloway rolled the idea over in his mind a time or two, then, in defiance of his better judgment, he agreed to the trust. Mike Starnes said that Bill and Jane Browning would provide thirty thousand dollars to set up the trust. That amounted to six thousand dollars apiece for each of their five children. In fact, six thousand dollars were all that any man and his wife could invest without paying a gift tax.

As co-trustees, both Pat Holloway and Mike Starnes were required to sign any document or check on behalf of the trust. One couldn't do it alone, which made it necessary for Starnes to approve everything done by the Browning Children's Trust. Even though it was permitted for him and Holloway to receive payment for their positions as co-trustees, neither of the two men ever withdrew a cent from the trust.

Pat Holloway promised to spend the entire thirty thousand dollars buying leases for the Browning children. He still didn't like it. But he did it.

In his life and in business, Pat Holloway had made mistakes of all shapes, sizes and denominations. He had, however, just made the largest mistake he ever made. It could ruin him.

●

The months passed far too quickly. Pat Holloway immersed himself in business with more preparation than production, sorted through a variety of details that always had a way of becoming tangled up at the last minute. He was not expecting the phone call when it came. The news was devastating. Pat Holloway continued to hold the telephone to his ear long after the brief, somber message ended, and the dial tone began ringing. He had heard the message. He did not believe it. No. He did not want to believe it.

Bill Browning was dead. Suddenly. Unexpectedly. Far too young. A man in good health. Everybody said he was. A man in the prime of life. A husband. A father. Wealthy. Respected. A community leader. He had it all.

His heart failed while he was jogging in the mountains of New Mexico, and no one even knew it was worn out. He was forty-six years old. Holloway glanced at the calendar. The month would forever be etched in his brain: September, 1976. He sat back in his chair and closed his eyes. He suddenly felt tired and a little worn out himself.

Bill Browning had been more than a partner. Bill Browning was his friend. Holloway poured himself a whiskey and drank to the memory of a good friend while the memory was still warm.

By morning, Pat Holloway found himself running a one-man operation with the obligation to buy thirty thousand dollars worth of leases for a bunch of Browning kids so they could beat the government out of an estate tax. He would have rather been working with Bill. He knew Bill. Bill Browning had never been afraid to fight the good fight.

●

Down in Houston, the officials at Exxon were holding a series of closed door meetings with their attorneys. They had been wronged, they said. Some little upstart oil exploration company in Dallas had stolen their name, and Exxon claimed that their name was worth millions of dollars to them. Their name stood for strength and quality and integrity, and they wanted it back. The trade name of Humble Oil & Refining Company had been on the books since 1917, and it had a revered place of honor in the annals of Texas oil history. Forget the fact that the oil giant had spent more than twelve million dollars in advertising and promotion to announce worldwide that it had changed its name to Exxon. It no longer wanted to employ the name of Humble, but Exxon would fight like a wounded tiger to keep anyone else from using it.

Despite having twelve million dollars thrown at television, in print, and on radio, much of the country still regarded the company purely and simply as *Humble*. People had grown up with the name and had probably filled the tank on their first cars with Humble gas.

They gathered around their radios and went to the games with Humble, listening as the legendary Kern Tips broadcast the top Southwest Conference football clash on those brisk Saturday afternoons in autumn.

At least, that's what Exxon officials claimed, and they weren't about to let some two-bit lawyer named Pat Holloway, who owned a two-bit oil company, steal their precious and glorious name. In a stern letter, Exxon demanded that Holloway give back the name.

In a letter just as stern, Pat Holloway said, more or less, to hell with Exxon. As far as he was concerned, Exxon had, by its own volition, abandoned the name of Humble. If company officials didn't believe him, all they had to do was drive around the country and check the name on company service stations. Exxon.

That's what the signs said. Exxon. Not a damned one of them said Humble. The only place any of the officials could find Humble was on his business card: Humble Exploration Company.

Exxon, trying to avoid a public skirmish, made an effort to settle the problem the only way it knew how. Exxon offered Pat Holloway a million dollars if he would agree to drop his use of the name and merely go away.

He was a small fish. Exxon owned a big pond. Company officials decided it was worth a million dollars just to rid themselves of a nuisance. One well could produce a million dollars worth of oil by sundown or at least by the end of the week.

Pat Holloway refused to negotiate. First, he told them, "I don't need a million dollars."

Secondly, he said, "It would be a lot of trouble for me to go around and change the name of Humble Exploration on all of the wells and lease signs I have."

"We'll still give you the million dollars," Exxon said, "and we'll pay for all of the expenses you incur changing the name you've placed on your wells and on those legal documents associated with your leases."

Pat Holloway smiled. "No deal," he said.

"Humble is not your name," Exxon said.

"It is now," Holloway said.

He knew he was bound for court. Had known it all along. Exxon would not stand for someone telling the company no and hell no. Exxon did not like it a damn bit. Exxon had a fight on its hands.

Exxon fired the first volley with a threatening letter, no doubt written by some lawyer who didn't believe that anyone had enough money to go to battle with a giant. He did not know Pat Holloway. Within legal circles and behind the closed doors of a judge's chambers, his rambling answer became recognized as a classic. It was pure Pat Holloway. He calmly explained why he and Bill Browning had originally chosen the name of Humble Exploration for their oil company:

When Bill and I decided to go into the oil business one evening over drinks after temporarily exhausting the subject of women, we agreed that while our many virtues and various attributes were undoubtedly sufficient to assure our success in the oil exploration business, both of us could, in all honesty, be somewhat deficient in humility, and we decided that while this might be no handicap in the pursuit of women, it could conceivably prove to be a detriment in the pursuit of hydrocarbons, particularly since neither of us had any prior experience in that field. We decided that it would be advisable not only to adopt an attitude of humility but also, as an added safeguard, to remind ourselves daily of the desirability of that particular attribute by reference thereto in our corporate name.

Pat Holloway's letter also addressed Exxon's grave concerns that the similarity between the names of Humble Exploration and Humble Oil & Refining might result in great public confusion. He wrote:

We were, of course, aware of the former existence of Humble Oil & Refining Company and that it had changed its name to Exxon. To avoid any possible confusion on anyone's part between our company and the former public identity of Humble Oil & Refining Company (which your company had then recently spent untold millions of dollars changing over to "Exxon"), we did not include in our corporate name any reference to "Oil" or "Refining" or "Gas" or "Petroleum" or "Hydrocarbons" or "Energy" or any other such word as might conceivably lead to confusion between the two organizations.

The principal reason we chose "Exploration" was because it aptly described our principal proposed (and to date actual) activity. A subsidiary or affiliated reason was that it was most likely to eliminate any possible confusion between us and the former name of your domestic affiliate since (1) the word "Exploration" has never (so far as I know) been included in the name of any of your vast menagerie of subsidiaries or affiliates, and (2) your company, in the years immediately preceding 1974, had not exactly been noted for its exploratory activities in the contiguous United States (where we intend to operate exclusively) except for your domestic exploration efforts offshore.

Pat Holloway fully explained that Humble Exploration was a "very privately owned company with only three shareholders, and no salaried employees. Zero. It does not sell any products or services or deal with the general public in any way. It does not do business with any trade or industry suppliers who could confuse us with you."

However, Holloway was forced to admit, without any hesitation, that one troubling instance of confusion did apparently exist.

He wrote:

I must confess that I did receive a call last fall from an irate lady demanding to know (1) what the heck I had done with Kern Tips, (2) did I or did I not intend to broadcast the Southwestern Conference football games on the radio this season and (3) if not, why the heck not. I tried to refer her to Exxon, but she would have none of it. She insisted that she had never heard of Exxon, and after a while I believed her. I tried patiently to explain to her about the change of your name, but she accused me of trying to put some big con on her.

As I recall, her exact words were, "I think you are spoofing me, young man." Considering this remark judiciously, in its entirety, and being 45 years old, I decided to accept it as a compliment to my youthful albeit non-existent guile rather than as an insult to my integrity. I had the definite impression that if I could have given her any kind of encouragement whatever about a possible forthcoming resumption of football broadcasts, she would have turned her radio up full blast, continued her reminiscences about Sammy Baugh, Davey O'Brien, Ki Aldrich et al., and happily motored forever.

However, Pat Holloway made it perfectly clear to all parties involved that he had no intention of changing the name of his company, pointing out that "the public has gone from Humble Oil & Refining Company to Exxon, not come to Humble Exploration." As he said so eloquently, 'We have grown accustomed to our name and somewhat more strongly, we doubt we would be willing to make an even swap of names with you even if you were to make such an offer. We simply have always preferred Humble to Exxon." He did write:

I trust you are not offended by our preference to our name over yours. Just because we think you made a mistake in changing your name does not necessarily make it so. And even if it was a mistake, we think you are now big enough to survive even more than one little mistake like this. Overall, we admire you greatly. In fact, we believe you guys have reached the point where you are probably going to make it in a big way. In all respects other than changing our name, we remain your humble and obedient friend.

If any of the foregoing arouses your ire or offends your dignity to the extent that you decide to revoke my Exxon credit card, please at least reissue to me in lieu thereof my old Humble credit card so that I can purchase on credit some of the products and services that you presumably still market under the (Humble) trademark registrations.

Pat Holloway knew that the company's Board of Directors had passed a 1972 resolution calling for the continued use of HUMBLE after the changeover to EXXON.

To do so, Exxon instituted a trademark maintenance program for the trademark by delivering packaged Exxon products to pre-arranged customers with the Humble name. It also formed three corporations – Humble, Inc., Humble Gas Transmission Company, and Humble Oil & Refining Corporation – to sell bulk Exxon gasoline and diesel fuel to selected customers with the name HUMBLE printed on the invoice.

It was, Holloway reasoned, all a scam and nothing else. Total sales from those so-called package products hit $9.28 in 1973, zero dollars in 1974, $140.12 in 1975, and $42.05 in 1973. The three corporations, in spite of their powerful and holier-than-thou Humble name, only had sales totaling $395,814 during the seven-year period from 1973 through 1979, not much for a corporate giant with worldwide business to worldwide customers.

Pat Holloway knew the inevitable was coming, and Exxon did not disappoint him. Exxon headed to court as quickly as the company could find a judge to hear the lawsuit.

In his deposition, Holloway, his face the portrait of diffidence in a gray flannel suit, was the iconoclast. He had more fun than any other attorney in the room. Amidst a crowd of grim-faced corporate suits, he told Exxon: *Your letter of January 11, 1977 addressed to William W. Browning, as President of Humble Exploration Company, Inc., has come to me because my friend Bill died last September, and, while we have spent considerable time since then worrying about where he went, at least one fact is certain. He left no forwarding address with the U.S. Post Office.*

Under pressing examination, Holloway admitted that Exxon's old name and his new name did provide some bewilderment. He said:

A couple of years ago, your people here in Dallas through postal error received one of our run checks, but they were kind enough to send it on to us after meticulously and exhaustively satisfying themselves that it represented production from a lease in which neither you nor any of your predecessors, subsidiaries, affiliates, etc., ever had any interest. The Exxon man apologized for opening our mail by mistake, explaining rather wistfully I thought, 'You know, we used to be a Humble Company.'

Holloway sought to cement the idea that Humble Exploration was too small and insignificant for Exxon to even worry about. He said:

Where we have not ventured, not being big enough to swim, although we have waded around a little in South Louisiana and in a Texas bay – and nearly drowned financially in just a few feet of calm water when we struck our dobber in the dirt, differentially, three times and had to sidetrack each time.

Pat Holloway even told the nervous panel of lawyers, with a degree of humility that only he could summon up at times like these, that his grandmother might well be the reason behind Exxon's success, pointing out:

When my grandmother was running Gulf's (and prior thereto Guffey's) operations in Texas from Beaumont during and after

*Spindletop, she hired some kid geologist who went on to find a bunch
of oil for your predecessor and ended up as President of Humble Oil
& Refining Company. The Lord only knows where you would be now
if Grandmother hadn't hired that kid, trained him, and then advised him
to switch companies because Ben Bolt and some other older geologists
said they could work up all the prospects they had budget enough to
drill. But maybe, just maybe, you would have ended up like Mobil,
forced into selling ladies' ready-to-wear, or like Gulf, bereft of
meaningful reserves or control of crude both in the Permian Basin and
in the Middle East, and, to boot, probably faced with increased premium
costs on their directors' and officers' liability insurance policy.*

Pat Holloway was through. He leaned back, propped his feet up,
folded his arms, and grinned defiantly. Exxon officials and attorneys
had no idea what they were going to do with him. They only knew they
would see Holloway in court. He was not concerned. Exxon's attorneys
began to sharpen their verbal swords. Pat Holloway's were already
honed to a razor's edge. The battle, however, would come another day.

Holloway knew and understood the court system. He might or
might not lose the name of Humble Exploration Company, but it would
be a long time before anyone knew for certain. Once the lawsuit
entered the mold-scented bowels of the courthouse, then tried to
shuffle its way blindly through the maze of an appellate court, any
permanent decision or ruling didn't have a chance of surfacing or
seeing the light of day for years.

In the meantime, Humble Exploration Company, in all of its glory,
with Exxon officials and attorneys seething in Houston, was on the way
to gamble in a play that was far too small for Exxon. Besides, an
independent operator could drill a well for upwards of two hundred
thousand dollars. The same well would cost Exxon a million and a half
dollars. Too much fat. Too much overhead. Too much fine print and
red tape.

At the moment, Pat Holloway had never heard of the Austin Chalk,
and Giddings was nothing more than a dot on the map that, until now,
his travels had always managed to avoid.

14

Pat Holloway had never before concerned himself with the trials and tribulations of drilling in the Austin Chalk. However, his father's cousin, J. B. Lovejoy, had bought a farm and retired near the Lost Pines of Bastrop. He invited Holloway to drive down for a visit that would be partly social, he promised, but mostly business. Lovejoy had come across an odd little black box that he swore could find oil. Just walk across the earth and read the meters, he said. That's all you have to do. If oil were indeed in the ground, then his little black box had all the technology it needed to make a radiometric survey of the land and locate the hydrocarbons beneath your feet. It all sounded like black magic to Pat Holloway, not much different from the divining rods and doodlebugs used by oilmen in earlier decades. Didn't cost much. Didn't find much. He would have laughed off the absurdity of such an idea if he had not known J. B. Lovejoy as well as he did.

During the 1920s, Lovejoy had been vice president in charge of geology for the Gulf Oil Corporation in Fort Worth. For more than a decade, he had been responsible for conducting the company's seismic work and choosing those drilling locations that helped generate the great West Texas oil boom. When the No. 1 Worley-Reynolds well brought oil and prosperity to the high plains, it triggered the development of a far-reaching field that stretched for a hundred and fifty miles across six Panhandle counties. It was a long time before anyone again cursed the harsh and barren landscape that would hold more than six thousand oil wells, as many as two thousand natural gas wells, and twenty-five plants that produced seventy-five percent of the world's carbon black.

Drill bits battled deep for oil, cutting through a maze of prehistoric graveyards, digging beneath towering derricks that stood like lone, lonesome skeletons silhouetted against a West Texas sunset. It was a country that J. B. Lovejoy knew well. He had mapped it. He had read its seismic logs. He had found so many of the producing wells. The West Texas oil patch was home.

When Gulf Oil tried to move him to Pittsburgh, Pennsylvania, in 1924, Lovejoy picked up his papers, marched out of the company's office, walked down the street, and took a job with Sid Richardson, who promised him an override on every oil-bearing site he could find. Locked within his brain, Lovejoy had information from all of the geology and seismic work he had conducted in West Texas. Sid Richardson had not hired him for what he could do. Richardson wanted the knowledge that the geologist already possessed.

Lovejoy again surveyed the staked plains he knew so well. He found the fields. His work made Sid Richardson a fortune. By the early 1950s, Gulf Oil was considering whether or not the company should buy all of Richardson's holdings. A young engineer was sent down to study those vast West Texas reserves. He didn't stay long. He drove back to the home office and said, "You better not try to buy out Mr. Richardson because his reserves are greater than the ones owned by Gulf. You might be biting off a lot more than you can chew."

J. B. Lovejoy would have no doubt found the oilfields for Gulf if the company had been wise enough to leave him alone and not try to send him to some northern city where he had no intention of going. Gulf lost. Sid Richardson won. And now Gulf Oil was facing the sudden realization that it would not be able to issue enough stock to raise the money necessary to purchase Richardson's company. The reserves were too great, the price too step even for a conglomerate like Gulf Oil.

●

Pat Holloway was on a lonesome highway headed to Giddings. If anyone else had come to him touting the possibility of a radiometric survey having the technology to find oil, he would have listened politely, cut them short as quickly as he could, and ridiculed such an audacious idea over whiskey at the Petroleum Club. But J. B. Lovejoy was a rare and different breed. Some had merely searched for oil. J. B. Lovejoy found it. A lot of it. Maybe there might be something to this little black box after all.

"How does it work?" Holloway wanted to know.

The science behind the little black radiometric box was not the easiest to explain. It was a single channel gamma ray spectrometer using a sodium iodine crystal detector that had the ability to find anomalies beneath oilfields.

The earth's crust contained uranium, thorium, and potassium, primordial radionuclides that were randomly laid down during the creation of the planet. They and the deposits around them emitted highly energetic gamma rays in the course of their radioactive decay. Hundreds of millions of years after the radionuclides had been layered into the earth, hydrocarbon deposits began to form. Many geologists had long believed that low gamma-ray levels existed above anomalies where deposits of oil could be located, and some insisted that radiometrics could detect surface radioactivity and therefore have a greater than fifty percent success chance in their ability to forecast the potential of hydrocarbons being discovered at differing depths.

Pat Holloway stared at the little black box that Lovejoy was holding. The idea was unconventional, perhaps. Far-fetched? No doubt. But when Lovejoy explained it to him, the concept sounded reasonable and plausible. He was a geologist. He studied the earth. Science was always changing and always changing the way men looked for oil.

"Has anyone proved the theory?" Holloway asked.

"Not yet," Lovejoy answered. "But they're working on it."

"Have you used the box yet?" Holloway wanted to know.

"I've stuck it on the front of my jeep and drove down a few country roads around here," Lovejoy replied, a smile playing at the corners of his mouth.

"Find any oil yet?"

"Won't know till we drill," he said. The smile faded, and Lovejoy became serious. "Pat, if you invest a little money in the project, I can go ahead and do some radiometric surveys. I believe there are Wilcox gas fields just about anywhere I go in the Bastrop, Washington, and Lee County areas."

"How much money do you need?"

"Just enough to get started."

For days, Pat Holloway and his father's aging cousin drove the jeep from one end of the country to another. Rolling hills. Brushy knolls. Baked farmlands. Dry creek beds.

Lovejoy came back home at night convinced that he had seen some anomalies that might indicate the presence of oil, especially down on the border of Lee and Fayette Counties.

"Do you really think there's oil in this part of Texas?" Holloway asked.

"There is if you can squeeze it out of the Austin Chalk. The chalk's got an awful good grip on it."

"Anybody had much luck?"

"Not many."

"And you think radiometrics can make the difference?"

"In the oil patch," Lovejoy said, "the man with the best science always wins. If you know anything about oil, Pat, you know that as gospel."

Holloway couldn't argue.

Over a plate of barbecue brisket and sausage at the City Meat Market, Holloway listened while the populace of Giddings passed along gossip as easily and often as they passed the toxic hot sauce. They did not own an oil well, nor had they ever drilled for oil. But oil had become their primary topic of conversation.

Oil was money in a town where men were born broke and tried to make their way through life without losing any ground. An oilfield could change their lives for better or worse, and none of them knew how it could get any worse.

He overheard a conversation about a couple of oilmen out of Dallas who had drilled a well just outside of Giddings. Pretty good well, too, with no signs of dying or giving up the ghost. They had unearthed the secret of the chalk.

"Know who they are?" Holloway asked.

"Max Williams is one of them. He owns U.S. Operating up in Dallas. Irv Deal is the other. I believe he runs Windsor."

Holloway smiled. So Irv Deal had taken the plunge and immersed himself in the oil business after all. He guessed that a bad real estate market could persuade even a sane man to do almost anything when the money started drying up.

"They do any good?" Holloway asked.

"Hit the biggest damn well anybody in this country has ever seen," he was told.

Pat Holloway wondered if they had a little black box to read the anomaly for them. Guessed they probably didn't. Guessed they had never heard of radiometrics. Guessed they could do damn well without it.

The next few sentences in the conversation startled him and rattled him to the core. "Those old boys made a good well because they had themselves a doggone good geologist," the farmer said. "He beat the chalk. Nobody ever beats the chalk. But he flat did it."

"Does that geologist have a name?"

"Ray Holifield. I believe that's what it is."

Pat Holloway felt as though he had just been hit between the eyes with a ball peen hammer. Ray Holifield. Damn. What was he doing in Giddings? No. The better question was: why was he working for Irv Deal and Max Williams? Sure, Holloway remembered, he had once told Deal to hire a good geologist. He might have even mentioned Holifield by name. He didn't remember. But, damn, Holloway always assumed that Ray Holifield would give him the opportunity to participate in any good field he was exploring. That was part of the deal.

He and Frank West were still shelling a thousand dollars a month to pay part of the geologist's salary, and, by all rights, Holifield was their man. He may have been tucked away in an office over at LaRue, Moore, and Schaefer, but his soul belonged to West and Holloway. Holifield had either forgotten that fact or was choosing to ignore it and keep them in the dark. He had not said a word about trying his luck down south in the Austin Chalk. He hadn't even had the decency or the courtesy to give him a call and tell him there was a new play in Texas. Well, damn Ray Holifield. Holloway had been left to ride a jeep and play with a little black box on some country road that had nowhere to go and was in no hurry to get there. *Damn*. He said it again.

Two questions were troubling him. He could not get them off his mind. Why had Ray Holifield allowed himself to be stolen away by Irv Deal and Max Williams? And was there any more oil in the earth below Giddings?

He might never find out. It would not be because he didn't drill.

Holloway listened as the same names, day after day, meal after meal, were kicked around while the men sopped up the last batch of barbecue gravy in their plates. They had all drawn the same conclusion. Sure, Windsor/U.S. had struck oil. Sure, Irv Deal and Max Williams were the oilmen of record and no doubt growing richer with every rising and setting of the sun. But Ray Holifield was the man. He had conquered the chalk. He had found the oil. He was the genius behind it all. No one knew or ever talked about the starts, the stops, the mistakes, the failures, the gambles, those endless nights of doubt and anxiety on the rig and in the chalk. Sure, they admitted, Max Williams and Irv Deal might have borne the risk and had the most to lose. But without Ray Holifield, they would have probably come up dry and driven out of Giddings as busted and disappointed as the oil operators who came before them. If you didn't believe Holifield was the top dog out there, said one of the farmers, just ask him.

Pat Holloway had not yet acquired any leases in the chalk trend or talked to any property owners who might not have a problem with turning over an acre of land for a new or wrinkled dollar bill. As a result, he did not yet have any drilling prospects, possess any wild ideas about where to drill, or even if he should drill. When an oil well carried an expenditure of two hundred thousand dollars, usually more, it was necessary to make every hole count. Unlike some fields, a man could not throw a beer can and drill wherever it landed.

On the surface, one acre looked pretty much like the next one. Pat Holloway needed a geologist who could read the strata and decipher the odd array of formations that disturbed the tranquility of the chalk. The primary difference between good fortune and misfortune, he believed, lay in a geologist's ability to make sense from a scientific set of mumbo jumbo. He certainly did not understand those assorted faults, fractures, and anticlines, but Holloway would be willing to pay dearly for someone who did.

He asked around town, and he didn't have to ask long, until someone directed him to the motel where Ray Holifield, on rare occasions, grabbed an hour or two of sleep. He knocked on the door. Politely at first. Then loudly. It had unsettled Pat Holloway a great deal when he learned that Holifield was on the ground and serving as the underground eyes for Windsor/U.S., and now his simmering contempt was beginning to burn. When the door opened, Holloway was looking at the geologist with a cold stare usually reserved for the death angel. His jaws and his fists were clenched tightly, his face as hard as the chalk. He did not have time for any pleasantries. His words went straight for the jugular.

"Dammit, Ray, I understand you're down here working for Irv Deal and Windsor," Holloway said.

"I am," Holifield answered softly, not quite certain why Pat Holloway was standing at his doorway in the darkness of night. He paused, then continued, "I'm working for him and Max Williams both."

"How did you get tied up with those two?"

"I guess you could say that I'm down here on loan from LaRue, Moore, and Schaefer." Holifield shrugged matter-of-factly. "Irv and Max decided to go into the oil business," he said, "and they came up to the office, wanting to hire a geologist. John LaRue thought I could do the job. Here I am."

Holloway's eyes narrowed. He felt like an attorney with a hostile witness on the stand. He did not know what the full menu of facts might be and was trying to fish out the truth as he went along. His voice softened as he said, "I hear by the grapevine that you've been able to figure out the chalk and find some pretty good wells."

A curious silence hung between them while Ray Holifield tried to decide what Pat Holloway knew, how much he knew, and how long he had known it. He and the attorney had met but had never struck up much of a friendship. Pat Holloway wasn't the kind of man to collect a lot of friends, unless, of course, they had money and he could figure out a way for them to invest it in his drilling funds.

He worked. He schemed. He planned. He worked some more.

He was strong-willed, passionate, and intimidating, especially in the reverent business of law. His briefs fought with the tenacity of a junkyard dog, had the uncanny ability to dance around any facts he didn't particularly like, and Holloway could charm the gloss off of a photograph.

Ray Holifield did not know whether to twist the truth or just go ahead and level with the lawyer. He decided it was an issue he could not dodge. "I'm sorry, Pat," he said, "but I can't talk to you about what we're doing around Giddings or how we're doing it. Technically and legally, that wouldn't be right."

"Why the hell not?"

"I'm working for them."

"That doesn't make any difference."

"I'm afraid it does." Holifield frowned. "In a lot of ways, I'm no different from you, Pat," he said. "You have your attorney-client privilege. I have an obligation to my clients as well. It would be a conflict of interest if I told you anything that might be misinterpreted as me giving away any of our trade secrets. Irv and Max paid for them. They are trusting me to keep them locked up tight."

"What secrets?" Holloway wanted to know. "An oil well is an oil well. You find a field. You drill a hole. You drill the next hole just like you drilled the last one. There's nothing secret about it."

"In the chalk, there is."

Pat Holloway folded his arms and rocked back and forth in his boots. He smiled and changed his tactics within a single breath. "Hell, Ray," he said quietly and reverently, "I'm the reason you're down here working for Irv Deal in the first place. I'm the one who recommended you. Deal asked me about getting into the oil business, and I told him if he wanted a damn good geologist, and he shouldn't drill without one, he should come and see you."

"That's well and good, Pat, and I appreciate the recommendation. I really do. But," Holifield continued, "I have a confidential deal with Irv and Max, and I'm not allowed to say anything to anybody about our operation or the field where we're working. Not even to you. If you're down here in direct competition with them, then I can't help you."

Holloway turned to leave, but Holifield stopped him. "Do you have any acreage?" the geologist asked.

"Not yet."

"Then why the hell do you even need a geologist?"

"I might have some acreage any day now."

Ray Holifield gazed up into the faint glow of an early night sky. The moon was hanging like a gold dollar above the Giddings water tower, ablaze in the last reflections of sundown. "Pat," he said softly, as though he were talking to no one in particular other than a ghost in the shadows, "if you get yourself some acreage, then come back and see me. I can't help you a damn bit until you have some leases."

That's a helluva note, Pat Holloway thought as he walked across the parking lot of the Sands Motel. "Windsor Energy and U. S. Companies had come to Giddings," he would remember, "and they were down there with my geologist. Ray Holifield took our money, and we weren't receiving any of the benefits. Irv and Max owned the field. I didn't. They were here, and so was I. Giddings had oil, and, if necessary, I would go out and find it without the genius of Ray Holifield." Then again, maybe not.

Ray Holifield was a troubled man as he watched Pat Holloway drive away. He had been careful to keep the oil discoveries under wraps as much as possible. He did not go around town bragging about the wells he had found for Windsor/U.S. although he had heard others boasting about his exploits.

No one could keep a secret in a country town the size of Giddings very long, but he doubted seriously if anyone beyond the boundaries of Lee Country had heard much at all about the strike.

Ray Holifield had not published any professional papers explaining his theories, old and new, about finding oil in the Austin Chalk trend. Max Williams had time and again discussed his constant fears that larger companies with more experience in the field might come charging into Giddings with pockets full of cash and devouring all of the leases adjacent to their wells before Windsor/U.S. had been given a chance to secure them.

Holifield was bright, all right, but he had not cornered the market on intelligence in the oil patch. He realized that, sooner or later, some other hot shot geologist could well march into town with the knowledge and technical expertise he needed to read and understand those fractures in the chalk as well as he did.

At the moment, Ray Holifield had a monopoly in the Giddings field, and he liked it that way. He had no reason to share the secrets he had uncovered down below the earth.

He remained discreet and reticent. When anyone asked him about his ability to locate and hit great pockets of oil, Ray Holifield merely smiled and kept on walking.

He was, in the words of the oil patch, a *tightholer.* Frankly, he did not want competition tramping across land that bore his imprint.

Of course, there wasn't anything either he, Max Williams, or Irv Deal could do about the here-today, gone-tomorrow, paycheck-to-paycheck cadre of landmen, company men, completion men, roughnecks, roustabouts, rig builders, or tool pushers who were out spreading the gospel of Giddings oil across the state.

They had worked a lot of places. They knew a lot of people. They liked to blow their own horn when standing ankle deep in oil, and, more likely than not, they were quite willing to take credit for every drop that hit the ground.

Yet, Holifield knew, most legitimate oilmen had been deeply ingrained with a heavy dose of cynicism and skepticism when it came to the Austin Chalk.

They might trek into the field, but they wouldn't be in a hurry to throw their money away. It would take more than a few producing wells to grab and hold their attention.

But Pat Holloway was another story. Holloway had never seen an opportunity that he couldn't claim as his own. He always aimed high and seldom if ever fell short. He had the quick and nimble mind of a lawyer and the nerve of a riverboat gambler. He was not the kind of man to let the reputation of the chalk ever bother him or drive him away from Giddings unless the chalk broke him.

If Pat Holloway ever did lose money, it would certainly be money that had been gathered from somebody else's pocket. He was a competitor.

If Max Williams and Irv Deal had two thousand acres under lease, Pat Holloway wanted five thousand acres, or as many as he could get his hands on, even if he couldn't locate oil in the fractures.

He was a player. Giddings was the play. Pat Holloway could no longer resist the urge to wash his hands with crude the color of honey.

15

Buddy Preuss had a front row seat to the biggest show and most curious cast of characters to ever roll, swagger, or stumble through Giddings. As the country editor of the weekly newspaper, he did not see a boom coming, shrugged off any reports or rumors that it might be on the way, had no idea how wild it would become, and kept his pages packed exclusively with the critical news of the day that made a difference in the lives of Lee County.

Buddy Preuss did report in 1976 that Windsor Oil wanted to drill inside the city limits, and, like everyone else, he hoped an oil strike might generate some new business in town and hush the economic death rattle that haunted the region. But none of them was willing to wager on it.

The city, Preuss reported, was far more concerned about its well water beginning to smell like dead chickens and taste like iodine. He reported that some believed it was healthier to drink beer than the water. Crews shocked the water well with two hundred pounds of chlorine and flushed it out. It was good as new again, and, even on a dry day, water, good or bad, was more plentiful than oil.

As the days passed, Buddy Preuss became more intrigued in the cautious search for oil that was slowly spreading out in all directions across the farm lands of Giddings, especially since Windsor/U.S., operated by Max Williams and Irv Deal, had discovered that huge well filled with honey-colored crude within the town limits. Back when Windsor/U.S. was faced with the procedural problems associated with drilling inside Giddings, Preuss wrote: *I'd heard rumors that an oil well couldn't be drilled any closer than 300 feet from a building in Giddings. So I decided to check it out and found that there is a city ordinance, which states that a well can't be drilled within 330 feet of a building unless the driller has written permission from the owner of the building. As far as I'm concerned, they could drill through the roof of my house if they'd promise me a good producing oil well.*

Preuss, however, did not want to get his hopes up. They had been dashed by failed attempts to find oil in the past. He knew the odds were against Giddings.

The chance of finding oil was no different from trying to draw to an inside straight and needing two cards. As he wrote: *It's a big gamble, especially since it costs hundreds of thousands of dollars to drill even a small well. I've heard that for every well which has commercial quantities of oil, six others are dry holes. A man's got a better chance on the roulette tables in Las Vegas.*

He even wondered about the longevity of Windsor's M&K well. Had Williams and Deal actually hit a reservoir, he asked, or was it just another small pool in the chalk formation? Only time would tell. And time would be measured in days and weeks, not minutes.

The Giddings News & Times took note that Delta Drilling Company of Tyler was setting up a rig at a deep test site on the Arthur Joyce farm just north of the city limits. It was expected that Delta would take thirty-three days to complete the well. Houston Oil and Minerals had begun leasing as many lots in downtown Giddings as the company could get its hands on. Houston Oil & Minerals was convinced that the sweet spot lay in the earth below the town. Didn't know how long or wide it was. But there was no reason to drill any place else. In fact the county clerk's office found itself swamped with the search for leases, and Preuss reported that no end was in sight. County Clerk Joyce Hamff had become so cramped for space because of the sudden flow of oil activity that she was forced to move part of her office down into the basement of the courthouse.

By early September, news indicated that the Joyce well had begun to make a good showing, and the rig had been moved farther south to the Droemer Farm. Wildcatters had searched the farm for oil in earlier, more troubled, decades and gone home disappointed. Then again, it just might be different this time Maybe this actually was the beginning of something after all. But, alas, twenty-one days later, an article in the newspaper grimly announced: *The reports we are getting about the wells dug south of Giddings are all negative. Neither the Joyce nor the Droemer wells are looking too good right now. Houston Oil & Minerals has stopped the leasing of lots in Giddings right in their tracks. All leasing has ceased.*

As always, the oil boom had come in a hurry and left the same way. Buddy Preuss lamented in his column: *It's hard to figure out why we can't get another couple of good commercial oil and gas producing wells in Lee County. With a little luck, this whole area could someday be a large producer of gas. But don't hold your breath because wildcat well drilling is a chancy business ... With the price of oil tripled and quadrupled in the last two years, a good producing oil well can be quite valuable to a landowner, even though he only gets one out of sixteen barrels produced. In fact, the last well drilled in Giddings was only about a block away from my house. I'd sure like to convince them to drill the next well in my backyard. There was some talk that the next well might be drilled on property at the Giddings Elementary School in East Giddings. But we'll just have to wait and see where they set up the rig.*

The school board may not have been skeptical, but, in a regular meeting, it took action on twenty items, including a workshop for bus drivers, reports on lunchrooms, the class activity fund, a teacher being granted a leave of absence, ordering school supplies, and results on achievement tests before ever getting around to deciding whether or not to lease the school campus in case some reputable company wanted to drill or dig for oil, gas, or sulfur. After discussing the district's opportunity to improve its fiscal status, the board said it would be fine. The board was looking for all of the additional tax money it could get.

Buddy Preuss had always known he wanted to track down and write the news in small town Texas. He even thought he might be an editor someday, but he never expected to own a newspaper. He was a senior in high school when Lawrence Pope dropped by the principal's office one afternoon, and said, "I've just bought the *Giddings Star*, and I would like to hire a young man who wants to learn the newspaper business. Right now, he will only work part-time, a couple of hours after school, and serve, more or less, as a printer's devil. Pay's not real good. But the hands on experience he would get working deadlines at a real newspaper might be invaluable some day."

The principal nodded and said, "I have just the boy for you. Good student. You can't work him too much. He likes to work, and he's pretty diligent at everything he does. He's a real good writer, and if you ever need to use him selling subscriptions or advertising, I believe that boy could sell a snowball to an Eskimo."

"What's his name?"

"Buddy Preuss."

Pope laughed out loud. "With a name like that, I guess his roots run pretty deep around here," he said.

"They do indeed."

"Tell him to come by and see me."

Buddy Preuss, not quite sure whether he should feel impressed or frightened, sat in Lawrence Pope's office and said, "I really do appreciate the opportunity you're giving me, sir, but I'm the team manager, and I won't have any free time to work on the paper until after the football season. My afternoons and especially my Friday nights are already pretty well taken."

Pope shrugged. "Come as soon as you can," he said.

Preuss walked out of the newspaper office and wondered what secrets lay behind Lawrence Pope's eyes. "They were," he said, "the most piercing eyes I had ever seen. They could look right through you and would certainly startle a man on a dark night."

Buddy Preuss didn't quite get there soon enough. He never did go to work as a printer's devil for Lawrence Pope.

A few weeks later, Central Texas was stunned when an armed robber, carrying a .38 caliber snub-nosed revolver, had the audacity to rob the banks of Thornton and Schulenburg on successive Saturdays in October of 1960. These weren't what anyone would call normal, traditional, stick-a-gun-in-somebody's-face, fill a bag with loose cash, and speed out of sight in a waiting get-away car kind of robbery. No. It was nothing like that.

The bank robber didn't seem to be in much of a hurry at all. He calmly took time to read over the ledgers to make sure he knew the amount of money in the bank's cash drawers, then he forced bank employees to remove their clothes while he casually took photographs of them – old and young, all as naked as the proverbial jaybird – in assorted lewd and suggestive positions. He locked the unfortunate souls in the vault and threatened to provide the photographs to newspapers if any of his victims dared step forward to identify him. The robber escaped with only seven thousand dollars from both banks and would say, "It wasn't so much a matter of me being desperate for money as it was just being real damn mad at bankers." He was disillusioned. He was angry. He had exacted his measure of revenge at what he regarded as fraudulent and unethical banking practices. Any bank would do. The ones at Thornton and Schulenburg were merely handy.

Buddy Preuss, like everyone else, assumed that Lawrence Pope, the guiding light of the *Giddings Star*, would be out with his press pass, covering the robberies and writing about the arrest of the culprit. He might have, too. But he couldn't. Lawrence Pope was the culprit. Long before he ever thought of buying a newspaper, Pope had worked as a national bank examiner, investigating financial institutions in Texas, Oklahoma, New Mexico, and Louisiana. He had served as a bank cashier in Abilene, vice president of a bank in Houston, and, along with three other investors, became part owner, as well as president, of the West National Bank in West, Texas. Without bothering to tell him, however, his partners unloaded their stock shares to a swindler in Dallas, and Pope walked in one morning to discover his bank facing serious financial difficulties. Bank examiners were running amuck and finding uncovered marginal loans. Lawrence Pope was the only one left standing to blame. He was fired and rode out of town under the humiliating cloud of scandal.

Working in a bank was the only business he had ever known, and Pope thought he was pretty good at it. But, he realized, a career in banking was out of the question. Word would get around, he knew. The storm of controversy at West would dog his footsteps no matter where he went. In reality, he bought the *Giddings Star* cheap for the sole purpose of using the newspaper's printing press to produce banking forms that some of his friends, sitting behind executive desks of various financial institutions, had promised to buy. Pope quickly discovered that friends had a way of disappearing when a man carried the taint of scandal on his shoulders. Overnight, he had become a stranger to them, and they just did not purchase forms or any other merchandise from strangers.

Lawrence Pope simmered in anger. He rolled out of bed one morning and decided he wasn't going to let the banking industry abuse him or kick him around anymore. To hell with his future, if he had one. Lawrence Pope reached for a snub-nosed .38 revolver and a camera. He would make somebody pay, and he didn't care which bank he hit first. He later told police, "Bankers have stolen more than all the criminals have stolen."

Pope never made any bones about his guilt.

He was sentenced to fifty years, and none of them would be spent at the *Giddings Star*.

Lawrence Pope went to prison. Buddy Preuss went to Blinn Junior College but quit school when the lady who owned the *Giddings News* offered him a job to run the editorial side of the publication. Buddy Preuss became the youngest newspaper editor in Texas. "In those days," he said, "life was a lot like riding on two different tracks. I was on one and wondering what it would be like to be on the other."

He received his journalism education on the job, covering theft, burglaries, city and county government, car wrecks, train derailments, fires, obituaries, barbecues, rodeos, chamber of commerce banquets, and courtroom trials.

Almost every one of his Viewpoint columns found some reason for him to brag about or lament the weather. Too much rain. Too little rain. Hail. Lightning strikes. An occasional tornado. And what difference did they make to the harvest of peanuts and the sale of cattle?

Buddy Preuss was the eyes and ears, if not the conscience, of Giddings and Lee County. But what could he say about the new search for oil? He couldn't ignore it. Then again, Preuss felt a little uneasy about giving too much coverage to those wildcatters and oil operators who were occupying motel rooms in the town because wildfire rumors and unconfirmed reports about oil exploration and oil strikes had burned the town before.

Over the years, Buddy Preuss had become as jaded as the rest of Giddings. He was not a man who hopped on wayward bandwagons. He dared to mention a few of the early drilling exploits simply because his readers had the right to know, but he would not write seriously about oil until it came running down the middle of Highway 77.

●

Within eighteen months after the OPEC nations announced their oil embargo, the price of oil had more than doubled from four dollars a barrel, enough to allow any well producing as many as fifty barrels a day to be considered commercially viable. The City of Giddings No. 1 was regularly cranking out three hundred barrels a day, and the M&K, drilled by Max Williams and Irv Deal, was showing even better results with no signs of slowing down or ever giving up. Houston Oil & Minerals had leased a few scattered lots inside the city limits but had decided against drilling. Robert Mosbacher of Houston and the most noted wildcatter of them all, Clayton Williams from Midland, had sent teams of landmen across Lee, Burleson, and Fayette Counties to acquire large blocks of acreage for wildcat ventures almost as soon as the rigs were brought into Pearsall.

If those gardens of chalk did possess any oil, they wanted to be ready to move as soon as the first drop came out of the ground. No hurry. Robert Mosbacher and Clayton Williams were content to sit back and wait, to see what would happen, if anything ever did. To both oilmen, dollar-an-acre leases were little more than cautious bets in a penny-ante poker game. They stayed at home and let others go to the expense of testing the Austin Chalk one more time, maybe the last time.

In Pearsall, many of the operators wound up broke, and their investors found some solace in the benefit of large tax write-offs. Only the oilfield service companies had managed to earn an appreciable profit, providing the drilling equipment and stimulation treatments for the wells. When the drilling began to shut down, however, those service companies suffered right along with the rest of South Texas.

Chuck Alcorn would never be satisfied with one well, even though the City of Giddings was a giant. He got lucky once. Alcorn thought he had a franchise on luck. He sought out a college classmate, Joe Walter, who just happened to be in charge of Houston Oil & Minerals, regarded as one of the hottest public oil companies in the history of the stock market. He had a proposal for Walter that might prove beneficial for both men and both companies. Alcorn said he was willing to transfer his twenty-two thousand acres in the Austin Chalk to Houston Oil & Minerals on a farm out agreement. He would take a lesser, but substantial, financial interest in any production without having to invest his own capital in the drilling costs. He didn't have the money. Houston Oil & Minerals did. He had access to the land that Houston Oil & Minerals needed. No reason to negotiate. No reason to worry. It was a sound deal, and Joe Walter agreed.

The men signed the necessary papers, and Alcorn waited for the oil money to start rolling in. Houston Oil & Minerals did its best. The company, without any hesitation, drilled three wells on choice locations within the twenty-two thousand acres, but all of them went snap, crackle, and fizzle. A little oil. Hardly enough to cover expenses. It was all a mistake, Houston Oil & Minerals decided. Company officials believed they should have concentrated their efforts solely in and around the town limits. That's where the chalk was hoarding its oil. The City of Giddings No. 1 and Windsor's M&K had proved it beyond a shadow of a doubt.

At the moment, however, no one at Houston Oil & Minerals was willing to throw away any more money to determine if their theory was correct. Many knowledgeable, experienced oilmen privately expressed their fears that the City of Giddings well was merely a freak, found strictly with blind luck. And they went about their business while waiting for the M&K to play out. Good for awhile. Would never last. Wells in the chalk never did. Chalk it up as gospel and open up another beer, cold, stale, or otherwise.

16

*T*he land map Pat Holloway placed on his desk was filled with confusion and a myriad of disappointments. It appeared to him as though the whole trend was already under lease. Texas Osage Royalty had purchased the mineral rights on thousands of acres back during the 1930s when oilmen believed they had uncovered a way to squeeze the oil out of the chalk. They hadn't. But Texas Osage held on to those mineral rights like a clasped fist around a gold nugget. Opportunities may have been slim, but a few of them existed, and Holloway jumped on the first one he found.

Like others before him, Holloway believed that the City of Giddings No. 1 had probably worked its way into the largest fault in the chalk. The problem was, no one had yet been able to calculate just how much underground acreage had been consumed by the series of fractures, and there might be thousands of them. Max Williams and Irv Deal had apparently followed the fault outside the town limits, not too terribly far, but far enough. Their strategy had obviously worked. They had the oil to prove it. Oil was, Holloway knew, like a wild animal. Whoever captured it, owned it.

Pat Holloway, however, was convinced that the broadest section of the oil-bearing fault still lay beneath the streets, buildings, and sidewalks of Giddings. He had no science to back his theory. It was merely a gut hunch. If he leveled with himself, however, it was because those downtown blocks contained the only remaining acreage that he could find to lease. Without any fanfare, which was out of character for Pat Holloway, he went to Southern Pacific Railroad and worked out a deal to lease two hundred feet of right of way running for ten miles and down both sides of the railroad tracks as they cut through town in all four directions. No one had ever before considered the land along the right of way. Maybe they overlooked it. Maybe no one wanted it. Then again, maybe the piece of land was worthless to everybody but Southern Pacific.

Holloway quietly maneuvered his way around town and began leasing blocks held together by sidewalks, neighborhoods, and assorted storefronts. If the fault did happen to be large enough to form the foundation of Giddings, he had the right to all of it, he and the landowners at least. Didn't need any new dirt roads to some isolated rig stuck out in the middle of nowhere. His leases were surrounded by as many streets as he would ever need. And he paid for them with the thirty thousand dollars from the Browning Children's Trust. He had promised Mike Starnes and Bill Browning he would. He kept his word. The trust fund account was bare.

Pat Holloway, by his own admission, knew absolutely nothing about the Austin Chalk, other than it had a checkered past, a bad reputation, and honorable oilmen were scared to death of it. As he told some friends back in Dallas, "Personally, as far as any oil exploration is concerned, I don't think the chalk is worth a shit."

Then Max Williams and Irv Deal brought in the M&K and showered Giddings with oil, and, Holloway said, "I found out in a hurry that shit could be pretty valuable."

As he later admitted, however, "When I first came to Giddings, I really didn't have any intention of looking for oil, much less finding any. Not really. Of course, I had hopes that other operators would strike it rich big time. I was in it strictly for the lease play. I wanted to buy leases cheap, probably pay no more than ten dollars and acre, wait for Giddings to turn into a boomtown, then sell the leases for a ton of money and make a killing. No drilling costs. No production costs. Just money for leases, and, when you look at the cost of producing a well, good or bad, that was pocket change."

Holloway was gambling on land rather than oil. Not much of an investment, but the potential return, he said, had a chance to be worth millions, provided he could lease enough land that didn't already bear someone else's signature.

From a distance, Pat Holloway kept a cautious and a watchful eye on the drilling exploits of Max Williams and Irv Deal. Of course, Chuck Alcorn was still in the field. And Houston Oil & Minerals was dabbling in the chalk. But Windsor/U. S. was making the most noise. Wherever Williams and Deal touched the dirt, it paid off. It was as though they had the only treasure map in existence, and the sweet spots were already numbered.

The more oil they found, the less Pat Holloway thought about selling the leases. Why make a dime when he could make a dollar? Then again, he might go home broke someday, but it wouldn't be because he didn't drill. A man could make some good money flipping leases. He could make a fortune if he found oil.

●

Pat Holloway was not a patient man. He could wait no longer. There was an oilfield slowly building on a godforsaken patch of raw land in front of him, the play was brand new, word had gotten out, but it had not gone too far, Speculation was running like wildfire across Lee County, and he knew the time had come to take the investors in his drilling funds to Giddings. Passing thoughts of Montana and the Dakotas began to fade in the background. Oil had been good to him thus far. It might get even better. His drilling funds were solid, and his investors wouldn't care what he did as long as oil lay beneath his boots.

Max Williams and Irv Deal were not old-school oilmen. They had been in the real estate business, for God's sake. And if they could locate oil, Holloway had no doubt that he could find more of it in more places and during a shorter period of time. He already had a track record, and, after all, the lust for oil was a family trait. He had been stricken with it all of his life.

●

Irv Deal had even approached him about investing in the M&K, and Pat Holloway toyed with the idea of getting involved with the venture. He studied the papers Deal handed him. "What am I supposed to do with these?" Holloway asked.

"Sign them," Deal replied. "It's a standard contract."

"I can't sign these."

"Why not?"

"I wouldn't be able to sue you."

Holloway laughed. Irv Deal figured he was dead serious.

If nothing else, Holloway wanted every deal weighted heavily in his favor. He was an attorney and was a genius at rearranging the fine print to take full advantage of any legal document.

In reality, Pat Holloway did not want to be an investor. He wanted to be an operator. He stood up, told Irv Deal, *no*, and probably, *hell no*. Deal could find his money somewhere else. It may have been a mistake.

●

Holloway had eyed a handful of potential leases and driven down to the county clerk's office to run a title search. Joyce Hamff led him to a row of filing cabinets filled with records, and he noticed that the inside of the classical old Romanesque courthouse was virtually empty. The only people around were the usual employees, and they spoke mostly in hushed tones and whispers. It sounded a lot like the inner sanctum of a library. The files were dusty as though his hands were the only ones to have opened them during the past ten years or so. Not much of a land rush. Not as much oil business going on as he had surmised. If Giddings really did reside on the threshold of a burgeoning boom, landmen would already be stacked three deep, hanging out every window, and fighting over every scrap of information they could find, worthless or otherwise. Names were precious. Land was gold.

Holloway was elbow-deep in a pile of sepia-tinted records, crumbling around the edges and dating back for decades, tracking down landowners and making sure that titles to the properties were clear or could easily be cleared. He scribbled down brief notes on those parcels of real estate where families and heirs, not all of them still speaking to each other, had scattered like seeds in the wind, where back taxes remained on the books as unpaid, where ownership had fuzzy lines that had no doubt been crossed and erased one too many times, where mineral rights had already been swindled, lost, or sold, probably to the Texas Osage Royalty Company.

Pat Holloway heard the muffled sound of footsteps in the room behind him and suddenly realized he was no longer alone. He looked up into the soft, pudgy face of Benny Jaehne. A young man. Probably not thirty yet. Crew-cut hair. Weighed on the north side of three hundred pounds. But his face was stern, and his eyes had a purpose.

"Are you one of those guys who's going into the oil business?" Jaehne asked.

"There's a good chance I am."

"Is there gonna be an oil boom around here?"

"I sure as hell hope so."

"Then you're the man I want to see."

"What can I do for you?"

"I want to learn something about the oil business."

Holloway leaned back in his chair and sized up Benny Jaehne, who looked more like a field hand than an oilman. His hands were rough, his fingernails broken, his face heavily tanned by the sun.

"Are you looking for a job?" Holloway asked.

"I'll work for nothing if you teach me about the oil business."

"You live around here?"

"All my life."

"Then I bet you know most of the people in this part of the world."

"If they live around here, I know them," Jaehne said. "If I don't know them, you can bet they're just passing through."

Benny Jaehne was not bragging. It so happened that he owned a welding shop, a hay baler, and had worked, at one time or another, for almost every farmer in Lee and the surrounding counties. He and his trusty welding apparatus had repaired their metal gates, cattle guards, and farm implements, which were always breaking and always breaking at the wrong time. Whenever some farming family needed a good welder, Jaehne was just a phone call and a few miles away. He traveled the roads both marked and unmarked – paved, gravel, dirt, and narrow ruts carved through the bramble brush – to every farm and ranch house within striking distance. He cut, baled, and hauled their hay. They knew him. They depended on him. They trusted him. He was one of them.

In a quiet country cautious and suspicious of strangers, Benny Jaehne was a recognizable face with a recognizable name. Holloway decided even before he stood up that Benny Jaehne would make a perfect landman and leasing agent. Those farmers and ranchers, who could see someone coming for miles away, might not bother to answer the door if some slick, sophisticated, somewhat flamboyant lawyer with a North Dallas address came knocking. They would welcome Benny Jaehne as though he were a long-time and welcomed friend. He was.

Then again, there was a good chance that none of them had any land available. "What do you know about leasing land?" he asked.

"It's been done before."

"Can you do it?"

"Nothing to it."

Holloway clasped his hands beneath his chin and said, "I've been looking over a land map pretty good, and it doesn't look to me like there is much acreage left to lease."

"That's a bad map," Benny Jaehne said. "Been out of date for a long time."

"How much land do you figure is available?"

"Well, I don't know for sure," Jaehne said. "But if this county has fifty thousand acres, then I'd bet you can get your hands on forty-five thousand of them."

"It's that wide open."

Jaehne laughed. "Folks have bought a lot of leases around here," he said, "but they're glad to give it back when the lease runs out. Most of them just drive out of town and let the leases die long after they're gone."

Pat Holloway held out his hand, and Benny Jaehne shook it. The deal was struck quickly. Why not? Holloway thought. If nothing else, the price was right. Here was a man not looking for a daily, weekly, or monthly paycheck.

Holloway said, "I knew that every oil company's success ultimately depended on landowners. I instructed Benny to work with all the landowners when we drilled on their land, take care of them, do everything they wanted, pay them any damages that might occur, within reason, leave them the water wells, and spread the drilling mud anywhere they could use it as fertilizer. I did not want to waste time with litigation, and I realized that their good will could get us leases from other landowners. Benny knew how to handle it. He was a landowner himself. The landowners were his friends. He knew that a satisfied landowner would make leasing other land for Humble much easier. I gave him an override on every well we drilled on one of his leases. Benny didn't have a lot of money at the time. But he certainly understood the art of making it."

Benny Jaehne, when he wasn't baling hay or at his welding shop, began driving from one end of the country to the other, leasing land for Holloway's initial oil and gas foray into the Austin Chalk trend. He was authorized to pay ten dollars an acre for the lease, guaranteeing the landowner a one-eighth royalty on production. He pocketed five dollars an acre for his trouble and earned a one percent override on any oil pumped from beneath the leased acreage. It was a good deal for Benny Jaehne, a financial godsend for those who generally reaped little more than hard times from their land, and had a chance to be extremely profitable for Pat Holloway, who, with a handshake and the promise of a formal, written agreement, was in the oil business in Giddings. So was Benny Jaehne. Well, at least they were in the leasing business. If Jaehne were right, and Holloway had no reason to doubt him, they would be able to get their hands on a lot of raw acreage, but whether any of it had oil in the chalk would be determined when a drill bit reached nine thousand feet.

When the sun rose that morning, the two men could have walked past each other on a downtown street and simply wandered off in separate directions. Maybe one of them would have nodded or perhaps said hello. Probably not. One had family roots in the soil, and the other was the newcomer. One belonged. One didn't. And now they were hooked to the same yoke with a singular purpose in mind. Drill. As far as Holloway was concerned, investors were not even a formal consideration. He would have no trouble finding the money.

He walked to the front portal of the courthouse and gazed across the street toward downtown Giddings. Buildings in need of repair. A dying population. A few old pickup trucks running here and there, leaving the empty streets veiled in their exhaust. It would never be his home, but he had chosen to stake his future – good, bad, or indifferent – in the raw land of Lee County.

Pat Holloway had been told time and again that the odds were against him ever finding a drop of oil in the chalk. It did not bother him. The odds were what you made them. At the moment, he had placed his trust in a stranger to bring him leases. He might never see Benny Jaehne again. A lot of men talked a good game. Not all of them wanted to play when the game turned sour or against them, and, sooner, or later, the game always did. His wait ended and his worry dimmed when Benny Jaehne met him at the City Meat Market and said, "I know for sure I can get you forty acres out on Highway 290."

"Who owns it?"

"I do." Forty acres. Not much. But it was a beginning, Pat Holloway was willing take every piece of acreage he could get, even a patch of hard ground lying alongside Benny Jaehne's farm house.

Pat Holloway had patched together another curious assortment of leases and was again knocking on Ray Holifield's door, making sure his face remained in the shadows of night. He had no idea what kind of contract the geologist had with Max Williams and Irv Deal and how tightly it bound him to Windsor/U.S. He was a lawyer, perhaps, but sometimes a *wherefore* or *thereto* in legal matters got themselves lost in gray areas that only a judge could figure out if he had the time. He did not need Ray Holifield full time, but he didn't want to go into the ground unless Ray Holifield had picked the hole.

The door to the motel room opened. Holifield didn't say a word. "Can I come in?" Holloway asked.

Holifield turned around and Holloway followed him inside. The bed bore the shape and imprint of the geologist's slender frame. It was obvious that he grabbed what little sleep he could without bothering to turn the covers down.

Holifield waited for him to speak.

"I have some acreage now," Holloway said.

"Where do you have it?"

"The leases stretch out along both sides of the railroad track, running north and south, as well as east and west."

"Farmlands?"

"Railroad right-of-way."

Ray Holifield did not know whether to laugh at Holloway's ignorance or cry with frustration because he had never thought of leasing the right-of-way.

"What do you want me to do?" he asked.

"Find me an oil well."

Ray Holifield shook his head.

"Look," he said, driving home the point, "it's like I told you before. I can't do any work for you around the City of Giddings. That's where my clients have their acreage. But you don't have to stay here, Pat. It's not Giddings. It's the Austin Chalk, and the trend runs all the way from Mexico to Louisiana. If you want to fight the chalk, you can lease some acreage somewhere else."

"I can't," Holloway replied.

"Why not?"

"I'm already here." Holloway shrugged. "And for the last year," he said, "I've been helping pay your salary. You're on my retainer. You may not owe me much, Ray, but you owe me something. It's just the railroad right-of-way, for God's sakes. It's not like I want to start drilling in Irv Deal's backyard or back pocket. You didn't recommend the acreage. I bought it on my own. All I want from you is a little advice."

Holloway's argument was a sound one, maybe even a reasonable one. Holifield leaned forward on the bed and thought it over. The seconds on the clock turned into minutes. Finally he said, "What you need to do now, Pat, is shoot some seismic."

"Who can I hire to shoot it?"

"A lot of folks can do it," Holifield said, "but none of them have any idea about reading the chalk."

"And you can read it."

"It has a language all its own." A slow grin crawled across his face. "I'm getting pretty good at it," Holifield said.

"How much will the seismic cost me?"

Holifield gave him a ballpark estimate.

"When can you do it?"

Holifield didn't answer.

Pat Holloway grinned. He knew by the look in Holifield's eyes and the broken pattern of his speech that he would not wait long to see if oil really did exist down somewhere in a broken fault line beside the tracks. It's not that he was disloyal to Max Williams or Irv Deal, or that he was in the market for a new client. Ray Holifield was simply a geologist in search of oil, never happy unless he was in the field, trying to resolve the next great mystery far below his feet.

He had been spending Pat Holloway's money for a long time now. He guessed Holloway was due a payback. Before the week was out, on his own time and while Max Williams was back in Dallas, Ray Holifield drove to the railroad tracks and began shooting seismic.

He read the logs and marked three locations on the right-of-way. It never crossed his mind that Max Williams might find out and fire him. Hell, he thought, Max Williams needed him, and so did Irv Deal and Pat Holloway. There was, Holifield reasoned, enough oil in Giddings for all three men. There was enough oil in Giddings for everybody.

The seismic blasts rocked downtown Giddings. Find oil, and no one minded the noise. A rig rose above the town and cast a giant shadow across both US 290 and US 77. The coming of Humble Exploration ceased to be a secret. Holloway was no longer merely leasing. Pat Holloway was going into the ground.

17

Max Williams and Irv Deal moved quickly after the huge success of the M&K. Chuck Alcorn, with a dose of old-fashioned good fortune, had brought in the legendary City of Giddings No. 1 but had not been able to make another well. He had thousands of acres leased but little else. Other drilling endeavors had been sporadic and afflicted with dry holes and used equipment left behind for the salvage crews. A few oil companies and a handful of fly-by-night operators had looked hard at the land but were scared off by the reputation of the chalk. They cautiously backed out and shut down their operations before ever giving the field a decent chance.

Windsor and U.S. Operating, in fact, represented the first companies to come in, set up shop, and stay in Giddings. Max Williams had known from the day he set foot in Lee County that his venture would focus on one well at a time. Strike enough oil, and the investors would answer his phone calls. Find the good wells or go home. Max Williams had no intention of leaving.

In the beginning, he and Deal could not afford many if any bad wells. The success of each operation would be the catalyst to find sufficient financing to drill the next well. Max Williams was certainly aware of his tenuous position. He and Irv Deal were still small-time gamblers in a high-stakes game and betting on the outcome.

Ray Holifield and Max Williams, ever the closeologist, moved the rig away from the M&K and tucked it in as close to the old, dried-up Knox well as they could get. Even though the old Knox well had never produced any oil – the crew had never drilled completely through the chalk – it must have fractures, Williams reasoned, or it would not have had enough pressure to blow out. The well was still located on a straight, crucial line that connected the City of Giddings to the M&K.

"You think the fault runs this far?" Williams asked Ray Holifield.

"I'm almost sure that the fault does," his geologist answered. "We'll find out soon enough what kind of fractures it has beneath us."

"Can you hit them?"

"The fractures?"

Max Williams nodded.

Ray Holifield shrugged. "It all depends," he said. "In the chalk, you may be drilling toward the largest collection of trapped oil you ever saw. But miss it by six inches, and you don't wind up with a damn thing. The difference between a rich man and poor man in the old chalk is sometimes the width of a splinter."

Within the deep earth below Giddings, Holifield had seen the same kind of faults and fractures he had discovered during his years in Iraq and Algeria. All he had to guide him there were well logs, and now he was studying well logs defined from the City of Giddings No. 1 and the Knox No. 1 drilled by Dan Hughes. The innards of the deep earth on the far side of the world had a striking resemblance to limestone formations beneath fields of peanuts and cattle pastures. No one to Holifield's knowledge had ever before drilled a well aimed at hitting a fault in located fractures. It was far too risky, a hit and miss proposition, and the chance for cutting into a small fault nine thousand feet below the surface was miniscule at best. He had been fortunate on the M&K. He was ready to read the fine print in those well logs and try again.

The Schkade No. 1 would be the second of three wells drilled by Windsor/U.S. as rapidly as they could sink the pipe in the ground. They attacked the chalk fearlessly. Max Williams had convinced himself but few others that Giddings was possibly the hottest spot for oil exploration in Texas. Others were more skeptical. While he kept on drilling, most were content to sit hunchbacked over a chicken fried steak at Schubert's Cafe and wait for him to fail. The beer had grown warm and finally stale. They were still waiting.

Max Williams had the right geologist and the right acreage. Failure for him was not even a consideration. In December of 1976, Windsor/U.S. drilled the Schkade well, and it came roaring in at a hundred and five barrels of oil an hour as crew members, in the dark of the day, danced in the headlights of their automobiles. After so long a time, the ground was finally giving up its oil the color of pure honey.

Ray Holifield had been in a hotel room in Lafayette, Louisiana, following the chalk trend, when Randy Stewart called him. "It's unbelievable," he said.

"How good is it?"

"Looks like it'll settle down to about seven hundred and eighty barrels a day."

"That's unheard of in the chalk."

"You've heard it now."

Holifield could almost hear Stewart grinning on the other end of the line.

●

The M&K well had been the best producer in the field, and now it was lost in the glorious shadow of the Schkade. Historically, the chalk had never been a field for natural gas, but the Schkade was showing the potential for a million cubic feet of gas production a day. No one had been prepared to control it. Frankly, no one had expected to loosen much, if any, natural gas at all. The M&K had been fairly quiet as far as gas production was concerned, and Max Williams had no reason to believe that the Schkade well would be any different.

He and Irv Deal faced a new dilemma they had not fully anticipated. From a financial point of view, they were overwhelmed about the burgeoning potential of natural gas. Unfortunately, there were no pipeline connections for gas anywhere in the county.

From a realistic point of view, they were not prepared to capture or regulate it. Flares were their only answer, and Max Williams watched millions of cubic feet of gas escape into the atmosphere. He was watching money leave the field in flames and knew he would never be able to get it back. He immediately filed away the need for finding a major pipeline company in case more natural gas rose to the surface of a well. He might not ever need one. Then again, his efforts might ultimately be doomed without one.

●

The Schkade was in. Williams had a few days less than a month to drill his third well in order to keep his farm out agreement with Hughes & Hughes intact. The pressure was mounting, and, on occasion, was almost suffocating. Max Williams could deal with pressure. He realized that business was never as good as it looked when things were going well and never quite as bad as it looked when things began turning sour. He had a job to do. He squared his shoulders and did it.

He had Ray Holifield at his side, and, thus far, his geologist had been a magician in the chalk. John LaRue said he was good. John LaRue was right. An occasional room at the aging and modest Sands Motel in Giddings was the only comfort Max Williams could find, that and barbecue ribs over at the City Meat Market. Most of the time, he was on the road, meeting with investors, telling them the story of Giddings, and the story was getting better with each passing day. Max Williams had chalk dust on his boots, and Irv Deal was in Dallas working the numbers, making preparations for Windsor/U.S. to drill the Carmean No. 1. He left the field to Williams. The drill bit would touch Giddings soil again without him.

Even before work began on the Carmean well, Max Williams realized that good luck seldom followed anybody for very long. Once had been enough. Twice was far more than he expected and probably deserved. Until now, he and Ray Holifield had merely tried to determine where the fault line ran from the City of Giddings well through the M&K and on to the Schkade. Gut feelings and a lot of guesswork were about all they had working for them, and both men were on the verge of running out of hunches. They had plenty of opinions, more than a few ideas, and even a handful of disagreements. But hunches were in short supply. It did not matter. This time, they decided to exchange luck for technology and gut feelings for science. Williams was still not ready to part with the cash he needed to shoot seismic, even though he recognized its importance.

Instead, Ray Holifield convinced Williams to purchase some old 2-D seismic data from Hughes & Hughes, the company that had earlier moved some rigs across the chalk, drilled a few test wells in the search of oil, and failed miserably. He carried the seismic log to Western Geophysical in Houston and asked the company to re-process it. Newer technology had made the archaic, traditional way of shooting seismic virtually obsolete. Williams did not have the money to pay for any high-tech processing, so Holifield had only the old, out-of-date, and fading 2-D seismic to study. He said he could not guarantee the accuracy of the data. After all, he hadn't shot it. He didn't particularly trust it. Yet it was all he had, and he was gambling that somewhere within those curious lines he could find the key to a lost world of oil and gas.

The original seismic readings had been based on the resonances of sound waves generated by twenty-pound dynamite charges planted ninety feet below the earth. Technology allowed the vibrations to be printed out on paper as a series of wavy lines, each one layered on top of the other, each one reflecting and recording the various depths of those subterranean rock layers. The data at least gave him a better understanding of the formations lying beneath the rig, and it meant that, for the first time, the string of drill pipe would not be going down blind.

Ray Holifield carefully read the seismic hieroglyphics. A lot of faults had bent and broke, creating a lot of fractures. The big ones collected oil. The little ones had been known to ruin oilmen and chase a few of them into a business where data made sense, and the final success of an operation didn't require the guts and guile of a gambling man.

Ray Holifield thought he could detect the traps that held the oil, and the size, shape, and angle of the formations gave him the evidence he needed to direct all future drilling operations once the Carmean had been completed.

He had no doubts about his ability to find that honey-colored oil, and Max Williams was content to let him select whichever location on whichever acreage he chose.

Ray Holifield had not missed yet.

Of course, Holifield had not yet dared venture far past the city limits of Giddings. The site of the Carmean would be located alongside FM 141, headed north to Dime Box. In time, it would be within two hundred yards of a pair of trailers that held the offices of U.S. Operating. Once again, Williams and Holifield were attacking the decisive fault line that had delivered them so much oil at the M&K and Schkade. Their fate was placed firmly in the rough, experienced hands of Lonnie Donald, drilling field superintendent, Red Livingston, the driller, never seen on the rig without his trusty cowboy hat, and tool pusher Charlie Adams.

Adams had four sons on the rig. All were roughnecks on or off a well site. If a fight broke out in a Lee County beer joint, chances were good that the Adams boys were involved. If there was no one else to fight, they fought among themselves. It had not been a good night if they went home without the taste of beer and blood in their mouths.

One night on the rig, suffocated with boredom, they persuaded Randy Stewart to climb with them to the monkey boards on the crown of the derrick. It was wet. It was cold. Stewart had nothing better to do, so he tagged along after them up the metal ladder. He had no idea how high the crown was until he looked down. Nothing but darkness. Empty. And black. It was as though the damp clouds had swallowed him. He was totally ignorant of the fact that far beneath them all, the blow out preventers on the well, for whatever reason, had been erroneously installed upside down.

"If the well had blown that night," Stewart said, "we would have gone sky high."

●

A self-acclaimed closeologist like Max Williams would not feel particularly comfortable with an orphan well stuck out on a remote location where the only traces of drilling operations lay lost and abandoned at the bottom of dry holes. The Carmean was being drilled well within his comfort zone. It all exploded in his face.

Without any warning, the well suddenly broke loose and violently shook the rig with a blowout of enormous proportions. The ground around them felt as though it was tearing apart. The crew frantically tried to close the blowout preventers and couldn't. And roustabouts were fighting furiously to tame a reckless and unruly well that was becoming unpredictable and potentially deadly. The mounting pressure boiling down at the bottom of the hole was threatening to blow oil, mud, pipes, rocks, chalk, and drill bit out of wellbore. It was man against the might of nature, and man was losing badly. Just fight it. The crew had no other choice. Day after day, night after night, just fight it. Don't let the well get the best of you. The rig shuddered again, and some thought it might shatter around them. The hot innards of the earth were showing little mercy and giving no quarter.

Randy Stewart would later describe that night in a letter to Windsor Energy investors. He wrote:

"It wasn't raining, but the threat of same hung as heavy as the dough-thick clouds being kneaded by an unseen hand above the rig lights. It was cold. As a whore's heart. As a December night during a Texas Norther. Which it was. Monday the thirteenth. Ten-twenty P.M.

"Lonnie Donald is a stout bear of a man. He is not tall, but thick. He broke into roughnecking at the age of fourteen and has worked iron ever since, in one capacity or another. Iron is an essential part of the environment in the oil patch. It is the tool and the material used in the search for hydrocarbons. It pervades lives and vocabulary. When a man gets crosswise with a piece of iron, it's a damn sure thing the iron doesn't bend, the old hands admonish the fledgling roughnecks.

"Lonnie Donald is in his forties, and he hasn't worked the rig floor in years. There is some padding now over the muscle, but the core is still there. Iron hard. On that night, Donald was working for Windsor/U.S. as a consultant, supervising the drilling. The depth of the well was approaching eighty-four hundred feet.

"Donald is very good and makes very good money at what he does. He has only been home thirty-three days in the last year. In the cocoon warmth of the mud logger's trailer, his eyes were on the gas detector unit, an electronic device that keeps a running tab on the background gas units present in the wellbore. The units are indicated in idiot's scribble on a scaled graph. They had remained steady for several days, lulling with monotony. No sweat. Nothing drastic had been predicted by the geologists, the rock-doctors, the slide-rule drivers, but the mud logger kept watch, and Donald did not let the graph get too far out of his sight for too long. It was never out of his consciousness. Gas causes blowouts and blowouts are the monsters-under-the-bed in the oil patch.

"Donald noticed that the needle had climbed on the scale. That happens. The well will kick a little gas and then settle back down. This time the needle continued to climb. It crossed the markers on the scale – one thousand units, fifteen hundred units, two thousand units.

"'Watch your gas,' Donald snapped to the mud logger.

"The inexorable march of the indicator pulled Donald to his feet.

"'What the hell?' he said.

"The indicator went off the end of the scale.

"Donald didn't see the marker making impotent jiggles in the space beyond the graph. With a bellowed, *sonuvabitch*, he exploded from the trailer door and charged toward the derrick. The mud logger emerged on his heels but headed in the opposite direction. No one would want to be under a tin can with a firecracker.

"Donald took twelve steps up to the rig floor, three at a time, and without the benefit of a railing. He rushed past the floor hands standing frozen and staring at the wildly spewing Kelly bushing. His objective was the heater in the doghouse, the small shelter attached to the rig wherein the roughnecks changed their clothes. It was an open flame heater, and if the gas reached it, it would set off a holocaust. He shut it off. In that instant, the geolograph caught his eye. The well depth was eight thousand, four hundred, and one feet.

"'Raise the Kelly,' Donald shouted to the driller. 'Get the rams on the preventer closed.'

"The hexagonal Kelly is screwed into the drill pipe and turns it by power from the rotary table. The Kelly had to be raised so that the rams of the blowout preventers could be closed onto the drill pipe. When the Kelly cleared the bushing, the mud, impelled by the gas, roared in a brown geyser to the monkey bars, eight feet above the floor.

"It could have all gone then. At any time. Released from its subterranean confinement, the gas hovered like a threatening bully, daring the laboring men to make a mistake. Just one mistake. Just one spark from a dropped wrench, from a frayed wire, from a cigarette dropped or placed down before the eruption, and the rig, the hole, and perhaps some lives would have been lost. They got the mad sonuvabitch closed in.

"The rams on the blowout preventers were closed, but before relief could cross the tension-tight faces of the men, a new menace threatened. An ominous hiss coming from somewhere on the lower preventer grabbed their attention like a clanging alarm. There was a leak, but now it couldn't be helped.

"Donald knew that encroaching gas was gathering beneath the rig floor and spreading, but it was too dangerous to attempt a repair. The gas had to be stopped at its source.

"The massive drilling rig with its soaring structure traced by strings of lights, with its rumbling engines and squealing machinery, is ordinarily reminiscent of a Midway ride at the State Fair. But for the remainder of that cold and nervous night, it exuded menace and danger. Its substructure housed the mud-layered blowout preventers like an altar around a threatening pagan idol. Gas hissed from the hidden leak and permeated clothing with a petroleum odor that would survive many launderings.

"By eight-fifteen of the following morning, Donald had begun to marshal his forces to attack the gaseous adversary. At his call, the Halliburton Company, whose employees would do yeoman service in the ensuing battle, sent Glenn Caroway, supervisor, with his trucks and crew to mix and pump cement. He ordered Steve Akin, an engineer with Trinity Mud Company, to send out an urgent call for additional lost circulation material and chemical mud. Caroway and Akin would be key allies in that they supplied the ammunition necessary to battle the rambunctious Carmean No. 1.

"The rig's tool pusher was Charlie Adams. He is as spare and rugged as the Palo Pinto rock hills in which he was reared. Jug-eared and rawboned in an age gone by, he might have trailed Charlie Goodnight's beeves north. Now he ramrodded a drilling crew that would be in the vanguard of the coming effort.

"The initial task was to kill the well with mud. Kill in this case would be a misnomer. Suppress or confine would be more accurate. It would entail putting enough weight in the form of drilling mud on the underground formation to equal the pressure of the gas being expelled.

"The mud was pumped down the annulus (the space between the suspended drill pipe and the wall of the wellbore), and it worked. For the moment, the opponent was subdued. The leak in the blowout preventer was located and fixed. Long clenched muscles in delicate bodily areas tentatively relaxed.

"The men had arrived at a standoff with the irritated burrow, an unstable truce threatened by another serious eruption should the balance between mud-weight and pressure be disturbed. Strategy was discussed.

"The daylight had been almost used up; the wind and cold were numbing and unrelenting. The interior of the mud logger's trailer resembled more than ever the field headquarters of a military assault. Bodies, bulky-wrapped and muddy, milled in and out, faces different but commonly marked with small, tight lines of concentration. Their fuel intake was now refined to high test – cigarette smoke and black coffee. Keep the nerves jangling to keep the body awake. Donald was there and then gone, rushing from one trouble spot to another, then back inside. One of Windsor/U.S.'s owners, either Irv Deal, Max Williams, or company president, Charles McLeod, was always present. Big money was being spent, and there was no time to telephone when decisions had to be made. The initial solution was approached. Cement the drill pipe in place right where it stood in the hole. Go in with a charge and blow the bit off the end. Perforate it across any pay sections. Produce through the drill pipe and be done with the dangerous bastard.

"Ted Ferguson, just arrived from another well in a different part of the state, objected. Most of Ferguson's working life had been spent in the oilfield, and he was an expert in the techniques of completing and producing wells. His purpose in being present was to see that the techniques employed to control the Carmean No. 1 did not result in a successful operation but a dead patient. It would fall on his shoulders to see that the tamed well ultimately paid for its mischief – and then some. Although it could be done, the problems of producing through drill pipe on a long-term basis would be tremendous. The alternatives were weighed and examined; consequences were subjected to consideration and reconsideration, speculation – and meditation. It was decided to attempt to get the one and three-quarters mile of drill pipe out of the hole and case the well.

"The mud was the key. Ordinarily a utility performer, essentially but routinely used to lubricate the drilling bit, to circulate the cuttings to the surface, to plaster and maintain the sides of the hole during drilling;

now it must be the star. It would have to be right. Heavy enough to hold back the gas, but not so heavy that it would break down and provide access for more gas; light enough so that it could circulate, take down the material needed to seal off the offending formations, and bring out the gas units still in the wellbore.

"The procedure was complicated because there were at least two trouble spots widely separated. The blowout had occurred when a gas zone was tapped at the total depth of eight thousand, four hundred, and one feet.

"A higher zone, from eight thousand and fifty feet to eight thousand, two hundred, and twenty feet also was porous and contained gas and oil. Unfortunately, the mud weight fund necessary to restrain the deeper gas was too much for the more shallow zone to bear.

"Donald hoped that the solution to this dilemma was to raise the mud weight very slowly and cautiously, adding more and more lost-circulation material such as walnut shells, cottonseed hulls, and mica to shore up the weaker formation and allow more weight to be put on the lower zone.

"For over forty-eight hours, he nursed the mud into the unruly well, seeking to find the proper compromise. But it could not be done. When a weight was attained that would hold the lower gas, the upper zone would begin to take the mud as fast as it could be mixed.

"At twelve noon on December 18, it was decided to pump a slug of barite, a mixture designed to set up into a consistency akin to heavy clay, into the bottom one hundred and sixty one feet of the hole. Hopefully, this would bridge off the erupting lower zone.

"Down it went, and then, mercifully, there was nothing that could be done for the six hours it would take for the plug to settle out. Men stopped, gave out where they sat, stretched out where they could. For those directing the fight, it was the first sleep in days other than purloined catnaps.

"At the pits, the shift-working roughnecks kept conditioning the mud, building the volume, preparing for the next assault.

"It was three hours before dawn on that Lee County hillside. The surrounding black night crouched at bay at the edge of the glare grown by the rig lights. On the rig floor, Charlie Adams prepared to pit himself and his machine against the grasping fingers of the gnomes – that fabled race of dwarf-like creatures, which lived underground and guarded hordes of treasure.

"It was time to start out of the hole with the drill pipe, and as Charlie took a firm grip on the control levers, he knew that it would not come easy – if it came at all. For over ninety-six hours, the string of pipe had been shut in the hole. The formation around it had been blowing and crumbling; heavy mud and a mass of lost circulation material had been forced down around it. He tentatively applied power to the drill string, watching the weight indicator, feeling the cables tighten, hearing the engines labor. The pipe was stuck. No one had expected anything else, but still there was disappointment. He tried again, harder this time. Nothing moved. If the drill pipe was irrevocably stuck, all that had been done until that point was wasted. All the planning. All the effort. By God, if it was going to come, it had to come now!

"Charlie revved the diesel engines and through the levers commanded his rig to raise the pipe. The wire rope snapped taut, the engines roared with their effort. The weight indicator swung toward its red line, registering well above two hundred thousand pounds. It indicated the derrick was withstanding the maximum weight that it could bear, but Charlie seemed impervious to its warning.

"He had become part of the iron that he was working. His sinews held the impossible weight. His muscles strained against the earth's hold. His concentration bound him to every foot of his trapped straining steel. Observers with fainter hearts had started to edge toward the rig's ladders when Charlie's experience told him: now! He released the brake lever, and the relieved pipe clanged downward, sending a jolt to its deepest joint. His hands flew like a maestro's from lever to throttle as he jerked the tortured pipe again and again, and suddenly it was free.

"Donald disappeared into the trailer and anxiously watched the gas detector unit. The kick it indicated was a heavy one. As he had suspected it might, the violent shaking of the drill pipe had dislodged some of the material packing off the gas in the upper zone. A giant bubble had forced its way into the wellbore and was charging to the surface. Quickly, he had the rams on the preventer closed. The gas, stymied in its charge, would be circulated out over a period of time through the choke manifold.

"Now they knew that even though the drill pipe was free, an attempt to bring it out of the hole in a normal fashion would create a swabbing effect that could result in another blowout. So, although their extended nerves and bodies cried to be through with this job, they chose a method of bringing out the pipe that would not allow their opponent another chance at escape. As each stand (two joints) of pipe was pulled, four barrels of mud was pumped into the hole to maintain the pressure on the formation. It was slow, but it was the only safe way.

"The stack of drill pipe in the derrick grew with maddening slowness through that endless night. The days and the tensions had taken their toll on the men. Like actors fatigued by an interminable script, they plodded through their performances. Bizarre occurrences flickered across their consciousness like the kaleidoscopic scenes in an old movie: Charlie Adams, always taciturn, becoming loquacious in his grief upon learning that his sister had been shot and killed in the Young County town of Graham. Two Bohemian drivers, fresh pulled drunks from a pre-Christmas party, arriving in giant tanker trucks full of mud and miring first one truck and then the other one again in the bog that the road had become – providing slapstick comic relief to a stark night.

"Then, at last, only a few joints of drill pipe remained in the hole. The casing had been delivered and lay in waiting on nearby racks. The special crew that would run the casing into the well stood by in readiness. When the last joint of drill pipe left the wellbore, the well would be restrained only by the weight of a column of mud – the barite plug and the lost circulation material jamming its formations.

"The last joint cleared the hole and was stacked. For a moment, the men on the floor looked down into the open mouth of their opponent. It was the moment when the bull in the ring is mesmerized. When it has been bedeviled, confused, and exhausted by the elusive matador and, for a moment, stands immobile, trembling with pent-up power and almost tangible anticipation as the man before the bull leans forward, hoping that fate has not marked him on this afternoon. In that moment, the lead joint of casing was stabbed into the hole, and then the next and the next.

"A dawn arrived, calm and in pastels, and foretold the first sunny day of the entire ordeal. Finally at 12:30 P. M., on December 22, the lowest joint was rested on the bottom. The well was harnessed.

Preparation was made to cement the casing in place. Thousands of feet below, the giant reservoir, trapped and refined over millions of years of time, shrugged disdainfully. Five hundred units registered on the detection graph."

For days, the men had been standing on a bomb. They could hear it ticking. Pipe by pipe, they managed to dismantle it. No one expected to die. Then again, perhaps, no one expected to get out alive either.

●

The Carmean No. 1 might not have been Max Williams' first rodeo, but it was definitely his first blowout. Time and again, Max Williams – standing with Lonnie Donald, Charlie Adams, Charlie McLeod, and Ted Ferguson – thought the well had been brought under control. Time and again, the angry Carmean tried to blow out in their faces. Time and again, Williams kept asking the same question. What do we do now?

The answer never changed. Pump in a heavy pill of mud. Always, it was pump some more mud. Max Williams remained on the rig floor for eleven days and nights without ever going to bed. The crew worked in eight-hour shifts.

Some were able to sleep while others battled to throttle down the pressure. Then they changed places. When Williams slept at all, it was sitting on a chair. To the crew, the Carmean was merely a job. To Max Williams and Irv Deal, it was a financial lifeline.

The Carmean, in spite of its explosive genesis, would never be quite as big or give up quite as much oil as the M&K or Schkade, but it provided Max Williams, Irv Deal, and Ray Holifield with a startling new vision and interpretation of an unpredictable field that had overnight become more provocative than either of them ever imagined. Initial tests predicted that the Carmean would have the ability to produce almost two hundred barrels of oil a day from the Austin Chalk and another hundred and fifty barrels a day from a deeper layer known as the Buda formation. Just as intriguing, perhaps, was the fact that the Carmean appeared to have the potential of three hundred million cubic feet of natural gas a day.

Holifield looked hard at the data. Just maybe, he reasoned, the ultimate secret of the Giddings field lay in its ability to connect an operator to *multipay* zones of oil and natural gas. Just maybe, the region was more valuable than anyone had ever dared to believe it would be. Maybe the chalk only rewarded those who had faith in it and didn't come to the field drilling scared.

The time had finally come for Max Williams to begin scrambling to find a good, solid, legitimate pipeline company. He and Ray Holifield feared that the well might blow sky high if the escaping gas ignited. If it did, God help them all. Millions of dollars worth of oil and gas both would be burned and lost. An oil well fire was a terrible thing. Men's lives were potentially at stake, and they were depending on Max Williams to find the right company and make the right deal, by dawn if possible, and everyone knew that it wasn't.

One by one, Williams made his pitch. The pipeline companies all politely listened to him, apologized, and said, no, they had absolutely no interest in wasting their time in the chalk, which had never shown a propensity for producing natural gas.

One discovery, no matter how significant, did not guarantee a profitable gas field. Only a fool would take such a risk. The chalk could be a killer. None of the pipeline companies had the resources to gamble on building a natural gas line across a field that was notorious for its dry holes and broken hearts.

Their investment would exceed hundreds of thousands of dollars. And, besides, just who, they wondered, was Max Williams? Never heard of him before. Didn't even know he was in the oil and gas business. Must be a novice or he wouldn't be in the Austin Chalk. The experts were deathly afraid of it. The experts had all gone somewhere else to drill. The experts had lost out.

In the back of his mind, Max Williams remembered seeing the name of Perry Gas Products on a pipeline running across Schleicher County in West Texas, and he placed a telephone call to the company's home office. He did not have a name. He only had a number. He would talk to anyone who answered the phone.

None of the big companies had been concerned about his plight at the Carmean. Maybe a smaller pipeline company would express far less cynicism and have a greater interest for acquiring business, any business, even business down in the cursed, old chalk.

Joe Feagan heard his name, and asked cautiously, "Are you the Max Williams who played basketball at SMU?"

"I am."

"I went to Texas Tech," Feagan said.

Bad news, Williams immediately thought. Bad blood. Maybe he had called the wrong company after all. Joe Feagan quieted his concerns. Yes, Feagan told him, Perry Gas Products had been talking about the possibility of developing another gas line in Texas. Giddings just might be the place to go. It would certainly give Perry a strong foothold in a place where no one else had yet ventured. The idea was intriguing. So was the potential. He wasn't quite as sure about the investment dollars. Could be a lot. Perry was successful, but the company did not rank among the big boys. "Let's talk about it," he said.

Joe Feagan met Williams in Dallas, and they began hammering out the details of a plan to connect the wells of Windsor/U.S. to a Perry pipeline. If the field in Giddings did become as big as Williams thought it could be, then Perry would have a prime location just down the road and around the corner from every new discovery, ready and in an enviable position to link up with any new well that began flowing natural gas. Feagan estimated that the pipeline would cost Perry as much as three million dollars. Perry would ultimately spend thirty million dollars in the Giddings field, and, when the time was finally right, the pipeline was sold for ninety million dollars.

While Perry was building its pipeline, the Texas Railroad Commission, against its will and better judgment, allowed operators in Giddings to continue flaring their gas. But Williams had no intention of losing a fortune to the flames and watching his hard-earned profits cast to the four winds. The harsh, sun-seared landscape was already hot enough. The heat from the flares almost made it unbearable. Max Williams was determined to keep the Carmean producing, and, Lord, it was producing even better than he had hoped it would. He and Perry would deal selling the natural gas as soon as the pipeline was built and finally connected to the well site.

Max Williams drove across the length and breadth of Lee County. He spotted a rig here, another one there. He heard the distant blasts of a seismic crew working beyond the next knoll. An oilfield couldn't keep a secret no matter how hard it tried. Word had reached every oil camp in Texas and maybe even the Southwest. Oil in the chalk was no longer a geological myth. Sure, a well might play out in a hurry. Some did. Then again, it might not. The good wells, the rumors said, all had fortunes at the bottom of the hole. Big risks. Big rewards. Nobody was playing with table stakes.

That night, he sat back in a booth at Schubert's Cafe and read the column Buddy Preuss had written in the town newspaper: *Lee County may possibly be on the verge of the biggest oil and gas exploration boom in its history. At least six different oil exploration companies have swamped the office of County Clerk Joyce Hamff during the past two weeks, checking oil leases and land deeds.*

Giddings Times & News sources indicate that oil company geologists feel there could be large amounts of oil and gas in the Austin Chalk formation which runs through the county. Sources indicate that these companies plan to lease all of the land in the Lee County area. Some of these companies are said to be paying as much as five dollars-an-acre bonuses to landowners for the first year lease, but are leasing the land for five to ten years. It was about a year ago that the leasing of lots in Giddings was going full blast until suddenly leasing came to a halt, apparently caused by the poor showing of a test well south of Giddings on three sites. Oil and gas activity in the Lexington and Tanglewood areas, plus excellent production over the past several years at the City of Giddings well, has spawned new interest.

Since the City of Giddings well is also producing a very large amount of propane, as well as oil, and since some gas has been found up in the Lexington area, some of the interest could be trying to find commercial supplies of natural gas.

Max Williams sighed and was suddenly aware of an inescapable fact that he had not paused long enough to consider. He and Irv Deal no longer had the Giddings field to themselves. And he had no idea that Pat Holloway was right behind and closing fast.

18

Max Williams had no complaints, no second guesses, no doubts. He was living in the vortex of fate and circumstance, a moment in time when the fields of Giddings had finally conspired to part with their oil and make him the beneficiary. His drilling efforts were thus far three for three, if anybody was keeping score, and those oil companies on the outside looking in were making note every time a drill bit touched the ground.

The M&K. The Schkade No. 1. And now, the Carmean No. 1. They were all flowing Windsor/U.S. oil. For the most part, life had always been good to Max Williams. A few hard knocks along the way, perhaps, but nothing he couldn't overcome. Now, on a patch of parched landscape above the chalk, life was getting even better. In the spring of 1977, he waited patiently, without a known care in the world, while Ray Holifield plotted and calculated the location for the Molly C. Davis.

Max Williams had begun spending more of his time in his Dallas office, driving back to Giddings once or twice a week for a quick check on the status of the operation. If and when trouble arose, he would be heading to a back room in the Sands Motel full time again. His crew probably didn't need him anyway unless they were staring in the face of trouble that had a chance to spill over into disaster. One of his key investors, June Collier, flew in from Alabama to help him set up his accounting books, making sure he had up-to-date data on debits and credits, expenses and revenues.

Dollars were coming in and going out at a furious pace, and Max Williams was moving almost as fast, maybe too fast, he sometimes thought. Without someone keeping a careful and watchful eye on the business end of the venture, it would have been quite easy for drilling, location, rig, and seismic costs, as well as his payroll expenditures, to veer out of control in the blink of an eye.

Back in Dallas, Irv Deal's Windsor Energy was making formal arrangements and signing contracts with drilling contractors and those independent companies he had hired to drill and complete the wells. Deal knew that it was vital for his accounting department to make certain that interest payments, royalty payments, and a various assortment of override payments went out in the mail on time. Money on time kept a lot of people happy.

The job of connecting percentages was not unlike making a patchwork quilt. The landowners received their share. So did the geologist, Ray Holifield, Hughes & Hughes, and the Knox brothers, who had taken a small override instead of their usual dollar an acre for the lease. Their fortuitous decision would earn them millions of dollars on the eight thousand acres they represented, the acreage Hughes and Hughes had leased to Windsor/U.S on a farm out agreement.

It was vital for payroll to be made in a timely and officious manner to the drilling superintendent, the company man, and crew members, whose names were always changing, and payments must be kept up to date for that never-ending parade of oil service companies. The more successful Windsor/U.S. became in the Giddings field, the more of a headache the paperwork became for Irv Deal and his company.

June Collier served as the business eyes that Max Williams had in the field. He trusted Deal explicitly, but he wanted to know, at a moment's notice, if he were making or losing money and how much. So often, he was on the road, leaving Giddings, meeting with investors, then traveling back into the oilfield at all hours of the day and night. His time was no longer his own. He had no idea whether he was winning or losing. He depended on June Collier, and she was figuring out who owned a sixth of the well, who had an eighth, a twelfth, a sixty-fourth, and who was responsible for which working interest.

How big was payroll? And how often did it change from well to well? The bottom line was simple, blunt, and to the point. There was nothing personal. She did not second guess any of the expenses, nor did she need to. It was just good business. Max Williams preferred the black side of the ledger.

He himself resembled the cowboy who had jumped on a horse and ridden off in all directions at once. He started his days early and ended them late.

He was constantly dealing with investors, both old and new, keeping Irv Deal informed of every move, raising money, securing new leases, working with Randy Stewart who was tracking down land titles, and watching as the wells were drilled into the chalk. After awhile, he and Irv Deal both were living in a fog that never lifted.

June Collier was an astute businesswoman, and he left her alone. When she finished a set of books, he knew, they were as solid as the chalk itself. To Max Williams, during those early days, she was an invaluable resource. Smart. Loyal. Trustworthy. He could not have had a better friend looking over his shoulder and after his interests.

Williams would break away during the week, drive down to check on the Molly C. Davis, walk out to the rig, and ask, somewhat cautiously, "How does it look, boys?"

"Looks great."

"Any problems?"

"Everything's running smooth."

"Like the Schkade?"

"As good as the Schkade."

"Are we getting any shows of oil?"

"Not yet. Not quite deep enough. We'll know pretty soon."

There was no reason to worry, he thought. Williams had drilled three winners in a row, and Ray Holifield had masterminded them all. Now, Holifield was in charge of the Molly C. Davis as well. Just give it time, Williams thought. Other geologists in the chalk were shooting wildly in the dark. Hit and miss. Mostly, miss. Holifield was the only one of them who could take a handful of seismic data and see deep enough into the core of the earth to find the faults, the fractures, and ultimately the pay zone.

●

Max Williams was on top of the world. It suddenly shuddered and began to erode away beneath him. He had been right. His concerns had been justified. Good luck would not be around forever. In fact, like an old girl friend, it was already walking out on him. Sooner or later, it happened to everybody in the oil game. Williams had always known it might happen to him someday. He just wasn't expecting it when good luck finally decided to split Giddings and leave for parts unknown.

The drill bit reached the depth where the chalk was known to hold its oil, and the crew ran its usual electric logs, lowering a device with a set of electrodes down to the bottom of the hole to take a continuous reading of the strata layered far below the peanut fields. The electrical current traced a pattern on a strip of paper creating a log, printing out the data as parallel lines on a chart. As one old geologist had said: "When you take the log from the well, it's a tremendous emotional experience. It's almost like going to an execution block." Ray Holifield leaned against the rig as the day dried up the remaining rays of sun and glanced quickly over the log of the Molly C. Davis, checking to determine where the spontaneous potential line and the resistivity line were bulging out, indicating to him the presence and location of oil-or gas-bearing zones.

He paused and looked again. Harder this time. He did not like or even pretend to understand the raw data staring him in the face. Those critical lines on the chart did not waver at all. They were running as straight as railroad tracks. No bumps. No bulges. No promises. No sign of oil. No sign of gas. No sign of anything but failure.

"I don't know how, but I must have made a mistake," Holifield said. His voice was hollow, devoid of all emotion. He hated to make mistakes. He hated even more to admit them.

"It happens," Williams said.

"I thought I had the seismic figured out."

Reading seismic was more than just a science and hardly ever an exact science. In this case, the drill bit had missed the fault. Williams didn't really understand the strange hieroglyphic markings of the log, but he studied it anyway. Empty. Dry. What now? What next? Why not? And what happened? Questions were plenty. He had as many answers as he did drops of oil from the Molly C.

Max Williams took a deep breath, his face stoic, his voice calm. But deep inside, the pain of disappointment gnawed at his gut. He took one last glance back at rig, standing forlorn in defeat. Men had gone busted spending their last dollars to revive a well that had drawn its last breath. He couldn't afford the risk. He ordered the crew to plug the well, walked to his Blazer, turned toward Giddings, and moved on. He realized he had no other choice. Three times he had beaten the chalk. Now the chalk had struck back with vengeance.

●

By now, Windsor/U.S. was shooting its own seismic. No longer did the company have to rely on second-hand data generated by somebody else's dynamite blasts. During the late night hours, Ray Holifield kept reading that confounded seismic log of the Molly C. Davis with all the intensity of a preacher man studying the scriptures for his Sunday sermon. Then he read them again. The desperate search for answers only left him with more questions. It galled Holifield to make such a mistake, especially one that cost his employer more than three hundred thousand dollars. He saw the faults charted in the data and knew that the faults created fractures. Simple science. Science could be a lying bastard.

Holifield wasn't sure what had gone wrong, but he learned that Max Williams was not the kind of man to hold grudges or stand still for very long. Those oilmen who fretted too much and too long about their losses never survived the tough times, and they were all playing a game that eventually told them how tough they really were. Max Williams wanted another well, the sooner the better. The quicker he washed the bad taste of the Molly C. Davis out of his mouth, the better he would like it.

Ray Holifield checked the seismic one final time, looked for some glaring flaws in the data, didn't find any, chose a location that revealed all of the proper geologic signs. The showing astounded him. It was on paper, but Holifield was staring at the largest fault yet encountered on any seismic data he had shot in the chalk.

The crew huddled on the rig and quietly began preparations to drill one more time, stepping out seven miles from the site of the Molly C. Davis. Holifield was hoping against hope that the Max Fariss No. 1 would turn out better for him and Max Williams than their last venture had been.

He had seen dry holes before. But the Molly C. Davis, in spite of the giant fault pictured on the seismic reading, was as dry as any well he had ever been around. His only concern was the fact that the well would be spudded in seven miles to the southeast. The fault might have been cataclysmic when it occurred eons ago, but had it been large enough to trap oil so many miles away? The locations within spitting distance of town had historically been good to them. What lay in the uncharted territory beyond?

●

Max Williams gazed out at the Max Fariss No. 1 and wondered what had happened and how he and Holifield could prevent it from happening again. Had the seismic data lied to them? Or had Ray Holifield merely read it wrong? Did they make a mistake by stepping out from the fault line that linked together the City of Giddings, the M&K, and the Schkade wells? Would it have been better to stay on strike? Don't tempt fate and turn your back on good fortune. That was the wisdom of an oilfield, and they had ignored it.

Max Williams had paid dearly. Now, he was daring to step out a second time. But was he in danger of making the same mistake again? Was the field long and narrow? Was it just small? Had he already found the only significant vein of oil in the field? Should he throw good money down the throat of another hole that might go bad? Should he have gone ahead and fracked the Molly C. Davis?

He had let his geologist talk him out of it even if Holifield had only temporarily abandoned the idea. Maybe he should have stood his ground. He was, after all, gambling with his investors' money, win or lose, and he regarded it as his own. It would certainly not happen again. If the Max Fariss balked, Williams vowed to himself, he would send out for the fracking trucks without the slightest hesitation or second thought. They were expensive.

So was a dry hole.

Ray Holifield , the geologist, had always been supremely confident in his ability to find oil. It was a rare gift, and he had it. But Ray Holifield, the man, was beginning to have serious doubts. Nights were always longer when a man couldn't sleep, and he could not sleep for thinking about those straight lines on the electric logs of the Molly C. Davis. He had expected a few difficulties. The chalk was always cranky. Watching the rig as it moved into a new place made him nervous.

The Max Farris No. 1 went into the ground, then slowly into the chalk. The well was important to Max Williams. After all, it was a three hundred thousand dollar wager for him, for Irv Deal, for all of his investors. Landowners were carefully watching every rotation of the drill bit. They had a lot riding on the Max Fariss, too. In reality, Williams also had an overriding interest in seeing if another good well could help him determine the actual size of the Giddings Field. A producing step out well was crucial.

Maybe the rumors, always the rumors, had not been the stuff of fiction, the half-stupor figment of someone's imagination gone wild. Maybe the fractures had only broken up beneath the land surrounding the town.

Maybe the layers of chalk across the rest of the field remained solidly packed together, un-cracked and uncompromising. Oil, he realized, lay trapped in every foot of the chalk. Without the fractures, however, it might as well be in a vault. Neither he, Ray Holifield, nor anyone else had the right combination for the lock. The bit could slice through the layered veins of the chalk, but if they didn't bleed, he might as well take his oilfield operation somewhere else. A month ago, he had no intention of ever leaving Giddings. Now he wasn't so sure. He watched the drill bit turn. The stakes were growing higher with every passing day and every rotation of the pipe.

The drilling had gone smoothly and without any complications, but Ray Holifield was wracked with the realization that something wasn't quite right about the Max Fariss. The log looked eerily like the one pulled from the pit of the Molly C. Davis.

Déjà vu.

His fingers traced the spontaneous line, then moved over to the resistivity line. Again, all he saw were straight lines, those same old railroad tracks going up and down but nowhere near any collections of gas or oil.

He was convinced that his ideas on seismic in the chalk were sound and based on years of experience in the Middle East, but they kept leading him down a false trail that mocked his every effort. He wadded up the log and threw it to the far side of the room.

Ray Holifield was depending on seismic to be his guide. The ability to read the chalk had been his secret, one he guarded so closely that he didn't even bother to educate his clients. Being able to read the defiant and elusive Austin Chalk made him the king of the field. His crown was suddenly resting uneasily.

He had told Max Williams, "The seismic tells me that the Max Fariss is sitting on top of the largest fault I've ever seen in the Giddings chalk."

He was convinced he had hit it? He had no doubts. But where was the oil?

"Maybe the string went down a little crooked, Williams said. "It sometimes happens in the chalk, you know."

"Wouldn't have made any difference," Holifield said firmly. "The fault's so big, there's no way we could have missed it. I am absolutely certain we hit it."

Oil had eluded them. Maybe the seismic was screwed up. Max Williams didn't mention it, but he was beginning to wonder if his geologist might be screwed up as well. Holifield had looked like a million dollars on the first three wells. He had been a wooden nickel on the last two. Williams would not be able to survive on dry holes. For the first time, Holifield admitted he was scared to death. "What happens if the Max Fariss doesn't come in?" he asked Williams.

"We may have to shut the operation down."

"For good?"

Williams shrugged. "I've been broke before," he said.

"I don't like it."

"In this game, it's the chance you always take."

They watched the drill bit slowly and methodically cut as far down into the chalk as it was supposed to go.

"Find anything?" Holifield was asked.

He nodded.

"What?"

"More chalk," he said.

No oil. No gas. Nothing but chalk. And it was dry.

●

In a dimly lit room in the Sands Motel, Max Williams, Ray Holifield, and Lonnie Donald, the company man on the rig, sat alongside investors Ben and June Collier, all of them quietly contemplating the fate and future of the Max Fariss, if perchance it had one. Daylight had faded away.

Williams felt his stomach burning, and it wasn't from the chicken fried steak at Schubert's. A spider crawled up the wall. The light bulb flickered. Thus far, they had all kept their ideas, their thoughts, their fears to themselves.

Lonnie Donald finally leaned forward and said, "The well don't look good to me, Max. You may be chasing oil that's not in the ground."

"I'm not giving up yet," Max Williams answered softly.

"Tell you what," Donald said, as though he had seen the end and had no way to stop it. "I'll carry out all the oil this well ever produces in a wheelbarrow."

"Ray and I believe we'll make a well if we frac it." Max Williams shrugged.

"Maybe." Donald looked up and shrugged. "Sometimes, that's about the only way you can skin a cat in this chalk," he said.

Ray Holifield swore that he had hit the fault, but it was devoid of any traces of oil. A smart man, he figured, would just walk away from the Max Fariss, write it off, and go somewhere else. But no one was quite yet ready to plug the well.

Williams glanced at the Colliers. A lot of their money had vanished in the Molly C. Davis, and even more had gone down the wellbore of the Max Fariss. He wondered how they must feel, sitting in a sad little room in a sad little motel in a sad little town, hearing men who should know the oil business argue about whether or not they had financed another bad well and a potential dry hole.

He grabbed Lonnie Donald's arm and nodded grimly toward Ray Holifield. "Let's go outside," he said. Williams opened the door, and they followed him into the darkness. Standing in the Giddings night, his face partially lit by the pale neon of a Sands Motel sign, Williams told them, "You can't make comments like that in front of our investors. They don't want to hear that the well doesn't have enough oil to fill up a wheelbarrow."

"Well, it's the truth," Donald said.

"It may not be a lost cause if we frac the well." Williams said defiantly.

"It would be damn costly."

When raising money, however, Williams always included the money he might need for fracking a well on every oil deal he put together in the chalk. He had not needed it on the first three wells, but it was definitely a gamble that Windsor/U.S. was willing to take. He and Deal would frac the well. There would be no argument and no discussion. At the moment, his only regret was that he and Holifield hadn't decided to frac the Molly C. Davis when they had the chance.

Holifield grinned. "Well," he said, "if it would make you feel better, Max, we can go back and frac the Molly C. Davis, and we can do it now."

Williams thought it over a moment, then replied, "The rig is standing at the Max Fariss, Ray. We're here. We're not there anymore."

Williams watched Lonnie Donald walk away and wondered if he should go right along with him. Maybe his company man was more astute than the rest of them. Maybe the well did only have a wheelbarrow full of oil, if that much. Maybe only a bucket full. Maybe Williams was only being stubborn and hard-headed because of the success he had experienced with his first three wells. Failure, he always believed, was not an option and never had been. He shrugged. Lonnie Donald could go ahead and walk out if he wanted to. Max Williams knew he couldn't leave. It was already too late for that.

The neon in the vacancy sign was not as bright as it had been.

19

*R*ay Holifield did not take time to feel sorry for himself and his failure to find the oil. He was mad, mad at the Max Fariss well, mad at the Austin Chalk, mad at the seismic data, mad at himself. He was still confident that the seismic data had been correct. He had been in charge of shooting it. Holifield went back to his motel room while Max Williams made preparations to frac the well.

In the back of his mind, Williams had always planned to bring the frac trucks to the Max Fariss and probably the Molly C. Davis as well. When he saw those dreaded straight lines staring back at him on the electric log, he forgot about everything but those stacked layers of chalk that defied him and refused to release their oil. His mind had been so absorbed with trying to comprehend the problem that he failed to grasp the obvious solution.

In the chalk, the difference between a good and bad well often resided in the hands of the crew hired to frac it. Williams was convinced of it, and Irv Deal believed more strongly than any of them that the men who knew how to pump that high-priced, magical concoction of water, sand, fluid, and mud into the fracture would ultimately make the difference between their getting rich or going broke in the gardens of chalk.

As Ray Holifield explained to Max Williams, the chalk contained a series of fracture systems, both large and small. That was fact. Oil was found where it had been trapped and collected in the fractures. That was fact. The Molly C. Davis and Max Fariss had both been drilled in the chalk, which, by all rights, should have been webbed with fracture systems. If so, why hadn't they found any of them?

Though he had no data to back his belief, Max Williams was convinced that the fractures were close enough to the wellbore to be reached by a frac Maybe the oil was there but couldn't migrate to the wellbore without the fractures or conduits. If he were able to artificially fracture the chalk, removing debris and mud from the cracks, oil would be able to flow freely into the wellbore. He didn't even need to invent a new process. It was already in place. The few good wells in Pearsall had remained unproductive until crews completed them with hydraulic fracturing, known in the field as fracking.

The process had been used in earlier days to create fracture systems throughout layers of hard rock when crews were trying to drill their way past the rock and into oil-bearing sands. It was certainly possible to frac the last two wells, the only duds he had found in the good earth of Giddings, clean out the formations, and open up clear channels where oil could flow through the fractures and into the wellbore. Max Williams was down to his final pile of chips. He hoped that he and Irv Deal had made the right bet. He ambled back to his room at the Sands and waited for morning.

Fracking was expensive, but so was plugging a well after all of his money had been poured down the hole. The job would cost Williams another eighty thousand dollars, and he was somewhat apprehensive about spending eighty grand he did not have to lose. He and Irv Deal were already over budget on the last two wells, and they had nothing to show for them. Williams believed he had one chance to get it back, If Windsor/U.S. abandoned the Max Fariss like it did the Molly C. Davis, there was a good possibility that the company had drilled its last hole in the chalk.

Nobody believed the devil had much oil anyway. Investors, Williams knew, would be extremely skeptical of a man who had dry holes back to back. He could talk all he wanted about the great discoveries of the M&K, the Schkade, and the Carmean, but all anybody remembered were the dry holes. That's the way it had been since time began. What have you done for me lately? He sat down and telephoned Irv Deal in Dallas. The two men weighed the facts and discussed their options. Eighty thousand dollars was a lot of money. "I raised enough extra money and put it in the budget," Williams told him.

"Then do it," Deal said.

As soon as he knew someone would be in the office, Max Williams telephoned the geology and petroleum engineering firm of LaRue, Moore, and Schaefer in Dallas. His question was quick and to the point. "I need to frac a well," he said, "and I want to know which company you would recommend for me to use."

"You've fracked wells before, haven't you?" John LaRue asked.

"Down in Pearsall."

"Who'd you use?"

"Halliburton."

There was a moment of silence, then LaRue said, "Halliburton's a good company and has had a lot of success. But it's always seemed to me that the Western Company offers a frac method that works a whole lot better in the chalk."

"Who runs it?"

"Eddie Chiles. He's the president." Then LaRue mentioned, "If you remember, Max, he's the guy who says in his ads: If you don' have an oil well, get one."

"You have a phone number?"

John LaRue did.

There was no hesitation. When Max Williams made a decision, it was time to hit the ground running and never look back. He only had regrets when he didn't move as quickly and decisively as he should have. He quietly chuckled to himself, but there was no humor in the thoughts troubling him. Being down three hundred and eighty thousand dollars wasn't much different from being three hundred thousand in the hole. Numbers and dollar signs. That's all it was. He could stand pat, he knew, but his money would be lost forever. Williams believed he owed it to his investors to make one final gamble. He at least had an outside chance of getting their money back. For him, a frac job was not unlike making a half-court shot with time running off the clock. Max Williams shrugged. He had done it before. Then again, with a basketball in his hands, he was in charge and in control of the situation, no matter how futile it might seem. In the Giddings field, the Austin Chalk was in charge. Always had been. But maybe this time, he would be able to outsmart the old chalk.

Max Williams promptly placed a call to Eddie Chiles, who, a secretary said, was not available. The head man seldom was in any business. "Well then, please let me talk to someone who can help me get a well fracked," he said.

"What's your name?" came the response.

"Max Williams."

"Do you have an account with us, Mister Williams?"

"No."

"A line of credit, perhaps?"

"If I don't have an account with you, I sure don't have a line of credit," Williams said softly. He might be angry or frustrated. He never let it show.

"If you would like, you can apply for credit," said the polite voice at the other end of the line. "Getting an okay may take awhile."

"I don't have awhile."

Max Williams hung up, shoved another quarter in the pay phone, and called W. O. Bankston, one of his strongest investors and supporters back in Dallas.

"Can you do me a favor," Williams said.

"Whatever you need."

"I'm betting you know Eddie Chiles."

"He owns the Texas Rangers baseball team. I'm a season ticket holder. And," W. O. Bankston said, "he and I have worked in and around a lot of business deals together."

"I bet he'll answer your phone call."

"He always does."

"Well," Williams continued, "I need his company to come down to Giddings and frac a well for me, and they won't move until I have a line of credit established. The lady says it'll take at least seven days to get one approved, and frankly, W. O., neither you nor I can afford to have the rig shut down and sitting idle for seven days while somebody's doing a credit check."

W. O. Bankston laughed. "Don't worry," he said. "Just sit tight."

A few minutes later, Bankston called the pay phone number that Williams had given him. "The deal's done," he said. "I'm giving you a man's name, and you call and tell him where you want the trucks sent."

"How close are they?"

"I seem to recall that they have a yard in Bryan, just up the road from you."

Max Williams made the call. The fracs, he knew, were highly engineered, and their success would depend greatly on Ray Holifield and his field superintendent, Ted Ferguson, being able to give the Western Company a better idea of the physical location of the well, its position in the field, the depth of the fault, and the proper amount of mud and mixing agents needed for the process.

Within hours, trucks from the Western Company were heading south and on their way to Giddings. Good friends. High places. It always helped. The Western Company had been a pioneer in both acidizing and fracking oil wells. Nobody could do the work better. There was, however, one slight difference in the two processes. Fracking was ten times more expensive than acidizing.

As Ted Ferguson explained to Williams in June of 1977, while they waited for the trucks to reach the Max Fariss, the fracking operation would be akin to putting on a big opera. A lot of moving parts. A lot of drama. The plot was always changing. Williams had seen it all before, but never on such a grand scale.

A half dozen Western Company trucks rolled up to the rig, and a crew promptly began digging a water-holding pond near the well. Three large yellow water tanks and a long, yellow sand bin were hauled up beside the Max Fariss. A special blender machine hooked the tanks, the sand bin, and the wellhead together with a network of pipes. The odd puzzle was becoming more confusing by the moment. The pumper trucks drove up and were methodically connected to a long pipe running from the blender to the well. The frac van, housing the crew boss and the control panels, eased into a tight space alongside the blender. Each member of the crew wore headsets, staying in constant communication with the van. When the crew boss gave the signal to stimulate the well, they activated the blender, the water tanks, and the sand bin, pumping thousands of gallons of jelled water and sand – under enormous pressure – into the hole. It was a precise, professional, well-orchestrated operation. The noise was deafening, the continuous clanging of metal on raw metal nerve wracking. It went on for hours, and even the ground beneath their feet felt as though it were throbbing.

Water began to rise up out of the hole. The crew shut it down. Thus far, the frac job had gone well. Now Max Williams and Ray Holifield settled back to wait the long wait. The moment of truth was at hand. It was similar to watching a jury file slowly back into the courtroom. Suddenly, the defendant did not want to hear the verdict. It might be bad. The wait dragged on into the late afternoon and spilled over into the night. Williams felt worn down to a nub. He had not slept in two or three days, had been afraid to leave the rig, wanted to make sure the frac job had been completed. The Max Fariss sat there in the darkness, flowing water. Nothing but water. And when it stopped, Williams said, his heart stopped.

The Max Fariss was stubborn all right. But did it have any oil? With the frac job completed and the weight of the unknown settling down upon his weary shoulders, Max Williams climbed into his Blazer and began driving back to Dallas. He had done all he could do. He had poured all the money he could pour into the well. Now, it was up to God and the Western Company. He left the praying to Ray Holifield. Williams stopped just long enough on the edge of Giddings to telephone June Collier. "Can you come on back down here and keep an eye on the well for me?" he asked.

"I'd love to."

"I need a break," Williams told her. " I'm leaving for a few days and need somebody at the rig to keep an eye on the operation."

"Sure. What should I be looking for?"

"Oil."

"How will I know when I see it?"

"You'll know." Max Williams rubbed his eyes. "Just watch Ray Holifield," he said. "He doesn't hide his feelings very well. If he's not depressed, we still have a chance. If he goes crazy, we have oil."

"What if he goes out and cries in his beer?"

"I don't want to think about it."

June Collier immediately took the next flight back to Texas. She grabbed a rental car at the airport and worked her way toward Giddings. The two-hour flight had been far shorter than the drive.

Max Williams reached Dallas during the late night hours. He caught a few hours of sleep, then headed west down I-20 toward Abilene to play in a tennis tournament. It would give him time to free his mind of the worries, the troubles, the plight surrounding the precarious status of the Max Fariss.

Williams pulled his motor home near a pay phone that had been placed next to the Abilene Racquet Club and alongside the tennis courts. He wrote down the number, made a quick call, gave it to June Collier, and told her, "If anything important happens down there, call me."

"How will I know if it's important?"

"Don't worry, June. You'll know."

He walked toward center court and left the tribulations of the Max Fariss to June Collier. For the next few days, she became a fixture in the field. After hours of drinking silver bullets – gin and seven-up – she would casually wander out during all hours of the night, her hair and nightgown blowing in the hot wind, to check on the well.

By day, she painted large smiley faces on the sides of tank batteries. She gave the rig and the Max Fariss a feminine touch. But no one underestimated her, doubted her, or defied her. She might not have known what fracking an oil well was all about, she had no idea what a flow back did or did not look like, and she was careful to stay away from the work and out of everyone's way. But everyone knew she was the eyes and ears of Max Williams. And, frankly, the crew was more nervous around her than him.

●

Max Williams was in the middle of his first match, and the pay phone rang. He finished the point, heard it ring again, and excused himself from the court, even though it was a highly unethical and probably an unsportsmanlike thing to do.

He picked up the receiver and heard June Collier say calmly, "They tell me the water's showing a little oil."

"What's it look like?"

"More like honey than oil."

"Much of it?"

"I don't know how much, but you're right, Max. You can certainly tell it's oil. Is that a good sign?"

Max Williams grinned. "It's the best sign we've had yet," he said. There was hope after all. He grinned again, hurried back to he court, and waited for the serve. Sorry, he told his opponent. He wasn't sorry at all.

●

By now, on an empty patch of farmland near Dime Box, there was more oil than water flowing from the ground, oil the color of honey. Ray Holifield had his strut back. He felt as though he and his reputation had been vindicated. He knew he had properly read the chalk. He said all along he had hit the fault.

There had been doubters, but not anymore. The Max Fariss was beginning to talk a language Ray Holifield understood, and oil had an accent all its own.

Williams was six games into his second match when the pay phone rang again. He was a little perturbed about the interruption, and he thought seriously about ignoring it. The phone kept ringing. Loud and urgent. He decided it would be less of a distraction if he went ahead and answered it.

He excused himself again. He apologized again.

He picked up the receiver and did not have to say a word. On the other end, June Collier was screaming, "Max, there's oil blowing all over Lee County."

"How long has it been blowing?"

June Collier was breathless. "I've watched it for a good ten minutes," she said, "then I decided I needed to come and call you."

"You did the right thing," Williams assured her. "Now I want you to go see if you can find somebody who can tell you how many barrels of oil a day the gauge says the well has the ability to produce. Come back to the phone, wait for me, and when the match is over, I'll call you."

"I hope it doesn't take long," she said.

"What's that?"

"The match."

Two quick sets, and Max Williams was on the pay phone again. "What does it look like?" he wanted to know.

"They say it's flowing a hundred barrels."

"A day?"

"An hour."

That, Williams thought, was unbelievable. "Keep me posted," he said. He placed the phone on the hook and ambled back toward the tennis courts with the *thomping* sound of racket strings on tennis balls ricocheting all around him.

He decided he might as well try to win the tournament and leave the cranky, old Max Fariss to the mercy of June Collier. She seemed to have brought back the good luck that left him.

For the rest of the afternoon, the pay phone rang without fail every hour on the hour. Each time, he heard the voice of June Collier, and her message was always the same. "We've got another hundred barrels," she said.

By the time the day ended, the gauge had calculated initial production for the Max Fariss No. 1 as more than seven hundred barrels of oil a day. Ray Holifield had told him all along that, according to his seismic readings, the drill bit was cutting into the largest fault he had ever found below Giddings.

Holifield had read the logs correctly. The fault wasn't a myth after all. It did exist. It was exactly the way the geologist had pictured it, exactly what he hoped to find. Holifield knew it was there and had never lost sight of it.

The gut decision Max Williams and Irv Deal had made to spend another eighty thousand dollars to frac the well had been the difference between the penthouse and the poorhouse. Clean out the clogged fractures, break up the chalk, and the oil would come. That had been his mantra on the Max Fariss. Clean out the fractures, break the chalk, and oil began pouring from the ancient fractures in abundance. It was as good as Max Williams and Ray Holifield had felt in a long time.

The oil was so pure and so thin that, by morning, the winds had blown it across the wheat fields, and the mist rising up from the oil hung like a fog above the fields. It was the first and only time Williams had seen oil on the hard ground of Giddings.

So much for dry holes, Williams thought. The Max Fariss had almost chased him and Ray Holifield out of town. Men wiser than they would have probably left. But the oilman and the geologist sucked up their disappointments and stayed. The chalk could never keep a good man down, much less two of them. Maybe now, the Giddings field would go on. If nothing else, Max Williams had seriously broadened the size of the field. Oil did lie beneath the town. No one disputed it. Big fractures, however, could also be found down other roads and across other goat pastures.

All it took was a good frac job to blast out those confounded fractures and let the oil rise up in the well. Maybe the chalk wasn't mad at him anymore.

Ray Holifield reached for another cigarette. Didn't want to light it. Too much oil. Too dangerous. He just wanted to chew on something strong and bitter. A little whiskey could wash away the tobacco stains. He needed a good whiskey. Needed it bad. He didn't have a chance to celebrate the Max Fariss the first time the string of pipe went down. Not a damn thing to celebrate. Dry holes could leave a man thirsty.

When Max Williams drove back up to the rig, June Collier was waiting for him. Without a hello, she said, "It was a great decision, Max. If you had walked away, you would have left hundreds of thousands of barrels of oil in the ground." She smiled and hugged his neck. The warm oil throbbing through the pipe felt a lot like money.

Ray Holifield simply wanted to know, "What's next?" He had already selected the next locations and was ready to drill again. More wells. More oil. More money to pocket. It was a formula he well understood.

"I think the decision has already been made for us," Williams replied. His mind had been made up long before he left Abilene. "We'll go back, unplug the Molly Davis, and frac it, too. If there's oil here, then there's oil beneath the Molly Davis as well. The hole's already down. I have no intention of leaving the oil behind."

He moved the rig. He called the Western Company. And the Giddings earth again felt the pressure of water, mud, and sand. The water flowed. The pressure increased.

Then came the oil. Honey-colored oil. The Molly C. Davis, considered a failure and a lost cause, struck with a violent thrust and came in producing more than two hundred barrels of oil and almost a half a million cubic feet of gas a day. Not as big as the M&K, the Schkade, or the Max Fariss, but a solid money maker just the same. Neither Eddie Chiles nor anyone else at the Western Company was worried about Max Williams having a line of credit anymore.

Max Williams and Ray Holifield gathered their considerable talents around them and moved farther away from town. There was no time to waste. They had already shot seismic from one end of the area to the other. Windsor/U.S. had access to the leases. Randy Stewart, working with the maps and documents tucked away in file cases at the Lee County Land and Abstract Company, had completed the tedious title work. All they had to do was drill, acidize a well if necessary, frac if needed, and drill again.

●

Max Williams was, in the words of Irv Deal, a great promoter and an even better salesman. "He made promises I would have been afraid to make," Deal said. "I heard him tell one potential investor that drilling for oil in the Giddings field was like shooting ducks on a swimming pool. It was a gut cinch. In the chalk there were no gut cinches."

Max Williams no longer feared the chalk. He and Irv Deal were making more money than they could spend, and Windsor/U.S. had already doled out almost three million dollars. They were running a step ahead of debt. And debt was losing ground.

"I had a good friend named Bill Hutchinson," Deal said. "He was such a good friend that I did not want to ask him to invest in one of our wells. I would have felt responsible if we sank his money in a dry hole. It didn't bother Max at all. He went around my back and called on Bill personally."

Hutchinson liked gut cinches. He invested. Deal held his breath. On the day the well came in big, Bill Hutchinson was seated in Schubert's Restaurant with a chicken fried steak – the size of a steering wheel – on his plate. Eat it all, the advertisement said, and the steak was free. Hutchinson grinned. And took a bite. When he finished, his plate was clean. Even the grease had been sopped away.

Here Hutchinson sat. He owned a piece of a multi-million dollar oil well. And he had choked down a chicken fried steak that wouldn't cost him a penny. Life would never be any better. That, he thought, was absolutely a gut cinch.

●

Schubert's Restaurant was little more than a traditional small-town, home cooking diner that sat perched next to the Sands Motel on the eastern outskirts of Giddings. It was old. It was quaint. It had the ragged edges of linoleum peeling on the floor. It also had two signature dishes, and everybody in the oil patch could tell you what they were: chicken fried steaks and homemade pies, both washed down with endless cups of coffee.

Schubert's served real round steak, often with the bone embedded, hand dipped in batter and smothered with milk gravy containing the right amount of lumps. The silverware had been bent and tarnished with time. The plates sometimes showed a crack or a chip or two. No one cared as long as they held together long enough to hold the steaks and pies.

Max Williams walked in with Ben and June Collier, trailed by Lonnie Donald and Ray Holifield. They all slumped down into a back table. Sleep had become a rare commodity. Their eyes were red and bloodshot, their backs weary, their boots covered with a fine layer of gray dust. Suddenly Donald looked up and saw a flame shooting up through a crack in the wall behind a rack of plates.

"There's a fire back there," he shouted.

"Where?"

"Looks like the kitchen."

The men stumbled out of their chairs, raced frantically across the dining room, and spilled out onto the streets along with the regular

Schubert's lunch crowd. Williams counted heads. "Where's Ben?" he asked. Ben was the only one missing.

Smoke was pouring through the door and windows as Williams ran back toward the restaurant. Inside, he could see the faint image of Ben Collier's heavy girth barely visible in a heavy charcoal haze boiling up from out of the kitchen.

"Ben, get out of there," Williams yelled.

No answer.

"Ben," Williams yelled again, "what in the world are you doing?"

From behind a veil of smoke, he heard the unmistakable sound of Ben Collier's gruff voice. "I'm saving the pies," he said.

●

From the beginning, Williams found himself confronting a problem with the sinking of the Schneider No. 1. Ray Holifield had found the fault. He was a genius at finding the faults. "I can hit it," Holifield said. "Hit it dead center, sure as the world."

It sounded good to Max Williams. The problem was, the fault lay beneath a farmer's hog pen. He was proud of his hog pen. The farmer motioned to the unplowed acreage behind his barn and said, "Boys, you can drill on anything you see out there."

"I want to drill here," Holifield said.

"Can't." The farmer was adamant.

"Why not?"

"Don't want you disturbing my pigs."

"A good well could make you a lot of money," Max Williams said.

The farmer shrugged and walked away. "I know a lot about pigs," he said. "Don't know a damn thing about oil."

Argument over.

Williams turned to his geologist. "What'll happen if we leave the hog pen alone and drill as close to it as we can get?" he asked quietly.

"I know where the fault is," Holifield replied, "and it looks like we have a little wiggle room. I think I can get us close enough to hit it."

"Without messing with the man's pigs?"

"Not unless they get splashed with oil."

"Let's do it."

The farmer went about his business. So did the pigs. They ignored the drilling operation until the Western Company fracked the well, stepped back, and watched the Schneider come roaring in as a big-time producer of oil.

The farmer turned his back on the pigs. He hadn't known a damn thing about oil, he said, but he thought it was beginning to smell a little more profitable than pigs. And one was about as messy as the other.

Ray Holifield folded his arms and watched great amounts of oil splashing through the pipe on its way to the frac tank. "That's what I like about these wells," he said. "They're getting better all the time."

"I think we have ourselves something," Williams said.

"What's that?"

"I think we have ourselves a genuine oilfield."

Max Williams turned away, his boots freshly stained with oil the color of honey, and headed toward a pay phone on the edge of Giddings. Irv Deal, sitting back in Dallas, had struck it rich again. He didn't know it yet. He would find out soon enough.

Frankly, Max Williams thought to himself, he was growing weary of Irv Deal living the high life and banking a good chunk of the oil money while he was on the road, pitching investors, and bringing them down to the metropolitan areas of Giddings and Dime Box to gather as close as they could to the edge of the work. He wasn't selfish. He didn't mind sharing any wealth he was able to draw up out of the ground. He just thought it was about time for Irv Deal to become part of the team or leave it. Didn't know what it would cost him if he and Deal split the blanket. He figured it would be a lot and, by the time he reached the phone, he had decided the price might be worth it.

But today, he had good news. Oil was flowing again, and oil had dollar signs attached to it. The storm of oil had indeed come in after the lull. Any decisions about the future of Windsor Energy and U.S Companies, either working together or apart, could be made later. Confrontations, civil or otherwise, should take place face-to-face, man-to-man. That was the only way Max Williams and Irv Deal knew how to conduct business.

20

Pat Holloway studied the history of the trend. The City of Giddings No. 1 was a barnburner. It was flowing at least three hundred barrels a day and, since its discovery, the well had given up more than three hundred thousand barrels of oil. It had long been the envy and the icon of the Giddings field.

Max Williams and Irv Deal, if rumors and newspaper articles had not slanted the facts, had brought in a half dozen good producers, maybe more. But the rolling landscape across Lee County – the high ground, as well as the meadows – was littered with the sad remains of dry holes that had rid themselves of every drop of oil they possessed in a single day or week.

Giddings, over a number of star-crossed years, had become a field of broken promises. A few oilmen employing radio metrics had stumbled upon small amounts of gas tucked away in the Wilcox formation, but in spite of the strong faith his father's cousin had in the little black box, the science had not yet unearthed any great and productive reservoirs of oil. Neither had the mediums and divining rods of years past.

Until Max Williams and Irv Deal moved in, apparently to stay, only the City of Giddings No. 1 had actually delivered on the promise of the chalk, and that was the result of good fortune and not good science. Hell, Holloway thought, Chuck Alcorn wasn't even drilling when oil came rushing to the top of the ground. He was simply ripping out a few old pipes to sell for salvage. Alcorn just happened to in the right place and the right time.

The sudden successes of Max Williams and Irv Deal, a couple of rank amateurs in the oil game, greatly puzzled him. What did they know that the others had never learned?

●

The oil business had long been a driving force in Pat Holloway's near and distant family. Oil, he believed, was a destiny from which he would never escape. His father had been an oil and gas attorney. But his grandmother, Holloway said, was the reason he had oil running thick in his blood. Lydia Hanszen had been a bookkeeper, the oldest of five children, and she had assumed the task of shepherding her siblings through life after their parents died tragically in a Jefferson City, Missouri, fire.

By the turn of the twentieth century, Lydia Hanszen had taken a precarious route to South Texas, and she was working in the office of Guffey Oil, which had journeyed to Beaumont because of Patillo Higgins, a man who had long been smitten with a barren, ghostly kind of place that rose up in a dome just outside the town limits. St. Elmo's fire could be seen dancing in the moonlight. Placid pools of yellow, blue, and green water were collected in the hollows, and, if a man stuck a hole in the ground with his finger and lit a match, the air would burn brightly for a minute or two on a dark night. By 1889, Higgins, a real estate developer, was convinced that oil lay waiting for him somewhere deep within the rise. The government geological reports did not agree with him, saying there was absolutely no oil-bearing rock in all of Texas, and, thus, no oil – only foolish men who lied to themselves and dreamed they could find it.

Patillo Higgins remained undaunted. He went door to door and was able to round up a few Beaumont investors who provided two hundred thousand dollars worth of stock to underwrite his ingenious scheme. Higgins only wanted to find a little oil, then use the strike to attract people to a model industrial community he called Gladys City, named for an eight year old girl who happened to be the daughter of his financial partner.

A crew dragged its drilling equipment atop Sour Spring Mound and pounded its way into a bed of quicksand and a type of mud peculiar to the region called gumbo. Some estimated that oil, if there was any at all, lay more than a thousand feet below the surface of the big hill, and no drill bit in the United States had ever gone that far down before. It couldn't be done, were the whispers around Beaumont. Higgins had lost his mind.

Patillo Higgins ignored the cackles of Beaumont laughing behind his back and tried to interest the Rockefellers of Standard Oil. They responded with a short note rejecting his offer to visit the dome at Spindletop. There was simply too much guesswork involved, they said. Besides, those well versed in the ways of oil realized that crude lay elsewhere, pumped out of fields that stretched from New York to Ohio. In fact, those fields hoarded as much as ninety percent of the nation's petroleum supply, and Standard Oil controlled so much of the market that the company essentially set the price on every barrel sold.

In desperation, Higgins advertised in an engineering trade journal for someone who had the grit and gumption to sink a deep well in return for a substantial share of the mineral rights. The only answer came from Captain Anthony Lucas, an Austrian mining engineer who had just enough money to drill one hole. One brave engineer and one good well were all they needed, Higgins said.

The well collapsed at five hundred and seventy-five feet. But before the hole caved in for good, Lucas was able to recover a few gallons of oil from the sands that his drill penetrated. Higgins had been right all along.

Captain Lucas, his money drying up, was ready to walk away from the onerous venture, but his wife urged him to stay long enough to put one more hole into the earth. Lucas drew no salary. He sold furniture out of his Beaumont home for enough money to keep his family fed, and he managed to obtain financing from a Pennsylvania wildcatting team – James Guffey and John Galey, who borrowed four hundred thousand dollars from Philadelphia banking magnate Andrew Mellon for the chance to battle the quicksand and gumbo of Spindletop.

The morning of January 10 broke cold and clear. Not a cloud spoiled the sky. The worn and blunted bit was replaced, and thirty-five sections of pipe were sunk seven hundred feet into the well. Down below, the mud suddenly exploded high up the derrick legs as it fell harmlessly over the rotary table. Gas rushed out of the hole. The noise was deafening. Six tons of four-inch pipe shot skyward, blasting the crown block off the top of the derrick. The pipes plunged to earth like odd metal sculptures hammered into the ground by the relentless force of nature. From deep within the earth there came a growl, a low rumbling, and a six-inch column of oil – thick and green – burst out of the earth with the roar of a heavy cannon shot, a geyser of oil shooting more than a hundred feet above the derrick with the force of a volcano unleashed, and scattering across Spindletop like a hot, filthy rain.

Pat Holloway had listened to his grandmother tell the story hundreds of times as he grew to manhood. She had been there. She had watched it. She had lived through it, taking a job with Guffey Oil Company and wrestling with the payables and receivables, as well as riding shotgun on a pay wagon carrying silver and gold coins from Houston to Beaumont. Earlier, the pay wagon had been robbed and a driver killed. No one, however, wanted to tangle with the pretty little lady who said she had never fired a shotgun before.

Within a year, the sour creek dome at Spindletop was ranked as the nation's third largest oilfield, making it possible for the United States to replace Russia as the world's leading producer of petroleum. As many as six hundred oil companies were chartered, but few of them had staying power and quickly vanished, including the Higgins Oil and Fuel Company. The world had suffered an unfathomable glut of oil, and prices began to plummet.

Day after day, Lydia Hanszen kept watching James Guffey's money drain away. Many considered him to be the father of the Spindletop field, but he was losing money every time a barrel of oil splashed on the ground. He bundled up a set of financial statements and wrote a frantic letter to Andrew Mellon in Pittsburgh, requesting a quick infusion of cash, preferably several million dollars, in order to survive and fully exploit the field. Guffey knew better than to give Mellon a true and accurate account of his predicament, so he played strange and assorted games with the numbers, cooking the books without bothering to show any financial liability to the royalty owners. On paper, he was rich.

Guffey asked Lydia, his accountant and bookkeeper, to certify the statements. She politely refused. "It's a lie," she said. Before the day ended, Lydia Hanszen walked into Guffey's office and handed in her resignation as bookkeeper and office manager. With a stiff upper lip, she gave him a copy of the letter she had already mailed to Andrew Mellon. It was brief, to the point, and carefully underlined the falsehoods and miscalculations that Guffey had sent along with his bogus financial statements. She signed it *L. Hanszen*. In those days, there were few telephones, and most correspondence was conducted by either mail or telegram. As bookkeeper, she always signed her name as *L. Hanszen*. In those days, bookkeepers were almost always men. Nobody in oil dared to have women working anywhere near the rig or the business. Bad luck, they said.

Andrew Mellon read her letter and compared her well-chosen words to the devious information that the honorable James Guffey had mailed him. Guffey braced for the worst. Lydia Hanszen's letter had nailed the lid shut on his financial coffin at Spindletop.

Andrew Mellon surprised them all. He did not call off the deal. He couldn't. He already had invested too much money in the Guffey Oil Company, and he could not afford to waste it regardless of how rich he might be. He was, however, quite impressed with a bookkeeper who had the nerve to stand up and tell the truth even if a job was hanging in the balance. He was quite impressed with L. Hanszen, someone he did not know and had never met. He immediately wrote a letter that offered L. Hanszen a position as vice president in charge of exploration and geology for a six state region. It was, he said, one of the most prudent moves he had made in the Texas operation. L. Hanszen was worth every cent he paid to give his bookkeeper a promotion. Years later, he rode his private railroad car into Baton Rouge, and, at a scheduled stop, a group of Louisiana oilmen walked on board to discuss the state of the oil business with the great Andrew Mellon. One congratulated him on that fine lady he had hired to run his operation in Beaumont.

Mellon was stunned. "What lady?" he asked.

"Lydia Hanszen," he was told.

It was the first time that Andrew Mellon knew he had someone wearing a skirt in charge of geology and exploration in the states surrounding Texas. All he could do was laugh. She had developed such a fine reputation in the oil patch that he kept her on with Gulf Oil.

At a later point in her life, Lydia Hanszen could count the presidents of five oil companies – Texaco, Humble, Shell, Magnolia, and Gulf – who began their careers by working in oil exploration under her supervision. They called themselves "Lydia's Club," and, as long as they lived, they honored her once a year with dinner and wine in Dallas. They continued to meet long after she was no longer among them.

Lydia Hanszen did all right. When she resigned from Gulf, she and a couple of lady geologists traveled to West Texas during the 1920s in a Model T. They were looking for salt domes like Spindletop, did not find any, but saw a series of rises on the flat lands that intrigued them a great deal. They purchased the mineral rights and tried to persuade Gulf to drill on their leases. Gulf refused. Gulf had lawyers who told the company to stay far away from those surface highs. Dry on top. Dry down below. Lydian Hanszen never blinked. She turned around and leased the land to Sid Richardson. He did not have the same lawyers. He drilled. Sid Richardson became a multi-millionaire. Lydia Hanszen sat back and watched her overrides make a lot of bankers happy. Gulf Oil tried to forget.

●

Pat Holloway would forever be indebted to his grandmother. She instilled in him the value of land that no one wanted, and he learned from her that oil never gave itself freely to anyone. You had to go out and find it. You had to take it with your own bare hands. It was not a game for the weak of heart or anyone fearful of taking a risk. You could not do it from behind the comfortable confines of a desk in Dallas. Sure, he had made some money. Sure, he would make a lot more. But Holloway's most prized possession was the royalty on a handful of oil wells that he inherited from Lydia Hanszen. That's something nobody can ever take away from you, she told him just before she died.

He drove down the empty roads that linked together the quaint little communities surrounding Giddings. All around him were flat land, knolls, mesas, pastures, hardwood thickets, wet creeks, dry ravines, farms, barns, and barbed wire fences, old, rusting, and busted. Serbin had been settled by the Wends who left Lusatia in East Germany. They did not come to Texas for the promise of land or money or even opportunity. They only wanted a place where they had the freedom to practice their own religion and speak their own language. They journeyed from the port of Galveston in oxcarts, bought land for a dollar an acre, and lived in small dugouts while surviving that first, hard winter. They had fled the harsh, imposing rule of the fatherland, but, in time, they began marrying off their daughters to German farmers plowing Texas land. In the land of the Wends, the brides always wore black on their wedding day, a color that symbolized the hardships a wife would have to endure upon the prairie.

The Wends continued to cling to their religion, but their culture and their language began to slowly wither away.

The town of Warda grew up amidst stands of post oak and pines, not far from the rich bottomlands and banks of Rabb's Creek. For generations, the cornerstone of Warda had been Falke's Store, a relic of 1874 that carried everything from groceries to furniture, from clothes and buggies to farming implements. It also housed a post office, a doctor's office, and a bowling alley. The last anyone knew for sure, the population had dwindled to ninety-eight, and the post office, with few letters to send and receive, had been carted on down the road to Lexington.

Old Dime Box had originally been known as Brown's Mill. But the name was changed. Blame it on those old Czech and German farmers who loved to chew tobacco. They would leave a dime in their mailboxes, the postman picked it up, and the next day he left off a pouch of tobacco. About the only person of any importance to come out of Dime Box had been Tyler Dee Bell, a guitarist who was known as the godfather of the Texas blues. In the 1920s, he was something special. He played an electric guitar, and when he took the stage of Austin's famed Victory Club, he limited himself to three songs a night. Don't give 'em too much. That's what he believed. Never give 'em too much. He certainly wasn't in the oil business. Dime Box gained national notoriety when it became the first town in the nation to have one hundred percent participation in the March of Dimes campaign. It was only fitting.

Pat Holloway drove through the little communities but paid little attention to them. He could go from one end of town to the other in a hurry. What they all had in common was a church or two, mostly Wendish or Lutheran. Holloway had a deeper interest in the land on which those little hamlets had been built. Chalk was a good foundation. But, Lord, what else did the chalk beneath them hold?

Pat Holloway stood alongside the highway and gazed across a goat pasture that separated him from the crumbling downtown of Warda. The land was baked, parched, and brittle. No salt domes, but plenty of chalk.

God, he said, and it may have been a prayer, what I need is another Spindletop. He wished his grandmother had been there beside him. She could read the land, the top as well as the bottom of a hole. But she was gone, and he still wasn't sold on Lovejoy's little black box. It reminded him too much of the accoutrement of a doodlebug man. All he had left to guide him was Ray Holifield. Holloway knew without a shadow of a doubt that he rightfully owned a piece of Holifield. But, hell, Ray Holifield was spending all of his time searching for oil in the damned old chalk for somebody else.

21

*T*he joint operation of Windsor Energy and U. S. Companies had drilled eight wells in the chalk, and Max Williams was beginning to feel more like the raggedy man than an oilman. He was caught in a web where time and miles were the demons he could not exorcise. Driving back and forth between Giddings and his Dallas office had become a constant occurrence from which there was no escape.

Raising money was a never-ending venture, but Williams preferred to station himself on the rigs to help breathe life into every well. He was there at all hours for the hits as well as the misses. Mostly, they had been hits.

More and more, he and Irv Deal had turned the day-to-day responsibilities of Giddings over to Randy Stewart. He was still their legal mind in the field, the man they trusted to buy leases and clear titles. Stewart was a fixture in the offices of John and Bob Knox, and there were times when he thought he might have touched or at least studied every land title and abstract in Lee County.

Like Williams, Randy Stewart was a prisoner of the highway. He drove back and forth between his Dallas office and Giddings at least twice a week. He monitored the drilling and production, selected the seismic shot points for each location, contracted to have the roads and rig pads built, drank heavily with the field hands, and had a passing acquaintance with the Down Hole Bar, where, he said, they checked you for a knife when you went in. And if you didn't have a knife, they gave you one because you'd damn sure need it before you came out.

It was often a struggle for a young lawyer who was learning the oil business from the ground up while usually shooting fast and from the hip. He was constantly searching to find ways that would save Windsor/U.S. money and ensure that the company drilled more efficiently. He kept a watchdog eye on the crews, constantly replacing those who didn't bother to show up for work on some mornings. Hangovers cost a lot of men a lot of work in the field.

On many occasions, Stewart would drive all night and meet with Ray Holifield to discuss potential seismic locations as they parked beside an Albertson's Supermarket just as the first crease of sunlight broke behind the distant skyscrapers of downtown Dallas. Both men lived in the nearby Irving suburbs.

Ironically, they saw more of each other in the city than they did in the barren pasturelands of Giddings. Stewart would then leave Holifield in the parking lot and drive to Irv Deal's office, bringing him and Williams, when he was in town, up-to-date information on the field operation, which was ruled in the chalk by Ted Ferguson and later Clarence Cheatham.

Williams kept bringing in the big dollars, and Deal oversaw the business end, but, for the most part, he left Windsor/U.S. in the capable hands of his CEO Charles McLeod and CFO Terry Harper.

For Max Williams, wells, either good or bad, cost money, big money, and it was vital to keep his base of investors updated on the last turn of the pipe, the last drop of oil, the last stubborn gamble in hard ground, even when he wasn't out selling production overrides and working interests to finance the next hole in the ground.

His body had worn down, his muscles ached, and he could not enjoy the benefits he reaped from bringing in one well for worrying about the precarious status of the next one. There were no sure bets, no gut cinches in the chalk, in spite of what investors might believe. Only price tags.

And they were growing larger with each new drill bit that went into the ground.

The success of Windsor/U.S., especially in the chalk, was viewed as a gift from Providence, a once-in-a-lifetime phenomenon in the oil business. As Irv Deal would tell *Forbes Magazine: We're not basically a drilling fund. We don't have a sales force and don't make money if we don't find oil as drilling funds often do. Our current drilling budget is roughly six million dollars. We have seven wells that are producing seventy-five hundred barrels of oil and twenty-five million cubit feet of gas a day. I couldn't even talk to one of those real old-timers. I'm just a businessman in the oil business. The great reward I've felt is building things up from absolute zero.*

He had started at zero. And now Windsor/U.S. was touching millions of dollars. He and Max Williams had built a strong, profitable business, but their relationship was becoming as precarious and as fractured as the ground beneath their wells.

The long hours and lack of sleep gnawed at Max Williams. The unending pressure of finding investors, raising money, and drilling wells, working day and night to keep the operation financially solvent enough to expand the fields of chalk, had become a weight lying heavy on his shoulders. He and his crew were capable of drilling and making a well in eighteen days, but it took months before the oil was ever translated into money. It was his job to bridge the tenuous gap between production and payout.

All the while, Ray Holifield was poring over land maps until his eyes resembled the tiny red roads intersecting on the paper before him, reading seismic logs, looking for bulges that indicated the potential presence of oil or gas, walking across leased acreage, and telling Williams and Irv Deal to keep the faith. He controlled the field. He had the ability to find reservoirs of oil in the fractures while everyone else was destined to pull up buckets of dry chalk.

The more Max Williams drilled, however, the fewer hours he had to sleep in a genuine bed, even at the Sands Motel, at night. More and more, he found himself falling to sleep, against his will, sitting in a chair or leaning against a rig at midnight. After eight wells had been completed, Williams sat down one hot afternoon and put the numbers to paper. He had raised slightly more than seven million dollars. Irv Deal had not yet raised a cent on his own. One investor from Deal's real estate past contributed three hundred thousand dollars, but not until Williams called on him and worked out the details of the investment

Irv Deal kept telling him, "Don't worry about it, Max. It may take me a little longer, but when I do raise some money, it will come in a big chunk. I have a group of investors in Chicago, and those old boys have no idea how wealthy they are. Oil is the kind of game they like to play."

Max Williams no longer listened to him. He had heard about Chicago investors for a long time, but he had never seen their names, their addresses, their phone numbers, or their money. He was tired of doing the work for two men when one of them wasn't in the field or on the phone working at all. Well, he was no doubt working, and every business did need a man in charge of pushing numbers, but, as far as Williams knew, Irv Deal certainly did not have any investment money on his side of the ledger.

Max Williams began to make mental preparations to move on in the chalk without the benefit of Irv Deal and his sophisticated business operation in Dallas. Windsor/U.S. had control of a lot of acreage in the Giddings field, but Williams had no idea what might happen when the two companies went their separate ways. He knew he would lose some of the wells and a lot of the leases, but Williams had made up his mind.

He began the mechanics of building his own U.S. Operating Company, preparing to fly it solo, before he even confronted Irv Deal about their impending divorce. He had no idea that Deal had planned for the separation from the start and hoped that the ultimate split would be clean and amicable, free of any verbal fights, threats, or acrimony.

He quietly met with Holifield and said, "Ray, I need some more acreage."

"For Windsor/U.S.?"

"Just for me."

"What about Irv?"

Williams didn't answer.

It was, Holifield knew, the beginning of the end.

Williams and Deal had made a great team and a lot of money. But not even great teams last forever. And there was money enough for both of them in Giddings. Frankly, they no longer needed each other. But both needed Ray Holifield.

Every day, virtually every time the phone rang, there were geologists – old friends of his – oil operators, and lease holders, trying to persuade Holifield to find someone with more cash, credit, investors, and expertise to take their land on a farm out basis. Many of them had drilled in the chalk, brought in a few chalk wells, none of them commercial, and were hoping that they might attach their overrides in a good deal and take financial advantage of Holifield's uncanny talent for finding good wells in Lee County.

Their drilling efforts had failed or come up miserably short. His hadn't. "I didn't have a gift," Holifield would say, "but I had a little luck and a whole lot of technology on my side."

While surreptitiously searching for potential drilling locations for Pat Holloway, he had become enamored with the potential for oil beneath land that sprawled north of Giddings, cutting a wide swath past the shuffling little dust-blown town of Dime Box. He discovered that the thickness of the chalk decreased from about six hundred feet to less than three hundred feet as it edged farther northward, and, in Holifield's estimation, those thin layers of chalk spilling across both banks of Yegua Creek were bound to possess a lot more fractures and therefore a lot more oil.

He met with the officials of Prairie Producing and made arrangements for Max Williams to acquire a traditional farm out arrangement that would give drilling rights exclusively to U.S. Operating. However, since Prairie Producing had offered two additional blocks to anyone unafraid to tackle the foibles and pitfalls of the chalk, Holifield went ahead and, with Irv Deal's financial approval, sewed up the remainder of the farm out acreage for Windsor/U.S.

Until the break came, if it was destined to come, both companies were still drilling together under a single banner. Until the break came, Holifield kept them supplied with good locations. Who knows, he thought. It may have just been a bad day for Max Williams. Maybe the break would never come. Ray Holifield had his hopes. He wasn't betting on them.

●

On one of his return trips to Dallas, while the nagging ache of drilling the last well drove like a knife between his shoulder blades, Max Williams met with Irv Deal to deliver his regular report on their activities around Giddings.

Some good news. Some bad. Mostly, it was good.

"Will you be in Dallas for awhile?" Deal asked.

"No."

"Headed back down to Giddings?"

"No."

"Then where are you going, Max?"

"I'm going deer hunting," Williams said, sagging in the chair. The emotion was gone from his voice.

"You can't do that." Irv Deal's face was suddenly creased with concern.

"Why not?"

"You need to stay up here and raise more money," Deal said as he shrugged. "I have a business to run. The operations end is becoming more complex all the time. We have more acreage than ever before. We have wells to make, and we need the financing."

A deathly silence hung like a shroud between them.

Max Williams leaned across the desk, braced himself, and said through clenched teeth, "When you put together as many dollars as I have, Irv, I'll come back and start raising money again. As near as I can figure, you're down some. Seven million to nothing."

Irv Deal had not said another word by the time Max Williams quietly shut the door on his way out of the office. The end had not come with a bang or a whisper. It simply came. In reality, the end had arrived long before either man was willing to acknowledge it.

Irv Deal had not been surprised. He had known from day one that two hard-nosed, stubborn, I-want-to-do-it-my-way entrepreneurs could not exist together for a long period of time. Each man possessed different ideas and business practices. Failure had broken up a lot of partnerships. So had success. The more oil they made, the greater the tear in their relationship. Williams wanted Irv Deal down in Giddings on a regular basis, or at least he wanted Deal out raising investment dollars. Deal didn't see any reason why he should waste his time in the field. It had been his decision to remain in Dallas and manage the business end of oil exploration. It was what he knew best, and he had a knack for it.

Besides, he thought, Williams only kept traveling the long road to Giddings for one reason. He wanted to show off the big wells to prospective investors. Williams needed to know what was going on so he could keep them all informed. He looked like an oilman. He talked like an oilman. He knew the vernacular as well as anyone working on the rig. He told a great story, and investors bought every word. As far as Deal was concerned, however, standing around and watching a drill bit touch a fracture with oil did not make Max Williams an oilman.

Irv Deal felt a measure of relief. He wasn't sorry at all to see Max Williams walk out the door. The two men had never been particularly close anyway. The only tie ever holding the relationship together was money, and they certainly did not need each other to make money. Now Deal was free to do as he wanted, whenever he wanted to do it. So was Williams. The field was big enough for both of them. Neither would ever live in each other's shadow again.

Within days, Max Williams and Irv Deal sat down together in a peaceful state of unspoken acrimony and agreed that they could live better separately than together. The grievous and untimely divorce of Windsor Energy and U.S. Operating came to fruition in October of 1977. The details were left to the lawyers. The two adversaries did, however, maintain joint custody of Ray Holifield, who seemed to be the only geologist around with the ability to locate oil in the Austin Chalk.

Ray Holifield, with the flourish of two signatures, became a man who lived at the mercy of three masters, He didn't mind. He liked all of them. Besides, he had an override on every barrel of oil from every producing well that he and his seismic science found.

With Max Williams and Irv Deal deciding to head off in different directions, there was a strong possibility that he could double his money in the Giddings field. Together, they had drilled eight wells. Apart, during the same period of time, they might well drill sixteen. It was worth a try anyway. Of course, stuffed away in the back of his mind, he knew there was a third master he could not dodge or escape, not that he even wanted to.

Pat Holloway had those leases along the railroad track right-of-way. But Ray Holifield was not talking about him, not aloud or in public anyway. He had no reason to mention the name of Pat Holloway. He may have been a geologist, but he also considered himself to be a good businessman who was always open to more business. That was the American way. Holloway would give him as much as he needed.

●

Max Williams and Irv Deal might each be afflicted with an assortment of deep-seated grudges and hard feelings, but socially, they tried to keep any disappointment, anger, or bitterness bottled up inside of them. The self-styled oilmen – one a money raiser and the other a business manager – agreed to divide their holdings down the middle: the leases, the money, the debt, and the producing wells. In the mix were the last two blocks of acreage Windsor/U.S. had been able to acquire from Prairie Producing.

Max Williams believed it would be more fortuitous for him to keep his oil operation pointed north, tying any new leases together with his share of the Hughes & Hughes farm out, as well as the leases he had personally acquired from Prairie Producing.

When the two men met in Dallas to officially divide and separate their holdings, however, Irv Deal announced that he wanted rights to the whole Prairie Producing farm out.

"I'm afraid you won't be able to do that," Williams said.

"Why not?"

"We're splitting everything right down the middle, "Williams said flatly. "I'm taking the acreage on the north side of Highway 290, headed up toward Dime Box, and you can have the farm out on the south side."

"Maybe I want the north," Deal said.

"You haven't been to Giddings or Dime Box enough to know which acreage you want or don't want." Williams said, leaning back in his chair and folding his arms across his chest. "Besides," he argued, "the chalk is the chalk, and the chalk has oil in it. As long as you're still attached to Ray Holifield, locating oil won't be a problem. It will, in fact, be the least of your worries."

Irv Deal thought it over. Williams had a sound argument, he conceded, but he wondered what the south side of Giddings looked like. Then again, if Holifield knew, he decided, it really didn't matter to him. Land was land. It all pretty much looked alike. He didn't need to see the land. The dirt. The rigs. Or know a whole lot about faults creating the fractures beneath Lee County.

He preferred to see the checks, the more zeroes the better. Irv Deal and Max Williams formally shook hands for the last time and headed in opposite directions.

Only time, in its infinite wisdom, would decide who wound up with the most productive acreage.

●

Max Williams, by all accounts, was finally in a position to devote more time to the oil business and less to the arduous, pressurized chore of raising money. What he needed, Williams decided, was a single major investor to finance his oil explorations in Giddings. Larger risk, perhaps. Greater reward. A big-money player could own the whole deal, and Ray Holifield had thus far removed most of the risk.

He went to see Bunker Hunt, the wealthy son of H. L. Hunt, who had founded the family fortune in the great petroleum fields of Arkansas and East Texas. The very name of Hunt conjured up the mythical image of the Texas oil rich. Williams thought he was giving Bunker Hunt a chance to be on equal footing with his illustrious father.

Max Williams gave his best sales pitch, backed up by the impressive production figures from the M&K, the Schkade, the Max Fariss, and the Molly C. Davis wells. Big strikes. A lot of oil coming out of the ground. He had not yet scratched the surface. He talked of opening up the Giddings Field and explained how Bunker Hunt, following in his father's footsteps, would have a chance to become a major name in a new oil boom long before the full brunt of the boom descended on Central Texas.

Bunker Hunt did not write down a note or even bother to scan the figures lying on the desk in front of him. Instead, he said bluntly, "My daddy told me many years ago about the Austin Chalk. He said the wells come in like a lion but go out like a lamb."

"That was then," Williams said politely. "What I'm talking about is now. These days, we have the science, the technology, the knowledge to make the chalk wells pay off. No more of those old-time sizzles and fizzles. And, as you can see, we have the production figures to prove it. These wells hit big, and they're still big."

Hunt never changed his expression. He leaned forward and propped himself on the desk with both elbows. "Max," he said, his voice growing softer, "believe me when I tell you this because I'm as serious as I can be. The three most overrated things in the world are home cooking, home pussy, and the Austin Chalk. Good oilmen stay away from the Austin Chalk. That's the way it was. That's the way it is."

Max Williams walked out the same way he walked in, empty-handed. He had no choice but to begin raising money again. It was all so time consuming, and his time had become a precious commodity. His days were all blending together. He would begin the journey from Giddings to Dallas sometime around midnight, usually arriving home and falling in bed about five o'clock in the morning. He grabbed a few hours of sleep, took his children to school, and drove to the office, devoting the rest of the day on the phone with potential investors. Promptly at four-thirty in the afternoon, Williams finished his last call, walked back to his car, turned south, and headed toward Giddings and the wells again.

Shortly after midnight, he slumped into his Lincoln Continental, wiped the sweat and grime from his face, and was on his way back to Dallas. The cycle had begun again. Day after day. Night after night. The only thing that ever differed was the amount of oil pumping out of each well.

●

Irv Deal, with little ceremony, replaced Max Williams with Red Livingston as his partner in the Giddings field. Deal had the ability to provide the financing, out of his own pocket if necessary, and Livingston knew how to drill a well. Deal had no interest in the nuances of turning a drill bit in the earth, and Livingston had rather be managing the drill bit than money. Together, they made a formidable team.

Randy Stewart remained with Irv Deal, he said, simply because he already had an office inside of Windsor Energy headquarters in Dallas. Besides, he knew Deal needed someone on the ground in Giddings to handle his leasing, his legal work, his title work, and monitor the scope of the operation. Deal knew business. Stewart understood the fine print of the oil game. Irv Deal removed Terry Harper from his accounting department and named him president of Windsor Energy, and Harper, ever mindful of the numbers, left Dallas and headed south from time to time to immerse himself in the wild, wicked, wayward ways of the oil business.

Now, however, Deal did have a reason to make his occasional presence known in Giddings. He always walked cautiously and gingerly across fields of peanut vines and oil dirt, wearing new boots and a new pair of jeans. According to the whispers behind his back, whenever Deal did decide to make the long trek and look over his chalk holdings, his assistant would have to go out and buy him a new pair of boots and jeans. He would no doubt wear them once, take them home, and forget where he stashed them. The suave, sophisticated Irv Deal did not wear boots and jeans inside the proper social circles of Big D Dallas.

Deal had access to a lot of acreage, but the terms and conditions of the Prairie Producing farm out required a lot of holes in the ground. The demand was daunting. Irv Deal was playing with his own money now. He said, "I was raising hell all the time, trying to keep everybody in line and our production moving forward."

He was becoming more frantic by the moment. The responsibility of it all was suffocating. He had to drill six wells a month. The overhead would drown most men. He said, "As soon as I got a check on production, I paid the investors as fast as I could and prayed there would be enough money left over to keep drilling." The worries, however, started to fade when his income began averaging a million dollars a month.

●

The success Max Williams had experienced in the chalk had ceased to become a well-kept secret, reserved only for the downtown streets and street-side bars of Giddings. He was no longer a stranger living among strangers in a wayward and disheveled motel in an adopted town,

It sometimes seemed that almost everyone who knew him, met him, drank coffee with him, tried to buy his lunch, and offered him whiskey had land to lease or acreage just waiting for his rig.

He learned quickly to smile and say, "No thank you, I'm on a well, we already have our acreage leased, and I don't have access to any more rigs," or he kept to himself and out of sight.

He never drank their whiskey, smoked their cigarettes, or chewed their tobacco.

Such vices had never tempted him.

Williams did, however, pour far too many cups of coffee down his throat, eat too many chicken fried steaks at Schuberts Cafe, devour too many barbecue ribs at the City Meat Market, but never did he drill enough oil wells.

He had no doubt that multitudes of independent oil operators would someday follow him, but, at the moment, he and Ray Holifield, along with Irv Deal, exploring the acreage of Prairie Producing on the south side of town, ruled the Giddings oilfield. It was a point that no one in town or across Lee County ever debated, discussed, or argued.

The phone rang. Max Williams heard a voice from the past, but not the distant past. It belonged to Ted Clifford, a left over from the field in Pearsall.

He was genuinely a nice man, a congenial man, short, little rotund, a professional glad-hander, a big talker, a happy Irishman who had a knack for telling everyone he met how great they were.

Most were glad to see Ted Clifford headed their way. Max Williams wasn't so sure. He did not approve of Schedule D operators who were known to employ a one-room, bucket shop of telemarketers tracking down small-time, penny-ante investors to earn his oil money. Clifford drilled a lot, but finding oil was the least of his worries.

"I hear you have some pretty good acreage up around Giddings," Clifford said.

"It's been good to us."

"Do you have more than you can drill?"

"Maybe."

"Tell you what, Max," Clifford told him, "I'll make the same deal with you that we had in Pearsall. If I like what you have, I'll buy the leases for fifty dollars an acre and give you twenty-five percent of production. You can't get a better deal than that."

Max Williams nodded and a solemn frown shadowed his face. He had heard it all before, particularly in Pearsall.

"I'm willing to talk about it," Williams said.

"Come on over to my office," Ted Clifford said jovially, "and bring your map and Ray Holifield with you. Let's see what you have that might interest me."

"There's other land around here that you can get your hands on," Williams told him matter-of-factly.

Clifford laughed. "From what I've been told," he said, "you and Holifield have nailed the big sweet spots and know where the rest of them are. I can drill all day long and twice on Sunday, but I prefer going where I know there's oil." He laughed again, louder this time.

The next afternoon, Max Williams, accompanied by Ray Holifield, sat down at a desk across from Ted Clifford. They spread out their land map, and Williams said, "We've shot the whole county with seismic pretty good."

"You like what you're seeing?"

"I like it a lot," Holifield answered.

Ted Clifford studied the map for a few minutes, then asked, "What's this square over here, the one you've left blank?"

Williams looked at Holifield. Holifield shrugged. "That's the Keng property," Holifield said. "We've got a promise on the lease and are signing the deal early next week."

Ted Clifford nodded, and his eyes moved on.

The next day, Max Williams received an urgent telephone call from his landman. Worry clouded his voice. "I'm afraid we won't be able to get the Keng lease," he said.

"Why not?"

"He's already leased his land."

"Why would he do a thing lot that?"

"He was offered more money."

"Who got it?"

"Man named Ted Clifford."

Inside, Max Williams was seething.

His hand was still strangling the phone when he placed an immediate call to Clifford. "What gave you the right to go out and lease Keng's land?" he wanted to know.

"I'm sorry, Max." Clifford was as congenial as ever. "I had no idea you wanted that piece of acreage," he said.

"Sure you did."

"What makes you say that?"

"You stole it off my map," Williams snapped as he slammed the phone down.

Ted Clifford drilled.

It didn't do him a lot of good.

"Ted Clifford could drill all right. Ted couldn't hit the faults," Max Williams said. "Ted Clifford did not have Ray Holifield. Land maps and leases were worthless without him."

22

*T*here were days, some more turbulent than others, when Pat Holloway resented the fact and second-guessed himself for not going ahead and investing with Irv Deal in the Max Fariss well when he had the chance. He had the drilling funds at his disposal. Money wouldn't have been a concern. Ray Holifield had chosen the location, which, most people in town would swear, made the Max Fariss a solid bet even in the Austin Chalk. But Bill Browning – his partner, his ally, his friend, his largest investor – had died, and Holloway, a man who never hesitated, had committed the unpardonable sin. He hesitated. And it cost him. He vowed he would not make the same mistake again.

Hell, he thought, the damnable old chalk hadn't scared off Max Williams or Irv Deal, and it certainly would not keep him out of Giddings, not for long anyway.

He might have lost a considerable fortune when the Max Fariss erupted with great amounts of oil, but, regardless of how much he regretted his decision, Pat Holloway realized he could not go back and erase any errors of judgment from the past. He would tackle the Giddings field in his own way and on his own terms. He sat down and began working on his game plan. Money was no object.

There was a legal war brewing in Giddings, but no one except Pat Holloway knew that the preliminary skirmish was on the verge of exploding. Holloway had fought legal wars in the past, but only with pleadings and briefs. He quietly formed an ad hoc group called the Lee County Royalty Owners Association and fired his first volley, aiming squarely in the direction of the only active operators drilling wells in the chalk. It wasn't personal, Holloway said. It was strictly business. He played hard. He played hardball. He did not care who might fall by the wayside. He was always looking for an edge.

The controversy centered on the distance that operators could place between one well and another. In the near past, U.S. Operating, Windsor Energy, Chuck Alcorn, and Houston Oil and Minerals had all been drilling under field rules that required wells to be spaced forty acres apart. However, as Max Williams said, operators feared that by continuing to jam the wells so closely together, they all faced the probability of draining each other's fractured reservoirs. As a result, Williams and Deal had filed a formal application with the Texas Railroad Commission, requesting new field rules that would establish a hundred and sixty acres of separation between the wells.

If the Railroad Commission granted their request, Holloway knew, it would kill his operation before it ever began. He had not yet drilled a well, and his land holdings at the moment were not much more than twenty acres of leases in town, as well as leases on the right of way running along both sides of the railroad tracks. It was his opinion that a new set of field rules could well be a potential death blow to his game plan in Giddings. It would forbid him from drilling a sufficient number of wells to profitably develop his handful of leases.

Pat Holloway struck back. Others were drilling wells. He was fighting for survival. Under the direction of the Lee County Royalty Owners Association, whose membership consisted primarily of Pat Holloway and no one else, Holloway promptly hired Dallas landman Sam King, who bought a full-page advertisement in the *Giddings Times & News*. It was a well-calculated counter-offensive, depicting the request for a hundred and sixty-acre spacing as a daring *conspiracy* designed by the *major oil companies* to deprive Lee County landowners of their rightful revenues. Wider spacing meant fewer wells on a property owner's acreage. Fewer wells meant less money. It was not hard to sell the plan to Giddings farmers and ranchers even though those so-called *major oil companies* were, in reality, only a handful of small, independent operators. They did, however, have access to acreage covering the length and breadth of the Austin Chalk. Landowners, on the other hand, only possessed the few hundred acres they had bought or inherited, and now most of their land would be lying above reservoirs of oil that no major or minor oil operator would ever be allowed to find.

It was a problem that property owners had never considered, but the more they thought about the impact of new field rules on their own potential royalty payments, the more they felt a new surge of anger running through their veins. Pat Holloway and Sam King had no trouble loading up a bus and transporting the *concerned citizens of Giddings,* most of them seething and as mad as a hornet with its stinger missing, to a date with the Texas Railroad Commission hearing in Austin. Holloway even provided each passenger with a fried chicken lunch.

Railroad Commission members looked out across the gathering crowd. Some faces were stoic, others scowling. Eyes were hard and glaring. They resembled, more or less, a mob without shotguns. Commission members dutifully and politely listened to the calm, reasonable arguments of both sides in the conflict. But they knew where public sentiment lay.

Four out-of-town oil operators had dared cross a bunch of good old hog farmers, cattle ranchers, and peanut harvesters. And the Railroad Commission, if nothing else, was political. The crowd of concerned citizens obviously carried the most votes. But those oil operators had the most money and might even help bankroll a campaign or two. With the wisdom of Solomon, the Commission issued a compromise ruling that allowed an eighty-acre spacing with an option for forty-acre spacing.

Pat Holloway and his wheeling and dealing had managed to protect the immediate future of Humble Exploration Company. He did not get everything he wanted, but it was close enough. He was in business with a clear track in front of him. He had leases, most of them small and either jammed together or scattered like misplaced orphans, and he had brand new field rules that permitted him to drill enough wells to make his Draconian sojourn in the Lee County field profitable. In addition, Holloway had forever endeared himself to the landowners of Giddings. If they had acreage, he would no doubt be their lessee of choice. He had stood up for them. He had fought for their rights. None of them ever suspected that Holloway might have had a selfish motive or two behind his actions. If they did, they didn't care.

Irv Deal knew there had been a problem, but he preferred to stay in Dallas and let his men on the ground in Lee County worry about it. Chuck Alcorn was still living off his working interest in the City of Giddings No. 1 and trying to find another well just like it. Houston Oil & Minerals would drill awhile, stop awhile, hold a meeting to think over its options, drill again, and stop again – spending as much time driving away with a rig as it did bringing in a rig. Max Williams had an enemy. He and Pat Holloway had never met, and, with the sun setting on the Texas Railroad Commission and its controversial ruling nailed in place like a commandment in stone, Williams preferred to keep it that way.

Pat Holloway overnight became the demagogue of the Giddings field. It didn't particularly bother him. Lawyers had been called worse. He was not the kind of man to wait around, however, and worry about those operators he had angered. They were his competitors, and if he could not outwork them, Holloway was convinced he could surely outsmart them.

●

Houston Oil & Minerals made the decision to follow as closely as possible in the footprints left behind by U.S. Operating and Windsor, keeping a critical eye on the City of Giddings No. 1 as well. Why continue drilling blindly in the field when you could play off of someone else's success? That was the company's way of thinking anyway. A well was spudded in on a town block lease that Houston Oil & Minerals had purchased years earlier. The bit touched down at a depth just below nine thousand feet, and the well took an unexpected kick. The rig began shaking and shuddering.

Pipes were rattling, and oil and gas shot out of the ground and out of control, threatening to blow out at any minute. Unfortunately, the mud weight had not been heavy enough to overcome the hydrostatic pressure generated by drilling in the chalk. The crew frantically and hastily slammed the blowout preventers shut, and the rig sat for four days while officials ran a log of the hole and shipped the data to the home office in Houston.

Geologists did not see a lot of oil traces in the log, but they were fascinated with an amazing show of gas in four hundred feet of Wilcox sand blanketing the chalk. The possibility of oil was suddenly not nearly as important to them as it had been. Houston Oil & Minerals, in the past, had made millions of dollars drilling for gas in Wilcox Sand across Texas, and some were boldly predicting that Giddings sat perched on top of a billion-dollar gas field. Let others fight the chalk for oil. Let others gamble on the sizzle and fizzle wells. Houston Oil & Minerals would be quite satisfied to earn its fortune in the rich Wilcox Sand.

Company officials immediately made the decision to move forward as rapidly as possible on the acquisition of more leases in downtown Giddings before rumors of their great natural gas discovery reached the corporate offices of their competitors. The trouble was, Humble Exploration already owned most of them, and Pat Holloway, it seemed, was trying to tie up the rest. Did he know about the gas in Wilcox Sand as well? Or could he still be simply looking for land near the City of Giddings No. 1 that might enclose oil-bearing formations?

Landmen from both companies butted heads time and again in a mad race to secure every inch of available downtown acreage they could find. Pat Holloway even began concentrating on tracts that ranged across the perimeter of town, telling anyone who wanted to listen that he was merely *trying to head Houston Oil & Minerals off at the pass.* Lease prices rose from fifty dollars to a hundred dollars a lot and were threatening to go even higher.

Pat Holloway was still in the dark, trying to figure out why in the world Houston Oil & Minerals, sitting with a well that wanted to blow out, could be so interested in leasing all of those town lots. He had no knowledge of the logs, the natural gas, or the rich promise of Wilcox Sand. He watched and waited in the wings to see what Houston Oil & Minerals would do next. He did not have to wait for very long.

One of the company's junior landmen tracked Holloway down and made an offer to buy his leases. Holloway refused. More money was placed on the table. The refusal stayed the same. Finally, the young landman, brimming with frustration, blurted out, "You don't understand, Mister Holloway. I have instructions to get you out of Giddings."

"The whole field?"

"Just the town."

Houston Oil & Minerals was becoming more desperate by the day. But why, Holloway wondered as he tried to make sense of it all. He thought back and realized that Houston Oil and Minerals had not logged its well inside Giddings since that fateful day when the blowout preventers were shut down. The rig was silent, activity was non-existent, and, from all outward appearances, the well had been abandoned. There was no apparent interest at all in going ahead and completing the well. So what had Houston Oil & Minerals found that didn't require a crew to run another log?

Then the answer hit him.

Natural gas. It had to be natural gas.

That was the only sane explanation.

And there had to be a lot of it.

"They're only fooling themselves," Ray Holifield told Holloway. "When the well was shut down, that old Austin Chalk gas came up and drained into the Wilcox Sand. That's what Houston Oil & Minerals geologists must have seen on their log. Nothing unusual about it. Happens all the time out here."

"So you don't think there are any great deposits of natural gas under Giddings?" Holloway asked.

Holifield grinned and said, "There's some gas in the chalk. In places there is a lot of it. Anytime you drill, you have to deal with gas, which is why Max Williams had to have a pipeline built. Flare it, and you're wasting a lot of money. But the Wilcox Sand beneath downtown Giddings isn't rich in natural gas, and it beats me why those big shots down in Houston haven't figured it out yet. What they probably did is take one look at the log and believe the whole Wilcox formation is packed with gas. Since the sand is hundreds of feet thick, somebody worked out a complicated volume metric calculation of the reserve and, I'm sure, came up with billions of dollars worth of natural gas. But Pat, let me be honest with you. It's not there."

"You sure?"

"Dead sure." Ray Holifield only smiled.

He had been wrong before. But not in the chalk. At least, not lately. Maybe never again.

Pat Holloway did what a man had to do. He sat down with Houston Oil & Minerals and said, "I won't sell you my leases in downtown Giddings, but I might entertain the idea of working out a trade."

Company officials nodded. They tried to keep a straight face, a solemn face, one that was all business. Holloway's proposition was certainly worth considering.

"How much land do you have leased around Giddings?" Holloway asked.

"About twenty-five hundred acres."

"How far is it outside of town?"

"About ten miles."

"Do you know where Windsor and U.S. Operating are drilling?"

"We do."

"Is the acreage located anywhere near the land they've leased?"

"No."

Holloway frowned, stared out the window, and appeared to be deep in thought. In business, he thought, he was a damn good poker player. In reality, the twenty or so town lots he owned were scattered and disconnected from those other scraps of acreage he had managed to patch together, and, frankly, they had become somewhat of a nuisance, not much more than a good idea gone sour. His business sense told him that those orphan lots would never be of any use to him under any circumstances.

Holloway finally said, "Okay, let's cut a deal. I'll trade you the leases on my downtown lots for the leases on your twenty-five hundred acres. I'll work up the legal agreement and get it back to you before the week is out."

"Can you do it any sooner?"

"How about this afternoon?"

Houston Oil & Minerals was all smiles. "We have the whole downtown," officials said among themselves, "and it's sitting on top of the richest natural gas deposit any of us have ever seen. And poor old Pat Holloway, bless his unfortunate soul, is walking away with a bunch of worthless acreage on some worthless farms that have trouble growing grass during the sun-baked days of summer."

And Pat Holloway was thinking, "Those fools think they have a billion-dollar gas well, and I know they don't. They have twenty-five hundred worthless acres, which means I now have twenty-five hundred acres out in the chalk," which made his odds a hundred and twenty-five to one. Pat Holloway was gambling that oil had backed up beneath every one of them."

Besides, Holloway had an ace up his sleeve. Ray Holifield had once told him that he wouldn't be able to handle any of his geology work or choose any of his locations as long as Holloway's leases were in direct competition with U.S. Operating and Windsor.

Holifield had a legal and a financial obligation, as well as confidentiality commitment, to Irv Deal and Max Williams.

Sure, Holifield had shot a little seismic along the railroad track for him, but that was on the sly, off the record, and had never amounted to very much. Holloway had never drilled on any of the locations, so, in the machinations of the lawyer's own legal mind, his brief dalliance with somebody else's geologist didn't really count. Holloway had no trouble understanding Holifield's reluctance. He didn't like it, but he could understand it. Now, however, he had managed to eliminate any hesitation that might be pricking Holifield's conscience.

His tract of twenty-five hundred acres was far removed from any play either Windsor or U.S. Operating had in the chalk. He could not be accused of competing with them, not directly anyway. They were miles away and miles apart, drilling into different fault lines. Hell, Holloway thought, why should anybody care if he borrowed Holifield from time to time?

●

Sure enough, the deposits of natural gas began seeping out of the Wilcox Sand and easing their way back down into the layers of chalk. Lots of sand. Hardly any gas. Not enough anyway to be produced commercially. The logs had lied, and Houston Oil & Minerals made the mistake of believing the lie. It cost the company dearly.

In time, Humble Exploration would produce millions of dollars worth of oil from those twenty-five hundred acres that Pat Holloway had acquired in the swap. Houston Oil & Minerals thought it was more like a swindle. Maybe. Pat Holloway even agreed. But he preferred to believe that Houston Oil & Minerals had swindled itself.

23

*T*he oil exploration business was gaining steam in Giddings, and, as always, there was a dread of failure around every hole that went into the devil's landscape. By 1977, the town had grown familiar with disappointments. A fear of distress and discontent had become an everyday part of life itself. Buddy Preuss wrote in a series of his weekly columns:

It was disheartening to hear that the Arnold-Rheinhardt No. 1 well about five miles south of Serbin was plugged. Prairie Producing had high hopes for the well, and there was a fairly good showing. Final production tests just didn't indicate enough for commercial production. They even tried drilling on down in the Buda limestone in hopes of finding enough gas for production, but that didn't pan out either. Possibly, the well was just a little too far outside the Giddings field where oil and gas production has been significant.

Of course, there is always the possibility of hitting a dry hole here and there, even in a fairly proven field.

That's why oilmen have to be big gamblers and some go broke trying to strike oil and gas.

The oil crews working in the Giddings area have certainly helped stimulate business at local motels, restaurants, taverns, and grocery stores. Most of the motels put out "No Vacancy" signs shortly after dark. They are filled to capacity. Giddings is reaching the critical stage for any kind of rental housing – houses, apartments, or just a room. Even mobile home parks are feeling the impact of the influx of new people. Those who might invest in new apartments are taking a wait and see attitude.

Will the oil boom really get rolling?

I wonder if a person could make any money buying a bunch of army surplus tents and setting them up on an empty lot, then renting them out by the night. Giddings schools are embracing for a big increase in students if the boom really comes.

Most wells being drilled in Giddings are a hit and miss situation. Every operator in the area is anxiously awaiting test results of wells now being drilled. Quite a bit of oil leasing activity is going on at the Lee County courthouse.

Most of it is tracking down missing heirs on various tracts to get a clear title before any drilling can be done.

In case you wonder why drilling for oil is such a risky situation, Prairie Producing spent nearly four hundred and fifty thousand dollars trying to bring in a well. And it was a dry hole. They had to walk away, leaving four hundred and fifty thousand dollars stuck in the ground. There's no way to recover it.

A bundle of money was spent drilling the Kappler No. 1 well, then another sack full trying to rework the well and even perforate it to get it to produce. That also failed. Hundreds of thousands of dollars gone.

It would be interesting to find out how much additional revenue the county of Lee gets from taxing oil wells to help repair and rebuild some of the roads being torn up by the heavy trucks now using them.

●

There was a good reason why oil exploration companies, time after time, came back to test their luck in the Austin Chalk. Years earlier, a consulting engineer told the Texas Railroad Commission that there were four hundred million barrels of oil in the trend. Some geologists estimated that as many as three thousand wells would be drilled if anyone ever learned to outwit the chalk. Unfortunately, the wells had a long history of behaving erratically, which had frightened off the major oil companies and left the field to the risk takers, to men like Max Williams, Irv Deal, and Pat Holloway.

As one major oil company official said, "A good Austin Chalk well will produce thirty-three thousand barrels of oil in six months, thirty-eight thousand barrels in twelve months, fifty-seven thousand barrels after two years, and seventy-two thousand barrels after three. I just can't afford to tie up that much money for so long a period. I figure it will take me fifteen years to double my money, which, I have to say, is no great deal."

Randy Stewart, serving as Windsor's attorney, pointed out, "We didn't have big oil companies drilling in our area. The majors weren't that thrilled about drilling in the Austin Chalk formation. They would rather drill deeper, more expensive wells and get much higher production. They thought big and expected big profits. Small independents were the only ones willing to take a chance."

Ray Holifield had been recognized as the guru who kept right on outwitting the chalk, and the wells drilled by Windsor/U.S. had been blockbusters. They were not saddled with a disappointing thirty barrels of oil a day. Their wells were bursting at the seams, producing hundreds of barrels a day, with each new day either as good or better than the day before. That translated into millions of dollars. It was difficult to keep the good news quiet and locked inside the parameters of Lee County. Then again, perhaps only Irv Deal, Max Williams, Ray Holifield, and Pat Holloway wanted to keep the news quiet.

They had their claws in the field and did not want other operators coming in to take the chalk away from them. They realized, however, that it wouldn't be too long before the town and surrounding landscape was filled with crews and rigs.

Booms begat people – all kinds of people, professional and drifters alike. Men looking for work, men with families, men on their own, men willing to sweat from sun up to sundown, men in search of a quick buck, legal or otherwise.

Rumors about the great oil strike may not have gone too far, but they had definitely reached Austin.

Reporter Kay Powers spent a few days in town, then went home to write an article in the *Austin American Statesman*. It read:

You can hear it in the jingling of cash registers at eating places, grocery stores, and other businesses all over town. You see it in the no-vacancy signs at motels and in the drouth of rental property in the town weekly. You feel it in the throbbing thump of drilling equipment in a dozen different locations. Giddings has got itself an oil boom going, and with more than a dozen wells already producing, leaseholders say they've only just begun.

At the bank, the feed store, and the country club, conversation that once centered on the cattle market and peanut crops is now permeated with terms like seismograph, workover rigs, royalties, and barrels per day. On the five acres, which Bill and Dot Brademan bought ten years ago as a horse pasture, there's a drilling rig at work right now. On the land Horace Moore moved to with his parents back in 1906, there's already a well producing an estimated two hundred barrels a day. That well, known as the M&K, is in an eighty-acre pro-ration field. Said Jim Kirchnalk, the K in M&K, 'We did get a new car, and everyone immediately said we must have gotten a check, but we haven't received any royalties at all.'

Horace Moore rests his lanky frame in an old chair, tired from hauling a hundred bales of hay by himself in ninety-degree temperatures. 'Money' he asked. 'What money? People are talking about money. I haven't seen any yet. If you ever have to deal with these people, you'll be sorry. They cut your land all up. They promise to fix it back, but they ain't done nothing yet. Money? I'd sure rather see it than hear about it.'

All across Lee County, landowners were becoming concerned because so much time had passed and still they had not received any royalty checks.

They thought they had a goodly amount of money coming their way, but none of them knew for certain. They had not yet seen it, felt it, spent it, or buried it in the bank or in a fruit jar out back. They had heard about landowners in other booms being cheated and scammed in the past, but the operators were still around and still in the field. They hadn't skipped town, but still the fears lingered. Oil was money, but money remained nothing more than a rumor.

As Kay Powers explained in her article: *A tremendous backlog of paperwork at the title companies, at the courthouse, and at the attorney offices of the oil companies has held up the royalty checks. Some may take a year and a half.*

It didn't make Horace Moore feel any better. "I may not still be around in a year and a half," he said. He was. And after he saw the number of zeroes on the check he received, Moore forgot all about being disgruntled, and he didn't mind going out and fixing up his land himself. "This is a lot of money for one well," he said.

"It's just the beginning," he was told.

"What do you mean?" Moore asked.

"You'll receive a check every month."

"For how long?"

"As long as the well keeps producing."

"Any signs of her quitting?"

"She's not even slowing down."

"Well, I'll be damned," he said. He laughed out loud. "Well, I'll be damned," he said again.

Horace Moore was an oilman, and he no longer cared if some operator drilled on every acre he owned. He had enough money in the bank to buy up most of Lee County, but he didn't expect anybody was foolish enough to be selling the land, not at any price, not anymore. He left the hundred-pound hay bales where they were sitting. A rich man didn't haul hay anymore.

●

Far too many landowners, however, were disappointed to learn that, by law, they would be forced to share their lease money with the Texas Osage Royalty Pool, whose representatives came drifting through the county during the Great Depression of the 1930s, buying up to half of the mineral rights on thirty thousand acres.

The company didn't simply hold the lease for a limited number of years before having to renew the agreement. Texas Osage owned the mineral rights for all eternity, and the company had a legal right to hold up or stop the drilling on property where it had a vested interest. Landowners and oil explorationists learned what J. Paul Getty had known all along: the meek might inherit the earth, but not its mineral rights.

One oil company built an expensive road and pad for an oil well on land south of Giddings, and its crew was ready to haul in a rig and drill. The law drove out and shut down the operation. The company, it seems, had failed to properly lease the other half of the property's mineral rights from Texas Osage.

In its defense, the oil company claimed it was totally unaware that Texas Osage owned any of the mineral rights. Signed documents and assorted legal papers had a way of becoming lost, misplaced, or thrown away as the years passed. The operator was unable to negotiate a deal agreeable to Texas Osage, so the crew loaded up, left the expensive pad behind, and drove away down the expensive road it had built. The farmer was out of luck.

By July of 1977, oil related businesses were moving into Giddings at an alarming rate – about one a week. Many of them were being forced to locate their offices outside the city limits. Most of the vacant buildings and warehouses in downtown Giddings had already been rented, and more rigs were on the road, coming from all directions and headed to the gardens of chalk and the field of broken promises.

●

Giddings began to feel the harsh and sometimes grim reality of an approaching oil boom. It had long been a quiet, remote, out-of-the-way little community whose peace and tranquility were hardly ever broken or even disturbed, much less shattered.

It was all about to change. Giddings knew it was coming. Still Giddings was not quite ready for it. Buddy Preuss wrote in his column: *I had been sleeping for several hours Wednesday night when I was awakened by what I thought was a clap of thunder. A minute or so later, I heard what sounded like motors starting up on the Brademan oil well being drilled about a half mile from my house. So I went back to sleep, thinking nothing of it.*

Others who heard the noise got up. They said the sky was pink or red with fire. The Brademan well blew out due to gas pressure. One roughneck had his clothes blown off. Elwood Sump said the explosion shook the ground like an earthquake. He was afraid to look out the window, afraid everything might be charred black outside. Some who lived in nearby houses were evacuated.

The Brademan isn't a good gas producing well. It had come in the day before. There is always a danger of explosions when drillers hit a pocket of gas. They had just penetrated the Austin Chalk when gas built up to nearly twenty-five hundred pounds of pressure. Roughnecks find drilling in the Giddings field more nerve-wracking and dangerous because they never know when or if they are going to hit gas in the chalk. It comes suddenly and without warning.

I had just been out to the Brademan well the day before the explosion, walking around like a big shot. Later, when I saw what could happen, it sent chills down my spine. Before I go traipsing out to the next well site, I plan to get myself some asbestos underwear and a pair of dark sunglasses – just in case.

●

Joe Goodson understood the impending dangers of a boomtown, provided Giddings was truly destined to become one. Boomtowns brought in the wheelers and dealers, the riff raff and scalawags, drunkards and gamblers, hustlers and thieves right along with roughnecks, roustabouts, and tool pushers who were merely looking for work. They all looked the same. It was difficult to tell who would be spending Saturday night in a bar or Sunday morning in church. Goodson knew one thing for certain, however. Lee County would not become a lawless town.

In 1976, Joe Goodson, a welder by trade, had made a run to succeed his father as county sheriff. He had the right name. He was a little short on experience as a lawman. He lost the race to his father's chief deputy. Even then, Goodson was aware of the changing faces of those communities in his county. Men were digging for oil, and oil begat money, and money, at least the lust for it, had always been the root of all evil.

Calm streets were on the verge of becoming mean streets. A sheriff no longer spent a goodly portion of his days and nights driving the back country roads, listening on his radio for the occasional report of a wreck, fire, cattle running loose alongside the highway, suspected drunken driver, or shop lifter. The calm had faded before the storm. As Goodson said, "We were in the midst of having ourselves an oil boom in the chalk, and things were starting to go crazy. They certainly weren't getting any better."

The new sheriff had his hands full. The job, he found out, was not what it had once been. It certainly wasn't what he expected, and he had worn a badge for years.

Night after night, he kept answering calls to the slew of little bars and honky tonks shoved to the side of the roads. Now, old Germans and Czechs had the propensity to drink all night and still be able to walk a straight line and pontificate on Sunday morning without a slurred word in the stories they told. The newcomers took one drink, sometimes two, and wanted to fight.

After a bottle of hard whiskey, the opinion was generally: "You big ones line up and you little ones bunch up because I'm gonna whip every damn one of you anyway." The new sheriff grew tired of the constant confrontations he encountered with an unending supply of oil workers with busted knuckles and confidence men on the prowl with a scam to turn an easy dollar.

He resigned toward the end of 1978.

County commissioners did what the voters had failed to do. They installed Joe Goodson as the Lee County Sheriff. His father would have been proud. If there was one man in the right place with the right attitude to keep an oil boom from getting out of hand, it was Joe Goodson. He looked like a mythical Texas high sheriff – tall and heavy in the shoulders. He would have appeared undressed without his Stetson hat and holstered Colt pistol. He was strong-willed. His eyes but not his voice were hard. He was fair. He was a straight shooter. He could not be bought and was seldom fooled.

Lawmen in central Texas were linked by a personal bond of duty. Shortly after Goodson took office, he was visited by Nig Hoskins, the veteran sheriff from Bastrop, who brought with him a simple message. Hoskins said, "You know me and your daddy had a thing going, Joe, and we might as well keep it going. You go in my county any time you want, and I'll come over to yours. You don't have to contact me if you're chasing somebody. You go get him."

As Sheriff Goodson said, "I was tough. My trade made me that way. I had been handling heavy metal all of my life." He would walk into a bar during the midnight hours and never say a threatening word to a pair or a mob of men trying to remove each other's head or pound somebody into the back side of oblivion. He simply motioned them to follow him.

Sheriff Goodson turned around and walked out. They fell in step behind him. None of them would have dared to defy him. In the darkness of the parking lot, their faces awash in the ricocheting glow of neon, Sheriff Goodson told them, "I really don't care how much you fight. You can try to beat each other to death every night of the week for all I care. But every time you do, it'll cost you."

"How much?"

"Two hundred dollars."

"That ain't much."

"It adds up."

"I make more than that in a day."

"Fine." Sheriff Goodson remained unperturbed. "Go ahead, work all day, and earn it, then along about this time every night, if you're fighting, I'll be around to collect."

"What are you gonna do with it?"

"Keep new tires on my car," Sheriff Goodson said, "because I'll be wearing the old ones out coming down here just to watch you fight. I can stop it early, or I can wait until you're as bloody as a stuck pig. Doesn't matter to me." They might test the sheriff a time or two. He had not lied to them. In Lee County, they discovered, a man could go broke fighting. Word made its way from bar to bar. It didn't matter who won the fight. Sheriff Joe Goodson would win in the long run.

Attorney Mike Simmang realized that oil might not mix with water, but it worked quite well and often with whiskey. Traffic was thick, especially at night. Cars and trucks were traveling as if they had no speed limits. Roads were wearing out. Bars and beer joints seldom ever closed until the last drunk stumbled out the door. Highways and backroads were littered with wrecks.

Speed and alcohol, mostly alcohol, were the culprits. Simmang noticed that Lee County was averaging as many as thirty DUIs a month and asked the county judge about the fine.

"What does it cost a man to get drunk, head down the road in his car, and get caught?" he asked.

"The fine is two hundred dollars."

"State of Texas says you can charge them up to five hundred dollars." Simmang grinned. "The county can make itself some money," he said.

The fine was raised to five hundred dollars. When the state legislature increased the maximum fine to two thousand dollars, Lee County did the same. Throw in court costs, and that came to just under thirty-five hundred dollars for the privilege of a man getting arrested in his car with too much alcohol in his blood.

"It didn't particularly deter anybody," Simmang said. "Oil was flowing. Money was flowing. The men usually paid their own fines, peeling off thirty-five one-hundred-dollar bills and handing them to the judge. Like the old song, they were dead set on living fast, loving hard, and dying young. They chased life from well to well, from one end of the field to the other. When they caught it, they didn't turn loose until somebody pulled them from a wrecked car. On too many occasions, on too many wet roads, on too many curves, on too many crippled bridges, the price they paid was far greater than thirty-five hundred dollars." Alcohol claimed more victims than violence.

"We had a lot of theft in the oil patch," Simmang said, "but not many shootings and hardly any killings at all. People had a healthy respect for each other. Everybody carried a rifle in his truck. Loaded. And it didn't take long to cock the damn thing. They didn't shoot each other, but they pretty much wiped out our deer population in a single season."

Pat Holloway was on a roll and picking up speed. Humble Exploration, owned by a lawyer who had never banked a barrel of oil from the chalk, was growing larger with each passing day and every new lease that Benny Jaehne brought him. His early flirtation with the lots of downtown Giddings was behind him and forgotten, which for hard and impatient drivers like Pat Holloway could happen within twenty-four hours.

Drilling stopped on the railroad track right of way with the completion of the Southern Pacific No. 1, a farm out for the Browning's Children Trust. It was drilled on the one big fault Holifield had unearthed beneath the tracks and made a decent but not spectacular well.

Holloway said, "I was scared to death that the well would blow out right there in the middle of Giddings. I bought all the insurance available and called Red Adair. I told him the situation and lined him up in advance to help if the well blew out. The edge of the drilling platform was so close to one house that the homeowners could not sleep at night. Humble paid for a motel room and sent them to LaGrange for the duration of the drilling. They couldn't stay at the Sands. The Sands was all booked up."

The well stayed steady. It did not blow. It kept oil inside the pipes and the bore. The strain had been too much. Holloway lost interest in the railroad tracks. He was fearful that drilling anywhere downtown might trigger a blaze from which Giddings would never recover, and, besides, Holifield had uncovered only one fault, and it had been drilled. The land running along the railroad tracks had been fine when it possessed the only leases he owned, but now his vision was expanding. Holloway had the leases he had obtained from Houston Oil and Minerals, but he began investigating other ranch and farm lands that sprawled beside a myriad of paved and gravel roads that led beyond the town limits. He had no idea which way he should go or how far he dared venture into the taunting and treacherous chalk trend. The play, at first glance, seemed to be in and around Giddings, but Holloway feared that it might be a dangerous business decision if he viewed those potential prospects with a narrow mind.

Ray Holifield, was no longer working in the shadows for Humble Exploration. Perhaps, he never had been. Everyone, even his early-day clients, realized that he had lent his vast knowledge of the chalk to Pat Holloway for a fee. The geologist pulled down a land map and suggested that Holloway look seriously at a package of scattered wildcat leases that stretched virtually to the Caldwell County line.

"That's the acreage you want," Holifield told him.

"Why?"

"I've got a good feeling about it."

In reality, Ray Holifield didn't have a feeling good, bad, or otherwise. He had learned what others would find out much later. There was no hidden or mystical secret to finding oil in the chalk. All of the chalk held oil. It was just a matter of locating the faults and, if necessary, fracturing them with mud and water. That's what Windsor Energy and U.S.

Operating had done. If the formula worked for Irv Deal and Max Williams, it should work for anybody.

"How many acres?" Holloway asked.

"Thirty-five hundred."

"Who owns them?"

"Robert Mosbacher."

"The oil operator down in Houston?"

Ray Holifield nodded.

"Why doesn't he want to keep them?"

"Mosbacher's too big to play in the chalk."

"Or too smart."

"He thinks so."

Pat Holloway thought it over a moment, then asked, "What will they cost me?"

Holifield shrugged. "I bet you can get them on a farm out basis," he said. "Won't cost you anything but a little working interest on the wells."

Pat Holloway knew he could handle that.

Robert Mosbacher was born the son of a wealthy New York stock trader who had the good sense to cash in most of his holdings before Wall Street crashed in 1929. He was able to ride through the Great Depression virtually unscathed economically. He owned a few oil investments in Texas, and that brought Robert Mosbacher as a young man to Houston. By 1954, he had founded Mosbacher Energy Company and found a million-dollar natural gas field tucked away upon the remote landscape of South Texas. He thus began a lifetime accumulation of wealth and key political connections that reached all the way to Washington, D.C. In time, Mosbacher would feel as much at home in the White House as most Presidents.

He had purchased leases in the northern quadrant of Lee County as a favor to his former college roommate. They cost him ten dollars and acre, and, he figured, any good friend was worth at least ten dollars an acre. Mosbacher now possessed leases on thirty-five hundred acres but had no idea what they were worth, what he should do with the leases, or how he could dispose of them without taking a loss. Mosbacher was simply resigned to the fact that he had no choice but to hang onto them. After awhile, he rarely thought of them at all.

Pat Holloway called and scheduled an appointment. He had an oil company, he said, and wanted to discuss the possibility of perhaps taking the Lee County leases on a farm out basis. No one at Mosbacher Energy had ever heard of anybody in the oil business named Pat Holloway, and Mosbacher certainly did not know who he was. Probably didn't care. A meeting with Holloway, he decided, would be nothing more than a ten minute glitch on his afternoon calendar.

Holloway, if nothing else, had a handle on the hard truth of the matter. "I was a lawyer, for God's sake," he said. "I didn't have any background or much experience in the oil business, and I'm sure Mosbacher probably knew it. He might not have any reason for wanting to keep the acreage for himself, but he was a high-powered operator, and he sure wouldn't be tempted to turn those leases over to some damn lawyer who was still waiting to sink his first hole in the Giddings field. He probably felt like other oilmen, at least the sane ones, who still did not regard Giddings as a bona fide oilfield."

Only the courageous or the desperate cast their fates to the Austin Chalk. The smart ones watched from afar. Those who had been burned or broken by the chalk before found some place better, or at least someplace else, to go.

Pat Holloway was well aware of Robert Mosbacher's political connections and knew that he was great friends with another Houstonian, who happened to be residing in Washington as Director of Central Intelligence, George Herbert Walker Bush. Holloway had been a freshman at Yale when Bush was a senior, and when Bush entered politics in an attempt to become the new Texas Senator in 1964, Holloway served as his campaign manager. The two men had forged a lasting friendship. Holloway, playing the odds and feeling as though he had nothing to lose, called Bush and told him about his plan to work on a farm out agreement with Robert Mosbacher. "He doesn't know me," Holloway said, "but he knows you."

George H. W. Bush laughed. "Don't worry, Pat," he said. "By the time I get through with Robert, he'll think he knows you, too."

Robert Mosbacher was relaxed and cordial when Holloway walked into his office. No, he said, he didn't have a lot of time, but he could always make time for the friend of a friend. Yes, he said, he would welcome the chance to work with Pat Holloway on a farm out of the leases near Dime Box. He would consider it an honor to be working with a man who had been one of George Bush's political allies. Yes, he had heard that a few new oil wells were giving Giddings a good run for its money these days. No, he didn't have any interest in entering the Austin Chalk himself. He was far too cautious for that. He would be quite pleased to let Pat Holloway do it for him. They agreed on the farm out deal, and Mosbacher handed down a restrictive deadline. "I'll let you keep the farm out on those thirty-five hundred acres as long as you me drill two wells," he said.

"That's fair."

"I want the first one drilled inside of ninety days and the second one drilled ninety days later."

"That's not much time."

Mosbacher smiled. "It is if you're an oilman," he said.

24

Pat Holloway had his back to the wall, working on a short time frame and faced with the dilemma of drilling two farm out wells within three months. By late November of 1977, he had quickly moved outside of town and ten miles up old Highway 141 toward Dime Box. It was a speculative undertaking that carried him into the great unknown of Elder Burttschell's farm.

Many of the sweaters congregating over coffee at Schubert's Café believed that the land holding the giant producing wells drilled by Max Williams and Irv Deal were nudging against the town limits of Giddings and probably the outer limits of the field. It was too great a risk to go much farther out. Those reservoirs of oil did not go on forever. Somewhere they stopped. And there was talk that Ray Holifield already had found the last fault north. It was almost within spitting distance of Schubert's, and it lay at the bottom of a Windsor/U.S. well.

Humble Exploration was headed even farther north, on the edge of Dime Box, to begin drilling operations on Robert Mosbacher's leases, so far away from town, in fact, that the Burttschell No. 1 was regarded as a step out well, a wildcat attempt that would ultimately extend the boundaries of the chalk play or suffer severe and dire consequences if Pat Holloway had stepped on the wrong and forbidden side of the boundary line.

Autumn hit hard, bringing with it the cold, the winds, and a chilled rain pounding the earth around the rigs like an irregular heart beat. As Holloway waited for the string of pipe to head down into the Burttschell, he heard that a wave of relentless thunderstorms had triggered the collapse of a workover rig at the Dwight Davis No. 1.

The rain-soaked ground shifted, the outrigger broke when the weight of the derrick changed positions, and it all came tumbling down into a soggy heap. Houston Oil & Minerals managed to limp away with a hundred and twenty thousand dollars in damages, more than half the cost of putting a new well in the ground.

Another search for gas in the Wilcox Sands had gone terribly awry.

Holloway glanced at the sky. Dark clouds. More rain. He felt the ground move slightly beneath his feet. If the chalk didn't beat them, the weather certainly could. The rain felt like ice pellets when it peppered his face. No reason to quit, he thought. No place to run. The string of pipe slid deeper into the hole.

Just before Christmas, the day broke with a bitter cold draped around Holloway's shoulders. The chill worked its way into his bones. He ignored it.

His eyes did not leave the rig.

The end was near, and no one would dare predict whether the chalk was ready or not to give up its oil. He had a lot riding on the Burttschell. No. 1. He had everything riding on the Burttschell.

Ray Holifield had told him that the fault down below was the largest in the whole field. But then, Holifield had a reputation for keeping an operator upbeat and optimistic, regardless of the mounting problems he might be facing in the hole of a step out well. He had told Max Williams the same thing.

Every fault Holifield found seemed to be bigger than the one before. Some ridiculed him behind his back, but Holifield had not lied. He was dead serious, and, what's more, he was right.

"The field was filled with faults, and some of them were damn big," Holifield said, and he knew where most of them were. He and his seismic data would locate the rest. No doubt about it. The ridicule stopped every time another well roared in and kept on roaring. Little faults didn't do that. Little faults coughed up their oil in a hurry and died quickly without a whimper.

Then it happened. Amidst the cold rains of December, it happened, and no one was expecting it.

Pat Holloway saw the drill stem suddenly drop four or five feet as though it had fallen into a massive hole, and oil rose up from the inner sanctum of the Burttschell like an old-time gusher, shooting a raw stream of honey-colored oil over the top of the crown block like a steady current of liquid money. The crew was bathed in oil. The countryside around the rig was splashed with oil. It fell on Holloway like a hot but gentle rain. He knew others had found the pay zone of the Giddings chalk before. None of their wells had come in as a gusher. Damn Ray Holifield.

He was right again. The fault must have been a giant.

Then it happened. Amidst the cold rains of December, it happened again, and no one was expecting it. The Burttschell turned abruptly into a defiant, renegade blowout, a genuine, oil in the sky and oil on the ground blowout. The crew lost control and was at the mercy of the well as a small fortune of the precious commodity spilled haphazardly across the landscape. A constant threat of fire hung over the men as they fought desperately to rein in a well gone berserk. All it would take was a single spark. The Burttschell had them all in its grasp. The drill bit had unloosed a monster.

Holloway ran to his drilling contractor and asked, "What the hell do we do now?"

"It's not my call."

"Whose is it?"

"Yours." Oil was dripping from drilling contractor's hard hat. Even in the cold December rain, he was sweating profusely and breathing heavily.

Pat Holloway was stunned. The Burttschell No. 1 looked like a ticking bomb. It was not the first well that Humble Exploration had operated, but those had been out of the chalk, and Holloway had never witnessed a blowout before. He had no idea what to do or how to do it. He kept waiting for answers. His crew was waiting on him to provide one. He waited for the well to settle down. It refused.

The blowout threw honey-colored oil across the landscape, probably no more than a few hundred barrels, and it only lasted a few thunderous minutes. It might as well have been a lifetime. For ten long and backbreaking days, Holloway's weary crew would struggle to restrain the well and bring it back under control. They had struck oil all right, but what good had it done them? The oil was going to waste. The driller had immediately shut the blowout preventer and the pipe rams, cutting off the flow of oil, or it could have been disastrous.

He turned to Pat Holloway. "It's up to you to tell us what you want done next," he said.

Holloway had no idea what to tell him. The Burttschell simmered. Holloway glanced over the driller's shoulder and wondered if it were going to blow again. He waited for the worse.

Pat Holloway, bone tired and frustrated, drove to Schubert's restaurant and sat at a table, drinking coffee to thaw out and perhaps warm his insides. Two oilfield workers, hired by U.S. Operating, pushed away plates of chicken fried steak as they listened to his plight. One told him, "That's a situation for your drilling superintendent to figure out."

"That may be the problem," Holloway said.

"What's that?"

"I don't have a drilling superintendent."

Pat Holloway had gone into the ground on a budget, trying to cut every corner he could, and it had suddenly become a painful cost to bear. One of the oilfield workers grabbed a pencil from his pocket and drew a diagram on the napkin. "First, you have to increase your mud weight," he said. "Do you know what that means?"

"No."

"Drop a pill in the well."

Holloway nodded as though he understood every word, but he had no idea what mud weight was and had never heard the word *pill* mentioned before. The man might as well have been speaking to him in unknown tongues. Holloway realized that oilfield vernacular was so foreign that he couldn't even carry on a decent conversation, much less ask the right questions. He kept his mouth shut, which was a chore for Pat Holloway.

The oilfield worker finished his diagram on the napkin and handed it across the table. "If somebody on your crew can read it," he said, "this should give them a pretty good step-by-step strategy for getting the well under control. Basically, just get yourself a fifteen-point-five-pound pill and drop it in the well."

"You sure it'll work?" Holloway asked.

"Always has."

"Worked a lot of blowouts before?"

"Personally, I wouldn't hire a man who hasn't."

Pat Holloway sat at the table alone, memorizing words he did not comprehend. He studied the napkin as hard as he would the case file for a trial. Legalese, as odd as it was, made a lot more sense. Holloway drove back to the Burttschell and wandered through the rain until he found his tool pusher.

He spit out the words exactly as he had heard and read them. Didn't know what they meant. But he had them all in the right order. His tone had the authenticity of a man who had handled blowouts all of his life.

"Here's what you do," he said. "Let's get a fifteen-point-five-pound pill and drop it in the well."

The tool pusher raised an eyebrow in surprise. Where and how, he wondered, did a rank amateur oil operator like Pat Holloway learn to stop an oil well still suffering a hangover from a blowout? He was impressed. He smiled. "I think that's exactly what we ought to do," he said.

Ten days after the Burttschell No. 1 embarked on its wild rampage, the blowout was finally brought under control when the crew dropped super-heavy drilling mud pills down the hole. After the kicking subsided, a test revealed that the well had the potential to produce a thousand and eighty-four barrels of oil a day, with a potential gas production of almost a million cubic feet a day. Such numbers were almost heresy in the chalk.

Holloway went to sleep that night convinced that his drilling contractor and tool pusher had both known what to do when the well blew out. "But," he said, "they were smart enough legally not to tell me what to do. They didn't want me to sue them if their ideas and suggestions didn't work."

All Pat Holloway knew for sure was that too much honey-colored oil lay on the ground. No way to recover it. No way to sell it. The oil represented the fragments of a small fortune running with rainwater down the gullies and ravines that sliced through the upper reaches of Lee County. By now, everyone knew that Giddings was definitely an oilfield. The Burttschell had taken the play ten miles outside of downtown Giddings and proven, beyond a shadow of doubt, that the field might well be larger than anyone could have imagined or predicted. With the year coming to a wet and chilly end, only Houston Oil & Minerals still had an interest in downtown leases. For Pat Holloway and operators who came before and after him, the field had no limits.

Columbia Gas Exploration Company had been one of Pat Holloway's first and largest financial supporters when he moved surreptitiously into the Austin Chalk. The company's president and top geologist had driven down from their Houston office and were watching oil blow over the crown block as day broke on a Sunday morning. Both were mesmerized, and neither could believe what they were seeing. The president told Holloway that they had never before participated in an on-shore oil well. Mostly, they had been involved in offshore oil and gas plays in the Gulf of Mexico. The Burttschell was their first oil discovery on land.

In the so-called petroleum nerve centers of Houston and Dallas, where the economy rose or fell depending on the price of crude, the high-octane and close-knit fraternity of major oil companies and those well ensconced within the oil industry remained cautious to a fault. The risk takers were in the field. The smart money stayed at home. Sure, they had heard about the Burttschell No 1. Sounded pretty impressive. Probably wasn't.

Sure, they had heard about those hundreds of barrels of oil flowing from the M&K, the Schkade, the Max Farris, the Molly C. Davis, and the Carmean. Somebody got lucky. That was all. Luck had probably run out by now. Always did. And none of them were on the phone trying to lease rigs or even contemplating the thought of heading up or down the roads to Giddings. It was a field that couldn't be trusted. Often the men who didn't drill wound up with more money in the bank than the ones who did.

Those wells would dry up before those boys ever cashed their first check. That was the general consensus among the oil lords who sat in fancy, high-rise offices. The chalk had them fooled one more time. Poor bastards. There wasn't any reason to be tempted. That's what the major oil companies thought. The land in Lee County was all gone, they said. Leased up. That's what they had been told. That's what they believed.

Somebody had lied, and neither Pat Holloway nor Max Williams nor Irv Deal planned to tell any of them anything differently. The independents began easing their way into the field by early 1978, as many as sixteen of them. They had no place better to go. Couldn't afford offshore drilling, and the majors had a monopoly on offshore drilling anyway. Superior Oil made the decision to test the wiles of the chalk. So did the Ada Oil Company of K. S. "Bud" Adams, who had used his early-day oil money to buy such playthings as the Houston Oilers.

A new wave was on its way, coming amidst the tumult and the shouting, but no one considered it a great land rush, and only a few newspapers ever got around to calling Giddings a boomtown. The quiet, little farming community may have felt like one with its sidewalks inundated by a conglomeration of strangers, drifters, scalawags, and men wearing hard hats, which indicated they might be working or looking for a job, any kind of job, somewhere in the oilfield. Traffic at the signal light connecting Highways 290 and 77 were jammed up at certain times during the day. The sound of engines dragged on for all hours of the day and night as trucks carrying rigs and oilfield equipment rumbled down patchwork country roads in weather both good and bad. The Sabbath offered hardly any relief from the noise. Out on some of the better wells, trucks had to load up with oil three times a day just to keep the storage tanks from overflowing.

New faces kept changing every week. No need to remember a man's name until he had been in town for at least a couple of weeks, or at least long enough to change his socks. Some had jobs. Some took jobs. Some had experience in the oilfield. Some were merely looking for a paycheck. Others were only passing through. It was not all wine and roses in Giddings. The Lee County courthouse had more DWI cases than normal on the docket. Illegal drugs had found their way to back alleys and beer joint parking lots. The sheriff's department was regularly working assorted shootings and stabbings at the Blue Lilly Tavern on the south side of Dime Box. Theft had become as popular as the search for oil. Cars. Cash. Clothes. It didn't matter. Easy come. Easy go.

Twenty-one year old David Rankin was on the D&B rig twelve miles north of Giddings, pulling pipe out of the well when the cable snapped. Block and tackle tumbled down the rig, and two sections of pipe flew out of the hole. He was in trouble before he saw it headed his way. The pipe struck him in the head, and knocked him off the platform. Twenty-one year old David Rankin did not live to see the well come in, stained with a thick mixture of oil and blood.

Max Williams received an urgent phone call. At least to him, it was urgent. He heard a voice from Prairie Producing on the line. "Max, do you remember the farm out acreage you got from us?" George Watford said.

"I do."

"You need to come see us about it."

"What's the problem?"

"You have the black squares on the outside of the checkerboard, and another company is ready to give us a check for the inside," Watford said.

"How much do you want for the leases?"

"A hundred and fifty thousand dollars."

"Maybe I want the inside of the checkerboard, too," Williams said.

"That's why I'm calling." There was a hint of apology in Watford's voice. "I always thought you deserved first shot at the leases," he said, "but, Max, I'm afraid somebody has beat you to it. Prairie Producing doesn't want to wait or negotiate. Right now, it's been decided to take the money and give the farm out to another company."

"This is kind of sudden," Williams said.

"They've brought us a helluva deal," Watford replied.

Max Williams was thoroughly perplexed. He knew that the oil business had always been fraught with troubles, hang-ups, and snags, but this was a complication he had not expected to encounter. He felt as though he had a gun to his head. He wanted both sides of the checkerboard, and, from out of the blue, someone had leaped into the fray and was trying to snatch a lot of good acreage away from him.

It didn't matter who the perpetrators might be. It only mattered that they were elbowing their way into his playing field. He didn't like it. He would fight for it.

He already knew the cost, and, at the moment, he was oil rich and cash poor. The silence hung as thick as a river bottom fog as Max Williams contemplated his options and wasn't quite sure he still had any options.

Finally Watford said, "You're already out drilling on the land. You've taken on the risks and made some good wells. I believe you deserve the chance to acquire the rest of the acreage, and, that's the reason you need to come see us as quickly as possible."

Williams sighed, trying hard to control his anxiety. Or maybe it was just a case of irritation gnawing at him like heartburn. "We're getting started on a new well," he said. "It's difficult for me leave, so I don't think I can get down to Houston until next week."

"We're expecting you no later than tomorrow."

"Can't make it."

"Max," George Watford said confidentially and in a hushed tone, "the other company is ready to give us a check. Neither one of us can wait until any time after tomorrow."

Max Williams hung up the phone and, by the next morning, was headed south to Houston.

He didn't want to go or have the time to go, but Williams did not want to lose a valuable parcel of land.

He could feel the white squares of the checkerboard beginning to evaporate and slip from his grasp.

When he signed his original farm out agreement, Prairie Producing had divided the land north of Giddings into a checkerboard, much as Hughes & Hughes had done on the acreage that held the first wells drilled by U.S. Operating and Windsor. One half of the squares were left white, the other half shaded black.

Max Williams had taken the black squares from Hughes & Hughes, hit big wells on the farm out, and had no intentions of tempting the wretched consequences of fate. He wasn't superstitious, he told himself. Then again, maybe he was. Once again, the black squares had been good to him.

U.S. Operating recorded another major strike on the three thousand-acre ranch owned by Garlan Gerdes. It became the hottest, most productive well Max Williams had drilled at the time, with the Gerdes No. 1 topping out at more than a thousand barrels a day and becoming the cornerstone for a new wave of oil exploration that was destined to descend upon the length and breadth of the ranch.

Before it pulled up stakes and left, U.S. Operating had drilled ten wells, and all of them together were pumping a minimum of two thousand barrels of oil a day. The family had never seen anything quite like it.

Then here came Pat Holloway to drill ten more wells, and the Gerdes property was crisscrossed with thirty-five miles of underground pipelines. When the wells began paying out, the family did not want to face the dire financial problems associated with inheritance taxes on the patriarch's estate. Instead, a royalty check for two hundred thousand dollars, sometimes more, found its way every month to the Gerdes mailbox – shared by Garland himself, his wife Ruby, son Gary, daughter Betty, or a family trust.

In many circles, the good, old German Gerdes name symbolized the promise and the payoff of homegrown millionaires in the Giddings field. Hard luck, hard ground, and hard times today. Hard cash money tomorrow. Would the riches ever end, why had they taken so long to get here, and what the hell were we gonna do with it all?

●

Max Williams never thought he could be beaten, but oil was a rough game that had no rules, no whistles, no fouls, and no time outs. His nerves were churning when he sat down with George Watford at the company's home office in Houston. There was no time for small talk.

He went straight to business. "What'll it take for me to acquire the entire farm out?" he asked.

"As I told you, the other oil company has a hundred and fifty thousand dollars on the table," Watford replied.

"Which company is it?"

"I'm not at liberty to say."

"What are my chances?"

"Match their offer, and the white squares belong to you."

Max Williams stared across the desk, feeling as despondent as he had in a long time. He said, "As you know, George, I have a lot of money committed to the wells we're now working on, and we're drilling most of them on your farm out. Frankly, I don't have access to a whole lot of cash. I'm putting every dollar I have in the ground."

"I understand, and I'm sorry," Watford replied, "but, unfortunately, I'm not in any kind of position to negotiate. If you want the inside of the checkerboard, you will have to let us know today. Tomorrow about this time, we'll take their check."

"This is awful short notice."

"It's the oil business." Watford shrugged. "Unexpected things happen in a hurry sometimes. You have to move fast or get left behind," he said. "It's not my decision, Max. I'm just the messenger."

Hiding behind his best poker face, Williams thought it over. He had the black squares, and, back when he first discussed a farm out with Prairie Producing, Holifield told him that one side of the checkerboard had as much oil as the other.

For a hundred and fifty thousand dollars, he would have the black squares and the white squares both.

But that was the rub.

Where would he find a hundred and fifty thousand dollars lying around unused and at his disposal?

Oil was a demanding game. Table stakes were out of sight, and the ante kept getting bigger all the time.

Max Williams excused himself and left the room. He placed an immediate phone call to Grant Hollingsworth at the Texas Bank & Trust in Dallas.

"I need some money," he said.

"How much?"

"A hundred and fifty thousand dollars."

"When?"

"Now. This afternoon."

There was a brief moment of silence on the line, and Williams could hear his banker whistle softly and low under his breath. Finally Hollingsworth asked, "What are you doing down there, Max?"

"I have a chance to buy the whole checkerboard from Prairie Producing," Williams told him. "The outside, the inside, the whole thing."

Hollingsworth was not interested in checkerboards of raw land. He wasn't even sure what it all meant. He asked the only question that concerned him. "Can you pay me back?" he wanted to know.

"I can."

"Write Prairie Producing a check," Hollingsworth said, resigned to walk with Max Williams every step of the way in Giddings, "and I'll make sure the money necessary to cover it is put into your account as soon as we hang up."

When Max Williams drove away from Houston, he felt the pressure mounting. He had wanted the farm out, all of it, and that's what he had bought. With the deal, however, he was facing a whole new set of problems. He had to drill a new well every ninety days on the black squares. He had to drill a new well every ninety days on the white squares. The investment would be outrageous, but it was, he guessed, a good problem to have.

Max Williams and U.S. Operating would ultimately drill a hundred wells on his Prairie Producing farm out. All of them hit, the whites as well as the blacks. There was not a dry hole among them.

●

With the oil from the Gerdes No. 1 still wet on his hands, Williams moved farther down the road to spud in the Hilliard No. 1. The Texas Railroad Commission had set the allowable of oil on an eighty-acre tract at three hundred and twenty-eight barrels a day, The agency, however, gave operators the option of tying two eighty-acre units together in a bold attempt to let them double their allowable, provided, of course, the wells had the capacity to produce that much oil. In the chalk, it was a rarity. No. It was non-existent.

His faith in those black squares of Prairie Producing land was about to pay off. Max Williams took a gamble, not a big one, perhaps, but a gamble all the same. He linked up two eighty-acre tracts, filed the necessary papers, and drilled. He now had trust in the chalk, in the seismic data, and in Ray Holifield's genius at reading it.

The Hilliard was virtually ready to burst open by the time the drill bit touched the good earth. According to Holifield, the fault was the size of a canyon, or at least a gorge. He marked the spot in the field, and, as Williams said, stabbed the heart of the fault. The well blasted its way in with six hundred barrels a day, and it was only getting started.

"The well can do better," Holifield said.

"How much better?" Williams asked.

"If we don't choke it down," Holifield confided, "I seriously think the Hilliard fault is big enough to produce as many as two thousand barrels a day."

Thank God for the gamble, Williams thought. Thank God for the two connecting eighty-acre tracts. They allowed him to produce six hundred and fifty-six barrels a day. Stephen Bassock had invested twenty thousand dollars in the Hilliard No. 1, and, over the next two decades, his investment would be paid back fifty-eight times, totaling more than a million dollars. Wells came and went in the Giddings field. The Hilliard kept right on pumping. As far as Williams was concerned, the well had emerged as the undisputed king of the Giddings field. It might not stay on top for long, but the Hilliard's production had passed Pat Holloway's famous Burttschell No. 1, and the farmers drinking early morning coffee down at Schubert's restaurant had been saying for weeks that the Burtschell was as good as it got. Wait until they saw the Hilliard.

Max Williams smiled.

●

Irv Deal and Windsor finally struck a tenuous deal to drill on the farm of an elderly gentleman, who wasn't certain he needed an oil well and didn't quite know what he would do with one if he had it. The old farmer said he already had just about everything a man could possibly want. A little land. A little house. A tractor. He did, however, need a shed for the tractor and agreed to lease his acreage if Windsor built him one.

Randy Stewart, in addition to his land and legal work, was locating and clearing access in and out of the drill sites selected by Ray Holifield, as well as trying desperately to keep the land titles clear in front of two, sometimes three, relentless drilling rigs. He needed help. Irv Deal asked Jack Killian, a heavy equipment operator, a true dirt man, to come out of retirement, head down to Giddings, and build pads for the rigs on Windsor's locations.

When he reached the farm, Killian sat down and tried to ease the old man's mind. The farmer had great fears that a bunch of city-slick strangers were coming out to mess up his land, destroy his crops, and probably leave him in the throes of utter ruination. He had heard the horror stories. Hadn't seen any of the damages. But had heard the stories.

"We'll take care of the land as if it was our own," Killian assured him.

"How do I know you haven't already messed up your own land?" the farmer wanted to know.

Killian didn't have an answer. But, on an impulse, he headed into town, stopped by Protho's department store, bought the old man a hundred dollar gift certificate, and drove back to the farm. The farmer looked the gift certificate over, frowned as though he had never seen one before, and chances were he hadn't, then asked, "Am I gonna have to spend it all at one time?"

"No, sir, you won't."

It took the old man ten trips to downtown Giddings before he finished running through the gift certificate.

By the time he spent his last dollar, he had an oil well. Didn't look like much. But he had one.

"I guess you'll probably buy a larger house now," Killian said.

The old farmer shook his head. "Don't need a new house," he said. "There's plenty of room for me to rattle around in the one I got."

"A new car, maybe?"

"Don't need a new car. The one I got runs just fine."

Killian laughed. "What are you spending your money on?" he asked.

"A new shed."

"We just built you shed."

"Ain't big enough."

"Your tractor fits in it just fine."

This time it was the old farmer laughing. "Young man," he said, "You ain't seen my new tractor."

Windsor defied the logic of drilling north of Giddings and eased down south toward the Wendish community of Serbin. Randy Stewart wrote of the venture, the past and the present: *From its rise, the tower of the grand old Lutheran church overlooks the offspring of its founders, their children and the children's children with names like Kappler, Krause, Prellop, and Dunk, Becker, Noack, Mertink, and Zoch, same names on the mailboxes as on the tombstones in the churchyard – continuity of life. To this enclave of the past, Windsor Energy came with its geology and seismology and racket machines to test the temper of the rock – to pursue the fickle hydrocarbon. But carefully, carefully, it approached these folks and cleared the way with respect for their place and promises to do as little harm as possible and maybe some good if such be the fate ordained.*

So the Saint Paul's Lutheran Church Well Number One came to be, and from beneath the acres set aside for church purposes by those weary travelers so long ago, oil now flows to serve their heirs. The clanking intrusion of the drilling rig is gone, and the scars it left are smoothed. The sound of the flowing oil and gas blends with the wind's rush through the oaks. Rhythm reestablished, the area is at peace with its visitor from the twentieth century.

●

Giddings was definitely beginning to experience the sights and sounds and impact of an oil boom. *Flowline Magazine* reported: *Oil rigs are frequently erected near private homes and operated amidst cows, peanut patches, basketball hoops, tractors, and an occasional stray dog with nary a complaint from nearby dwellers.*

Says James Hoffman, City Council member and owner of Hoffman's Gulf Service Station, 'This county was at one time broke.

Then the oil came in. The revenue from the oil industry here has brought more tax money and helped the schools. I've benefited a hundred percent here at the station with all the new business I'm getting. Why, just the other day I was offered a hundred and fifty thousand dollars for this station and all of my inventory, which would have been unbelievable a few years ago. Well, of course, I turned the offer down. This oil business has created many new jobs. People here have never made these kinds of salaries before.

More rigs, even though they were scarce and hard to find, were on the road and headed toward Giddings. As soon as oil exploration in Pearsall leveled off and began to decline, service companies pulled up stakes and marked the route to Lee County.

Giddings was in the midst of a new day, which was just as well because cattlemen were suffering from falling prices and a serious lack of rain, and peanut farmers did not foresee much of a crop at all. The bad times had gotten worse. Giddings was depending on oil, and Giddings was depending on the poor boys to find it. It was definitely an oilfield that should not have been. No big oil companies were yet on the ground. It would be years before they found enough nerve to test the chalk.

As one tool pusher pointed out, "By the time the majors finally started hauling their equipment into Lee and the surrounding counties, the mavericks had already gobbled up the good acreage and were drilling deep into the sweet stuff."

The majors would be forced to take the leftovers. In reality, however, the boom had not yet boomed.

25

*P*at Holloway had not rested on his laurels after the Burttschell blew in and blew out, staining the land around him the color of honey, the rich color of Giddings oil. He quickly drilled twice more in northern Lee County. His good fortune was running a hot streak, and he was determined to strike as often as possible until his luck turned cold. Besides, he needed to drill another new well every ninety days to keep his farm out from Robert Mosbacher intact.

Backed by investment money from Columbia Gas, Humble Exploration completed the Perkins No. 1, which initially showed a lot of promise with a hundred and fifty barrels a day before bogging down with disappointment. Within only a few days, production began a slow and steady decline. Holloway, forever the optimist, expected the wells to all be as good as the Burttschell. He felt as though he had been sucker punched. The curse of the chalk had struck again. Pat Holloway loaded up his rig and moved another ten miles farther north and just inside the Burleson County line. It was virgin territory, and Ray Holifield had chosen a location as far away from Holloway's first big well as possible without leaving the Mosbacher leases.

Holloway drilled the Kocurek No. 1, and the well made him forget all about the losses that still lay down in the cursed abyss of the Perkins hole. Oil had thundered to the surface of the Kocurek, producing more than a thousand barrels a day, almost as much as the famed Burtschell. The oil game was a lot like poker. Until the money runs out, keep on playing. Wait for the luck to change. Holloway was glad he had stayed to see the next card. The Robbie No. 1, named for his wife, had a potential of almost six hundred and fifty barrels a day, and the Jimmy Kuehn No. 1 began flowing a thousand barrels of oil and a million cubit feet of natural gas a day.

Pat Holloway told Buddy Preuss, editor of the *Giddings Times & News:* "This can perhaps be explained on the basis that we are just plain lucky, which for sure is better than being smart. On the other hand, there is at least some possibility that we actually know what we are doing, which is the next best thing to being lucky."

●

Pat Holloway was relieved. The discovery had further solidified the size and the importance of the field in the vast terrain north of Giddings. Columbia Gas Exploration had paid one-half of the cost of the well, and Pat Holloway had purloined one of Max Williams's prime investors, Mary Kay Ash, and American Petroleum Partners, a Wall Street firm, to cover the other fifty percent of the Kocurek No. 1.

The president of Columbia Gas was perplexed. "Pat," he said, "I'm afraid we have a problem."

"What's wrong?"

"Our company doesn't have any area of interest in our operating agreement," the president said.

"No, it doesn't."

"That means you can just go out and buy all of the acreage around these wells you want, and you don't have to share any of it with Columbia Gas."

"That's right."

"But we paid for half of these wells."

"You did at that."

"Then why are you leaving us out in the cold, Pat?"

Holloway shrugged. "That's the way I intended it," he said.

He definitely did not need Columbia Gas to help him lease any more land. He had Benny Jaehne for that, and, as he said, "Benny never cheated any of them on baling their hay, so they figured he wouldn't cheat them on an oil deal either. Farmers did not like to negotiate with outsiders. Columbia Gas was an outsider."

The president thought it over, then said, "Pat, we don't want to compete with you, so let's strike a gentleman's agreement. You go ahead and buy all the acreage you want in Lee County, and let us go buy land over in Burleson County. Let's split the world into two counties. You keep Lee, and we'll own Burleson."

Pat Holloway left the president long enough to confer with Ray Holifield, who told him, "The Austin Chalk gets awful thin in Burleson County."

"Is that good?"

"I don't think it'll be worth a damn," Holifield said.

When Holloway returned, he was ready to make the deal with the president of Columbia Gas. Nothing written. Just a handshake.

"If he stayed off my turf," Holloway said, "then I would respect his right to lease in Burleson County. However, I'm not sure Columbia Gas in Houston ever found out about our handshake deal. The president talked his father-in-law and brother-in-law into forming a company. He resigned from Columbia Gas, went over, and leased up all of Burleson County. He was drilling his own wells now, and the field turned out to be pretty good. Not nearly as spectacular as Lee County, but pretty good all the same. When the price of oil went up, the old Columbia Gas president got rich. I heard he became a multi-millionaire."

Pat Holloway had the instincts of an oilman. But more importantly, he had Ray Holifield showing him where to drill. It gave him the bravado to confound those other operators, which he enjoyed as much as drilling a well, and head off in directions where no one else had either the nerve or a reason to go. During the summer of 1978, even though he had struck two major wells far to the north, Pat Holloway turned around and began a journey into the unfamiliar lands lying south of town on the road toward Fayette County. La Grange, only a couple of years earlier, had served as the home of the storied and notorious Chicken Ranch, a brothel of good standing that was frequented regularly by students from Texas A&M and The University of Texas, as well as by state senators and representatives who needed a quiet, intimate place to freshen their minds and sharpen their wits when the legislature was in session.

The profession of prostitution in LaGrange could be traced back to 1844 when a widow came to town and settled down in a small hotel with three young women from New Orleans. Unfortunately, during the Civil War, the madam and her girls were chased out of town and branded as Yankee traitors. Miss Jessie Williams revived the business in 1905 when she bought a small house of business on the banks of the Colorado River. She admitted politicians and lawmen, but drunkards never made it past the front door. During World War I, prostitutes dutifully and patriotically mailed packages and letters to soldier boys fighting on foreign shores, and the sheriff was known to hang around every evening to pick up information about criminals who had a propensity for visiting the whorehouse to brag about their deeds and misdeeds.

When the economic pain of the Great Depression began hovering ominously over the country, the parade of gentlemen callers seldom knocked on Miss Jessie's door, and her girls were suffering from hunger. She fought the hard times her own way. She began the "poultry standard" for her house with a new piece of internal legislation that charged *one chicken for one screw*. The girls were never hungry again, and Miss Jessie managed to supplement her income by selling eggs to the good citizens of La Grange. From that moment on, her house was forever known as the Chicken Ranch.

When Miss Jessie grew old and feeble, Edna Milton arrived to take charge of the business, and she ran the brothel with an iron hand. She walked the hallways at night, and if she heard someone abusing one of the girls, she ran him out of the establishment with a metal rod for a weapon. Miss Edna gave money to the civic causes of La Grange, and she was recognized as the largest philanthropist in town. Soldiers joined college students and legislators in the lobby and backrooms of the business during the 1950s, and one nearby military base even arranged for a helicopter to transport the men to and from the Chicken Ranch, which appeared to be nothing more than a whitewashed farmhouse alongside the Houston and Galveston Highway. For many, it was the end of a pilgrimage on their way to manhood. No cursing, smoking, or partaking of alcoholic beverages were permitted on the premises, and as near as anyone could tell, the establishment was earning an income of almost a half million dollars a year.

In 1976, however, it all began to fall apart. A holier-than-thou consumer affairs reporter named Marvin Zindler, posing as a crusader from KTRK-TV in Houston, ran a week-long expose on the Chicken Ranch, as if no one in Texas knew its name and reputation. He claimed that the brothel was guilty of taking its money straight from the bedrooms to pay off corrupt state and local officials. The adverse publicity persuaded Governor Dolph Briscoe to shut the doors of the brothel forever. By the time the law stepped up on the front porch of the Chicken Ranch to deliver his edict, Miss Edna and her girls were gone. She married, moved on toward the Sabine River, and opened up a restaurant, serving the best little chicken in Texas. The business was similar. Only the side dishes had changed.

Pat Holloway, a rebel who didn't really need a cause, decided that the well he was spudding in on the outskirts of La Grange should pay tribute to Miss Jessie, Miss Edna, and the legendary house of ill repute. He named it the Chicken Ranch No. 1. Holloway had originally thought about naming the well after the landowner, who had one of those hard to pronounce and even harder to spell Czech names. "I knew oil people would never be able to write it correctly on a run ticket," he said. "So I called it the Chicken Ranch No. 1 for luck."

There was nothing subliminal about it. And, no, it was never intended to be a monument to any underbelly exploits of Pat Holloway's past. The well brought him luck all right. Bad luck. His Humble Exploration crew reached the total depth of the well and ran a log. There were no shows, no signs of faulting, no bulges in the formation, nothing but those dastardly straight lines that looked like railroad tracks bound from nowhere to nowhere without any detours along the way. Pat Holloway was devastated. He pointed out, "Under normal circumstances, you wouldn't have even bothered to set pipe if you'd looked at the log. You would have plugged the well, gone off, and left it. If I had shown the log to my partners, they would have voted to forget it and go on. It was always better to bust a little than bust a lot."

Ray Holifield was not nearly as concerned with the data. He had seen those same railroad tracks before on the logs at drilling locations he had selected for U.S. Operating and Windsor Energy. The straight lines had fooled him the first time. They couldn't fool him again. "There's a fault down there," he said with a nonchalant shrug.

"Where?" Holloway asked, holding the test log closer to the light. "I sure as hell don't see the damn thing."

"On down a little farther," Holifield said, rubbing his hands together. "The problem is, you stopped your drilling too quickly, and we came up a little short. The fault's down there all right, and if there's a fault, you'll find fractures full of oil."

"How do we get the oil to the surface?"

"We'll set pipe on the well and frac it."

"That's a helluva gamble to lose."

"If you walk away, you've already lost."

Pat Holloway glanced again at the log. "What will it cost me?" he asked.

Holifield grinned. "When you hit the oil, you won't care how much it cost."

Cost overruns could be the death of an independent oil operator. It didn't do the major companies any good either. But they had a deeper pool of money, and mistakes wouldn't kill them financially. Could hurt them all right, but not kill them. Unlike Max Williams, Pat Holloway had not figured the cost to frac a well in his budget. He would be forced to go back to his drilling funds for more money, which made even the savviest of investors a little nervous.

Pat Holloway put his trust in Ray Holifield. What else could he do? His options were limited, and his geologist had not failed him yet. Even the disappointing Perkins No. 1 would give back enough oil for them all to break even. He no longer felt like an attorney. He felt like a juror, who judged guilt or innocence with a single decision. He had a single decision to make. "Let's take it down," he said.

By early September, mud and water had broken into the fault, the frac had done its job as advertised, and the Chicken Ranch No. 1 was, in the words of Pat Holloway, a real barn burner, becoming Fayette

County's most productive ranch property since Miss Edna and her girls departed a shuttered whorehouse. What the test gauge revealed was staggering. The well had the potential of thirteen hundred barrels a day. Holifield had been right. Why, Holloway wondered, would anyone dare to doubt him?

The strike was colossal in its own right. Perhaps, more importantly, the Chicken Ranch No. 1 marked a significant extension of the Giddings chalk field, moving it, as the crow flew, at least thirty miles south of the Kocurek No. 1 near the Burleson County line.

It was a new day. Raw land that had been forgotten or ignored in Burleson and Fayette Counties were suddenly the rage. Independents who feared the chalk, cursed the chalk, and never had a good word to say about the chalk, suddenly wanted to be drilling in the chalk. Wherever oilmen went, the cry was the same. *Let's go to Giddings*. The rush was on.

As *Time Magazine* reported: *The sleepy farm town of La Grange, Texas, has not had much to brag about since 1976 when a nosy investigative reporter helped close down the Chicken Ranch, the famous brothel celebrated in the Broadway musical,* The Best Little Whorehouse in Texas. *But now, La Grange has a different kind of natural resource: Chicken Ranch No. 1, an oil well that is producing low-sulfur crude. Hamlets like Old Dime Box and La Grange have turned into boomtowns. In Giddings, the epicenter of the oilfield, houses that rented for seventy-five dollars a month now go for three hundred dollars, and one entrepreneur is converting old oil-storage tanks into motel rooms and renting them out for twenty dollars a night. That is exactly what the girls at the old Chicken Ranch used to charge.*

●

Giddings did not yet realize that it was on the threshold of becoming a genuine boomtown, but it had become, as *Time Magazine* said, the epicenter of the oilfield. The town liked the money. It was not wild about the hassle of it all. Buddy Preuss tried to sum up the situation in his Viewpoint column: *The oil in Lee County may not do a whole lot to solve the worldwide shortage of oil or turn our nation's balance of payments around on oil imports, but it sure is putting a lot of money into the local*

economy. Landowners are making a nice chunk of money and oil
operators and those servicing the wells have big payrolls in the county
and are spending lots of money.

With the boom now centering in the area between Giddings and
Dime Box, on over toward Deanville and Caldwell, and down to La
Grange, the entire Lee County area is now beginning to feel the
economic boom. Oil people are having to find housing in Lexington
and Dime Box since Giddings just doesn't have anything much left to
offer. Even surrounding larger towns like La Grange, Brenham,
Caldwell, Rockdale, Bastrop, and Smithville are having to house people
who are working in the oil business or oil-related businesses. Some of
those wells are potentially five hundred to over a thousand barrels of
oil a day and lots of natural gas to go along with it. So the oil boom
continues in our area with no end in sight.

No one in Houston or Dallas was reading the *Giddings Times &
News*. It was just as well. Giddings already had more problems than
the town could handle. Bad weather – rain, cold, and soggy ground in
winter and a blistering, suffocating heat during summer months –
hampered drilling. The cost of building pads for the rigs had gone up
from ten thousand dollars to forty thousand dollars, depending on how
many miles of new road an operator had to build across somebody's
pasture. Oil wasn't always conveniently found next to the highway. On
one side of the county, wells were being drilled. On the other side, they
were being plugged and abandoned. A few wells were blowing out,
sometimes throwing the cement casing out of the holes and roaring, it
was said, like a freight train. The constant hit-and-miss of oil exploration
reminded a lot of the old-timers of the 1930s. Some of them shook their
heads in dismay. History was repeating itself all over again, they said.
They had survived it once. They guessed they could live through it
again.

A suit was filed against one oil company that, a farmer said, had
messed up his land and caused him to lose a year's worth of peanut
production. Yet another man stood beside his farm house and told a
reporter for *Flowline Magazine*: "All my life I had to work like the devil,
and now Houston Oil & Minerals comes in and drills here, and I just
can't believe it. You see this wooden walking cane I've got? Well, one
of those boys who works for Houston Oil & Minerals gave it to me. Why,

I got my first royalty check, and I was able to buy my wife a diamond ring for Christmas. It's the first time I could buy my wife anything nice. It sure feels good."

Pat Holloway had always been sure of himself and his decisions in court or in the oilfield. He was viewed as arrogant. He liked being viewed as arrogant. It was part of his image and persona in the Austin Chalk. All he needed was his own intuition, Ray Holifield, and a driller who knew his way down to the limestone faults. There had been a time when Holloway was desperately looking for leases. No more. Now he could pick and choose. He only wanted the best.

John and Bob Knox at the Lee County Land and Abstract Company sent him a lease to sign. Pat Holloway signed it all right. In his mind, the Knox brothers were asking too much for the acreage. He stamped *bullshit* all over the lease and sent it back. Pat Holloway was no doubt the only oilman in town who had his own rubber stamp that said *bullshit.*

Early on, even before the boom ignited, Holloway had placed a top lease on the Schkade acreage. Simply put, it meant that he had the right to the lease if Windsor/U.S. decided to walk away. If Max Williams and Irv Deal chose to make a well, however, he would have to release his right to the acreage. Randy Stewart contacted him by phone. "Windsor/U.S. are about to commence drilling," he told Holloway. "They'll need your release signed."

Williams promptly received a note from the lawyer turned oilman. It said, "But I had the time, I would give you a lesson in oil and gas law. But I have other interests at this point in time. Here is your chicken shit release."

As one operator said of Pat Holloway, "He's the kind of oilman who'll get in your pocket and mess up your change."

An elderly African American gentleman walked into a bank with his royalty payment check. "I'd like to cash it," he said. "It's for a hundred dollars."

"No, sir," the bank teller told him. "It's not a hundred dollars."

"It's a good check, isn't it?"

"Yes, sir, it is."

The old gentleman frowned, somewhat bewildered. "Then I'd like my hundred dollars," he said. "Lord knows I need the money."

"Sir, I'm afraid I can't cash the check for a hundred dollars."

"Why not?"

The bank teller answered with a smile, "It's for a hundred thousand dollars."

"What am I gonna do with that much money?"

"I don't know," the teller answered. "But I'll put it into an account for you. I'm afraid I can't cash it."

"Why not?"

"We don't keep that much cash money on hand."

The old gentleman cocked his head and rubbed his chin as he looked around at the sign on the wall. "This is a bank, isn't it?" he asked.

"Yes, sir."

"I sure would like to have a little walking around money," he said.

He walked out clutching a hundred dollars in ones, fives, and twenties, wondering if he still had the rest of his money, or if he had lost it somewhere between the check and the deposit slip. All he had done was trade one old piece of paper for another. He sure would have liked to take a good, hard look at all of that money. Never in his seventy-six years had he seen a hundred thousand dollars stacked up on top of each other. But if the man behind the window had been right, the old man thought, he was a damn sight richer than the bank.

●

As Buddy Preuss wrote: *Whenever an oil well is brought in anywhere in Lee County, and it only produces seventy-five or a hundred barrels of oil per day, landowners seem to be a little disappointed. The reason for this is because so many wells are producing a hundred and fifty to three hundred barrels a day or more. Quite a number of the oil wells completed recently in the Giddings Field farther south in the Northrup-Serbin area have been put on pump to help get more oil out of the ground. Some of these wells wouldn't have produced more than forty or fifty barrels of oil a day without a pump,*

but with it, some are pumping a hundred and fifty to two hundred barrels
a day, which ain't bad.

A do-it-yourself operator in the Clay Creek field near Brenham had
hooked his oil well to a tiny pump, powered by a small electric motor.
It only pumped two barrels of oil a day. Someone snickered. Someone
else laughed.

"That's not much," he was told.

"No," the operator said, "but I'm pumping seven hundred dollars
worth of oil out of the ground every month. What are you doing with
that farm of yours?"

"Not much when I'm waiting on the peanuts to produce."

"In that case," the operator said with a weary shrug, "I think the
wrong one of us is laughing."

●

Reinhardt Richter had known about the confluence of volcanoes
and those fiery gates of hell beneath the surface of his family farm long
before Max Williams, Irv Deal, or Pat Holloway knew about oil in the
chalk. He made his way from one oil company to the next.

He was looking for a job, said they needed him, said he had been
probing the earth around Giddings for oil since the 1960s. Reinhardt
Richter was a massive man. He owned a farm, had a daughter, often
seemed to walk on the outer ridge of reality and sanity, and could never
figure out why those so-called, self-respecting oil companies refused
to hire him as a consultant.

Hadn't found oil, he said. But he had experience. "Not many of the
locals around here's got experience," he said.

Reinhardt Richter had indeed searched for oil with an old cable
tool rig, a strange and rather dilapidated relic from another era. He
didn't drill.

The rig had a great hammer that slowly rose up into the rig derrick
and dropped heavily to the earth, delivering a mighty blow, pulverizing
the packed dirt, and literally pounding the string of pipe down into the
ground. Richter never made an oil well. He only reached twelve
hundred feet. He came up short.

The chalk lay another eight thousand feet farther down.

A wary Barry Rodstrom came driving into Giddings, not unlike hundreds of other oil patch veterans who chased the drill bits from field to field and had been lured to town by the promise of jobs in the Austin Chalk. He knew his way around a rig. For years, he had worked on drilling, completion, and production crews, primarily in the rich sands of West Texas. He did not battle the chalk until he reached the straight-hole wells of Dilly and Pearsall. Another thousand dollars a month could persuade a man to change jobs in a heartbeat. In the chalk, he found much to his dismay, that bearings wore out on the bits about every sixteen hours. In the sand, he only needed to replace the bearings every five or six days. A crew could drill a thousand feet a day in sand, but only three hundred feet a day in the rock layers of limestone. Rodstrom had dropped strings of pipe down several wells before he discovered how deeply the chalk could break an oilman's heart.

He went to work as the field superintendent for Thomas D. Coffman of Austin, who had drilled his first producing Lee County well on the outskirts of Northrup and Serbin during 1977. Over the next eighteen months, Coffman emerged as a new player who kept to himself and went his own way. Drilling almost one a month, he completed seventeen more wells and became one of the very few operators in the region who had a measure of success without attaching himself to the geologic readings of Ray Holifield.

Thomas Coffman had his own in-house staff of geologists, and they developed their own parallel methods for interpreting the odd array of seismic pictures snapped deep in the chalk. Rodstrom knew they were exchanging a lot of information with anyone who had ever explored the limestone formations, doing a lot of corner shooting, and, as much as possible, offsetting good wells that were already producing in the field. Among the oil explorationists, there was no magic and very few secrets. Shoot. Drill. See what happens. And drill again. Each new day was much like the last. As Rodstrom said, "By 1978, there was so much seismic going on with dynamite blasts rocking the innards of the earth that the whole countryside sounded as though it had gone to war."

Coffman moved his operation out into Fayette and Burleson Counties. Around Giddings, Rodstrom knew, the faults were so large and so much oil was draining into the fractures that he could bring in a well if the drill bit managed to reach anywhere close to the pay zone. In Fayette County, however, it was an altogether different struggle. Wells were difficult to make simply because the fractures were so small. Rodstrom realized he would have to hit his mark dead on or run the risk of missing out entirely. He just had to be careful.

Back in 1897, a gas well had been struck in Fayette County, about four miles southwest of LaGrange. The bit only reached a hundred and twenty-four feet when gas erupted and caught fire. The hole had to be filled half full of dirt before the flames were extinguished. An oil company in the area had intended to reopen the well and go down a considerable depth. Nothing ever happened. He left a fortune untouched in the hole.

Thomas Coffman did not believe that a truly dry hole existed in the chalk. As he told Rodstrom, "All you have to do is set the pipe and we'll find oil. Then we just sit back and wonder how long it'll take before the oil plays out."

Barry Rodstrom found a definite contrast going from one boom to the next. "In Pearsall," he said, "all of the companies had been friendly and cooperative. In Giddings, on the other hand, oil for the operators became a cutthroat business. With a lot more money at stake, the arguments were bitter, the feuds without end, the competition fierce, and the battles always one sudden spark away from turning deadly or at least winding up in court."

By day, operators and landmen fought tooth and nail for leases, for rigs, for land, for farm outs, for royalties, for overrides, for deals. Any deal would do. At night, they gathered at the bar nearest their rigs and drank whiskey together. Whiskey may not have settled any of their feuds or quieted any of their bitterness, but it served to exact a tenuous truce that separated war and peace. Barry Rodstrom said he enjoyed those nights so much and so often that once he walked away from the oil patch, he didn't have a drink of good or bad whiskey for the next fifteen years.

●

With the Tom Brown Drilling Company, every day was a new adventure. Rig number eight was old and powered by aging engines that ran on propane or natural gas. It was a pile of worn-out junk that had been brought to the chalk from Odessa. When parts needed to be replaced – and most of them were held together by rust and always falling apart – they had to be built from scratch in a machine shop. The parts had grown obsolete and could no longer be bought off the shelf.

Nobody had any luck making the balky old rig work. It had trouble with sand. The chalk was impossible. Barry Rodstrom drove up and looked around for roughnecks. There weren't any to speak off. Tom Brown Drilling Company didn't hire many, would have liked to hire less. His tool pusher was an older man named Johnny Henderson who wore a wooden leg to replace the one lost in an oil-field accident.

Rodstrom checked the old man's work schedule. Henderson would be on the rig for thirty straight days, then receive two days off. He would drive home to the far side of Abilene, nine hours away, eat supper, sleep in his own bed for a night, grab a little breakfast, and head back to Giddings.

"This is a killer," Rodstrom said.

"Not to me it isn't," the old man replied.

"Why not?"

"This is the first job I've ever had where Tom Brown's given me two full days off at the same time." Johnny Henderson grinned. "I'm happy as a dead pig in sunshine," he said.

Old rig number eight might have had trouble working. Johnny Henderson never missed a lick. He and Barry Rodstrom hauled the piece of junk from one end of the Giddings field to the other. They cursed it every step of the way. They used it to drill thirty producing wells. They weren't great wells. Some called them poor. But they were producing.

26

Virtually overnight, an honest little boom became an unruly quagmire as a new assault was unleashed on the Lee County Courthouse by an invasion of landmen and lawyers working to clear up titles that, far too often, only a miracle had any chance of clearing. Much of the land had passed too many times through too many hands and too many generations, and at least once or twice through too many divorces. It had been sold, traded, auctioned, and scattered by judges, lawyers, and families no longer speaking to each other. Heirs were lost or missing. Often, not even their families knew where they had gone or remembered exactly when or why they had left.

Large sections surrounding Dime Box were owned or at least had been settled decades ago by poor African American families, who lived in houses, cabins, and shacks but did not have any legal papers declaring whether or not they actually had title to the land or the mineral rights. *Mama lived here. Grand mama lived here. And her mama came here by wagon. We've been here a long time. I guess the land belongs to us.* Nobody knew for sure. Until oil began rushing out of the ground, no one cared.

People were simply people living next door or down the road. Neighbors were neighbors. And a person's birthright was more important than a set of legal papers, which no one outside of a lawyer could understand anyway. As one landowner said, "The fine print said so much to say so little and was always against us." Even Pat Holloway admitted, "The standard lease maps for the area were all screwed up."

If it hadn't been for the Knox Brothers and their Lee County Land and Abstract Company, the lack of organized or even disorganized titles might have shut down the burgeoning boom of Giddings for good. John Knox, Sr., had long been revered as the county surveyor and proprietor of the abstract company. During the early part of the twentieth century, he meticulously created and maintained two sets of land maps, giving one set to the county and keeping one in his own private office in the basement of the courthouse. John Knox was something of a perfectionist, and he kept his maps current and in good, chronological working order.

The county maps, however, were in disarray and badly out of date. Some had disappeared altogether. The earliest documents, according to timeworn rumors, had been lost when the courthouse burned. Maybe the fire had taken them. Then again, maybe someone else had scooped them up from the ashes and carried them away. Until now, it had not ignited much of a controversy. The idyllic way of life in Giddings was changing with every new parcel of land leased, with every new hole in the ground. No longer would it have a *live and let live* existence. Once, a handshake was as good and as binding as a contract. Now it took a lawyer.

When John Knox, Sr., died, one son, Louis, replaced him as the county surveyor, and twin sons John and Robert inherited their father's abstract and title company, which included the possession of his land maps. In the early days of oil discovery, lease hounds generally found what they needed in the county clerk's office, but by the late 1970s, an army of landmen and lawyers were beginning to realize that some of the most critical records they needed were contained in the abstract office owned by John and Robert Knox.

Their files held the keys to a vault. The Knox brothers understood the value of good land maps, especially their own, and began using them to cash in on oil lease title work while the boom raged up and down the streets of Giddings. Title work was one thing. Oil was quite another. One paid a little. One paid a lot.

It would not be long before the brothers made the obvious decision to become landmen themselves, assembling oil lease blocks for operators who came to town and did not have any idea about where to go next.

John and Robert Knox felt as though it was their birthright to acquire a piece of the action. After all, they and no one else had full access to the missing pieces of the land puzzle. A few overrides here, a handful of royalty checks there, and they could wind up doing quite well for themselves.

It was legal, above board, and had the potential to be extremely profitable, a rare opportunity for a small-town abstract company in a town that had been born into poverty and chose to remain there.

Most of the early day oil exploration firms, especially Windsor Energy and U.S. Operating, used the records in the Lee County Land and Abstract Company. There was one exception. Neither John nor Bob Knox liked Pat Holloway. They would not allow him or his people, even the trusted Benny Jaehne, in their plant.

As early as 1977, the Lee County Commissioner's Court had grown weary of the steady complaints instigated by Pat Holloway. He was constantly berating harassed county officials about their missing maps, their out-of-date maps, the various and sundry deed and title records that had been misplaced or somehow allowed to fade into oblivion. If the county did possess the ancient records, Holloway said, they were in absolute and total disarray, generally filed out of order, and stacked in the wrong places. He had trouble finding them. The files were a grab bag of uncertainty.

The Commissioners passed a resolution that called for Louis Knox to make certain that Lee County had custody of all the maps, plats, and surveys that it rightfully owned. They also made a formal request for John and Robert Knox to provide the court with all of their father's working papers.

The Knox brothers replied with a letter, explaining that, unfortunately, their father had never kept any working papers, and the commissioners might be better off consulting with the county deed records if they were determined to bring their land maps up to date.

County Judge Carey Boethel, financed and encouraged by Pat Holloway, was stung by the lack of cooperation he received from John and Bob Knox. He promptly brought the matter to the attention of Texas Attorney General John Hill, but his complaint – because it had no merit – was allowed to expire without any formal action ever being taken. The confusion over the displaced and uncorrected maps and title records had suddenly become even more confusing.

John and Robert Knox thus retained their monopoly on the only current land maps that could be uncovered anywhere in the whole of Lee County. The brothers continued to faithfully maintain and update them. At a singular glance, it often appeared to landmen that Windsor Energy, U.S. Operating, and Humble Exploration already had tightly locked up the best and biggest parcels of acreage in the area. What, if anything, was left?

That was the burning question facing operators who were cautiously easing their way into the field. Within the confines of the Lee County Land and Abstract Company, the Knox brothers, for a fee of course, could give them the answer they were seeking.

Max Williams, Irv Deal, and Pat Holloway had explored the region first, tying together great packages of leased land. But they had not yet scratched the surface. The Knox brothers had perhaps the only business in town that knew who owned or had rights to the most valuable minerals in the county.

●

The boom had quietly begun with a handful of operators inching their way, acre by acre, across the field. No one had to look over his shoulder. Max Williams, Irv Deal, and Pat Holloway all knew what each other was doing, where each other was drilling, which piece of land each one was leasing, and what, if anything, each other had found. In reality, only Williams and Holloway were actually keeping an eye on each other.

Deal was still in Dallas, but he wasn't content to merely earn royalties from the production of wells acquired in his split from U.S. Operating. Windsor had three rigs working, and he had Randy Stewart in the field. Stewart was familiar with every backroad, crossroad, county road, and dirt road in Lee County. He had driven them and had been lost more than a couple of times. But, even more important, he had absolute access to both the records and the historical knowledge of John and Bob Knox.

They trusted him implicitly. His eyes saw records and old maps that few if anyone else ever viewed. Nothing escaped him. Now that he was no longer drawing a paycheck from Max Williams, Randy Stewart gave Irv Deal the edge that no one else possessed.

As Pat Holloway said, "The fierce competition for leases was a curious and often bitter mixture of war and peace, and peace was nonexistent. I'd cut their throats to get leases, and they'd stab me in the back if I was in their way. It was business. It was also personal. That's the way we played the game." After Benny Jaehne, Holloway's landman, finished looking through records, he would leave the books open on the wrong page in the County Clerk's office, knowing that someone would be along shortly, trying to discover which patch of land Holloway wanted. Jaehne was doing his best to lead them astray down a bad road and in another direction.

Williams and Deal had come to Giddings as partners, but now they had gone separate ways. Bad blood had risen between them, and their feud could not be settled or negated.

It was every man for himself, and winner take all, or as much as he could get.

Pat Holloway viewed himself as the lone ranger, the iconoclastic renegade of the field. He depended on Benny Jaehne to handle his legwork, but the Dallas lawyer became quite proficient at handling his own title and abstract work. In the beginning, he had paid ten dollars an acre for a lease. The fee had grown to twenty-five dollars an acre. The economics of the boom were getting out of hand, but the price for oil was on the rise, and the market had eased its stranglehold on operators.

Jaehne kept bringing him blocks of five hundred acres, and Pat Holloway kept shelling out the money necessary to lease them. Before the end of the decade, he would have in his possession more than a hundred and seventy-eight thousand acres spreading across the reaches of Lee, Fayette, and Gonzales Counties. He was, without question, the largest leaseholder in the field.

Max Williams held a deep personal grudge against Pat Holloway primarily because both operators were using the same geologist, Ray Holifield. Neither man wanted to share Holifield. Neither wanted to give him up. Holifield, despite his success, became a constant thorn in their sides. He had a good read on their leases, prospects, and chances, good or bad. No matter how hard Williams and Holloway tried to keep them, there were no secrets in Giddings.

Max Williams was burning because he had paid a million dollars or more to shoot highly technical 2-D, then 3-D, seismic throughout the field, and he had come to believe that Holifield was guilty of using the same seismic data to select drilling locations for Pat Holloway. Williams was slow to anger, but he had just about reached his limits. He cornered his geologist and angrily told him, "Ray, you just can't do that. I paid for the seismic, and it's confidential. It's proprietary. I own it. It is the edge I have out here, and nobody else is allowed to use it."

Ray Holifield was not perturbed in the least. Max Williams, he knew could not read the seismic. If Holifield weren't around to point out what all of those squiggly little lines meant, Williams wouldn't be able to tell the difference between a fault, a dome, or an anticline. Williams needed him.

"Since Pat Holloway is dead set on making waves in Giddings, let him buy his own seismic," Williams snapped.

"That's what he's doing."

"I keep hearing that you and Holloway used my seismic to locate his wells."

"He paid for his own," Holifield said, his eyes smoldering. "You owned the original seismic. I shot it. But you own it. There's not even a question about it. But I shot seismic again for Pat even though I knew the data wouldn't tell me anything different."

"You choose his locations?"

"I read the data for him."

"Is Holloway taking your advice?"

"If he's smart, he will."

Max Williams frowned. The riddles that lay nestled underground and locked in the devil's own chalk now belonged to Pat Holloway as well. Williams simmered. He had hired Ray Holifield. Why would his geologist even think about freelancing for a competitor? At the time, and for years later, Max Williams had no idea that Holloway, even before the lawyer ever thought of coming to Giddings, had been paying part of the salary that Ray Holifield collected each month from LaRue, Moore, and Schaefer.

The anger burned deeper. He would have fired Holifield on the spot. He thought about it. He couldn't. Ray Holifield was still the only geologist consistently finding big fractured reservoirs of oil in the chalk. He hit his mark dead on every time. It was as though he had a supernatural gift. Williams sighed and tried to cool the burning anger inside of him. With Ray Holifield, he guessed he would just have to take the bad with the good.

●

Max Williams and Pat Holloway had an odd relationship. They fought. They very seldom spoke to each other. They didn't want to be seen on the same street or in the same café together. They were waging their own private little undeclared war. But when one was in trouble, the other came to his aid. Good wells had a knack for exploding to the surface, making a sudden impact, and flowing fast before anyone expected it. High pressure in the chalk created a constant threat for a blowout or a fire. On at least two occasions, massive balls of flame shot from Humble Exploration wells and lit up the Giddings sky.

Drilling on so many locations at the same time, the operators were constantly in danger of suddenly coming up with serious shortages during critical junctures of drilling. Williams and Holloway swapped and shared their mud, pipe, equipment, and even an occasional roughneck or roustabout in times of crisis. If a well happened to blow, their crews raced frantically to the troubled rig and would fight all night to save the well and rescue the men who had worked so hard to bring it in. By morning, their feud would be just as heated and tempered as it was before. But cease fires were commonplace in the Giddings field. The threat of blowouts haunted the rigs. Fighting one was like walking a tightrope without a net. It was a constant dread, and failure was not an option.

Buddy Preuss drove out to Windsor's B. J. Stork well on an early Saturday morning to witness the remains of a big blowout. He wrote:

That was some sight to behold. Natural gas mixed with powdered cement shooting up thirty to forty feet into the air and roaring like a freight train. They tell me that several thousand dollars worth of natural gas escaped from that well every hour during the nearly day's time that it was blowing gas. Fortunately it never caught fire or they might have had to call Red Adair down from Houston to put out the fire. They tell me old Red charges a cool million dollars just to go to the site of an oil well fire and much more than that if it takes any length of time to put it out. The well was finally capped by Halliburton crews who forced water down the hole into the casing and cemented the well shut.

●

As a rule, Pat Holloway and Max Williams stayed away from each other in town and in the field. That's why Williams was somewhat stunned to look up from a plate of barbecue ribs and see Holloway grab a chair and sit down beside him. He should not have been surprised. So many from the oilfield kept pushing their way into the City Meat Market for lunch that Williams began calling it the Giddings Petroleum Club.

He said, "I'd bring some potential investors down from Wall Street and take them through the line picking up barbecued brisket, sausage, and ribs all smothered in homemade barbecue sauce. They would grab a hunk of cheese and a raw onion and find a table in a haze of smoke from the cooker. By the time they finished eating, they couldn't wait to invest. Giddings was different from any world they had ever seen before."

Williams had glimpsed Pat Holloway plowing through brisket on brown butcher paper at other times, but they had never before sat at the same table. Holloway looked as serious, as perplexed, as Williams had ever seen him. "Max, you and I have drilled a lot of wells around here," he said. "I need to ask you a question."

"Go ahead."

"Are you making any money?"

"I'm doing all right." Williams would have never dared to say otherwise.

"You have a gas contract?"

Williams nodded. "I'm selling mine to Perry Gas," he said. "I've hooked a gas line to every well we've drilled."

"They cheating you?"

"They've been pretty good folks to work with."

Holloway shook his head. "My problem," he said, "is that I don't have a gas contract, and I need one. I'm having to flare all of the gas I find."

"You're wasting a lot of money."

"Probably so," Holloway said, "but I don't trust the gas pipeline companies. Every damn one of them will screw you."

"Maybe," Williams answered, "But, Pat, if you keep on flaring your gas, you're screwing yourself. You're losing millions of dollars."

"I don't trust the bastards".

"What choice do you have?"

Pat Holloway shrugged. "I guess I'll build my own pipeline," he said, standing up and walking away with the smell of barbecue smoke thick around his shoulders.

It had not been difficult to determine that Holloway was probably losing a fortune and tempting the wrath of the Texas Railroad Commission by flaring the gas. The whole countryside around his wells was ablaze in the darkness at night. Some even swore that the flares were so bright and so numerous that a man could park anywhere inside the Humble Exploration field and read the fine print in a newspaper during the middle of the night. It was almost like daylight.

●

Field operators were constantly trying to guard themselves and their resources against theft. Greed was an accepted way of life. Theft was a sin without redemption. Pipelines had not yet begun to catacomb the field, and most companies were relying on trucks that rolled into their locations, often at night, to pick up their oil and deliver it to buyers, mostly faraway and out of state.

Operators found themselves at the mercy of the gaugers. Thank God for the honest ones. Some gaugers were guilty of falsifying reports on the amount of oil they found in the storage tanks and stealing enough crude to double their salaries each month. They might take an inch of oil from each of several tanks. No more. Just an inch. Not enough for operators to miss or even realize it had vanished. Corrupt gaugers were skimming the bottom and playing a felonious game of fractions. That single inch of oil in a five hundred gallon tank was roughly equivalent to twenty barrels of oil and worth in the neighborhood of three to four hundred dollars. A thief might not get rich. But he kept his pockets filled with somebody else's money. A few pipeline companies were culpable. Lots of gravel roads. Lots of tanks. Lots of oil. Trucks rolling in the dead of night. The temptation was just too lucrative to resist.

Some, on the other hand, had unwittingly hired crooked men to haul the oil. Either way, operators had been robbed as surely as if some unscrupulous and renegade oil hauler had held a gun to his head. In a bitter attempt to fight back against the loss of oil and revenue, field operators began hiring and dispatching their own gaugers to keep an accurate account of the oil in their tanks. The really ingenious sleight-of-hand thief, however, had the ability to steal oil with somebody looking over his shoulder or staring at him eyeball to eyeball. The professional cheats never blinked.

Pat Holloway even went so far as to persuade his twenty-one-year-old daughter Marcy to quit her job at an Austin bank and join him in Giddings. She drove into town and immediately acquired a certain amount of notoriety as the only woman working in the Austin Chalk oilfield. Marcy had no idea what a gauger was or did, but she became one. As she said, "My family had been in the oil business for generations. I looked around and decided I was the heir apparent to follow my father into the field." She had already worked as a landman for Humble, although no one ever mistook her for a man in or out of the land. She cut a striking figure in a field occupied mostly by hairy-legged old, beer-drinking roustabouts, roughnecks, and pipeline men. She was young. She possessed the natural good looks of a celebrity, and Marcy turned a lot of heads, especially those belonging to truck drivers and oil service company employees who happened to cross paths with her in the field. They were used to men, old and broken down long before their time, with dust and grime trapped in the sweat on their faces and breathing the fumes of cheap whiskey. The lovely Marcy Holloway was a breath of fresh air.

She and her truck drove all over Lee and Fayette Counties, traveling to fourteen producing wells each day, taking measurements in the tanks, making sure there was no hint of oil missing, and checking out tank batteries and production equipment. It didn't take her any time at all to master the techniques of climbing storage tanks, operating oil tank measuring reels, and starting up heater treaters. No one treated her as though she was the boss's daughter. Oilfield workers treated her like an old hand in a hurry. She earned their respect. Marcy was her father's watchdog, and whenever a professional thief saw Marcy headed his way, he blinked and began backing up. He might get away, but he wouldn't be hauling any stolen oil with him.

As Pat Holloway told Max Williams, he was desperately in need of a gas pipeline contract. By continuing to flare his gas, he was casting millions of dollars to the mercy of the winds, but he had little regard for any of the pipeline companies he had encountered.

He only trusted one man in the oil patch. Holloway trusted himself. He tracked down a steel mill in Alabama that was agreeable to selling him pipe on credit. He hired a pipeline supervisor to put together the nuts and bolts of a company and signed an agreement with Purvin & Gertz, pipeline engineers who had the expertise to extract natural gas from deep sources, and, the chalk was productive at twelve to thirteen thousand feet. Holloway borrowed enough money to finance the operation from a bank in Illinois. All he had was his word, a few good oil wells, an idea, and the genius to make a deal sound convincing no matter how absurd it might really be. He approached each negotiation the same way he built an argument in his courtroom briefs. He was sincere and believable. The truth could take a holiday.

Pat Holloway built his pipeline. No longer would he be flaring gas and watching money burn in the sky above the field. No longer could a man read a newspaper around Pat Holloway's wells in the darkness of a night draped with clouds and lit only by the faint glow of a new moon. Now he got rid of his natural gas with a piece of pipe instead of lighting a match. The pipeline cost him, but Pat Holloway slept well at night. No one could cheat him. He kept his money in his own lockbox and knew where he hid the key.

27

Max Williams had new rigs coming to the field, old rigs moving to new well sites, and he was on the phone, scouring the country and looking for more rigs. His had long ceased to be a one-man operation. By now, back in Dallas, he had five men working for him and raising funds for his various forays into oil exploration.

Richard Flashnick came from the real estate world and was on board early, generating his first dollars in 1976. Jim Hammond had played basketball with Max Williams at SMU. Cliff Harris had gained enduring fame as an All-Pro safety for the Dallas Cowboys. Investors went out of their way to do business with Cliff Harris simply because he was Cliff Harris. He had worn a star on his helmet, and, in Dallas, that was as close to knighthood as anyone could get.

Baron Cass and Bob Swisher had both been connected in the high-powered world of finance with the global investment and banking firm of Bear Stearns. Williams paid them five percent of the cash they raised, plus one-thirty second of production after payout of the wells.

Once a week, Williams gathered his staff together in Dallas and gave them an updated review of U.S. Operating and the successes, as well as the problems, he was facing in the field. He then let each of his fundraisers stand and report on the amount of money he brought in for each new venture into the chalk. It was an old technique he had learned at the real estate company. The pressure of finding out that someone else had been more successful that month was a powerful form of motivation. Nobody wanted to be last. It was part of Max Williams's business policy to have the money banked a month before he spudded in the well. If his money men came up a little short, Williams made up the difference and bought an interest in the well himself.

Williams made it a point to let his whole team, from secretaries to landmen, earn overrides, even allowing them to buy into the good wells he knew he had in the ground. His staff was loyal to Max Williams because he had been loyal to them. They watched the manner in which he conducted business. If an operator needed money, he could go to Williams with an oil deal and know he would not be cut out. Max Williams was a rarity in the field. He was a wildcatter with a conscience.

The cost of drilling a well had risen dramatically from two hundred thousand to three hundred and fifty thousand dollars, and Max Williams would soon have the financial burden of as many as fifteen rigs all running at the same time. He had great chunks of acreage in the Giddings field and was looking for more, even though he had been stretched thin physically and financially. Not enough hours in the day. Not enough money in the banks.

Although Williams had more than enough work to keep him occupied between Giddings and Dime Box, he could not turn his back on the opportunity that had arisen down in Dimmit and Webb Counties, sprawling south of Carrizo Springs and on toward the Rio Grande. He heard that an operator was suffering financially and might be willing to sell his leases on the Gates Ranch. The play was already in progress. And it was out of the chalk completely. Max Williams drove down, met with the operator, struck a deal, and left with the leases on the ranch. The operator wanted out as much as Williams wanted in, which made the deal a perfect fit for both men. Williams already had three or four rigs running, and he had more than four million dollars in the ground.

Regardless of how good the production might be, Williams had a lot more money going out than coming in, and he realized it would take at least four hundred thousand dollars to capitalize his newest venture in South Texas. He had the leases. He had the prospects. He did not have four hundred thousand dollars in his hip pocket.

Max Williams was playing tennis one afternoon with Bobby Stewart, chairman of the board for First National Bank in Dallas. Between sets, in casual conversation as the two men wiped sweat from their faces, Williams mentioned that he had acquired an oil prospect that his geologist and petroleum engineer really liked.

"How good is the field?" Stewart asked.

"It already has about twenty producing wells on it."

"In the chalk?"

"No."

"Sounds promising."

"My people think so."

"I have a couple of customers in our trust department who are looking for a good investment deal," Stewart said. "Maybe this is it."

"Can you set up a meeting?"

"Whenever you want."

Max Williams was introduced to Bill Farriss and Ernie Barnett, both petroleum engineers who worked at the bank. They were looking for an investment for Southwest Bell Telephone Company's profit sharing and pension plan. They liked the potential of the oil prospect Williams presented them. The financial arrangement was quickly nailed in place. Lots of fine print, but most of it was standard legalese, and there was hardly any bargaining at all. Williams retained fifty percent interest in the wells drilled on the Gates Ranch, with the profit sharing and pension plan taking the remaining half interest.

He now had the money he needed to hire a crew, lease a rig, and begin drilling down south, but he and his partners in U.S. Operating were required to sign a note, which guaranteed the payback of those four hundred thousand dollars regardless of what happened with the wells. Williams did not hesitate. He had no qualms about placing his name on the document, and he carried it to Dick and Alan Gold for their signatures. Back when Williams made his move to the oil business, they had bought a one-third interest of U.S. Operating. He had needed a substantial amount of working capital then. He needed it again.

Dick Gold looked at the note and balked. "Alan and I didn't mind putting up money to buy a third of the company," he said. "We thought that was all we would ever have to spend. We did not anticipate having to borrow more money as we went long. That's a lot of debt for us to handle."

"We've made good wells in the chalk," Williams argued.

"But the chalk's the chalk," Gold replied. "Nobody trusted it when we went down to Pearsall. Nobody trusted it when we came to Giddings. I still don't know if I trust it. Just when you get a handle on the chalk, you want to leave it. The oil business is a crapshoot, Max. Even now, Alan and I really don't know that much about it."

"It's an expensive game," Williams said. "You can make a lot of money in oil, but you have to spend a lot of money if you want to find it and produce it."

Dick Gold's mind was made up. He shrugged apologetically and said, "I don't think Alan and I want to sign the note. It's just one more risk in a game full of risks."

"I'm committed to the wells," Williams said.

"And the four hundred thousand dollar note?"

"I am."

"How can we get out of it?" Dick Gold asked.

Williams, without argument, hard feelings, or any cross words coming between them, separated out the Gold's one-third share of U.S. Operating. The brothers were no longer liable for any production costs or debt incurred by the firm. They were, however, allowed to keep one-third of the working interest on any wells Max Williams discovered. He now owned a hundred percent of U.S. Operating, and he personally signed the note for four hundred thousand dollars, didn't consider it much of a risk at all, and accepted the fact that spending big chunks of money was a necessary evil in the oil game.

Max Williams had all of the work he could handle in Giddings. But an oilman was never satisfied with the oil he had in the hole. He suffered from an unquenchable thirst to find more. It was a business. It was an addiction.

Dick and Alan Gold had no doubt been hesitant to take on any more financial obligation because, after the success U.S. Operating had with the M&K, Schkade, Max Farris, Molly C. Davis, and Carmean wells, they believed they were riding a hot streak that would possibly never end. They had been feeling courageous and confident enough to back the Matthijetz No. 1 with their own money. No other investors were needed. They felt destined to hit the proverbial jackpot on their own. They had cash on hand and the guts to roll the dice.

The well rushed in at a hundred and seven barrels a day, but, within seventy-two hours, it barely showed any faint seepage of oil in the pipe. Not much more than a stain on the tank. Small fractures. Quickly drained. The Matthijetz was a lost cause, not even promising enough to frac. One unexpected and heavy loss had dampened all of the good times. Their confidence had been shaken.

In the long run, it didn't matter. Williams permitted them to retain their one-third working interest in his wells, and, before the decade of the 1970s ended, they would each be earning a half million dollars a month in production payments. Only God and a good accountant could have figured out the amount of money they would have pocketed if they had signed the note that Max Williams paid off before he finished drilling his tenth well on the Gates Ranch. The Southwest Bell Telephone Company profit sharing and pension fund considered those ten wells as good as any investment Bill Farriss and Ernie Barnett had ever made.

●

When Max Williams returned to Giddings, he had an appointment to meet with Jack Dreyfus and Elmer Heubeck, who owned a three thousand acre horse ranch not far from the acreage that held the Gerdes No. 1. The two men had selfishly kept a tight rein on their land, watching the boom crawl like shadows at sunset across the farmlands, and it was crawling their way.

Jack Dreyfus may have walked the streets of Giddings as just another stranger in a town full of them, but, in New York, his name was revered on Wall Street. He founded the billion-dollar Dreyfus Fund and became widely publicized as the man who invented the commonplace mutual fund.

Life Magazine even referred to him as the most singular and effective personality to appear on Wall Street since the days of Joseph Kennedy and Bernard Baruch. He was as much at home at a horse racing track or a gin rummy table as he was strolling the hallways of the stock exchange.

Elmer Heubeck passed himself off as a savvy old horse trader from Florida. Dreyfus had the money and liked to bet on the ponies. Heubeck, if nothing else, had the expertise and the knowledge to make them run and, hopefully, to the winner's circle. On the ranch outside of Giddings, they planned to breed, raise, and train thoroughbreds. Oil got in the way. "We've been told you guys are the best," Heubeck told Williams.

"We've had our share of successes."

"How many wells have you drilled and made good?"

"Close to twenty-five," Williams answered. "Maybe a couple more."

"I know Garlan Gerdes," Heubeck said. "You made him a pretty wealthy man."

"He's not hurting any for money."

Heubeck laughed. "The oil business is like horse racing," he said. "We only want to run with the best."

Heubeck talked and finagled until it was time to strike a deal, then Jack Dreyfus took over. He knew Max Williams wanted his acreage. Max Williams knew Dreyfus wanted to lease it. It was just a matter of agreeing on the details. Hammering out the details was what Jack Dreyfus did best. He drove a hard bargain.

Williams didn't budge. He liked the land where fine horses grazed between the fences. The acreage sat atop the thick layers of chalk that had appealed to Ray Holifield when he directed U.S. Operating to keep moving north, always north.

Jack Dreyfus backed off of his demands. He discovered in a hurry that money was the only thing mutual funds and oil had in common.

Max Williams might be able to drill enough on the ranch to make him a lot of money, but the operator had no intention of paying much up front for the leases. Dreyfus decided he didn't really need the lease money. It was pocket change. He wanted to cash checks with a lot of zeroes on them. He wanted to rub his hands in pay dirt from the bottom of a rich hole.

Max Williams leased the ranch land cheap, far below the going rate, and made immediate preparations to drill the Harriet No. 1. His business was already wildly out of control, and, perhaps, the only man in Giddings who faced a more hectic schedule was Ray Holifield.

The geologist was running back and forth between U.S. Operating, Windsor Energy, and Humble Exploration, day and night, holidays and

Sundays, when the dust blew in his face, when rain turned the dust to mud. As one company man said, "The deals kept falling into place, and Holifield was all over the field. He kept showing up in the middle of the night knee deep in mud to look over his logs one more time but never one last time." He slept wherever he could catch a wink. He ate Vienna sausages from a can. He wished for the good old days when he only worked eighty hours a week. He did not have a day off or a day to rest."

Serves him right, Williams thought. The geologist had become an irritant not unlike a speck of dust in his eye, but still, Williams knew that he owed Ray Holifield. More than twenty-five years later, production from the horse ranch would still be paying Jack Dreyfus and Elmer Heubeck both a hundred thousand dollars a month. Oil was, Williams told Dreyfus, the gift that kept on giving.

●

Pat Holloway, without anyone realizing it, had a sudden change of heart. Almost two years earlier, he had established a small and short-lived organization called the Lee County Royalty Owners Association, loaded the landowners in a bus, traveled to Austin, and argued vehemently against a proposed new field ruling that would require wells be spaced a hundred and sixty acres apart. It was his contention that the wells should only be separated by forty acres, just as the old rule had mandated.

Of course, at the time, Holloway only had leases on twenty blocks of downtown Giddings. The new ruling would have suffocated his operation. He did not have access to the same acreage as Windsor Energy, U.S. Operating, and Houston Oil & Minerals. Now he did. Now, he was drilling on vast tracts of acreage and he, too, was aware that wells spaced too closely together had an inherent danger of draining each other's reservoirs. It was a losing proposition to invest almost a million dollars to drill three wells that might all be pumping oil from the same fault.

Pat Holloway was back before the Texas Railroad Commission, which earlier had mercy on him and established a compromise field rule that provided a spacing of eighty acres between the wells. Then, he had been satisfied. It had been enough. Now, it wasn't.

Pat Holloway, the self-appointed gunslinger of the Giddings field, was demanding a spacing of a hundred and sixty acres. His arguments bore the same passion. They possessed the same logic.

But this time, as Holloway admitted with a slight shrug of his shoulders and a wry grin, he was able to prove conclusively exactly what he had disproved conclusively before.

He got what he wanted, and he was convinced that what was good for Pat Holloway was good for Giddings.

Operators kept competing against him.

Sometimes a business, sometimes a war. Some operators did not trust him. Others believed that there was a finely drawn line between a shrewd businessman and a crook, and Pat Holloway was as shrewd as any of them had ever seen.

28

*B*ill Shuford's venture into the Giddings oilfield had been as circuitous as it was unpredictable. He had, by his own admission, driven fast cars, chased fast girls, drank hard whiskey, and ridden a wild streak as far as it would take him. Giddings, on the other hand, was such a tame little town that stray dogs seldom crossed against the light. *Marked down* and *discount* were considered brand names down at Protho's department store, and its life after dark was a far cry from the temptations and promises offered around SMU's campus, where Shuford hung out until he realized that going to class was a requirement, not an option. Much to his disappointment, hustling girls until the hours before daybreak was not part of the curriculum either.

Bill Shuford had an eye on a business degree but dropped calculus four times and said he was running on little more than a hope and a prayer. Not knowing what else to do, he decided to join his father in the life insurance business. Didn't like it. He jumped into the world of real estate. It was worse. Shuford found himself on a fast track to nowhere, and he was having trouble finding any way to get off. He spent his evenings with a bad crowd, he said, and never planned for day after tomorrow. Wasn't quite sure he would ever see day after tomorrow. Bill Shuford existed only in the moment, which wasn't, he thought, a bad place to dwell. Shuford was devoid of ambition and still living in a little room behind his parent's home. It bothered him but not enough to move out.

His father was playing golf one afternoon with a couple of friends who worked for SEDCO in the oil and gas business. Bill Clements, the man who would be governor, ran the company, and he had launched a program designed to hire bright young men for management training overseas.

Bill Shuford received a call from his father. The phone jarred him. It woke him up. Good Lord, he thought, it's not even noon yet. Shuford heard his father saying, "I've found a job you might be interested in."

"What is it?"

"Let me mention three words," his father said. "Oil. Gas. Overseas."

Shuford was suddenly awake. He seldom listened to his father. This time, he did. To be truthful, he had never thought about the oil and gas business, but the chance to live in some exotic foreign locale at somebody else's expense appealed to him a great deal.

The next morning, Shuford walked confidently into the SEDCO office of Rabbit Wilson, wearing the proper attire, a coat and a tie, and made his formal application for the management training position. "Thanks for coming," Wilson said, "but we don't have any openings right now. I'll give you a call if we do."

Shuford grinned wickedly. His reputation had obviously preceded him. SEDCO must know more about him than he knew about SEDCO. But that was okay. He wasn't particularly looking for a job anyway.

Two months passed. Shuford knew he was up to his eyeballs in debt. He felt stifled. He was troubled. Debt was piling up faster than he could pay it off.

He sat down at dinner with his family one Friday night, and the meal turned into a heated discussion about Shuford's future, or, to be more exact, his lack of one. The discussion shifted from a verbal sparring match into a fight.

"It was," he said, "an old-fashioned knock down, drag out altercation with angry tempers running out of control and the central theme centering around my worthless existence as a derelict."

The phone rang. The fight stopped. Shuford answered it. "I'd like to speak with William Shuford, Junior," the voice said.

"That's me," he answered, curtly and rather rudely.

"This is Rabbit Wilson," the voice said. "We've had a cancellation in SEDCO's next management training class, and I'm calling to see if you're still interested."

"Yes, sir. I am."

"Great." There was a slight pause, then Wilson continued. "There is a slight catch," he said.

"What is it?"

"You have to be in Beaumont Sunday afternoon."

"No problem." Bill Shuford would have been ready to head out for Beaumont the next morning if possible. At the moment, he only wanted to get away and did not care where or how far away he might be going. "I knew if I didn't do something pretty soon, I'd probably wind up in prison," he said.

He turned and glared at his parents. "I hope you're happy now," he said.

"Why?"

"I have a job."

●

By Sunday morning, Bill Shuford was on his way to SEDCO's facilities in Beaumont. His father loaned him ten thousand dollars and, along with the money he earned selling his car, Shuford paid off his debts. Six weeks later, he was flying across the Atlantic Ocean. Shuford had not known anything at all about oil and gas, and here was SEDCO spending good money to send him out and find it. His original assignment would have shipped him to Iran. The mission changed abruptly at the last minute, and Shuford was on his way to an offshore rig in the North Sea. No one else wanted to go, he found out. He had not been given a choice.

The rig manager picked him up in Aberdeen, Scotland. They boarded a helicopter and headed for parts unknown, at least unknown to Bill Shuford.

"How long will I be over here?" he asked.

"Two years."

"No. I mean on this trip. Out on the rig."

"Two months."

"Before I come back?"

"Before you go anywhere."

Shuford contemplated the answer a brief moment, then asked, "What's there to do on the rig for two months?"

"Work."

"Anything else?"

"Stay out of the way of the storms."

"Just how do I do that?"

"You don't."

Bill Shuford began on the rig as a roustabout and worked his way up to the status of a roughneck, provided a roughneck had any status. He worked twelve-hour shifts, all days the first week, all nights the second. The work was hard. It was tough. It was dirty. The seas rolled. The storms blew. Rain hammered his face. He found shelter from the turbulence and the elements only when he slept. No drinking was allowed. Apparently, neither were women. Much to his dismay, he was never able to find any.

Shuford wound up in Aberdeen during the early 1970s, living in a nice apartment, earning thirty-five hundred dollars a month, saving most of it, and traveling Europe when he had a few days off. He was promoted to derrick man, then to the position of assistant driller, and he worked in the freezing cold, often until the dead hours of morning, covered in grease with the wind coming in so hard it was blowing the rain sideways.

Bill Shuford had fled his hometown of Dallas to grow up. On those lonely, wind-battered, never-ending shifts aboard an offshore rig, he became a man. He became his own man. He did not particularly like the North Sea. He was intrigued by the North Sea. He signed up for another two-year hitch. He worked twenty-eight days on and twenty-eight days off, and during those long spells when he had time on his hands, Bill Shuford was able to travel anywhere he wanted to go. He went home to Dallas. He and his family no longer had any serious reasons to disagree. It was accepted that he had a future, maybe a tenuous one, but a future nonetheless.

●

At the country club, Bill Shuford chanced to sit down with two of his father's biggest insurance clients, Harold Clark and Harold Dunk. They talked for a long time, and the conversation never strayed far, if at all, from oil and gas. Clark and Dunk had made their fortune by turning raw land into housing developments, and they had been investing, they said, with a former Dallas real estate salesman who was dabbling in the oil business, Max Williams.

"Where's he drilling?" Shuford asked.

"Giddings."

"Never heard of it."

"He's trying to outsmart the Austin Chalk."

"Had any luck?"

"He's found a mint for all of us," Clark said.

"Is he looking for a good man who knows a thing or two about finding oil?"

"From what I understand," Dunk told him, "good hands in the oilfield are hard to find. Everybody down there is looking for somebody with experience, and I'm sure Max is no different from the rest of them."

"Then maybe you can tell Max about me," Shuford said. "I've spent about as much time overseas as I want, and I'm ready to come home again."

The message Harold Clark and Harold Dunk carried to Max Williams was brief and to the point. They had a good friend whose son had been working on a rig out in the North Sea for a couple of years. He had learned a lot. He was a fine young man. He missed Texas. He wanted to stay in the oilfield, but he would like a job closer to home. Did Williams have any suggestions? Or did he need a good hand?

"Who has he been working for?"

"SEDCO."

"That might be a problem."

"How's that?"

"I'm working on a deal with SEDCO, and I sure would hate for them to think I was stealing one of their men."

Clark and Dunk laughed.

Max Williams was dead serious.

He and Ray Holifield had been trying to expand the chalk play, which ran from Giddings, across Mississippi, and down to the gulf. Williams had put together leases on three hundred thousand acres, worked out a ten-million-dollar investment deal with Don Carter, and mentioned his expansion plans to Steve Mahood at the end of a tennis match.

Mahood, serving as legal counsel for SEDCO, knew all about the successful wells Max Williams had found in the chalk and saw a chance for his company to move into the trend as well. "You need to go back to Carter," he said.

"Why?"

"See if we could give him an override to step aside." Mahood sat down on a bench beside the court and wiped sweat from his face. "Max," he said, "you should let SEDCO do the deal."

Don Carter was certainly amenable. He was freed from any investment money up front, SEDCO was responsible for gambling the ten million dollars, and he would be receiving an override on any oil production discovered in the acreage. He liked his odds. He liked them a lot.

Max Williams telephoned Steve Mahood to check out the possibility of hiring Bill Shuford. "I certainly don't want to create a problem with SEDCO," he said.

"You won't."

"What kind of job did he have for you?"

"He was a roughneck out on a North Sea rig, " Mahood answered. "Feel free to hire him if he wants to get back to Texas. The North Sea can take its toll on young men. You won't affect our relationship at all."

Max Williams wanted Shuford to understand the Giddings field before making any kind of decision that would drastically affect or alter his life.

He telephoned Shuford and said, "A couple of my friends have recommended you for a job. It's down in the chalk. I don't know what you have planned for tomorrow, but if your schedule is free, I'd like for you to fly down and take a look at the operation."

Shuford certainly had nothing better to do. Giddings was a lot closer to Dallas than the North Sea had been. Surely, it wasn't as remote or isolated as an offshore rig. Sure, he would go.

He boarded the Citation jet that Williams had bought and paid for with oil money and headed south. He had the plane to himself. Williams was already back in the chalk. A company man was waiting for him. Shuford was driven up one gravel road and down another, traveling from rig to rig. They were scattered all over the field, and it did not take him long to realize that Giddings had absolutely nothing in common with the North Sea.

The wind was blowing, but it was a dry, hot wind. More like a furnace. The ground didn't swell and roll beneath the rigs, and, from all reports, it had not rained more than a good spit in months. Bill Shuford ordered a chicken fried steak at Schubert's, and by the time he climbed back on board the plane late that afternoon, his mind was made up.

If Max Williams offered him a job, he would take it. Williams did.

"What do you want me to do?" Shuford asked.

"I want you to work under Jim Brim," Williams replied. "He runs my operation down here, and I want you to learn all that you can about the oil business in the Austin Chalk. Right now, I own three rigs, and I have all of them running. Turbo Dixon has one. J. E. Traweek oversees one. I'll turn the third rig over to you."

"What kind of salary are you offering me?" Shuford asked.

"What kind of salary do you want?"

Bill Shuford told him.

Max Williams thought it over, played with the numbers in his head, and came to the conclusion that if a man was more than satisfied with his paycheck he would do a better job, especially when running his own show. Williams offered him more money, which placed Bill Shuford in an immediate quandary. He had one job. He had been offered another. One was five thousand miles from home. One was two hundred miles away. One didn't have much of a night life. He doubted if the other one did either. Shuford looked at Max Williams and asked, "Can I sleep on it?"

"You'd be foolish not to."

Bill Shuford did not sleep much at all that night. He did not want to face SEDCO and tell anyone that he was resigning. He had just signed another two-year contract. But in Giddings, with the chalk giving up so much of its oil, Max Williams might just make him a millionaire. In a big company like SEDCO, he could get lost in the shuffle. In a small, aggressive firm like U.S. Operating, the sky was the limit. He could start at the bottom and still be within striking distance of the top.

He drove to see Rabbit Wilson, explained the deal Max Williams had offered him, and, with regrets, handed in his resignation.

"I think you're making a big mistake," Wilson said.

"You may be right," Shuford answered. "And if I am, I'll be back."

Rabbit Wilson shook his hand and watched him walk out of the door to his office. He could read young men pretty well, and he knew Bill Shuford would not be back. He took the resignation and filed it away in a folder of forgotten resumes.

●

Max Williams sent Bill Shuford to W. O. Bankston's automobile dealership and told him to pick out any car on the lot. Might as well get yourself a good one, he said. You'll be spending most of your life in it. Shuford selected a hot, new, 1978 Lincoln Cougar and drove toward Giddings. He had never been around a land operation before and did not know quite what to expect. The excitement of a new job, a new location, a new challenge was daunting and lost in a complex set of ragged nerves.

He wondered if Rabbit Wilson had been right. Had he made a serious mistake, and did he still have time to rectify it? Those offshore rigs were massive and expensive. He had worked with the best equipment money could buy. By comparison, the land rigs looked small, maybe even fragile. In the North Sea, his job was to simply maintain equipment that had already been built and pump the oil somebody had already found.

Giddings was in the midst of a boom. Seismic blasting day and night. Roads locked up with rigs on the move, coming and going and never staying in one place for very long. Pump jacks coaxing oil out of the dark recesses of the earth. Mad and often futile attempts to bring in the next well before the last one played out or hope Ray Holifield figured some way to keep it from playing out.

Hell, Shuford thought, he wouldn't be able to maintain or pump a well unless somebody drilled deep enough to bring the oil out of the ground. The equipment he had seen throughout the field was mostly junk. Still, Max Williams had to drill a new well every ninety days to keep his farm out agreements intact, and he had too many farm outs, too many leases, too many prospects, too many deadlines, and too much drilling going on at the same time.

Bill Shuford drove straight to the DB Rig Number 7 without stopping. At least, he told himself, he wouldn't have to work all night.

He was wrong.

●

Bill Shuford had been in Giddings three days when he chanced to run across a young lady who lived just down the street from his trailer. She was cute, had a winsome smile, and was single. For Shuford, it was a winning combination.

She invited him to a dance at the SPJST Hall in Dime Box. It wasn't Highland Park in Dallas, perhaps. But it was a dance, and, until now, he had not been sure whether or not Giddings had any attractive or available women, and he was more than delighted to meet one. The lonely nights might not be so lonely after all.

The hall was crowded. The dance floor was jammed, no place to move, just enough space to sway and tightly hold a date, which, Shuford thought, was not at all bad. The noise of the music pounded off the wall, and he knew that somewhere between the beats, there must be a melody. Bill Shuford had just wandered up to the bar and ordered a beer when he heard those dreaded words: *Better look out.* It was not the first time he had heard them in his life.

He glanced over his shoulder and saw a renegade posse of five men headed his way, all of them a little too tall, a little too wide, a little too muscled, a little too pissed off. And that made them a little too dangerous. One elbowed Shuford on his way to the bar. "Excuse me," he said gruffly. He did not mean it as an apology.

"Can I help you?" Shuford asked. The tone was condescending.

The man pushed him again, harder this time.

"Here I was," Shuford recalled. "I was the new guy in town. I had been in Giddings three days. And already I new I was in the middle of a barroom brawl."

He broke a beer bottle on the top of the bar. Shuford turned and hit one of the men. It was the best shot he had. He knew he might not get another one. That left four, which, in a barroom brawl, was always four too many. They surrounded Shuford. He waded into them. After awhile, the fists no longer hurt. He felt them. They were no longer afflicted with pain. Maybe he was just numb, Shuford thought.

One of the burly, broad-shouldered men throttled him by the neck and asked, "Why the hell won't you quit?"

"I can't," Shuford answered. "I have no place else to go."

One was a big Giddings football player, thick, rawboned, tough as nails, calloused knuckles. He had fought before. He liked it. Pain was a familiar way of life. The angry and frightened girl grabbed his arm. She nodded toward Bill Shuford, bloodied but still standing, and said, "This guy's all right. Don't bother him any more."

The men smirked. But they backed away.

"The ringleader of the posse was a man named Rocky Spacek," Shuford said. "He quit fighting long enough to go to work for us and stayed for twenty-five years." Shuford shrugged and said, "That's the way it was in the oilfield. If a man showed up, somebody wanted to find out how tough he was. You learned to fight. You might not win, but that didn't matter. You just never backed down. Men in the oil patch wanted to know that, when it got rough, you wouldn't quit on them."

●

Pat Holloway had left the neon lights of Dallas far behind in his rearview mirror and was on his way back to Giddings. A long week in his law office was about all that a sane man could take. He was running late on a Friday afternoon, and the sun was casting its last dim glow across the brittle croplands. The road cutting into Lee County was flat, straight, and he was running wide open. Pat Holloway was always running wide open.

Jimmy Luecke was waiting on him. But, damn, Jimmy Luecke was always waiting on him, parked in the darkness alongside Highway 77 just north of the Lee County line. He had known Holloway would be coming when he pulled his highway patrol car over next to the barrow ditch. It was dark. It was Friday. Holloway would be driving fast and belly low to the ground. Sure enough, he recognized the car by the time it topped a gentle rise coming out of Rockdale. He grinned, calmly reached over, and flashed his lights.

Sheriff Joe Goodson might have been the law in Lee County. Jimmy Luecke owned the rights to the highways. He was ruthless, every move was well calculated, and some doubted if he had a conscience. Luecke never listened to or paid much attention to sob stories. Being down on his luck did not give a man the right to drive fast, haul stolen merchandise, drink bad whiskey, or be in hurry to get from some honky tonk woman's bed to his own.

Luecke believed that any man breaking the law behind the wheel of a car was guilty until proven guilty. Innocence was never part of the equation. Drive long enough around Giddings, old-timers said, and sooner or later you'd get acquainted with Mister Luecke. A few cars even dared to sport a bumper sticker that said: *Will Rogers Never Met Jimmy Luecke*, and Will Rogers claimed he had never met a man he didn't like.

Pat Holloway moved over to the shoulder and eased to a stop in front of the patrol car. He could see Luecke's broad shadow in the moonlight as the highway patrolman swaggered purposely toward him. Holloway rolled down his window. Luecke's shadow blotted out the moonlight. "You were driving eighty," the patrolman said.

"I'm drilling a well down here," Holloway explained as politely as if he was addressing a judge, "and I was in a hurry to get to the rig."

Silence.

Then Luecke asked, "You're Mister Holloway, aren't you?"

"Yes, sir."

"It looks like I'm gonna have to haul your ass to jail."

Holloway stared at him incredulously. He searched for the right words of protest but couldn't find them for fear of making the patrolman even angrier than he already was.

More silence.

Luecke spoke again. The silence shattered like ice crystals. "I might let you go," the patrolman said, "if you let me buy you a cup of coffee down at Schubert's."

Holloway grinned. That, he knew, was probably as good a deal as any driver had ever been given by the cantankerous Jimmy Luecke.

The patrolman eased back out onto Highway 77, and Holloway followed him to the café. The dark road, for a Friday night, was virtually empty.

It was not their first introduction. Weeks earlier, Holloway had gone with his landman to meet the highway patrolman while Bennie Jaehne was trying to track down good leases near the old Luecke home place. Both men were well aware of each other's reputation. The oilman and the lawmen. One reigned over the oilfield. The other ruled the highway. One was always looking for good land. The other had it wrapped up in his family's name.

Jimmy Luecke ordered a cup of black coffee at Schubert's, leaned heavily on the table with his elbows, and said, "Mister Holloway, the reason I stopped you for speeding is because you speed every time you come down here. I've been watching you. And I'd like for you to slow down. No use dying on the highway. Speed can do that to a man."

Holloway nodded.

Luecke took a sip, waited while the coffee warmed his throat, then said softly and confidentially, "But what I really want to do is make you a deal."

Holloway waited.

"Tell you what," Luecke said, "I won't throw you in jail or even give you a ticket if you agree to lease my parents' land for an oil well."

Holloway was an old pro at making snap judgments. "I'll lease your parents' land," he said, "if you help me lease all of the land your neighbors own."

Luecke nodded. "Then I guess I'm in the oil business," he said.

"You deal with Benny Jaehne," Holloway said. "He's my landman. And when he brings me back all of those leases, I'll drill you a well."

Luecke nodded, stood up, and strode briskly out of Schubert's. The patrolman had promised to buy the coffee. He didn't pay for it. He left Pat Holloway holding the check for fifty cents. Holloway didn't mind. From what he had learned from Ray Holifield, Jimmy Luecke's acreage possessed the only Wilcox field in the Giddings play. The Wilcox formation was shallow sandstone and packed full of oil. It would make Jimmie Luecke a wealthy man. It would make Pat Holloway even wealthier. But as he always said, a man isn't really rich if he can still count his money.

●

Danny Anderson, in 1976, had been laboring for Otis Engineering in the Austin Chalk that formed the precarious foundation for Pearsall and Dilly. He was delivering some equipment to Ted Ferguson, a completion specialist and company man for Windsor Energy, when he glanced for the first time at a new oilfield unfolding in the gaunt shadows of Giddings.

If Max Williams and Irv Deal had not been drilling a test on the M&K well, Giddings would have been just another country town that existed solely for Friday night football, the crowning of a homecoming queen, cold beer, hot barbecue ribs, and the annual parade of John Deere tractors in the peanut festival. The only thing going on after dark was the red light changing colors above the intersection of Highways 290 and 77.

During the next few years, Danny Anderson watched Pearsall fall into a minor state of depression.

The capture of oil in the chalk was facing a serious downturn, the boom was grinding inexorably to a stop, and the lights were going out in Pearsall.

Danny Anderson was wondering what he should do next when the telephone call came. It was Ted Ferguson offering him a job at Windsor/U.S. "It's more money than Otis is paying you," Ferguson said.

"How about the hours?"

"Fewer hours than what you're used to," Ferguson promised. "Why, you'll be able to drive back home every evening."

It was definitely an appealing offer. Danny Anderson had a new wife but no personal life at all. He was working as many as a hundred and twenty hours a week for Otis Engineering.

The hours were killing him.

His boss at Otis only laughed when Anderson turned in his resignation "You shouldn't waste your time in Giddings," he said.

"Why not?"

"It'll be just like the Pearsall boom," his boss said. "It'll be over in a year, maybe two, and you'll be out of a job."

"It's already been going on for more than a year and half."

His boss shook his head. "It'll be ready to quit by the time you get there."

Danny Anderson prepared to drive to Giddings early Monday morning.

"You need to pack some clothes?" his wife asked.

"No need to pack," Anderson replied. "I'll see you this evening. Probably before the sun goes down."

His wife did not see Danny Anderson again until the next Friday night. Work in the oil patch was unpredictable at best. Sometimes, a man had to fight a well all night. No. A man almost always had to fight a well all night. Oil did not keep a timepiece.

Danny Anderson climbed up on the rig platform and did not climb down for five days and four nights. Ted Ferguson had told him he could have his life back.

Ted Ferguson might have lied.

29

*C*layton Williams had been in no hurry to tackle the Austin Chalk. He arrived late and, on those days when the unpredictable play threatened to dismantle his operation and his sanity, feared he might be too late. Williams did not particularly doubt or distrust the chalk. He was simply stretched too thin. His oil and gas exploration business was already committed to too many fields covering too many miles and far too much terrain. Clayton Williams had made and lost a few fortunes in cattle and oil, and he was, without question, the most widely known and respected oilman of any stature to make his way to Giddings. His presence legitimized the field. He would be the talk of the town, and he liked it that way.

Max Williams, Irv Deal, and Pat Holloway were considered novices who struck oil simply because they ignored the so-called petroleum experts who predicted that the chalk would take their money and leave them high and dry, particularly dry. They did not care if the field was regarded as legitimate or not. They were only interested in making money, and they were making a lot of it. A boom was trailing along in their footsteps.

Clayton Williams, who preferred to be called Claytie, was different. He was not a big or imposing man, but he possessed a larger than life personality. Those who made the mistake of underestimating him paid dearly. He was a barroom brawling, hard-drinking, plain-cussing wildcatter at heart whose oil patch gambles usually kept him in limbo and dangling somewhere between bank loans, banked riches, and bankruptcy. He liked the risk and did not mind the wild, precarious ride on a financial roller coaster.

When it was all over, and not until it was over, would he look back and decide if he had won or lost.

Clayton Williams once said, "I ran my company like Christopher Columbus. When he left Spain, he did not know where he was going. When he got here, he did not know where he was. When he got back, he did not know where he had been. And he did it all on borrowed money. "

Clayton Williams first heard about the Austin Chalk play in Central Texas from Bill Haverlah, an old friend, a former employee, a top-notch landman who had traded a life in the oil patch for a ranch down in South Texas. "The play's been around for years," Haverlah told him. "I don't know whether you want in on it or not. It covers a lot of land, but it's never been very economical."

"Are the leases expensive?" Claytie wanted to know.

"Not in the chalk."

"I might be interested in the play if you'll go back to work for me," Claytie said. "I've done a little research on the potential of the chalk. I like it. But it's an unknown field, and you're a damn good landman. I'd feel a helluva lot better if you were down there with me."

"I won't go back to work for a salary," Haverlah said adamantly. "I'm not gonna be a hired hand and your personal servant. I'll work for you, but I want a commission and an override on everything I do."

"That's tough."

"That's the way it is." Haverlah was spitting out his words. "There's no way I can work for you, Claytie. You're too damn hardheaded. I'm hardheaded, too. I've had one round of that, and that's enough."

Clayton Williams smiled. He knew without a doubt he would see Bill Haverlah in Giddings.

●

During the mid-1970s, Clayton Williams, without any fanfare, tested his luck in the Giddings field and came up disappointed. He drilled five wells. Four of them were classified as non-commercial. The chalk had not beaten him.

The chalk had merely defied him, and Claytie drove quietly out of town and headed back to West Texas, where his fields in Ward County were as strong and productive as they had ever been. He silently cursed himself for straying so far from the rich oil and gas production in the Permian Basin and falling, even temporarily, under the God forsaken spell of the Austin Chalk.

As far as he was concerned, the potential of Giddings looked so bleak that he made an all-out effort to sell the leases on those two hundred and twenty thousand acres he and Bill Haverlah had acquired in the Austin Chalk trend. The price of oil in 1978 had withered away to only seven dollars a barrel. The game had become harder to win.

Claytie drove to Houston to meet with an oil company that was still stricken with the promise of the chalk. He was determined to ask for twenty dollars an acre. Fair price, he thought. Make a little profit. After all, he had originally leased the land for a dollar an acre. He might negotiate but not much. Claytie was ready to forget Giddings, go on back home, and stay in the fields where he belonged. Clayton Williams had it all figured out.

He waited in the lobby, his eyes impatiently watching the clock. The appointed time for his meeting with the company president arrived, then passed, and the doors did not open. Ten minutes slipped away. Twenty minutes came and went. Clayton Williams had never been a patient man, and he was losing the little scrap of patience he had.

The clock ticked off another ten minutes. Claytie sighed wearily and stood up. He was a damn good horse trader himself, and he realized immediately what was happening behind closed doors. The oil company president had his strategy all mapped out, Wait Clayton out. Make him sweat. Keep him anxious. Steal his land. Well, he was damn wrong. Clayton Williams was not that desperate. He walked out and never saw a soul.

He and the oil company president both stayed grumpy for a long time. Claytie said, "We needed each other, could have used each other, and let a couple of damned old hard heads get in the way. He was bound and determined to outsmart me. I wanted to outsmart him. We outsmarted ourselves."

Time would prove, he said, that circumstances, once again, had protected him from his own ignorance. He was still in Giddings whether he wanted to be or not.

●

Clayton Williams was born in the cowboy country of Fort Stockton, Texas. He was at home in the great outdoors and, while growing up, never figured that life would take him much farther than the next cattle herd. He dutifully studied agriculture at Texas A&M University, but his father sold the family farm and ranch, which left Claytie on the road and without a job.

He had always planned to run the operation someday, but fate turned him toward another direction. He toyed with the idea of becoming a lawyer and was even accepted by The University of Texas Law School.

But, hell, that was the wrong school and, if nothing else, Claytie had learned in the holy, sanctified hallways of Aggieland to detest – no, hate – the dreaded University of Texas. The military came calling, which was just as well. As he said, "If I'd gone to law school, I'd be just another damn lawyer."

The life insurance business seemed like a fairly lucrative job alternative when his military discharge became final, and Clayton Williams was convinced that it provided the best training he could find. "Imagine," he said, "if you can talk some old boy into taking his beer money, and instead of drinking beer, buy a life insurance premium so when he dies his wife can live happily ever after with another man using his insurance money to buy beer. That's selling."

Claytie did quite well selling insurance to friends until a few months later when he ran out of friends.

He tried to buy a farm and wound up in the oil and gas business with the man who had been trying to sell the farm, Johnny May. They became lease brokers and promoted a few wells, struggling through two years when bad luck far outweighed the good. They did, however, manage to build a small pipeline to carry natural gas to farmers from a well in Pecos County and named the little enterprise Clajon Gas. It was destined to one day become the largest independently owned gas company in Texas.

Claytie and May drilled a dry hole, but with desperation and determination, held on to a one-sixteenth interest in a well that hit fairly big not far from Fort Stockton. Clayton Williams thought he was rich. Big oil. Big strike. He opened his first check. It was for thirty-five dollars. It was enough to make a man seriously consider going back into the life insurance business. Oil, he thought, might not be what it was cracked up to be.

It all changed when the Merrick No. 1 came thundering in with fifty barrels an hour. Claytie and May owned half interest, and the success of the well established their credibility and their reputation throughout the Permian Basin. Once and forever more, Clayton Williams was an oilman to be reckoned with.

He learned quickly that oil could kill men as easily and ruthlessly as it could make them rich. His Sibley No. 1 turned out to be a major discovery in the Coyanosa field, but the deep well was having major pressure control problems. At ten thousand, five hundred feet, it was churning and rumbling and threatening to blow. Fifteen minutes after Claytie departed the rig's platform, the casing collapsed and ignited. A huge explosion shook and rattled the ground. A ball of flame shot across the landscape. Five men died, two of them cremated. A hundred or more cotton pickers in surrounding fields were burned, many of them severely. Clayton Williams himself had come within fifteen minutes of dying on the parched Coyanosa field. A man, he knew, could be careful, and still it might not do him any good.

Clayton Williams drilled for oil the way he lived, hard and reckless. He was a wheeler-dealer in every sense of the word, building a company cemented on the risky proposition of OPM: Other People's Money. *The Associated Press* once described him *as cunning as a coyote and often as wily. He rose from a ten thousand-dollar-a-year insurance peddler to oil millionaire in a life punctuated with good luck, bad luck, hard work, cold beer, and the competitive, indomitable spirit of a pit bulldog.* For Claytie, it was a rambunctious, wind-in-your face, gun-to-your head ride.

He once came storming into the office of Bernie Scott, a long time employee at Clayton Williams Energy Company, and he was mad as hell. He severely reprimanded Scott for having the audacity to turn down an offer to join in the development of an oil well. The well was good. Claytie was on the outside looking in, and he did not like it.

"Why the hell did you reject the offer?" he demanded to know.

"Because that's what you told me to do," Scott said.

"You should have known better than to listen to me," Claytie snapped as he turned and brusquely left the office.

●

On many nights, Claytie had gone to sleep, believing he would be broke when the sun rose again. As he swore, in the oil business, it's usually ninety percent boredom, five percent unbridled excitement, and five percent fear. Panic. Or depression. He knew them well. They had been constant companions. But as a typical Aggie, Claytie said, "I always tried to drill my way out of trouble." He kept believing that the next new well would pay off the last old debt. Drill. Hit one. Miss one. Drill again. As long as he kept a hole in the ground, there was hope.

"Between 1977 and 1979," Clayton Williams said, "we were in the twilight zone in Giddings. Knew it was there. Had tried my luck. Came up empty. Thought about going back. Wasn't sure it was the wisest move. But the play kept looking better and better. Those old boys in Giddings were making it look easy. I decided to try it again."

The price of oil suddenly began to turn in the oilman's favor during early 1979. The nation was facing a shortage of petroleum as Iran became embroiled in revolution while facing open hostilities with neighboring Iraq. The countries had two of the largest oil reserves in the world, and now they were more interested in killing each other than keeping their pipelines open and their oil supply flowing to the West. Oilmen struggling to make ends meet on seven dollars a barrel, watched the price of oil inch its way up to twenty dollars a barrel, then sharply rise beyond all expectations, reaching forty dollars a barrel. Wells roundly cursed in the chalk for only producing five to ten barrels a day were suddenly viewed as money makers. What's more, the Natural Gas Policy Act, less than six months old, gave the price of newly produced gas a significant boost. The door was flung wide open for the Giddings oil and gas play.

It was madness in Giddings. The illustrious Clayton Williams was in town, and he wanted everyone to know it even if he had to face challenges of Biblical proportions. This time, he did not slip in or have any plans for slipping out. With oil selling for forty dollars a barrel, he couldn't miss. Even a bad well wasn't all that bad.

He threw a big barbecue for the city of Giddings to announce his arrival, wiped the sauce off his face, and went to work. Clayton Williams, however, did not immediately drill and would not drill for another year. There was a time when he may have been a go-for-broke wildcatter, and he still possessed the tenacity, the spirit, and the audacity of a wildcatter. But since those early wind-blown days in the Permian Basin, he had become a businessman. Claytie was content to let the get-rich schemers and operators string their pipe in the chalk while he firmly established his company and his presence on the ground in Giddings.

No longer would he hit town flying by the seat of his pants. Those times were past. He built a ten-thousand-square-foot office complex east of downtown, complete with a yard to hold equipment and pipe, a workshop, and a helicopter pad. He made a decision early that he would not commence operations in Giddings unless and until his people had a place to live. "My friends were my employees, and my employees were family, and I liked it like that," he said. "I was determined that none of us would ever have to operate out of a syrup bucket."

To provide his employees with a home during those scant and varied hours when they weren't stationed on a rig, Claytie created a trailer-house town, placed it on the back end of his forty-two-acre company complex, and called the eighty-five trailers, with a certain amount of pride, *Williamsville*.

His decision to wait instead of drill, however, cost him to miss at least two years worth of good prices. He would never recoup lost earnings. He never looked back. It was not, he said, his first rodeo in the oil patch.

Williams was flush with bank credit that rose proportionately with the value of his oil and gas reserves. He still owned leases on those two hundred and twenty thousand acres that fate had kept him from selling to a Houston oil company.

He was finding oil long before most of the operators in the chalk had ever bothered to read any oil and gas journals. So many of them were new to the oil business. He was an old hand. He had been tested and tempered with experience.

Clayton Williams was at last ready for Giddings. Was Giddings ready for him?

An oilfield hand walked up to Claytie on a downtown Giddings street and asked him, "Are you gonna use Ray Holifield to find your prospects for you?"

"No," Claytie replied, "I have my own geologists."

"Have they been in the chalk before?"

"They have."

"Drill anything?"

"Five wells."

"How many dry holes?"

"Four."

The field hand shook his head. "Without Ray Holifield, "he said, "it's gonna be a long, hard ride."

30

*T*he second coming of Clayton Williams may have legitimized the scope of the Giddings field, but it was the *New York Times* that legitimized the impact of the boom. How in the world did the famous *New York Times* find Giddings, Texas? That's what everyone in town wanted to know. Sure, the home folks had witnessed a bunch of odd and wayward outsiders drilling across an untold number of acres, a lot of oil was flowing, and the pastures flickered with an unholy light of gas flares at night. But they doubted seriously if anyone north of Dallas and certainly no one east of Houston had heard about a little old boom in their little old town. Giddings had suddenly become front-page news on the fashionable streets of Fifth and Madison Avenues. Who would have ever guessed it?

William Stevens wrote in the bastion of American journalism: *What has been going on lately in Giddings is a throwback to the early glory decades of the oil era: Muddy boots, black gold, and greenbacks are everywhere. Roughnecks have been cutting loose in the bars at night and paying their way out of jail in the morning. Newcomers have been sleeping in the park, in cars, wherever they can. Instant millionaires have watched their royalties roll in.*

Texas has not seen anything quite like it in years, and it has the folks of this formerly tranquil little farming community, on the fringe of the oak and cedar-clad Hill Country, shaking their heads. It is all because of the Austin Chalk, a limestone formation eight thousand to ten thousand feet deep, stretching in a great, diagonal underground slash across Texas from the Mexican border almost to Louisiana. Parts of the chalk are full of innumerable little pockets of oil, much of it so clean, so sulfur-free and golden that it looks like honey, or twenty-weight oil. It is premium stuff, and experts say a billion barrels of it – some say five billion – is ready for recovery. By comparison, the Alaskan Slope's estimated yield is nine billion barrels.

According to City Manager Larry Pippen, the sudden and unexpected growth of Giddings had been unreal. "The town's population had more than doubled to an estimated fifty-one hundred in the past two years," he said, "and we're afraid it's going to explode in our face" The bucolic, small-town atmosphere that Giddings residents once prized had been swallowed up in a pit of fresh oil. No forests of derricks rose above the streets. Signs of the boom were subtle. No one announced that it was coming. No one announced it had arrived. It just happened much like time itself. Darkness. Then a faint hint of daylight. In an instant. No one was quite sure when one had replaced the other.

Each day at noon, Dub Dixon opened the buffet line at Schubert's, dishing up three vegetables and one selection of meat for two dollars and seventy-five cents, plus tax. At the City Meat Market, not much more than a hole in the wall flavored with barbecue smoke, Hershel and Lillian Doyle were piling ribs, brisket, pork, pork chops, chicken, and sausages on brown butcher paper. No plates. Just plain old brown butcher paper. No menu. A man had no idea what a meal would cost him. He simply took as much meat as the cook stacked up, had it weighed, and paid so much an ounce or a pound. The saying was: *If you could afford what you ordered yesterday, you can probably order it again today.*

The floor of the City Meat Market remained thick with oil men and oil operators who generally came in with their lawyers or landmen, spreading documents or land maps on the table tops and cross cutting deals that might make them or break them there amidst the sauce. *The hard-bitten men of the oil patch slouch, swagger, and stomp in, baseball caps on many heads and beards on many faces. The dried mud on their boots leaving no doubt about where they work.* That was what the *New York Times* said.

Some families came in day after day without a dime or the hope for a nickel to their name. It didn't matter. Herschel and Lillian Doyle kept them fed. It was no sin to be poor, Lillian Doyle said. Every one had been. At least everyone in Lee County they knew had been. It was a sin to let somebody go hungry.

●

Lee had been classified by those who delved into such statistics as one of the poorest counties in Texas. But suddenly, bank deposits in Giddings were growing by a million dollars a month, and the cost of living, especially for those men hunting jobs as diligently as the explorationists were hunting oil, was surging out of sight. Before the boom, a meal costs less than three dollars at the best restaurant in town. Now menus were changing. The same meal was touted for five dollars and sometimes six dollars, depending on the night of the week and the size of the crowd outside. Groceries went up, and so did gas, caps, flannel shirts, and denim jeans. One retailer was embarrassed to admit, "The only things I have to watch my prices on are beer and cigarettes. The oil people don't know what anything else is supposed to cost."

From her perch behind the teller's cage of the bank, Diane Zoch witnessed the dramatic changes that oil had on Giddings and on the multitudes who believed the lies and the promise that oil told them. She said, "When the rumors of a boom finally erupted into the reality of a boom, people from all over the United States descended on Giddings. One week, I knew everybody in town. The next week, I hardly recognized anybody on the streets. When the bank opened in the morning, a crowd was already waiting out on the sidewalk. The lines were long at every teller's window. An unbelievable amount of cash was going in and out every day. Supervisors came in on Fridays and cashed checks for their hired hands out on the rigs. The men didn't have time to take off work. Couldn't do their banking themselves. I saw a lot of my friends quit the bank and start looking for jobs in the oilfield. My father kept telling me not to follow them. He said, 'Keep your job at the bank, Diane. The bank's gonna be here when the oilfield is dead again.'"

Oil was a blessing. It was a curse. One worker came in every Friday and cashed a check for twelve hundred dollars, Diane Zoch said. By the next Thursday, he was back in the bank trying to borrow twenty dollars until he got paid again. People living in shacks became rich overnight. It was not really unusual at all for an African American sharecropper to come in wanting to cash a royalty check for a hundred dollars, then be told it was actually worth a hundred thousand dollars. Never had a bank account. Lived out of his pockets. Had no idea what to do with a hundred thousand dollars. Had no idea where to spend it. He probably went home and stuck it under his mattress. Slept good for a long time. Bill collectors didn't knock on his door anymore.

"One of the first wells around here was drilled on a poor family's farm," Diane Zoch remembered. "The folks suddenly had money. Lord, they had never seen that much money in one place. But the lady of the house was diagnosed with cancer. She had no insurance. Oil may not have saved her life. But it saved her from suffering. My father invested in a few wells and earned so much money one year that he had to pay eighty-nine thousand dollars in taxes. If he had invested his money, we would have all been rich. He didn't. He gave it all away. Said money had never made him happy. Using his money to make other people happy did."

●

As the *New York Times* pointed out: *Everywhere there is money, though the town's undoubted multimillionaires tend to keep quiet about it. Bank deposits have grown from thirty million to a hundred million dollars in two years. You don't see bankers walking around here with frowns on their faces.*

Emmett Hannes had gone to work at First National Bank as a cashier, and by the time the boom thundered across the Giddings landscape, he was occupying the office of the president. "It seemed like every person walking into the bank wanted to borrow money to go into the oil business," he said. "Most of them had absolutely no security or collateral. They were betting that they could find an oil well and wanted the bank to bet with them."

Hannes sat down with one potential oil operator and said, "I've checked with the banks you've done business with in the past."

The man nodded, totally unconcerned.

"Frankly," Hannes said, "you still owe them a lot of money."

"I know," said the man. "That's why I need the loan."

"What do you mean?"

"I want the money to pay off my old loan so I'll have good credit." The operator sat back, shrugged, and said confidentially, "If my credit is good in Giddings, you'll be able to loan me enough money to make a well."

On some, especially those who had farmed the land for years, Emmett Hannes took a chance. He had been in the banking business a long time. "After awhile," he said, "you could read men and knew who was good for a loan and who wasn't."

He let them sign their names and borrow good money, and he said, "I held my breath."

Emmett Hannes had seen the maps of the Austin Chalk and realized that his land probably wasn't anywhere close to the heart of the field. It lay off to one side, a little too far off to one side. Still, he said, he got excited when a operator leased his five hundred acres near Dime Box. The driller said he had looked down into a cesspool and spotted a little oil floating on top of the water. He liked his chances. He drilled. He trudged back into the bank and told Hannes, "I've never seen anything like it."

"You hit a good one?"

"I do believe it's the driest hole I've ever drilled."

At the bank, Emmett Hannes kept everyone else's oil money. None of it belonged to him.

●

Oilfield workers were finding their families shelter wherever they could, sleeping in cars, in parks, in condemned houses, even in oil tanks that Dub Dixon turned sideways, welded together into individual sleeping units, and rented for twenty-four dollars night, including meals at Schubert's. New housing was being leased before it could be built, and no one even bothered to inquire about those smoke-filled rooms, mostly in disarray, at the town's four motels. They were rented by the day, the week, the hour, either day or night, and were lit by the neon of *No Vacancy* signs.

The pages of the *Giddings News & Times* advertised for experienced gang pushers, roustabout crews, backhoe operators, truck drivers, lease records clerks, dirt movers, and oilfield supply salesmen. If a man had ever seen an oil well or heard rumors that oil was pumped from the ground, he had a job in town waiting for him. No questions asked. Show up. Show up on time. Stay late. Stay often. Don't drink hard liquor unless you can work with a hangover. Kiss your wife goodbye and send her pictures so she won't forget you. Those were the only qualifications a man needed to work the oil patch. He could use his own or somebody else's name. He was allowed to give his home address or invent one. It didn't matter. Giddings was overrun with three kinds of strangers: those looking for a job, those working, and those being run off a rig. Yet the field was still drilling more wells than it had people in town to man the rigs.

Attorney Mike Simmang recalled one man who owned a liquor store not far from downtown Giddings. The gentleman sold a little whiskey and a lot of beer. But he earned most of his money cashing payroll checks. Like any good man in the oilfield, he charged an override of one percent.

On Friday morning, he would venture over to the bank and borrow two hundred thousand dollars in cash money. No collateral was needed. His word was good enough. On Friday afternoon, the workers received their checks and headed to the liquor store. Some were here today, gone tomorrow drifters, wandering from job to job, from town to town and never staying anyplace long enough to darken the interior of a genuine financial institution. They preferred to do their banking in a liquor store.

On Monday morning, the man stopped by the bank on his way to work. He paid off the two hundred thousand dollar loan and added another two thousand dollars to his own personal account. He was earning more than a hundred thousand dollars a year and had never drilled a hole in the ground nor needed to. Even so, oil was making him rich, and wealth could make even a liquor store owner respectable in a Sunday morning church pew.

A lot of weekend paychecks were cashed at the drive-through window of a convenience store. One afternoon, a car pulled up, and the owner looked down to see a shotgun pointed at him. "Hand me the money," came the demand.

The owner went for his pistol.

The shotgun fired. Nervous fingers could be deadly fingers when attached to the trigger of a shotgun. The blast blew away most of the window. It took a chunk out of the store owner's shoulder. Within days, he had patched his window, his shoulder, and was back at work. There were checks to be cashed. And most of them were stained with oil.

The Houston Chronicle wrote: *Wildcatters have honed in on the scent of easy oil and quick money. New folks – strangers and oil people – are milking the earth for its precious but once ignored slugs of oil and natural gas. Prices have skyrocketed. Land is leased up and has tripled, even quadrupled, in value. Giddings is swarming with new pickup trucks, and the floors of every bar and café and bank are covered with dried red mud toted into town on the roughnecks' steel-toed boots. It's probably the most excitement this town has seen since 1878 when special trains brought folks from Houston for the hanging of Bill Longley.*

●

Tank trucks created traffic jams on Highways 290 and 77. Some were carrying acid used to frac a well and break the oil loose. Others were hauling oil to the refineries. The beds of flatbed trailers were stacked with pipe. And expensive sedans carried CB antennas, oil company logos tagged their doors, and mud caked their underbellies. The trucks roared past, going one way or the other, for twenty-four hours a day, and almost fifteen thousand vehicles circulated through Giddings between sunup and sundown.

Traffic may have been inconvenient downtown. Those outlying farm and county roads, particularly FM 141 winding north to Dime Box, were deadly. Headlights from trucks and cars glared wearily down narrow stretches of rutted pavement all hours of the day and night.

Sleepy drivers. Drunk drivers. Drivers in a hurry. Drivers going home. Drivers never getting there. Within eighteen months, FM 141 would witness thirty-five accidents and three fatalities. Those who tackled the twenty-mile ribbon of nightmares, lined with gas flares and oil wells, began calling the twisted and twisting roadway *Death Alley.*

●

The Houston Chronicle reported: *Old people who used to lollygag in the middle of the main street now have to hasten across so as not to be flattened by the stream of huge trucks ... All of the highways are lined with new metal buildings and temporary trailer offices of drilling contractors and their supporting service companies. Many long-time citizens have jumped ship from their traditional low-paying jobs to work for the oil companies. The boom owes its life to a geological stratum, the Austin Chalk. The chalk was badmouthed for years, light with its oil and gas, and about as much of a sure thing as a long marriage to Zsa Zsa Gabor.*

For Giddings, an uneasy labor situation was growing more desperate by the day, and City Manager Larry Pippen realized that he was facing a dilemma that could easily and quickly escalate into a full-blown crisis. Jobs in the oilfield were paying eight dollars and fifty cents an hour. City workers were earning just a few cents above minimum wage. Pippen had to squeeze his meager budget dry in order to give his sanitation employees a raise to five dollars and fifty cents an hour just to keep them from walking out and going to work on an oil rig, doing God only knows what but earning good enough wages to eat good meals at Schubert's instead of sitting on their running board by the side of to the road and opening another Vienna sausage can. A town with garbage on and in its streets was earmarked for condemnation.

Chamber of Commerce Manager John J. Socha could be as passionate about the potential of the boom as he was about the promise of salvation in the pulpit of his Trinity Lutheran Church in old Dime Box. He liked to mention that the Austin Chalk, as difficult to understand as the prophecy of Ezekiel, possessed at least four thousand million barrels of recoverable oil that were up for grabs. "This was not wildcatting talk," he said. "What we get are reliable figures from petroleum engineering reports. With fifty-two potential drilling sites, at a rate of two thousand wells per year, they could be drilling here for the next twenty-six years."

This was a prophecy that made sense to him.

Randy Stewart moved down from Dallas. At the moment, he still represented Windsor Energy, but in time, he would establish his own oil company. He now looked out on Giddings from the window of his newly opened law office. He said, "We didn't have any Cadillac or Lincoln dealerships in town before the boom. We didn't have any Cadillac or Lincoln dealerships in town after the boom.

"They would have starved no matter how much oil we pulled from the ground. The folks around here drove Fords and Chevrolets and mostly pickup trucks. However, we did know who the overnight oilfield millionaires were. They were the ones paying cash and buying new John Deere tractors, usually two to a farm."

Of course, the Knox twins, John and Robert, were driving Lincoln Continentals, but they had to leave Giddings to buy them. They were definitely society members of the new rich, the new guard, the new money in town, and they wanted all of Giddings to realize just how much those wrinkled old land maps and survey abstracts had been worth. They may not have inherited the earth, but with a few up front deals, back room deals, side deals, and sweetheart deals, they had inherited their share of wealth from the oil beneath it. For the Knox brothers, the boom was not unlike a stiff game of poker. They may not have held all of the cards, but they did hold the maps.

Early on, they had the opportunity to lease land for a dollar an acre to operators making their way into town. Instead, the brothers opted for a one-thirty-second override for wells found on the acreage they leased. The override could have easily been worth nothing, and they would have been left to lament their failure to earn at least a few dollars for their trouble. Fortunately, the overrides made them millionaires, and not once did they have to invest their own money or sweat out the potential failure of an old chalk well. Play the oil game of Giddings their way, or an oilman had a hard time playing at all. The Knox brothers took a fistful of dollars from a boatload of operators. Small percentages did add up. They could not have done much better with holes in the ground.

Mayor Robert Placke had seen his welding and blacksmith shop dramatically increase its business with the boom, but he understood the inherent dangers of a town that had more strangers than home-bred farmers and ranchers walking its streets. "Before the discovery of oil," he said, "you never had to lock your car or your house. Other than the one we used to turn on the ignition of our car, we didn't know what a key was. We trusted everybody. We felt safe sleeping with our windows up at night. Now everybody was after our land or our money, and a lot of them didn't care how they got it. They just took it." Mayor Placke gazed down sidewalks no longer empty and sadly shook his head. "I guess the prosperity outweighs the grief," he said. Still, he wasn't entirely convinced.

●

Leonard and Margaret Kriegel owned a clothing store for men and women when the exploration for oil was a distant memory of the thirties and an unsubstantiated rumor of the seventies. They had bought Heck's Clothing Store on faith, knowing full well that the tight-fisted German farmers of Lee County only purchased one suit during a lifetime, no matter how long or short it might be. They were commonly buried in the same suit they wore on their wedding day. If it didn't fit, who gave a damn? Hard to tell in a casket.

After oil began to paint the town the color of new money, the Kriegels were not nearly as trusting as they had once been. Business became an open conflict between the good, the bad, the bold, and the worse. The boom brought all sorts of people to Giddings, and most had no plans or any reason to stay longer than their last paycheck. "A lot of them were wonderful," Margaret Kriegel said, "and some of them were plain scoundrels. In those days, we sold on credit. When I expected them to pay their bill at the end of the month, it was like trying to pry blood from a turnip."

As far away as Germany, *the Stuttgartner Zeitung* was reporting: *The oil bosses from Houston and Dallas came in hordes to get a slice of the cake. There were geologists and lawyers, as well as knights of fortune and prostitutes. Giddings had thirteen churches but only four small motels, and these were not able to handle the onslaught.*

The rigidly virtuous citizenry, its backbone reinforced by the German-Lutheran faith, did not permit itself to be corrupted. The police force expanded from four to ten, saw to it that the questionable fun of the questionable characters was spoiled. Only those interested in serious work were tolerated. What is precisely the thorny question for Giddings is whether the temptations to fall prey to the seductions of the new wealth will, perhaps sooner or later, become unavoidable.

Back when the sidewalks rolled up early, prayer meetings were the last things in town to die down at night, and Grand Juries had far less to do, police had been called on to break up maybe two fights a year. With roughnecks and roustabouts swarming the easy come, easy go places in town and elbowing their way into the saloons scattered randomly across the county, lawmen found themselves in the middle of two fights a night, even on slow nights. It seemed as though every street corner in Giddings had a grocery store, and every grocery store served beer and whiskey in the back. Disorderly conduct was on the rise. Simple assaults were as commonplace as stringing pipe. Good times often meant hard time as soon as a judge was brought in to survey the damage.

●

Historically, booms – oil, gold, silver, and otherwise – became overnight hell holes for backroom gambling and houses of ill repute. Both were games of chance, and Sheriff Joe Goodson knew they were on their way long before they ever settled down on the wrong side of the tracks. Both sides were sometimes wrong. The sheriff kept his eyes open and his nightstick loaded. He never had to shoot anybody. He never needed to. One look in his eyes, and a man could sober up in a hurry or lose interest in any games he had come to play – illicit, banned, or felonious. Sheriff Goodson's eyes weren't lethal, but neither did they possess a lot of empathy. They always had a faint hint of amusement aimed at anyone foolish enough to defy them. Jail was inviting for a man down on his luck only when it had the last empty bed in town.

Off the beaten track, far out of town and out of sight, the sheriff discovered a couple of vice trailers trying to set up the only game in town never called on account of either darkness or rain. No red lights needed. Red lipstick worked just fine. Hostesses were dime-a-dance girls without any music and pretty enough if a man wasn't particular or hard to please. The trailers were too small for dancing, and, besides, dancing wasted too much time when no one was interested in pleasantries, small talk, or light conversation. They were, however, spacious enough to accommodate configurations of love by the hour, provided anyone had an hour's worth of time on his hands. Joe Goodson cracked down before the girls had time to get properly undressed, and the rolling whorehouses rolled out of Lee County before their engines had time to cool.

●

The major oil companies had not yet gathered up enough nerve or daring to come to Giddings, but a lot of their employees had found the road to town. Some resigned. Some just didn't show up one day. For so many of them, the sudden expansion of activity in oil exploration created immediate expectations of instant wealth. An ever-increasing number of them were gambling their security, their pension, and a regular paycheck for an outside chance to get rich quick with honey-colored oil.

When oil reached thirty-five dollars a barrel, said Kenneth Hooper with the Texas State Securities Board, "Everybody and his damn dog was out there getting into the oil business." A great number of them were descending in force on Giddings, arriving by airplane, freight train, and automobile. The streets and highways were thick with tractor trailers, Broncos, and pickup trucks. It did not matter how a man reached Giddings as long as the last oil well had not been drilled, and there were still jobs for the great unwashed. The field had become a haven for geologists and geophysicists, landmen and lease hounds, promoters and lawyers, tool pushers and completion men, pipeline crews and logging crews, mud crews and frac crews, acid crews and operators hoping against hope that they were not battling the tempestuous old chalk in vain.

The young, the inexperienced, the desperate hired on as roughnecks, and the job was as rough and demanding as it sounded. Most were in their twenties or early thirties, usually long-haired Anglos who intermingled with undocumented Mexicans. Language was no barrier. The oilfield had its own vernacular anyway. *Drill, dammit, drill* could only be translated so many ways, and all of them required a crew that knew when to pray, when to curse, and when a well was about to blow. A few who hit town had even been veterans of oilfields in Louisiana, Alaska, and the Rockies.

They knew what a boom was all about. Hell, they could drill a well in their sleep and half drunk. They had done it before. The chalk would bring them to their knees

A newcomer, ignorant of the ways of the hard-rock limestone formations, asked Ray Holifield what the chalk looked like so far beneath his feet.

"A concrete floor," he said.

"Where's the oil?"

Holifield took a brick, dropped it on the concrete floor and let it splinter into bits and pieces.

"The oil is where the chalk has shattered," he said.

31

Wherever there was a profit to be made or squandered, some promoter or scam artist could generally figure out a way to make it, and few worried about whether or not their scheme was illegal, immoral, or unethical. Nowhere did the fanatical lust for filthy lucre grip a man's soul like a boomtown oilfield. Investors could not wait to get in with money borrowed and sometimes stolen.

They would throw their family's last dollar down a hole and pray there was oil instead of chalk in the fractures. Said Mike Armstrong of the State Securities Board, "These promoters will tell investors they have hit twenty out of twenty-two wells, which they may have. But what they don't tell investors is that it will take them twenty years to recoup their money."

Some promoters sold interest in oil wells that did not exist. Some peddled drilling ventures even when there was absolutely no reasonable possibility of ever finding oil. A few never got around to sinking a hole or making a bona fide effort to even find a decent prospect to drill. They lived off of too many phony reports and the regret of dry holes.

One promoter proved that investors were so eager to be part of an oil boom that they didn't take time to read either the large or the small print of a prospectus. He listed *God Almighty* as a director of his oil exploration company. He wrote in the literature he used to seek investors:

If and when thou art ready, willing and able to invest large sums of cash money in the greatest, biggest, hottest, wildest, most exciting, and most profitable oil and gas boom anywhere on this earth up to the present time, the wisest and best move thou couldest possibly make, in pursuit of good investments, is a mailing of thy good checks for substantial amounts of cash money unto GOD & SON at the above address; without any further stalls, delays, excuses, questions, provisions, requirements, directions, or instructions, hanky panky, or any other sort of idiocy.

As strange as it seems, he raised money. God may have been on his board. He didn't use God as his geologist. He should have. God knew where oil lay beneath the ground. He didn't tell the promoter.

●

Danny Anderson had seen all kinds of characters in the oil patch. The good. The bad. Those passing through. Those who had nowhere else to go. Those who would cheat a slow man and kill a fast one for big money and sometimes take his last dollar and regret not being around to steal his first one.

He said, "People were throwing a lot of money at the Austin Chalk, and there were crooks standing on every street corner ready to take their money. The field was full of corruption. It was easy to make a dollar, easy to lose it, and easy to steal it."

A few dishonest landmen were told to offer property owners twenty-five percent royalty on oil produced from a lease. They would give the landowner twenty percent and keep the other five percent for themselves.

If a landman could speak German, he had a chance of talking a poor old farmer out of anything.

Those old farmers had possessed very little in their lives, and now they didn't even have an honest deal.

One promoter raised a million dollars on each of twenty wells, hid the money, declared bankruptcy, and walked away without paying any of his bills.

He had thousands of small-time nickel and dime investors scattered all over the country, and they simply thought they had the misfortune of putting their money in another dry hole. They never realized they had been swindled, and none of them thought it was worth the cost of hiring a lawyer to get back their five-hundred-dollar investment. A lawyer would charge them that much money to pick up the phone and talk to them.

The price of oil was spiking. More money was flowing from the Austin Chalk. Times were getting better. And more and more strangers were casting dubious shadows across the Giddings field.

Danny Anderson figured he might have a problem when he saw the truck pull off the main road and ease slowly down the ruts and in his direction.

He didn't recognize it, and he knew just about every vehicle being driven in Lee County. Who owned it, who drove it, and, even more importantly, what it was doing at one of his U.S. Operating rigs.

The man with an unfamiliar face stepped out and looked casually around. He was all smiles, which was always dangerous. "Who's the man in charge?" he asked.

"I guess that would be me," Anderson said, his tone clipped but polite.

"How many of these workover rigs do you have running?"

"Five."

"Who's your well service company?"

"Alcorn."

"I have a better deal for you."

"I like Alcorn."

"Well," the stranger said, handing Anderson a business card, "we're new to Giddings and trying to get our business jump-started." He was straight-forward, cock sure, and to the point. "We're looking for ways to introduce our services as quickly as possible to as many companies as we can."

Anderson didn't say a word, just watched him. A man's character was reflected in his eyes, not in his words. Anderson saw the eyes shift.

"Here's what we can do," the stranger said. "There will be a hundred dollars a day for you for every rig you call us to service. That's five hundred dollars a day. Not a bad little bonus." The stranger grinned.

Danny Anderson's eyes narrowed. He had seen scams before and certainly knew what this one was all about. The company's standard service call was probably no more than a hundred dollars. This one, however, was scheming to charge Max Williams two hundred dollars, then split the invoice fee with Anderson. The stranger probably knew that U.S. Operating had so many invoices coming in and payments going out that no one back in the office would ever know or suspect the difference.

"It's not right," Anderson said.

"What's a few hundred dollars a day to an oil operator?"

"Not as much as my good name."

Danny Anderson threw the stranger off the site.

"You don't understand," the man said as he wiped the dust off his face and stumbled back to his truck. "That's the way people do business in Giddings."

"Not here they don't," Anderson said.

If he had carried a gun, he might have shot the man. Danny Anderson grinned. Hell, he thought, in this desolate, God-forsaken country, no one would have ever known. He was a stranger. No one would miss him. The bottom of a dry hole would be a damn fine place to hide a body. Nobody ever went back to dry holes in the chalk. If the well couldn't be fracked, it was forgotten. A body buried was a body gone. Too much land. Too many holes. Too deep for the vultures to find. He doubted if he was the first one to ever think about it.

It got worse. Oilfield theft was reaching epidemic proportions as gangs and freelancers alike roared in under the cover of darkness and roared out with stolen trucks, tools, pipe, bits, oil, and even drilling mud. Sheriff Joe Goodson estimated that oil companies were losing several thousand dollars a month because of the illicit oilfield traffic. Operators were so busy pumping that honey-colored crude out of the ground that few ever took the time to worry about theft. They were making millions.

They were losing thousands. Frankly, it was not worth their trouble. A great number of the thefts were never reported, recorded, or investigated. Crooks ran rampant with no one around to slow or gun them down.

All across the Giddings field, more payments were made under the table than across the top of it. A trucker would come in to have his ticket signed and surreptitiously leave a hundred-dollar bill beneath the paperwork. A grin. A wink. He was gone.

Salesmen preyed on the oilfield, constantly searching for a man's weakness. They supplied alcohol to the thirsty, money to the greedy, and women to the deprived.

"It was nothing," Danny Anderson said, "for company men to show up at a rig early in the morning and have bottles of whiskey, shotguns, rifles, pistols, and sometimes boxes of old and wrinkled cash waiting for them."

Painted women knocked on their trailer doors at night, or found their motel rooms. No names exchanged, no money needed. Business was business. Secrets were kept as secrets. What a man said behind a closed door remained behind a closed door.

As Anderson said, "If anybody with any authority in the oil patch ever gave in to one of those high-dollar hustlers and proved he could be bought or was willing to take an illegal payment, here they all came on a dead run. Crooks ran in packs like wild dogs."

Wild dogs were more civilized.

●

Clayton Williams had no regard and little patience for anyone inside or outside his company who tried to cheat him or feloniously take his money. He hired good people, he gave them the responsibility and authority to do their jobs, and he did not want to lose time looking over somebody's shoulder to keep the man from drifting too far from the straight and narrow. He did not have the luxury of time.

He was constantly on the ground in Giddings, headed back to West Texas, in the air to Florida, developing prospects in the far reaches of the country, moving rigs around like pawns on a chessboard, borrowing money, drilling new wells, balancing his financial statements with ulcerated bankers who could become depressed and dysfunctional for months over the news of a dry hole.

Clayton Williams could not escape the rumors. He had drilling people taking kickbacks. Somebody was selling stolen bits to his company. He had been invoiced for the same equipment twice. He had paid the same bill more than once, maybe more than twice. He had been invoiced for tools he didn't receive. He had paid the bills and still needed the tools. Landmen were on the road buying leases for him and placing some of the leases in their own names. He did not have tight controls. He and his company were moving too fast in too many corners of Giddings and the world to maintain tight controls.

"Crooks," Claytie said, "were drawn to an oil boom like a magnet. They could not help themselves. Money was rampant. The temptations were too great. Stealing was far easier than drilling and a damn lot cheaper."

Clayton Williams fought it the best way he could. "If my employees were cheating and hurting me, I fired them," he said. "If they were cheating and hurting somebody else, I had them thrown in jail. I didn't care how badly they begged for mercy, I let the law deal with them and forgot they ever existed. By the time I caught a man dealing crooked, he had already had his second chance and usually his third. The best thing I could do for the Giddings oil patch was keep him off the streets and make sure he didn't steal from anybody else."

Secrets were difficult to keep in the oil patch. The guilty were tried and convicted and the innocent often indicted by word of mouth alone. Max Williams had heard the talk and the seamy innuendos. He did not want to believe the veracity of the rumors. But then, he was afraid not to track down the allegations and find out if they were fact, fiction, or just the end result of a jealous man spreading his discontent.

One of his trusted employees was on the take. Williams had heard the idle gossip make its rounds one too many times. "Don't know what all he's doing or how he's doing it," the informer said, "but I think he understands everything there is to know about kickbacks, and he agrees with most of them. He's made a lot of improvements to his place, the kind that costs a lot of money. He doesn't make that much money. If you haven't seen it lately, you wouldn't recognize it."

The words stung. Here was a man Max Williams had trusted with his oilfield. He was like family. Williams placed a phone call. "I'm coming out to your house," he told the man.

"You can't."

"Why not?"

"Let's meet somewhere in town," the man said. "I'll buy lunch."

Max Williams hung up. He drove straight to the man's home. Nice place, he thought. No. It was a brick short of being a mansion. A high-dollar chain link fence encircled more than fifty acres of land. Exotic animals, imported from Lord knows where, roamed the pastures. They had not been cheap to buy. Nor were they cheap to transport. And down beside the road, several old buildings, which hadn't been much more than abandoned shacks, had been repaired, renovated, and remodeled. One was being used as a private office. "It looks to me like you're taking kickbacks," Williams told him bluntly without any pleasantries or small talk.

"Max," the man argued, "you know I wouldn't do that."

"I know what I pay you," Williams replied. "You can't afford all of this."

The man had been taking bids from companies who wanted to build rig pads for U.S. Operating. A company entered a bid. It was accepted. It became the only bid the U.S. Operating accountant ever saw. Meanwhile, the same company, unencumbered by any conscience, entered a second bid, substantially lower, quietly, covertly, and under the table. The employee simply pocketed the difference. The difference could be tallied in thousands of dollars. He had pocketed his last dollar for U.S. Operating.

As gossip said, "Max found the cheat and scoundrel on a train. Max made a mistake when he didn't leave him on the train."

Sheriff Joe Goodson had been staked out most of the night. He wasn't alone. With him were highway patrolmen and members of the Texas Railroad Commission, the Texas Rangers, and Giddings Oilfield Security, set up as a lone-wolf act by Clayton Williams in a defiant move against those bold enough to think they could confiscate his oil and get away with it. The January darkness descended around them early, and a bitter cold seeped into their vehicles. There were no trees to hide them, only the night itself. Temperatures were hovering around eight degrees, and a northerly wind was sweeping across a barren countryside. There would be sleet and snow and thunder before sunrise.

Hundreds of thousands of barrels of oil had been stolen from wells in Burleson and Lee Counties. Many oil companies had no idea they were being robbed, even though thieves were hauling off thousands of dollars worth of oil every week.

Charles Sebasta, the Burleson County District of Attorney, pointed out, "There's not a lock that can be made that these individuals can't cut. If they're brave enough to go to the lease, they can steal the oil. It hurts operators. It hurts landowners. And the state loses tax revenue every time a tank truck crosses the Red River and drives into Oklahoma with illegal oil."

An anonymous telephone call to Don Chamberlain, chief of operations for Giddings Oilfield Security, provided the crucial tip which led Goodson and the law enforcement agencies to stake out several key oil lease and distribution points. For the past three months, they had slipped into the field each night.

A car dealer in Giddings provided the vehicles for after hours surveillance, but thus far, luck had abandoned them. The stakeout had been a bust. Thus far, the nights had provided darkness and little else. Tonight, it would all change.

Shortly after eight o'clock, a truck eased out of Henderson's Cafe's parking lot just north of Giddings. Sheriff Goodson tailed the truck to Burleson County but decided to turn back when it cut sharply down a dirt road. He couldn't follow. He was in danger of being seen. It was odd enough for a single pair of headlights to be cutting through the darkness of a lonely road. Two pair of headlights on the same remote stretch would have aroused suspicion.

Goodman knew he had one chance to catch and convict the thieves. He had to wait until the truck was filled with stolen oil. He eased back to Henderson's Café and waited. It was a long night. The wait dragged on until the minutes seemed like hours. At four o'clock, he watched the truck return out of the darkness and head back toward an oil storage tank behind the café. Sheriff Joe Goodson grinned. The wait was over.

The truck was filled with three hundred and thirty-one barrels of oil stolen from the Fillipone Leases, owned by Columbia Gas & Development Company. The storage tank had another truckload of a hundred and eighty barrels, and both shipments were on their way to Oklahoma. The drivers had been told they were hauling recycled drilling fluid, or so they claimed. Goodson thought they probably knew the difference. He doubted if anyone could prove it.

The thieves had been ingenious in their reasoning. They had centered their illegal activity in Burleson County, which only had three deputies and no one with a badge patrolling the back country roads after dark. In Burleson County, they could run hot oil all night without anyone around to wonder what they were doing at such curious hours.

Lee County, on the other hand, had eight deputies and a night patrol strung out on desolate roadways, driving from one oil lease to another. Odds of stealing oil and getting away in Lee County were a long shot. The thieves were not desperate enough or arrogant enough to take such a desperate and arrogant chance.

They did, however, make one serious mistake, and it cost them. They operated out of a storage tank tucked away in Lee County. It took Joe Goodson nights of surveillance, but when he and his task force struck, it was sudden and effective. One oil thief admitted, "Stealing was so easy, so damn easy, I couldn't believe it. It was a pretty good way to make a pretty good living."

"How about jail?" he was asked.

"How's the food?" he answered.

A meal was a meal. A bed was a bed. In jail, he didn't have to work nights.

A trucking company executive told the press, "I may have sent the trucks out, but I never told anybody to steal oil. I didn't know anything about stolen oil until the raid." When he testified before the Grand Jury, however, he sat back, confidently placed his hands together, and pleaded the Fifth. It didn't matter.

Indictments were handed down to seventeen people, including the presidents of two corporations, company executives, truck drivers, a restaurant owner, and his wife.

Charges ranged from felony theft of crude oil to receiving and concealing stolen oil. It was estimated that at least two hundred thousands dollars worth of misappropriated crude had passed through the storage tank behind Henderson's Café.

District Attorney Charles Sebasta had his own idea about ending the flagrant thefts. "We need full-time patrols that drive from lease to lease day and night," he said. "Every time they see a truck, pull the driver over, check whether or not he's supposed to be on that particular road at that particular hour, then make a notation of the driver, the truck, the company he's working for, and the lease he's on. If it doesn't check out, see if the oil has been stolen. If it has, you've knocked another thief off the highway."

32

*F*rom inside the cramped quarters of an old Gypsy trailer, Bill Shuford watched the darkness slowly dissolve into the new light of another day. He shivered. Outside, an early frost lay on the ground. Inside, there was no heater. Of course, during the blistered days of summer, there hadn't been any air conditioning either. He was at the mercy of the weather and a victim of temperatures that could be frigid or parched, depending on the time of year and often the time of day. The bare walls were closing in around him, but it was home. It might as well be a jail cell. It was that confining.

Shuford had been working for U.S. Operating for less than a year – it seemed longer – and still he had not had a day off. The rig. The trailer. Brown butcher paper piled with barbecue. A chunk of cheese, A jalapeno. A dusty road. A cranky well. A second-hand workover rig. A beer, cold or otherwise. Another bottle of whiskey. Another dog cussing from a roughneck with a hangover. Another dollar. And damn few of those.

He kept asking Max Williams for a raise. Every time he saw the boss man, he asked for a raise. But there was nowhere to spend any of it. Too many nights alone. Well, not every night was spent alone. Giddings definitely did not have Dallas girls nor as many of them, but it did have its nightlife if a man was willing to look for it, and Bill Shuford was. However, the intimate, candle-lit dinners lost some of their romance when shared over a bowl of chili or a can of sardines. And true love seldom lasted longer than a bottle of beer and three songs on a jukebox. That was life. No. That was his life.

Bill Shuford did not know whether to be mad or simply feel sorry for himself. So he directed his anger and frustration toward Max Williams and U.S. Operating. They had, with malice aforethought, stranded him out here on an island devoid of water and any kind of sensibilities.

They were responsible for his woes. He was certain of it. Nights. Days. Only an hour or two ever separated them. Work. Sleep. And whatever he did between the two. After awhile, they all ran together.

At SEDCO, Bill Shuford had been stationed in the fabled North Sea, living the high life in Aberdeen, Scotland, working twenty-eight straight days, then free to travel for the next twenty-eight consecutive days, and earning fifty thousand dollars a year. Now he was trapped in Giddings, Texas, of all places, wasting away in the chalk and earning fifteen hundred dollars a month.

Hell, he thought, it was peanuts. Any fool or derelict could make fifteen hundred dollars a month and still get two days off at the end of the week. Eight-hour work days were a bad rumor.

He had thought that, with any luck, he would wind up with a few good overrides that might potentially make him a millionaire. But somewhere along the line, the dreams he had for himself, the promises he had made to himself, had all been lost or misplaced in translation. He kept asking for the next raise. He kept waiting for the next raise. The numbers on his paycheck never changed.

Don't worry, Bill Shuford kept telling himself. Be patient. No hurry. Take your time.

It's all just a learning experience. He could still remember when he believed the lies, or least a twisted version of the hard truth, he told himself when the nights were long and the days were either too damn hot or too damn cold. He was killing himself and did not have enough time left over in the day to die.

Shuford was growing more disgruntled by the day, and Max Williams dreaded his visits to the rig. He already knew the first question he would be asked.

Finally he relented and handed Shuford a piece of paper. On it, he had written down a new set of numbers. "Will this salary make you happy?" Williams asked.

Shuford grinned. "It's perfect," he said.

"I hope so," Williams said. "If I hear another word about another raise in the next six months, you're fired."

Shuford wadded up the piece of paper and stuck it in his pocket.

He grinned out loud. Tonight he would celebrate. The oil business was paying off quite handsomely after all.

●

Bill Shuford stumbled out the trailer, fell into his Cougar, and headed for the rig. The coffee would be hot and a little too strong, the drill bit turning, mud in the hole, oil in the fractures, each new hour looking eerily like the last one. He was never far from J. E. Traweek, who, as much as anyone, understood the assorted day-to-day mechanics and the complexities of a good land operation from drilling to completion. Shuford observed, listened, and placed each detail, no matter how insignificant it sounded, into the deep abyss of his memory bank. He wanted to learn as much as he could as fast as he could before the oil began to play out in the chalk, provided, of course, it ever played out. The lust for oil had gripped him. The North Sea had spoiled him. Giddings would never let him go.

It wouldn't be long until he was running his own show, Shuford thought. He was more comfortable working in the midst of the big picture, leaving the details to someone else, someone like J. E. Traweek. Shuford might indeed become a millionaire someday, he decided, but if he did, he would have to go out and find that million-dollar payoff on his own. Bill Shuford was impatient. He was restless. He did not like being chained to a rig virtually twenty-four hours a day. His body and soul belonged to the company. About all he owned anymore were his own thoughts, and, more and more, his thoughts were on leaving. Good terms. Or bad. It did not matter.

Shuford wanted to be out and on the go, meeting people, leasing land, looking for prospects, putting deals together, and pumping his own oil out of the chalk. A good crisis, from time to time, a bitter fight, all hell breaking loose never bothered him. He was not afraid to make decisions, sometimes right and sometimes wrong, and stand behind them.

What troubled him was boredom, the day-to-day monotony of keeping a rig running and a bit boring deeper. The landscape did not change. The job did not change. The paycheck never changed, not more than a few dollars anyway.

Lord, it was tedious, unrewarding and unforgiving work. In his heart, he understood the reality of the situation confronting him. He would never be able to work for somebody else. It wasn't his nature. He wanted to be his own boss even if it meant he was working for the meanest sonuvabitch in the Giddings field.

●

Ray Holifield drove up to the rig bright and early every morning. He knew Bill Shuford would have a pot of stout coffee handy, and Shuford was beginning to wonder if Holifield ever slept at all. The geologist was wired day and night, had a nervous twitch in his eyes, and some in the oil patch considered him downright eccentric. He kept showing up at the oddest of times for the oddest of reasons. It was not unusual for Ray Holifield to sit out on the mud pits and talk to Shuford all night long. Might as well. Neither one of them had any place better to go.

They discussed the business, the chalk, and Shuford remarked about how unjust and unfair the Giddings field had been.

"What do you mean?" Holifield wanted to know.

"Some get rich down here, and some don't," Shuford answered.

"Don't blame the field."

"Why shouldn't I?"

"If a man doesn't get rich in Giddings," Holifield said, "it's his own damn fault."

"I'm not rich."

Holifield grinned. "It's your own damn fault," he said.

Shuford nodded and glanced up at the midnight sky. A new moon hung like a fragile splinter above the clouds. "I think I can do this," he said at last.

"What?"

"Run my own oil business."

"Nobody's stopping you."

"I need a good geologist."

"That's always a good starting point."

Shuford leaned forward and asked, "Ray, if I leave U.S. Operating and form my own company, will you do the geology work for me?"

Ray Holifield sat back, deep in thought. Max Williams and Irv Deal had hired him, then they split, and now he was working for both men. Hadn't been a problem. Neither of them had complained. Pat Holloway needed him, so, as fate would have it, he was now finding good, producing wells for all three operators. Nobody liked it, but, hell, nobody had chased him off. He could find enough oil in Giddings to satisfy everybody who wanted to drill.

Holifield reached over, poured himself another cup of coffee as thick as fracking mud, and stared at the kid who wanted to stand toe-to-toe and battle it out with the big boys. Well, he reasoned, the big boys had Ray Holifield. Shuford might as well have his services, too. Nobody was going to fire him. They might all get cross with each other and fuss a little.

They might even sulk or yell at him. But nobody was going to fire him. Not Ray Holifield. Ray Holifield was the lone untouchable in the Giddings field.

"I'll do it," he said and drained his cup of coffee.

●

Bill Shuford wanted to be his own boss. But leaving the security of a paying job for one filled with dread and uncertainty would take a major leap of faith, and he wasn't quite ready to make such a precarious leap without a safety net beneath him. He saw Max Williams coming his way about the time the first hint of daylight began crawling across the peanut fields. The new salary he had liked so well? Well, he didn't think it was nearly as much as he probably deserved. Bill Shuford took a chance. A man couldn't acquire anything without asking for it. He asked for another raise.

"How long have you had this job?" Max Williams asked.

"Almost a year."

"You won't have a second year," Williams said.

Bill Shuford was startled. "Are you firing me?" he asked.

"No." Max Williams shrugged, turned, and walked slowly away. "You fired yourself," he said without emotion. "I drew a line in the dirt, and you stepped over it."

Bill Shuford knew Max Williams and his reputation well. No more discussions. No more negotiations. Max Williams was right. It was over. Then again, maybe for him, it was just the beginning. Finally, whether he was ready or not, Shuford was free to attack the chalk and do whatever he had enough savvy and nerve to do. He was in charge, the ramrod of his own outfit.

Of course, it wasn't really much of an outfit. Bill Shuford was an oilman without a crew or any money to drill a well. He was a one-man operation who didn't even own a shovel. Of course, he had Ray Holifield. But how could a geologist, no matter how good, locate prospects in land Shuford had not yet leased?

In the end, Williams and Shuford felt a slight bitterness toward each other. Some was business, and some was personal. In time, they became strong, defiant competitors in a field where men spent so much time desperately fighting the chalk that they seldom had time to battle each other. They kept apart even when their rigs were in sight of each other.

Bill Shuford knew he could make it on his own. Max Williams already had.

●

Bill Shuford was immediately on the phone with his father back in Dallas. "I've left my job," he said.

"You think that's a wise move?"

"I've decided to start my own oil company."

His father had been a child of the Great Depression. He still remembered when families had to scrape for a handful of coins and eating three meals a day was out of the question. Get a good job. That had been his father's philosophy. Work hard. Be loyal. Make as much money as you can, and be happy.

He had worried when his son left SEDCO. Now, barely a year later, his son was walking out on another good job and headed down the same empty streets again. The boy always had grandiose ideas, but now he might be biting off more than he could chew. He had plans to found his own company in a business where only the strong survived, the weak quit along the way, and the timid went in some other direction. Lord, help him. Lord, help them all.

"How are you planning on getting started?" the elder Mr. Shuford asked his son.

"That's why I'm calling," Shuford said. "I know a lot about the oil business. I know my way around Giddings well enough to find some good leases, and I'm pretty good at drilling and completing a well. But I need money. I need some good investors."

"They'll want to see your track record."

Bill Shuford sighed. He had made some tracks along the way. But he had no record at all to brag about, not in the oil patch anyway. He found his first investors in Harold Clark and Harold Dunk. They knew a lot about the riches of the Austin Chalk. They trusted it. After all, they had been quite successful by investing in wells drilled by Max Williams and U.S. Operating.

They listened to Shuford's game plan, saw the unbridled excitement in his eyes, and politely left the room.

Clark went straight to the telephone and called Max Williams. "I want to ask you about a situation we have," he said. "It might be a conflict of interest."

"I'm listening."

"You know Bill Shuford?"

"He used to work for me."

"He's wanting to put together a few leases and is talking to both Harold and myself about investing with him."

"It's your money," Williams said. "I certainly won't tell you how to spend it."

"We've been friends for a long time."

"We have."

"Would it bother you if we invested with Bill?"

"I wouldn't care at all," Williams said and chuckled. "This is business. All is fair in love, war, and the oil business."

Harold Clark and Harold Dank walked back into the room and gave Bill Shuford a line of credit worth a half million dollars to buy leases.

Bill Shuford was in business. "It was me," he said. "I was the company."

He was on his way back to Giddings to rent an apartment, track down a few scattered acres of land, more if possible, find a rig, hire a crew, sign an agreement with Ray Holifield, and officially establish an oil and gas corporation he would call *WCS* for William C. Shuford.

●

His was no longer an unfamiliar face in a town filled with unfamiliar faces. Bill Shuford was part of the oil crowd, ambitious and assertive, a young gun determined to prove that Max Williams, Irv Deal, Pat Holloway, and Clayton Williams neither owned nor controlled all of the oil beneath Giddings. Shuford had already determined which sections of the field he wanted, and Ray Holifield provided him information about choice locations. Holifield should know. He possessed seismic logs that had already ripped away the mysteries of underground chambers where large pay zones were clustered together. Raise a little money. Lease the land Holifield told him to lease, then drill where Holifield told him to spud in a well. It wouldn't be that difficult, Shuford figured. The Giddings field was no longer a riddle. Holifield had turned it into a science.

Bill Shuford settled in at the courthouse, memorized the land maps, searched for acreage he wanted to lease, personally tracked down data on landowners, both past and present, followed cold case leads to missing, forgotten, or buried heirs that often seemed like wandering down lost roads to dead ends, finally pieced together the information he needed to clear titles, and typed up his agreements on an old manual typewriter. They may not have looked official. They were.

Shuford, however, realized that it was probably time to hire an attorney, but Jim Robertson was the only name he knew. Robertson had a reputation for being the best damn lawyer there was in the business. Jim Robertson, however, was doing the legal work for Irv Deal and Windsor Energy, and Bill Shuford wondered whether the attorney had an attachment to Max Williams as well, or even if Robertson was allowed by law to represent two different and competing oil companies in the same field. Then again, he had watched from afar and wasn't sure if the oil business had ethics, morals, scruples, rules, commandments, or even laws to guide it.

Generally, in the struggle to find oil, it was every man for himself in a dog-eat-dog environment, and the victors walked away with the spoils. Common sense, however, told Shuford that he was undoubtedly walking a fine line, so he met with Robertson's partner, Bruce Stensrud.

The operator and the lawyer had a lot of similarities. Both were young. Both were aggressive. Neither worried about challenges or obstacles standing in their way. Neither ever thought about backing down or quitting. It was not their nature. And both could see the untapped potential that still existed in a field even after it had been heavily explored and drilled, provided that Shuford had the financial strength and backing to survive in the cutthroat world of oil, particularly Giddings oil.

Stensrud was intrigued, fascinated, and concerned. He liked the deal. He liked Bill Shuford's straightforward tenacity. However, he recognized immediately that he might be immersing himself in a conflict of interest – morally if not legally.

"I don't foresee it as a problem, "Shuford argued. "Jim Robertson sticks with Irv Deal. You do my work. The firm keeps everything separate and apart. The twain never meets. Legally, I'm confident that you can figure out a way to protect all of us."

Legally, Bruce Stensrud knew he could. But he did not want to take a chance on a new client without a track record at the risk of losing an old and successful one in the oil patch. He carefully studied both sides of the problem, balancing the pros against the cons, the good against the bad, the right against the wrong.

He could effectively justify either side of the equation. It was indeed a sticky situation and a tough decision, but he was paid to make tough decisions. Bruce Stensrud made one.

He telephoned Bill Shuford. "I'll take your company on as a client," he said.

Bill Shuford left U.S. Operating, and that was bad enough. But he ran off with Max Williams's geologist, made a deal with two of his prime investors, hired one of his drilling superintendents, J. E. Traweek, and now had engineered a deal with his old partner's law firm. Such was the harsh realities of the oil business.

Sometimes a man could count his money much longer than he could count on his friends, even when the money was going bad. Max Williams turned back to the land, forgot about lawyers, and refused to dwell on his losses, real or imagined. It was more profitable to drill than commensurate with the recent and sordid past.

Bill Shuford surveyed the great Giddings oilfield. He had the lease. Ray Holifield had the location. All that kept him from spudding in the Patricia Smith No. 1 in Burleson County was four hundred thousand dollars to cover the cost of drilling. Shuford didn't have to wait long. He played his trump card.

"Ray Holifield is my geologist," he said.

"He choose your location?"

"He did."

As Shuford said, "I no longer had any worries. I simply sat back, and the money raised itself." Ray Holifield's name had not lost its magic.

The Patricia Smith No. 1 only added to his legend. The well came thundering in with two hundred barrels of oil and more than three million cubic feet of gas a day.

WCS Oil & Gas was up and running, and it was running hard. Other companies had come before him, and even more were on their way. But Bill Shuford had made his mark, and he had only just begun.

Before the year ended, Shuford had drilled seven successful wells, and, he said, "I wouldn't sign my name to any piece of paper without Bruce Stensrud telling me it was all right. I handled the fieldwork. He handled the legal work. Between us, we had all of the bases covered, and still there was so much of the Giddings field yet to cover."

33

*F*or Gary Bryant, the oil business had been a long, hard, and steady climb. At the age of twenty-six, he seriously thought he had been condemned to life without parole in the dreaded insurance business. Make a telephone call. Make an appointment. Make his pitch. Make his sale. Sign on the dotted line. Earn a premium or two. Wonder how long the premiums would keep rolling in until somebody let his policy lapse, and the selling cycle would begin all over again. In reality, the cycle never stopped.

Bryant, with great reluctance, dialed every number. He was extremely shy, he said, and sat down with a bottle of whiskey beside the telephone. He would pour himself a glass, take a sip, make a phone call, ask for an appointment, take another sip, and dial again. "If I had not left the insurance business," he said," I would have probably become an alcoholic." He and whiskey made a lot of calls together. Whiskey never made a sale.

Gary Bryant secretly wanted to emulate his brother-in-law. Ted Clifford was in the money business. "Whatever he did," Bryant said, "he made money."

Mostly what he did was drill oil wells from Oklahoma to South Texas and at a handful of places in between. He offered Bryant – who had never seen a well drilled, completed, or producing – a job in the never-ending exploits of oil exploration.

"Where?" Bryant wanted to know.

"Big Spring."

"Big Spring's a long way from Amarillo."

"That's where I'm drilling."

"We've only been in Amarillo for two weeks."

"Then there's nothing to keep you there," Clifford said.

"My wife just took a job teaching."

"She'll have to quit."

"She won't like it."

"Wives never do."

Gary Bryant struck out for Big Spring with the promise of an eight-hundred-dollar-a-month salary, a company car, travel expenses, and hospitalization insurance. What more could he ask? He wasn't on top of the world, but he knew where and how far away the top was situated.

Bryant had never finished college. It no longer mattered. A man did not need a degree while fighting sand storms or standing knee-deep in mud, battling for every drop of oil the land had to give him.

Mostly, Gary Bryant remained in the office, reading files, working with an accountant, doing whatever odd job Clifford asked him to do.

He was learning the oil business on the go and on the job, and by the time Gary Bryant walked out the door and away from Ted Clifford's operation six years later, he had saved enough money to establish his own company.

He called it CAG Petroleum, using the first letter from the names of his three small sons – Chad, Aaron, and Gary.

●

Gary Bryant was facing a formidable task. It did not bother him. He and formidable tasks were old cell mates. He had spent twenty months in Vietnam with mortar shells raining down around him almost every night. He had survived the onslaught of the Tet Offensive when, he said, "All hell broke loose and threatened to take me with it." He was wearily surprised every morning when he saw the sun and realized that the darkness had been night instead of death, and the two seemed so disturbingly similar.

Exploring the countryside for oil might be difficult. It might even break him. It would not kill him. Gary Bryant drilled his first well for CAG in a cotton patch outside of Snyder in far West Texas. He had watched Ted Clifford coax a drill bit into the earth many times. He knew and understood the regimen. Nothing like the oil business, he reasoned. Drill a hole. Strike oil. Make a little money. Drill again. Let the good times roll.

He drilled a hole all right. It was dry. There wasn't even a promise deep in the ground. Gary Bryant could not believe it. He was only just beginning. This was not the way it was supposed to end. Not yet anyway. "I sat down and cried," he said. "Maybe I wasn't tough enough or good enough to be in the oil business. Maybe I needed to just go back to work for somebody else and let them deal with the problems of raising money and hitting dry holes." Bryant wasn't drowning in self-pity. But he was close.

Gary Bryant had a choice to make. He could quit. Or he could put the dry hole behind him and move cautiously forward. He found a little oil still spilling out from the badlands around Snyder, enough to keep CAG in business, then headed toward the ominous and uncharted tracts of Lee County where a Midland lawyer had purchased leases too far away and too erratic for him to consider keeping. Maybe the lawyer knew something he didn't. Others had tackled the chalk, but it was still virgin territory for Gary Bryant.

"I'm an attorney, not an oilman," Larry Flynn told him. "I no longer have any interest in this deal and simply want out of it. If you're buying leases and don't particularly care where you go, I'll sell them to you."

"How much?"

"The same as I paid for them."

"What's that in dollars?"

"Twenty thousand."

Bryant did a quick calculation in his head. It had not been difficult to memorize the numbers in his bankbook. They weren't nearly as large or cumbersome as they had once been. A dry hole could do that for a man. He did, however, know he had at least twenty thousand dollars left over in his savings account. The leases would drain him financially. He was not in the oil business without them. He took what he could get.

The two men shook hands, and Gary Bryant began the arduous task of raising four hundred thousand dollars to drill the Marburger No. 1 on a patch of ground near Dime Box. He was unknown in Giddings, in Lee County, in the chalk, and the old chalk, the incarnation of the devil himself, could be unpredictable and unfaithful. Investors already knew it. Newcomers had better beware, and Bryant was as new as they came. The chalk would siphon off a man's blood in dollars and cents, then rob him of his soul. No one made a bargain with the devil, and the chalk wasn't negotiating.

The high rollers, those whose bank accounts were already saturated with oil, were all signing checks with Max Williams, Irv Deal, Pat Holloway, and Clayton Williams. It appeared that Tom Coffman had Austin investors sewn up. And Bill Shuford had quickly carved a nice and rich little niche for himself. Gary Bryant's name did not have a lot of clout behind it.

"Who are you?" investors wanted to know. "What have you done?" And, more importantly, "What have you done lately?"

"Giddings was an odd little town," he said. "Speculators heavily promoted the oilfield, making money whether they made oil or not. The streets were filled with greed, gossip, and men who wouldn't loan you a dime or give you a piece of advice. I've seen many of them stagger into small roadside cafes and order a six pack of beer for breakfast. Oil was a steep price to pay. It made some families millionaires. It ruined others. Fathers and sons, brothers and sisters fought tooth and nail over leases and royalties. Husbands were kicked out of good homes and usually for good reasons. Wives left, but not without alimony that came from a field of producing wells. People always told me that blood was thicker than water. Maybe so. But blood was never thicker than oil. A lot of friends didn't bury the hatchet. They just buried their friendship. And here I was in the middle of a town where oil was a magnet that drew the desperate and the depraved. Oil and money never changed a man's character. It only magnified what he already was."

Bryant patched the four hundred thousand dollars together and kept the names of his investors written on a scrap piece of paper and stuffed down in his wallet. The night the Marburger No. 1 began flowing oil, he hurriedly drove to a pay phone beside the railroad tracks in Giddings and called every one of them.

"Yes," he said, "we have oil."

"How much?"

"The gauge indicates four hundred barrels a day."

His grin was almost audible. His breath came in short bursts.

"That's right," he said. "Four hundred barrels a day. Roughly speaking, that's about eight thousand dollars a day."

"That make us rich?"

"It'll certainly keep you in new socks."

Gary Bryant was not an unknown any longer. Those who had investment dollars were knocking on his door, calling his phone number all hours of the night. It took him thirty minutes to raise the money for the second well. The sudden euphoria might not last forever, but it was damn good while it lasted.

●

Gary Bryant's second lease was purchased from an elderly couple of Bohemians, he said, descendents of those German Lutherans who rolled by wagon into the region a century earlier. They were brother and sister, both somewhere in their seventies and worn down by hard work on land that did not always grow what they had planted. Their farm had been handed down through generations, and they clung to it like life itself.

Bryant wanted the leases to the land.

"We won't sell," they said.

"I just want to lease the acreage to drill."

"What happens if you find oil?"

Bryant shrugged. "You make some money," he said. "I make some money."

"How much?"

"Depends on the well."

"What happens if you don't find any oil down there?"

"You plant it in peanuts next year."

"We've lost a crop."

"We all take our chances."

Gary Bryant still didn't have any cash on hand. He was on the telephone when he offered them thirty-five dollars an acre for two hundred acres.

The old man was not impressed. There was silence on the phone.

"What's wrong?" Bryant asked.

"I want fifty-five dollars an acre," the old man said.

"I can't afford fifty-five dollars an acre," Bryant told him.

"Then you need to lease somebody else's land."

Gary Bryant learned that desperate men have the capacity to do desperate things. He loaded up his wife and children in Dallas and drove them out to the old man's farm.

He introduced himself.

The old man's eyes narrowed. "You're the man who's trying to steal my land for thirty-five dollars an acre," he said.

Bryant said. "I came out here because I want you to meet my wife."

"Why?"

"She's Bohemian, too."

"What's her name?"

"Deborah Dolezal."

The old man's face brightened. His eyes lit up. He didn't look quite as old as he did when Bryant turned into his driveway that afternoon. "For a Dolezal," he said, "I'll lease the land for thirty-five dollars an acre."

The well came in as Bryant hoped it would. It wasn't as good as the Marburger No. 1. But it was good enough. It paid better than a good harvest of peanuts. "For thirty-five dollars an acre," Bryant said, "it was as good a deal as I ever made."

"For thirty-five dollars an acre," the old man told his friends, "I found out what real money looked like. It spent the same. It just took longer to spend."

Gary Bryant, by his own admission, was a two-fisted tightwad. While drilling in the old Snyder field, he had bedded down on rented cots and occasionally slept beneath the town's underpass at night. Hardships were a way of life. He continued to maintain an office in Dallas, working nine or ten hours a day, then driving to Giddings and arriving at all hours of the night. On more than one occasion, Bryant would be so tired as he sped down Highway 77 between Rockdale and Giddings that he had to pull off the road and walk around the car, letting the cold wind slap him in the face to wake him up. His back ached. His shoulders sagged. His eyes burned.

One night as he drove toward the chalk, he looked down the road and saw two culverts. One was a blur. One was real. For the life of him, Gary Bryant had no idea which was which. He could see the lights to somewhere, a dim glow beneath the clouds. No moon. No stars. Just the dim lights to somewhere. He hoped it was Giddings. It took him forever to get there. Five miles, on a weary, Godforsaken night, could seem like forever.

Bryant refused to waste money on motel rooms. He found a little, out-of-the way hole in the wall where he could rent a bunk bed by the hour and have access to a shower, sometimes with hot water. He hired his crews from the men staying there. He hired some and didn't even know their names. They were willing to work, and that was all he cared about. Neither Bryant nor the men on his rigs knew the difference between being broke and tightfisted. "A man had to be a tightwad to survive those limestone fractures," Bryant said. Any dollar they saved was a dollar they didn't have to spend. For a lot of oilmen, the Austin Chalk had been and would always be the kiss of death.

Bryant lived from pay phone to pay phone. "I knew where all the good ones were," he said. "I knew which phones had lines of lonely men waiting to talk, which ones were used by oil operators trying to conduct their day-to-day business, and which ones never had anybody around. I didn't have time to stand in line. I figured that losing time was a lot like losing money."

●

For Gary Bryant, the Giddings field was either flush or flustered. From the first morning he walked across the raw land, he sensed that he was drilling with blinders on, gambling that the chalk had fractures beneath his rig, gambling that the fractures were large enough to contain reservoirs of oil, never knowing whether the next well would be better or worse than the last.

Oil baron J. Paul Getty had once said, "Without the element of uncertainty, the bringing off of even the greatest business triumph would be dull, routine, and eminently unsatisfying." Maybe. Then again, maybe not. Gary Bryant knew all about uncertainty. It stuck to his soul like mud from a slush pit.

He was having enough success to stay in the game. He realized that Giddings had its high stakes players and its penny ante gamblers. Drilling a well cost the same for both. The high stakes players had good prospects to drill. The penny ante gamblers were hoping for the best. And the difference between them had nothing to do with strokes of good or bad fortune.

The high stakes boys owned Ray Holifield. Gary Bryant didn't. "Ray Holifield was the secret, or at least he possessed the secret," Bryant said. And his expertise in solving the complexities of the chalk was confined to the drilling operations of Max Williams, Irv Deal, Pat Holloway, and Bill Shuford. Holifield wasn't difficult to find. He was everywhere. Just stand on a street corner or drive down County Road 1612, which was so rough it was better known as Hemorrhoid Road, and, sooner or later, at any hour of the day or night, the eccentric and enigmatic Ray Holifield would wander past.

Bryant met with him. Holifield would sit down and discuss oil exploration with anybody and usually did. He might not remember the names or the details or even the conversations, but he liked his status as the oracle of Giddings.

"I need a good geologist," Bryant said.

"There aren't many good ones down here," Holifield replied bluntly.

"I want to hire you."

"It shows you have good sense."

"I'll make you a great deal."

"I already have all the clients I can handle."

"I'll give you a better deal than they did."

Ray Holifield smiled apologetically. "I've already made enough people mad at me," he said. "There's no use in me upsetting the rest of them, too." Gary Bryant was out of luck.

●

He, like Bill Shuford, was working the operation of the oil patch alone, and it could indeed be a lonely ordeal. Sure, there were a handful of hired hands, but, for the most part, each of them worked in solitary confinement, and the job was sucking the life out of them. Shuford almost killed himself coming back from his rig in the dark hours of early morning. He was tired, his mind was numb, it was difficult to keep his eyes open, the long hours had battered him, and his car left the road without ever slowing down.

Shuford climbed out of the metal wreckage, a frightened and, in some ways, a changed man. He wasn't quite sure if he wanted to be the lone gun in the Giddings field any longer.

Gary Bryant sat down with Bill Shuford and, amidst leftover barbecue sauce and jalapeno pepper seeds, placed a proposal on the table. Nothing elaborate. Nothing out of the ordinary. Nothing that couldn't be worked out. "Let's partner up," Bryant said.

"How will it work?" Shuford wanted to know.

"I'll raise the money," Bryant said. "You put the holes in the ground. If we make some money, we'll split it up."

"Fifty-fifty?"

"That's the way I figure it."

"And that's all there is to it?"

"Plain, down and dirty, and simple."

By the time the last of the meat had been gnawed from the rib, Gary Bryant had a partner. Even more importantly, he now had access to Ray Holifield.

He had not been able to hire the geologist. So he struck a deal with Shuford to acquire him. No longer would he be operating in the chalk and in the dark. Holifield would make the difference.

As he said, "As long as I had Ray Holifield's name attached to a prospect, it wasn't necessary to go out and spend a lot of time raising money. I took orders. In those days, if you had Ray Holifield, you had investors."

More rigs. More seismic. More good locations. Lord, Ray Holifield had access to it all. All Bill Shuford and Gary Bryant had was the oil. They didn't ask for anything more.

●

In March of 1980, *The Dallas Times Herald* wrote: *Giddings is in the center of one of the hottest booms in Texas, a drilling spree that has spread over four counties. More than sixty rigs are at work, and they are being snapped up as fast as they become available. At least four hundred wells have been drilled in the area and most of them have found some oil or gas. The wells are coming on line faster than pipelines can be built to gather the natural gas.*

The once-quiet town has doubled in size, experienced a sharp increase in crime, and been overrun by pickup-driving, beer-guzzling roughnecks sleeping in trailers, cramped motel rooms, and even tents. Now you can't find a parking space anywhere, said Bennie Jaehne, who, like many other Giddings natives, gave up his old job for a more lucrative one with one of the several oil-related companies that have built new office buildings there. As in Giddings, the key to the nationwide drilling upsurge is higher prices for oil and gas, new exploration and production techniques, and luck.

Four hundred wells had indeed been drilled, but not all of them proved to be commercial. By the end of 1980, the Giddings field boasted a hundred and fifty producing wells, and seventy-five of them had been drilled by the three principal clients of Ray Holifield – Max Williams, Irv Deal, and Pat Holloway. Bill Shuford, Gary Bryant, and West Texas oilman Clayton Williams might be coming hard and on the dead run, but they were only beginning to scratch the opportunities of the chalk.

●

Others ventured into the field, some cautiously, some quietly and some full bore. Thomas Coffman, Champlin Exploration, and Keith Graham had all experienced a good deal of success. Houston Oil & Minerals had struggled, using the money from good wells to finance its operations in bad wells. Houston Oil & Minerals was a lot like the gambler who walked out of a racetrack one day after betting on the ponies and said, "Well, I broke even today and Lord knows I needed it." Not everyone had found the cursed old chalk to harbor get-rich-quick drilling operations. It was a slow climb to the top, and not every venture had a top.

While Ray Holifield's major clients were collectively pumping twenty thousand barrels and cashing in the equivalent of three hundred and fifty thousand dollars a day, with another hundred million dollars awaiting them in the chalk, a field full of operators were simply struggling to survive. A lot of wells. A lot of disappointments. Hopes on the rise. Hopes dashed. Mostly, those who drilled in the chalk without the seismic data, the prospects, the advice, and the geologic expertise of Ray Holifield drove away from dry holes, and not all of them came back.

The statistics were staggering and difficult to believe, especially for those who looked on Giddings from afar and predicted the boom would die within a year. With Holifield choosing their locations, U.S. Operating, Windsor, and Humble Exploration struck oil in nine out of every ten wells they drilled. Seven out of ten were commercial producers. Such results were unheard of in any field, especially in the cantankerous and defiant chalk.

The reason for their phenomenal success? Most came to the same conclusion, and their answer was simple: Ray Holifield. He could see faults in the seismic hieroglyphics, understand which faults had most likely created fractures, and knew which fractures had the best chance of carrying the oil. He was the magic man. Some had Holifield. Some didn't. He upset a lot of people. He crossed a lot of people.

He was arrogant. He was the kingpin of the Giddings field, and he knew it, and he knew that everyone else in the field knew it as well.

Curse him. Condemn him. Or praise him.

It did not matter.

Ray Holifield found oil.

34

*F*or C. J. Halamicek, it was coming home again. He had taken an uncertain and sometimes unstable path that led him into the dangerous and often disgusting underbelly of Military Police work at White Sands Missile Base in New Mexico and as a guard for a federal prison outside the drug-infested streets of El Paso. He had existed far too long among the worst that mankind had to offer, heard all the threats, suffered through all the various rages of violence, but now he had made his way back to a peaceable kingdom, the farmlands he had inherited from his father, and settled down at the end of a dirt road outside of Fayette, one of the few places on earth, he said, where most everybody could correctly spell and pronounce his last name.

Halamicek took a series of odd jobs, trying to rehabilitate himself from those dark days patrolling the cellblocks of a prison where a man kept his friends at a distance and his enemies on the other side of the bars. The nine years had left a dark stain on his soul, and he felt depressed even when he was in a good mood. He ran a front-end loader for a gravel contractor for a time, even learned to fly an airplane, but the days of boredom and frustration were beginning to weigh heavy on his shoulders. In either direction he traveled, the roads simply took one detour too many and ran out.

C. J. Halamicek was explaining his plight to his attorney in LaGrange when Mike Klesel told him, "Folks are looking for a lot of oil and gas around here. Can't drill without leases. Why don't you consider becoming a landman?"

"I don't know anything about it."

"Don't need to," the attorney said with a grin. "Believe me, any idiot can be a landman."

"How would I get started?"

"Nothing to it," Klesel said. "Go down to the courthouse. Find the county clerk. Tell her you want to talk to Dana Morris. He's been a landman for thirty years and can tell you everything you need to know about the business. He knows who's looking, who's being fired, and who may have a position to fill. Dana can help you get a job."

Dana Morris did. Lots of land, Lots of oil. Dana Morris was not particularly concerned with another competitor in the field. He had lasted for thirty years.

He didn't know whether or not C. J. Halamicek would last the weekend. There were three kinds of landmen. Those looking for overrides. Those lost in the maze of frayed courthouse records that dated back decades, even a hundred years or more. And those who were looking for the road to another job where they did not have to argue, cajole, or plead with stubborn German farmers for a tract of land that might be rich or might not produce anything but suitcase sand, so dry it was time to pack the suitcase and leave.

Robert Graham hired him to work for Clayton Williams Energy.

It was a good move, Halamicek thought. Graham was kinfolk. He said he was Claytie's cousin. He had ties to the top.

The next day, Halamicek received the bad news, which was almost always more plentiful than good news in the oil patch.

"There's been a little cutback," he was told. "I'm afraid you've lost your job."

"What about Graham?" Halamicek wondered.

"You can forget him."

"Why?"

"Graham's no longer around either."

Humble Exploration had become the giant of the expanding Giddings field, and Pat Holloway was feverishly moving in all directions at the same time, waiting for the next bolt of lightning to strike and gambling it would strike twice in the same place. He had money, all he needed, which was never enough. He needed good leases. He would hire any landman worth his salt, and, as far as he was concerned, C. J. Halamicek could go out and negotiate with every landowner in Fayette County. The country was rife with Germans and Czechs and Wends who settled the region. With a name like Halamicek, C. J. could be a godsend.

Holloway's new landman shoved his way into the courthouse and realized quickly that there was barely enough room in the County Clerk's office to stand and certainly not enough room to work. He began thumbing through indexes of oil and gas units, dreading to find any that said "HBP," *held by production.* It meant that some other company owned the lease, even if all they had was a crippled old well coughing up a barrel of oil a day. If nothing else, it allowed them to legally possess the acreage as long as a drop of crude kept climbing out of the pipe. "For every good well drilled in the chalk," Halamicek said, "there were always six or seven dogs, but even the dogs kept the land held hostage in somebody else's hands."

Finding new leases took long hours and the uncanny ability to immerse himself in record after record, document after document, piecing together aging transactions that often led to nowhere, tying lost limbs back on family trees that had been split apart for generations, finding who owned the mineral rights, who had sold them, who had bought them, and who had lost them in a game of cards or a messy divorce. Oil, perhaps, produced the money, but leases made the wealth possible. Without leases, operators had nowhere to drill and no way to get to the oil.

●

Landowners became suspicious. So many of them leased land for pennies on the dollar, watched a well flow in, assumed it would keep producing forever, went out and paid top prices for new pickup trucks, new tractors, new plows, new barns, a new herd of cattle, and new homes. They wasted little of their time in buying up acreage from their neighbors next door. More land meant more leases. More leases meant more money. It was a kind of math that even the poor and uneducated could understand. When the oil suddenly dried up without warning or died off within the first six months, they were left entangled and embroiled in debt, harassed by the tax man, and could find no viable way to dodge or escape financial ruin. So many feared the chalk. So many came to fear the landman.

In Fayette County, it was even worse. The chalk wells were being drilled on the Edwards Reef, Halamicek said. There were a few producing wells scattered in isolated areas of the region, but operators discovered they had to drill twelve to thirteen thousand feet just to hit the chalk, which was layered like pancakes.

Most of them found salt water. Time after time, they saw the latest in technology get whipped by the hard rock that Mother Nature left behind.

A lot of drill bits broke off or wore out. Pump rods were bent and twisted, and they headed out in crooked directions in the chalk. Seismic might tell a geologist where the fracture lay in hard ground, but it was virtually impossible to drill a hole straight enough to hit it.

In one lease he secured, Halamicek said, he drove to the site and found the driller angry, the farmer confused, and the geologist adamant and wringing his hands.

"The geologist had read the seismic," C. J. Halamicek said, "and he knew the exact spot where the reservoir of oil lay encased in the ground."

It was beneath the barn. "I can't drill through the barn," the driller said.

"Bulldoze it down," the geologist said.

"You can't bulldoze my barn," the farmer said.

"We'll build you a new one," the geologist said. "But it is absolutely vital that we drill to a precise location."

The barn came down. The drill bit tore into the earth. Twelve thousand feet. Then thirteen thousand. A million dollars was in the hole. The hole was dry. The driller had aimed for the precise location all right. The drill bit missed by two hundred feet.

The chalk could be a tough nut to crack.

●

The games became deadly serious. In Austin, the Texas Railroad Commission ruled that wells must be drilled twelve hundred feet apart on the same lease, or four hundred and sixty-seven feet apart off each lease boundary line.

Pat Holloway sent teams of undercover agents out hidden by the darkness of the night. He dispatched them to trespass into enemy territory, armed with tape measures, and make sure that other companies had not drilled too close to his own wells. If they did, he would go to court. If any new drilling operations defied the space requirements regulated by the Texas Railroad Commission, he would shut the operators down, which would then allow Holloway to drain the area with his own wells.

Halamicek, as well as other landmen working for Humble Exploration, invested time running down titles on leases owned by other companies. Sometimes a company might have missed a few outstanding percentages of the mineral rights. It was not that difficult to sneak in and steal them away. Pat Holloway had become ingenious at stealing them away.

"The oil companies played King of the Hill," C. J. Halamicek said, "and they were all trying to knock each other off the top of the hill. There were a lot of big dollars and big egos involved. They reminded me of the street drug gangs in El Paso trying to protect their turf."

Giddings had plenty of turf wars. Winner take all. Pat Holloway was always looking for an edge An unquenchable thirst for money tended to keep men on edge. Then the big companies came into the field. They didn't play games. "If anything was amiss or had gone awry," Halamicek said, "they simply picked up the telephone and said, let's make a deal." They had rather spend money than fight, and Pat Holloway was quite content to let them spend money. Poor people were crazy. That was the general consensus. Pat Holloway was eccentric.

C. J. Halamicek had only looked through a few assorted records and could tell immediately that he was in the midst of turmoil and trouble. He was trying to lease land around Lake Somerville in

Washington County. The territory was hot. The land beneath was bubbling with oil.

Pat Holloway was ready to drill. He needed a clear title, and he needed it now.

In every file that Halamicek could find, the heavy cloud hovering darkly over the title became a little thicker and a lot more confused. Two brothers had owned the land back in the 1860s. They were slave traders. They had families and children, a lot of children.

Some of the heirs were white. Some were black. Apparently, the distance between the main house and the slave quarters had been close and easy to negotiate on cold or fevered nights.

When the government bought the land so that the Corps of Engineers could build the lake, the heirs of the inside children received the money. They were white. They owned the land. It had been part of the family estate. The heirs of the outside children filed suit in federal court in Fort Worth, moving far beyond the boundaries of Washington County. They were black, and they had a solid legal claim.

C. J. Halamicek was stumped. There was too much he did not know and even more he could not find. He was eating at a Mexican Restaurant one night with his wife, Chic, complaining about the legal entanglement of the situation and the myriad of problems he was facing. His effort to clear the title had met one frazzled end after the other.

A man sitting at the counter alone turned around and said, "You won't find it."

Halamicek looked up. He had never seen the man before. "Find what?" he asked.

"The information you're looking for."

"I guess I can drive up to Fort Worth and check with the federal court," Halamicek said.

"Not anymore."

"Why not?"

"I've already been to the county clerk's office." The man shrugged. "I may have the only copy," he said. "When the government and the Corps of Engineers took the land, they didn't pay enough people. Whoever manages to untangle and clear up that land is going to cough up a small fortune. "

"How do you know?"

"My company has already sorted out the details, and they are as sordid as they can get," the man said.

He handed C. J. Halamicek the folder. He didn't have to. But he did. "Good luck," he said. "I don't need it anymore. It's too rich for our blood."

Halamicek knew better than to ask fate any questions. He took the folder. "Let me buy your dinner," he said. It was a cheap price to pay.

The next day at lunch, Halamicek carefully read through the intricate details of the federal lawsuit, which were as sordid as promised, drove to Humble Exploration's office in Giddings, and told his story. No one in the room smiled. No one in the room wanted to touch the file. "You'll have to show it to Pat," he was told.

"What do you think Pat will do?"

"Well," the office manager said, "he's real good at doing one thing."

"What's that?"

"He knows how to kill the messenger."

C. J. Halamicek took a deep breath and headed toward Dallas. He sat down with Pat Holloway and said bluntly, "We have serious problems at Lake Somerville."

"What are they?"

"You can't drill."

"Why the hell not?"

Halamicek told him.

Holloway went ballistic. "I already have a rig in place," he said. His voice was one decibel below a scream.

"The land's tied up in court." Halamicek shrugged. "It all happened a long time ago," he said. "Too many white children. Too many black children. Everybody says they own the land, and nobody owns it. Pat, you and I will both be in a box before that title is ever cleared."

The next afternoon, C. J. Halamicek drove past Lake Somerville. The rig was gone.

●

During the Christmas season, Pat Holloway hosted a party in Dallas and brought all of his employees up from Giddings on a chartered bus. There was barbecue. Beer. Lots of beer. And a dance band. "Everybody there was nervous," C. J. Halamicek said.

There was one truism found throughout the oil patch. When a company threw a big party with mountains of barbecue and free cold beer, it was time for the hired hands to start looking for another job. The company was probably one bad well or one dry hole away from going out of business.

"We might not get fired that night," Halamicek said. "But the door was being shut." It's just that nobody had yet heard it slam. The devil's chalk would nail it tight.

35

*C*layton Williams was in a desperate mode, trying hard to make up for lost time. For too long, the turbulent Giddings field had gone on without him, and no independent oilman in Texas had the ability to outthink, outwork, outsmart, outwit, or out-drill him. Clayton Williams was sure of it.

Giddings was already swarming with operators and an ever-increasing number of small oil companies, but there was always room for one more, especially when the last one, or at least the next one, was as much of a mythical giant in Texas as oil. So many of those battling the Austin Chalk were undercapitalized, hoping that the next well would pay off the drilling costs of the previous one. Too many were largely unlearned and untutored in the wicked wiles of the oil patch.

They were the dreamers. Clayton Williams was the top gun, and no one doubted or disputed it. He had acquired his knowledge of the business the hard way. He was savvy. He was relentless in his oil exploration ventures. He had been to the bottom more than once but had never considered quitting or giving up. He knew what to expect in the oil patch, and, perhaps more than anyone, Clayton Williams knew that every day would not be a payday.

He recognized immediately that the vast oil and gas reserves found deep within the chalk represented the fortuitous holdings of a major U.S. field. He had invested a year of his time getting ready for Giddings. He could not afford to wait any longer. Ready or not, Clayton Williams attacked the field with conviction and vengeance. From 1979 to 1982, he drilled more than a hundred wells in the Austin Chalk, each of them costing him substantially more than six hundred thousand dollars. His philosophy was simple: find land, sign a lease, and keep on sinking wells until he looked around one day and all of the land was gone. Claytie could find more money.

He could not manufacture any more time or dirt that led to fractured chalk. He had been allotted only a certain number of days in life, and he was not about to waste any of them.

Unlike most of the operators whose sole interest and last dollars were confined to the netherworld of the Giddings field, however, Clayton Williams continued to intensify and multiply his oil explorations across the nation, leasing more than four million acres, opening up new offices in Denver, Oklahoma City, and Houston, and expanding his old operations in Fort Stockton, Midland, San Antonio, and Jackson, Mississippi. Within two years, he said, Clayton Williams Energy magnified the unpredictable and erratic foibles of the oil game.

He went from thirty-eight employees and thirty-eight million dollars in debt to twelve hundred employees and debts exceeding five hundred million dollars.

Blame it on Giddings, he said. Blame it on the chalk. Blame it on the rise and fall of oil prices. They were unreliable. They were often the illusion of a market manipulated by politics rather than genuine supply and demand.

In 1979, while Claytie and his band of explorationists were gathering around the outskirts of Giddings like the harbingers of an approaching storm, the price of oil soared to forty dollars a barrel. Giddings never looked better.

Even small wells apologetically producing a mere twenty-five to fifty barrels a day were worth the risk. In years past, such wells would have been considered failures, plugged, and forgotten. Not anymore. Bad wells had suddenly become decent wells, and no one was afraid to drill.

Clayton Williams leased thousands of acres of land and boldly dragged his rigs across horse and cattle pastures, atop bald knobs, on the far side of cedar stands and oak groves. His geologists dutifully read their seismic and pinpointed their locations. The fear of the Austin Chalk had lost its grip on big-time operators. Claytie was no stranger to the oil patch, and he saw little difference between Giddings and the other fields where he had worked. He would suffer the consequences that had trapped and beaten so many who had stumbled into the field before him. He greatly underestimated the chalk.

He drilled one dry hole. Then another. As he said, "We had a lot of land and a lot of leases. We didn't have any of the sweet spots." He had been warned against drilling in the farmsteads around Giddings without the genius of Ray Holifield to guide his exploration efforts. On two separate occasions, Clayton Williams negotiated deals to work with the geologist, but, at the last minute, he always changed his mind, disgusted at Holloway's arrogance, and never executed either of the agreements. His business was not large enough or bold enough to hold two egos that big.

Clayton Williams had never used Holifield in any of his other endeavors. He certainly did not need the geologist now. It was his belief that the great Ray Holifield no doubt had everybody buffaloed, a man who had been in the right place at the right time and stumbled across the right formula for solving the enigma of the chalk. There was nothing ingenious about it. Luck played a bigger role. That was his reasoning, and he stuck to it.

Clayton Williams may have been wrong. His costs were soaring and out of sight. He had very little to show for the millions he had poured into the earth, which, he decided, might as well hold the boiling mass of fire and brimstone that Reinhardt Richter was always talking about. It sure as hell didn't hold any oil. Not for Clayton Williams anyway. He was at the mercy of the chalk.

●

Max Williams made an overture. He was willing to trade. Clayton Williams had sewn up so much of the land. Max Williams knew how to find oil. It might be beneficial for both of them, he said, if they teamed up. Max Williams was seeking a farm out arrangement that would allow him to drill on five thousand acres of Claytie's leases. He placed a land map on the desk with the farm out acreage outlined in red. "This old chalk's tough to figure out," he said.

Clayton Williams agreed.

"If you let me take a farm out on the acreage," Max Williams said, "you can go along with us, see first hand how we interpret the seismic, and find out how we pick our oil and gas locations. We've had a lot of success in the chalk."

Clayton Williams glanced over the land map. "Sounds like a deal that might work," he said. "Let me get back to you."

When he did, he offered Max Williams a farm out arrangement on acreage in Pearsall more than a hundred a fifty miles away. It was in the Austin Chalk all right, but nowhere near the boom. "It's the best I can do," the Midland oilman said.

Max Williams was disappointed. He had played the game in Pearsall before. He had no intention of going back. "We prefer to stay in Giddings," he said.

"In Giddings," Clayton Williams said, "I'll drill on my own land. I don't need anybody else doing it for me."

"I thought it might give us a chance to help you get started," Max Williams said. "The chalk's an expensive undertaking if you don't have the right locations."

Clayton Williams leaned across the desk, his dark eyes burning like coals. "You don't have a monopoly on brains down here," he said.

The two men never again sat down to discuss a deal, They remained friends. They remained competitors. They remained rivals. Clayton Williams needed a break. He was up to his neck in debt and bad wells. Max Williams had offered him one. Clayton Williams was too stubborn to take it.

●

Terry Stembridge was in the midst of broadcasting the 1978-79 season for the San Antonio Spurs. His life had become a whirlwind. Mostly, he was on the road, living out of a suitcase, and, after awhile, all of the towns and all of the late-night, post-game hotel rooms began to look alike. He was seldom at home and had decided long ago that he was destined to live life behind a microphone until his voice gave out and, with any luck, it never would.

He loved basketball. His ability to paint pictures with words and describe action as though it were lines of poetry, filled with imagery and punctuated by a frenetic grace known only to the rhythms of sport, had made him legendary in the field of radio broadcasting. He was serious about his craft. He never took the game lightly. It wasn't life or death, but he had a front row seat, and his eyes were the eyes of those thousands throughout San Antonio who could visualize the action on the court simply because of the words he chose to describe it. He was thin and built like a razor. His friends in the media called him *Stick*.

From out of the blue, Terry Stembridge received a call from Max Williams, who had first hired him as a play-by-play announcer during the inaugural season of the Dallas Chaparrals, long before the team ever thought about moving south to San Antonio. Since then, their paths had taken starkly different directions.

One continued on a grueling and circuitous route to the basketball capitals in America. The other ambled down a pockmarked road to forge the foundation of an oil empire virtually unknown throughout the civilized world. Few were even inclined to argue or accept the fact that Giddings had managed to remain borderline civilized.

Max Williams explained that he had established a burgeoning oil operation in Giddings, and he needed some good people to help him build it. Stembridge, he knew, was loyal. He was detailed. He did not mind hard work or long hours. He was honest, which was often viewed in the oil business as a lost or ignored trait. "The next time you come through Dallas," Williams said, "let's get together and talk about the possibility of our working together again."

The two men met during the late fall of 1978 in the midst of a long road trip, the kind known only to the NBA, and by the time he left, Terry Stembridge had come to the conclusion that his days courtside and behind a microphone were coming to an end.

He had only one request. "I want to finish out the season," he said.

Max Williams expected nothing less of him.

"He put our deal in writing," Stembridge said, "and he honored every word of it. He never left me stranded. Even on those wells where I could have easily and rightfully been excluded, Max always interpreted our agreement in my favor. He gave me an office and a telephone. He let me sit in on negotiations. He allowed me to look for deals on my own. He knew if they were good, I would bring them to him."

Within six months, Terry Stembridge had placed three different oil opportunities on the table at U.S. Operating. He thought they were good. On the surface, they certainly looked and sounded good. He did not know for sure. He still regarded himself a neophyte in the oil business, and he was learning on the run. Not all deals, he realized, were what they appeared to be. There were wheelers and dealers in the oil patch who would look you straight in the eye, never blink, and lie. The bigger the lie, the easier it was to believe. Not all facts with big dollars attached to them were truth. "But Max Williams had a gut instinct, a sixth sense, about deals," Stembridge said. "He could tell the good from the bad and determine which ones were worth a gamble and which ones should be left alone."

Stembridge drew a salary for fifteen months. As soon as the big wells roared in, he paid back every dime he had received in his paychecks and was quite content to live off his overrides, never believing they would last forever, always searching for the next lease, the next field, the next gamble, the next well. He was not driven to strike it rich for himself. Terry Stembridge believed that if he could strike it rich for U.S. Operating, Max Williams would take care of him. After awhile, he no longer remembered what the fine print of their original agreement had been. After awhile, it didn't matter. Max Williams would not forget.

"In the chalk," Stembridge said, "it was a numbers game. We had rigs running all over the field and never felt like we had a dry hole even if the production was bad or considered a disappointment. Max simply squared his shoulders, rolled up his sleeves, moved his rig to another lease, and said, "Let's go find another well." For him, a dry hole was not the end of the world. A good well, he knew, paid for a lot of mistakes.

●

Joe Green was bitten by the oil boom. He had been a high school Ag teacher in Beaumont, and his brother, attending Texas A&M, kept calling and telling him about the ungodly amounts of oil coming out of the ground just down the road at some little place known on the map as Dime Box. Giddings was the hub. Dime Box, it sometimes seemed, had oil running down its streets. It's just a hole in the wall, his brother said, but everybody who goes in poor and drills comes out rich. Ag teachers did not get rich.

As soon as the school year ended in 1980, Joe Green was on the road and headed toward Bryan/College Station. His brother had an idea that just might make them both wealthy. It was an old Conoco recipe, concocted and developed in the Midland oilfields during the 1960s – a patented bond coat that stuck to the outside of the cement casing and prevented oil from flowing outside the pipe, seeping back into ground, and becoming lost forever in other formations. Wasted oil could sound the death knell for an oilfield. It was expensive to find and expensive to produce. An operator could not afford to lose a barrel or even a bucket full because the casing wasn't sealed tightly enough to keep it shooting through the pipe. In Giddings, where no one could ever predict whether a well might last for a night or a decade, every drop of oil was a precious commodity. The bond coat could be a difference maker. David Green was sure of it.

Since his family, years ago, had been licensed to sell the innovative bond coat, he and Joe brought the product into the Giddings field, purchased a building on Highway 77, just south of town, and nailed up a sign that said, simply enough: *Bond Coat Company.* Nothing fancy. Just workmanlike. And effective.

Danny Rogers gave them their first job on a well being drilled by Tom Coffman. The results kept them in business, virtually night and day, for the next nine years. The casing in hundreds of wells would be stained the color of the Green brothers bond coat.

"Danny Rogers was a company man for at least eight to ten different exploration firms," Joe Green said. "He was an independent consultant. He hired the crews. He was in charge of the rigs. He kept them all running at the same time, and they stretched from one end of the field to the other. He often worked twenty-four hours a day." Daylight and darkness were only separated by a fine line that tired men could never quite distinguish, and the hands on a clock meant nothing to him. He seldom ever shut down before a well did.

Rogers sat up his office at a corner table in a Winchester beer joint better known as Shorty's Place. He was jammed up against a jukebox on one side and a pool table on the other. He ate sandwiches when he was hungry and received his calls on the pay phone beside the bar. Danny Rogers, however, left the drinking to others. Neither hard whiskey nor beer ever touched his lips. His drinking days were behind him. Waitresses answered the phone and wrote down his messages for him when he was out on a job. It was the least they could do. Danny Rogers, far and away, was the steadiest customer they had.

He was thin and lanky. A felt cowboy hat covered his long hair. He didn't have time for barbers. Didn't need any barbers. The hat kept his hair out of his eyes.

He was a deeply religious man, but it took God and whiskey-drinking men both to keep the oilfield from blowing up around him. He knew where to find them. One was on his knees. The others held court at Shorty's.

●

Joe and David Green drove the bad roads, sometimes only ruts in a stray pasture, traveling from one rig site to another, peddling their barrels of patented bond coat. They were armed with references and testimonials. The bond coat worked. No doubt about it. A lot of good drilling superintendents and operators said it did. The bond coat kept the money flowing out of a well instead of draining out of the pipe and soaking back in the ground.

Early one morning, as the first hint of dawn crept atop the bare knoll behind him, David Green drove up to a lone rig, looking for business, usually finding it at the edge of the earth, at the end of the road. He glanced at the rig. Men were on the platform and working. They had probably been there all night. None even looked up when his truck rumbled to a stop. David Green stretched his muscles, tried to work the ache out of his shoulders, and walked to the trailer where the company man stayed. He knocked on the door.

Silence. Faint footsteps. The door opened. And there the company man stood in all of his glory, the first rays of an early sun splashing his face. He was at peace with himself and the world, not unlike the way he had come into the world. He was buck naked. David Green stared at him. He stared back.

David Green finally cleared his throat, squared his shoulders, and, with as much dignity and aplomb as he could muster, said, "I am sorry, sir. I have obviously caught you at a bad time."

The company man didn't say a word.

David Green could not think of anything else to say. He even forgot his sales pitch. He drove away and never looked back. He regretted having looked in the first place.

The dust kicked up by the tires of his truck blocked his view. He was grateful. It was one job that the Green brothers did not get. The company man needed clothes a lot more than he did a bond coat.

36

*I*t was not the first or the last time that Clayton Williams would be bent but not broken. He was at his best when his back was against the wall, and his back had become a permanent fixture against the wall in Giddings. However, as he would often say about the risk of finding locations for oil wells, "I don't know how to pick them any better than anyone else, but I know it's a numbers game. Let's roll the dice."

By the autumn of 1980, Clayton Williams was in the process of making a radical and tactical change in his approach to Giddings. A loyal graduate of Texas A&M, a man who bled maroon and white and even flew Aggie flags atop his wells, hired the number one and number two graduates in geophysics from the A&M graduating class. It was a gritty and a revolutionary decision.

Matt Hammer and Steve Pawelek were only twenty-three years old, and Clayton Williams brought them sight unseen into the heart of the Austin Chalk and armed them with a bold mission. Shoot the seismic. Read the data. Read the chalk. Forget everything they had learned about textbook drilling in an orthodox field. Giddings, although Claytie was loathe to admit it, was obstinate, unpredictable, and different. "The oil is down there," he said. "Find it."

Matt Hammer and Steve Pawelek did. Not right away, of course. It took awhile. But, within the strange hieroglyphics of their seismic data, they began to detect the same irregular and unconventional phenomena that Ray Holifield had been able to discern years earlier. They promptly chose a hundred locations. And Clayton Williams drilled. He never doubted them. Again and again, he drilled. Eighty-five of the holes became completed and productive wells. Immediately, Clayton Williams felt as though the chalk had unloosed its dastardly grip and set him free. The great Giddings puzzle no longer puzzled him.

With so much activity rocking the Giddings field, however, Claytie began to fear that the increased drilling endeavors of competitors – and there were at least a hundred of them, some coming, some going, and some staying for the duration – could potentially drain his newly discovered reservoirs of oil.

In his mind, there was only one solution. Drill more. Drill faster. Drill more often. Get to the oil before anyone else hauled it out of the ground. Clayton Williams had the largest leasehold in the trend, more than six hundred thousand acres, and he took a gamble that only a very few would have the guts to take. He went into debt two hundred million dollars in order to keep eighteen rigs all running at the same time. A sane man probably wouldn't have done it. Clayton Williams never thought twice about the consequences.

He was ready to slug it out with the banks, his competitors, his own chief financial officer, and the Austin Chalk. He thought he had a better than average chance of winning.

●

Oil was booming, and Clayton Williams was riding the crest of good fortune. He had drilled forty consecutive commercial wells and was caught in an unending search for more rigs. Forty-dollar oil had suddenly made them the most sought-after commodity in the nation's oil patch. His wells were producing fifteen thousand barrels of oil a day from acreage that stretched a hundred miles long and, at some points, thirty miles wide.

Expenses were climbing. Equipment was difficult to track down. Companies were working twice as hard and falling farther behind, constantly fighting and bidding against each other in a losing effort to find laborers to work the rigs they had. Once they had looked for experience. Now warm bodies would do. The experienced oilfield hands already had jobs or had retired. Clayton Williams even hired three Texas A&M engineering graduates and began training them while searching for professionals. Men were looking for jobs. They would work for whatever wages they could get, and oil companies were hiring anyone who might show up on time come Monday morning. They had no choice. They possessed a lot of hand-written resumes, thrown together in the dim light of a beer joint jukebox, that generally omitted any facts or confessions about drugs, theft, or prison time, sins that could all be washed away by oil.

Clayton Williams, as a last resort to prevent a rampant outbreak of oilfield theft, established Clayco, an oil-field trucking company that would collect, purchase, and resell his Giddings oil. Perhaps, he thought, drivers wouldn't be so eager to steal from him if he were signing their paychecks. They rumbled across the field day and night, a cadre of inexperienced drivers traveling at breakneck speeds down narrow, gravel country roads whose obstacles included holes, ditches, and sharp turns. Top-heavy trucks, laden with oil, had a habit of wrecking, often overturning on isolated stretches of bad road. Several drivers were seriously injured. Several drivers died.

Claytie's idea had been sound and reasonable. He built his own personal trucking firm in an effort to eliminate crime and corruption. He could not afford the losses. He had grown tired of depending on men who simply weren't dependable. Then he checked on his own drivers. Nine of them were ex-convicts. He hired one drilling superintendent who, everyone said, was a nice guy, a hard worker, and good at his job. The man had framed one certificate and hung it on the wall of his office. It was his pardon. He was, he said, damn proud of it.

Clayton Williams had another drilling superintendent who was tough, mean, and, downright nasty even on his good days. "He wore a sneer, a snarl, and had a menacing presence," Claytie said. "He had a bad habit of harassing and intimidating the men I had working for me. They kept leaving, and I needed them more than I needed him. I fired him. He didn't like it. Hell, he didn't like me. He didn't threaten me, but I knew the thought had crossed his mind."

Clayton Williams slept at night in his little Williamsville trailer with a knife beside his bed. Strange noises outside kept him awake.

●

Mike Dudley had learned early that the oilfield possessed triumphs for a few and tribulations for many. He generally regarded himself as part of the tribulations crowd. He watched his first oil well come on the harsh, desolate flatlands of West Texas, where a workingman's success seldom lasted much longer than a tumbleweed blowing south in a cold blue norther. He hoped that his next paycheck would pay off the sins left behind by his last one, and he wondered what might have become of his life if he had gone on to law school after graduation from Texas A&M.

But frankly, Mike Dudley had grown tired of schoolrooms, classes, and books, particularly textbooks, and he preferred the long hours of solitude, spending time as a roughneck on wells outside the sand dunes of Monahans. The wages weren't particularly bad. The hours were tolerable, even though there were weeks when he was on the rig for forty-eight straight hours before ever seeing the road home again.

When a job played out, Mike Dudley tacked his name and phone number on an old board inside a truck stop that happened to be on the road to almost every oilfield in West Texas.

A company man trying to find a good hand, would stop by for a cup of hot coffee, shuffle through the well-worn collection of oil- and grease-stained cards, locate either a roughneck, a roustabout, a derrick hand, a tool pusher, or a driller, depending on which position he needed to fill, make a phone call, and say, "Bring your lunch pail and come on." That's all it took.

No one cared where the job was or who the company was, only that a paycheck would be waiting at the end of the week. It was like religion. Men lived, worked, and survived on faith.

Oilfield hands, especially the experienced ones, had a tendency to be filled with a dose of wanderlust, and jobs, even the good ones, did not last. As Dudley said, "When you were stopped at the end of the day, pulled aside and told to pack your boots and hard hat, you knew you weren't coming back the next day."

●

Mike Dudley, on the spur of the moment, suddenly quit roughnecking in the middle of a hard afternoon. He was tough. He could take a lot of harassment. But this time, the blasphemous trash talking had gone on a word too long. It had been a brutal day. A hot day. Suffocating. The man in charge of changing out the mud was constantly yelling. Complaining. A curse word or two managed to escape his lips. "He was downright nasty," Dudley said. "Mean. The hotter it got, the madder he got, and the madder he got, the meaner he got. I was twenty-four years old, and I didn't need his attitude. I packed my boots and my hard hat and walked off the job. He thought I was coming back, but I was a gone man walking. I thought about going to the nearest bar. Cold air. Cold beer. It sounded good. I went fishing instead."

The next afternoon, a truck from the Baroid Mud Company pulled up at the rig. "Where's Dudley?" the driver asked.

"He quit."

"He coming back?"

"Hasn't yet."

"Know where I can find him?"

"I know where he hangs his card."

A day later, Mike Dudley became a mud engineer, earning six hundred dollars a week. " I thought I was cutting a fat hog," he said. "It was as close to being rich as I had ever been and might ever be again."

However, he did not like the car Baroid gave him to drive. It was yellow with a red roof, and it was, he said, "the ugliest piece of worthless, worn-out slab of junk I had ever seen. I was embarrassed for people to see me coming and ashamed for them to see me leave." The road, filled with strange twists and a few odd turns, grew longer, darker, and more precarious. The miles led him away from the windstorms that tortured West Texas and toward the windstorms that dusted Giddings. He came rolling into town as a card-carrying mud man for the Buckeye Mud Company out of Midland, and he learned in a hurry that the chalk was, if anything, a bastard oilfield. It was different and far removed from the outlying boundaries of the ordinary. It was unsanctified insanity.

The Austin Chalk was littered with the empty footprints of oilfield workers who walked away long before they planned to leave and hardly ever had any intentions of coming back. The chalk beat a lot of good men into submission. Those who stayed were just too broke or too stubborn to turn their back on the field. It was hard. It was ruthless. It was intemperate. It was a living.

●

In West Texas, Mike Dudley drove a little truck filled with hand-packed mud. In Giddings, the trucks were larger and carrying so much mud they had to be unloaded with a forklift. Attacking the chalk was not unlike storming the Bastille. It was do or die and definitely not for the weak of heart. A man could find a thousand reasons to leave if he didn't need a paycheck.

"The chalk was a bitch," Mike Dudley said. "The fractures were deep. A lot of them were thick. While the drill bit kept on turning, we mixed mud with water and pumped it down the hole. What we wanted to do was coat the walls of the hole and stabilize it, then bring up the cuttings made by the bit. The mud had to be delicately weighed so it would keep the well from kicking and possibly even blowing out. However, if it was too heavy, the mud had a habit of breaking down the formation and going out into the zones where we were drilling. A lot of times, the chalk demanded a lot more mud than one of those little old trucks could carry. A little truck was as worthless as a four-card flush."

Dudley left Buckeye to fend for itself back in the Permian Basin and partnered with Ace Barnes, who had fought rampaging oilfield fires around the world with the famed duo of Boots and Coots, to form Ace Mud Company. Hard, disagreeable work, personal disagreements, and the chalk all took a brutal toll, and sometime during the next two years, he said, the romance of their partnership turned sour. Both men wanted to rid themselves of each other.

Bill Shuford of WCS finally turned his attention from drilling long enough to buy out Ace Barnes and establish Rebel Pump Services. He kept Mike Dudley running six trucks, six forklifts, eighteen mud engineers, and working as many as twenty-eight rigs on any given day.

The Giddings field, no matter how hard it tried, could not out-grow him or drill a well Dudley could not find. And when oil came busting out of the fractures, the chances were good that the walls of the wells had been sealed with Rebel mud.

●

The geographic face of the field kept changing every time a new sun rose and a new pad was built for a new well. If a man happened to be a day late, he might be lost and on the wrong road headed for someplace he had never been before or could not find again. The frantic activity sprawling wildly across the chalk waited for no one.

Clayton Williams wanted a straight-hole well drilled. The pad had been built, and he was ready to go. The drilling contractor was on his way to the site with hand-written directions tucked firmly into the pocket of his khaki shirt. Turn on County Road 182. Set up the rig on the first pad he found on the left side of the road. Drill.

Clayton Williams would not be there. He had too many rigs running and, try as he might, he could not be at all of them at the same time on the same day. It didn't matter. The drilling contractor was an old warhorse. He knew what to do. By now, the great chalk field was as familiar as the stray array of lines on the palm of his hand, all running in different directions and never winding up in the same place. He turned on County Road 182. No problem. He found the first pad on the left side of the road. No problem. He set up his rig. He drilled. No problem.

The drilling contractor had reached five thousand feet by the time Clayton Williams, ripping and roaring, mad as a rained-on rooster, turned sharply off the pavement and spun his car to a stop beside the rig. Damn, the contractor thought. For a rich man, Clayton Williams sure did look upset. Might even be angry enough to bite the head off a hammer. He was. The driller had gone five thousand feet all right. He had drilled the wrong well on the wrong pad. Clayton Williams did not own it.

From the time the drilling contractor had received his directions until the time he and his crew turned down County Road 182, some operating company had come in and, virtually overnight, built a new pad. The contractor didn't get paid. Then again, he didn't get fired either. It was just a wasted day and wasted night.

●

Benny Waddlington was in trouble long before he knew it. He had been drilling the Baron well in Fayette County with seven-inch casing, carefully studying the samples that came from the micro-fractures on top of the chalk. He had gone down ten thousand, four hundred, and twenty feet. The mistake he made would cost him. He stopped ten feet short. Waddlington had not yet hit oil. But he found all of the natural gas he could handle.

Gas had come boiling out of the well, the pipe string had begun to shudder, men were working and men were running, and five thousand barrels of mud exploded out of the wellbore, covering the rig in a blanket of cedar fiber and cotton seed hulls all mixed up like a thick batch of chocolate pudding. Waddlington was on the phone, trying desperately to track down Mike Dudley. He wanted more mud. He needed it now. An hour from now would be too late. How fast could Dudley reach the well site?

Dudley drove up and surveyed the situation. Immediately, Dudley saw that Waddlington was right. He was in a bind that might be irredeemable. He needed all of the mud he could get and a lot more than Rebel had on its trucks. Mike Dudley drove to the nearest pay phone, spread the word, and mud companies began filing in from as far away as Bay City, down on the Gulf.

Waddlington knew he was ten feet short, and he was determined to keep drilling.

"You can't," Dudley said. It was a warning.

"Why not?"

"You set your pipe ten feet too high," Dudley argued. "Drill another foot and, with all of that gas down there trying to get out, you'll burn your damn rig up."

Dudley lost the argument. Waddlington drilled. Maybe a foot. Maybe two. It was hard to say. Natural gas burst out of the ground with volcanic force. It caught fire, and, as Dudley said, "You could see the flames for forty miles. Here we were. It was two o'clock in the morning, the sky had been as black as the inside of a hog, and now the field was suddenly as bright as broad daylight."

Bill Fenn, who had producing wells scattered throughout the field, came driving up and made a quick assessment of the well. A lot of gas. Gas was pretty damn profitable. Probably a lot of oil. Wild. And out of control. But, hell, it looked like a winner if it didn't burn them all up. The price of oil was as good as it had been in a long time.

Bill Fenn sidled up to Dudley, his face blackened with mud and smoke, and said confidentially, "Mike, do you think we can keep this a secret?"

"Why?"

"I want to get back to town and start leasing some more land around here."

"Bill," Dudley answered, "just look around you."

"Why should I do that?"

"There must be a hundred cars parked around the rig." Mike Dudley grinned. "We have every operator from four counties out here watching the fire," he said.

"So?"

"Damn hard to keep the well a secret."

By morning, Bill Fenn was out on the road trying to lease the land. He was too late. Bill Shuford had already gone from door to door and grabbed up every acre in sight of the flames.

"Shuford," Mike Dudley said, "was known in the field as a pretty good corner jumper. He would find or hear of a good well, lease every inch of land he could find around it, and begin drilling offset wells."

That's the way it was in the chalk. One good fault could make a lot of men rich.

37

*C*arol Dismukes looked around at the burgeoning number of landmen crowding their way into the County Clerk's office and had no idea where she would put them all. There were new faces and old ones, young men frantically trying to figure out what they were doing while they were in the midst of doing it and grizzled old veterans who could merely glance at the records and know almost immediately if a title was good, legitimate, cleared, or flawed beyond all reasonable doubt.

Landmen were crammed shoulder to shoulder in the hallway and falling all over each other in the office – pushing, shoving, scrambling, often on the verge of fighting in determined and desperate efforts to find the next scrap of land that could be leased, the next scrap of land that might be blessed with oil.

The going rate for a lease, good or bad, was going up every day as farmers spent as much time with calculators as plows.

Carol Dismukes could remember when her office was nothing more than a small, clean, well-lighted place where people came and spoke in hushed tones as they checked through a maze of records for dates and information on births, marriages, deeds, deeds of trust, and death.

She always said, "We kept all transactions of a person's life from his first breath until his last."

She had worked for years in the County Clerk's office, spending day after day writing, recording, and indexing all certificates and documents by hand, wrapping band-aids around her fingers because they would become too sore to hold a pen or a pencil. In 1977, the county clerk unexpectedly resigned, virtually drowning in a morass of chaos, consternation, and confusion unleashed by the sudden and unforeseen discovery of oil. There had simply been too much work and not nearly enough help. In 1970, there had only been fourteen hundred instruments filed. By 1977, that number had risen to more than four thousand and, within five years, it would be topping the seven thousand mark.

The workload had become enormous, the hours from can till can't, the size of the staff unchanged. Lee County didn't dare increase the budget. The tax revenue from oil was tremendous. But how long would it last and when would the last well belch dry and when would the next wells be dusters and working men on the road out of town? When would the motels be empty again, the restaurants closed down, the service companies pulling up stakes, the gravel roads less traveled then left to the weeds and the bramble brush?

For Carol Dismukes, life took a surprising turn and would never be quite the same again. Lee County Judge Carey Boethel offered her the position of County Clerk, and she immediately inherited the headaches and troubles that came with shuffling landmen from pillar to post every morning. They came early and had to be asked to leave when the clock struck five o'clock. The day only had twenty-four hours. The landmen needed more. They were loud. They were obnoxious. They were annoying. They could be a terrible nuisance. It seemed like every time one of them took a big book off the shelf he was in danger of hitting somebody else in the back of the head.

They might fight over the same piece of land, but not about the inconvenience of their close quarters. The records, the documents, the instruments, the titles, the transactions from first breath until last possessed the hidden nuggets that kept them and their oil companies in business. As Carol Dismukes said, "The oil they helped discover poured a lot of tax revenue into one of the poorest counties in Texas.

Those landmen could be demanding and often frustrating. But we needed all of them, and it was my job to be good to them. When the door opened, mine was always the first face they saw. It was important for me to smile, no matter how tired I was, and do what I could to make them feel as if I were glad to see them."

On Friday mornings, she and her assistants brought handmade breakfast tacos for the landmen. They might not work or darken the doorway of the County Clerk's office all week long. They never missed Friday mornings.

●

Carol Dismukes moved forward with the steadfast common sense approach of her heritage. As soon as she took office, she sat down and wrote a letter to each of the major oil companies operating in the Giddings field. Her proposal was simple and direct.

"We need you in Lee County," she said. "You need us. More importantly, you need easy access to our records. We are overworked, understaffed, and trying to benefit your efforts with a very old, outdated, and archaic system. It's indeed antiquated, but it's the best we have. I am asking you for whatever donations or financial contributions you can provide so we can afford to place all of our records – the records you need – on microfilm. It will save us time. It will save you a lot of future and unnecessary delays."

When the mail began arriving the next week, it brought thousands of dollars from oil companies to the County Clerk's office. Critical records were immediately placed on microfilm, which did indeed save both space and time."We were isolated in our own little world," Carol Dismukes said. "None of us was involved in the wheeling and dealing of the oil business. But we saw the aftermath. We felt the impact of the dollars when they reached our treasury and our people. We worked to make life easier for the oil companies. They certainly worked just as diligently to make life easier for us."

One landman told her with a wry grin, "If the well comes in, I'll give everybody who works here a party." She laughed and forgot it.

He didn't. The well came in, and day later, the invitations to a party arrived. Wear whatever she didn't want stained with oil.

Carol Dismukes followed the exact and demanding letter of the law unequivocally and with absolutely no exceptions. Pat Holloway had become the most wildly fanatical icon of success in Giddings. Few dared to confront him, and no one refused him or stood in his way. Early one morning, he swaggered into the County Clerk's office as though he owned the place and asked to have a legal document filed.

Carol Dismukes refused.

"Why not?" he asked.

"The notary didn't sign it in the right place."

"That's not particularly illegal."

Carol Dismukes shrugged. "I'm sure it's just an oversight," she said. "But if you want the document filed in my office, you'll have to bring it back properly and correctly acknowledged."

Holloway was adamant. "I don't have the time to mess with small things like that," he said. He was convinced he was special, he had the money to prove it, and he expected special treatment.

"Then you don't have time to have the document filed," she told him.

Pat Holloway shook his head and looked at her as though he were facing a hostile attorney in closed door debate. "Carol, I am really disappointed in you," he said.

She stared without flinching. Her eyes smoldered. The tone of her voice was hard as nails. "You would be a lot more disappointed in me if I did it your way, the wrong way," she replied. "I follow the rules, and the rules apply to everybody, even to Pat Holloway. That way, no one can complain."

He grinned, winked, and walked away. "I'm officially complaining," he said.

"Perhaps," Carol Dismukes told him, "but no one is listening."

●

Ron Newton was in Giddings, and there were times, like most nights and virtually every morning, when he wasn't quite sure how he had the good or misfortune to find the road to such an out-of-the-way town in such an out-of-the-way place. Then again, Ron Newton was well acquainted with out-of-the-way places. After graduating from Texas Tech, Ron Newton said he tried the wild side of life until he grew tired of it, and, in the fall of 1972, enrolled in SMU's law school. He took courses in business, tax, and real estate, as well as oil and gas, and he stayed in the library until they kicked him out at midnight. A wrong turn here, a dispute there, a job he didn't want, a job he didn't like, a brotherhood of attorneys he didn't trust, and Newton wound up working in the law firm of John Roach, an old SMU football player who was handling the oil and gas work for Max Williams in Giddings, which, the young lawyer said, "made Lubbock look like the Garden of Eden."

In time, his became one of the most recognizable faces in the oil patch, and Ron Newton would spend the next twenty-two years of his life living in motel rooms, working through stacks of records in the Lee County courthouse from eight o'clock in the morning until five o'clock in the afternoon, then driving to Caldwell and continuing his search of Burleson County documents far into the night. He had persuaded the Burleson County Clerk to leave the door unlocked even after the courthouse closed down for the day and everyone else had gone home. His became a life of solitude, dusty shelves, and musty records.

A few hours of sleep and a breakfast taco at Taco Bell were about the only luxuries Newton had. On Friday nights, he drove back to Dallas and closeted himself during the weekend writing title opinions. He shuddered whenever he thought about the number of hours he spent on the road. He trudged his way through old land grants from the Republic of Mexico, dating back to the 1840s, tried figure who out did and who didn't own mineral rights to the land, straightened up titles, and validated leases by meticulously researching unwieldy bound volumes of documents that held deeds of trust, marriage licenses, divorce decrees, liens, and mortgages. He was a lawyer among a room full of landmen, stuffed in quarters so cramped he either had to work on a radiator or steal a place at a table when someone else left to look for another document. In the County Clerk's office, squatter's rights were usually understood and respected by everyone in the place.

"We were running title searches blind," Newton said. "A man might have bought the land in 1880. He had five legitimate children and two illegitimate children. By the 1980s, he may have had five hundred heirs, some legitimate and some from the bastard side of the family. It took a lot of math and a lot of long hours to figure it all out. If a title wasn't clean, it was useless and the lease was worthless. A lot of oil stayed beneath a lot of land because we could never reach a legal conclusion on who owned it. Tracking down titles could be impossible for the inept and a nightmare for those who had wandered down those trails before."

Ron Newton saw oil operators buy backwoods leases from backward landowners, he said, for five dollars an acre and a box of chicken wings. He knew lawyers who had lost their scruples in the slush pit of a good well. "If you needed a good lie and could afford it," he said, "they certainly knew how to deliver. They would do anything for a dollar, and there were a lot of dollars lying loose around Giddings."

He kept a file on those operators who would drill, then forget to pay overrides. Some drove out of town under the cover of darkness. Some were run out of town. A few stayed and became pillars of the community. He knew who was eccentric and who was simply regarded as odd and whom he could trust with his last dollar.

He felt the grief when the sons of rich men, those who had ventured into Giddings and struck it rich, died of a drug overdose or put a shotgun under a chin and pulled the trigger. A second generation of wealth was a hard burden to bear. It robbed young men of their ambition and found all sorts of expensive ways for them to wreck their lives. Oil money built families. Oil money could ruin them. Divorces were hardly ever filed because of love, lost or found. They mostly had to do with bank accounts, mineral rights, surface rights, royalties, and overrides, large or small, real or imagined. Always, husbands and wives were at the mercy of the lawyers, and the best team always won. The facts were generally wrapped in a greasy piece of brown butcher paper at the City Meat Market and thrown away.

Ron Newton went wherever his clients asked him to go and eventually knew his way around the courthouses in the counties of Caldwell, Brazos, Burleson, Bastrop, and Gonzales. During his sojourn in the Giddings field, Newton did legal and title work for U.S. Operating, Bill Shuford and WCS, Gemini Oil & Gas, operated by Jim and Robert Edsel, and Browning Oil Company.

He could drive across the Giddings field and, in any direction, see rigs, pump jacks, slush pits, and gravel roads that had been built because he delivered cleared titles to operators and landmen.

They all looked alike. His title work had been responsible for so many of them.

Ron Newton had watched the field come in with a distant rumble, then explode. He saw millions made and millions lost – the little guys who struck it rich, the little guys who poured their last dollars down empty holes that gave them nothing in return. They might have good geologists to read the land. They had worse luck reading people. Bad leases. Bad titles. Bad luck.

So many thought oilfield hands were simply oilfield hands and all alike. They were wrong. They would simply drive from beer joint to beer joint at night and hire whoever was sober enough to sign up for a job – drillers, as well as roustabouts and roughnecks.

The successful operators found professionals.

So many hired oilfield trash and suffered the consequences. Ron Newton had seen them come and go. Mostly, he had seen them go.

●

C. J. Halamicek had closed in on the land he wanted, the lease he needed. He had been told by Humble Exploration to make a fair offer. He did. The farmer was in his sixties, had been worn down by hard work on hard ground, and had heard all of the sordid tales about the oil business. They'll take your land. They'll steal your oil. They won't give it back. The bastards will cheat you. The last one is no better than the next one. Don't trust a damn one of them.

The farmer heard the name *Halamicek.* It belonged in Fayette County. That's what troubled him even more. Even his own kind was turning against him. C. J. Halamicek was a landman and not to be trusted.

"We'll pay you fifty dollars an acre," Halamicek said. "The lease is for three years. And we will give you a one-sixth royalty."

The old man narrowed his eyes. He coughed. "I want a one-eighth royalty," he said.

Halamicek was flabbergasted. "Why?" he wanted to know.

"It's bigger."

Halamicek waited for the old man to laugh. He didn't. He was dead serious. "I'm sorry, sir," Halamicek said softly. "But a sixth royalty is quite a bit larger than an eighth."

"You think I was born yesterday?"

"No, sir."

"You trying to play me for an old fool?"

"No, sir."

C. J. Halamicek could have easily changed the figures on the agreement, given the farmer the one-eighth he wanted, shook the man's hand, and been on his way. He could not bring himself do that. He did not want the old man to be guilty of cheating himself. He thought it over for a moment.

How could he explain it so the old man would understand without being offended?

Finally, the landman asked, "Does your wife have any pies cooked?"

"Apple."

"How many?"

"Two of them."

"Place them on the table," Halamicek said.

The farmer did.

"Now cut one into six slices."

"Okay."

"Now cut the other one into eight slices."

Again, the farmer did as he was told.

"Now," Halamicek said, "which pie has the largest slices?"

The old man grinned.

"The one with six pieces," he said.

"Let's do the deal."

The farmer signed the agreement. He had not been cheated after all. He kept both pies for himself.

C. J. Halamicek knew that the field was filled with a dishonest array of dry hole people. They weren't looking for oil, he said. They were drilling people's pockets. One of the two-bit operators sold four hundred percent of a well. He banked a lot of money. Then he drilled.

"The only choice he had was to hit a dry hole," Halamicek said. "If he struck oil, he couldn't pay off everybody who had invested. He might even go to jail. He did real well with dry holes. He wasn't alone. When his lease expired, he would hire another landman to go in and buy a cheap lease on the acreage in the name of another company. He re-entered the dry hole. He had plugged it with cheap, porous concrete. It was easy to drill out. He fracked the well, and it became a good producer. He knew it had the potential to make a lot of oil when he pulled out his pipe the first time."

The operator made his money two different ways: The wrong way, and the right way. Bank a little money. And run. Run quickly, and he might not get caught.

Who would ever complain? The investors?

They didn't know each other or any difference. To them, the well had merely been a bad investment. They lost a few thousand dollars. Nothing serious. Nothing to upset or alarm them. True innocence was never knowing or realizing they had been swindled.

"His was like a lot of the hundreds of small companies that hauled their rigs into the Giddings field," Halamicek said. "Some were honest and forthright. Some were built on dreams instead of cash, heavy investment backers, or drilling funds."

The chalk welcomed them all.

Some struck.

Some struck out.

Within a few years, most of them had disappeared like smoke on the wind.

38

T o most, Giddings was an oilfield. To Clayton Williams, it had the faint aroma of natural gas, which smelled a lot like money. Traditionally, wherever he happened to be drilling, Claytie always built pipelines to gather his own gas while competing to purchase the natural gas of other major producers in the field. According to the Texas Railroad Commission, a company was not allowed to flare its gas for more than ninety days after the completion of a well. If an operator did not have access to a pipeline, he would not be permitted to produce either his oil or his gas. It was that simple. The business of oil and gas was a losing proposition if it was forced by regulations to sit untouched in the hole. Pipelines became a company's financial lifeline.

Clayton Williams knew it was imperative for his company to gather the casing head gas as quickly and as efficiently as possible. He had the oil. He had the natural gas. He was frantically building his own Clajon pipeline across the faults, battling against rising expenditures and constant rains that pounded the farm and ranchlands without pity. For two weeks, Claytie's pipeline crew had doggedly fought the downpour. They were beaten down. They were bone tired. Some were ready to quit.

Clayton Williams did not leave them in their misery alone. He drove to the field and crawled down into the mud trenches with them. "With the boss on the ground, we got it going," Claytie said. "I always believed that the best fertilizer in the world were the footprints of the owner. If the boss was in there suffering with his men, they would stay and do their job. Without somebody leading the way, they sometimes wouldn't."

The work was demanding and performed in deplorable conditions. Hour after hour, men dug out the trenches, often standing ankle deep in cold water. Time dragged. Days were as gray as the night. Clayton Williams didn't flinch. He had been rained on before. The pipeline was slowly moving in a haphazard fashion from well to well. It would eventually weave its way for more than fifteen hundred miles across the Giddings field. It was useless, however, a wasted exercise in futility if Claytie did not find a company to buy his gas.

For years, especially when gathering natural gas throughout West Texas, he had worked with LoVaca, but the company found itself bombarded with a rising number of lawsuits and regulatory problems. Drowning in a morass of trouble – legally, financially, and otherwise – LoVaca had changed its name to Valero, and Clayton Williams drove down to San Antonio to outline his proposal for Dan Eldridge, a smart, hard-nosed trader with the firm.

Eldridge knew all about Giddings and specifically the Austin Chalk. He was not impressed. The field had only produced a small volume of natural gas, or so he had been told, and it was scattered over hundreds of square miles. A good field today. A ghost field tomorrow. No guarantees. Such were the folk tales of the chalk.

●

Of course, the ultimate financial risk for gathering, processing, and delivering the gas lay with Clajon, and Clayton Williams understood the consequences of the impending gamble as much as anyone. There was no question he was facing the erratic peculiarities of extracting oil and gas from the forbidding chalk. That was cut in stone. The exorbitant cost of construction and acquiring so many miles of pipeline right-of-way could at times be damned discouraging. Claytie, as was his nature, fretted about the durability of a field where production could be expected to deplete by forty to fifty percent a year. Yes, he understood the gamble. It was all his personal gamble. Valero faced hardly any risk at all.

The sticking point, as always, was price.

Clayton Williams wanted more money. Valero was offering less. One meeting between Don Eldridge and Robert Lyon, Claytie's hired trouble shooter, only led to another. One was argumentative. Another was contentious. Then the discussions became acrimonious. Eldridge and Lyon finally worked out a deal that they thought would be acceptable. Clayton Williams rejected it. The deal died. Maybe it was dead before negotiations even began.

Dan Eldridge recalled, "Clayton was pulling for more and more money, and we had people in the middle saying that there wasn't any gas in Giddings, that there would never be any gas in Giddings. So here was our dilemma. How do you pay a guy for building a big system up front and still not overpay if he's right and Valero's wrong?"

●

Eldridge met with management one more time and argued them out of a few more dollars. He called Clayton Williams. "A while back, I gave you a final offer," he said.

"And I turned it down."

"It seems the offer wasn't final after all," Eldridge said. "I have a new one."

Claytie listened. He scratched the figures on a scrap piece of paper to see if he could make the numbers work. It wasn't what he wanted. It wasn't even what Clajon deserved. He was running out of time. Clayton Williams broke the silence. "We have a deal," he said.

The Valero Contract more than validated the gamble Clayton Williams had taken in Giddings. It turned out to be worth millions of dollars to him.

With Rick Boring and Clarence "Quatie" Wolfshohl managing a complicated and sometimes convoluted pipeline system that twisted and turned like a drunken pretzel across the chalk, Clajon, by 1982, would be recognized as the largest individually owned gas company in Texas, delivering two hundred and fifty million cubic feet a day.

Robert Lyon was well acquainted with the pitfalls of the oil business. He had worked for Mobil for almost seventeen years, and one too many times, the company sent him someplace he didn't want to go. One too many times, the company told him to do a job he didn't want to do. He was the puppet. Someone else was pulling the strings. There's no future in this, Lyon thought. Mobil owns me. Mobil owns my soul. He wanted his life back. He quit.

Robert Lyon had no interest in ever working for a company again. He preferred being his own hired gun and handing out his own assignments. He became an oil consultant and, after a few years, he spent so much time working for one man and one company that he had to let his other clients go. His one single client: Clayton Williams. His business: collecting and selling natural gas.

After awhile, Robert Lyon became a hired gun for Clayton Williams as well. He had a heart-to-heart with himself, resigned from his own business, and walked down the street to a waiting office with Clajon.

Clayton Williams and Robert Lyon were flying back to Giddings from West Texas late one afternoon. They were cold and tired. Too many long and distant miles, even by air. Too many hours stuffed into the same old company plane.

They were drinking from bottles of Pearl beer and eating hamburgers. Greasy hamburgers. Cold hamburgers. Soggy French fries. Heartburn was only a bite or two away. Robert Lyon turned to Claytie and said, "I only have one thing to say."

"What's that?"

"Isn't it nice to be rich?"

Only an entrepreneur like Clayton Williams had the nerve to build a pipeline in a strange field across a strange landscape, laying pipe to wells that, as likely as not, would produce as much sand as oil. To him, taking risks were as normal as breathing. The major gas companies all based their decisions on the statistical projections of engineering reports. His competitors, working strictly off the bottom line, did not dare construct a pipeline unless the field had been tested and they were satisfied it was productive and would be profitable for a long time. Clajon did not wait for the results of any scientific or engineering reports.

Clayton Williams immediately began buying right-of-way and laying pipe – often to fields not yet explored or to wells yet to be drilled. He was confident that certain areas would be productive, and he wanted to have the pipeline in place by the time gas reached the top of the ground. He only lost money when the pipe was stretched across dried peanut vines and dried ravines and dried ponds on the way to dry holes,

Clayton Williams said, "If we hit a dry hole, we simply shook the old boy's hand, wished him better luck next time, and forgot our own bad luck. Giddings was a big field. A commercial well and a dry hole often sat right across the road from each other. Every foot of pipe we put in the ground carried us closer to somebody else's well. We were already there while the big boys were back in their offices and still trying to make up their minds about coming."

Said Robert Lyon, "Clayton Williams was a friendly dictator and an impatient man, It was his money. It was his company. If he wanted to build a pipeline, by damn, he went ahead and built it and did not care if a market already existed or whether he was simply betting that the field would eventually turn out all right."

The other gas gathering companies were counting revenues. Clayton Williams was counting miles. He had a team buying right-of-way, and Clajon had more than three hundred employees crisscrossing the Giddings field with ditches full of pipe. "We had a distinct advantage," Robert Lyon said. "It didn't take us long to make a decision and get something done."

It wasn't easy. There were more than a few angry threats aimed at the pipeliners. A judge occasionally had to condemn those long ribbons of empty land that Clajon needed.

The acreage was worthless, barren, uncultivated, and had been damned for generations. If some fool wanted to buy an oil lease or needed to cut any right-of-way for a string of pipe, however, landowners and their lawyers suddenly viewed the tawdry patch of ground as a precious and a priceless commodity.

Clajon never wanted property owners to feel cheated, and, besides, it was far less expensive to work out a deal with landowners than pile up exorbitant legal fees.

Condemnation rulings begat violence. There were even rumors of shotgun blasts in the night. Claytie had to dig his ditches at his own risk, financial or life-threatening, and some said his pipeliners should have received hazardous duty pay. Maybe even combat pay. A lot of crusty old landowners would no longer speak to Clayton Williams. But, in the end, they did not mind cashing his checks.

●

"As a rule," Rick Boring said, "Clajon hired people who lived in Giddings to go out and buy the company's right-of-way for pipelines. They were neighbors dealing with neighbors." No fights. Only a few feuds. The feuds weren't new. Some hadn't liked each other for a long time anyway.

"Clajon did not need or take a lot of land," Boring said, "just the long, narrow strips it required to hold those never-ending sections of pipe." The company did not cut through pastures. Instead, it eased along back fences. "And when we took a fence down, we put it back up," Boring said. "We built it better than the fence the farmer had in the first place." It wasn't simple policy. It was law according to Clayton Williams.

Rick Boring made it a point to sit down at four o'clock on many mornings and have breakfast with a farmer or rancher on whose land he was working. Mama kept the coffee hot and didn't fry the eggs until he knocked on the door. "They got mad if I didn't show up," he said.

Representing Clajon, Boring drove to Caldwell one night and delivered a check for ten thousand dollars to the hospital. "It's for taking care of the children," he said.

No one had ever done such a thing before. Clayton Williams had not felt obligated to sign the check.

It was something he wanted to do. Clajon, in spite of those rumors about shotguns being fired in the night, was rapidly becoming part of the community.

Collecting his own natural gas was critical to his operation, but Clayton Williams realized he would never maximize Clajon's profits unless he was also able to tie up gas from other wells in the field. He was competing against the big boys.

They did not worry him. He was confident. He was fearless.

Clayton Williams dispatched Travis Lynch and his team of gas buyers to every near and remote corner of the trend. They were the new boys, the new faces in the field. They were the unknowns. They had to sell themselves to a variety of gas producers, large and small, then sell the benefits of Clajon. "We run an honest meter," the team told them all. "And we'll get out and pick up your gas quickly so you won't have to keep your wells shut in because of the no-flare orders."

Robert Lyon wrote the contracts, and, he said, "I could make deals that lawyers didn't have to approve. Big companies worked under the dictates of a legal team. I did not have that problem. In the field, we were our own boss. Make it happen. That's all Claytie ever wanted. Make it happen."

Clayton Williams turned them loose and stayed out of their way. He recalled, "I used to say this about Travis and Aubrey Price, our pilot. Don't tell them to go kill somebody and then change your mind the next day because that somebody will already be dead. They had two attitudes: 'We can do it and we will get it done.' They hustled so much that we bought nearly all of the gas. The workers in the field and the gas buyers up front formed a solid team and kicked ass. Our aggressive attitude combined with our geology made us one hell of a competitor." They were, as the bumper sticker proclaimed, busting their ass for Clajon gas. Oilman Charlie Perry simply acknowledged, "Claytie outworked everybody and out-traded everybody."

By the time the early 1980s rolled around, Clajon was gathering sixty percent of the natural gas uncovered in the Austin Chalk trend, and Clayton Williams had built two gas-processing plants in Giddings.

Robert Lyon said, "We were out on the road, buying every compressor we could find. We were buying so many compressors and had so many compressors running that I had nightmares about waking up some morning to discover that, overnight, we had become the world's largest owner of used compressors."

Clayton Williams may have owned Clajon, but he never considered himself a pipeliner.

"I was a driller," he said. "And I survived the oil patch in Giddings because of my growing up days in West Texas. On my father's ranch, on my own ranches, I had already fought hailstorms, windstorms, droughts, floods, and boll weevil attacks on our cotton. I knew what a heavy dose of reality looked like. It made me mad sometimes. It no longer scared me. Bad times? They were sure to come. But a man couldn't wish them away. He had to deal with them. I didn't always like it, but I dealt with them."

●

Clayton Williams arrived in Giddings with a splash. He was a genuine oilman of mythical proportions, and nobody would ever be able to figure out if he had just made his next million dollars or lost his last one. Clayton Williams rode into town wearing a nine-hundred dollar pair of alligator boots, stained with crude, his cowboy hat pushed back on his head, and the wry smile of a man who owned six ranches, had leases on three hundred thousand acres, and a net worth exceeding two hundred million dollars. He would tell *Forbes Magazine*, "I'm not a billionaire yet, but it's nice to have a goal."

Clayton Williams had chosen to move his oil and gas exploration business to Giddings, and the town felt humbled because a legend had chosen to walk its streets.

He hauled in a lot of rigs. He put a lot a people to work, including landmen, geologists, seismologists, rig crews, truck drivers, mud men, pipe men, chemical men, specialists, and technicians of all stripes and pedigrees. He put every roughneck, roustabout, and tool pusher he could find on the payroll. Damn, he said, sooner or later he would need them all.

He never saw the cattle herds, the grazing horses, the peanuts waiting to be harvested. He looked out across the rolling farmlands and envisioned an empire. But then, Clayton Williams had earned his reputation the hard way. He started at the bottom. He rode the highs, suffered through the lows, was knocked down, beat down, left for broke, and left for dead. He never gave up. He was proclaimed as the benevolent dictator of the Giddings field before he ever left his first boot print in hard ground or spudded in his first well.

The town, and especially those he hired, all got together and whipped up a big barbecue dinner down at the old fireman's hall in his honor. He was the man of the hour. Ribs gnawed down to the bone were piling up in the trash cans. A truck was kept busy hauling out empty kegs of beer and hauling in new kegs of cold beer. Empty whiskey bottles were piled almost as high as the ribs. After awhile, no one remembered how cold it really was, and the night chill was dipping dangerously close to thirty-two degrees.

Men were shooting dice. Some were inside playing pool. The clock slipped past midnight. It inched on toward two o'clock. Somebody saw the red glow of the blaze before anyone smelled the smoke, and it hovered above the dark streets of downtown Giddings.

Fire!

The dreaded word was yelled, then yelled again. Round up the fire department. The cry was desperate.

"Won't be hard."

"Why not?"

"We're all here."

Giddings had a fire department all right. It was made up of volunteers.

"We may have all been drinking a little too much," Mike Simmang said, "but I knew what the manual said, and, fortunately, we didn't have any rules against fighting a fire while we were drunk. If we did, somebody would have thrown the manual away. Or burned it. We all climbed aboard our little old antiquated fire truck, spun out of the gravel driveway, and began racing madly toward the fire."

A beer joint was burning, which, in the middle of an oil boom, was almost as bad as a bank going up in flames.

The roof was collapsing.

"We recognized immediately that it was gone," Simmang said. "We immediately made plans to try and pump enough water to save the buildings around it."

Embers were flying. Smoke was suffocating. The wind was blowing water in all directions. Mike Maas, who had been slicing up good barbecue brisket at the City Meat Market since he was sixteen years old, glanced up amidst the smoke and flying embers and saw Curtis Christiansen up on the burning roof, battling the blaze with his hose. It was a fight he could not win. The fire kept inching closer, Christiansen kept retreating as the fire scorched his face, and he suddenly realized that another man was on the roof with him, helping him hold the big hose steady.

Christiansen snapped around. It was a face he did not recognize, a grim face blackened by smoke, a blistered face sweating profusely in the frigid chill of the night. "Are you with the fire department?" Christiansen yelled.

"No," the man yelled back.

"You goofy sonuvabitch, get off the damn roof." Christiansen was in his face shouting now. "You're gonna get yourself killed up here."

The man crawled over the edge of the beer joint. Christiansen followed him to the ground as the flames devoured the last patch of wooden rafters where they had stood.

Rusty sheets of tin tumbled downward, pockmarked with glowing red embers. Curtis Christiansen was still holding one end of the hose. Clayton Williams, wearing his nine-hundred dollar alligator boots, held the other. "I think we could have put it out," he said.

Of course, Clayton Williams had never seen any job, no matter how daunting, he didn't think he could finish.

Mike Simmang only grinned. "Claytie had drunk so much whiskey he thought he was a firefighter," he said.

Clayton Williams did admit he had a damn good time, so good in fact that he reached into his pocket, grabbed a pen, and, on the spot, in the dim fire light of a beer joint crumbling to the ground in ashes, wrote a check for fifteen hundred dollars and gave it to the Giddings Volunteer Fire Department.

39

Jimmy Luecke had grown weary of the road. For a man sworn to combat crime, he was in the right place. He watched the traffic increase on the highways coming into and out of Giddings. He kept an eye on his share of oil thieves. As soon as the what-nots, ne'er-do-wells, and scalawags hit the open highway, they belonged to him. A badge and a gun and a bad attitude had made Jimmy Luecke the most feared man in several counties.

As the boom began to sprout oil wells as thick as sunflowers in summer, he wrote his final ticket, hauled his last felon to jail, and prepared to hand his highway patrol car over to another officer. Somebody else could keep the law and order in Giddings. Somebody else could endure the pleasure of breaking up barroom brawls. Somebody else could drive fast with his siren screaming in the night. His interest had turned to oil.

Oil was money. Jimmy Luecke liked money. He hated like hell to spend it. He loved making it. Luecke was no stranger to the oil business. He had already packaged some of his family's land together, leased the acreage to Humble Exploration in lieu of dragging Pat Holloway to a backroom cell, and experienced a slight taste of the potential and massive fortune that lay at the bottom of a good well. It had whetted his appetite, and Jimmy Luecke wanted more. Too much might not be quite enough.

●

The field was still quite young, and Randy Stewart continued to handle legal work in Giddings for Irv Deal and Windsor Energy. He had developed a pretty good reputation for troubleshooting problems that arose in the field, and he even took a few of the serious disputes up to Dallas to be settled by lawsuits.

Lawyers lived for courtroom battles, the bloodier the better. Stewart preferred the chalk. It could be just as bloody. For a lot of operators, however, it sometimes seemed that as much oil was won or lost in the courtroom as in the oil patch itself.

When Ray Holifield branched out as an operator, as well as a geologist, Stewart worked with him to pinpoint his drilling sites in the ground while moving rocks, earth, and stubborn landowners to make sure drilling rigs could get back to the locations. In addition, as Windsor Energy's rigs continued to penetrate the chalk, Irv Deal, heavily burdened by the need for more money to finance more wells and keep his farm out agreements intact, began asking Stewart to help him raise critical investment dollars.

Throughout Lee County, it was no secret that Randy Stewart was showing some interest in the prospects of locating oil wells he could sell, so it did not surprise the young attorney when the telephone rang. The frantic days of the boom had kept it ringing. Potential investors, salesmen, service supply companies, scam artists, drilling contractors, lease hounds, and landmen all had his phone number. Odd hours of the day or night were inconsequential. Got a deal, call Randy Stewart. Got a problem, call Randy Stewart.

Charles McLeod, Windsor Energy's CEO, was on the other end of the line. "Randy," he said, "we've had a call from Jimmy Luecke. He wants to talk to someone about investing in a well. I don't think he can afford it, but we sure don't want to piss off some lawman who could interfere with us moving our rigs between locations. Will you talk to him and let him down easy so there are no hard feelings?"

What a waste of time, Stewart thought. But what he told McLeod was, "Sure, I'll set up a meeting."

He walked down to meet Jimmy Luecke in front of the sheriff's office and wedged himself into the front seat of the highway patrol cruiser.

"I want to invest in an oil well," Luecke said. He was not a big believer in either small talk or formalities.

"It can be awfully expensive," Stewart said.

"Don't care."

Stewart certainly did not want to offend the man who ruled the highway with a badge, a gun, and a particularly onerous attitude. Stewart drove the same highways. He did not want to keep looking into his rearview mirror in case Luecke might be persuaded to hold a grudge. Don't cross Jimmy Luecke. That had long been the common sense belief around Giddings. Luecke never forgets. He always gets even.

Stewart, however, felt that an oil venture could be a little too risky for a highway patrolman's salary. He did his best to discourage Jimmy Luecke, painting the worst and bleakest picture he could conjure up in his mind. "It's a big investment," he said, "and an even bigger gamble."

The chalk, he explained, could be an absolute killer. A lot more people went busted than got rich in oil. Of course, you seldom heard about them. Mostly, you only heard rumors about little old farmers walking around town with hundred-thousand-dollar checks stuffed in the bottom of their work boots. The odds were bad and definitely against him. Randy Stewart told Luecke that, as a friend, he would not and could not, in good conscience, recommend such a risky investment.

Jimmy Luecke didn't budge. "I want to invest," he said adamantly.

Randy Stewart used the one undeniable, indisputable fact that he believed would clench the argument and make Luecke see the folly of his ways. "Jimmy," he said softly, "the smallest investment share in one well costs thirty thousand dollars."

Luecke did not hesitate. "Okay," he answered. "Let's start with three wells."

Stewart wondered if the patrolman had heard the number correctly. "That's a total of ninety thousand dollars," he said.

Luecke didn't blink. "Do I write you the check?" he asked, "or do I make it out to somebody else."

Randy Stewart realized that he had no choice and no chance of talking the patrolman out of the foolish venture. Ninety thousand dollars were probably the man's life savings. He reluctantly took Luecke's check and hated to see someone not schooled in the precarious ways of the oil business run the risk of going broke. He hoped that the man with a badge, a gun, and a known bad attitude would not blame him personally if something went wrong and the wells were dry. Big-time investors in the oil game knew what they were doing. Luecke was a novice, a dreamer, a beginner, and Stewart figured the check no doubt included the last dollar that the highway patrolman owned. He did not sleep well that night.

Windsor Energy drilled the three wells. Two of them hit big. Maybe, Randy Stewart thought, the ninety thousand dollars had not been such a big risk after all. Jimmy Luecke might not be rich yet, but he would never have to worry about being poor again. He kept his gun handy but retired his badge. The bad and onerous attitude remained optional.

There were those in the oil patch who were crooked. There were those who were straight shooters. Jimmy Luecke, Stewart said, was renowned for his good luck. No science needed. No geology required. No engineering necessary. Whenever he managed to tie a few leases together and drill a well, an investor could wager his last dollar that the land had a lot of oil beneath it. Jimmy Luecke didn't care who got the oil as long as he got the dollar.

●

Jimmy Luecke had not always patrolled the highways. He was raised a farm boy on two hundred acres just outside of Giddings and was known far and wide as a cattle and mule trader long before oil changed the complexion of the region. His mentor had been the original owner of Schubert's Restaurant, and Luecke learned about the land, its livestock, and the incongruities of life by hanging around the tables and listening to Lee County farmers and ranchers talk, argue, and pontificate as they drank their way into the late hours of a Saturday night. When the doors finally closed at Schubert's, they would all stumble down the street to a nearby beer joint and drink until the last neon sign went dark. Even then, they weren't ready to call it quits.

"Let's go on over to LaGrange," a farmer said one night.

"What's open at LaGrange this hour?"

"The Chicken Ranch."

"The girls still up at this time of night?"

"Those girls will get up anytime you knock on the door."

One rancher shook his head. "I guess I'll go on back to the house," he said.

"Why do a fool thing like that?"

"I got more woman than I can handle at home."

"Then let's go to your house," the farmer said as he tossed his last beer bottle into the gutter.

Life was what a man made of it in Giddings, Texas.

●

The hardships connected with finding oil could bring people together or drive them apart. Jimmy Luecke and Randy Stewart formed a fast friendship, which would, in time, lead to a business partnership, Tex-Lee Operating Company. It was only the latest in a long line of hard-nosed operating companies begat by the boom.

Tex-Lee, however, was different. Tex-Lee was home grown and pure Giddings. Stewart handled the legal aspects of the oil venture – leasing acreage and securing land titles – and Luecke handled all field operations. The drilling and fracking operations were placed in the experienced hands of Clarence Cheatham, who had once served as field superintendent for Windsor Energy. It was Stewart who had originally recommended him to Irv Deal, and Cheatham had been the man whose key decisions, made with dictatorial authority, resulted in a number of big producing wells for Windsor.

Clarence Cheatham never forgot Randy Stewart and had a soft spot for Tex-Lee Operating. He was a bull-of-the-woods kind of man, physically imposing and a born leader. He knew a lot about the fine art of drinking whiskey, could find a party or start one, regardless of the hour, and he sometimes acted as though he had invented oil just so he would have an excuse to drill for it. He only had a high school education but was smart and wily enough to one day become the mayor of a town in Oklahoma. He did confess, with a certain amount of humility, that he knew as much about the oil business as anyone living or dead or caught somewhere between the two. During any kind of negotiations, Randy Stewart made sure he ran his assortment of ideas and options past Clarence Cheatham before ever making a final decision. The old oilman might not always be right, but he damn sure thought he was. Every new play in the chalk had its own peculiarities.

Stewart continued to raise investment dollars, and he no longer worried about whether or not a venture might be too risky for a former highway patrolman's salary. If needed, Jimmy Luecke could write checks with the big boys now. However, he remained tightfisted and conservative by nature. As one operator said of him, "You're never going to find Jimmy on the leading edge of risk."

Together, Stewart and Luecke began leasing a lot of acreage on the *up dip* side of the trend. Most operators had shunned it. The business, so often, had a follow-the-leader mentality. Drill where the other rigs are running. Stay away if the land was vacant and devoid of activity. The chalk was perilous enough. Don't ever venture out alone into an unknown field. It was a sin without redemption.

Randy Stewart and Jimmy Luecke found themselves virtually alone in a remote, untested, and unproven corner of the trend. But the leases were cheap. Certainly no one was bidding against them for the acreage, and property owners were simply glad to see someone willing to take a long-shot chance on their land. Most feared that the boom had either overlooked them or passed them by.

Stewart possessed inside knowledge that no one else had learned. He had known Ray Holifield from his days at Windsor, and Holifield told him to go ahead, lease all of the land he could get, and go for broke if he had to. "I don't think the wells will produce a lot of oil," the geologist said, "but as long as the price of oil stays above twenty-five dollars a barrel, they should be profitable. In the past, I've spotted a little oil around the Navarro Sand. It's fairly shallow, not much more than five thousand feet deep. It won't cost you much to drill, not like it would in the chalk anyway, and at forty dollars a barrel, you can own that whole section of the field."

Holifield was right.

Stewart was introduced to Bill Noble, a former band director who had traded in his baton for a chance to strike it rich. Noble raised enough money to drill one deep well in the chalk. The hole was dry. The money was almost gone. Noble might have enough left, he said, to drill one last well, if it were shallow and cheap, just to see what the earth might be hiding, provided, of course, anything of value lay in the hole between the peanuts and hell.

Randy Stewart knew what was there: Taylor Sand, It was ground where Ray Holifield had spotted traces of oil. Stewart made Bill Noble a typical farm out deal. "If you make a well," Stewart said, "we'll give you the option to get some more."

Noble discovered oil at five thousand feet. It only flowed at sixty barrels a day. But, as Ray Holifield had predicted, at that depth, there was enough oil to be profitable as long as the price stayed favorable for the oilmen. Bill Noble drilled twenty wells. But, as Stewart said, "He wasn't going fast enough for us."

Tex-Lee farmed out more of the land. Randy Stewart found a number of other operators to drill the land they had leased, with Tex-Lee taking cash and a nice override in each barrel that the acreage produced. Stewart and Luecke picked up a handful of investors along the way, and they began drilling their own wells. They bet a lot of their own money on the development of the field.

When a well threatened to break loose, some competitor's company man could be seen driving up every thirty minutes or so to study the cut of oil.

He immediately headed back out as the bearer of good or bad news, the kind that helped him keep his job or find a better one. A man who knew first where the next strike was on the verge of occurring was a valuable commodity. One decent well, especially shallow and in the sand, was sure to bring in other rigs.

By the time Randy Stewart and Jimmy Luecke walked away from the field, they had personally drilled, participated in the drilling, or negotiated the farm outs of more than seventy producing oil wells. They had left big footprints in a field ignored by most oilmen, a field that sputtered from time to time but always came back with a vengeance just when the so-called experts predicted again that it lay on the outer edge of dying.

Jimmy Luecke liked to make deals. He never hesitated to give up percentages, if necessary, to make sure that a deal was tightly drawn together and workable. As he told Randy Stewart, "If a well is good, owning a little bit is enough. If the well is a dud, it doesn't matter how much of the deal we own. If somebody has gone to the trouble of leaving a hole in the ground, it's surely worth something, and we may as well try to get it cheap." Tex-Lee bought a lot of wells – in both chalk and sand – where other operators had finally lost hope and left them orphaned and abandoned.

Frac them. Rework them. Squeeze them dry. Jimmy Luecke believed in sucking out the last drop of oil he could find in the earth. On the road, as a highway patrolman, his word had been law. In the oilfield, his word still carried the same authority. Whatever he did, right or wrong, Luecke did with conviction. If a competitor, an investor, or a hired hand did not like his decisions or the way he operated his oil company, Jimmy Luecke had no qualms about showing him the quickest road out of the county. He knew all of the roads. Some said Jimmy Luecke knew who was buried beside a few of them.

Luecke did not spend all of his time on a backroad or in the oilfield. He wisely invested in a couple of housing developments in Giddings and decided to purchase the venerable old Schubert's Restaurant so, he said laughingly, he could keep his wife off the streets. He spent most mornings at the cash register, presiding over the regular breakfast crowd, and it hardly ever changed. "This is a good place to get together with my friends," he told *Texas Monthly's* Harry Hurt III. "When I get up in the morning and handle a little cash, it makes me feel good."

It had happened years earlier. Randy Stewart could not remember all of the sordid details, but an oil promoter, peddling promises filled with vim, vigor, and excitement, had stood eyeball-to-eyeball with him, his face as righteous as a Lutheran minister on Sunday morning, and told him a bald-faced lie.

The promoter had cheated another man, lied to him, and acted as though it were just another typical day in the oilfield. No need to get upset, he said. In this game, the truth was never as important as the money that could be made. Oil, as far as he was concened, was nothing more than a high-dollar game of liar's poker. The promoter laughed and shrugged it off. He considered his deals similar to street corner shell games. You pay your money. You take your chances. The hand is always quicker than the eye.

Stewart didn't laugh or even smile. He unceremoniously ushered the promoter out of his office. "Don't come back or call," he told him. "We won't ever be doing business together."

The promoter didn't really consider himself a scam artist or even a confidence man. He just liked to play loose and fast with the facts and, in the next breath, alter whichever facts he might need to revise in order to make a bad deal sound infinitely better than it was.

Years later, Randy Stewart received a phone call in his office and immediately recognized the tenor of the voice, filled with vim, vigor, and excitement. He had heard it all before.

"I've got a deal," the promoter said, brimming with confidence.

"I know all about your deals."

"How's that?"

"You offered me one of your deals several years ago," Stewart said, "and you're the sorry sonuvabitch who lied to me."

Silence. "Was that you?" the promoter asked.

"It was."

"Sorry to have bothered you," the man said. "I didn't recall your name."

"In the oilfield," Randy Stewart said, "you kept running into the same old promoters over and over again."

Some good. Some bad. All of them were looking for a quick buck. Some tried to pick your pocket while shaking hands with you, and they would cheat you every day of the week if they thought they could get away with it.

They didn't have an ounce of guilt on their conscience.

They were the flotsam of the boom.

40

*I*rv Deal had a big decision to make. He had been involved in Giddings since the discovery of the field, and Windsor Energy continued to rake in a healthy profit. By 1981, according to *Forbes Magazine*, Windsor Energy's annual revenues were exceeding a hundred million dollars a year, and his holdings had been valued upward from eighty-five million dollars. He still preferred handling his substantial oil deals from the comfort of a Dallas office, realizing that his operation had done quite well without him ever staying for long on the ground in Giddings.

However, almost a quarter of Windsor's acreage had been acquired from Hughes and Hughes, which retained a thirty percent interest after the wells drilled on those leases paid out. Landowners received their royalties, geologists earned their overrides, and Irv Deal was left with only a relatively small net working interest.

In spite of his enormous success, before and after his split from Max Williams and regardless of Windsor's sterling reputation, Deal was always forced to raise new money to finance each new well. It was a grueling and a constant challenge.

New oil meant new dollars. New dollars meant new telephone calls. New phone calls meant new meetings. And no end at all was on the horizon. Deal stared out the window of his office. He glanced at the calendar. Time was moving faster than ever, and the dates were closing in around him with the pressure of a metal vise. His agreement with Hughes and Hughes was airtight and irrefutable. If he did not drill seventy-five more wells on the acreage by the summer of 1982, he would be faced with the financial agony of forfeiting the leases. Deal was not sure he could find that many investors and drill that many wells in the next eighteen months. Maybe, he thought, it was time for him to leave Giddings and possibly on his own terms.

But first things first. He had money to raise. He had wells to drill. The burden of it all was stifling. Irv Deal said, "My reach, and it was a pretty long one, had exceeded my grasp. I had thirty-nine thousand acres leased and could not drill them all. I had more commitment than capacity to drill. I knew I could sell and get out from under the burden, but I didn't want to deal with any of the get-lucky, get-rich millionaires already working in the Giddings field."

Instead, as always, he met with his self-confessed Patron Saint of the oilfield, Frank West, who was now working with Santa Fe Minerals. The two men had long ago been classmates at Stanford University. "I need to sell off some of my acreage," Deal said.

"What's the problem?"

"I can't handle it all."

West laughed. "That's what you get for being the most over-achieving sonuvabitch I've ever known," he said.

"Are you interested?"

"I am when you're ready to sell the whole thing."

Irv Deal knew how to play poker. He kept a straight face. His eyes showed no emotion. "Maybe that's what I'll do," he said.

"Give me a price for your existing wells," West said.

"Okay."

"Give me a price for your undeveloped wells."

"Okay."

"And give me a price on your undeveloped acreage."

Deal nodded.

The undeveloped acreage was what intrigued Frank West the most.

The price came to fifty million dollars. The negotiations did not linger long. Frank West looked at his old friend and said, "We'll take it." By the early summer of 1981, the arrangement had been consummated. Irv Deal closed his books on the Giddings field. Leases and their potential, especially their potential, he found out, were as valuable as the oil. He slept that night without a care in the world. He had no more money to raise, no more wells to drill.

He read a short time later that Santa Fe Minerals had sold his wells and acreage to the national oil company of Kuwait, and Frank West was on the phone immediately. "I'm embarrassed," he said.

"Why?"

"We sold the wells and acreage for a hundred million dollars."

"You have no reason to be embarrassed," Irv Deal said. "I don't care what you and Santa Fe Minerals made on the deal. I'm happy with what I got."

He hung up. Case closed.

The Middle East had discovered Giddings. The Middle East would be drilling on acreage that had threatened to consume and maybe even bury him. Irv Deal did not care one way or the other and doubted if Giddings would ever know the difference. Irv Deal didn't. Irv Deal was a free man.

●

The ramifications of the boom fell on rich and poor, sophisticated and unwashed, alike. The drilling of oil wells had raged like a wildfire blown by an unpredictable wind and moving in ragged patches across the solitary faces of Lee, Burleson, Fayette, Washington, and Gonzales Counties. Tired old roads were battered and cracked, worn by years of use and abuse, no longer able to outlast or even survive the constant turmoil created by oil trucks and tanker trucks in a hurry to get loaded and out of town. New ones, fashioned from gravel and dirt, cut haphazardly across a landscape once reserved for cotton pickers, weed choppers, peanut gatherers, mule teams, and tractor tires.

Old roads faithfully followed the clearly marked right-of-ways, never disturbing any acreage held in holy reverence by the last in a long line of generational farmers. New ones showed little respect for the land.

They led to well sites, rig sites, slush pits, oil tanks, and pipelines. Once a new road had been carved into a farm, it left a lasting imprint, more of a scar on the terrain than anything else. Little would ever grow where the tire tracks went. The aftermath of a grand and glorious boom fell into the hands of the disgruntled poor and the disgruntled rich.

During those first few years after Max Williams, Irv Deal, and Pat Holloway had discovered, developed, and cast their fate with the promise of Giddings oil, the chalk had fewer than thirty companies exploring the field. It would take them time to figure out what Ray Holifield and his clients, by trial and error, by luck and an uncanny ability to read confusing cross sections of seismic data, had already learned. Giddings bewildered and confounded them. It was much different from any oilfield the professionals had ever before encountered. Historically, operators had consistently found natural gas *up dip,* or closer to the surface, and oil and water *down dip,* far deeper into the earth. Giddings, on the other hand, defied them and tested their resolve. In Giddings, the laws of nature were turned upside down. Drill bits bore into water and oil *up dip* and gas *down dip.* And the oilmen, at least in the beginning, could not figure out why.

Harry Hurt III wrote in *Texas Monthly: The newcomers realized that the Giddings field was not a continuous underground layer of oil-producing areas but a garden of sweet spots, some interconnected with other fracture systems and some more or less isolated. Each well was like its own separate field. Instead of being either horizontal or vertical, fracture systems containing oil tended to lie at an angle like the fingers of an up-reaching hand. The fracture systems could be two hundred feet thick, depending on the thickness of the chalk, but they were very narrow targets, perhaps only two hundred to three hundred feet wide. For that reason, wells had to be drilled exactly above the spots where the seismic data indicated the fault or fracture systems to be. Closeology did not necessarily work. A dry hole could easily be drilled within a few yards of a terrific producer.*

As soon as operators and geologists began to solve the riddle of the chalk, oil companies descended on Giddings like a pack of turkey vultures. Almost overnight, as many as a hundred of them were crawling across the field, grabbing up every inch of unclaimed and unleased land. A majority, as always, were independents, but such giants as Exxon had begun to poke around the confines of Lee and surrounding counties to see what the fuss was all about. It wasn't surprising that a major company had embarked on its own exploration for oil in Giddings.

It was surprising that a major oil company had waited so long. Most of the big boys still believed that the devil's chalk was a trap waiting to strangle them with bad wells and worse debts. To those majors, the lure of Giddings was little different from a beautiful woman who had quietly retained an alimony lawyer long before the engagement was announced. Sooner or later, a man could wind up broke and bankrupt.

●

Austin Chalk oil, by 1980, had become more predictable but less of a profitable venture. Exploration and drilling remained an edgy business, a vocation for those who knew and understood the risks but had the nerve and a few spare dollars to take a chance anyway. President Jimmy Carter, who certainly knew a lot more about peanuts than oil, imposed a windfall profits tax, and, in effect, the price of oil – even new oil that sold at world market value, the kind that came from the chalk – fell from thirty-nine to thirty dollars a barrel.

No one backed away from Giddings. The boom was still in play. But companies became much more selective about where they chose their drilling locations. The price of crude might have been down, but drilling expenses had exploded in their faces. For example, Max Williams had drilled the M&K, the first new big well in the field, for as little as three hundred thousand dollars. Now, shallow wells cost six hundred and fifty thousand dollars, and the deeper ones were being earmarked at a staggering million dollars. Operators were battling to break even, hoping for a big payday down the road.

For roughnecks and common field laborers, Giddings had jobs. Giddings was a godsend. All a new hand had to do was show up for an early breakfast at Schubert's or Dub's Grill, and he would have work by the time the butter had melted on his toast. Crew bosses, on many mornings, lined up in front of the eating establishments, trying to catch the attention of any hard-working soul who happened to pass by. They hired newcomers off the streets or tried to steal those who already had jobs. They would simply ask, "How much money are you making? I'll double the size of your paycheck no matter what it is."

No experience was required. They were merely looking for bodies to put on a rig. They could teach them their jobs later. Most of the new laborers would need replacing by the end of the week anyway. The money was good. The work could break a man down in a hurry. Some were cut out for the oil business. Others couldn't take it, wouldn't take it, or couldn't get away from it soon enough.

Drilling for oil could stagger a good man standing.

Men in the oilfield conducted their work by automobile, by pay phone, and over breakfast, lunch, or dinner in Schubert's. Tool pushers made their reports. Landmen and landowners consummated lease agreements. Salesmen drifted with their brochures from table to table. Representatives from service supply companies handed out business cards. Money under the table was available to anybody who would take it. Operators and their lawyers finalized the intricate fine print of their farm out deals. Acreage was sold, leased, turned, and flipped as often as the dishes were washed.

Danny Anderson pointed out, "If you sat at Schubert's from six o'clock in the morning until one o'clock in the afternoon, you'd run across almost everybody doing any kind of business, legal or otherwise, in the Giddings field."

●

By the end of 1979, the chalk field held two hundred and fifty producing wells with fifty rigs running day and night. Within the next twelve months, more than seven hundred producing wells clustered across the landscape, and the rig count had reached eighty. They covered the entire countryside, as far as the eye could see, as though they were pieces on a grandiose chess board. The Texas Railroad Commission had spacing requirements that did not allow the wells to stand within striking distance of each other, much less toe to toe.

Drilling had even spilled across the lines bordering Bastrop and Brazos Counties. An oilfield that had been predicted to die and be forgotten within a year continued to grow and expand and spread its enormous wealth.

With the riches came the complications and troubles. For generations, Giddings and surrounding counties had been the domain of stoic, tight-fisted farmers and ranchers of German, Czechoslovakian, and Wendish descent. The land was their heritage. Their ancestors had come to a new world to find it, homestead it, improve it, and live on it. Now all of those oil companies and all of those trucks and all of those drill bits were threatening to destroy their most prized possession. Oil was the wealthy but wicked and ugly stepsister.

Oil was making some of them rich, a few of them filthy rich, but they had begun wondering aloud if the personal price of their heritage had become too steep to pay. They criticized, judged, and condemned oil companies for ravaging a proud and ancient landscape with absolutely no regard for a fragile environment that, for so many years, had remained untainted and unspoiled. Until now, only a plowshare had dared disturb the good earth. But oil companies, they swore, were guilty of carving deep, ragged ruts and calling them roads, breaking fences, tearing strands of barbed wire from its posts, knocking down trees, polluting creeks, filling ponds with trash, turning pastures into mud bogs, leaving old rotting junkyard equipment and pipe behind for somebody else to salvage or haul away, and, God forbid, spoiling their deer stands.

Pipeline companies, they charged, were the worst culprits of all. Pipeliners came marching across their lands armed with the legal powers of eminent domain, grabbing up the strips of acreage they wanted, and no one had the right or the authority to keep them from bringing out their big earth moving equipment and digging up farmland so they could bury their underground lines. The sacred soil was splintered with the leftovers of excess greed.

What would happen, they wondered aloud, when Perry Gas built that natural gas processing plant near a cluster of residential ranches just outside the Giddings city limits, or when Texas Refining constructed a ten thousand-barrel-a-day oil refinery? A few more jobs? Maybe. A few more newcomers in town? Probably. A few more headaches? No doubt. Oil was suffocating the very life it had breathed into Giddings.

Property owners, maybe a handful, maybe more, began banding together and forming formal ad hoc protest groups to oppose oil and gas companies, but most just stood around, bitching and complaining on front porches and street corners and over chicken fried steaks at Schubert's. Harry Hurt III wrote in *Texas Monthly: One Lee County lady who lived barefoot in a shanty out in the country beat a pair of big rocks together to express her outrage when oilmen crossed her property. Several Lee County landowners pulled guns on – but did not shoot – alleged trespassing oil workers. Fallout from the oil boom also spilled over into Fayette County. V. A. "Boss" Hrbacek, owner of the Cottonwood Inn in La Grange, told a reporter for* The Austin American-Statesman *that he'd rather have the Chicken Ranch any day than pipeline trash. Some good citizens of Giddings who supposedly welcomed the influx of oil money allegedly conspired to ostracize what they considered oilfield trash from church and social positions.*

The people welcomed the prosperity of the oil boom. Many also welcomed the oil boomers. But they still had serious reservations about the way oil was changing their towns and their lives. One Giddings storeowner expressed this ambivalence succinctly when he exclaimed, "Damn the oil companies! Damn the pipeline companies!" And in the very next breath he said, "I have nothing bad to say about the oil people. Their checks are almost always good."

The residue from the boom had touched them all. Only a few landowners were cashing checks, and they did not expect to cash them for long or forever. Money had a way of running out in Lee County, they said.

Oil would not last as long as the peanuts, and men were going broke planting peanuts, raising cattle, praying for rain, and praying harder that it would not flood the pastures when the rains finally descended to the earth.

Attorney Mike Simmang remembered the old truck driver who worked hard all of his life, saved his money, and built a beer joint beside his home on the road from Dime Box to Giddings. A well was drilled on his place, and he watched day after day as tank trucks drove in and ceremoniously hauled off the oil. He waited for his royalty check. It did not come. Week after week, the tank truck drivers kept hauling off his oil. Still no royalty check. He grew tired of waiting. "Where's my money?" he demanded to know.

"It's coming,' he was told.

"When?"

"Soon enough." The operator grinned. "Don't worry," he said, trying to reassure the old man. "The oil business is tough and it's a slow, laborious process. We have to get a lot of oil out of here before the money ever makes its way back to us. Make sense?"

It didn't. The operator, as the lease agreement allowed him to do, moved in another rig and began drilling his second well. He and his crew drove up one morning, and the gate to the property was closed. And locked. The old man was sitting atop a bulldozer that had been left beside the fence. He cradled a deer rifle in his arms." Nobody's coming in or out," he said, "until I get my money."

"You can't keep me out," the operator argued. "I have a well to drill."

The old man cocked the deer rifle.

"I'm wasting money," the operator said.

The old man nodded. "It's my money," he said.

"The money's in Dallas," the operator said as a last resort.

"Get it."

"I'll have to make a phone call," the operator said. "The phone is on the rig."

"There's a pay phone in town."

"That's a long way to drive."

"I don't care if you drive to Dallas." The old man shrugged. "Nobody steps through that gate or past this fence until I get my money," he said.

The next morning, the operator returned with a check for eight hundred thousand dollars. As Mike Simmang said, "The old man was merely practicing the doctrine of self-help. The operator may have had the law, the fine print, and a lawyer on his side. The old man had a deer rifle. Lawyers are real good in court. They don't argue worth a damn with a deer rifle."

●

The rumors persisted. Every inch of the old chalk was saturated with oil. But not everyone who lived above the chalk had found their fields saturated with oil. Many of the property owners had the misfortune of farming and ranching around dry holes. Some had lost half of their mineral rights when destitute families fighting the economic hardships of the Great Depression sold them to Texas Osage Royalty between 1929 and 1930. They had oil all right, but others were dividing up the financial spoils.

Leonard and Margaret Kriegel watched the boom impact Giddings through the front window of their department store. They reaped dividends because oil meant jobs and jobs meant money and money meant that families could afford to buy clothes again.

All around them was oil and rumors of oil. The temptation became too great for them to resist any longer. Leonard Kriegel threw caution to the wind, reached into his bank account, and took out enough money to invest in a well. It was a risk, he decided, but so was life. Giddings was booming. He and Margaret might as well join the parade and go along for the ride. Besides, it seemed that every new customer brought the same old news when they walked into the store. Someone had struck it rich again.

Within an hour or two, Leonard Kriegel bet the money it had taken him years to save. He counted the days until the drill bit to hit the chalk. Within three weeks, he would know whether or not anyone had found a show of oil in the ground. Drilling had become an exact science. The bit carved its way deeper.

It hit. Nothing. A crew fracked the well. Nothing. The hole was dry. Leonard Kriegel heard the news with stoic silence. His expression never changed. Someone on that day had not struck it rich no matter what the old news said when a new customer walked into the store.

God made some men to drill wells. He made others to sell clothes. Leonard Kriegel went back to his suit rack. Along about the same time he lost his money, he lost interest in oil.

Ken Weiser found himself caught up in the oil fever sweeping through Giddings. All a man needed in order to have an oil well was land, he thought, and, if nothing else, he had a little land. Years earlier, Weiser had purchased seventy-one acres to make sure that the old homestead remained in the family. Within a week after he had leased it for twenty-five dollars an acre, an oil company was dragging a rig out behind his father's store.

Four holes went into the ground. Only one showed signs of oil, and the well came limping in, making a hundred and fifty barrels a day. It wasn't strong.

It would never be a great producer. But it was steady. For years, the well settled down and pumped twenty-five to fifty barrels a day without missing a beat. A man couldn't get rich, perhaps. He didn't go hungry either.

Ken Weiser, from behind the desk of his bookkeeping service, witnessed the trials and tribulations that afflicted so many landowners who had never expected to be in the oil business and had no idea about handling wealth that the chalk suddenly heaped upon them. Weiser sat down with an aging farmer and glanced over his financial statements. The man's income for the year had totaled just a fraction over one million dollars.

"You've done pretty well this year," Weiser said.

The farmer nodded apprehensively. "I guess I'll have to pay the government a little of it," he said.

Weiser worked as many deductions as possible into the equation, figured the total taxes that were due the Internal Revenue Service, wrote the number on a piece of paper, and pushed it across the desk.

The farmer's face turned red, then went pale. "I can't pay that much," he said. His voice was sanded to a whisper." I don't have that much money anymore."

"Don't worry," Weiser said, trying to reassure him. "The bank will let you borrow against your certificates of deposit to pay the taxes. Banks do it all the time."

The farmer's face lost all of its color. "I can't do that," he said.

"Why not?"

"I don't have any certificates of deposit."

Ken Weiser's eyes narrowed. He had become as apprehensive as the farmer. "What did you do with the money?" he asked.

"We spent it all," the farmer said.

Landowners, as a rule, did not have much before oil was discovered beneath their fields. Royalty checks had not eased their pain. Easy come. Easy go. No reason to save for a rainy day. The rains had passed them by. They were rich. They did not stay that way. So many of them lost their homes, their land, and their holdings even while oil was still flowing freely from the chalk. Foreclosures often followed the riches.

Hershel Doyle thought that, with any luck at all, he might have a tax problem. It all looked good for awhile. He and Lillian leased out a hundred and seventy-five acres, picked up a pocket full of loose change, and watched the Gemini Company drill test their land. It's a good well. That's what Doyle was told. It's a damn good well. Without any kind of warning, something went terribly wrong. The chalk belched. The oil no longer reached the surface.

"What happened?" Hershel Doyle asked.

"Don't know." The operator shook his head, as bewildered as anyone else. "The well was flowing real good," he said, "and all of a sudden it just cut off and shut down. I sure as hell can't explain it."

"What can you do?" Doyle wanted to know.

"Guess I can drill someplace else."

"What about my oil?"

"Near as I can tell, you don't have any."

A few years later, Clayton Williams leased the land and tried again. He reworked the well. He had faith in it. The well stayed dry. "It looks like something broke off down in the hole," the driller said.

"Can you fix it?"

"About all I can do is plug it."

The operators, roughnecks, roustabouts, tool pushers, wheelers, and dealers who ambled in to the City Meat Market for barbecue every day left Hershel Doyle more oil on his table tops than anyone ever found deep in his ground. Of course, most of them bought on credit, and a few of them rode Doyle so long that he felt as though he probably owned a percentage of their business. Then he woke up one day and figured he owned it all.

Bad debts had found the road out of town and took it.

The family of Garlan Gerdes was the first and last great scion of the homegrown millionaires spawned by the boom. As many as twenty producing oil wells all clustered together atop the acreage surrounding the Gerdes farmstead, and the earth beneath was a metal web entangled with thirty-five miles of underground pipelines reaching out in all directions. During the height of the boom, the family hardly ever saw a month pass when its royalty check sank below two hundred thousand dollars.

"It paid to have a lot of land," Gerdes always said. It paid to have the right land. It paid to have Max Williams and Pat Holloway fighting to see just how many wells their crews could drill, and, Lord knows, they drilled enough to keep the whole lot of them fat and happy. Williams and Holloway, bitter rivals, were so focused on tying up the field that they seldom, if ever, realized they were drilling on acreage next to each other. Mad men, they were. If Garlan Gerdes could separate them and keep them apart, he had a chance to wind up with the richest parcel of real estate in the oil patch. He did, and he did.

A check for twenty-five thousand dollars a month came to Elder Burttschell, a former county official who, early on, had agreed to let Humble Exploration drill the famed Burtschell No. 1 on his property. At the time, the boom had not yet boomed. The boom was not even a whimper. But Pat Holloway could look a man dead in the eyes and persuade him to believe anything, and this time he was telling the truth. He said the land had oil. No. Ray Holifield said the land had oil. And Pat Holloway would blindly drill wherever Holifield drew a line in the dirt. No questions asked.

Elder Burtschell certainly did not dispute either one of them. If they hit oil, he would cash their checks. If not, he had never left the farm. He had nothing to lose and lost none of it.

Bennie Jaehne – young, rebellious, and ambitious – had left his job cutting hay to serve as Pat Holloway's first landman. He had no idea what he was doing, but he became real good at it, and he became real good in a hurry. Jaehne kept right on leasing vast sections of land, collecting his overrides from Humble Exploration, and he quit counting when his assets reached just north of a million dollars.

Pat Holloway, during a short period of time, drilled more often than anyone else in the chalk, and every well that came in on the land bearing Bennie Jaehne's signature stacked a few more dollars in his account. Jaehne was no longer an agrarian, a man of the soil. His hay cutter was coated with rust. He wore his hair a little longer to reflect the high fashion styles of a disco era, and, not unlike a lot of the new rich, Jaehne decided he no longer needed a wife, not the first one anyway. He stashed away a goodly portion of his money. A divorce ripped away a lot of it. A new wife took a little more. She dangled with diamonds. Benny Jaehne bought himself a new Lincoln Continental and made a two hundred and seventy thousand dollar addition to his Giddings home. He even brought in a hot tub, which was as far removed from the hay cutting business as a man could get.

Jaehne invested in an Austin furniture store and in a new movie house for his hometown. He had become a man of style and leisure, haunted only by thoughts of the battles he had waged and the landmen he had angered to acquire so much land, so many leases, so much money, so many enemies.

Max Williams received a confidential phone call that asked him to meet John and Robert Knox down at their survey company. They had found a man who needed them. They had found a man in trouble. They sat together and talked of Quentin Donovan, a poor African American farmer who lived on the wrong side of the tracks and the road. He owned some prized acreage in the field.

U.S. Operating had already drilled on the lease and struck a heavy producer, a well capable of flowing four hundred barrels of oil a day. At the moment, however, the title had not been cleared. The oil money was being held in escrow by the operator, who happened to be Max Williams.

Randy Stewart was frantically trying to track down the missing and misplaced heirs, and Donovan's note with the Production Credit Association was in default. He was several months behind in his payments, and, without his royalties from the well, he might not ever be able to catch up. Only the Good Lord knew how long it would take before the title was cleared, and the money released to Donovan and his heirs. No one knew the value of it all better than Max Williams. The well might be worth a fortune. But for the moment, the landowner's money was untouchable.

Quentin Donovan contacted the Knox brothers, which wasn't unusual. A lot of African Americans came to see John and Bob Knox when they had a problem. They had all lived together in the same hometown for a lot of years, and there was an unspoken bond of trust between them.

Randy Stewart was asked to look at Donovan's Deed of Trust and determine if there was any way to postpone a foreclosure until his title was cleared.

Stewart came back with the bad news. There was no way.

The Knox brothers called Max Williams because he owned and operated the well. He had the ability to purchase the note and prevent a mortgage company – or one of its principals – from gaining a windfall for a pittance of what the mineral interest would be worth when Stewart, working out of the Lee County Land and Abstract Company, finally cleared the title. He knew he could, but it would just take time, and time they didn't have.

Quentin Donovan had borrowed money, using the land as collateral, and, at the moment, he was oil rich but cash poor. He was in danger of losing both his land and his royalty. The lender, everyone knew, would not carry him forever. Quentin Donovan was at the mercy of the financial system. He had never had any money in his life anyway. He was a stranger to the finer things in life.

Neither Max Williams nor the Knox brothers saw any reason for any institution to take advantage of an old man drowning in money problems. Williams listened intently as John Knox outlined the plight facing Quinton Donovan.

He knew there was no time to waste.

Williams headed straight to the Production Credit Association, and, before the day ended, he wrote a check for more than twenty thousand dollars, which brought the note current. It immediately alleviated the burden hanging like a noose over the troubled head of Quentin Donovan.

Williams would say, "I knew that as soon as Randy cleared the title, there would be plenty of money around for Donovan to make his monthly payments. The old farmer would never need to be behind in his note again. The land was his. Neither I nor the Knox brothers wanted anybody to take it away from him."

Max Williams was right. The well became a steady producer, earning enough royalties to provide Quentin Donovan and those seven family members who shared the property an income of slightly more than a hundred and fifty thousand dollars a year.

Quentin Donovan had indeed been a stranger to the finer things in life. Even he would admit that.

However, Quentin Donovan built a new one-story brick home in the backyard shadows of the ramshackle white shack where he had lived as boy and man for most of his seventy-nine years.

He kept the shack intact. He could not bear to lose it.

But he and his family moved themselves and their meager belongings to better surroundings.

Quentin Donovan might still live on the wrong side of the tracks and the road. It no longer seemed like he did.

He farmed.

He was no longer a farmer.

Quentin Donovan was an oilman now. Just like Max Williams and the Knox brothers, he was in the oil business.

Production Credit had their money. He had more, and that's the way it should be.

41

*G*ary Bryant was drilling a well, living behind the rig in a mud logger's trailer shack, stuffed with bunk beds. He glanced out the window one afternoon about three o'clock and saw a man ambling toward him. He was wearing a badge on his shirt. A pistol dangled from his belt. The constable opened the door to the trailer and blotted out the sun, Bryant said. He was a big man, broad shouldered, weighing at least two hundred and fifty pounds. His face was grim, his eyes hard. He was the law and no one disputed it. He looked like the kind of man who carried a pistol for one reason. He wanted a cause or a reason to use it.

"Where's Gary?" the constable asked.

Bryant thought about lying, then thought better of it.

"That's me," he said.

The constable leaned against the door frame and draped his arm across the butt of his pistol. "I want to talk to you," he said.

"What about?"

"An oil and gas lease."

Gary Bryant exhaled and felt himself take a decent breath for the first time since the constable walked into the trailer shack without knocking. It was his introduction to Jim Dobos. The two men drove down to a little, ramshackle eating joint just south of the railroad tracks. Bryant looked around as he walked through the door. He and Jim Dobos were the only two white people in the room. No one bothered to look their way.

They ordered coffee. Hot. Black.

"I have two places to lease," Dobos said. "Clayton Williams already has one of them. If you like, I can lease the other acreage to you."

"It may take awhile before I can drill," Bryant said.

"I'm in no hurry."

"I'll pay a hundred dollars an acre."

Dobos nodded. It was the going rate. The deal was done before the coffee turned cold.

●

Jim Dobos lived in a little shotgun house beside the railroad tracks near Old Dime Box. He had been born into hard times and never left. His wife Betty drove an old Beatle Bug into work at the Giddings hospital early every morning, and, it seemed that, at least once a week, the aging, decaying car broke down alongside the highway. She had to hitch a ride with whichever oilfield hand happened to drive past on his way to town. It wasn't an easy life. She seldom complained.

During the Christmas season of 1979, Gary Bryant bought a new Cadillac in Dallas and, on his next trip to the field, offered to sell his Monte Carlo to Dobos. "Buy it for your wife," he said. "It's about time she had some reliable transportation to drive into work. I'll charge you only fifty-eight hundred dollars."

"I'd like to, but I can't," Dobos said.

"Why not?"

"Constable pay is the pits," he answered, "and, frankly, I just don't have that kind of money."

"Don't worry," Bryant told him. "You can pay me when you get some."

Jim Dobos shrugged. "I'm not expecting any money until either you or Clayton Williams bring in a well," he said.

"I'll wait."

There was no signed contract, only two men making a verbal agreement. They may or may not have shaken hands. In late January,

Gary Bryant turned his Monte Carlo over to Betty Dobos. Clayton Williams didn't strike oil until August. As soon as the constable's first royalty check arrived, Jim Dobos was back at Gary Bryant's door. This time, he knocked. "Here's your fifty-eight hundred dollars for the car," he said.

Bryant would have torn up the contract. He didn't have one.

Months later, Jim Dobos telephoned Gary Bryant at his Dallas office. "I have us a deal," he said.

"What kind of deal?"

"I know where we can lease a thousand acres in Burleson County. Won't cost us a lot. Might be a real steal."

"Any production around it?"

"The land's got oil. I'm sure of it."

"Keep an eye on it," Bryant replied, "and when I get back down to Giddings this weekend, we'll go over and take a look at it."

"I'll be here."

Bryant started to hang up, then asked, "Can anybody come in and steal it out from under us?"

"I'm the only one who knows where it is," Dobos said.

That was good enough for Gary Bryant. He drove into town late Friday and ran across John Driver, an old friend, who, like himself, had been brought to Giddings by the temptation of oil. During casual conversation at dinner, he mentioned that he and Dobos were heading out early the next morning to check on a potential lease near Burton.

"How much land does it involve?" Driver asked.

"A thousand acres."

Driver sat for a moment in silence, then said slowly, almost apologetically, "You're too late."

"What do you mean?"

"Dobos and I leased the land last week."

The food began to taste sour, the coffee bitter.

Jim Dobos and John Driver knew absolutely nothing about the science of drilling and completing an oil well. They brought in a third partner who did. They ignored and possibly forgot Gary Bryant altogether. A few months and a dozen or so wells later, Jim Dobos and his partners sold the wells, the leases, and the reserves for fifty-three million dollars.

"It was my one chance to get rich in a hurry," Bryant said. "Dobos was loyal only to the next dollar that came his way. This time, the quickest dollar won. He couldn't wait for the weekend."

Lost deals, lost chances, lost leases, lost wells, and lost millions were the curse of the Giddings chalk. Money would make Jim Dobos a miserable man.

●

Gary Bryant stared at the remains of the well. It had oil in the bottom. No doubt about it. He would never produce it. Hope had vanished as soon as the casing fractured. It had been faulty and rifled with holes when the Japanese manufacturer shipped it. Bryant did what any good operator would have done.

He squared his shoulders. He rolled up his sleeves. He sued. He was asking for ten million dollars.

On the witness stand, the defendant's high-dollar, big-city attorney began to hammer Gary Bryant hard. He leaned forward, only inches from the operator's face, spit spraying and punctuating every word, and said in a condescending tone, "How long have you been drilling down here?"

"Several years now."

"You know all about the bad reputation of the Austin Chalk."

"I do."

"You know then that there is no well in the chalk worth ten million dollars."

Gary Bryant smiled. He glanced up at the judge, who had been an investor on the wells in Burleson County that Jim Dobos had peddled for fifty-three million dollars.

"Don't ask me that question," Bryant said.

"Why shouldn't I?"

"Ask the judge."

"Why ask him?"

"Three months ago, he sold a well worth ten million dollars."

No further questions. Some out-of-town attorneys had no business in the chalk.

●

Jim Dobos made a brave effort to change his lifestyle. He had always been poor. Now he had money, and he could not figure out how to spend it. Not wisely anyway. He stayed in the oil business. He bought a six passenger Aerospace CL helicopter. He hired a Vietnam marine veteran to fly it. The copter skimmed along two hundred feet above the ground with Dobos leaning out the side and shooting running coyotes with a .357 Magnum pistol.

"He could hit them right below the left ear," Gary Bryant said. "He was the damndest shot I ever saw."

Jim Dobos loved poker. He loved sports. Mostly, Jim Dobos loved to bet on them. He never met a bookie he didn't like.

"Dobos did business with one oil company, then another. He met operators all over the country, and the smart ones," Gary Bryant said, "kept him as a cash-only customer. It's not that he refused to pay his invoices, it's just that Jim Dobos wanted to keep his money for as long as he could before losing his grasp and seeing it leave town in somebody else's hip pocket. A dollar gone was generally not a dollar coming back."

One operator in Dallas answered the doorbell late one afternoon and received an unexpected UPS package from Jim Dobos. He opened it. He found a *Texas Monthly Magazine* tightly tied together with strings. The operator cut the strings. The magazine flopped open. Stacks of hundred dollar bills began falling to floor. The pile totaled ten thousand dollars. The operator immediately called Jim Dobos. "What's all the money for?" he wanted to know.

"I need you to pay my bookie for me."

"How could you owe the sonuvabitch that much money?"

"I bet one time too many."

Dobos hung up the phone. He wasn't coming to Dallas. He didn't want to face the bookie himself. Giddings was a good place to hide.

Jim Dobos had a reputation, and it wasn't sterling. He wasn't good about paying his bills or keeping tabs on his money. Bankruptcies had a tendency to follow in the wake of his business deals. Gambling debts were staggering. And after awhile, he began having trouble finding partners or investors in the oilfield. Get your money up front. That was the warning. Get it quick. Jim Dobos could make it disappear. Not even Dobos knew where it had gone.

Gary Bryant kept telling him, "You have to be a tightwad if you want to survive the limestone fractures."

The chalk giveth. The chalk taketh away. Jim Dobos was losing it quicker than the chalk could take it. It cost him his life.

By early autumn of 1991, the bottom had fallen out of the petroleum business. A barrel of oil was barely worth more than a barrel of spit. The oil patch was suffering. No one could see a light at the end of the tunnel. No one could find the tunnel. Only a short, narrow bridge separated wealth from poverty, and it was crumbling. Oilmen who went to bed rich weren't sure they wanted to wake up the next morning and face another day of turmoil in the chalk.

At first someone only saw the smoke pouring from the roof of a mobile home parked back behind the office of the Dobos Corporation just off Highway 21 on the outskirts of Old Dime Box.

It was a Monday afternoon, and fires were a dime a dozen in the oil patch. Firemen burst inside and found Jim Dobos lying across a bed. His mother, seventy-four-year-old Magdalene Kati Dobos, was seated in a living room recliner.

Both were quite dead.

During those first brief moments, it was believed that mother and son had probably died tragically from smoke inhalation. An autopsy told another story: gunshot wounds from a high-powered pistol, a .357 Magnum, the kind Dobos once used to shoot down coyotes running two hundred feet below his helicopter.

The pistol was found near the body of Jim Dobos.

A representative from the State Fire Marshal's office determined that a liquid substance of some sort had been poured in a bedroom closet and ignited. Texas Rangers privately suspected foul play. The gossips around Giddings thought it was an odd and uncharacteristic way for Jim Dobos, the former constable of Precinct Six, to die.

Maybe he had crossed one man too many, they whispered. Maybe he was involved with a bookie, who preferred to be paid on time, a bookie with a gun, a bookie who had access to the .357 of Jim Dobos.

Maybe a bad deal or a lost deal or a stolen deal in the oilfield had simply claimed another victim. The former constable could count his friends on one hand. His enemies were legion.

The Travis County Medical Examiner was not swayed by the intrigue. Suicide, he ruled. No note. No matter. There was a definite history of bad health. The mother was a victim of Parkinson's disease. The son had recently suffered two strokes. It was, at best, a depressing set of circumstances.

Jim Dobos, he reasoned, simply went home one afternoon, set fire to a mobile home to destroy the final traces of his existence on earth, put his mother out of her considerable misery, lay down on the bed, jammed the muzzle of a pistol against his head, pulled the trigger, and splintered his skull.

For a split second, he knew what the coyotes felt.

42

*I*t was a curious cast of characters who drifted through the ragged edges of the Giddings field. Reinhardt Richter never stopped shuffling from well to well, always talking about the great furnace far beneath his farm, that solitary location where all the burning, churning lava from every volcano in the world collided with the gates of hell. Always looking for an oilfield job. Seldom ever finding one.

Most of the time, Richter collected junk to stack on top of each other behind the Giddings peanut mill. He never fed his cattle hay. He waited until a road crew cut the grass and weeds alongside the highway, then drove out, piled it in the back of his old truck, and carried it out to the pasture. His cattle didn't eat well. Then again, the herd didn't starve to death. He was indeed a frugal man.

Richter had his own philosophy about the search for oil, developed during the 1950s when he began hammering the ground with his little cable tool rig. "Something must be good beneath this land," he said. "It ain't worth a damn on top."

As the years dragged on, Reinhardt Richter began spending more of his time trying to convince the poor, lost, and wayward that it might be more fortuitous to forget about oil and search for a hidden cache of

Confederate gold bullion buried, like the lava, below the acreage across his farm. He never found the gold. In the dog days of August, however, when a blistering sun bore down from a scorched sky, he had no trouble at all selling his theory about the unforgiving heat of the volcanoes devouring the land.

Tobo Dixon never drove to a well unless he had Crown Royal stuffed in a little sack back under his car seat. Couldn't drink and make a well, the operators told him. Hell, thought Dixon, he couldn't make a well without a drink. Not much. Just enough to keep his heart jump started. What operators didn't know certainly would not hurt them. Crazy Joe lived in a house without electricity and rode the gravel ruts hell bent for leather on a motorcycle, wearing boots and a single spur.

Mike Dudley was the recognized peacemaker of the devil's chalk. No, he said, he was the *Dear Abby* of the Giddings field. The angry and the hurt would talk to him when they were too upset to confide their secrets or vent their frustrations to anyone else. "In the oil patch," Dudley said, "everybody was getting screwed, but nobody ever found the guy who did the screwing. He was a piece of smoke. But every time I drove up to a rig in my mud truck, somebody wanted to pull me aside and tell me his problems. They all had a gripe, and all I had to do was listen and act like I cared."

It kept him in business. If you're mad, call Mike. If you need mud, call Mike. Dudley did real well mixing mad and mud in the Austin Chalk.

Early on, a banker from Dime Box could not resist the temptation of oil. He sold his motorcycle for a hundred and fifty dollars, peddled his helmet for fifteen dollars, took out a loan for a hundred and seventy-five dollars, and used the cash to make a small down payment on land.

He was in the oil business. He leased the acreage. He saw the oil flowing. He started cashing royalty checks. He thought he was smart. Those who knew him knew better. He was lucky, they said.

The banker collected his earnings and established his own oil company. If he did it once, he thought, he could damn well do it again. He hit a dry hole. Then another one. He lost his land, his leases, his oil, his money. He was broke.

Greed had taken another oilman down.

●

Claude Flippin farmed the top of the land, and it hadn't always been kind to him. A good plow might scar the acreage, he knew. But a drill bit and a rig and a slush pit had a good chance to ruin it.

He was content to leave the land the way he found it. Poor and unspoiled if a man didn't count the peanut crops. Oilmen had tried to invade his domain before.

He stopped them. It took a shotgun. But he kept them on the other side of the fence.

Claude Flippin, after a great deal of complaining and negotiating, finally relented and leased his land to U.S. Operating. He watched with doubting eyes as the big rig was rolled into place, and he walked down to meet the man in charge of digging a hole in the middle of his farmland.

He sat down in the grass beside Danny Anderson, who was toting a paper sack. It held a batch of homemade beef jerky and two six packs of beer.

By the time the second six pack was empty, the farmer no longer carried a grudge against either the company or the oilmen clearing his land, building a pad, and dropping one string of pipe after another into the hole. Flippin had never seen so much pipe in his life. He didn't think the string would ever end.

U. S. Operating might find some oil. Then again, it might not. But there sure were a lot of people coming and going, going and coming, at all hours of the day and night.

Claude Flippin didn't know a lot about oil. He did know people. They were all around him, and every last one of them looked like he harbored a powerful thirst in the middle of a hot summer afternoon. Sweat creased their brows and dropped like running water from their chins. A bitter dryness lingered amongst the dust in their throats. Pockets were full of cash. It was a convenient combination.

Claude Flippin opened a beer joint by the side of the road. Behind him, the well came roaring in as a strong producer, and it made him a lot of money, almost as much money as the beer he sold. He trusted the beer trucks to keep delivering longer than the chalk.

From out of nowhere came the illustrious and notorious Al Pampell, nicknamed "Hollywood" because, back in high school, he drove wildly around town in a hot car blessed with extremely loud and extremely overbearing Hollywood mufflers. Pampell considered himself a player, even though he had absolutely no familiarity with any facet of the oil business.

He quickly became a major player. He was tough, tenacious, and a great negotiator. He never broke or bent any rules. Al Pampell did not have any rules. He played fast and loose. He discarded any trace of law or morals on the highway from Houston to Giddings.

Gary Bryant said, "Al Pampell was a man who proved that, out in the oilfield where big dollars were being bet, won, and lost with the speed and audacity of a roulette wheel, you did not necessarily have to like or even trust somebody to do business with him."

Pampell had family roots and a little farm in Fayette County. He was no stranger to the region, even though he had made an inordinate amount of money by building new houses in Houston. Big Al Pampell was rough-hewn, raw around the edges, and didn't make a deal until he knew he could win. He had a solid reputation for buying wood, shingles, and concrete for a fistful of dollars and peddling them for a wheelbarrow full of cash. He didn't particularly cheat anybody. He just knew how to take advantage of a man's weakness and exploit his faults.

Al Pampell had an eighth grade education, or at least that was the gossip in the field. He was a self-made businessman who decided that oil was a better deal than real estate. He was notoriously grumpy and disheveled even on his good days.

"He talked rough and had a vocabulary as coarse as anyone I ever heard," said Bruce Stensrud of WCS. "His undershirt had holes. His socks had holes. His clothes looked like they had been handed down from somebody who wore a different size. He had one belt his entire life, and it was wearing out. His shirt always bore grease stains from the barbecue he devoured while running the road between Houston and Giddings."

If he were awake, Al Pampell was chewing tobacco. He even chewed tobacco while eating a chicken fried steak at Schubert's. Tobacco juice and cream gravy went down the same way and mostly at the same time. Unless a prospective lease was on the table, few could stomach sitting with him over lunch, and dinner was out of the question.

"Al Pampell treated everybody the same way," Stensrud said. "He did not make any exceptions. He treated everybody like shit."

But he had a swagger when he walked. He possessed a devil-may-care attitude. He made every effort to look like the underdog, the mistreated, the victim. He wanted people to underestimate him, feel sorry for him, maybe even pity him, but everybody in the oil patch knew better. Al Pampell was a marked man. High school was long past, but he still called himself *Hollywood.*

●

According to Bruce Stensrud, Al Pampell had a reputation as a hard trader, and he regarded himself as a tough negotiator. He would take a stance, reach an agreement, then, at the last minute, always demand more.

That was his style of doing business. He would spend days trying to figure out some way to screw somebody out of forty cents. He loved to make a deal, but he hated to complete one. Pampell lay awake at night, always fearful that he had left behind good money he might have earned if he had negotiated a little harder and a little longer. Al Pampell cursed himself as much as everyone else in Giddings did.

He knocked on the door of Randy Stewart's room at the Sands Motel one night as the boom was beginning to seriously heat up. Stewart opened the door and gazed into the face of Al Pampell, standing like a grotesque apparition beneath the faint glow of a neon *vacancy* sign. Short. Fat. He had a towel wrapped around his neck. He had bought sausage at Chapel Hill and ate it as he drove to Giddings. He had as much grease on his shirt as he did in his mustache. He dropped a lot of sauce, thought the towel would catch it. He was wrong.

"I hear you're in the oil business," Pampell said.

"I am," Stewart replied.

"That's where I want to be."

"Where?"

"In the oil business."

"Okay," Stewart said. "Let's see what you can do and how fast you can get it done."

He wasn't about to turn his back on anyone. In the oil business, he knew better than to judge a man on first impressions alone. As the days passed by, Pampell put some acreage together, and Stewart arranged for him to meet with Irv Deal and his Windsor Energy CEO, Charles McLeod.

Deal tried. Deal tried hard. But neither he nor McLeod could not pin Al Pampell down. Hollywood never had a plan. He simply flew low and by the seat of his pants. If it felt right, do it. He was never quite sure when it felt right.

"What do you want?" Deal asked him.

Pampell did not admit it, but he didn't know.

"What will make you happy?" McLeod said. "Let's figure that out, then work our way back from there."

"It was," Stewart said, "like throwing blood on the water."

Pampell closed in for the kill. He made Irv Deal an offer, and Deal, weary from the long negotiation, was ready to accept. Pampell could see it in his eyes, and that immediately began to bother him. If Irv Deal accepted his proposal that quickly, he thought, then he must have left too much money on the table. He had screwed himself, and Lord, how he hated to screw himself.

Pampell fumed. And fretted. He immediately placed a second offer on the table, It was even better. Not for Irv Deal. But certainly for Al Pampell. Windsor needed acreage, and Deal was ready to strike any kind of bargain he could get, good or bad. Where's the deal? Where do I sign? Do you want cash, check, or money order?

Charles McLeod excused himself and led Irv Deal from the room. Out in the hallway, he said in hushed tones, "That's a terrible offer, Irv. He's asking way too much money. Even if you sell that deal, you won't have anything left. He's taking the profit and leaving you with all the work."

Irv Deal nodded. He could not dispute anything McLeod said. He walked back into the room and told Pampell, "I'm afraid we'll pass."

Pampell was dumbstruck. "You can't do that," he said.

"Why not?"

"I've got good leases, and you need good leases."

"You're asking for way too much money."

Pampell did not flinch. "I'll take the first deal," he said.

"No," McLeod said, we'll pass on that one, too. Let's just part friends, and we wish you the best of luck."

Al Pampell never forgave either one of them. Nor did he ever do business with them. Nor did they ask to do business with him.

●

William Shuford and Bruce Stensrud probably knew better, but they decided to drill wells on eleven scattered prospects that Pampell had managed to patch together. "He had picked up a bunch of leases," Stensrud said, "and he bought a lot of them for a handful of sausages. We had developed a fifty-fifty partnership with Robert and Jim Edsel, and we had the money to drill. We needed leases, and we knew that Pampell had acreage in some good sections of the field. We realized from the beginning that he would be a hard man to deal with. We knew what kind of man he was. We figured that Pampell would be gunning for us by the time we walked through the door. But his leases were critical. In business, you weigh the risks, and then take the bad with the good."

Al Pampell agreed to meet them all in the board room of the law firm where Jim and Robert Edsel did business in Austin.

It was four o'clock in the afternoon when Shuford, Stensrud, and the Edsel brothers all arrived and seated themselves around a conference table.

Pampell walked in late, as usual, his clothes as wrinkled and disheveled as ever. He looked more like a hobo who had been thrown off the morning train than he did an oilman. He had tobacco stuffed back in his cheek. He had tobacco stains on his chin. They may have been permanent. Maybe not. Pampell did not like old stains. He preferred making new ones.

His attorney was nowhere in sight. Al Pampell was alone. He did not need a lawyer, he said. He could negotiate quite well without one. Pampell was carrying copies of the leases in an old file folder stuffed under his arm.

Everyone thought that he would bring a written agreement. He didn't.

Stensrud recalled, "That was Pampell's style. He didn't want to spend money on a lawyer. He wanted us to prepare the documents. Our time. Our money. His deal. He had it all worked out."

The men began hammering out an agreement. Some give. Some take. A few small compromises along the way. The dollars kept changing. Pampell wanted more. He was offered less. He always held out for more.

The agreement wasn't cut. Nor was it dried. The hours dragged late, and then slipped into the darkness of night. As each section was completed, the paper was faxed to Bill Shuford's office in Dallas where a secretary was working overtime to type the document in its proper form.

Stensrud was amazed. Pampell kept stuffing tobacco into his mouth, one plug after another. He never spit. Not once did he spit. It was an awful lot to swallow.

During the midnight hours, the five men patched together the last key critical components of their deal. Al Pampell would receive forty thousand dollars up front for his acreage. He would be paid an additional twenty thousand dollars for each well drilled on the eleven prospects under consideration.

He would receive an override on production, then earn twenty-five percent of the working interest after each well had been paid out. All Pampell had to worry about was making sure that the titles to the leases were clear.

The partnership forged between WCS and the Edsel brothers was responsible for a hundred percent of the drilling costs.

It was not an easy negotiation. Al Pampell thought Robert Edsel was a crook. Robert Edsel was certain that Al Pampell was a crook. Neither kept their thoughts a secret or their accusations silent. At last, the final hand-written sections of a twenty-page agreement, plus another forty pages of exhibits, were on their way to Dallas. They would be formally typed and the originals flown back to Austin via Southwest Airlines. Daybreak wasn't that far away, and the men were bone tired.

"Pampell's goal had been to wear us out," Stensrud said. "My goal had been to wear him out. Al Pampell didn't wear out."

The plane landed. The agreement arrived. A couple of signatures. That's all they needed. Then they could all go home. Stensrud reached for his pen. He was ready to sign. Shuford was rubbing his temples to relieve the stress and tension. Stensrud yawned. The Edsel brothers were slumped with sagging shoulders.

"I don't like the deal," Pampell suddenly said.

"What?"

His words were as sharp, as deadly as a pistol shot. Everyone was suddenly wide awake. "Don't like it," Pampell repeated. "I want twenty-five thousand dollars for every well you drill."

"You agreed to twenty thousand dollars," Stensrud argued.

"Twenty-five thousand dollars," Pampell demanded, "or I walk."

"To hell with you," Robert Edsel said.

"To hell with the deal," Pampell replied.

Edsel stomped angrily out of the room.

Pampell folded up the papers, tucked them under his arm, stuffed a new wad of tobacco into his mouth, and headed for the door.

Shuford was stunned.

"We don't want to lose this deal for a mere fifty-five thousand dollars," Stensrud told him in a whispered voice. "It could be worth millions."

"God almighty," Jim Edsel said, "he's got us by the gonads. The sonuvabitch has nailed us." Al Pampell had been carrying the nails when he walked into the room.

On the back of the agreement, Stensrud wrote by hand that Pampell would receive twenty-five thousand dollars for each well drilled. He initialed the amendment.

Pampell signed.

Tobacco spittle was running down his grizzled chin as he grinned and left the room.

Lord, Al Pampell loved the oil business.

●

The landowners of Giddings learned a hard lesson early in the boom. They no longer trusted Al Pampell. He talked a good game. He was a whirling dervish in the field, making every deal he could find and leasing every rock that had not been spoken for. He was known to show up at a farm to sign a lease deal, then suddenly offer a thousand dollars less than the original agreement. Take it or leave it. The farmers usually took it. By then, they were tired of arguing and just wanted as many of the dollars as they could get. Maybe they could make up the difference on production royalty.

Al Pampell, however, had one basic character flaw. He would lease land and hardly ever drill. Property owners were stuck. There was little if any drilling.

There were few if any prospects of money.

There was nothing that property owners could do about it. The lease might last for ninety days, which meant that Al Pampell had a legal, if not moral, responsibility to begin clearing the land and making preparations to drill a well within ninety days, or the landowner had the right to reclaim his land.

Al Pampell had no intention of losing the land. On the eighty-ninth day, he would haul a bulldozer out to the site and move a little dirt around as though he might be building a rig pad.

He had fulfilled his obligation. He had earned another ninety days on the lease. He would leave the land untouched until the time came when he had to haul the bulldozer out again and, maybe this time, work on a slush pit.

Property owners were up in arms. Some sued him. It was not a wise decision. Now, Al Pampell could hold onto the land until the lawsuit was settled, and that might take two or three years within the slow-moving machinations of the court system. Landowners faced one delay after another.

Chances were, the suit never reached a courtroom. If nothing else, Al Pampell knew how to work the legal and judicial system to keep his leases alive.

"He was," Stensrud said, "a sly old fox."

Property owners hated him. Some wanted to kill him. A few thought long and hard about it. Al Pampell was always running around town, and, Mike Maas at the City Meat Market remembered, "He always had a bunch of land maps rolled up under his arm. He treated them like found money." None of them were worth a damn. Or a dime.

He never got around to paying one little black lady her royalty, said Maas, and she sued him. She sat down proudly in the witness stand, her head held high.

Her attorney asked, "Is the man who wrote your lease in the courtroom today?"

She squared her narrow shoulders, lifted her chin in a defiant, yet dignified manner, and said with as much sophistication as possible,

"There's that sorry ass little sonuvabitch sitting behind the table right over there."

In the end, property owners had no choice but to instruct their attorneys to add an official *Pampell Clause* to their lease agreements. Bruce Stensrud had written it himself, and, simply put, it stated that if Al Pampell – any members of his family, any heirs, or any potential heirs – were connected in any way with the lease, the agreement was null and void, probably more void than null.

●

Al Pampell may have appeared to be a buffoon, but he knew what he was doing. At least, he was successful while doing it. He would take seismic from several prospects to five different geologists and pay each of them twenty-five hundred dollars to grade the data. He added up their scores, determined which prospects graded out with the greatest potential, and drilled.

He farmed out his best acreage to Endrex, and the company hit thirty consecutive wells – all of them drilled at locations personally chosen by Pampell and based on his grading system.

All thirty of them were extremely productive.

WCS had a standing agreement with Al Pampell. Whenever the company was ready to plug a well that had been drilled on his acreage, WCS would have to give him the well back for its salvage value. Let Pampell go to the trouble of pulling out the casing, tubing, pumps, jacks, and batteries.

Somebody had to do it.

On good days, Pampell had a chance to walk away with as much as twenty thousand dollars. On other days, he was fortunate to break even. When a well was on the threshold of running dry and only pumping a few barrels of oil a day, it was a losing proposition for WCS. The cost for keeping the well in production far exceeded the revenue.

For Al Pampell, however, it was money in the bank. He had a habit of taking every well he could get and squeezing every last nickel out of it.

Now he had overstepped his bounds, and Bruce Stensrud was mad. He wasn't upset. He was mad as hell. After working together for all of those years, Al Pampell had the unbridled gall and audacity to sue WCS for fraud. He charged that WCS had violated Rule 37 in the oil patch, the one forbidding operators from drilling too close to someone else's lease line. He claimed in court that WCS's offset well had not been located far enough away from Pampell's lease line. It was a fraudulent act, he said. The well was draining oil from beneath his lease. He wanted satisfaction. He wanted it in cold, hard dollars. He wanted a lot of them.

It was an asinine claim. Stensrud was sure of it. Stensrud would never forgive him. It cost him more time than money in court. Pampell did not care. He had plenty of time. He did not mind waiting for the money.

In earlier days and better times, Al Pampell owned a lease on the Rohde farm, gave WCS a farm out to drill the well, and kept a big override for himself. Nothing unusual about that. It happened all the time.

Ten years later, however, the well was rapidly running down, barely spitting out two barrels of oil a day. WCS was losing money. WCS made the decision to plug it. Al Pampell, of course, had absolutely no objections. "In our agreement," he told Stensrud, "if you decide to plug the well, then I get it back – plus an assignment of the leases."

"No," Stensrud said. "In this agreement, all we have to do is give you the wellbore back. We don't have to assign you the leases. If you want the leases, make us and our partners an offer."

Stensrud was still mad. He was slow to forgive. He didn't mind a lawsuit every once in awhile. They were part of the territory. He was an attorney. He expected them. That was just the danger of doing business in the oil patch. But fraud? He wasn't just mad. He was bitter. Bruce Stensrud had a personal vendetta against Al Pampell.

Pampell was adamant, however. "Our agreement says I get the leases back if WCS proposes to plug the well," he repeated angrily.

"No, it doesn't."

"It always has."

"Those terms aren't in this agreement."

"Why not?"

"I took them out this time."

"Why the hell did you do that?"

"You sued me for fraud." Stensrud snapped. He waited a long moment, then continued, "You should have read the agreement instead."

"You cheated me."

"You signed it."

Pampell was livid.

Stensrud grinned. He liked it when Al Pampell was livid.

WCS gave him the well but not the leases. Stensrud warned him: "You have to buy the leases from about twenty working interest owners in the well, and there are three property owners in the unit. You need to contact them and pay them for their share of the production. Do that, keep Mister Rohde and the landowners apprised of what you are doing, and I guess you're back in business. You can operate the well, but it's gonna cost you. You won't get the leases for free."

End of warning. End of story. Well, not quite. As far as Al Pampell was concerned, the Rohde well had prospered for a long time before playing out, and he believed there was still oil at the bottom of the hole. Al Pampell had always regarded himself as sly as the devil was ornery, always looking for shortcuts, always trying to acquire something for nothing, always trying to squeeze an extra dime from a wooden nickel, never afraid to use delays in the court system for his own advantage. This time, however, he never got around to negotiating a new deal with the landowners or buying the leases from the working interest owners.

Pampell simply took over the well, and, for the next two years, produced as much oil as he could coax out of the ground. He collected the royalty check on his override with unerring regularity. It was a steady income if a man could earn it. Al Pampell did. Few took notice. Few ever did when Pampell was involved. He could fly under the radar like a ghost in a winter fog.

Bruce Stensrud received a phone call one morning from the landowner where the well had been drilled. "Why in hell is Al Pampell on my property?" Rohde asked.

Stensrud had no idea. The lawsuit for fraud was still bouncing around in the court system.

But he had, more or less, chosen to forget about Pampell. "What do you mean?" he asked.

"He's been out on my land and pumping oil for two years," Rohde said, "and I still haven't gotten my first royalty check from him."

"Nothing?"

"Nothing."

Stensrud contacted the other two landowners in the lease pool, and they all told the same story with the same unfortunate ending. No royalty checks. No money. Nothing at all. Stensrud felt himself consumed with anger all over again, and he told the property owners they had a decision to make.

For them, it was a tough decision. The vote was split. Sue Al Pampell. Or let WCS do it. Al Pampell hadn't stolen anyone's money. He just didn't pay anybody. The royalty payments had simply been held in suspense for two years. No one knew where to send the checks. And Al Pampell didn't particularly care if they had been sent or not. In reality, the well hadn't made a lot of money. But a few barrels a day had always been good enough for Al Pampell.

Stensrud recalled, "The property owners made a deal with WCS, and we hired an attorney to obtain releases of the old leases. Then we took new leases from the three landowners. Next, WCS obtained a temporary restraining order against Pampell for trespassing and had the sheriff chase him off the lease."

Al Pampell was aghast. He counter sued WCS. "I own the lease," he claimed. The fine print proved that he didn't.

Pampell claimed in court that the Rohde well was commercial, but, the fact remained, it had not been commercial for a long time. The lawsuit lingered on so long the pages began to mildew.

Al Pampell never heard a verdict. He never had his day in court. He died on the operating table two years later without any ruling ever being handed down by the court.

There was a large turn out for his funeral. It was agreed by those who hung around the cemetery that most had shown up to make sure the scoundrel was really dead. WCS settled the lawsuit with Al Pampell's widow. In time WCS would re-enter the Rohde well and drill a big horizontal well that became a huge success. WCS gave Pinky Pampell a two percent override.

"She was a classy lady," Stensrud said. "She stood by her husband for better or worse. Pinky Pampell deserved better."

43

*P*at Holloway walked the downtown streets of Giddings like a charismatic brush arbor evangelist. He may well have been the last of a breed in the oil patch – flamboyant, contemptuous, outspoken, and extravagant in everything he did. He had become a legend in the making and was doing everything he could to transform the myth and iconic status of his own existence into reality.

When he swaggered into the City Meat Market at noon, a strange hush fell over the congregation of oilmen, roughnecks, roustabouts, and tool pushers who had gathered over a brisket or rib, heavy on the sauce. In quiet tones and not always behind his back, Pat Holloway was referred to the H. L. Hunt of the Giddings oilfield. He was a man of cunning and controversy, owning a great sense of humor and, by the end of 1980, possessing a personal bankroll of almost forty million dollars, which was not bad for a man who drilled the first oil well he ever saw in the chalk, standing close enough to leave with mud on the bottom of his shoes.

He was a showman. Sometimes his presence took on the atmosphere of a circus act. He disdained a chapel or a church or even a preacher when he married Brenda Joyce "Brandy" Mohammodi-Manizani in 1982.

Holloway chose to repeat his wedding vows in the cockpit of his company's helicopter, hovering at ten thousand feet above the oilfield that had made him a rich man. In reality, he and Brandy said their vows more than once.

They stood reverently side-by-side in the Holloway ranch house outside of Giddings while County Judge Carey Boethel solemnly recited the standard litany of marriage.

Then Pat Holloway took a stiff drink and said, "Hell, that was so much fun, let's do again." As he said later, with a wry smile, "I've heard rumors that there may have been a little too much whiskey consumed that night."

Holloway, his bride, Judge Boethel, and best man Garlan Gerdes – a rancher and royalty owner who had leased a lot of land to Humble Exploration – all jammed their way into the helicopter and rose above a muted landscape as dark and veiled as the night.

The wind was calm. The moon looked away and hid its face behind a cloud.

Pat Holloway took Brandy's hand across the aisle.

He said, "I do."

She said, "I do."

And the pilot, at Holloway's request, suddenly cut the engine and placed the craft into a slow glide, descending silently toward the earth. No sound. No vibration. No cause for alarm. That's where legends begin. The gossip ran rampant around town. "Did you hear what Pat Holloway did?" That was the question on everyone's lips.

"Do you think it's true?"

"Holloway will do anything."

"Marriage is a sacred thing."

"To Holloway, nothing's sacred."

The *Giddings Times & News* even went so far as to report that "the ceremony was *further enhanced* as the helicopter drifted above the oil patch."

"Does that mean what I think it means?"

"Sounds like something Pat Holloway would do."

"He's a crazy sonuvabitch."

Pat Holloway even wrote a letter to a friend, explaining that *further enhanced was nothing more than a delicate German-American euphemism for consummated.*

Giddings nodded. The rumors had been accurate after all. Pat Holloway did, or so he said, exactly what he had been accused of doing. Nothing wrong with it, of course. It was just another wild and unpredictable ride in the wild and unpredictable number of rides taken by Pat Holloway. The quiet, unassuming, conservative, God-fearing little community of Giddings had never seen another like him and probably wouldn't again. Wherever he went, he left a storm in his wake.

●

By the time 1980 drew to a contentious close, Pat Holloway had parlayed his original drilling funds into oil production totaling more than six million barrels and gas production that surpassed six billion cubic feet, roughly equivalent to two hundred and fifty million dollars in revenues even after that damnable windfall profit tax. He had been better capitalized than most when he burst into Giddings, and Holloway was able to move quickly and aggressively while others were stuck on the road or on the phone raising money. As soon as he realized that the play lay beneath the peanut farms and cattle ranches rather than downtown, as soon as he persuaded Ray Holifield to guide his oil exploration endeavors, he became the unabashed kingpin of the field. Holifield always claimed that Holloway had emerged as the perfect client. "He never asked any questions or argued with me," the geologist said. "He simply drilled wherever I told him to drill."

Pat Holloway's Humble Exploration Company became the unquestioned leader in the Giddings oil game where the rules were always changing, sometimes bent, often broken, and sometimes buried in an unmarked grave. He was a magician, or at least an illusionist, with the rules. No one had thus far drilled more wells, pumped more oil, and trapped more natural gas than Pat Holloway.

Then the unthinkable happened. A legal sniper fired his first shot.

It had been two years since Bill Browning – his friend, his largest investor, his old drinking companion – had unexpectedly died with a bad heart. Browning had been beside him when Holloway formed

Humble Exploration and made his plans to attack the chalk. Holloway already had his drilling funds in place, but Browning pumped even more money into the venture, was given ten percent of the stock, and vociferously lobbied for a chance to be named president of the oil and gas company. He had no interest in running Humble Exploration, he said. He merely wanted his high-rolling, high-society friends to know that Bill Browning was firmly entrenched within the mystical Texas oil myth. It was all about ego and nothing else. Browning was already rich. It was important for him to feel important as well. Pat Holloway relented, regretted it, and gave him what he so desperately wanted. Browning, as he promised, stayed out of the company's business. He was little more than a card-carrying president. That was good enough, he said. Browning died suddenly while the field was still young and virtually unexplored.

Holloway did not slow down. He could not afford to. Everything was moving too fast and headed in too many directions – all at the same time. A funeral. A eulogy. A farewell. And Pat Holloway was back in the oil patch and drilling again. Since day one, Mike Starnes, Browning's right-hand man, had been on board to keep the accounting straight and up to date.

Early on, the family had invested thirty thousand dollars in a trust fund for the Browning children. The money was designated to buy leases in the name of the trust, a legal maneuver to relieve the heavy tax burden confronting the children in case the oilfield was as lucrative as Pat Holloway thought it would be and Bill Browning happened to die before his time. It was, and he did.

The thirty thousand dollars barely lasted a year as Humble Exploration rapidly expanded its holdings, but Holloway faithfully kept taking money from his company's account to buy lease after lease in the name of the Browning Children's Trust. He didn't have to do it. He was not indebted to the trust. In fact, he had asked Jane Browning, Bill's widow, to increase the trust's investment in leases. She refused. Holloway kept buying the leases because he desperately needed them. Neither he nor Starnes ever collected any kind of fee for serving as trustees. But Holloway felt a deep obligation to his old friend. He kept right on purchasing leases in the names of the children for no other reason than his timeless respect for Bill Browning. Under similar circumstances, he believed, Bill Browning would have no doubt done the same for him. The two men were that close. Death and nothing else could have separated them.

Browning's widow, Jane, did not agree to buy more leases for the children's trust, but she had approached Pat Holloway, asking if she might be allowed to purchase more stock in Humble Exploration. Mike Starnes, she knew, owned ten percent, and she had inherited ten percent from her husband. It was not enough. She was already rich, but the very wealthy always wanted more. It was an affliction of class and social standing that had been bought, not handed down as a birthright.

"I won't sell any more of my stock," Holloway told her. "I have eighty percent, and I want to keep it. I'm doing all of the work, and I'm taking all of the risks. I plan to hang on to what I have."

Jane Browning was not pleased. She was not accustomed to anyone refusing her. No one had dared to ever refuse her before. Bill Browning certainly didn't. Jane Browning decided to get even with the contemptuous Pat Holloway. She sued.

The day began badly for Pat Holloway. It ended tragically. He was served with the lawsuit sometime that afternoon, and word reached his daughter, Marcy, shortly before sundown. She hadn't thought her circumstances could get any worse. They did.

She had quarreled with her boyfriend, a pipeline man, and she angrily stomped out of his house after darkness had descended across the oil patch.

It was late, but not too late. A new moon dangled in the sky but did not cast any light on the narrow and winding ranch road. She was still mad at the pipeline man. It had something to do with him seeing another girl. Damn him. At least that had been the rumor, and he had given her no reason to doubt it.

The news of the lawsuit brought against her father had left her emotionally distraught. The whole sordid affair was unfair, she thought, unfair and unjust. Her father had worked so hard for himself and Bill Browning, and now a black widow was trying to take it all away. Damn

Jane Browning, too. It was Pat Holloway's life. It was his business. But it was her inheritance, her future, that was hanging in the balance.

Marcy's mind was in a state of anger and chaos. She was less than a quarter of a mile from home, driving hard and fast. The madder she became, the faster she drove. The cement pavement was a blur. There were no white lines or yellow lines, only a dizzying blur of gray turning black. Marcy never saw the sudden curve in the road. The Spider Fiat left the pavement on a dead run and flipped over and over. She was thrown free and lay unconscious beside the tangled and twisted metal.

The doctors who sewed her up at the Giddings hospital said she was a miracle. She should be in the morgue. They quickly shipped her to Austin, and the next ten days were distorted images of endless surgeries and drugs that tried to fight back against the unbearable pain. Accidents could happen in the snap of a finger. This one left her paralyzed from the waist down.

From the hospital to the courthouse became a journey bridged by emotions of depression and discontent. Oil money had been important to Pat Holloway. It was his ego stamped on a bank statement. His daughter was much more valuable. He forgot about himself. Marcy was the only one who counted, he said. Giddings had given him so much. Now Giddings was trying to take it all away.

●

Pat Holloway had never witnessed the face of pure, unadulterated hate until he watched the elegant, attractive Jane Browning come waltzing with her battery of pin-striped attorneys into the Dallas County Courthouse. He had what she wanted. Money.

Her husband, Bill Browning, had been Holloway's largest investor when he journeyed into the empty fields of Giddings to drill in the chalk. It had been a great friendship, an even better business relationship. But somewhere along the way, it had all gone wrong. Bill Browning had screwed him. Bill Browning had the indecency to die. Bad heart. Bad luck. Damn Bill Browning, Holloway thought.

His widow wanted every dollar that Holloway's Humble Exploration Company had squeezed from the dreaded and defiant Austin Chalk, and, in a few short years, he had pumped out a sizable fortune. She did not particularly want the millions for herself, Jane Browning said. It was for the children. All for the children. Always the children.

She had, in legal documents, accused Holloway of being a cheat, a liar, a fraud, a crook. She had charged him with everything except murder, and that might come later if her investigators uncovered any proof, and, Lord knows, they were trying.

Holloway stared at Jane Browning as the grieving, vindictive widow took her seat with a flourish of pomp and circumstance. Her eyes simmered. Her face was a mask. Hate had such a face. So did evil, he thought.

Jane Browning did not have a solid legal case. She knew it.

So did he.

"It doesn't matter," his lawyer told him. "She has the judge."

The law remained outside the courtroom when Jane Browning walked inside.

Back in the oilfield, Holloway had been a free man. The courthouse was stifling. His nerves had left the sour taste of bile in his mouth. Pat Holloway shifted his eyes from the hard face of Jane Browning to the judge strutting in from his chambers like a little Druid dressed in the robe of justice. Holloway knew all about staying awake at night. He felt as though he had been sleeping for too many days just outside the gates of Reinhardt Richter's hell, down in the devil's chalk. Holloway had his demons, too. His were inside the courtroom.

●

In court, Jane Browning squared her shoulders, tilted her head, let a tear leave a quiver in her voice, and, with all the gentle humility she could muster, claimed that she and the Browning Children's Trust owned a hundred percent of Humble Exploration. She wanted control of the company. No. She wanted Pat Holloway broke, beaten, ruined, bankrupt, on the streets, and preferably kicked to the gutter.

"The facts were definitely not in her favor. But she was not afraid to buy a judge," Holloway said, "She did not care what the cost would be, and she had enough oil money to pay off whichever judge her attorneys thought was for sale."

Hell had no fury like Jane Browning scorned.

In a billion-dollar lawsuit, she adamantly maintained that Humble Exploration had been created and established solely for the benefit of her husband. In her opinion, Holloway and others had nominally been holding a majority of the stock because William Browning believed he might need protection from any liability that might arise from the firm's operation.

Jane Browning saved her deadliest volley for a vehement and personal attack on Pat Holloway himself. She alleged, with malice aforethought, that he had been guilty of breaching his fiduciary duties as trustee by co-mingling the Browning children's funds with his own. Furthermore, she blatantly accused Holloway of embezzling millions of dollars in profits derived from his drilling operations throughout the Austin Chalk.

Giddings was in a state of disbelief.

The stately, elegant Jane Browning had drawn a line in the dirt, and Pat Holloway had stepped across it. The dispute should have all been over and behind them. Pat Holloway had millions of dollars in the bank, millions of dollars in his drilling operation, and millions of dollars worth of reserves still in the ground. For him, money was no object. According to an attorney for the Browning family, he and Jane Browning had already settled the disagreement out of court. They weren't on speaking terms. But they had been civil.

A settlement had been struck, the attorney said, and all had agreed that the terms were quite fair. Humble and Holloway would receive the entire lot of leases held in trust for the Browning children. The Browning family, in turn would be paid fifteen million dollars by Pat Holloway, the sum levied out over the next thirteen years.

Jane Browning agreed to walk away and leave both Pat Holloway and his Humble Exploration alone. No more quarrels. No more condemnations. No more accusations. Both would be free of each other. The settlement was entered into court. Before the ink had dried, however, Holloway was notified that Jane Browning would seek the appointment of a receiver to manage the company until their claims could be resolved.

Pat Holloway went ballistic. He refused to pay the fifteen million dollars. That's what the attorney said. And all hell broke loose. Jane

Browning went straight for his financial jugular. She no longer wanted to settle. She would not be content with a mere fifteen million dollars. She wanted it all. Company. Wells. Reserves. Assets. And she wanted Pat Holloway to suffer the wrath of her righteous indignation. Her preference was watching him wallow in a state of abject poverty. Any hints of civility had flown the coop.

●

Jane Browning must really hate the bastard, gossips said. Some whispered that they heard Holloway had gone to bed with her. *He's married. He wasn't then*. Wild-eyed rumors were more common than leases. Among the giddy populace of Giddings, gossip passed around over breakfast and repeated at least twice during lunch was accepted as unmitigated fact by the time supper was on the table.

Pat Holloway struck back. First, he told the court that a lawsuit was out of the question because he and Jane Browning had previously settled their dispute for fifteen million dollars. That was all she had coming to her. The judge turned a deaf ear and dismissed the argument. Pat Holloway had not yet paid the fifteen million dollars and apparently had no intention of paying the fifteen million dollars, he said. The judge declared the settlement null and void. Jane smiled. Holloway looked to see if the judge was smiling, too.

Pat Holloway had made a lot of mistakes in his life. The failure to pay off Jane Browning promptly if not sooner would be his worst one. Holloway, however, went on the offensive, countercharging that Jane Browning was engaging in *a brazen conspiracy* to ruin him because of their disagreement over the extent of her late husband's holdings in the company.

He contended that a provision in the trust agreement for the children allowed him to act in his own interest while serving as trustee. Besides, Bill Browning had died in the high country outside of Rociada, New Mexico, at least a year before Holloway began to show signs of making his gamble in hard ground pay off. When Browning was buried, Holloway was still regarded as a rank beginner in the oil business, desperately searching for the right leases to hold his first wells. Within three years, however, his exploits in the field had already earned millions of dollars for Jane Browning and the trust established for her five children – Kathy, Averille, William, Fallon, and Robert, their ages ranging from twelve to twenty-two. Leave me alone and get out of my way, Holloway argued, and he would earn them a lot more.

He believed that he and Ray Holifield had discovered and owned a key to the oil vault of the Giddings field. A sizable fortune had already flowed into Humble Exploration, and he had yet to make a dent in the chalk.

Jane Browning was certainly not destitute, not by any means. The Browning family interests included more than eleven million dollars worth of real estate and gas and oil interests in Texas and six other states, almost two million dollars in a stock and bond portfolio that contained holdings in forty corporations – ranging from Mobil Oil to McDonald's – and the sole or majority ownership of several Dallas businesses, such as Precision Motors, SRO Clothing Company, and Piper Southwest, an aircraft distributing company.

Jane Browning had money. She had power. She was in the upper echelon of the upper echelon in Dallas. And Pat Holloway could not, for the life of him, figure out why she was so damn angry and so fiercely determined to tear him apart.

●

The litigation, in Pat Holloway's words, became a nightmare. He realized he was doomed from the time the first sound of a judge's gavel echoed throughout the courtroom like a gunshot. The silence was broken.

Pat Holloway certainly did not realize it, but he would soon be broken as well – financially and emotionally. His work, his life, his triumphs in the Giddings oilfield would all lie in shambles. He might as well have been a walking dead man. Pat Holloway would never lose his swagger.

He lost everything else.

"Before the first witness finished testifying and before we had a chance to begin our cross examination," he said, "the judge granted a receivership for Humble Exploration. The trial had barely begun, and the operation of my company had already been taken away from me.

I was treated like a common thief in my own place of business. My records, my files, my leases had all been grabbed by the court."

Holloway walked into his office late that afternoon and found the court-appointed receiver standing at the Xerox machine. The oilman's face was red.

His pulse beat heavily against his temple. Holloway looked over the man's shoulder and asked, "Why are you making copies of my leases?" It was more of a growl.

"So we'll know what the Brownings own when the trial's over."

"The Brownings haven't won anything."

"You don't understand, do you?" the receiver said, a strange grin playing across his face.

"Understand what?"

"When the trial's over, you won't have a damn thing." The receiver shrugged. "The judge is taking everything away from you," he said.

Holloway was stunned. Nothing made sense to him. "How do you know?" he asked. "We've barely gotten started."

"The judgment is all going to the Brownings."

"Regardless of what the jury says?"

"That's the deal."

Pat Holloway said that his attorneys told him confidentially, "From what we've been able to learn, the Brownings have two state district judges in their hip pocket, and this is one of them."

"How can they do that?"

"Campaign contributions," the attorney answered matter-of-factly. "A judge runs for office. The election costs a lot of money. He collects a lot of money. And, sooner or later, he pays off his debts – usually from behind the bench."

"That's not right."

"That's Dallas."

●

Early the next morning, Pat Holloway met with an executive at Republic Bank, where much of his oil money had been locked away. He explained his plight. "My mother and father were both attorneys," he said, "and they taught me a lot about law and the need to respect our judges. But neither one of them ever told me that state district judges in Texas have the right to be crooked."

The banker leaned across the desk and said, "Pat, it's well known in this city that the Dallas County courthouse has a lot of corruption in it. The Brownings probably do own a couple of judges. I wouldn't doubt it for a moment. And if they do, you don't have a ghost of a chance in that court. I imagine the judge has already decided who's going to win and who's going to lose, and, Pat, he'll figure out a way to take every cent you have to your name."

"He can't do that."

"He's a judge. He can do any damn thing that he wants to do." The banker paused a brief moment, then said, "Your only chance is to get this suit into the federal court system. You can get a fair hearing there."

"How can I do that?"

"Declare bankruptcy."

Pat Holloway laughed out loud. "I don't owe any debts," he said. "How in the world can I declare bankruptcy?"

The banker leaned back in his chair and smiled. "The Brownings claim they own everything, don't they?" he said.

Holloway nodded.

"And the Brownings claim that you don't own a damn thing," the banker said.

Holloway nodded again.

"My friend," the banker said as he shrugged apologetically, "as near as I can tell, if they own it, and you don't, then you're bankrupt. Go talk to your lawyer. I believe that the Brownings have given you a chance to get the suit out of district court. May not do you any good, but it's worth a shot."

Holloway's attorney listened to the strategy the banker had proposed. It was a little unorthodox and an intriguing legal maneuver, he said, and it might just work. But he doubted if a bankruptcy judge would ever be persuaded to try a major case that kept him and his courtroom tied up for months.

However, there was a chance he might agree to let the bankruptcy hearing be held in district court as long as a retired or visiting judge was brought in to preside over the trial. That's what the law said should happen anyway.

A retired or visiting judge was insulated from the need to raise money in Dallas County. He wasn't running for office or committing his soul and judicial decisions to some financial backer. He would be the best, the safest, and the only legitimate bet that Holloway had.

Pat Holloway sat in the darkness of his home that night and tried to bring some sense or order to the situation confronting him. It was, he thought, the damndest thing he had ever witnessed. He had paid a two hundred thousand dollar down payment on a 25-B Lear Jet. He was projecting that his oil and gas revenues for the year would exceed seven hundred million dollars, maybe more. He and a previous wife owned three Cadillacs, a Mercedes 450 SL, a Lincoln, a ski boat, a ten-carat diamond, and ranch lands filled with grazing cattle. Among Holloway's real estate holdings were a $1.3-million-dollar home in the Preston Trails area of Dallas, an eight-hundred acre Giddings ranch valued at eight hundred thousand dollars, a two hundred thousand dollar condominium at Matagordo Bay on the Texas coast, and one-third interest in a pecan farm that sprawled across Lee and Washington Counties.

Yet, he was bankrupt. Such was life in the fast lane. Such was life in the oilfield. Such was life in a courtroom.

Negotiations began as they must in federal court. Sure enough, the bankruptcy judge adamantly refused to be locked down by a case that he realized had the potential to drag on for weeks, maybe even months. He realized immediately that he was not being requested to preside over a simple bankruptcy hearing. It would be an all-out, full-scale war scattered with complicated legal tactics, personal attacks, and bitter confrontations.

He thought it far wiser to turn the trial over to some retired or visiting judge in a district court. Such a judge did not have a backlog of cases to worry about. He had time on his hands. He could sit back and let Pat Holloway and the Brownings slug it out for as long as they wanted.

The bankruptcy hearing, as expected, took a sudden and sharp detour and headed for district court.

Pat Holloway felt as relieved as he had in a long time. He had never feared the legal system, not when he had the facts and the law on his side. It could be flawed from time to time, but generally it was fair. He walked confidently into the courtroom and sat down to face Judge Dee Brown Walker. But something, he sensed immediately, was wrong. Walker was not a visiting judge. Walker had not retired. Walker was a state district judge, the kind beholden to campaign contributions, and he had suddenly stepped in out of nowhere to demand that the case be transferred to his own courtroom.

The federal order had been ignored. All previous agreements were set aside.

The negotiations had been for naught.

Holloway's attorney leaned over to him and whispered, "You know I told you that the Brownings had two judges in their pocket?"

Holloway nodded.

"This is the other one," he said.

The battle had begun. Only Jane Browning was smiling.

●

The case had originally been assigned to retired Judge Fred S. Harless. But as Rich Arthur, of *Legal Times,* wrote: *The gist of Holloway's allegation is that Jane Browning and her attorneys, (Jack) Ayres and (G. H.) Kelsoe, initially conspired to maneuver the case away from Harless and into Walker's court where Walker, Browning, Ayres, Kelsoe, and several other attorneys appointed by Walker staged a biased trial to wrest control of the company from Holloway. The alleged vehicle for getting Browning's claims before Walker was a suit filed May 26, 1982, by a group of investors (referred to as the APP Entities) that owned working interest in a large number of Humble's wells.*

The suit stemmed from a long simmering dispute between those working interest owners and Holloway. At this particular point, the working interest owners informed Holloway that he was no longer authorized to sell their oil, and Holloway immediately shut down production on approximately a hundred and fifty producing wells.

At the center of the fray, and lodged in the crosshairs, was Pat Holloway, who friends and foes alike described as a brilliant lawyer and businessman. However, they did admit just as openly that he was afflicted with a ten-gallon ego.

Said James Keahey, Holloway's attorney, "Pat was like the brightest boy in the class, grown big and rich but still mischievous. Pat had the ability to snatch defeat from the jaws of victory each time by being too smart." Even Keahey, however, agreed that Holloway's decision to shut down the wells was based on sound reasoning. Holloway no longer had any authority to dispose of the oil, and, what's more, he had no place to store it. He couldn't let it merely soak into the surrounding pasturelands.

APP Entities thought he was just being obstinate. APP Entities claimed he was a mad man. Holloway took the accusation as a compliment but claimed that the counsel for APP Entities had met with the attorneys for Jane Browning before filing the suit. He said that a deal was cut. Its purpose was to cut him out of his company.

The counsel for APP Entities merely shrugged and said that the so-called secret meeting was simply *a momentary commonality of interest between our clients and the Brownings, who also wanted the wells opened.*

In an interview, however, he did say he gave the complaint to G. H. Kelsoe to file, and Kelso admitted that he didn't remember filing it. He said he had no idea who filed it. The plot, already thick, began to thicken even more.

●

As Eric Miller wrote in *D Magazine: In the beginning, there was no fury, and there was no hatred. There were no claims of bribery and murder to FBI agents knocking on doors and no grand jury investigators chasing paper trails. There were no high-stakes legal contests or sordid public displays of private lives. In the beginning, there were just friends with ambitions founded in oil.*

It would never be that way again.

In Jane Browning's eyes, Pat Holloway had cheated her children out of their financial birthright. She would even tell the court that Holloway, during a meeting in her fashionable north Dallas home, had cursed and denigrated her for the Browning family's total lack of gratitude for a measly few million dollars he had poured into their coffers. She said he even threatened to destroy her and Mike Starnes unless they transferred their remaining stock interest in Humble Exploration to his name.

The trial became a war of words, accusations, and allegations, punctuated by a heavy dose of bitter and salacious testimony. It was getting ugly. Harry Hurt III wrote in *Texas Monthly: Browning regaled jurors with tales of how Holloway had threatened to destroy her, how he had reviled her as nothing more than Bill's dirty whore, how on Christmas Eve, 1978, he had walked into her house and crawled in bed with her – in his tuxedo, she did add.*

In Pat Holloway's eyes, Jane Browning wanted to steal the oil empire he had built with his own hands. Humble Exploration belonged to him and him alone. It had been built with his guts, with his guile, with his vision, with his sweat. He took the risks. He was due the rewards. Sure, Bill Browning was an investor. Sure, Bill Browning owned ten percent of the stock. Sure, Bill Browning had contributed thirty thousand dollars to create a trust fund for his children. But Holloway had kept the trust fund going with company revenue. Jane Browning had never invested another dollar. And the children had received every pile of money they had earned from Giddings oil. As far as he was concerned, socialite Jane Browning was a vindictive thief who wanted his money, his blood, his worthless soul, and she wanted to watch him suffer humiliation and the insufferable agony of defeat.

The feud became heated and filled with animosity.

She said.

He said.

Jane Browning said she had long been suspicious that Pat Holloway was trying to eliminate the family's stock holdings in Humble Exploration. He had, after all, sold all of the assets of Humble to Holloway Exploration Corporation, then merged Holloway with Humble. It had been a slick but an obvious maneuver. He wanted Jane Browning and her children as far removed from his oil business as possible. He had shared with them long enough. He wanted to cut them out for good.

When the original Humble Exploration Company was formed back in 1974, she said, both Holloway and her husband agreed that fifty percent of the stock would be kept in the possession of Robert Nance, a consulting geologist and a mutual acquaintance who lived in Billings, Montana. But the critical question had never been resolved. Was Nance holding the stock for Bill Browning? Or had Nance bought the stock outright? No one knew. Or no one would say.

Robert Nance did. Robert Nance quietly walked down the aisle of the courtroom, took the stand, and testified that, in order to eliminate any potential conflict of interest between Hanover and Humble Exploration drilling funds, he had personally endorsed the stock and transferred it back to Pat Holloway. To no one else. Just Pat Holloway. It was a simple fact known only to the one man who possessed the truth.

No one contradicted him, no one but Jane Browning. She claimed that the stock transfer had, in reality, gone directly to the corporation and not to some individual named Pat Holloway regardless of Nance's testimony.

Pat Holloway said he had bought the stock and sent Robert Nance a check for twelve hundred dollars, which was the amount the geologist had originally paid for his fifty percent of Humble Exploration. Pat Holloway was adamant when he said that none of the stock rightfully belonged to the Browning interests. In fact, when Bill Browning died, the corporate stock only reflected his ownership of two hundred and forty shares.

The estate, however, could never find any evidence that Bill Browning had ever paid a penny for his stock in Humble Exploration Company, which, by that time, was worth millions of dollars. If Browning had never paid for the stock, did he really own it? That was the simple question as far as Pat Holloway was concerned. Why wouldn't the court listen?

She said.

He said.

Mostly, she said.

Jane Browning said that Pat Holloway, on at least one occasion, had converted, embezzled, and misappropriated lease acreage belonging to the trust by mortgaging seventeen wells and leases – which he claimed to personally own – to a third party.

She said that Holloway's other companies – Sterling Pipeline, Austin Chalk Drilling Company, Flojo Trading Company, BP Fuel

Services, and Bar 7 Investments – all belonged to the Browning Children's Trust as well.

He said her charges bordered on being ludicrous. Pat Holloway did not know whether to laugh or cry. Jane Browning's wild and largely unsubstantiated allegations had become more radical and infinitely more ridiculous every time the jury heard her testimony. And she was, if nothing else, a credible witness, one who knew as well as anyone the art of portraying herself as the poor little victim of an avaricious and ruthless oilman.

Holloway had trusted Bill Browning and Mike Starnes, and now a very uncivil lawsuit was trying to gut him. He turned to his attorney and asked, "Why would anyone who is already worth more than a hundred million dollars lie under oath just to get some more money?" She had no need or any real use for it.

His attorney simply shook his head, looking at Holloway as though his client were a simpleton. He answered the question with a question: "What makes you think that any woman who is an alcoholic and a mean bitch would not lie to rake in another hundred million dollars?"

●

Pat Holloway, more and more, began to comprehend her relationship with Judge Dee Brown Walker. He was serving as Jane Browning's perfect ally. The judge promptly ordered armed guards to patrol Humble Exploration's headquarters twenty-four hours a day. It was their duty to keep anyone, particularly Holloway, from tampering with any documents while a court-appointed accountant deciphered the records for the receiver in the bankruptcy case.

Ugly suddenly turned chilling.

At least it did in the eyes of the jury. The threat of murder began to sweep through the courthouse hallways in hushed whispers. Nothing official, mind you. Nothing from the witness stand. Just another rumor on the loose, and rumors were crawling through Judge Dee Brown Walker's courtroom like cockroaches. Don't doubt it for a moment, some said. People have been killed for less. Somebody's making a grandstand play for the jury.

It was working.

Jack Ayres, one of Jane Browning's attorneys, reported to the Dallas office of the FBI that he had received an urgent phone call from a lady named Betty Gardner, who just happened to be Pat Holloway's mother-in-law. She appeared to be a little nervous and confessed that she had overheard a telephone conversation between her daughter and the oilman. They spoke of the bitter enemies they had. They whispered about getting rid of them. They talked of murder.

"Did you overhear any names?" Ayres asked.

"I did."

"Who did they mention?"

"Jane Browning," came the reply.

"Anyone else?"

"Judge Walker."

"Anyone else?"

"The third name I heard was yours, Mister Ayres."

Jack Ayres had formerly been a police officer. He might have routinely dismissed the telephone call as a crank. But he learned that Holloway's wife had recently completed a sentence at a Federal Correctional facility in Fort Worth in a conspiracy to blow up an automobile with dynamite. She had admitted her involvement and served her time. Jack Ayres had no idea if she were capable of murder. He didn't know the woman, only her recent history. But he had received scattered information that Pat Holloway – although a brilliant attorney and a successful oilman – had a dark side, a bad temper, and known to exhibit occasional outbursts of violence.

Pat Holloway did like his hard liquor, and when he drank too much, he did sometimes think he was invisible. By the time he was invisible, he thought he was invincible. By the time he was invincible. Holloway thought he was immortal. He could throw a punch and take a punch. No hard feelings. But was he capable of murder? Jack Ayres wasn't taking any chances.

The FBI investigated but never proved or disproved Betty Gardner's allegation. Agents could not corroborate her story, and the FBI never bothered to interview either Pat Holloway or his wife. Holloway believed it was all a fabrication, nothing more than a seamy scenario played out in the back recesses of an attorney's conspiratorial mind. But then, he said, the whole damn trial was a fabrication.

Judge Walker nevertheless tightened security in the courtroom. He had no reason to be worried about anything but his own integrity and nothing else, Pat Holloway said. The Brownings had a suite in a hotel across the street from the courthouse, and it was his contention that Judge Walker walked over and had lunch with them every day. "It was no secret," he said. "Everyone knew about clandestine meetings. During the trial, one of the attorneys representing the Brownings even acted as the bailiff, carrying popcorn and messages to the jury, probably answering any questions they had. I doubt if he ever spoke highly or kindly of me." A constitutional law professor at Harvard studied the proceedings and said he had never seen anything like it in his life. The trial made travesty sound like something of an understatement.

●

While the jury worked its way through volumes of testimony, data, records, and exhibits, a group of plainclothes Dallas County Sheriff deputies sat quietly on benches around the courtroom. Their eyes never left the crowd of spectators. They did not expect trouble. They were ready if it came.

After seven grueling weeks, the jury was ready to end it all. Harry Hurt III reported in *Texas Monthly: The jury reported its verdict to a courtroom guarded by armed bailiffs, who frisked Holloway. The jury treated him even more roughly, awarding Browning and her children seventy million dollars in actual damages and two million dollars in exemplary damages. A week later, Judge Walker also awarded Browning a hundred percent of Humble Exploration's stock, thereby hiking Holloway's total loss to an estimated eighty-two million dollars.*

Pat Holloway was devastated. The king was dead, at least financially. His business and his life were in ruin. "In reality," he said, "the end was just the beginning. That's what makes America's legal system so great."

The Brownings had won. But what the hell had they won and how long would it take them to collect it? They had not gutted him. They had gutted Humble Exploration. The millions had once rolled in for Jane Browning and the Children's Trust. Overnight, the millions were nowhere to be found. Pat Holloway prepared to wage another war.

44

Doug Jatzlau had watched the boom from its infancy, especially during those startling days when oil began to explode upon the farmlands around his hometown of Dime Box. Raw land. Empty land. He knew it well. He had walked its furrows most of his life, never realizing that the soles of his shoes were touching rich land. Armed with a degree from Texas A&M, Jatzlau began teaching in Giddings during the fall of 1975, earning a six-thousand-dollar-a-year salary and pocketing another five hundred dollars for coaching football, baseball, basketball, and track. "During those years when I grew up," Jatzlau said, "Giddings was as poor as any town in Texas. If a man didn't teach, he ran a garage or worked his daddy's farm. We were ten years behind the rest of the world."

He loved teaching, but, more and more, he began to notice that boys with only a high school education were headed to the oilfield after their senior year and making more money than he was in the classroom. No college education. No fancy diploma on the wall. Just big paychecks. It began to bother him a lot.

Jatzlau and his wife had been living in a 1957 trailer for nine years. It was clean. It was nice. It had obviously seen its better days. He decided to sell the trailer house and buy a larger one, so he placed a *for sale* ad in the newspaper for a Wednesday afternoon. It was lunchtime. The newspaper had barely hit the streets. His phone was ringing. "How much do you want for the house?" asked the harried voice on the other end of the line.

Jatzlau did not have a firm figure in mind, so he said, "I'll take forty-eight hundred dollars." He realized it was too much money. Nobody would bite on such an outrageous figure. He wished he had taken the time to think about it and come up with a more realistic asking price.

"I'll buy it," the man said.

"It's not worth that much," Jatzlau told him.

"I'll buy it anyway."

During a time when working men were sleeping in cars and under bridges, a mere forty-eight hundred dollars for a good trailer house was considered a bargain.

●

As summer of 1981 rolled around, Jatzlau went knocking on the door of Humble Exploration, vaguely aware that Pat Holloway and the Browning family were battling it out in court but realizing that the company had sixteen drilling rigs hard at work in spite of their differences. Jane Browning was out for blood and millions of dollars. All Doug Jatzlau wanted was a job.

He was offered one on the Friday afternoon when classes officially shut down for the summer. Jatzlau's game plan was to work in the oil patch for the next three months, pocket a few extra dollars, and then be ready to coach football again in the fall.

"Can you come in today?" the Humble official asked.

The Humble official was no stranger. Jatzlau had known him when the man served as the maintenance supervisor for the school district. He did not care whether an employee of the oil company owned a college degree or not. He was simply looking for a man who was not adverse to long hours and hard work.

"I'll be there," Jatzlau replied. He glanced at his watch. It was almost four o'clock.

The job was already waiting for him when he arrived at Humble Exploration's office. He was given a time sheet, report forms, and asked to sign a contract.

"We'll pay you a hundred and twenty-five dollars a day," the official said.

Jatzlau quickly did the math in his head. That was six hundred and twenty-five dollars for a normal five-day week, twenty-five hundred dollars a month, roughly thirty thousand dollars a year, or five times more than his teaching salary had been. Doug Jatzlau knew he had written his last lesson plan, coached his last play, and walked out of a classroom for the final time.

"When do we get paid?" he wanted to know.

"You get the first hundred and twenty-five dollars today."

"But it's almost quitting time."

"Doesn't matter."

Humble Exploration brought him several hundred dollars worth of tools.

"I can't pay for these," he said.

"Don't worry about it," the official replied. "They belong to you now."

Doug Jatzlau grinned and wondered why he waited so long to finally make his way into the oil patch.

He said, "I found out that I had been hired as a twenty-four-hour-a-day baby sitter for wells that had been fracked. My job was to monitor the flow black, watching as water and sand pushed the oil, then the natural gas, out of the rock and back to the surface with as much as three thousand pounds per square inch of pressure. The well was probably flowing as much as a hundred barrels an hour when it came in, but then it tapered off to only fifteen or twenty barrels. The fracking and the flow back operation were geared to return the well to its original status. Every drop of oil was money, and we didn't want to lose any of them."

Most of the wells did not yet have pipelines, and the escaping gas was consumed by flares that lit the night and cast a curious array of dancing shadows around the well. The first time Jatzlau caught sight of the distant flares as they blazed across the oilfield, the sky was overcast, the clouds were hanging low, and he thought that the whole town of Smithville was burning.

The next morning, John Korb, his supervisor, drove Jatzlau to a well where the frac job was being completed, handed him a two-way radio, gave him a couple of phone numbers in case of an emergency, and said, "Try not to blow yourself up."

Jatzlau waited for him to laugh. He didn't. Korb turned and walked away. So much for training. Doug Jatzlau was on the job twenty-four hours a day for forty-three straight days, sleeping in a pickup truck and occasionally leaving the well just long enough for a hot shower and a cold sandwich. Night and day, he was intently focused on the simple measurements of life in the Giddings field. Sand. Water. Oil. Gas. Pressure.

And, of course, trying to make sure he didn't blow himself up.

●

A week before his summer contract ended, Doug Jatzlau began his move up the company's precarious ladder. A pumper had been fired, and he was promoted to replace the man, finding himself in charge of the wells surrounding the towns and communities of Smithville, LaGrange, Muldoon, and Flatonia. The salary was good, and so were the benefits. He began driving his own personal pickup truck, and what's more, he learned that he would be receiving a substantial product incentive bonus. Humble Exploration tossed a nickel a barrel for every barrel of oil the company's wells produced into a pool, and the money was divided equally among the dozen or so pumpers roaming the field. Humble had hundreds of wells. Fifteen to twenty thousand barrels of oil a day added up to a lot of nickels.

Doug Jatzlau may not have been rich, but he was pocketing more money than he had ever imagined, and the dollars were wrinkled and stained with oil. He drove the oil patch, constantly on the move, heading down one set of tire ruts, then another, moving from well to well and doing his best to coax more oil from the ground. He no longer saw barrels of crude. He saw nickels. He had no idea that the world possessed so many damn nickels.

Jatzlau, however, was standing on a fragile precipice of the oil business. Prices would soon begin to crumble around him, and, like everyone else in Giddings, he was ignorant of a great, international political game being played far beyond the chalk that would threaten to undermine them all.

The boom was going bust.

●

In the midst of tenuous circumstances, Carey Boethel made the decision to step down from his post as Lee County Judge. In his letter of resignation, he wrote:

As you know, our county has undergone tremendous growth during the past several years. Unfortunately, despite the many blessings, the growth has brought with it serious challenges. They can be as mixed as alphabet soup and knotty as tangled twine.

The solution to these unfamiliar and feverish issues is time – time to think things out so that the best can come of it. It's like a ransom note or cement ready to pour – when you get it, you must be ready to know what to do.

Because of my personal lack of time to continue to meet the growing demands I described, I decided, some months prior, not to seek re-election as your county judge.

More and more, his legal mind had found itself devoted to oil, oilmen, an oilfield, and the exploration for oil. Lee County had outfoxed the chalk, and he knew it needed a full-time judge to oversee, supervise, and guide its business affairs. Besides, he was a lawyer. A man never knew when Pat Holloway would need another one.

●

Danny Anderson had awakened to better days. He sat alone on a rig floor in the late-afternoon hours, a blinding sun glaring down on the back of his head, and could not remember having ever felt so low, depressed, and despondent. His life in the oil patch had taken too many wrong turns, headed down too many dead-end roads, and he wasn't for sure if the decisions he had made along the way had been particularly smart ones.

He had worked for U.S. Operating until J. E. Traweek cut loose and changed his allegiance to Bill Shuford. Anderson had reluctantly followed his old friend to WCS. Oil was oil. The chalk was the chalk. He had left one good man to work for another. He had left because of his own insecurity. At U.S. Operating, there had been a change at the top in Giddings. Danny Anderson had worked for one president. The president was demoted, and another man had taken his place. An unknown name. An unknown face. At the end of a long, hard day, when dark shadows turned to night around the rig, Anderson began to wonder if he would even have a job by morning. The new president might replace him. He might replace them all. New presidents sometimes did things like that.

Anderson never talked to Max Williams. He knew he should have. But he didn't. He later found out that Williams was enraged to find him gone. "Maybe I should have stayed," Anderson told himself. "Then again, maybe I'm better off where I am." He did like Shuford's direct approach to oil exploration. "He told us where he wanted to go," Anderson said, "and we took him there."

Getting there was not always the easiest of tasks. The road never ended. One job became another. One crisis became another. Wells were unpredictable. If he left one, he might soon regret it. He slept whenever he could, wherever he could, but seldom at home. The long hours, the long days cost Danny Anderson his marriage. He was always gone. His wife wanted a divorce. He could not blame her. She walked out. He was alone. He began a night-after-night escapade of drinking and driving the highway, looking for the next party and knowing he could always find one somewhere in the oil patch. "I was living hard," he said. "I knew every hot spot between Bryan and Austin and when to be there." A party did not begin or end without him.

On the afternoon of his thirtieth birthday, Danny Anderson sat on the rig floor, dangled his legs off the edge, and contemplated the miseries of his life. "Here I am," he thought. "I'm thirty years old. I had a wife. I had two great kids. I was making real good money. In a heartbeat, it was gone." It was not a good afternoon to celebrate a birthday. No party. No cake. No cards. No presents. Nobody had said, *happy birthday*. He was dead broke. Good parties took a good deal of money, and there had been too many good parties. He could not remember them all. Hard whiskey would do that to a man. He felt as guilty as his conscience said he should. Danny Anderson bowed his head and, as unaccustomed as he was to praying, he whispered, "God, if you give me another chance, I promise to do whatever you ask me to do this time." He was at the end of his rope.

He sat by himself on a workover rig in the middle of nowhere. He wondered if God heard. He doubted if God had a connection to Giddings or even bothered to listen to reprobates like Danny Anderson. Five minutes later, he saw a black Monte Carlo bounce down the dirt road, a cloud of dust in its wake. The automobile slid to a stop, and a young blonde sales lady from a service supply company stepped out beside the rig.

She wore a big smile. "Happy birthday," she said and handed him a cake.

He was shocked.

"What are you doing to celebrate?" she asked.

"Nothing," he said softly.

"Good," she said. "I'd like to buy you dinner."

They ate that night in a Bryan diner. Anderson asked her for a date. She smiled again, tilted her head seductively, and said, "If you want to date me, you'll have to take me to church on Sunday." He did not see her again for a month. By then, he was ready to go to church. He was raised a Baptist. With her, he became a Catholic. Two years later, they were married. Anderson said, "I asked for a second chance. God gave me one. I had been greedy, ambitious, and constantly on the road in search of the next big payday. It cost me everything. That was a rough game to play. Some can do it and win. I no longer wanted to even try it."

Danny Anderson settled down as Operations Superintendent for WCS Oil & Gas. Bill Shuford was still telling him where he wanted to go, and Anderson always made sure Shuford got there. He remained humble. He was soft spoken. He was generous to a fault.

He wore a belt buckle with a big "A" on it. Most everyone thought it stood for the "A" in Anderson. It didn't. "It was for Asshole," he said. "In the chalk, we did a lot of handshake deals. We fired a few. We gave a lot of men a lot of breaks. We kept a lot of little companies in business. Without the cash flow we provided them, they wouldn't have been able to survive the tough times. When drilling shut down, we helped them over the hump. If Shuford found out that a little guy needed his payment within a week to keep from going out of business, he found the money to pay him before the week was out. It wasn't always easy. But we got it done. A lot of knockdown, drag-out, cutthroat competitors ran in the field, but when a man was down on his luck, there was always somebody around to pick him up again. If I helped him today, he might be around to help me tomorrow. People made mistakes. We tried to correct them. If they cheated us, however, we cut them down and didn't mind burying them."

When his company needed it, Danny Anderson could be tough. "As much as I'd like to, I knew I couldn't be everyone's friend all the time," he said. "Too often, people saw kindness as a sign of weakness. If they tried to take advantage of us, it was the last and only chance they ever had." Danny Anderson did not like hurting people. He made damn sure none of them ever hurt his company.

●

Tom James, the attorney representing Pat Holloway's former wife Robbie, was still startled, confused, and frustrated about Judge Dee Brown Walker's judgment in the Jane Browning lawsuit against the oilman. Trials, if legal books could be believed, were quests by honest men for justice, equity, and truth. The suit had been a theater of the absurd and, he would write, had "stripped Robbie of all her properties, including the separate properties she had acquired after her divorce from Holloway, as well as all her interests in their former community residence in Dallas, their former community home and farm near Giddings, and all their other former community property." Her separate and direct appeal of the Dee Brown Walker judgment had been dismissed. By taking all of Holloway's assets, the judge had coldly ripped away his client's assets as well.

Tom James wrote in his bill of review that during the legal odyssey known as the Holloway Case, "The courts of Dallas have never looked upon Robbie's case as having any distinction from that of her former husband. Her fundamental right to have her appeal thoughtfully considered on its own merits has been lost in procedural complexities generated out of Pat Holloway's federal court actions. Indeed, it is not without foundation to say that no appellate court has examined from

Robbie's special position the sordid record of the demonstrably corrupt and fraudulent trial before a clearly disqualified judge. Her direct appeal was dismissed with little explanation and less justification."

James sat quietly in his office and carefully began to load both barrels for the appeal with his opinions and interpretations of the cold, hard facts. The attorney did not like to see anyone accused or condemned either wrongly or unjustly, and, as far as he was concerned, Holloway had been a victim of greed and maybe even fraud. There was no doubt that he had been railroaded out of his rightful holdings.

In an application for Writ of Error to the Supreme Court of Texas, Tom James clearly outlined his contentions in a scathing personal attack against the presiding judge, Dee Brown Walker.

The judge's action against Holloway had effectively left Robbie financially broken as well.

It wasn't fair, he thought. It wasn't right. His client deserved far better than she had received from the courts.

In his bill of review, James wrote:

"Judge (Dee Brown) Walker unlawfully took nearly $100,000 out of Holloway's company Humble and paid it to his personal lawyers and personal accountant working for him personally in other unrelated matters without any other compensation. Judge (Dee Brown) Walker privately hired his own personal lawyer to represent him in the Browning case against Holloway, then paid him out of the funds of the Defendant Humble, Holloway's company, on the same day he transferred Humble from Holloway to the Brownings by his judgment. Judge Walker in mid-trial deprived the defendants of their lawyers, their accountants, their trial files, their evidence files, their documentary evidence, their business records, and their fact witnesses.

"Judge Walker set it (the case) for trial in his court on only twelve days' advance notice to the Humble-Holloway defendants. Then he refused to allow them to present any expert witnesses on the grounds that they had failed to give fourteen days advance notice before trial, a physical impossibility under the circumstances. But then Judge Walker waived such fourteen-day notice requirement to allow two undisclosed and undeposed witnesses to testify as experts for the Brownings, S.M.U. Professor McKnight and Judge Walker's own personal accountant, J. R. Hurt. At trial, Judge Walker refused to require the Brownings to produce as demanded any of the accounting or financial records of the $30,000 Browning Children's Trust (BCT).

"Having deprived the defendants of their fact witnesses, expert witnesses, lawyers, trial files, documentary evidence, accountants, and business records, Judge Walker then allowed the Brownings to continue to conceal their own records and evidence, which would have disproved their claims. The Brownings alleged that Holloway was a 'thief' and had 'embezzled' from the BCT. Yet Judge Walker allowed the Brownings to continue to conceal the financial and accounting records that would have disproved such charges. Robbie, as Holloway's wife, secretary, and bookkeeper during the time period involved, knows any audit of the BCT would reveal the following: Holloway never 'stole' or 'embezzled' anything from the BCT. Holloway never took even one penny of trustee's fees, attorney's fees, or any other compensation from the BCT. Holloway was never even reimbursed for all his actual out-of-pocket expenditures for the BCT. The leases Holloway bought for the BCT for less than $30,000 have actually produced oil and revenues of more than thirty million dollars. And Humble was never repaid any of the advances it made to the BCT at Holloway's direction when Jane Browning, after Bill Browning's death, refused to make an additional contribution to the BCT vitally needed to complete the purchase of the lease block, which now has so greatly further enriched the Browning 'children.' If any kind of audit would have supported in any way the Brownings' claim of embezzlement, fraud, and misappropriation, they would have produced some such audit at some point during the thirteen years of this litigation ...."

"At the time of trial of the Browning case, Judge Walker had an ongoing professional and financial association with Kelsoe and (Jack) Ayres, John Wright, Whitley Sessions, and J. R. Hurt." (Ayres was an attorney for the Brownings, in partnership with Kelsoe. Wright had been appointed by Judge Walker as the Brownings' receiver over Humble and the Holloways, and Sessions was the receiver's attorney, also appointed by Judge Walker.)

As Tom James pointed out in his bill of review to the Supreme Court of Texas: "One of these legal matters was the ongoing sexual harassment proceedings brought against Judge Walker by the Librarian of the Dallas County Law Library whom Walker had discharged. Judge Walker had been Chairman of the Dallas County Law Library Committee; Whitley Session had been its Vice-Chairman; and G. H. Kelsoe and John Wright were members. (The Librarian) charged that Committee Vice-Chairman Sessions had complained to her that 'the Judge' (Walker) was accustomed to making library decisions wrapped in the arms of the Librarian, and he was dissatisfied because he didn't get to do that.' Kelsoe, Wright, and Sessions were all representing Judge Walker in the matter without payment of any kind. 'It's all free for love,' said Judge Walker

"The jury three times found Humble belonged to Holloway; Judge Walker awarded it to the Brownings. The jury found for Holloway 22 times on Sterling Pipeline Company; Judge Walker disregarded all 22 of these jury findings and awarded Sterling Pipeline Company to the Brownings ....

"Judge Walker awarded $72,000,000 damages against Holloway and his companies. This was derived from jury findings based solely on the testimony of an expert witness (which the defendants were not allowed to rebut) as to a totally fictitious $500,000,000 reduction in value of Humble and Sterling Pipeline Company between the 1979 date of suit and the 1982 date of trial. The jury repeatedly found these companies belonged to Holloway, not to the Brownings. Holloway, Humble, and Sterling were thus held liable for damages to themselves, while by the same judgment all of their assets were transferred to (Mike) Starnes via constructive trust. The jury twice found that Holloway-Humble defendants had caused 'zero' damages to the Browning Estate ....

"Judge Walker did much more than just disregard all jury issues favorable to the Holloway-Humble defendants. He gave the Brownings not just everything they asked for in their pleadings; he gave them much more than they even attempted to show by any evidence. He imposed, on the alleged basis of a 'trust opportunity' of the $30,000 Browning Children's Trust created on December 31, 1975, a constructive trust for the Brownings on real property which had been owned by co-trustee Holloway's family for more than sixty years, the Holloways' residence in Dallas, their farm and home in Lee County, and several thousand oil and gas leases and several hundred producing oil and gas wells not described in the Brownings' petition.

The Brownings' principle witness Starnes had admitted on the witness stand that none of these 'constructive trust' properties had actually been paid for to any extent by any Browning money. Then Judge Walker amended his original final judgment two and a half months after its entry to divest the defendants of an additional one hundred and twenty-five (overlooked) wells. None of these were described in the Brownings' trial petition, no evidence about them had been introduced at trial, and there was no post-judgment evidence or hearing."

In addition, attorney Tom James wrote, an affidavit given by Louis P. Bickel, Humble's trial counsel, said that throughout the Browning litigation, "There were long recesses in both morning and afternoon during which time Messrs. Kelsoe and/or Ayres were in Judge Walker's chambers without the attendance of Humble-Holloway attorneys … Likewise, at the conclusion of court each day, a meeting between Judge Walker and Messrs. Kelsoe and/or Ayres in Judge Walker's office would commence … Throughout the litigation, I was impressed that Judge Walker had grasped and embraced the position of the Brownings and was determined to exert his every effort to favor and advance the Brownings' interests as articulated and urged by Messrs. Kelsoe and Ayres."

James pointed out that an affidavit given by Judge Robert H. Hughes said: "Judge Walker worked privately with the Brownings' attorneys on their jury issues, with no lawyer for the Humble-Holloway defendants present. At one of these attorneys' work sessions (on Saturday), Judge Walker stated that 'we are not going to give Holloway any special issues,' that 'under our theory of the case, he is not entitled to any.'"

Wrote James: "Then, after the Dallas Court of Appeals issued its subsequent opinion dated August 30, 1982, ordering the issuance of a writ of prohibition against Judge Walker to vacate the Humble receiverships, previously held unlawful, he met again Ex Parte with the Brownings and their attorneys to discuss how to avoid the writ of prohibition. This Ex Parte meeting was also recorded by the court reporter. At this meeting of the conspirators, Judge Walker said: 'We have control of Humble through all of the hundred percent of the stock. We are in control and we are going to stay in control.' At this meeting, Judge Walker approved the instructions of his armed guards, given by his receiver's attorney, to fire their shotguns at Humble's general counsel (a small, slightly built former law clerk to U. S. Supreme Court Justice William Brennan) if he put both feet on the steps leading to the Humble office in reliance upon the order of the appellate court. Sessions promised Judge Walker that 'somebody is going to get shot if they do that.'"

Tom James concluded in his bill or review: "So as far as Robbie can determine, no court of record anywhere in this nation at any time in the last 200-plus years, or in England in the last 400 years, has ever ruled that a judge who acted as Judge Walker did in the Browning Case nevertheless remained legally qualified to pass judgment in the case before him. On the contrary, every court has disqualified every trial judge who has done only a minor fraction of what Judge Walker did in the Browning Case."

The facts according to Tom James were in and undeniable. The strange and curious pilgrimage from courthouse to courthouse, from judge to judge, from appeal to appeal still had a long way to go, and the journey would become more bizarre with each passing year. In the end, Robbie Holloway's application for Writ of Error to the Supreme Court, like the one submitted by Pat Holloway, was refused without either comment or opinion.

Tom James began to wonder if there was anyone in the court system who even cared.

45

Jeff Carter had quite a story to tell, and he told it often. He was only twenty-nine years old, strikingly handsome, born with a silver tongue and a smooth, persuasive way of talking, and he came to Giddings from the great oil domain of West Texas. Midland had been his home base, but now he was expanding his operation into the chalk, intent on establishing his own mark in an oilfield made rich and powerful by the gambles and the exploits of Max Williams, Irv Deal, Pat Holloway, Clayton Williams, Bill Shuford, Tom Coffman, Gary Bryant, and, of course, Ray Holifield.

He had drilled forty-eight consecutive wells in the chalk, Jeff Carter said, and every one of them was productive. It was an enviable record. He was indeed an oilman to be reckoned with. Business associates, when pressed, as they often were, did admit that Jeff Carter's bold and excessive claims may have been somewhat overblown. Even Carter, when pressed, as he often was, reluctantly confessed that he had not actually been the operator on forty-eight straight producing wells. He had simply been one of several passive investors who had placed his money in a private drilling fund.

But Jeff Carter had set his sights on the big-time. He viewed himself as a player even if it meant creating an illusion that did not exist. He was passive no longer.

Carter went for broke. He bought an expensive house in Houston, began flying across Texas in a private jet, hired a public relations man to promote himself and J.E. Carter Energy, raised enough money to establish a multi-million dollar drilling budget, leased a couple of rigs, and began looking for more.

He signed a deal with Canso Oil & Gas Company of Canada to begin exploring leases in the Austin Chalk.

His was the new face in Giddings. He was rolling new dice with new money. Jeff Carter made such an immediate impression that the *New York Times*, in early 1981, ran a fascinating profile, quoting the young, self-proclaimed millionaire oilman as saying he had studied the lives of J. D. Rockefeller, John Paul Getty, and H. L. Hunt, and he had a goal to let Giddings oil make himself and his brothers one of the wealthiest families in the world.

He had his future planned. He had his strategy in place. He might have well succeeded until he realized that the noise ricocheting across the oil patch sounded a lot like a death rattle. Giddings shuddered. The price of oil hit rock bottom.

Jeff Carter did drill sixteen wells in the Austin Chalk, but, mostly, they were not commercial successes. He sold out to his partner, Canso Oil & Gas, which paid him about a half million dollars in cash and assumed two million dollars of indebtedness.

A year later, Carter would file for reorganization under Chapter Eleven Bankruptcy, listing eight million dollars in assets and more than thirteen million dollars in debts.

A former associate said, "I guess you've seen it in the oil business hundreds of times. Somebody makes a few wells, and they think they can do anything they want." He tried to tell Carter, "It's not how fast you get started. It's how well you hang in there."

Jeff Carter and his brothers didn't hang well and would never be one of the wealthiest families in the world or even in Giddings. The same glorious oil that had tempted them would ruin them. Oil had been such a sure bet. Oil was loaded dice.

Nobody won. Not even the house.

●

The distant signs of hard times were looming on the horizon, but no one had time to pay them much attention. When times were good, oilmen simply assumed they were bound to get better, and no one could convince them otherwise. Yet, the weight of new and perilous times was already falling heavily around them.

Throughout the country, rig counts had been rising every week. Then again, so were interest rates. For the first time in a decade, the world at large was experiencing an oversupply of oil, and, in the beginning, no one could quite figure out how or why. The price of crude was no longer spiraling higher. It had leveled off and had even begun to show a slight decline. The oilfield, however, was accustomed to long hauls of ups and downs, and many believed it was merely a temporary condition and discomfort.

Mike Maas watched it all from behind the barbecue counter of the City Meat Market. "Giddings was busting at the seams," he said. "If a man could find a clear piece of land near town, he hauled in a trailer house or built a shack. The streets were full of oilfield trash, and, for them, money was no problem. Spend it. Lose it. Don't worry. There's more. Always more. For awhile, it seemed like everybody who could drill a hole was out in the field fighting over land. Then the field went silent. The boom turned sour, and few realized the good times were over until they drove out to work one morning and couldn't find anybody drilling on the rig. Some collected final paychecks. Some didn't."

The reasons for a suddenly tighter economic period were varied: conservation, alternative fuels, a worldwide economic recession, new oil discoveries in far corners of the globe, the lust for war in the Middle East, and an American President who realized that time, fate, and circumstance had given him the chance he needed to leave Russia's Iron Curtain lying in rubble and ruin.

Ronald Reagan would destroy the Soviet Union. He wouldn't do Giddings any good either. The price of oil dropped to thirty-five dollars a barrel. Then, it slipped to thirty dollars and finally tumbled to twenty-three dollars.

Some operators in the chalk were beginning to lose their nerve. A grave situation was growing more serious by the day. Lower prices had begun to dramatically increase the risk of oilmen, big or small, in the devil's chalk.

Making a well pay out at forty-one dollars a barrel, or higher, did not take a lot of skill or knowledge. It was simply follow the trend and drill. Fracking could solve a lot of mistakes. It was, however, a lot harder to generate a decent or a livable profit at twenty-three dollars a barrel. If the prices fell again, the ominous sounds of silence echoing across the Giddings field would be deafening.Drill bits were still turning, but they were turning in quiet desperation.

When would the prices stop dropping?

That was the first and primary topic of conversation at either Schubert's or the City Meat Market. A second was just like it.

Would the prices stop dropping at all?

In reality, the price of oil had begun and would end with the confluence of crises and chaos in the Middle East. Back in the early 1970s, the oil business was barely getting by at four dollars a barrel when Saudi King Faisal joined an Arab oil embargo in a bold effort to punish the United States for appropriating $2.2 billion to pay for arms shipments to Israel. The king had been regarded as a friendly ally, a dependable supplier of oil, who had wilted under the intense pressure applied by his neighboring states.

In the midst of a bitter conflict, OPEC announced an immediate five percent cut in production, followed by continued monthly cuts until Israel withdrew its troops and retreated back to its homeland. The flow of oil became a trickle. Any of it reaching the United States came through Great Britain or France, countries untouched by the embargo.

America panicked. Long lines of automobiles wrapped themselves around gas tanks. The myth said that America was running out of oil, and most considered the myth as reality. The nation could no longer rely on an unstable and unfriendly corner of the world for oil. America must find more of its own. Even though the embargo did not last long, a new era of oil exploration exploded across the country and settled down around Giddings. Rig counts rose. So did the price of oil, inching upward until it slipped toward the high side of forty dollars a barrel.

Even the turmoil in the Middle East did not deter the growth of profits in the oil business. In the wake of the Iranian Revolution in 1979, the Shah fled the country, the Ayatollah Khomeini gained control of the country, Iraq invaded, and oil production in Iran and Iraq both was drastically reduced. A strike by thirty-seven thousand workers at Iran's nationalized oil refineries reduced production from six million barrels a day to only one and a half million. Reduced production. Higher prices. Increased profits. It was a simple formula for success in America's oil patch. The bust had been left in the dust of a new boom.

As National Public Radio reported: *Easy money, during the late 1970s, flowed like Perrier, and Americans had an unquenchable thirst for attaining fabulous wealth. This was the era of champagne wishes and caviar dreams.* Another reporter wrote that o*il is flowing like Texas tea. Millionaires are being created by the thousands. Everybody has an airplane or two. If you aren't wearing thousand-dollar cowboy boots, you aren't anybody. The booze is flowing almost as fast as the oil. Alcoholics are being created faster than millionaires.*

Giddings had been golden. The good times, however, were not destined to last. Good times in oil were hardly ever more than a delusion. They came to an abrupt and frightening halt in the early 1980s, and their demise had nothing to do with oil, the exploration for oil, the discovery of oil, or the production of oil. President Ronald Reagan decided that the time had finally come to end the Cold War. Russia, he privately decreed, must fall. He saw his chance, and he took it. Reagan would not attack with troops or guns. His strategy was far more subtle. He would create a troubled state of affairs that did not exist in the world, and oil would be the President's ultimate weapon.

With the price of oil skyrocketing because of Iran's struggle with Iraq, the Soviet Union was deriving a majority of its hard currency reserves from the sales of Red oil to the West. With mounting profits being stuffed into the Kremlin, Russia was able to build up its rocket forces, as well as purchase equipment used in the manufacture of anti-tank shells, rocket gyroscopes, and even timing devices for nuclear weapons detonators on the world market. The threat of world domination by the Soviet Union was increasing with every drop of oil drained from Russian ground.

Ronald Reagan had long viewed the Soviet Union as an evil empire. Even before he was elected president, Reagan was charging that the United States was quickly falling behind Russia in military strength. National Security would become his watchword. The fight against the portentous threat of Communism would become an obsessive focus.

The President and his Director of Central Intelligence, William Casey, made the decision to assault their enemy indirectly, avoiding a head-on confrontation. Their idea was as simple as it was effective. They decided to break the bank in Moscow with an attack on Russia's economic and political weakness.

They would employ strict covert operations, hidden diplomacy, the show of force in a build-up of the American military, and strategic policy maneuvers to sow political discord and dismantle Russia's ability to utilize its one great asset – oil – to further establish itself as a world power. They wanted to restrict the Soviet's access to Western credit and technology in a well orchestrated campaign to slash Soviet hard currency earnings by driving down the price of oil.

It was a risk taken in secrecy, a deal made with the powers of darkness. Reagan's clandestine diplomats, with a list of promises and guarantees, persuaded Saudi Arabia to ramp up its production of petroleum and flood the world market with oil.

The Saudis promptly opened the valves on wells that had been shut down in the rugged desert climes, and began pumping another two to three million barrels per day.

The market staggered as though it had been shot from a gun. Oil prices plummeted. Russia was devastated. Its oil was virtually worthless. The Iron Curtain fell with a thud. And American oilmen were knocked to their knees. At twelve dollars a barrel, no one had any interest or inclination to go out and spend a million fragile dollars to drill a new well.

Rigs were racked and stacked. Gang trucks were parked in the yards, provided, of course, that drilling companies could still afford to own a yard. Otherwise, they were sold as junk. Smaller oil companies bit the dust. Independents limped out of the field. Majors were fighting for survival and losing badly. If the phone did ring in the office of a supply service company, chances were good that it was probably a wrong number.

Drill bit makers managed to stave off financial discord by producing anti-tank shells for the U.S. military. The only businesses making money in the oil patch were the "plug and abandon" firms, those companies that pulled steel casing out of oil wells to sell as scrap. Once, they had simply rammed tree trunks, utility poles, or railroad ties down oil wells. Now, they pumped the boreholes full of concrete, which was better for the environment anyway. No longer was the high pressure stemming from gas and oil vapors popping out of wooden and rotting plugs to spark a fire. Concrete even lessened the chance of contaminating ground water with oil well brine.

A fortune in oil lay in the ground, perhaps. No one was looking for it. Not now. The crisis of the 1980s left Giddings paralyzed in a state of rigor mortis.

●

The price of oil hovered for a time around twelve dollars a barrel, then dropped to eight dollars. Pump jacks fell silent. Oilfield workers were out of work. There were no jobs for them. The nation convulsed with financial uncertainty. Banks – a hundred and five of them in Texas during a single year – closed down, traffic in the oil patch was sparse or non-existent, and prices had become far too high at the pump. Bankruptcy judges were swamped. Homeowners bailed out on their mortgages, and the market was glutted with houses that no one could afford to buy. In Houston alone, foreclosures on homes and businesses numbered three thousand a month. If that wasn't bad enough, the Savings & Loan industry was rocked by embezzlement and scandal.

It couldn't get worse was the common belief. It was getting worse. All across the oil patch, pickup trucks carried bumper stickers that read: *Lord, if you give me one more oil boom, I promise not to piss it away this time.* Randy Stewart said, "We all knew that the great oil boom in Giddings could not last forever. But none of us realized that it would end while we were out to lunch one day. I saw a lot of people just give it up. One day, they were drilling. The next, they were plugging their wells and out of work. Farmers woke up as oilmen and went back to sleep that night as farmers again. The boom came quick. It left the same way."

When Randy Stewart first made his way into the Giddings field, oil was selling for three to four dollars a barrel. "When it went to twelve dollars a barrel," he said, "we thought we were rich. Then we lived too long on thirty-and-forty-dollar-a-barrel oil. When it went back down to twelve dollars a barrel, we thought we were broke. No. We didn't just think it. We were flat broke."

●

Buddy Preuss had watched the boom fade to a bust from behind his desk at the newspaper office. He had written of successes and failures in the field, described the hopes and fears and disappointments that were all part of the oil business. He had seen operators come and go, watched oil explode from the earth, and seen dry holes plugged. He had smelled smoke from oilfield fires, witnessed the aftermath of wells blown out, and written the obituaries of those whose lives had been snuffed out by highway and oil patch accidents. He remembered stark days when oil prices were four dollars a barrel and saw them skyrocket to forty-one dollars a barrel.

Not once had Buddy Preuss been tempted to drill a well. The boom heaped riches on those around him. He remained content to collect his revenue from advertising sales and publish his newspaper once a week. His columns were the voice of reason, never offensive, always exploiting the good while trying to justify the bad. Most times, oil stories were an afterthought. Football games, weddings, school board meetings, civic club meetings, church suppers, controversial leash laws for pets running loose, firing coaches, hiring coaches, downtown parades, and community social events always took precedence.

Back a few months, when the price of oil was flirting with forty dollars a barrel, Buddy Preuss was being urged by Clarence Cheatham to become involved in the oil business himself. "Don't just write about it," he said. "Here, you have a chance to live it."

Preuss listened politely. Cheatham, he knew, had long been a solid fixture in the development of the Giddings field. He had been the drilling supervisor for an untold number of wells, maybe more, and by now,

Cheatham had a pretty good handle on the Austin Chalk. Preuss had a lease on some land near Dime Box, and Cheatham, armed with a little black box wired for radiometrics, began showing him some possible locations for oil. Nothing guaranteed, of course. But the little black box certainly liked the acreage.

"I'll think about it," Preuss said.

The price of oil dropped to twenty-seven dollars a barrel.

"I have a great idea for you," Clarence Cheatham told Preuss. "Nobody can find oil in the chalk like Ray Holifield. You know his reputation as well as I do. Why don't you go out and pick up some leases that Holifield chose for Santa Fe Minerals. Good leases. Good prospects. Nothing happening with them. I bet you can get them dirt cheap."

Buddy Preuss was almost persuaded to pull the trigger. However, he read that the National Oil Company of Kuwait, which had ended up with Windsor Energy, had warned its people that the price of oil was destined to drop to nine dollars a barrel, which would scare off even the most seasoned of oilmen.

Operators had already begun shutting down. Oil companies were idle. Rig builders were out of work. Trucks had ceased to run and ruin the back country gravel roads. Landmen had no trouble finding good land to lease but no one to lease it. The whole region was sitting back and waiting to see what might happen. Oil had always been the great temptation and often a greater illusion. Maybe the price would sink that low, Preuss thought, and maybe it wouldn't. Nobody dared predict the unpredictability of the petroleum business. He had never been a gambler, but he wasn't afraid to take a chance either. It was time, Preuss decided, for him to finally let Clarence Cheatham drill him an oil well.

He bought five of the best leases he could find. Cheap. He sometimes thought he had stolen the acreage. Clarence Cheatham was simply looking for a place to work. He did not have a rig or a drill, which was just as well He had no place to put them if he did.

Buddy Preuss did not raise money. He did not knock on doors. He did not run a bank of telephones. He did not try to even track down the first investor. Preuss went into the oil business the same way he went into the newspaper business – alone, and on his own terms. He methodically went from bank to bank and borrowed one and a half million dollars to finance a package of three wells. Everyone in town knew him. The gamble might not be solid, but Buddy Preuss was. He had the collateral he needed.

The banks dutifully told Preuss that he was making a terrible mistake. He was simply moving into the wrong business at the wrong time, rushing in where only fools dared to leave their footprints in the dust, and throwing himself into a brutal quagmire that could well ruin him. Preuss stood fast. Against their better judgment, perhaps, the banks loaned him the money.

Just before the first well was spudded in, Clarence Cheatham and Buddy Preuss walked into a meeting where representatives from fifteen field service companies were seated around a big table. Many of them had not worked in a long time. They had no idea why anyone would actually go back into the chalk, not with oil so precariously low and threatening to fall again at any minute. But they were certainly glad to see Buddy Preuss.

Cheatham pointed to the newspaper publisher and said, with a certain amount of pride, "Gentlemen, let me introduce you to the man with brass balls."

Three wells were drilled within a period of five months. Two of them hit and hit big, coming in at two to three hundred barrels of oil a day. It would be at least eight months before they began to slack off to slightly less than a hundred barrels a day. They were indeed strong producers, but Preuss only wondered if the wells were strong enough. He owed the banks more than a million and half dollars, he had regular payments due on the note, and the National Oil Company of Kuwait had unfortunately been right in its prediction. The price of oil had indeed gone into another freefall, plunging to nine dollars a barrel and threatening to tumble even lower.

"When we drilled the second well," he said, "you could go out at night, look across the skyline, and we had the only lighted rig between Dime Box and Giddings." It was a lonely rig. The rest of the land lay dark and silent.

Buddy Preuss felt as though he was the only man in the field.

46

T he sudden bust hit Giddings with the impact of a punch to the gut. The news around town and around the country was ominous and growing worse by the day. The early years of the 1980s would be devastating. As the *Giddings Times & News* reported: *Across Texas and the nation, problems facing small oil and gas producers are deficits, not profits, debts, not earnings. With an expanding oversupply of oil and gas, many exploration projects have been scrapped, deeply indebted drilling companies have been forced to mothball their rigs, and lenders have begun foreclosing on their loans. At least a hundred drilling and production companies have filed for bankruptcy ... As each new day goes by and crude oil prices continue to decline, thousands of Texas businessmen are scrambling to reassess how their companies will survive the most dramatic downturn the oil industry has ever seen. Optimism has completely vanished.*

There was a growing fear that the Saudis, in a surreptitious agreement with the U.S. government, would drop the price of oil to seven dollars a barrel, maybe even four dollars. Prices were falling the way they went up, and it was not in an orderly fashion. When oil was selling for forty-one dollars a barrel, operators, rigs, and money poured into Giddings, and each new day brought news of another strike. More than a few dog wells were over-promoted and drilled just because money was available and investors were eager to sink a hole. They couldn't get rich on oil without one. Bad times, however, were stalking their every move with a combination of oil gluts, declining oil prices, tight money, and new tax laws that made it considerably less advantageous to invest in oil and gas. There had been a time when high rollers had hardly any qualms about gambling in oil because good old Uncle Sam would pay seven out of every ten dollars they lost even if they hit a dry hole. Now, the best tax-write off investors could expect was five out of every ten dollars. Smart money had found other places to go.

During the boom, any self-respecting energy company could sell common stock to a pool of investors and raise capital for exploration. By the early 1980s, those same investors had literally slammed the door shut on public financing. It was going to be a rough ride.

Buddy Preuss wrote in his Viewpoints column: *The price of a barrel of oil has been going down instead of up this past year. And with many of the oil-producing countries trying to undercut each other's prices in recent weeks, it's no telling just how much lower prices will go this year. Even when the price of a barrel of oil dropped a few dollars, it really put a damper on the oil boom in the Giddings Austin Chalk. There are a lot of people out of work, and many more will be laid off if the oil price-cutting war really gets into full swing and the price drops like a rock. That could also trigger a big drop in the price of natural gas, which has already dropped from about seven dollars per thousand cubic feet to the deregulated market of four dollars. And if it drops much more, you'll see very little deep drilling in search of natural gas.*

Thus began, as Clayton Williams said, the wreck of the eighties. It would be monumental. The Giddings oil and gas industry was severely damaged, maybe even ruined, by foreign countries that did not even know, or care, that Giddings existed on the face of the earth. It was, the farmers said, a hell of a sad place to be.

Derricks were lowered from the drilling rigs, stacked alongside drill pipe, and lined up shoulder to shoulder in company yards.

A hard and inconvenient rust began to replace the limestone coating of Austin Chalk.

●

For awhile, according to rumors on the street, it appeared that Clayton Williams was moving steadily forward with a secret plan to gain control of the money in Giddings. His initiative would begin with a takeover of a bank that many in town had begun calling the Clayton Williams Bank. It was all news to Clayton Williams. He had problems enough in the oilfield.

Owning and operating a bank were out of the question. He needed a bank, he said, like a hog needed a Chicago packinghouse. He wondered if he could pay off the banks that held his loans. Even if he owned a bank, he sure wouldn't loan himself any money. Times in the oil patch were tight and growing tighter. To Clayton Williams, it was beginning to feel like a noose.

In order to quiet the rumors, the newspaper was asked to print a front-page story saying, in effect, that the bank was going to sell a big part of its shares to Lee County and Giddings citizens. Clayton Williams might be stockholder. Then again, maybe he wouldn't.

At the moment, he had other worries. His deal to sell natural gas to Valero had broken down, then fallen apart. No warning. No discussion. No further negotiations. Clajon kept gathering gas at the wells. The trucks kept rolling.

The payments suddenly stopped. Clayton Williams recalled, "When the price of oil and gas plummeted, Valero quit paying me. We had our words, our differences, and our grievances, but, in reality, Bill Greehey, Valero's chief executive officer, was fighting for his life, and I was damn sure fighting for mine."

Both would survive. Each would pay dearly.

●

Rumors had begun to circulate through the field that Clayton Williams was on the crumbling threshold of a financial collapse. Some said he was facing bankruptcy. Others predicted that he would simply sell out and leave town. The truth was lost in the shuffle. With eighteen rigs in operation, Clayton Williams, with an average production of twelve thousand barrels, had become the largest daily producer of oil in the Austin Chalk. He was second in gas production, delivering thirty-five million cubic feet of gas per day. He was aggressive. He had replaced Pat Holloway as the king. Then again, everyone had replaced Pat Holloway as the king, even Jane Browning. Especially Jane Browning.

Claytie's revenue, however, was having a great deal of trouble keeping up with his cash outlay. His drilling operation was on the books as costing him eighteen million dollars a month. His gas pipelines were eating up seven million a month. It resulted in his spending twenty-five million dollars every thirty days. In addition, Clayton Williams had a two-hundred-million-dollar development loan, and the interest alone was digging forty million dollars a year out of his profits.

He thought for awhile that maybe he should go public and raise money through a stock offering. But Clayton Williams was too independent to have shareholders harassing him and telling him what to do. He rejected that idea in a hurry. Clayton Williams was slowly and methodically cutting his losses, and he had a lot to cut. In January of 1982, he stunned Giddings by announcing that he would auction off half of his non-producing leases on three hundred thousand acres, as well as a hundred and fifty-two wells, primarily in Burleson County. He was battling to pay off bank loans and weather the downturn of a deteriorating oil and gas economy.

More rumors suddenly began bubbling up from the bars and cafes, the rigs and slush pits, the park benches and Sunday morning pews of Giddings. The gossips said that Clayton Williams was being stonewalled by severe financial problems that threatened to cripple both him and his business. The gossips made him mad.

Fifteen years ago, he had been a ten thousand-dollar a year insurance salesman, and now he was on his way to becoming a member of the Forbes Four Hundred list of the wealthiest Americans, and a bunch of fools were trying to portray him as a pauper. Damn them, he thought. Damn them all.

Clayton Williams was nowhere close to going out of business. Sure, he was facing a pot full of hard financial times. He was familiar with them. An oilman and hard times spent a lot of time together. However, he still owned seventy producing wells throughout the Giddings field, and he had five hundred and fifty thousand acres of non-producing leases scattered across Texas, the chalk, and the United States. He said, "I guess when you've done well in business, there are always a lot of people out there hoping you'll lose your ass. I've had people call me up and tell me they had heard I was broke. Well, I'm a long way from being broke.'

Clayton Williams angrily cancelled the auction. The word *auction*, he decided, had triggered all of the rumors anyway. He had four contract rigs working, which sounded good until someone realized that, a year earlier, he had been operating eighteen.

He continued to drill one new well a month, never quite sure how much longer he could keep a bit going deep into the chalk. He woke up every morning with only one thought on his mind: What's the price of oil today?

He put the package together, printed a brochure, and commissioned Lehman Brothers Kuhn Loeb, an investment banking firm, to handle the sale because, he said, "They're used to talking to corporate presidents, and I'm not."

In the midst of economic turmoil, Clayton Williams found a buyer. He hadn't needed an auction after all. He sold a hundred and fifty-two oil and gas chalk wells to the Denver-based Petro-Lewis Corporation for slightly more than a hundred and ten million dollars. The wells had proven reserves estimated at five million barrels of oil and seventeen billion cubic feet of gas. The deal was, he said, "the biggest sale I ever made, and it was the first time in seven or eight years that I had sold anything."

The rumors of his untimely demise in the Giddings oil business sort of drifted away and were forgotten before the gravy grew cold on a Schubert's chicken fried steak.

●

Everyone in the oil business was in dire straits, and Pat Holloway could not stay out of court. In 1982, he was still battling to prevent the Browning family from running off with his oil company, his leases, his wells, his reserves, his royalties, his ranch, and eighty-two million of his oilfield dollars.

He had filed a lawsuit against Phillips Petroleum for fourteen million dollars in actual damages and another twenty million dollars for exemplary damages, claiming that Phillips was paying Humble Exploration and royalty owners a lower price than it did for the natural gas it had purchased from other producers in the Giddings field. In addition, the lawsuit charged that millions of dollars were lost when Holloway was forced to flare his gas simply because Phillips failed to connect its pipeline to the Humble wells within the allotted time required by standard gas contracts.

As his attorneys wrote in the lawsuit, *these unlawful actions were done willfully and wantonly in conscious disregard of the rights of Humble and landowners and were fraudulent and with malice.* Pat Holloway had never trusted gas pipeline companies, believing since his first foray into the oilfield that one would someday cheat him. Now he was giving a judge the chance to prove he had been right.

However, a much larger fight was brewing. and, once again, Pat Holloway was in the middle of it. Fraud. Conspiracy. Theft. Money laundering. Somebody in high places was guilty of not paying twenty-eight millions dollars in oil production revenue to Humble Exploration, its investors, or seven hundred of its royalty owners.

That was bad enough. Now a Lee County court of inquiry, investigating the charge, was discovering that BRIO and CPI, two companies that took delivery of the oil produced from those wells, probably did not have the money available to make the payments. Twenty-eight million dollars did not hang around as long as it used to. A fortune had vanished like a wisp of smoke. Was it greed? Or merely the retribution of hard times?

Donald W. Womack, a former secretary of BRIO, testified before the inquiry that officers of the Dallas-based corporation were so deeply in debt that they used the revenue generated by the sale of oil gathered in the chalk to pay off their bills. Nothing had been left to pay the landowners. He said that BRIO used some of the royalty funds to speculate on the spot oil market – a very high-risk venture that proved to be a financial disaster for the company when the price of oil spiraled downward. The company was broke and had more creditors than dollars.

BRIO had a lot of subsidiaries, Womack said, and he often found it necessary to move funds, at the last minute, from one corporation to another in an effort to come up with forty to fifty million dollars a month in accounts payable. "But no matter how hard I tried, I just couldn't get it down," he said. "The money just wasn't there." CPI was in no better shape. According to the *Wall Street Journal,* "The company was having financial problems and asking for extensions on filing income tax reports." By now, CPI was drowning in debts totaling a hundred million dollars and was no longer in business.

Oil had left the chalk, and the money vanished overnight or, as some suspected, overseas. Foreign and offshore accounts did accrue a lot of ill-gotten gains. Womack did tell the court that he asked company executives about the nature of business being done by BRIO's international affiliates, and he said with a shrug, "It appears they were trying to hide something from me."

●

It was a strange, curious, and convoluted case, full of twists and turns, charges and countercharges, that was about to become even more bizarre. Pat Holloway testified that, beginning in 1978, he used one oil company to haul his crude but had problems getting the company to pick up the oil. Sometimes the tanks overflowed and spilled out into creeks and steams. He lost oil and lost money.

Holloway decided to begin using BRIO Petroleum and first became aware of the company's failure to pay royalty owners in early 1982. In February, Humble Exploration had not received its payments either. Holloway promptly called his Giddings office and left word to keep all BRIO trucks from driving onto Humble leases, and he made the decision to use CPI at the suggestion of an Abilene banker who happened to sit on CPI's board. Abilene National Bank was heavily involved with BRIO as well. In order to keep Pat Holloway from moving his business, the banker extended to Humble a line of credit for twelve and a half million dollars and also promised to pay the money that BRIO still owed Holloway for his royalty payments.

By August, however, federal banking authorities had taken over and orchestrated a merger between Abilene National and Mercantile Texas Corporation of Dallas. Abilene National had simply suffered too many devastating financial losses in the energy field. Holloway knew the end was in sight and managed to rescue a two hundred and fifty thousand dollar certificate of deposit from the institution. However, he testified that he lost the fifty thousand dollars he had invested in the bank's stock.

●

In his defense, the banker told the court that he did not realize Abilene National was suffering from grave financial troubles until federal bank examiners showed up one morning and directed the board to raise thirty million dollars to cover potentially bad and massive loans it had made to oil-related companies. Those firms were suddenly short of money and on the brink of bankruptcy because an oil boom had begun to collapse around them. In Oklahoma City, the enormously powerful Penn Square Bank had defaulted, and the examiners were running scared.

The entangled web of financial intrigue began to unravel. One of the bank's largest creditors was CPI with debts amounting to a hundred million dollars with much of it secured by letters of credit issued by Abilene National.

BRIO had also made loans, owed the bank, from time to time, as much as ten to fourteen million dollars, and had also been given substantial letters of credit. It seemed as though every principal in the lawsuit and in the courtroom had a briefcase packed with letters of credit issued by Abilene National Bank.

The banker stoically tried to distance himself as far as possible from the sordid affair. He was, if nothing else, an innocent bystander caught in the line of fire.

The district attorney asked him, "Have you ever received anything worth more than fifty dollars from BRIO?"

The banker admitted that, at BRIO's invitation, he had once sat in a box at Texas Stadium to watch a Dallas Cowboy football game.

"Do you know the price of the box?" the district attorney asked.

"Probably three to five hundred thousand dollars."

"I wonder," Charles Sebesta said, "if any of the money owed to royalty owners had been spent for one of those boxes."

The banker had no idea. The District Attorney did.

Judge John L. Placke did not particularly care about the trials, the tribulations, or the difficulties facing BRIO, CPI, and Abilene National Bank. The court of inquiry, he said, had a singular purpose. "What happened to the money?" he wanted to know. "And how were the royalty owners going to get paid?"

David Botaford, the attorney for BRIO's owner, L. Bob White, charged, "This whole thing is a kangaroo court." It was illegal, he contended. It was merely trying to crucify his client. It was an absolute travesty. Back in the comfort of Dallas, he had connections. Back in the comfort of Dallas, U.S District Judge Jerry Buchmeyer had issued a restraining order forbidding officials in little old Lee County from conducting its inquiry while the company was in bankruptcy.

Judge Placke was not impressed. The order signed by the district judge was highly improper, he said, and, what's more, he did not appreciate BRIO's lawyer interfering with the sanctity of his courtroom by even obtaining such an order.

Attorney David Botaford, who never suspected that a small town like Giddings would have the nerve to disregard the holy and sanctimonious ruling of a well-respected Dallas judge, sternly warned John L. Placke and District Attorney Charles Sebesta that both men would be held in contempt of the court if the inquiry did not immediately cease.

Judge Placke leaned back and folded his arms defiantly. If some out-of-town, out-of-county lawyer wearing a high-priced suit and spit-shined shoes was trying to frighten, intimidate, or threaten him in his own courtroom, the man had failed miserably. Placke's mind was already made up. The court of inquiry would continue. He did not simply ignore the district judge's order. He tossed it aside, and the hearing suddenly began to get very ugly. The war shifted its focus. Humble and its royalty owners still wanted their twenty-eight million dollars. BRIO and CPI remained at the mercy of a Giddings courtroom. But the real battle and bloodletting had erupted between judges,

Placke was mad at Judge Buchmeyer for trying to shut him down.

The district judge was mad because Placke had dared to defy him.

Didn't Placke know who he was?

Placke didn't care who the district judge might be. He and Sebesta were ordered to appear in a Dallas courtroom. Placke refused to go.

He hired an attorney to handle his legal problems in Dallas. A pissing match with a district judge was a waste of his time. He was too busy moving forward with the court of inquiry.

"Why?" the press wanted to know.

"I don't like seeing seven hundred landowners cheated," he said.

As Charles Sebesta argued, "A federal court, in bankruptcy hearings, did not have the right or the authority to stop a legitimate criminal investigation."

Judge Buchmeyer, obviously weary of the long-distance standoff, decided not to press the issue. He quit pissing. He knew that Placke would simply piss back. Placke, he realized, had no intentions of coming to Dallas, and Buchmeyer sure as hell wasn't going to Giddings. It was a waste of his time and gasoline. What happened in Giddings could remain in Giddings.

BRIO's lawyer filed a motion requesting that the dispute be settled in bankruptcy court. Pat Holloway, Humble Exploration, and the royalty owners could stand in line and add their claims to those of the other creditors. Botaford wanted his clients to stay as far away from Giddings as possible. He knew that a court of inquiry had the authority to ask potentially damaging questions that would never be allowed in district court.

●

Pat Holloway packed his overstuffed briefcase one chilled afternoon, walked out the courthouse, and didn't bother to come back. He saw no reason to darken its hallways again. He was angry, bitter, frustrated, and subdued. In Dallas, he had lost. He had lost it all. Even if a judgment did force either BRIO or CPI to pay off the missing royalties, the check would go to Jane Browning. He ambled past the City Meat Market on his way out of town and for the first time in a long time did not go in and order a plate of ribs. For an afternoon, the swagger was gone.

In the Lee County court of inquiry, Humble Exploration was now represented by W. R. Sessions, counsel to John Wright, the new court-appointed receiver for the company. For CPI, Pat Holloway had been a formidable foe. A new guy, like the receiver, was an easy target.

CPI promptly charged that Sessions and Wright had possession of a letter of credit from Abilene National Bank, guaranteeing payment to Humble and the royalty owners. However, the attorney said, Sessions and the receiver never did get around to presenting the letter of credit for collection. If the money had not been dispersed, CPI claimed, it was the receiver's fault or his counsel's procrastination. CPI was blameless.

"W. R. Sessions," he said accusingly, "was guilty of deliberately withholding evidence that dramatically underscored the sole reason why Lee County landowners had not been paid." It was a blistering argument.

Former CPI president, Dr. Jack Young, even testified that Sessions could have taken the letter of credit to virtually any bank in the country and received millions of dollars for the royalty owners.

Pat Holloway was no longer around. Now, it was Humble Exploration on trial. Jack Young cleverly and immediately shifted the blame of his company's demise to the contemptuous actions of the missing Pat Holloway. He told the court that CPI had been taking as much as four thousand barrels of oil per day from Humble wells and delivering them to such major oil companies as Arco, Mobil, and Standard.

In April, however, Humble had stopped trucks hauling oil for CPI from entering any of the company's leases. The contract was abruptly cancelled. Holloway's behavior, he testified, put CPI in a bad financial bind. Bob White was no longer able to honor his obligations to other companies. The money was gone. "We had to shut down CPI," he said, "because Humble destroyed our credibility in the industry."

W. R. Sessions and John Wright were caught in the middle of a game they had never played before. Holloway had lived the facts and been the triggerman behind most of them. Sessions and Wright had not yet figured out what had happened, who caused it to happen, or how to survive the desperate games that desperate people could play. It was all aces and eights, a dead man's hand.

John Wright, when pressed, argued without a lot of conviction that he had not tried to cash the Humble letter of credit for almost four million dollars because he was aware of the bank's precarious financial condition. He had fired back. It was, at best, a stray shot. If Wright or Sessions had known Abilene National was on the verge of failing, royalty owners said as they gathered outside the courtroom, why hadn't they promptly gone in and captured as much money as possible before it was all gone?

●

The District Attorney began fighting back as he continued his examination of the former board chairman of Abilene National Bank. In a hushed courtroom, he looked the banker straight in the eyes and said, "According to BRIO's attorneys, Mr. Sessions, representing the royalty owners, has a letter of credit from your bank in his possession."

"The letter of credit was issued solely to Pat Holloway and Humble Exploration," the banker replied.

"Did it cover the royalty owners?"

"No, sir, it did not."

"For royalty owners, it was a worthless piece of paper."

"Yes, sir, it was".

"Even if Wright or Sessions had cashed the letter of credit, royalty owners, all seven hundred of them, would have been left out in the cold." Only Charles Sebesta was looking after their interests. And even for him, it was probably too late.

Charles Sebesta was in a quandary. He began suspecting that a conspiracy existed between bank officials, BRIO, and CPI, and he wondered if the conspiracy might even have criminal overtones. He believed that Abilene National had obtained royalty money belonging to Giddings landowners for the purpose of covering oil company indebtedness, and he began trying to determine whether BRIO, CPI, and the bank had violated any state or federal laws.

The general counsel and corporate secretary for BRIO was called to testify, and he hid behind his attorney-client privilege. A former vice president of the bank took the witness stand and was asked if he knew of any possible criminal activity being committed by bank officers during his five years at Abilene National.

Silence.

Same question.

The former vice president had a decision to make, and he chose to plead the Fifth Amendment. He did not want to say anything, accidentally or otherwise, that might incriminate himself – even if he were innocent. All that he knew, if he knew anything at all, would remain his secret.

An angry Charles Sebesta was stonewalled. By late December, with Christmas only two days away, the court of inquiry still had not been able to determine what happened to more than seven million dollars in loans from BRIO to seven of its foreign subsidiaries. A company CPA said he and his records could not account for any of the missing millions.

As the calendar changed on a new year, Charles Sebesta announced that a Lee County Grand Jury would receive a preliminary report on the investigation. The District Attorney fully expected criminal indictments. The trouble was, he had to wait for a new Grand Jury to convene and make their way slowly and methodically through a morass of thefts, rapes, burglaries, robberies, forgeries, homicides, drugs, and aggravated assaults before it had a chance to decide the fate of those companies accused of stealing more than twenty-eight million dollars from Humble Exploration and its royalty owners.

The District Attorney might gain a measure of justice. He might even send somebody to jail. But none of the royalty owners expected any money. It was gone. Long gone. In October of 1983, a year after the court of inquiry had first gone into session, the Grand Jury finally handed down its indictments, and there were plenty to go around, especially when it came to felony theft in the disappearance of the royalty payments.

No money exchanged hands.

Royalty owners had been broke before the boom.

They were still broke.

47

Doug Jatzlau, by 1985, knew for certain that Humble Exploration would never be quite the same company again. Pat Holloway was in court fighting for his business life one appeal at a time. The Browning family was determined to take everything he had in the Austin Chalk and keep it, and a judge had ruled that the stately and elegant Jane Browning was entitled to the land, the leases, the wells, the oil, the royalties, and virtually everything else that Pat Holloway had ever touched or claimed to own.

The jury had long ago awarded the Brownings an eighty-two million dollar judgment. But Pat Holloway did not go quietly into the night. He headed back to court as quickly as he could get there, charging that the trial judge was crooked, had been bribed by the Brownings, and had cost Humble Exploration millions of dollars by taking control of the firm, yanking it out of his hands, and turning it over to an incompetent receiver. It was a bitter suit with a constant barrage of new beginnings and never any endings. Trials lingered on year after year, appeal after appeal. He said. She said. The attorneys said. The judge said. None of them were listening.

Doug Jatzlau did not have time to be concerned with the legal machinations of the court or the magic tricks conjured up by a parade of high-dollar attorneys. No matter how bad the economic conditions might be in the oil patch, he had a company that required his every working hour, which was usually before the sun rose and long after it fell beyond the oak thickets. The Giddings operations were his to run.

He supervised drilling, which he liked. He dealt with court appointees, which he didn't. Mostly, Jatzlau had to guide a company through the rigors of bankruptcy with an oil industry caught in the midst of death throes and a court-appointed receiver looking over his shoulder. "The judge and the trustees came from a good old boy network," he said. "The trustee hired a president and CEO, who always happened to be his good buddy, and these good buddies took turns appointing each other to whichever new paying position happened to come open."

●

Jatzlau had taken over the Giddings operations of Humble Exploration and really did not care who owned the company, who won the court fight, what the firm was called, or even if the name might be changed. At the moment, it was HECI – a bastardization of Humble Exploration Company Incorporated – since the courts, after such a long time, had finally ruled that Exxon, not Pat Holloway, still had formal and official rights to the *Humble* name.

Jatzlau had never known Bill or Jane Browning, although he would be working for the Browning name if all of those appeals fell on deaf ears. Pat Holloway was a legend in exile. He had been spending far more time in a Dallas courthouse than on his Giddings field leases, which he no longer owned. He had already lost his grasp on the present and future of the company he had founded. His friends, his competitors, his employees, his enemies all knew that Pat Holloway had drilled his last well under the Humble Exploration or HECI banner.

For several years, Doug Jatzlau had served as the company's field foreman, the man quickly called when a problem couldn't be solved. He was different from most of the other hands. He was older. He was educated. He was ambitious. His wasn't just a job, one that abruptly changed locations every time a new boom hit another corner of the country. It was a career. As much or more than anyone else at HECI, he understood the strengths and limitations of computers, which, for most in the early 1980s, were little more than curious offshoots of science fiction. Technology came easy for him. Working with trustee-appointed executives did not.

Frank Tye came first, and, Jatzlau said, "He had every intention of doing a good job. He was in the office a lot. He watched. He studied. He listened. He made a valiant attempt to learn the oil business. He was getting a pretty good handle on the operation when he died of cancer. It was definitely HECI's loss."

Then came a long succession of court-appointed jesters. They did not understand nor comprehend the nuances of the oil business and had trouble in the field dealing with unshaven, uneducated, and often untrained men who possessed a lot more knowledge and common sense than they did.

They were much more comfortable in the secure, cool confines of a metropolitan office or boardroom. Giddings, they thought, was hanging on the edge of the earth, and no one would miss it if the little town fell off. The sweltering heat, the bitter cold, the unquenched drought, the rainstorms that turned into floods were more than most of them could stand.

They simply cared about the bottom line. Nothing else. Profits. Numbers. Dollars. To hell with the employees. Lose one, and another would be standing in line to take his place. Forget the seismic, the drilling, the production, the day-and-night struggle against all odds to make those drilling efforts pay off in the chalk. They only walked into the office with two questions on their minds: "How much money are the wells earning?" And, "Why aren't all the wells producing the same amount of oil?"

Jatzlau came back out of the field late one afternoon and found a secretary softly crying at her desk. "What's wrong?" he asked.

"I'm afraid I'll lose my job."

"Why would you think a thing like that?"

"The new president wants a full production report for oil and gas on each of our wells, and we have at least three hundred wells," she said. "He wants the figures tabulated and on his desk by five o'clock."

Jatzlau cast a quick glance at the clock on the wall. It was already four. She had less than an hour. "That's impossible," he said.

"He told me that if I didn't finish the report, he would fire me."

Jatzlau turned and walked into the court-appointed president's office, sat down, and said, simply enough, "If you get me a computer, I can have the report finished for you first thing in the morning."

"You don't need a computer."

"I need one if you want the reports that quickly," Jatzlau replied.

"No." The president was adamant. "I worked at Amoco in the fifties," he said, "and we wrote the figures down by hand on ledger books, and we always had the reports on time."

"How many were working on the reports?"

"About twenty as near as I remember."

"Accountants?"

He nodded.

"I don't have twenty accountants," Jatzlau said. "I have one secretary out there. Her desk is piled with paperwork, and she's in tears."

The president smiled. "That's not my problem," he said.

"He thought he was tough," Jatzlau said. "He had fired employees before. He got a kick out of it. He liked the unmitigated exertion of power, and, if he were in the office, the president was always in the midst of a power play. He was quite aware of his own importance. He wanted to make sure that everyone else was able to recognize it as well."

Doug Jatzlau grabbed a list of the HECI wells, made sure he had the company's percentage for each individual well in a file folder, drove home, turned on his personal computer, hastily wrote a program, formatted it, plugged in the numbers, printed the reports with a dot matrix printer, and, within thirty minutes, ceremoniously dropped them on the executive-by-proxy's desk.

The president looked up. He did not smile. His eyes narrowed. For a moment, Doug Jatzlau thought, perhaps, that the president looked a little disappointed. It was quitting time. He had no one to fire that day.

●

HECI had been hell bent to reach the chalk on a well being drilled on the Luecke home place. Nothing but the chalk. That had been the battle cry. Drive on through the shallow Wilcox Sand. Hit the chalk. That's where the oil was waiting. It was the beginning of a miracle, and no one realized it. When a well was being pumped, the rods sometimes began rubbing on the casing because the hole was not particularly true. It was difficult to drill a straight hole when the chalk kept knocking the drill bit in different directions at different angles.

It happened in the Luecke well. It happened at just the precise depth where the welbore cut through Wilcox Sand. At about three o'clock in the dark of the morning, Albert Luecke, Jimmy's father, was suddenly awakened by an ominous and violent roar erupting from the well. It sounded like gas escaping. It sounded like hell was about to light up and burn. He immediately called HECI's field people. "You need to come out and check on your well," he said.

"Now?"

"Anytime later might be too late."

HECI was on its way.

They discovered that the Wilcox Sand was loaded with oil and gas, and the production people had no idea why it was there, how it got there, and how much was packed into the layers of sand. The well was immediately shot and tested. Wilcox Sand would prove to be as rich in oil and gas as the tight and troublesome limestone formations jammed thousands of feet below.

The devil's chalk lay deeper than nine thousand feet, but the Wilcox formation revealed a solid play at only five thousand feet. It was more of a traditional field with a gas zone lying above a reservoir of oil, both being pushed into the well by a pool of saltwater beneath them. In the chalk, historically, gas, oil, and water all mingled together within the tight fractures. The wells were costly to drill, and the recovery of either oil or gas carried an unreasonable price tag.

With financial hardships hovering around the company like vultures in search of new prey, the Wilcox Sand had been a godsend. It was easier to reach, less expensive to drill, and productive enough to keep HECI in business in spite of oil prices that had gone just about as low as they could go. The company moved quickly, drilled a number of wells in the Jenny Field on the Luecke farm, and controlled at least eighty percent of the field. The oil business remained a constant struggle, with bad times far outdistancing the good ones, but profits harvested from the Wilcox field made life bearable even when unpredictable.

●

In an oilfield, there were no unexpected problems. HECI had one, and it came right out of the blue. Doug Jatzlau said, "We had a good well, a dependable well, and one morning, without any warning, it began prematurely pumping saltwater instead of oil. We first thought that we had made a serious mistake, so we began running a series of tests and calculations, and we could not find anything out of the ordinary. We were puzzled. We were stumped. We could not figure out what had gone wrong, but something certainly wasn't right."

He and his crew gazed across the fence line. A deep-seated suspicion began to gnaw its way into their minds. A little renegade company had leased a long narrow tract of land just beyond the fence and drilled four wells. The first had been a dry hole. One had been located too far down structure in the water zone, and it was useless. Two were productive, even though repairs on a bad cement job in the wellbore had shut down one of the wells. The pores of the sand matrix had been plugged, the formation was severely damaged, and a repository of oil lay bottled up in a fracture. It could not escape.

"The Wilcox Sand was extremely sensitive," Jatzlau said. "If the daily production from a single well was too great, it could push a great deal of saltwater into every other hole around it. We weren't too particularly far away, maybe only a thousand feet, and we were pumping saltwater. We felt that the little renegade company had wrecked our well. But could we prove it?"

The Texas Railroad Commission had established an allowable of a hundred and two barrels of oil a day from each well. A quick check of commission reports revealed that the renegade company was on record as pumping a hundred and two barrels of oil a day from each of three wells. Jatzlau shook his head. It was ridiculous, he thought. No. It was impossible. Only one well was flowing a lot of oil, and Jatzlau speculated that it was pumping more than three hundred barrels a day into the tank while the company was hard at work allocating a hundred barrels to each of the two worthless wells.

The reports had been faked. The figures were wrong. Somebody was lying. Somebody was making oil with pen and ink rather than drill and bit, and his well was suffering the consequences. HECI was losing money at a time when no oil company could afford to let a single dollar slip through its grasp. HECI prepared to sue, but Doug Jatzlau realized that he needed more hard evidence than his own jaded speculation. He thought he was right. He certainly did not have enough proof to convince judge and jury.

For weeks, then months, he and members of his crew hid out behind a brush line near the fence and kept constant videotape surveillance on a little renegade company that kept on collecting three hundred barrels of oil a day as regular as clockwork. Jatzlau and HECI's pilot even rented a low-altitude airplane in Dallas and made passes just above the treetops, taking photographs of the operation. He felt like a spy. Hell, Jatzlau said, he was a spy. In time, HECI possessed a day-by-day, minute-by-minute video and photographic record of everything that took place at and around the well site. Not once had anyone stepped across the fence line or set foot on the lease.

A separate tank sat beside each of the three wells, and Jatzlau wanted to find out how much oil was actually being collected in each tank. He had an idea and put it into action. Using a pair of binoculars, he watched the pumper drive up and drop a little brass weight, attached to a metal tape measure, into the tank. He counted each turn of the crank and believed that the number of turns would help him properly calculate the depth of oil.

It wouldn't be an exact measurement. But it would be close, and it might be close enough to sway a jury's opinion. He tested the procedure in his own tank. Crank after crank. Turn after turn. His calculations were becoming more accurate by the day.

Reality would prove that it had all been a waste of time. He focused his binoculars late one afternoon, and the pumper had no idea anyone was watching him. A little brass weight was dropped into the tank of the one productive well, and the pumper cranked it up until the weight reached the top level of the oil.

He yelled loudly, "Six feet and four inches."

Jatzlau stared in disbelief. The pumper was yelling out the depth to make sure that his wife heard him. She was sitting in the pickup truck and writing down detailed notes. Jatzlau did not have to count the cranks. All he had to do was keep the videotape and sound recorder running. The pumper was giving him the calculations he needed, and they were exact. The man walked over to another tank, dropped the brass weight, reeled it up and yelled, "Two feet, three inches." It was all on tape, even the voice.

The company may have been trying to cover up its misdeeds. The calculations did not lie. One good well. Two dogs. Doug Jatzlau had been right all along. He could have acted immediately, but Jatzlau chose to bide his time and wait until his video camera was able to catch a company executive on site when the pumper called out his self-incriminating measurements. Otherwise, he knew, the blame would be piled on the pumper's shoulders, and he was simply a hired hand doing his job. *It wasn't our fault, the little renegade company would tell the judge. The pumper made the mistake. He's at fault. Not us. We had no idea what he was doing.* The days passed. No hurry.

Doug Jatzlau knew when he saw the big blue Suburban headed toward the well, kicking up a cloud of dust, that his wait was finally over. The pumper was hard at work. The vice president of engineering had arrived, and, now, there was nowhere for the little renegade company to run. Jatzlau and the video camera had them dead to rights.

HECI filed its suit. The judge heard the evidence and made his ruling. The judgment was for four million dollars. "We knew from the beginning we would never get any money," Jatzlau said. "The little company didn't have any money. It was going broke. It was desperate. It was merely ignoring the law and trying to stay afloat. But we did manage to prevent the company from over-producing its one well and ruining ours. We weren't trying to put anybody in jail or take their last dollar. All we wanted to do was protect our interest, and we did."

In time, HECI would purchase that long, narrow tract of land, keep the good well pumping a hundred and two barrels a day, drill a second productive well, and fix the bad cement job so there would be a third well making its allowable, too. When trapped in the shadows of harsh and unforgiving economic times, every drop of oil was viewed as a fistful of dollars the company needed to survive.

48

*D*uring the first trial, Pat Holloway had been on the defense and on his heels. Primarily it was accuse and deny. Jane Browning made the accusations, and judge and jury regarded them as cold, hard, and indisputable facts. He was forced into repeated denials, and, after awhile, they began to fall on deaf ears. It was punch and counter punch, hit and run. The accusations carried a lot more clout. They always did.

This time, Pat Holloway was ready to strike back. He was on the attack. He had appealed the verdict, which was standard procedure, and he moved quickly to avert a looming disaster. Since Holloway had previously filed for Chapter 11 bankruptcy, he was able to obtain a federal court order preventing any sale or distribution of Humble Exploration's assets pending his appeal of the jury's decision. And he would appeal for a long time. The court had a lot of legal avenues for him to follow, and Pat Holloway tangled them up into a maze of complications, contradictions, and confusion.

He wasted no time in winning an appeals battle to get rid of the court-appointed receiver, who had been designated to run Humble Exploration's continued venture in the Austin Chalk. Judge Dee Brown Walker, with little regard for the law, blatantly ignored the ruling, however, and kept intact the receivership for Holloway's personal affairs. He prohibited Holloway from entering the company offices or having any access to any of the files.

For Pat Holloway, Humble Exploration was off limits. Not long before Jane Browning dropped her legal bombshell, he had been offered several million dollars for the company. It was not an offer that enticed him or even tempted him. In retrospect, he wished to God he had listened more closely and made a deal. He would much rather be in an oilfield than a courtroom. The chalk was contemptuous, but at least it wasn't crooked.

Judge Dee Brown Walker may not have overstepped the bounds of his judiciary authority, but he had come close. An appeals court directed the judge to *vacate all orders*, and, for awhile, Pat Holloway was convinced that the ruling had effectively overturned the jury's debilitating judgment against him. U.S. District Judge Barefoot Sanders, in fact, voided the jury's decision in Dee Brown Walker's court because, he said, the right judge did not hear the case. He expressed no opinion on the merits on the Browning's claim against Humble Exploration. For Holloway, it was a victory short lived.

As Eric Miller wrote in *D Magazine: Although the original verdict had the legal effect of turning control of Humble over to Jane Browning and her children, the widow soon learned that the Humble man had another card up his sleeve. As it turned out, she would never collect a penny of the seventy-two million dollar judgment. More importantly, she would learn that her victory in the state court would be negated in federal court later. A state jury had ruled, but in terms of the bigger picture, the jury was still out.*

●

As far as Pat Holloway was concerned, the appeals would take time, and, sooner or later, probably later, take care of themselves. In the meantime, he rolled up his sleeves and launched a multi-million-dollar federal civil rights lawsuit against Judge Dee Brown Walker. He blamed Walker as much as Jane Browning for his predicament.

He alleged that the Brownings and their attorneys had entered into a conspiracy to bribe the judge. He alleged that the judge held secret meetings with the attorneys representing the Browning family. He alleged that, in the past, Jane Browning's attorneys had represented Judge Walker, and one of them had at one time served as his campaign treasurer. He alleged that the Brownings and Judge Walker had conspired to violate his rights and had conspired to seize control of the company through the abuse of Walker's judicial office. It was his contention that the Texas Court of Appeals had handed down a mandamus order to refrain Walker from interfering in Humble's business, but the judge had defied the order. Judge Walker, he claimed, had appointed an incompetent receiver for the company and dismissed many of Holloway's personnel. Walker had forcibly and effectively taken over the company's headquarters building by posting guards, prohibited the release of corporate and legal files during the trial, and, in a hotel near the courthouse, conducted secret meetings behind closed doors regarding Humble's business and the trial itself. Pat Holloway charged that extensive damage was done to him and his company because of Walker's pernicious actions.

The crosshairs were clearly planted on Judge Dee Brown Walker's chest, and, as long as the courthouse doors were open and the courts had not yet thrown him out, Pat Holloway kept firing away. *Alleges* were the only ammunition he had.

Walker was an easy target. *D Magazine* would write: *Judge Walker is more than just a bad judge; he is a living legend known far and wide as the worst judge in Dallas County. Walker is bad on so many different levels it is hard to know where to begin. Take the way he runs his courtroom. He tells you that his court will reconvene at 1:30 after a lunch break, says one lawyer. That means you won't see him until three o'clock. It doesn't seem to bother him at all that he can let a simple proceeding drag on for days and days. He openly rules his court by whim, going off on self-serving, personal campaigns like his seven-year crusade to get former political adversary Charles Ben Howell jailed for contempt of court over an incident that happened in Walker's courtroom when Howell was representing a divorce case there.*

When U.S. District Judge Patrick Higginbotham recently issued a writ that kept Howell from going to jail, Walker, exercising his typical lack of restraint, called the federal courts just glorified justice of the peace courts. Walker is not even subtle about the fact that his likes and dislikes count much more than the law in his courtroom. If he doesn't like a jury's verdict, he will issue a judgment n.o.v. (judgment notwithstanding the verdict). That basically means to hell with what the jury thinks. We're gonna do what I think, says one lawyer. Only thirty-seven percent of the attorneys in Dallas surveyed in the Dallas Bar poll think Walker correctly applies the rules of procedure and law in his courtroom. Most astute lawyers know that Walker doesn't pay much attention to the fine points of the law, and they use that fact to their advantage.

Judge Walker, says one attorney, will issue a temporary restraining order against anybody for anything at any time. It's as easy to get a TRO in his court as it is to walk into Baskin-Robbins and take a number. One of his more infamous restraining orders enjoined KDFW-TV from broadcasting one of the parts of a consumer fraud series. Clearly an unconstitutional prior restraint of the press, his order was struck down by a higher court within a couple of days.

Walker has the demeanor of an old-time Southern sheriff. He is the original redneck. He once briefed a group of young attorneys on "how to handle your nigger witnesses," and once admonished a young girl who wanted to change her name to match her adopted father's name because "it sounds too much like a Mexican name."

Originally appointed to the bench by John Connally in 1963, Walker has benefited at the polls because of his notoriety. Most people have seen Judge Walker's name in the paper, says one of his critics, but they don't remember at election time that what they read about him is all bad. But it is.

In another year, *D Magazine* labeled him the *Biggest Buffoon* among any Dallas judges, quoting one attorney as saying, "*If Judge Walker knew two languages, he'd be bi-illiterate.*" The magazine went on to say that *Walker regularly receives among the lowest ratings in the Dallas Bar Polls. His docket is stacked up like Central Expressway. Lawyers say that trying a case in his courtroom is similar to being in quicksand. He is known for getting bogged down in complicated disputes and getting sidetracked.*

The judge was well known for cutting jury settlements in half or doubling them, depending on his own personal bias. In a personal injury trial, he stunned the attorneys and everyone else in the courtroom when the lawyer sought to obtain the medical records of a defendant. The judge said: *If the guy was a nigger, it would be more important to get the records because those guys have more VD than white folks.*

Judge Dee Brown Walker would be defeated by crusading television journalist Catherine Crier, who, in 1984, became the youngest elected state judge in Texas history. Her decision to run was based, she said, on how corrupting campaign contributions can be to the judiciary. As she pointed out, "Dee Brown was rated frequently at the bottom of the bar poll, but his campaigns were always well funded because he would sign those temporary restraining orders at four o'clock on a Friday afternoon when the other side wasn't there. To me, that just wasn't right."

●

Rich Arthur wrote in *Legal Times* during October of 1985: *The gusher of litigation that erupted from a 1979 dispute between the lawyer-turned-oilman, Pat. S. Holloway, and the heirs of his former client and business partner, William W. Browning, Jr., has been no less remarkable than the Cinderella success of the oil company they founded.*

As the court proceedings now stand, Holloway has lost his oil company and seventy-two million dollars to Browning's heirs under a 1982 judgment handed down by former Texas Judge Dee Brown Walker. Holloway, in turn, is pursuing claims against Walker, Browning's widow, four attorneys, and a number of other parties who were involved in the 1982 trial before Walker, claiming that they conspired to fix the outcome of that trial.

Confused?

So are many of the attorneys involved in the case, and there have been dozens.

"It's a most bizarre lawsuit," said Austin litigator Dale Ossip Johnson, who had been chosen to represent Pat Holloway. However, Johnson added with a chuckle, "It's not that amazing in Texas."

"It's been a wild case," noted J. Bruce Bennett of the Austin office of Reynolds, Allen & Cook, one of several attorneys who worked on Holloway's various appeals. "We've been dismissed time and again on procedural grounds," he said, "and our appeals have been thrown out on a lot of novel theories. It has been disheartening. Whatever Pat Holloway may have done, even the lowest criminals get better treatment in the courts than he's got."

Kay K. Pierce of the Reynolds, Allen & Cook firm said angrily, "All we've ever asked for is a fair trial. We'll take any judge in the country, put on the evidence, and if we lose, fine. The problem is, we've never had a fair trial."

What surprised them most, however, was one simple fact. Pat Holloway had a dogged determination. He refused to give up. He would spend all of his money in court before the confounded Jane Browning received a nickel of it. That was his attitude, and he was sticking to it.

●

For a time, said Don Navarro, the first court-appointed receiver, Humble Exploration was in shambles, its production was steadily declining, and its drilling program had virtually come to a standstill. The book containing board meetings was missing, but an investigator had found no evidence of *blatant fraud* by any Humble employee. Pat Holloway, he told the court, would at least provide him with informal updates on business decisions, but the Browning family refused to communicate with him.

"The fight is so emotional," he said, "I have not seen any grounds for settling it. This is one you live with day and night."

By 1984, however, the outlook began to show signs of breaking through a dark lining in the financial clouds. Humble Exploration had collected thirty million dollars in revenue, was operating a hundred and fifty producing wells, and Don Navarro was steadily traveling around the country, making business deals for the company.

Eric Miller wrote in *D Magazine: Humble employees continue to be well paid and enjoy such amenities as free breakfasts and lunches served in the Humble offices. Things seem to be going so well that it might even be easy for those who work at Humble to forget they work in the midst of a complex bankruptcy. On the other hand, no one will be able to ignore the gloomy shadows cast by the feud, at least not until the Humble man or the widow wins.*

Pat Holloway would have his day in court. No. He would have years in court.

He submitted sworn affidavits that:

- *The Brownings' attorneys, behind his back, clandestinely arranged to have the case set before Judge Walker.*
- *Judge Walker was known to be under the control of the Brownings' attorneys, and they often bragged about it.*
- *The Brownings' attorneys boasted about plans to gut Holloway in Judge Walker's court.*
- *Judge Walker engaged in numerous private conferences with the Brownings' attorneys regarding the Brownings' attempts to take control of Humble's and Holloway's other assets.*
- *The Brownings' attorneys and Judge Walker engaged in private conferences during trial in surreptitious circumstances and colluded to give the jury instructions favorable to the Brownings.*
- *Holloway and his attorneys were not given proper notice of meetings relating to the trial and were therefore denied the opportunity to attend.*
- *Holloway and his attorneys were denied access to the documents and files they needed for their defense by the receiver who removed the documents from Humble Exploration's offices.*
- *Holloway was denied the right to effective counsel by Judge Walker's mid-trial order discharging Holloway's and Humble's attorneys.*

The Fifth Circuit Court of Appeals admitted that those statements in the affidavits were clearly sufficient to establish collusion between the Brownings' attorneys and Judge Walker to deny Holloway a fair and impartial trial. The Court, however, never got around to making any formal decision or issuing any binding verdict on Holloway's assumption that he had been the victim of a fraud perpetrated by the actions of Judge Dee Brown Walker. They did not have to.

Walker simply argued that, as a judge, he was immune from any lawsuit. A district court dismissed Walker's motion, but the Fifth Circuit Court of Appeals, ruled that Judge Walker was indeed entitled to the protection of absolute judicial immunity and dismissed all damages, real and imagined, against him.

For eight years, Pat Holloway had kept firing away. Now, he was shooting blanks.

The trial, the appeals, and the legal maneuvering ranged from calculated risks to tales of the bizarre. One court finally ordered Holloway to pay the entire cost of his appeal because his attorney had filed four volumes, containing six hundred and forty-six pages of documents, including abandoned pleadings, temporary orders, notices of intention to take oral depositions of witnesses with written interrogatories attached, jacket sheets, jury lists, and briefs. Very few of the pages had any relevance at all to the trial at hand. The court simply referred to the abundance of files as a *reprehensible practice* from a *man of excess*.

In one desperate measure, and angry that a judge had judicial immunity, Pat Holloway sued, declaring that he should receive diplomatic immunity from any proceedings because he had been serving as an Honorary Consul of Bolivia. He said he even had a written proclamation, and neither the President of the United States nor the President of Bolivia had ever revoked it. No judge found any humor in Holloway's assertion. But then, Pat Holloway was dead serious. He even had the state department search through its records, and no official revocation or withdrawal of his position as an honorary consul was ever discovered. It was all a waste of time. A district court terminated his consul status for him.

During the long and tedious battle, there had been appeals. And judgments. Appeals were overturned. And upheld. So were judgments. It became a web so twisted and entangled that it was difficult to know whom the courts favored, and, after awhile, the courts favored no one. Justices had grown frustrated and disillusioned over the unceasing power struggle being waged between Pat Holloway and the Browning clan. The Fifth Circuit Court of Appeals began its 1985 summary by writing: *This unrelenting battle is a familiar fray to the court. It has been marched up the hill to us several times before. We march it back down once again ... In closing, let us say that we sympathize with all of the parties, all of the courts, and all of the judges, who have surely tired of these prolonged proceedings. We wish there were another course, but the case must be remanded for further consideration.*

Two years later, the same court, in weary resignation if nothing else, slammed the case shut. Justices titled their summary, the Hatfields and the McCoys, and they admitted: *Plenty of process has been provided to the parties in this dispute. It is fair to say that seldom have so many judgments decided so little. We conclude that the litigants have had their day in court and that it is time to end this dispute ... Justice Story once wrote,"It is for the public interest and policy to make an end to litigation (so that) suits may not be immortal while men are mortal." Little more need to be said.*

Pat Holloway won a few judgments and lost a few. One court would see it his way. A higher court wouldn't. The Brownings won more often than they lost, and, in the bitter, distasteful end, Pat Holloway would lose his company. Somewhere along the way, an appellate court finally got around to ruling that the name of *Humble* still belonged to Exxon. Pat Holloway, alas, could not call his company Humble Exploration anymore.

He laughed. Humble Exploration had ceased to exist anyway. Now it was Browning Oil & Gas. Exxon could go to hell for all he was concerned. Pat Holloway had walked out of the Giddings field for good. Jane Browning owned the empire he had built.

For her, it wasn't enough. She tried to have Pat Holloway jailed. Her charges were brought before a grand jury more than once. It was the one case she lost.

Said attorney Dale Ossip Johnson, "I've read this case from beginning to end, and this is the worst travesty of justice I've seen in twenty years of practice. As a former judge, I'm aghast at the conduct of that trial. It was a three-ring circus."

Pat Holloway, however, found no consolation or satisfaction in having his case dismissed by the Grand Jury. He was numb and callused by judicial hearings that had already taken everything good that belonged to him, including his ranch and the small royalty leases left to him by his grandmother. The jury had given away his business and his money. Judge Walker had stripped him of everything but his dignity. He had not let himself worry about a grand jury's decision. Being locked in prison was little different from being locked out of the Giddings field.

He couldn't go back. He could no longer drill. The H. L. Hunt of the Giddings field was broke. He could not afford to buy a lease or rent a rig if he found one.

Eight years had passed.

The field had changed.

A boom. A bust. A boom again.

Pat Holloway was no longer the king.

Pat Holloway had lost his leases, his oil wells, and his relevance.

He did not want anyone to pity him. He worked for a time as an oil and gas attorney in the Giddings office of friends Carey Boethel and Mike Simmang but was haunted by a landscape that held someone else's rigs and someone else's oil.

He had helped pioneer the boom.

It now belonged to somebody else.

Pat Holloway unceremoniously threw his law books in a suitcase, walked for the last time across the gardens of chalk, and left the oilfields of never-never land.

49

$\mathbf{M}$ax Williams had weathered tougher storms before, and he had not forgotten them. The inglorious downfall of the real estate market in the early 1970s had driven him to the oil business, and drilling on raw land had suddenly become as risky and perhaps even less profitable than selling it. All across the country, banks, both large and small, were scrambling to survive the harsh reality of the economic crisis, changing owners, changing names, changing their loan practices, and feverishly holding on to their money.

The oil patch took a look at the big, powerful NCNB financial institution and believed that it's initials stood for *No Credit for No Body*. Banks were failing and falling with stunning regularity. The real estate market was once again on the skids and being dictated by foreclosures instead of sales.

And just north of the Red River, the State of Oklahoma, long the beneficiary of riches in oil, announced that it was broke and could not pay its bills. As one of its state senators said, "We are headed for a financial disaster the likes of which has not been seen for years." He intimated that a financial crisis was on its way and moving closer. In the vast reaches of the Giddings oilfield, the bad times had quit circling like vultures with claws outstretched and had already landed.

Clayton Williams had suffered a series of financial disappointments and been forced to lay off seventy-seven employees. He was taking a wait and see attitude before deciding whether or not he would remain active in the Austin Chalk, He said that he had been as aggressive as possible for a long time but thought the day had finally come for him to step aside for awhile and catch his breath. His plans were to sit back and tighten up his operation, indicating that any future drilling strategies would be much more dependent on the status of the national economy than on the strict economics of oil. Of course, one, he said, could not be separated from the other.

An independent oil operator had been left with only two options. He could drill with his own money or not drill at all. The hole would cost a million dollars, and the price of oil was swinging back and forth between both sides of ten dollars a barrel. A man might not live long enough to make a well pay for itself no matter how productive it was.

When the real estate market crashed in the early 1970s, Max Williams found his financial savior in oil, and the chalk was his domain. However, by the middle 1980s, the price of oil was beginning to skid dangerously, and, more and more, it was a struggle to keep his Giddings operation running smoothly. The crisis in the petroleum industry had bludgeoned the economy, and a calamity of monumental proportions was taking a heavy toll in the chalk.

Max Williams watched oil from the Middle East flood the market. He knew it was bad. He did not know how crippling it would become. The price continued to wallow in its own misery. Drilling in the Austin Chalk began to wind down, fade away, and grow silent. It wasn't a mere economic hiccup this time. It was a death sentence handed down in Washington D.C. By the time it made its way to Giddings, the financial depression had reached epoch proportions. The rig count across the country dropped. Rigs were selling for a mere ten cents on the dollar, and companies were hiring night guards to keep them from being stolen and sold for scrap metal. More than three hundred people who had been drilling in the Giddings field were terminated. No drilling. No money. No paycheck. No job. It was a deadly formula. The future of oil looked so bleak that neither The University of Texas nor The University of Oklahoma had a single student majoring in geology. Good, experienced, knowledgeable oilfield hands walked away for the last time and would never come back. In Giddings, a feeling of uncertainty gave way to nausea, then panic.

Max Williams had no idea whether or not the price of oil would ever recover. Williams had built three rigs for seven and a half million dollars. He was forced to sell them for junk metal and collected only three hundred thousand dollars. It was quite a loss, but he was desperately fighting for the life of his business and needed the three hundred thousand dollars. It wasn't enough.

Max Williams knew life would be a lot easier if he simply let go, locked the doors on U.S. Operating, and drove away from the oilfield. Debts were mounting throughout the oil patch, and other oil companies were letting their creditors fight over the wells, the leases, the prospects, and the reserves, which were worth pennies on the dollars. His own assets had once propelled him into the *Forbes* Four Hundred List of Wealthy Americans. But the money was draining, and he was fighting to get it back. One thing, he knew, was a cold certainty. He would never recoup his money unless he stuck it out in the chalk. Giddings had been good to him. He made the decision to stay even though others were crowding the road out of town. It was a tough choice. He began to sell some wells, deal some leases, and peddle some property. Cash flow demanded it. But through it all, Max Williams managed to hang on to the most crucial of his Giddings holdings.

He did have to cut his staff. He didn't like it. It couldn't be helped. It was like a sad parting with members of his family. They had been with him through thick and thin. There was no thick anymore.

Max Williams had a critical decision to make. A few years earlier, he had hired David Latchford as the company's legal counsel. "He had a brilliant mind," Williams said, "and he was one of the best closers I had ever seen. A lot of good deals never got finished because somebody didn't properly do the paperwork. David Latchford could get the deals done. Early on, I did all of the detail work, but I didn't like it. Latchford liked it. And he was so honest, you could play poker with him over the phone. He never cheated anybody and would never be associated with anything that even had the hint of being unscrupulous or on the edge. He wanted both sides to be treated fairly. If they were, he believed, everyone would be ready to do business again." David Latchford was ready to go ahead and lose the deal if it wasn't done right, if both sides couldn't walk away from the negotiating table believing they had won.

Whether it was good or bad fortune, Max Williams had two men at the top of his organization – his company president and his legal counsel. He had to let one of them go. He terminated David Latchford. Within a month, he realized he had allowed the wrong man to walk out the door. The work slowed down, then stopped altogether. "Losing Latchford," Williams said, "was the worst mistake I ever made." It was a mistake that could be rectified. A short time later, he hired David Latchford back. "It was," he said, "the best move I ever made."

David Latchford had been Mobil's man in Libya and Venezuela. He knew his way around the oilfield. He was no stranger to foreign locales, and the wildly, out-of-control, catch-as-catch-can plotting, scheming, and business intrigue in the Austin Chalk made Giddings as foreign and often as bizarre as any place he had ever been.

Latchford knew good deals when he saw them and had the gut instinct to cut through all the smoke, figure out what a man wanted instead of what he was saying, and analyze an assortment of lies, promises, guarantees, and scams to ferret out a crooked deal while it still looked straight. Sometimes, the deal was straight and the dealer crooked. The primary difference between guilt and innocence almost always lay buried in the fine print. David Latchford had no equal when it came to refining the fine print.

During a sojourn in Austin, he had worked in government relations with the Texas Railroad Commission. At Mobil his focus on oil and gas had constantly taken him to Chicago, Los Angeles, Denver, and back to Dallas. Giddings was like a time warp.

●

The oil crunch was bad enough. But an old nemesis had raised its ugly head. As money from oil rolled in, Max Williams continued to invest in those real estate deals that he considered solid and potentially profitable. The market had greatly loosened up during the past half decade, and land, especially in North Dallas, had become a good bet once again.

A Savings & Loan approached Williams and Jim Hammond with an offer to buy a choice piece of real estate along a valuable corridor that was already in the path of expansion. The land could be purchased for only forty million dollars. The Savings & Loan would be their partner and be responsible for furnishing the capital. Neither Williams nor Hammond particularly liked everything about the deal, but the Savings & Loan persisted. It wanted the deal, and it needed a couple of real estate heavyweights like Max Williams and Jim Hammond to back the acquisition. Time, was a critical factor.

"We need to move and move quickly," the Savings & Loan president told them, "or we might lose a portion of the land, especially the frontage. And none of us can afford to see it wind up in somebody else's hands. It is simply too valuable to lose."

A lawyer, a CPA, and a secretary worked night and day, then stayed through the weekend, to make sure the proper paperwork had all been completed on time. The Savings & Loan attempted to show its appreciation. Its president said, "These people have done such a great job in the short time frame we had, let's give them a small percentage of the deal." Max Williams and Jim Hammonds certainly had no objection. A document was hastily drawn up, assigning a small interest to the lawyer, the CPA, and the secretary. Neither of them ever got around to signing it.

Williams and Hammond quickly assembled the land and buildings required of them for collateral. The Savings & Loan had been required to furnish the funds. The loan documents stated that it would be necessary to pay a fifteen percent liability fee or six million dollars. As a result, Williams dutifully put up six million dollars, and the deal was properly finalized.

The contract was in place. But disaster struck. Sudden. And without any notice. The Savings & Loan failed. It was broke and belly up. All across the country, financial institutions, large and small, had fallen on hard times and were going out of business. Nine of the top ten banks in Texas all went under. They would be sold and emerge in the marketplace with new names and new leadership. Only Frost Bank survived.

It signaled the virtual end of the Savings & Loan industry. The North Dallas real estate deal hung in the balance. Max Williams and Jim Hammond had not lost it. The Saving & Loan had. But the Savings & Loan no longer existed. And a contract worth forty million dollars was in default.

The Federal Savings & Loan Insurance Corporation promptly carried the legal documents straight to the courthouse, and U.S. District Judge Jerry Buchmeyer, a liberal icon who would serve on the federal bench for three decades, leveled both barrels at those who might still have money to pay off the loan.

Max Williams was never asked to come to court. He never met the judge. Their paths never crossed. Judge Buchmeyer simply handed down a summary judgment, which meant he considered the suit so one sided that he didn't even bother to go to trial.

Max Williams awoke under the weight of a forty-million-dollar judgment. As his lawyer argued, Williams had already paid six million dollars to protect him from personal liability. It was all for naught. Jim Hammond was also saddled with a forty-million-dollar judgment. The CPA and the secretary were each blindsided with two-million-dollar judgments, and they had never signed the document. That apparently did not matter either. The judge or one of his minions had seen their names typed in somewhere and went after them as well. Only the lawyer had inexplicably escaped financial liability, and that led to a lot of curious questions without answers.

The ruling was devastating. Max Williams knew that it could financially ruin him. He met with his attorney. "I'll appeal," he said.

"I'm afraid you will have to put up the full forty million dollars to appeal," the attorney said.

Williams was confounded. He desperately needed to keep U.S. Operating up and running. He did not have forty million dollars in cash lying around in the vault of some bank. Neither did Hammond. Williams had only one option left. He filed Chapter Eleven bankruptcy in an effort to reorganize and keep his company intact.

●

The reorganization had a stranglehold on Max Williams. He was trying to operate a company whose assets were held by a bankruptcy trustee, and the strain was becoming unbearable. The months dragged on. Both Williams and the oil industry had seen better days. The price of oil was still in the tank, the curse of Chapter Eleven was hanging over his head, and his hands had been tied by a decision of the court.

Max Williams received a call from the trustee. It was surprising, intriguing, and completely out of the blue. "We've checked you out thoroughly," the trustee told him. "We've searched high and low and every place where we thought you could have possibly hidden your assets. And we can't find any of them."

"There's a reason you didn't find them," Williams said.

"What's that?"

"I didn't hide any assets."

"Let's meet," the trustee said.

Williams agreed. He did not know what to expect. After the formalities had been completed, the trustee sent her lawyer out of the room. "I don't really understand it," she said, "but you are the only person I've ever known who filed Chapter Eleven and did not try to hide any assets."

Williams nodded. Such a devious thought had never entered his mind.

"I have developed a plan," the trustee said.

"Let's hear it."

"The judge probably won't like it because there is an awful lot of money involved," she said. "But here is my deal. For two million and four hundred thousand dollars, you will be allowed to buy your company out of bankruptcy. If you can come up with another six hundred thousand dollars, I can make everything else go away."

It sounded to Max Williams like a lot of money. It was, but nowhere close to the forty-million-dollar judgment. "I can get the six hundred thousand dollars," he said. "That's no problem. However, it will take me awhile to come up with two point four million dollars. How much time can you give me?"

"I'll give you a year."

Williams nodded again. That was fair enough.

The trustee delivered her plan to the Creditor's Committee. She knew each of them quite well, and she respected their common sense approach to sticky situations.

The committee approved her plan without dissent. The judge, with a quick signature, made it official. Williams doubted if he even read it.

Max Williams felt as good as he had in a long time. He would feel even better if he could figure out a way to come up with two point four million dollars. He met with David Latchford and began to develop a game plan. It would not be easy, not with oil still selling for nine to ten dollars a barrel. He wasn't looking for miracles, but Williams was hoping for a short- and long-term strategy that would somehow save his company. After all, the bankruptcy trustee still had possession of his stock, his assets, and over ten million of his dollars. They were virtually worthless to him. Williams was shaken but not broken. For the first time in a long time, he knew how the story would end. No longer was he caught in the grip of an unknown. The bankruptcy trustee had shown him the way out. If he had any kind of chance to take back his company, he and David Latchford, with the help of his CPA, Curtis Leggett, would find it. All it took was money he didn't have.

Latchford closed the doors to his office, locked himself away, and carefully began appraising all of the properties that Max Williams had owned before the reorganization papers had been filed. It was more or less a jigsaw puzzle, and he was putting the pieces together on a far-sighted and complicated plan to salvage as much of the company as possible. With any luck, he thought, he just might be able to get it all back. It was not unlike playing poker with a pair of deuces, no hole card, and a pocketful of pennies.

U.S. Operating had three floors of a building in Dallas, tucked away alongside a prestigious location on Northwest Highway and the Toll Road. "We can't save the company if we pay that much rent," Latchford told his boss. Let's consolidate the business on one floor."

Max Williams nodded. "Do it," he said.

It was a start.

David Latchford met with the bankruptcy trustee. "You hold the stock owned by Max Williams," he said.

"I do," the trustee said.

"I would like to try and buy it back."

She nodded and gave him the price he would have to pay. No discounts. Full price. Latchford sighed. It was a steep hill to climb. He might as well begin.Latchford looked through the files, found wells in Lee County where production was low. However, they would require no drilling costs. The wells were already in the ground, and in at least twenty of them, oil had been found in the upper chalk.

The Hilliard, for example, began producing after the drill bit only cut its way fifty-eight feet into the limestone. Williams had launched a cost-efficient strategy of fracking the wells where he had seen traces of gas kicks on the mud logs, cracking the faults wider and much deeper, increasing production from ten to an average of a hundred barrels a day. Even at low prices, it made a significant difference. They would flow a little oil. They would flow a little money.

He sold forty wells, most of them outside of Lee, Fayette, and Burleson Counties, for a couple of million dollars, which were enough hard cash dollars for Max Williams to begin paying off his immediate debts and buying his stock back out of bankruptcy.

Latchford concocted a simple formula. He sold a percentage in each of the wells owned by U.S. Operating and used the money to buy back the stock.

It took awhile, but Max Williams looked up one day and all of the stock had been moved from the bankruptcy trustee back to him.

Now, David Latchford set about to resolve another dilemma. Max Williams had his stock back, but, in the process, he had lost most of his interest in the wells.

Undismayed, Latchford triggered phase two. He had carte blanche in developing his strategy. Max Williams trusted him implicitly. Whatever he wanted to do had immediate approval. Max Williams had one chance to escape from bankruptcy, and he would follow any route that Latchford laid out for him.

In a series of intricate and legal maneuvers, Latchford formed his own company, called it Roan, and methodically began making preparations to bring some much-needed cash back into the company. It would take a half million dollars for his company to buy a small interest in the forty wells and keep them producing for U.S. Operating, as well as for Roan. Silent wells in an oilfield were worthless assets.

David Latchford sat down with the officers at First City Bank and made his pitch for a half million dollars. He and Max Williams had done business with them for a long time. In the early halcyon days of oil exploration in Giddings, a loan for a half million dollars would have been chump change, a deal made with a quick phone call. But that was when oil was selling for more than forty dollars a barrel.

It was a precarious time for banks to deal. No offense, but the banks had federal rules and regulations they had to follow, especially when they were afraid to issue new loans because they were still mired in trying to unravel themselves from too many bad loans already on the books.

But the bank officers knew David Latchford.

They respected his reputation.

He walked in that morning, closed the door of the banker's office, would have locked it if he had a key, sat down, folded his arms, and told them, "Boys, I hope you have cleared your calendars for the day. I'm not letting you out until I get the money." Latchford outlined his plan. He needed to borrow money. He had an interest in forty producing wells. He was proposing to use the value of his interest in the wells as collateral.

The bank officer was abrupt and to the point. "We will loan you the money," he said. "Or we will loan Roan the money. But we won't loan Max the money. We can't. He's in bankruptcy."

"Roan will make the loan," Latchford said.

"Do you have an appraisal on the collateral?"

"I do." Latchford pulled the numbers from his folder.

"How much is the collateral worth?" a bank officer asked.

"The interest in the wells is valued at a little more than a million dollars."

"How much money do you want?"

"A half million dollars."

"Do you really think your idea will work?"

Latchford grinned. "You won't be disappointed," he said.

He walked out of the bank that morning with a half million dollars in his account. Max Williams would keep his company. It was up and running again.

Williams could have sold out at any time and to virtually any company in the oil business. He had his chances. He had never been tempted. He did not want to leave the chalk. Williams still had faith in the field, and he knew that the hard times would not last forever. All he had to do was hang on.

A better day was on its way.

Storms did pass.

"I placed my trust in David Latchford," he said. "I lost a little interest in the wells. But I knew if he and his partners in Roan had some interest in the company, they would take care of the business. A little of it belonged to them now, and Latchford made sure I didn't lose any of my wells or see U.S. Operating bite the dust. A lot of companies did go under during the bust. If they had David Latchford, it might have been different for them."

Latchford promptly sold a half interest in U.S. Operating's Fayette County wells to Union Producing for substantially more than a million dollars. He took the first five hundred thousand dollars, paid back the loan, and left a room full of happy bankers.

With David Latchford skillfully handling the legal and financial machinations of the business, Max Williams had been able to maintain control of his wells in Lee County, the heart of the Giddings field, and he had a little cash on hand to crank up his operation in the chalk once more.

Max Williams wasn't back on top yet, but he knew the distance from the bottom, and it wasn't nearly as far as it had been. His business would live to drill again. He called the bankruptcy trustee.

For her, it was intriguing and out of the blue.

"Can we meet?" he asked.

"Is there a problem?"

"No," he answered. "I have something for you."

"What?"

"Two point four million dollars."

Max Williams, after almost being ruined by a Saving & Loan that fell victim to a weak economy and its own poor decisions in a deteriorating marketplace, had the check waiting for her when she arrived. She was not surprised.

He had been a man maligned. He had borne the brunt of an unfair judgment. He had fought back.

Nothing personal.

Business was business.

The trustee kept her word.

She accepted the check, returned his company to him, and made the bankruptcy go quietly away.

Max Williams again had access to his money, his wells, and his assets. He cast his fate to the dusty farmlands around Giddings once more. In reality, he had never left.

50

*B*y all rights, Ray Holifield should have been the richest man in the Giddings field. He had been the mastermind who cracked the code of the Austin Chalk. He had personally triggered the nation's hottest oil strike, guiding those early explorationists, whose drilling exploits built one of the country's largest and most important oilfields. Geologists, even those on the payrolls of major oil companies, had been adamant about condemning the chalk and its bad reputation. Ray Holifield, after a time, had faith in it.

Others were looking for standard pools of oil beneath the earth. Holifield recognized that the oil lay encased in fractured schisms within the faults. The small fractures erupted with oil then fizzled out. The big ones made men rich. Ray Holifield figured out how to find the big ones.

Historically, he knew that faults were almost always cut into the earth at forty-five degree angles. In the chalk, however, he discovered that the seams of faults ran at sixty-degree angles. When a geologist selected a location, when an operator was ready to drill for oil, those fifteen degrees made all the difference in the world. It was the one single secret that Ray Holifield never shared with anyone. He was the guru and the genius of the chalk. Some said he was a man most fortunate. Some boldly said that the entire chalk was a rich maze of faults and fractures. Drill anywhere, they said. It didn't matter. And the bit would hit oil. Maybe. They left a lot of dry holes in the good earth. During the seventies, everyone in town said the same thing. "Want to drill? Hire Ray Holifield to find your locations. Want to go broke? Hire another geologist."

When Max Williams and Irv Deal brought Ray Holifield, along with their Windsor/U.S. companies into the chalk, he was dedicated and extremely loyal. Then he became famous. Or at least notorious. Holifield began dividing his loyalties. While still working for Williams and Deal, he began finding prospects for Pat Holloway and Humble Exploration, and Holifield made Holloway a rich man. He discovered wells on every side of Giddings, near and far, at a time when it was a common belief that oil could only be found beneath the town. He even dared to venture out into surrounding counties, and Holloway pumped so much oil that he hung a brass plaque on the side of his Giddings business office that said: *The House That Holifield Built.*

Bill Shuford came along with WCS and made Holifield an offer that the geologist could not refuse. Holifield decided that he might as well go ahead and provide the young man with some seismic logic, even choose him a few locations. After all, Shuford had worked for Max Williams, and Williams was a client, and Holifield did not see anything wrong with keeping oil in a big expanded family. Gary Bryant partnered with Shuford for a short time just so he would have access to Holifield's expertise in the chalk. Sooner or later, as time went by, any operator who wanted to make a deal – large or small, real or imagined, legitimate or counterfeit – found that Holifield was in the market for a deal. If a hole went into the ground and struck oil somewhere within the chalk, it more than likely had the name of Ray Holifield attached to it.

The geologist, the magician of the field, was always paid a two and a half percent royalty on every prospect that was converted into an oil well. It would have taken a team of accountants just to keep up with his wide array of royalties flowing in from every corner of the field. There was no telling how many dollars passed through his hands. Ray Holifield, by his own admission, had trouble holding on to them. Why try? He could always find more oil. For Ray Holifield, the Austin Chalk was no longer an unknown and never much of a challenge. The innards of the limestone formation were as familiar to him as his own face.

●

His early clients – Max Williams, Irv Deal, and Pat Holloway – already had more than fifty percent of the field under control by the early 1980s. Blessed with a little luck and some old fashioned, crafty ingenuity, they had worked with Lee County insiders to own the best and three largest acreage positions in the Austin Chalk trend. They would attack the play with a dedicated frenzy, drilling hundreds of producing wells, not really appreciating the success of one before heading out to find another.

During the first four years of the play, Ray Holifield collected as much as twelve million dollars in royalty payments, but he was still a working geologist on the payroll of LaRue, Moore and Schaefer. He was under contract, earning a salary, and obligated to hand over seventy-five percent of his override money to the engineering firm. He had not pocketed as many dollars as most believed he had.

In March of 1979, he went into business for himself, and his geological consulting company became a questionable and costly venture. Oil did not change Ray Holifield. It only made him the high-roller he had always wanted to be. He built a large house for his family in Dallas and leased the entire floor of an office building in Las Colinas, which, according to some reports, held as many as seventy-five members of his own geology team. Holifield, on the other hand, had little time for Dallas. He kept his car gassed and turned toward Giddings. He was devoting sixteen to eighteen hours a day in the oilfield.

He was a modest and unassuming man. He was never a lavish dresser, generally looking more like a field hand than a renowned geologist, regarded, even worshipped, as an icon in Giddings. His only weakness was a diamond-studded Rolex watch. He did not wear it to particularly impress anyone. He wore it solely because it had been a gift from Max Williams. It marked the first symbol of his unrivaled triumph in the Austin Chalk.

When the 1980s descended on Giddings, Ray Holifield had no reason to shoot or read any more seismic data. He had the length and the breadth of the oilfield embedded in his memory. He had watched operators earn fortunes while most of his royalties had been marshaled into the accounts of LaRue, Moore and Schaefer. He was considered wealthy. Others who had gambled on hard ground were filthy rich. If occasional rumors could be trusted, Max Williams had already banked seventy-five million dollars, including forty million dollars in 1981 alone. Irv Deal had sold out for fifty million dollars. And neither of them had pocketed as many Giddings oil dollars as Pat Holloway.

None of those clients could have attained so much wealth without Holifield. He was there with them in the beginning. But what if they no longer needed him, he wondered.

Ray Holifield watched them all drift quietly away. Pat Holloway was in court, and he would lose Humble Exploration to the Browning family. Holloway would never set foot again in Giddings and had no need for a geologist. Irv Deal took his money and ran as a wise man should. His name had once been an important fixture in the field, but now it would be forgotten and ignored by those who wanted to drill farther, faster, and deeper. Max Williams had long been simmering over his belief that the seismic data he financed was being used by Holifield to find locations for his competitors.

Pat Holloway, however, had always found Holifield to be very punctilious in not disclosing to him anything the geologist was doing for any of his other clients, especially Irv Deal and Max Williams. He said, "At times Holifield made me run seismic lines that lay down exactly over the lines he had run for them because they had not agreed for me to have the information. Later, he worked out agreements where we shared the cost of seismic lines that ran across or near leases held by Humble and his other clients. Even then, he was careful not to let me know about the results of seismic lines running across their leases. He told me only about the seismic data that affected our drilling plans at Humble Exploration."

Ray Holifield worked for a lot of competitors. He could keep their secrets to himself. Not everyone thought he did. But Holloway said he did. In the oil patch, right or wrong, truth or consequences, fact or fiction always lay in the harsh glare of perception, and perception was reality.

For Max Williams, the final, fragile straw holding together his tenuous relationship with Ray Holifield broke when W. O. Bankston, one of his original investors, called and told him that the troubled Penn Square Bank in Oklahoma City was trying to liquidate its oil and gas assets. The energy crisis had left the bank in financial ruins and on the brink of closing its doors. In the banking business, the powerful were beginning to fall.

"Let's get your geologist and go up there," Bankston said. "I have a good friend with the bank, and he says the oil and gas department will give us access to everything the bank owns. I think we have a chance to get the deals for pennies on the dollar."

Max Williams, Ray Holifield, and W. O. Bankston headed for Penn Square Bank and methodically went through a detailed list of oil and gas holdings scattered all over the country. Williams carried the information home to Dallas and began to study it.

A week later, Bankston was on the telephone and as mad as Williams had ever heard him. "What's going on?" he wanted to know.

"What do you mean?"

"That damn geologist of yours is back up at Penn Square Bank, and he's trying to sneak out with the assets you and I wanted to buy."

Williams began to boil. He sat down with Ray Holifield and asked, "Why did you go back to the bank without us?"

"I didn't think it had anything you were interested in," Holifield answered.

"You need to let us decide what we are and aren't interested in," Williams said. He left Ray Holifield sitting alone for the last time.

Bankston promptly called his friend at the bank. "Don't ever let Ray Holifield back in," he said. "Holifield doesn't represent us anymore."

Max Williams, still simmering, told David Latchford, "I'll never work with Ray Holifield again." The trust factor between the two men had been left trampled in the dust of the chalk. Williams hired a new geologist, Lloyd Hanson. The geologist had been trained by Ray Holifield.

Ray Holifield said he was at a loss. He could not understand the reason behind the anger that had persuaded Max Williams to cut him loose. He recalled, "For years, I had maintained an office in Oklahoma City. In early 1986, the oil and gas business was facing a total collapse.

My staff was reviewing oil and gas properties at numerous oil companies and banks, including the largest bank in Oklahoma – Penn Square Bank."

Holifield said he had no interest in becoming further involved with Williams and his partners on any new deals. His staff had been moving in and out of Penn Square Bank from time to time, but he certainly didn't bother to darken its doors. Williams may have found some oil and gas assets that interested him. Holifield never knew, and, frankly, he didn't care. He said, "It is for damn sure that neither I nor anyone working with me ever acquired any wells from the Penn Square Bank."

Ray Holifield had spent his life in the debt of others. He was ready to strike out on his own. The oil business may have been sickly. Some said oil was on its deathbed. But it would recover. Ray Holifield was sure of it. The price of oil and gas might be low. But so were the prices of wells and leases and assets that had bankrupted oilmen by the thousands. One man's failure could well be another man's gain. Holifield geared up to take advantage of the slump. Giddings was never far from his mind.

He had built his reputation in Giddings, which was recognized as the first field in the United States where faults and fractures – the result of a meteorite slamming to the earth in Mexico more than five million years ago – created their own reservoirs of oil and gas. Holifield's understanding of the non-porous, permeable rock formations, discovered during his work in the oil fields of Algeria and Iraq, made Giddings unique and changed the conventional wisdom about oil and gas reservoirs in the United States.

His geologic work had led to the development of the second largest oil and gas field discovered in the onshore continental United States during the last fifty years. Only the famed North Slope fields of Alaska were larger.

Mention the name of Ray Holifield, and investors in the oil business, he believed, would be quick to take notice and start writing checks. He had cracked the code of the chalk and helped open the field for Irv Deal, Max Williams, Pat Holloway, Bill Shuford, and Gary Bryant. His mark lay bold and deep in the ancient limestone. By now, however, everybody had the code or a reasonable facsimile.

Ray Holifield, more or less, had retired as a geologist. Why bother anymore? To him, the chalk was a mystery solved, and, what's more, he had an office full of geologists back in Dallas. Let those boys earn their keep. Ray Holifield wanted to be like those men who had been his clients. He may have read and interpreted the seismic. He may have located the wells. But they had reaped a greater share of the fortune from Giddings oil.

Ray Holifield became an operator.

There was nothing to it, he thought. Lease some land. Locate some prospects. Hire a crew. Drill some wells. Tank the oil. Run pipelines to the natural gas. Negotiate with the buyers. Find a bank. No. Find a lot of banks. Why not? He had enough personal money to finance his own oil exploration.

He might take on some investors from time to time, even make a loan or two, but he probably did not need them. The money generated by each new well would no doubt be able to finance a few more sorties in the oilfield. His mind was on go and ready to strike out on his own. He did not need a big car. He did not need his own private plane. But he did want to be a card-carrying member of the Big Rich in Texas. He had the title. He wanted the money.

Ray Holifield did not realize it, but he had already reached the top. There was no place higher for him to climb. His foray into the enigmatic world of oil operators and petroleum financiers proved to be disappointing, then disastrous. He poured out money like rainwater after a storm. After awhile, the bucket was empty. Holifield had made his mark and earned his reputation in the Giddings field, but he was struck with wanderlust.

He followed the chalk, and it carried him to places where no sane man should have gone. If the chalk had fractures filled with oil beneath Giddings, he thought, it might be even richer down toward the coast and across the lower plains of Mississippi. He bought a lot of leases. He drilled a lot of wells. He watched his money waste away. As Pat Holloway always said, "Ray Holifield had one basic fault. He trusted people too much." When business turned sour, he was the one left holding an empty bag.

The chalk beneath Mississippi coughed up a little oil, but it wasn't Giddings. Holifield paid more than he took, and the chalk took what was left.

The bust grew deeper, more painful, and threatened to crush him. He had a little money left. He felt as though he were broke. The wild, unpredictable, frenzied search for oil had robbed him blind, and three divorces did not help the finances any, although he married his third wife for a second time. The oil bust stopped Ray Holifield in his tracks. He came back home and found it a disquieting place.

The oil bust had crippled the Giddings field. An eerie silence hung over the deserted rigs. Even the bars had closed. The field hands were gone. The Austin Chalk was dead and lying in a calm repose. The only sound was made by the gear jammer on another truck leaving town.

Everyone except Ray Holifield suspected that Giddings had given up the ghost. He believed that the rumors of the field's tragic and untimely demise had been greatly overblown. He was convinced that the chalk still contained as much as a billion and a half barrels of oil, maybe two billion, and he hesitated to even guess the amount of natural gas remaining untouched and untapped in their underground chambers.

The problem was not finding it. He knew where it was. He had the seismic data and it was as clear to read as a road map. With the price of oil slipping below nine dollars a barrel, however, the secret was being able to develop a cost-effective and profitable way for operators to come back into the chalk and produce the oil and gas without the operation breaking them financially.

Holifield was convinced that, as a geologist, he had controlled the Giddings field for almost seven years. He did not want to lose it. But the price of oil was in danger of taking the fickle, unpredictable Giddings field away from him and everyone else who had ever believed in the validity of the chalk.

Holifield began toying with the idea of directional drilling, a rough-hewn, poor-boy technology that dated back to the 1920s. Historically, it had resulted in lawsuits, large fines, and criminal indictments when oil companies deliberately slanted their drill bits in an effort to tap into someone else's pool of oil.

During the early 1960s, the great East Texas Field had become rift with slant-hole drilling, and dalliances with the law led to more than two hundred indictments against forty-four defendants, including a county judge and the district judge. A Grand Jury condemned the practice as corruption, theft, and a devious way to make a *fast buck*. A legal version of directional drilling had been tried in Pearsall, but it wasn't profitable.

Holifield believed that the idea was sound. An operator would not necessarily have to cover the million-dollar expense of drilling a new well nine to twelve thousand feet below the earth. All he had to do was enter a wellbore already in the ground, then kick out the pipe, and, if his geology were correct, he could drill into a series of fractures. Holifield decided that it would be no different from drilling five different wells into five or more different fractures. Save a lot of money. Find a lot of oil. It made a lot of economic sense.

The idea was indeed intriguing, but no one had the technology. In the past, the length of a drilled horizontal shaft, even an illegal one, hardly ever reached fifty feet. Ray Holifield, however, could envision a revolutionary process that might travel underground for hundreds and maybe even thousands of feet. He was given his chance to find it.

51

By the time the first brutal signs of the oil bust cast an ill wind across the country, Bechtel had gained stature as one of the world's top engineering and construction firms with major projects in faraway corners of the globe, from seawater treatment facilities at Prudhoe Bay to the conversion of natural gas to gasoline in New Zealand, intricate gold and copper projects in New Guinea, and the massive billion-dollar clean up of Three Mile Island's Nuclear accident in Pennsylvania. As the country fought to endure the economic crisis of the 1980s, a Bechtel executive said boldly, "If we don't have a client, we get one. If there's no project, we assemble one. If there's no money, we get some."

In California, Bechtel invested twenty-two million dollars in the development of technology designed to trigger an innovative new wave of horizontal drilling in the world's oilfields. It may not have been a disaster, but it was considered an abysmal and a costly failure. Bechtel didn't simply walk away from an idea, however. It was ready to throw good money after bad, just not as much of it. The company turned to Bill Mouer, who had been a research engineer for Exxon before leaving to create a number of improved tools for use in the exploration for oil and gas. He was considered a genius by those who had known and worked with him.

Mouer was given almost two million dollars to conduct concentrated research on horizontal drilling. He immediately struck out in several convaluted directions, developing drill bits, mud motors, and an array of assorted drilling tools, while working to convince the manufacturer of atomic submarines in California to string five thousand feet of cable together so he could monitor the Russian efforts to build a new technology for directional drilling.

●

Back in Giddings, Ray Holifield had the basic idea for horizontal drilling rattling around in his head, but he was growing short of time and even shorter than he thought on money. At the time, Holifield believed he was fairly rich. But his focus on the concept of horizontal drilling broke him before he knew he had financial problems. He said, "I was pouring my own money in the ground. The tools kept breaking. During my first test of a horizontal well, I had to come out of the hole twenty-seven times, and each time cost me an eight-hour day. It didn't just happen once. It happened again and again. In my heart and on my drawing board, I knew that horizontal drilling could revive the Giddings field. It could recover millions of dollars worth of oil lying dormant in the chalk. But in order to get the technology perfected, I was losing my ass." It was gone before he missed it.

Ray Holifield kept a rig running, hoping against hope that he would find a partner who might want to invest in half of the well. There were no takers. The economic bust in the oil patch had everyone running scared. Holifield kept right on drilling. He kept right on testing. He kept looking for a mysterious answer that had thus far eluded him, attempting to successfully kick the bit out of the vertical hole without losing his pipe, working to turn the dreaded curve, fighting to drill sideways instead of down, trying to determine if he were still aimed in the right direction, and never quite knowing whether he would hit the fault or miss it. He was drilling blind. The tools kept breaking. Strings of pipe went into the ground. Strings of pipe were lost and buried in the ground.

It was costing him two hundred and fifty thousand dollars a month to drill. He said, "I was burning up money." His operation was moving slowly, plagued with starts and stops, mostly stops. The money was evaporating in a hurry.

●

Two oilmen journeyed into the field with very little money and very little to lose. They had already lost far too often but were willing to take one last fling with the chalk. They presented Ray Holifield with the idea of joining forces and forming a horizontal drilling company. They needed wells that could be easily re-entered, and Holifield had them or knew where they could be found cheap. Holifield was running out of options. He accepted their offer.

They persuaded a drilling company to bring its idle rig out to the well site. No money up front. The company would provide the rig and bits, then drill for an interest in the well. All of them were playing with too few cards in their hand or in the deck.

The two oilmen bartered with service companies. No one had any money. No one had any hopes of a job in the Giddings field. It was a risk, but the risk at least kept them occupied, which was better than staring at blank walls and unwritten paychecks. It was a foolhardy and probably a hopeless gamble, and all of them knew it. Very little cash changed hands. The drill bit cut into the earth. The first well was a disaster. The men frantically wrestled with crooked sections of pipe for three months. "Nothing worked," Holifield said.

The second well became a nightmare. The drill tried to turn the curve at six hundred and twenty-five feet and failed miserably. The tools had a life of only a few hours before tearing apart. A mud motor lasted for no more than five hours before burning up. All along, Holifield realized that he needed to drill long distances, striking more fractures, finding more reserves, cutting through the chalk for distances of two to three thousand feet in order to make a well pay out and pay off.

He kept coming up short. He couldn't make the turn. He missed the fractures. The equipment played out. Men were tired, frustrated, and beaten down. The gamble had been a long shot at best, and now the chips had all been stacked, wagered, spilled, and lost. The two oilmen spent their last dollar and drove away. The service companies went bust. But, in reality, they were already bust. Ray Holifield had been working without a salary, and he was right back where it all began. He thought he had been fairly rich. Now he was more certain than ever that he might, in reality, be fairly broke.

●

Bill Mouer walked out of his lab with a harsh realization staring him in the face. Bechtel's money was gone. He could not afford any more research. He was at his wit's end. He had an inventive mind, perhaps, but the elusive technology for horizontal drilling had thus far stayed beyond his mental and his material grasp. The search had placed him in a position he had never been before – confused, dejected, and defeated.

Bechtel in 1986 invited the old poor boy geologist in Giddings to join Mouer's team. Maybe, this time, two heads would indeed be better than one. Bechtel was well aware of Holifield's ill-fated attempts with horizontal drilling. He had met with failure. He was hurting financially. But, in the research business, it was important and acceptable to make mistakes, then learn from them. Bechtel was betting that Holifield had acquired as much or more knowledge in the field than Mouer had learned in the lab.

Ray Holifield liked the idea of joining forces with Bechtel. His optimism, even in the face of malfunctions and collapse, remained undaunted. He was ready to begin again.

Bill Mouer wasn't. He was weary, discouraged, and no longer convinced that an oilfield would ever be resuscitated by the concept of horizontal drilling. He closed down his lab. "I'm done," he told Holifield. "I created six companies trying to develop new oil fields, and all of them went under when the price of oil fell out from beneath us. I lost years of work. I'll never do this again in my life."

He turned his back on Bechtel. He was through. Bechtel looked at Ray Holifield, who was the only one left standing. The company and geologist worked out a deal that formed BecField Horizontal Drilling Services, combining the names Bechtel and Holifield. It may not have been the wisest move for Holifield, but he offered to buy fifty percent of the company. He wanted to share in the wealth, as well as the glory, and if he were able to piece together the right technology to harness horizontal drilling, he could. He thought it would be just a matter of time. But life itself, he said, was just a matter of time.

He agreed to pay Bechtel the one million, seven hundred thousand dollars that the firm had lost in the Bill Mouer research project. A lot of money? No doubt. In the oil business, he had seen that much money pissed away between one heartbeat and another. The money would be due in two years. Holifield did not flinch at the deadline. He may have been having trouble making ends meet, but two years down the road were a lifetime. He could make anything work in two years. Even horizontal drilling.

All he had to do was drill a few successful wells while testing the technology, then use the revenue from his oil discoveries to pay off Bechtel. His first ventures had ended in failure, but those were shoestring operations hammered together with bartered makeshift equipment and store-bought, sometimes second-hand tools. This time he would have Bechtel engineering behind him. Holifield liked his odds.

Bechtel told him, "Do whatever you want. You're in charge. You figure it out. If you have problems, give us a call and we'll help you build whatever tool you need."

It sounded promising. Ray Holifield, however, had no idea how long his odds really were.

Bechtel's money had been lost in its wager on Bill Mouer's research. Now the company would watch Holifield battle to come up with a million and seven hundred thousand dollars at a time when the price of oil was fluctuating somewhere between five and ten dollars a barrel, the oilfield was virtually devoid of activity, and the self-styled magician of the Giddings field was flying by the seat of his pants and trying to utilize a technology that did not exist and might even be an unattainable myth.

In September of 1987, Holifield found a likely prospect and drilled again. The attempt died in the ground. His operation was still primitive, his equipment not yet able to drive the bit on a straight directional line, his tools still breaking, and his strings of long pipe grinding to a halt and stuck in the chalk. But the results were better than they had been. Holifield stepped back and grinned his wry grin. "We just might get this sonuvabitch to work if we keep after it," he told the crew.

No one believed him. But they kept working. A paycheck was a paycheck regardless of what happened to the well. Ray Holifield had payroll. He had expenses. The drilling ventures were costing him twelve thousand dollars a day. Almost daily, however, he was on the phone telling Bechtel what had gone wrong with the tools. And BecField engineers, true to their word, kept modifying the tools, making them stronger, giving them a longer life in the earth. It was trial. And error.

"We drilled over and over," Holifield said. A tool would break down, and BecField would fix it, then improve it. Another trial. Another error. After awhile, the trials were still formidable, but the errors were fewer and farther between.

Ray Holifield continued to work the Giddings field alone. "The oil game didn't have any secrets," he said. "I wasn't making any money, and everybody knew it. That's why I couldn't find any partners. They weren't willing to throw their money after mine. A few thought I was crazy. The rest knew I was crazy. But we kept on drilling sideways."

The technology had gone from impossible to improbable.

In the autumn of 1987, Holifield, at long last, had his *Eureka* moment. He had managed to drill horizontally for almost as far as he thought he could possibly drill. He had never gone any farther. He kept waiting on a tool or a section of pipe or a drill bit to break or lodge itself in the chalk. Nothing did. He discovered that he was finally able to keep rotating the pipe one full turn per minute. It wasn't much, but it was measurable. Hour after hour, with a cautious, nervous, and apprehensive hand, he rotated the pipe one full turn per minute.

"All of a sudden," he said, "that sonuvabitch began drilling a lot faster. We became a lot more aggressive. The tools had not broken. The equipment had not shut down. We did not have to pull the pipe back out. I kept increasing the number of revolutions per minute."

It had taken him two years of debilitating work. He had reached two thousand feet. The well had cost him three hundred and twenty-five thousand dollars to re-enter, not a million dollars. He had hit several fractures, not one. The oil was flowing. He was on top of the world. The faint pulse in the throat of Giddings began to feel a little stronger than it had a month earlier. Once again, Ray Holifield had de-mystified the chalk. He had deciphered the riddle of horizontal drilling.

It would be a scientific breakthrough. But then, as Holifield said, the Giddings field had been the incubator of many new ideas and technological improvements that were transferred to other oilfields around the world. He, Bechtel, and the science attached to directional drilling would forever change the complexion of the oil patch. A new era had dawned, and Holifield was eager to prove that his success was not a one-time shot that happened to come up lucky.

In 1988, BecField drilled eighty-eight wells. "That got people's attention," he said. "And I pissed everyone off. I wouldn't give any of my secrets away. There were a lot of leaches in the oilfield. Operators had a penchant for taking without giving anything back. It was and always had been a cutthroat business."

One more time, one last time, Ray Holifield was recognized as the genius of the Giddings field. But there was no time for accolades. Bechtel was waiting. Bechtel wanted its million and seven hundred thousand dollars. The price of oil had climbed past twelve dollars a barrel, and Holifield, in order to finance his oil exploration, had been forced to sell large chunks of interest in his wells to doctors and lawyers, all gambling that the bust was coming to a belated end. On top of his mounting drilling expenses, the fee promised to BecField cost him two percent overriding royalty in each well, which could amount to millions of dollars.

Ray Holifield believed, however, that the science was worth the payoff. He was depending on BecField having the ability to drill horizontal wells on a sustained basis. One hole. Multiple fractures. Multiple payoffs.

How much did the gamble cost him? "I managed to spend my last five million dollars," he said. He was a man of triumph. He was a man in financial pain. He was in debt. Holifield had not been able to sell enough interest to cover his fee to Bechtel. Time was rapidly running out. He knew that if he were unable to make the payment, he would lose everything.

He felt as though he had to buy his way out of his own execution. He sold his half interest in BecField for seven and a half million dollars. Bechtel received its money and on time. Holifield paid off his debts.

He had won a little. Once again, he had lost a lot. "With a little luck," he said, "I figured I had broken even."

●

As always, the success of any venture in the oil patch, even one impacted by horizontal drilling, was dependent on the guts and gambling spirit of the man in charge of a hole in the ground. Ray Holifield was asleep in Dallas when the phone jarred him awake in the dark hours of morning. He glanced at his Rolex. It was three o'clock.

Who in hell would have the audacity to call him at three o'clock? It must be trouble, he thought. He answered the phone.

"Ray, we're running out of room," the drilling superintendent said in a harried voice at the far end of the line.

"What do you mean?"

"We can only drill another fifty feet until we reach the lease line."

A long pause. A longer silence.

"I'm shutting the damn thing down," the driller said.

"Have you found any oil?"

"Not a lot. Maybe a trace."

"And you have fifty feet left?"

"That's all."

"Don't stop and don't waste a foot of it." Holifield was adamant. "Drill until you touch the lease line," he said.

At thirty more feet, natural gas began to work its way into the hole. Just before the drill bit touched the lease line, oil exploded. The well came in at a thousand barrels of oil a day. Fifty feet had made all of the difference in the world.

Life in the field had changed abruptly for everyone. C. J. Halamicek said, "The problem we had as landmen was going out and trying to lease land ahead of the drill bit. We could not afford for it to catch us. And if the bit happened to change directions, our need for new leases did, too."

It was a mad scramble. The closer a horizontal drill came to some farmer's land, the bigger the price on the lease became. The farmer had the acreage and the leverage. The operator knew it was robbery. But he paid. He had no choice. Regardless of the price, he paid.

●

Horizontal drilling took Giddings by storm and shocked the oil patch back to life. Downtown and throughout the field, the scene was reminiscent of the mid-1970s when the first boom erupted, and good oil was flowing as thick as bad whiskey. Streets were again packed with men looking for a job. Traffic was thick and growing worse.

Roadside bars turned their neon lights back on. Jukeboxes rocked. Companies were out looking hard for men with any kind of experience, and experienced oilfield hands had all drifted out of town.

The reverberating noise of drilling again punctuated the days and nights above the chalk.

Oil companies such as U.S. Operating, Clayton Williams Energy, Browning Oil and Gas, and WCS had selfishly held on to their wells and their leases even when the crisis often threatened to leave them in bankruptcy and ruin. In difficult times, operators were never quite sure what they should do next. Drill? Stand pat? Hang on? Get out? Now they knew. They were going sideways.

Horizontal drilling triggered a brand new boom in the Giddings field, larger, more explosive, more pronounced, and even more profitable than the old one had been. In the past, operators drilled a single vertical well and were betting on the size and productivity of a single fracture. Miss, and it was over. Horizontal drilling penetrated multiple fracture zones. Miss one, and hit a half dozen more. The business was not nearly as complicated as it had been, and more oil than ever before was flowing from each well.

The price of oil had begun to feverishly climb its way back up, and a truck load of new oil companies was rolling toward Lee and the surrounding counties. New faces. New technology. New money. A lot of new money. Oilfields in the chalk had long ago been drilled. Wells completed. Oil drained.

Then along came horizontal drilling, and it allowed the same field to be used and re-used time again. Shallow. Deep. Even deeper. Each new layer, each new strata might offer a new entrance into a new reservoir of oil. Almost on a daily basis, old sections of the chalk were being redeveloped with new technologies.

Every drop of oil was a premium.

A new field had been created within an old field, using most of the same vertical wellbores already in the ground. The secret was to nose a drill bit along an oil-bearing stratum and stay within the pay zone's narrow and irregular boundaries. It wasn't easy. The use of 3-D seismic imaging made the revelation of targets much less of a shot in the dark, and, as time went by, the advent of computers greatly increased the probability of nailing a fracture dead center. Guesswork was no longer a critical and puzzling part of the equation.

For years, a driller would simply aim his bit in a certain direction, bore a few hundred feet, shut the drilling procedure down, and send an instrument mounted on a camera downhole to photograph a compass attached to the bit. He then removed the instrument, checked his location, realigned his bit if he happened to be off course, and began drilling again. He lost valuable hours, but, more or less, he stayed on line even in limestone.

Then came the introduction of an innovative measurement-while-drilling process. One or more instruments rode the drill bit into the hole, kept track of the bit's location, and sent back messages to the surface. Engineers added sensors to let drillers and geologists know the various conditions encountered by the bit as it tore its way through the earth or the chalk. The sophisticated, powerful, and high-tech array of sensors increased payoffs in the oil zones while generating faster and less expensive methods of horizontal drilling. Sensors, guided by computers, gave oil companies unflinching eyes in the hole.

They revived old fields. They increased recovery. They took much of the gamble away from oil exploration. As one completion specialist said, "In earlier days, an operator could leave fifty million barrels of oil behind because he might be guilty of bad practices, and yet he still had a commercial well. Times won't let him do that anymore. Today's empire builders in the oil patch are those who can find oil that others left behind and produce it." Horizontal drilling made it possible in Giddings and worldwide. The scraps from yesterday's table became today's meal. New technologies ushered in a brave new world.

In time, the Austin Chalk region became prolific once again with oil flowing from more than twenty-one hundred wells. For Giddings, happy days were here again. This time, they didn't end. There were slumps, to be sure, but, year after year, the chalk trend kept right on producing as drilling found new pay-zone layers at a variety of depths – in the sand, in the chalk, far below the chalk. More than two decades later, the notorious Giddings field, an oil patch with a bad reputation, a piece of ground that the major petroleum companies feared, great reservoirs of oil discovered by luck and produced by grit and fortitude, remained as strong as ever.

Millions of barrels of oil had left the field during the first boom. Because of horizontal drilling, millions more were on their way out of the earth the second time around. Ray Holifield had helped develop the technology. He did not share in its wealth. He sold too much interest in too many wells. He sold off his half-interest in BecField.

No great wealth from his directional drilling technology ever came his way. No one, probably not even Holifield himself, ever knew exactly how much money had slipped from his hands. He didn't mind. Not really. "I'd do it all again," he said, "and I would do it the same way."

He witnessed the boom erupt around him with the pride of a father watching a son grow to manhood. Holifield may not have birthed the field, but he was the midwife who brought it into existence. He outsmarted the chalk, which had outsmarted the geologists who came before him.

Chuck Alcorn, by chance, proved that the chalk was not a fluke. It did have oil and a lot of it. Max Williams and Irv Deal dared to chase a dream, and, even though they parted ways on less than favorable terms, they turned the chase into personal fortunes. Pat Holloway played for high stakes, the higher the better. He won, and he lost, but he played hard until the chips were taken from his side of the table.

Giddings lived. It died. It lived again. A lot of oil had been overlooked in the field. Horizontal drilling went back and found it. Horizontal drilling went back and produced it. In the farmlands around Giddings, horizontal drilling had become as common as patches of peanuts lying parched in the field.

Pat Holloway had never gone back to Giddings. But the play in the Austin Chalk never left his mind. He scanned a land map in his Austin office, drew a circle around the length and breadth of the field with his pen, and said, "Whenever it looked like the oil business in Giddings was ready to die and leave its ghost in the chalk, Ray Holifield always figured out some way to bring it back to life."

Epilogue

*I*t had been almost forty years since the Austin Chalk began reluctantly giving up its barrels of crude and a genuine boom spread across farmlands that had historically been known in the oil exploration business as *Heartbreak Field*. The chalk had broken a few hearts in its time, but then it broke the banks all the way from Houston to Dallas.

Chuck Alcorn started it all. He drove down to Giddings in 1972, bought a couple of worthless wells for their salvage value and decided to pump hydrochloric acid down the holes in an effort to clean out the rock crevices in case oil had been clogged in the pores of the chalk. It was a last-ditch attempt to collect a few barrels of leftover oil and make a little money before selling the equipment and pipe abandoned at the well site.

He brought in the famed City of Giddings Well No. 1, and it was a monumental moneymaker, steadily flowing three hundred barrels of oil a day for years. Within the next eight years, Chuck Alcorn produced almost six hundred thousand barrels from the well, generally considered a fluke or a freak of the chalk. It was not a bad return on the twelve-thousand-dollar salvage fee he paid Union Producing. Over a short period of time, he farmed out twenty-two thousand acres to

Houston Oil and Minerals, run by an old college classmate, receiving a substantial interest in any future production. He had no drilling costs. He would simply share in the profits. Houston Oil and Minerals promptly drilled three wells around Giddings, and all of them proved to be great disappointments.

Alcorn kept searching for another blockbuster like the City of Giddings No. 1 and finally found the Patterson No. 1 by extending the Austin Chalk play on down south toward Gonzales County in 1981. The well, one of twelve he had drilled in the area, produced more than a hundred thousand barrels during its first year.

Alcorn did stay close enough to Giddings to oversee workover rigs for U.S. Operating and Windsor Energy. He claimed to have a percentage in several hundred chalk wells, earned a small fortune on the first Big Well he had discovered through blind luck, and settled down in a mansion on thirty-five acres near the Victoria Country Club. He told Harry Hurt III of *Texas Monthly*, "I haven't gotten wildly rich like some of the other guys, but it's been the biggest thing of my career."

Irv Deal left behind Windsor Energy with Santa Fe Minerals, roughly pocketing fifty million dollars before paying his capital gains taxes. He chose to remain in Dallas, involving himself in the real estate market, which had always been his primary interest, but never turning his back on a good oil deal and never forgetting that honey-colored crude had pulled him out of financial depression when hard times struck down real estate during the bust of the 1970s.

Although he continued to drill for years in the Barnett Shale around Fort Worth, Irv Deal preferred to keep and manage a bulk of the revenue he received from Santa Fe Minerals in good, solid, and safe investments.

Irv Deal always possessed the devil-may-care spirit of an entrepreneur, but his days of wild, over-the-top risk taking were sins of the past. He liked the thought of long-term financial security. He had made a lot of money, lost it, and, with the wisdom of someone who had lived through the tempestuous gamble in hard ground, had no intention of losing it again.

●

Pat Holloway never drilled again.

He lost Humble Exploration, his wells, his leases, his reserves, his royalties, his ranch to the Browning family in court. He went back to a successful law practice, settling in Austin and using his legal mind to handle high-powered, high-dollar, often controversial oil and gas lawsuits across the country. Over the years, Holloway had known personally what it was like to be on both sides of a case and the wrong side of a judge.

Browning Oil Company, after wrestling control of Humble Exploration from Pat Holloway in a heated, celebrated lawsuit that lasted almost a decade, remained active in the Giddings field. Mike McWilliams became president of Browning during the 1990s, well aware of the Austin Chalk's bad reputation among so-called petroleum experts, not quite sure whether or not the dollars were still worth chasing down in Giddings. He said, "The first thing I wanted to do was bundle up everything the company owned in the chalk and sell it."

The growing success of horizontal drilling helped McWilliams change his mind. He kept a solid hold on the acreage, began to understand the enormous value of those reserves still untapped, and, instead of selling, began farming out some of Browning's leases.

"I'll never regret keeping the acreage intact," he said. "The chalk defied us all. We kept waiting for the field to play out and dry up, and it kept right on producing. It had some costly hiccups along the way, and it slumped from time to time. But always, a new technology would come along, and the field was up and running again."

Mike McWilliams was as staunchly conservative fiscally as Pat Holloway had been a shoot-from-the hip, no-holds-barred gambler. McWilliams followed two lines of thought. He tried to make money. He never risked a lot of money. Every decision was weighed heavily against the way it would affect the bottom line. His only goal was to build long-term value in Browning Oil.

Down in Giddings, Browning's production superintendent, Doug Jatzlau, watched the operation abruptly change with the passing of time. "When I came in 1981," he said, "it took a hundred employees to keep the company running down here. After awhile, we were able to do the same amount of work with eight people, a pocket full of cell phones, and a desk stacked with computers."

●

Bill Shuford and Bruce Stensrud never even considered pulling up stakes and taking WCS Oil and Gas out of the Giddings field. For them, the chalk had always been the center of their exploration efforts. They endured and survived the downturns in oil prices. They rode the good times to better times. WCS battled its way out of financial slumps by employing BecField Drilling Services and finding its share of horizontal payloads in the chalk.

As Shuford said, "We began small. We stayed small. I loved being small. We didn't have to answer to anyone, we were free to make our own decisions, and we could make them as quickly as we needed in order to get something done.

"There was a time during the early boom days of Giddings when it was every man for himself. The field was filled with operators we knew, operators we did not like, operators we did not trust, operators we had never seen before, and operators who showed up one day and left before the week was out. We fought. We competed. We argued. We battled over leases, over geologists, over hiring the right people, over finding the next prospect. And I'm sure there were some backs stabbed along the way. Every man was trying to get as much oil as he could as long as it was in the ground. Now, we know the oil's not running out. Now we all get along better and work together."

The oilfield wars had found a measure of peace.

Over time, WCS drilled as many as four hundred wells in the chalk. They brought Bill Shuford riches. One broke his heart. A blowout. A raging inferno. The flames wildly out of control. They took the life of his mentor, a trusted employee, his best friend. He buried J. E. Traweek, and Shuford would never be tempted to leave a field that still held the deep imprint of a memory.

Shuford was no longer on the ground in Giddings. He and Bruce Stensrud ruled their holdings from the corporate office in Dallas. They left the day-to-day Giddings operation of WCS in the hands of Danny Anderson. He was loyal. He was dedicated. He was dependable. Danny

Anderson understood the nuances, the trials, and the tribulations of the chalk as well as anyone.

Bill Shuford invested a good amount of his oil money in the development of a charitable program designed to work with men leaving prison in search of a new life. He taught them the basic facets of business during the last eight months they were behind bars. As they walked out and heard the big iron gates clang behind them, he gave them a hundred dollars, a change of clothes, and a bus ticket home. He mentored them and helped them find jobs. "If they were left on the streets," Shuford said, "they almost always found their way back to prison."

He remembered his own rough and rowdy days of fast cars, faster women, hard whiskey, and a world full of temptations. He watched as they departed prison and said, "There, but for the grace of God, go I."

●

Clayton Williams had taken the chalk by storm. His was the largest oil company operating in the Giddings field, and he became the largest lease owner with more than six hundred thousand acres. Yet he always viewed himself as nothing more than a working independent oilman, never afraid to get his hands dirty, as comfortable on the rig floor as he was in his Midland office. During the 1990s, he described himself as "an independent dinosaur that was damn near extinct." He once said, "You can be a man of achievement and not be an arrogant snoot. If I had to choose, I'd be on Bubba's side. Hell, I am Bubba."

It was always difficult to determine exactly how successful Clayton Williams was in the chalk. On a monthly basis, he made millions of dollars and lost millions of dollars, and somewhere in between was the real measure of his financial stature. His exploration for oil and gas carried his company to Louisiana, New Mexico, Mississippi, and across Texas. But his operation never strayed from the Giddings field.

He was always buying new leases, selling old leases, drilling new wells, selling percentages in old wells, maybe even selling the wells themselves, and forever building more gas pipeline. He threatened to leave. He dared to stay. He welcomed a new century by moving his drilling rigs up to Robertson and Burleson Counties, carrying the play farther to the north and investing more than twenty-one million dollars on prospects in the updip of the Austin Chalk.

His business was diversified into farming, ranching, real estate, banking, and Williams even tried his hand at long distance telecommunications. He ran for Governor of Texas and urged Hispanics to support him because he met his wife in a Mexican Cafe. His sense of humor was legendary. Williams, in or out of Giddings, remained an optimist. As the votes were finally counted in the gubernatorial election, he told his supporters, "I've got some good news and bad news. The bad news is that we lost. The good news is that it is not the end of the world."

He packed his bags and returned again to Giddings. His drilling and pipeline exploits there, he said, "were the biggest things I ever did. Life has been pretty good to me. I suffered through ten-dollar oil like everybody else, but I sure can't bitch about it."

●

Randy Stewart maintained his close friendship and partnership with Jimmy Luecke and controlled the business end of their Tex-Lee Oil Company. After selling all of their shallow wells, they still owned and operated more than eighty producing wells.

Stewart was easy to find.

He was the one dressed in a suit and tie and spending most of his time in the office. Luecke was the richest one. He looked more like a field hand or a drifter riding through on the rails.

Randy Stewart became one of the most revered and respected lawyers throughout Lee County. He had participated in the oil discovery, secured leases, and cleared titles on the first wells. He watched the rigors of oil from good to bad and back to better. He, as much as anyone, understood the ramifications facing those who were caught up in the legal confusion of it all. Oil deals. Gas deals, Lease deals. Deals gone awry. Divorces. Randy Stewart handled them all.

As opposed to most of the other pioneers and participants in the boom, Stewart remained as a resident of Giddings. He said, "I moved my family here by choice. We've been here longer than anywhere. I'll never leave. This is home."

Jimmy Luecke, the highway patrolman who negotiated with Pat Holloway to drill on his family's land, invested in more than fifty of Windsor Energy's wells, then, with Stewart, established his own oil company. Most would say that Jimmy Luecke became the wealthiest home-grown oilman in the chalk. No one would ever know it.

Jimmy Luecke liked to be known as the common man. The riches did not go to his head. They went to his bank account, and, in time, he became chairman and the largest shareholder of the oldest bank in Giddings. He was still driving a rusty, old, disreputable 1970s model Dodge pickup truck that did not have a radio, a heater, or an air conditioner. If the day was hot, he was hot. If it was cold, Luecke wore a coat.

Of course, by 2011, he did own a newer truck, but it was a relic from 1981, whose side had been caved in by a collision with a cow. The truck looked as though it just might be traveling crooked as it chugged down the highway. But the pickup ran, so Luecke kept on driving it. There was no reason to buy another. The engine worked just fine.

Jimmy Luecke was a man who lived for the sole purpose of working. He may have been a rancher, an oilman, and a banker, but he spent most of his daylight hours perched on a D7 Caterpillar bulldozer. His only weakness was buying more land. He patched together a jigsaw puzzle of five thousand acres down near Bastrop just so he could clear it and shape it, perhaps dig a pond here, and build an earthen dam over there.

Finally, with nothing better to do, Jimmy Luecke used the dozer to artistically carve his last name in bold block letters among the tall pines and hardwood. The line of each letter was four hundred feet wide, and it took a distance of two and a half miles to separate the "L" from the final "E." The name was best viewed and could always be seen on airline flights between Austin and Houston.

●

Ray Holifield sometimes felt like the hermit of Giddings. The other major players of the Giddings oil boom were all tucked away in their Dallas or Houston offices.

He and his Holifield Oil Company had planted roots in the field and left them there. He had been recognized as the geologist who unearthed the mystical secret of the chalk.

The first six hundred and forty-four wells he discovered for his clients, in fact, averaged almost a hundred and fifty thousand barrels of oil equivalent a day, which was almost five hundred percent higher than the average of all his competitors.

Holifield had even done his part to develop horizontal drilling and jump-start the heartbeat of a dormant oilfield once more. Even during tough times, his had been the only voice to preach that Giddings remained as rich with oil as it had ever been. Hold on, he always said. Hold on. Ray Holifield held on. After all, there had been a time when his income rose to a hundred thousand dollars a week. The bust drained him.

He firmly believed that, even as the crisis whistled across the farmlands like an ill wind, the Giddings field had at least another billion dollars worth of oil and gas reserves waiting to be recovered. He wanted to go into the shallow sands, the lower Austin Chalk, even down to the Buda lime, the Edwards shale, and the Smackover.

Even blessed with unbridled optimism, it had not been the easiest of times for Ray Holifield. By his own admission, he said he wasted his money on divorces, lost money on horizontal drilling and on oil exploration in Mississippi and in Russia, where he gambled that he could bring new oilfield technology to Perm, located a good thousand miles from Moscow. During the 1990s, it was a land filled with promise and potential but devoid of any expertise in the oil business.

He launched a pilot project to utilize bacteria in an effort to control paraffin in wells scattered throughout the Uzen field. Oil exploration was archaic.

The political situation was risky, uncertain, and often dangerous. The escapade cost him forty thousand dollars a month for three years. He divorced one wife and brought back a replacement from Russia with love. The divorce from his lady from Russia cost him another small fortune. In Russia, Holifield had no better luck with oil than love.

He thought that, somewhere below the cold surface of the Soviet Union, he might regain the wealth he had thrown away. He knew he would never recoup the years he lost.

His money ran out, and Russia, he said, became the biggest financial disaster of all. He had not had a winner since the glory days of early Giddings. It had been so long.

He trekked out of the Perm wilderness, caught a plane, and headed home. Giddings was waiting. For Ray Holifield, Giddings was always waiting. Oil companies, especially the new ones testing their luck in an ever-expanding Giddings field, sought out his services. His exploits in the chalk were almost mythical. Even as one century turned into another, his name was magic.

One more great deal. That was all Holifield ever thought about. He said, "I got rich and will again by keeping my independence and working as many hours per day as I can stay awake because I am just too good of an oil finder to keep down."

One more great deal. Time was growing short. Randy Stewart said, "Ray Holifield was the tragic hero of the chalk. He geologized hundreds of wells. Oil flowed. Flared gas lit up the sky across Central Texas. Then came the bust and the fall – wasted time in Russia, wasted money, tragic divorces, the tragedy of trying to become something other than an innovative, eccentric, genius of a geologist."

As oil continues to flow in prolific proportions from the chalk, Ray Holifield, as a close friend said, "is scratching a broke ass and looking for the next multi-million dollar deal. And who's to say he won't find it?"

●

Max Williams arrived in Giddings before any of the new breed. He drove into town in pursuit of the location of the Big Chalk Well that Chuck Alcorn had discovered quite by accident, the well that was consistently flowing three hundred barrels of oil a day in a field that usually traded barrels for buckets after only a week or two. Max Williams and his U.S. Operating Company stayed for the duration.

In partnership with Irv Deal and Windsor Energy, he established the field for others to follow. They showed the way by fracking their wells in order to crack and expand the faults, allowing them to release more oil into the wellbore. The science of fracking brought dead and dying wells to life. The secret to the chalk was not merely solving the mystery of finding the oil. Ray Holifield did that. It was figuring out a way to squeeze it out of the ground.

Max Williams – along with Irv Deal and Holifield – had the guts, the foresight, and the determination to find a solution. A small town, barefoot, basketball-playing boy from the metropolis of Avoca in far West Texas had actually defied the odds and become a millionaire. It was almost more than he could imagine.

He was working so hard in the chalk that he was rich long before he realized it. Oil was not a game for Max Williams. It was a business. A hard business. Yet, he never stopped to count his money. He was too busy, caught in the middle of finding his next well. Lease. Drill. Frac. Test. Oil for him was the great adventure. It was about money, to be sure. It was also about winning and losing.

As Max Williams told Harry Hurt III of *Texas Monthly* in the early 1980s, "I was broke. I was broke. I was broke. Then suddenly I was rich. There never was a time when I sat down to think about what was happening."

By the end of 1981, his U.S. Operating was the second-largest daily oil producer in the Giddings field as his wells produced more than nine thousand barrels a day. He was far and away the leading gas producer in the chalk with average daily volumes of perhaps sixty-million cubic feet – more than double the amount of anyone else.

And yet, he was only beginning. For many, the end time was at hand. The oil bust of the 1980s threatened to destroy the Giddings field. Max Williams watched others giving up on oil, on the chalk, on Giddings, on the business. The price of oil had spiraled below ten dollars a barrel. Money was scarce. For operators, oil had become a venture where nobody won. Soon, nobody was playing. Max Williams stayed. A bad real estate deal jeopardized his business. Oil saved him. Oil always did. Max Williams would drill more than five hundred wells, and he always had a desk drawer filled with a handful of more prospects. He always knew that great amounts of oil had been left behind in the ground. He always knew, that sooner or later, he would pump the old oil or find reservoirs of new oil.

There were those so-called petroleum experts and analysts who, for decades, had forecast the end of Giddings. The field would dry up, they said. The fractures would be empty. Max Williams only smiled.

"The oil was here when I came to town," he said. "It was here when my children grew up. It will be here long after my grandchildren have walked the field and gone. The oil experts have tried, but no one has ever been able to shut down the Giddings field. I sometimes doubt that anyone ever will."

The oil, he thinks, may last forever, encased in hard limestone rock somewhere between the coastal Bermuda pastures and Reinhardt Richter's volcanic gates of hell.

ACKNOWLEDGEMENTS

Buddy Preuss, editor and publisher of the *Giddings Times & News*, who, though he probably did not realize it at the time, was the official historian of the Giddings boom. The pages of his newspaper and his personal column, *Viewpoints*, provided the kind of week-by-week information that could not be found anywhere else.

Harry Hurt III, whose three articles in *Texas Monthly Magazine*, "New Oil: The Giddings Gamble," "Rich Man, Poor Man," and "Meanwhile, Back in Giddings," were an essential guide in better understanding the array of players who found triumph and trouble in the midst of the boom.

Mike Cochran, a complete reporter, an old friend, whose remarkable biography of Clayton Williams, "Claytie: The Roller-Coaster Life of A Texas Wildcatter," provided invaluable insight into one of the most important oilmen to walk above the chalk of the Giddings field.

Eric Miller, whose article in *D Magazine*, "The Humble Man Vs. The Widow," captured the essence and the hostility of the multi-million dollar lawsuit between Pat Holloway and the Browning family.

Rich Arthur, who, in 1985, skillfully wrote "Texas Oil Field Litigation Produces Prime Time Drama" and gave a legal perspective from attorneys involved in the famed Holloway-Browning lawsuit.

Reporters for *The Houston Chronicle*, *The Austin American Statesman*, *The Dallas Morning News*, *The Dallas Times Herald*, *The Fort Worth Star-Telegram*, *The Wall Street Journal*, and *The New York Times*, who all descended on Giddings as fresh oil exploded from the chalk and left a vivid portrait of a boomtown and its people.

Information on the status of boom and bust in the oilfield came from the following.

Publications: CanWest News Service; The Associated Press; *Time Magazine; The Energy Bulletin, World Net Daily, D Magazine, The Houston Chronicle; The New York Times; The Middle East Forum; The Washington Post; Improved Recovery Publications; Explorer; Audabon Magazine;* and *The Atlantic Monthly.*

Books: *Victory: The Reagan Administration's Secret Strategy that Hastened the Collapse,* Peter Schweizer; *Oil Booms: One More Boom,* Byron W. King.

Websites: Nationmaster.com; Dailyreckoning.com; Dallasfed.org;. National Public Radio; MSNBC Television Network.

Organizations: Energy Information Administration; U. S. Department of Energy, American Association of Petroleum Geologists, Business Services Industry; and an article by Dr. Eugene Kim at The Bureau of Economic Geology.

PERSONAL INTERVIEWS

Danny Anderson, WCS Oil & Gas
Otto Becker, former County Commissioner
Rick Boring, Clayton Williams Energy
Gary Bryant, independent oilman
Bill Buscha, Holifield Oil
Irv Deal, founder of Windsor Energy
Carol Dismukes, former County Clerk
Hershel and Lillian Doyle, City Meat Market
Mike Dudley, Rebel Pump Services
Gary Dunaway, oilfield consultant
Joe Green, owner of Bondcoat, a service company
Gary Gerdes, landowner
C. J. Halamicek, landman

Emmett Hannes, former president of Citizen's National Bank
Ray Holifield, Holifield Oil Company
Pat Holloway, attorney and founder of Humble Exploration
Doug Jatzlau, Browning Oil & Gas
Leonard and Margaret Kriegel, owners, a clothing store
David Latchford, U.S. Operating
Robert Lyon, Clayton Williams Energy
Mike Maas, City Meat Market
Michael McWilliams, president, Browning Oil & Gas
Ron Newton, attorney and landman for many oil companies
Kenneth Nye, Dallas attorney
Jim Plumlee, Texas Hot Oiler
Buddy Preuss, publisher, *Giddings Times & News*
Barry Rodstrom, drilling and completion specialist
William C. Shuford, founder of WCS Oil & Gas
Michael Simmang, attorney
Terry Stembridge, Southwest Operating
Bruce Stensrud, attorney, WCS Oil & Gas
Randy Stewart, attorney, Tex-Lee Oil Company
Ken Weiser, accountant and bookkeeping service
Clayton Williams, founder of Clayton Williams Energy
Max Williams, founder of U.S. Operating
Diane Zoch, former bank employee

Made in the USA
Coppell, TX
27 November 2020